THE BODY *of* MYTH

Perseus Slaying the Gorgon (Alinari/Art Resource, New York)

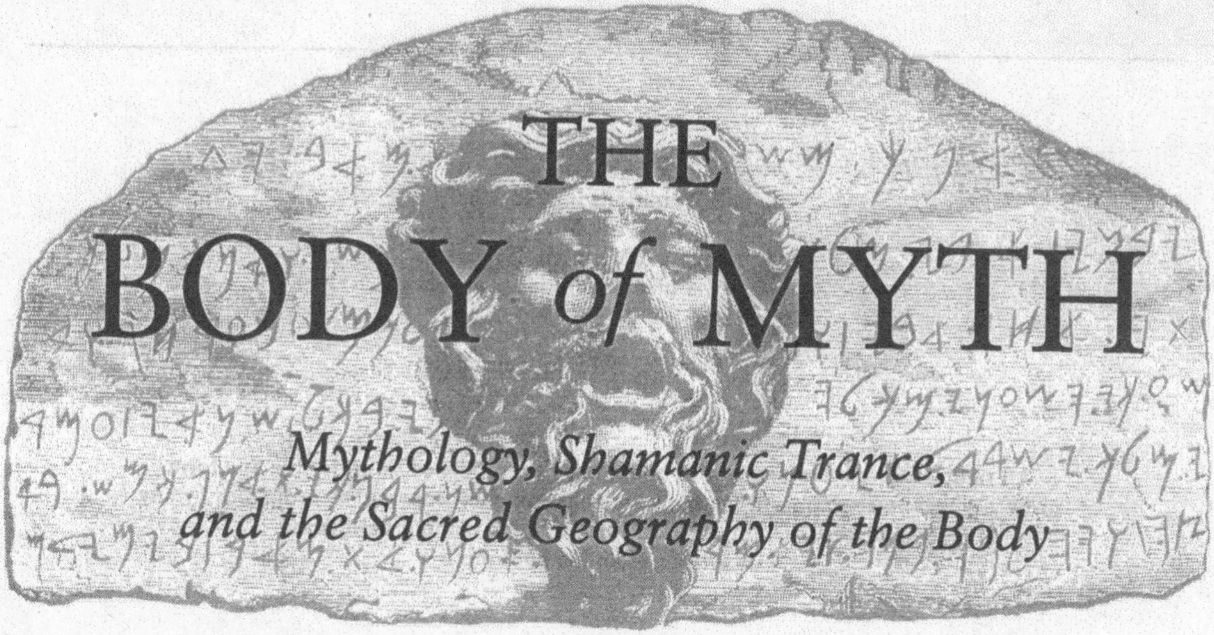

THE BODY *of* MYTH

Mythology, Shamanic Trance, and the Sacred Geography of the Body

J. NIGRO SANSONESE

Inner Traditions International
Rochester, Vermont

Inner Traditions International
One Park Street
Rochester, Vermont 05767
www.InnerTraditions.com

Library of Congress Cataloging-in-Publication Data
Sansonese, J. Nigro.
The body of myth : mythology, shamanic trance, and the sacred geography of the body / J. Nigro Sansonese.
p. cm.
Includes bibliographical references and index.
ISBN 978-0-89281-409-1
1. Myth. 2. Mythology. 3. Shamanism. 4. Trance.
5. Body, Human—Mythology. I. Title
BL313.S326 1993
291.1'3—dc20 92-46586
CIP

Text Design by Virginia L. Scott

Printed and bound in the United States

10 9 8 7 6 5 4 3

To Judith Elizabeth Kovach
. . . sine qua non

Every table of values, every "thou shalt" known to history or ethnology, requires first a *physiological* investigation, rather than a psychological one . . . .

Frederich Nietzsche
Genealogy of Morals 1.17

CONTENTS

List of Figures

ACKNOWLEDGMENTS

This book is *not* a manual of yoga. You can no more learn rāja yoga from it than you can horseback riding. Yoga, like all craft, can be safely learned only under the tutelage of a trained teacher—a guru, if you will—who was himself or herself trained by a teacher. As the Good Book says, the way into the sacred garden is blocked by an angel who wields a flaming sword. To avoid the necessity of sincere discipleship is at best futile, at worst dangerous.

I would be remiss if I did not acknowledge those special people without whose criticism I would still be toiling at this project. First of all, there is Judith Kovach, who provided me with guidance, inspiration, astute editing, and so many ideas that she is entitled to coauthorship. Early on I realized how invaluable was Judith's understanding of trance and myth, so I married her. I hope I have been half as useful to her in her own work. I would like to thank Dean Wicks, Steve Schmidt, and the late and sorely missed Veronica Schnittman for profitable hours of discussion on the science connection and to acknowledge the valuable help provided by my agent, Douglas Storey. Thanks are also due to Barbara Williams, Christine de Laage, and Ken Peterson for moral support during the difficult and hectic final days of preparing the manuscript; to Steve Larsen for his advice and encouragement in the early stages of writing this book; and to Cannon Labrie of Inner Traditions for his many helpful suggestions for elaborating and clarifying obscure passages. Finally, thank you to my mother for reading me *The Pokey Little Puppy*, my first book, and many, many more.

PROLOGUE

This Book Is about God

This book is about the gods of mythology, who long ago satisfied our need for the one god. Before religion, there was myth, the fruit of a special knowledge. We can discern that special knowledge in myth, just as, within the moon, we see the brilliance of the sun disguised. But to what category—faith or reason—does myth belong?

To answer that question, we must understand the secret of myth, and the secret of myth is that *you* are hallowed ground. Liken science to the sun, the moon to faith—in other words, echo the pretty poetry of myth—just remember that the place where all pretty poetries meet is you. In you are science and religion both. Electron and Sermon on the Mount—both are conceived in you. When understood from within that special knowledge, myth teaches us, in strange and archaic ways, that electron and scripture are not free creations of the mind. More fundamentally, they derive from the nature of the human body itself. Science has granted nature its power. Religion strives to give it love. Myth tells how it may in fact *be* love.

The existence of the one god is a vexed question, vexed because it is an individual decision not only how to answer it but even whether to answer. Yet history has demonstrated two things at least: The one god as concept is both various and dispensable. As need, it is from everlasting to everlasting.

INTRODUCTION

Mythology Resurrected

In 1987 American television viewers watched Bill Moyers interview the late Joseph Campbell on the ancient subject of myth. The seven-hour Public Broadcasting System series was remarkable for several reasons, but chiefly because it revealed an unexpectedly wide interest in myth among ordinary Americans. A hoary old discipline, mythology, hitherto the province of otherworldly Oxbridge dons and Ivy League classicists, a discipline largely done to death in the days of Sir James Frazer before the Great War, suddenly again had the power to claim the attention of millions.

◆◆◆

Why do myths intrigue us? What magic is there in Achilles girding on his armor that rivets us? When Perseus unveils the HEAD OF THE GORGON,* why do we pause, our minds simultaneously snatching at and recoiling from the image? Does a hidden part of us live in the open, if only momentarily? Does the maiden in each of us tug with Andromeda at her chains, or the mother weep with Niobe for her slaughtered children? Do we perhaps revel at the sack of Troy because rape and mayhem come so naturally to our kind? Or if we prefer to stand with doomed Hector, waiting for bloodthirsty Achilles, do we but acknowledge our mortality?

Reflecting upon the myths that have come down to us—Greek, Roman, Judeo-Christian—nearly same emotions grip us, presentiments of depth, mystery, and enigma. But what is a myth? Can it be understood systematically?

Many answers have been given to that question, beginning in antiquity. Even then, learned sorts knew quite well that whatever a myth was, it was something extremely old. The word *myth* is Greek .

*** Specific myths are set in small capitals at first mention in the text.**

(μυθός) and seems to mean simply "a story." In both Eastern and Western cultures the greater portion of surviving myth is an archaic anthology of pastoralists and hunters, creatures familiar with animals, horses especially, and inured to war. By contrast, agriculture plays a role in relatively few of the stories, an important fact in dating the origins of a specific myth.

The historical era in which a culture passes from pastoral to agrarian varies dramatically. Indeed, many cultures have never made the transition or have done it rather recently: most Native Americans, for instance. Indo-European Greeks and Romans, on the other hand, entered Europe on horseback four thousand to five thousand years ago, and by the fifth century B.C., the "classical era" of Greece, their descendants lived in cities, managed large farms, and traded over thousands of miles. An educated fifth-century B.C. Athenian probably could not have said just when the Greeks sailed off to Troy or recounted with any conviction the meaning of a Greek myth. In general then, distance from pastoralism means distance from myth.

To be sure, in antiquity* there was no shortage of theories about myth. The Euhemerists, for instance, speculated that myths were histories of actual people blown out of all proportion. Although Euhemerism did not originate with Christianity, it certainly appealed to a Christian writer such as Clement, bishop of Alexandria (d. ca. A.D. 211), because it neatly disposed of divine claims for Zeus and other figures of pagan myth that quite obviously were at odds with evolving Christian doctrine.

The Rationalists argued that the incredible stories of mythology had natural explanations. The centaurs, mysterious half-man and half-horse creatures of legend, for example, were explained away as mounted archers mistaken for beasts in the moonlight. Not surprisingly, the Rationalist approach in one guise or another persisted and has its adherents even today. There are those who confidently assert that the forty days and forty nights of rain depicted in Genesis (and other Middle Eastern myths) are a dim collective memory of the end of the last Ice Age, when, it is imagined, stupendous quantities of water released by melting glaciers inundated the earth.

In antiquity, people also thought a myth might be an allegory, although the idea never gained many adherents. Plato (d. 348 B.C.) denied to allegory any explanatory value for myth, almost certainly because he himself made use of allegories from time to time. Plato was an idolator of pure reason, which he called *Logos*. He distinguished between allegory, which is a carefully crafted story having a hidden moral susceptible to reason, and myth, a healthy exercise of the imagination. Myth, for Plato, was unsystematic and tainted by imprecision, even though, through the medium of Socrates, he made extensive use of myth in his dialogues, particularly in the *Republic* and the *Phædo*.

During the Middle Ages, the most influential ancient Greek writer was Aristotle (d. 322 B.C.), but of all the celebrated philosophers of antiquity, he was probably least interested in myth. *Anthropologia kai zoölogia*, "tales of men and animals," is a useful aristotelian summary of myth. The medieval model for myth was Æsop's *Fables*,† which survived as bestiaries, anthologies about animals with preternatural powers of speech and intelligence that were interpreted allegorically. The bulk of pagan myth—save for a few cases tendentiously reconciled with Catholic dogma—was suppressed, only to surface in the veneration of figures like Saint George and the Virgin Mary who have clear antecedents in mythology.

The Renaissance saw a renewed appreciation for certain exaggerated affections of antiquity, chief among them an egoism and a thirst for individual fame that cannot be separated from pagan hero worship and the abuses wrought by

* The several dozen centuries before ca. 700 B.C. are referred to as the Archaic Era; the words antiquity, antique, or the Antique Era are reserved for 700 B.C.–A.D. 500.

† Also the second century A.D. *Physiologus*, author unknown.

deification of Roman emperors. Although myth per se was but little appreciated, the Humanists glimpsed in the rediscovered literature of antiquity a cultural alternative to monolithic Christianity, which had squeezed the spirits out of the world and into heaven. Greek was a virtually unknown tongue among Italians, the creators of the Renaissance. Latin, however, was not only ancestor to Italian but a part of Roman Catholic rite. The initial impetus of the Renaissance was thus provoked by ancient Rome, not Greece. Not until after 1453, with the arrival in Italy of large numbers of Greek scholars fleeing the fall of Constantinople to the Ottoman Turks, did knowledge of classical Greek—and hence Greek literature and mythology—begin to influence the West. The Renaissance, for all its pretensions to learning, was basically a superstitious age. The pagan model was Augustan Rome, with its augurers, astrologers, and superficial metaphysics. The writers most admired were Horace, Ovid, Virgil, Tacitus, and above all Cicero. Pagan myth transformed art and literature, but because the hold of the Roman church was still strong, mythology could rise no higher than the plane of allegory. Myth became a virgilian wonderland of fauns, shepherds, and amorous dalliance, achieving no greater dignity than a Titian, a Donatello, or a Botticelli might give it.

By the late eighteenth century, mythology, adopted by the romantic movement, was a retrograde discipline relative to the scientolatry of the Enlightenment. The work of collecting and translating the classics that had been going on since the days of Boccaccio (d. 1375) continued in earnest, and the linguistic similarities among Greek, Latin, Celtic, Germanic, Persian, and Sanskrit—the Indo-European languages—were discovered. The artistic and literary legacy of the Renaissance continued to dominate studies of myth, but the bloodless rationalism of the Enlightenment also provoked an interest in myth as a symbol of the irrational impulses in human beings. The study of Greek poetry accelerated, at first of the pretty variety found in Anacreon, Longus, and Theocritus, then the weightier themes of Æschylus, Sophocles, and Euripides, finally Hesiod and that colossus of mythic poetry, Homer. Johann Joachim Winckelmann (d. 1768) began the vast work of archaeology necessary for a solid understanding of antiquity.

Nineteenth-century mythographers (those who collect myths) and mythologists (those who interpret them) behaved like proper colonialists. Like Victorian conquistadors, they took possession of the legends of the past and all but fatally corrupted them in the popular understanding, creating their own pernicious "myth," that of the superstitious savage who resorts to myth from ignorance and fear. Among them were F. Max Müller (d. 1900), the famous Sanskritist and translator of many Hindu scriptures, including the *Vedas*, the *Purānas*, and the *Brāhmaṇas*, Georg Friedrich Grotefend (d. 1853), the translator of Persian myth and Latin poetry, F. F. Adalbert Kuhn (d. 1881), who reduced myth to primitive meteorology, and Sir James Frazer (d. 1941), whose *Golden Bough* was for a long time the bible of many would-be mythologists. Mythology was being absorbed by ethnology, and nineteenth-century ethnologists tended to patronize their subject. The myth they knew, to which culture and education had indoctrinated them, was folklore, substandard cultural artifact. They were uncomfortable with mysticism in Christian religious themes, so they were not about to embrace it in myth. The nineteenth-century mythologists in large measure reduced the mythic to either the barbarous or the picturesque.

The work of translating and critically editing the manuscripts of Judeo-Christian myth was carried to new heights by men like the Abbé Migne (d. 1875) and Ernst Renan (d. 1892). Comprehensive Greek, Latin, and Hebrew Bible concordances appeared. The work of the nineteenth century was thorough, painstaking, and analytical, although the Christian scriptures were treated gingerly for the most part and with every attempt made to see in them the spiritual daylight to which benighted paganism must inevitably have succumbed. Later, however, biblical exegesis took a somewhat more skeptical approach to the literalness of the New Testament in the work of scholars such as Rudolph Bultmann.

The relation between mythology and nineteenth-century imperialism was deeply rooted. As an integral part of the study of Latin and Greek, myth had become the special interest of the upper classes of Europe, and nowhere was that more true than in England. To "take a first" in the Greek *tripos* at Cambridge was for centuries the most esteemed honor the university could bestow. In certain circles, it still is. And because of the close ties between Oxbridge graduates and Whitehall, the classics touched all the great leaders of the British Empire. Their response to myth was largely aesthetic and sentimental. The measured, high-minded treatment of myth such as one finds in Jacques-Louis David's *Oath of the Horatii* or *Death of Socrates* suited them. A good example is William Ewart Gladstone (d. 1898). A complicated man—he was a low-church zealot, with peculiar ideas about prostitutes, who favored home rule for Ireland—Gladstone was also a magnificent orator and talented classical scholar who wrote an undeservedly neglected three-volume study of Homer. He represented Oxford in parliament and four times rose to the rank of prime minister between 1868 and 1894, a period that saw the zenith of the Empire. In Gladstone's opinion the study of the Greek classics was an inalienable prerogative of the gentleman-statesman and indispensable to "the education of the youth of England."*

That long and somewhat dotty tradition was destroyed in the carnage of the First World War. Robert Graves has written movingly of the traumatic effect the Great War had on the ranks of Gladstone's gentleman scholars.† After 1914 it was no longer quite possible to idealize the heroics of Heracles, Achilles, or Æneas complacently. We may never know to what extent the ethos of myth had penetrated Victorianism before World War I, but after that horrific conflict it must all have seemed a little silly.

By midcentury, however, mythology had become complicated. Émile Durkheim (d. 1917) and Georges Dumézil wedded archaic religion to sociology. Psycholinguists such as Freud and Jung linked myth to the arcana of psychoanalysis. In their densely argued, deftly inscrutable opinions, mythical themes pervade the mind in somewhat the same way that girders sustain a skyscraper. To a psycholinguist, a myth is first and foremost a state of mind. And given the fondness of psychoanalysts for words and wordplay, carried to truly dizzying heights by Jacques Lacan and Claude Lévi-Strauss, the problem of explaining myth became the problem of explaining language.

The next, obvious step in the linguistic program for myth was to redecorate the antique notion of myth as allegory or symbol, as metaphor, as grand archetypal imagery of one sort or another. Such explanations are widely held today thanks in large measure to the efforts of Jung and Campbell, both extraordinarily prolific writers. A hallmark of modern theories (those of Campbell and Jung especially) is their insistence on mythmaking as a natural activity of mankind, an activity occurring even now, unconsciously or subconsciously, in convoluted ways, and subject to vaguely defined dynamics that are either unprovable or incomprehensible. But the intermingling of myth and meaning in the grand sense yields a solution that can grease a very slippery slope. In the guise of psychoanalytic jargon, truly mystical concerns are being reintroduced into the substance of myth, without any clear conception of mysticism accompanying the procedure. More than anything else, however, the revalorization of myth as psychological meaning has contributed to a resurrection of mythology. No longer is it necessary to master the endless complexities of classical Greek and Latin. One need only have strongly held convictions about "the self," which myth is said to mirror.

Psychoanalysis also fathered a temperamental bastardization of Freudian and Jungian mythology: deconstructionism. In a fit of psycholinguistic hysteria, the deconstructionists seek to murder the "self" of myth, which is deconstructed into pure literary formalism. Driven by sundry political agendas,

* W. E. Gladstone, *Studies on Homer and the Homeric Age* (Oxford, 1868), vol. 1, pp. 11–20.

† R. Graves, *Goodbye to All That* (London, 1923).

deconstructionists indict myth, place it in the dock, and interrogate it for signs of "phallogocentrism." Deconstructionism and its heirs have taken over academia to a truly alarming degree. As with all theories that see in language the alpha and omega of human existence, it must sooner or later disappear up its own diacritical backside, where, one supposes, it will discover yet another backside to welcome it and so on.

The central problem with all of the above theories—the patently silly ones excepted—is that they say far more about modern thinking than about myth. Instead of narrowing the cultural gap between ourselves and our mythmaking ancestors, such theories drastically increase it. They assume a philosophical turn of mind and a fascination with the manipulation of symbols that are themselves the products of thousands of years of advanced culture and closely allied with mature forms of writing and literature. Indeed, certain elaborate myths—the TROJAN WAR, for example—have played an incalculable role in the growth of both literature and philosophy from antiquity to the present, from Bronze Age oral ritual to PBS. To suppose that myth, which antedates civilization, literature, and systematic philosophy, also should spring from them—or from the sensibilities they require—is to suppose that myth is its own father and mother. Such a supposition, the sort of psycholinguistic conundrum in which intellectuals delight, is of very dubious utility in explaining what a myth was originally. Authentic myths are no more being created today than are sphinxes being built.

◆◆◆

There was simply no way that anyone in the media could have predicted it: Joseph Campbell was a hit. The average American viewer, recent surveys have shown, is hard pressed to give within a generation the dates of the Civil War, much less to explain to what era myth belongs. In fact, the average American viewer of the PBS series quite likely believed that Plato, Heracles, Socrates, and Helen of Troy are equally figures from history. Ancient learning—Greek history and philosophy, Roman history, not to mention the myths of the Hindus, Buddhists, and Muslims that Campbell so frequently alluded to—was, every jot of it, indescribably remote from the life of the average American television viewer. And to imply, as Campbell more than once seemed to, that the stories of the Old and New testaments were also myths seemed outlandish and more than a little sacrilegious.

Just as remarkable was the evident personal affinity among viewers for Joseph Campbell himself, a man who had been quietly writing about mythology for over forty years without attracting much notice outside a circle of specialists—specialists in fields uncountenanced and even unrecognized by the classical Greek and Latin mythologists of the Frazer school: depth psychologists and psychotherapists, sociologists, existentialists, and groups such as the Anthroposophists who are even further on the fringes of respectable opinion. There has always been an aspect of Campbell's work that appealed to the so-called New Age audience in search of cosmic identity, something with which Campbell himself was not entirely comfortable given the vocal anti-intellectualism of the 1960s.

On TV, Campbell came across as both charming and wise, a man with an endless fund of knowledge drawn from numerous cultures, a man who applied that knowledge to the ethical, philosophical, and religious situations in which "ordinary people" found themselves every day. Joseph Campbell, it appeared, had achieved that blend of insouciance and sagacity that marks the saint, whose opinions have an integrity drawn not solely from an analytical system but from experience as well. If, as Plato assures us, we shall do best when we remember that the unexamined life is not worth living, what was it that Campbell seemed to understand and how did he apply it to life?

From the start, Campbell combined a scholar's talent for toil and detail with the desire to understand the relevance myth held for his own life. Campbell realized that all the religions (therefore myths) of the world were far more similar than they were different. The myths of peoples as widely separated as Arctic Eskimos and Mediterranean Greeks bear uncanny resemblances. The Inuit of Greenland tell a story that is a carbon copy of JASON AND THE ARGONAUTS. Hundreds of such global correspondences could be cited. Yet no satisfactory explanation for the similarities has ever been put forth.

The inference Campbell drew was that the authentic subject matter of myth must be something fundamental to human experience. That something, he called the self. Above the entrance to the temple of Apollo at Delphi was inscribed "Know Thy Self." Campbell believed that mythic unity, when properly interpreted, could light the way to knowledge of the self—indeed, that myths were fundamentally about the self.

Campbell began his work in the 1930s, when psychoanalysis was legitimized as a theory of the mind and Sigmund Freud (d. 1939), the founder of psychoanalysis, reached an apogee of acclaim, if not influence. Yet it was not the writings of Freud himself that influenced Campbell most profoundly, but those of Freud's disciple, Carl Jung, who had early broken with "the master" with respect to not only the details but to the fundamentals of psychoanalytic theory and its meaning in human experience.

What Jung contributed so crucially to Campbell's search for the explanation of worldwide mythic unity was the concept of the universal *archetype*, something maddeningly difficult to define other than to say it is a meaningful symbolic image—for example, the Sage, the Witch, the Hero. The totality of archetypes make up what Jung called the collective unconscious of humankind. Thus, each individual, simply by virtue of being human, shares in and is affected by the archetypes, although usually in an unconscious or subconscious way.

From Freud, Jung had inherited the predisposition to think of archetypes as fundamentally *biological* categories; mystically inscrutable they might appear to be, but they were part of the life of the human body. If, then, as is extremely likely, the biology of a Hindu is not fundamentally different from that of a Greek, a Persian, an Eskimo, or a Trobriand Islander, the similarity of myths arising in different cultures is inevitable.

Unfortunately, Jung was not all that forthcoming about crucially important aspects of his theory of archetypes. In particular, the question of the biological basis of the archetypes—how, for instance, are they to be found in the body?—went begging. Indeed, the biology of psychoanalysis in general has been problematic from its inception. Freud's dream of converting psychiatry from a quasi-religious to a physical discipline, of changing the focus from the soul to the body, ended in a redefinition of the soul: the unconscious. When it was realized that the empirical evidence for the objective existence of the ego and the id would never be more than inferential, and nebulously so at that, psychoanalysis began its transformation into psycholinguistics.

The concept of the archetypes had come to Jung primarily through an exhaustive analysis of dreams reported by his patients in psychoanalysis, so the logical place to look for them was within the brain. But that would have meant, for Jung, the necessity of advancing a theory of the precise relationship of archetype to dream and sleep—in other words, of mind to body. Jung speculated that the archetypes might be genetically encoded in our nervous systems, but he went no further in spelling out the structural connections. As a psychiatrist, he was more interested in understanding the role the unconscious and its archetypes played in individual human behavior than as sources of myth. Myth per se was only a secondary concern of Jung's, significant only as evidence for the existence of archetypes. Rather than attempting to solve the ancient and probably insoluble mind-body conundrum, he set out to determine the effect that archetypes have on human behavior, particularly religious behavior.

Campbell too, as was amply demonstrated in the PBS series, was interested in individual human happiness, but for Campbell, more philosopher than physician, myths and archetypes were on a more equal footing as objects of inquiry than was the case with Jung. Campbell eventually showed an inclination to generalize from the archetypes, to out-Jung Jung, as it were. He came to understand the archetypes as deep metaphorical and symbolic "structures" of human consciousness. In time, metaphor in general came to occupy a central place in Campbell's thinking, because in metaphor the inert archetype is put into motion, so to speak. The legend of Parsifal, for example, is more than an archetype of the HOLY GRAIL. It somehow—metaphorically—describes a method of defining the Holy Grail personally and within oneself. Inevitably, such an approach requires, on the one hand and in general, demonstrating the equivalence of archetypal metaphors and the normative structures of religion, and on the other hand and in particular, conflating symbols with the search for meaning by individuals.

Campbell was also more biological than Jung. He recognized that the precise biological locus of the archetypes was the Achilles' heel of Jungian psychology. Where, apart from dreams, are these potent archetypes to be found? Here again, myth provided answers that Jung had neglected. The more ancient the myth, the more often do parts of the human body play an explicit role in the myth. ADAM'S RIB is the best example; the Egyptian myth of SET AND ISIS is another. In Campbell's work, the brain is only a part of the body, no more paramount than the liver, kidneys, or spleen in rationalizing human conduct. He tells Moyers at one point that myth is about the "war between the organs of the body." With each bodily organ, he seems to say, is associated an archetypal reality or state of consciousness, and it is with the integration of those states of consciousness, leading to happiness and "self creation," that the metaphors of myth concern themselves.

With Campbell, one either intuits his meaning or moves on. Few of the terms he uses are particularly well defined. For example, consciousness is not a "thing" in any conventional understanding of the term. Hence, how can it have a structure? Campbell has been criticized more than once for his gift of talking around objections to his ideas, for airily assuming that the meanings of controversial terms like consciousness, mind, and archetype are perspicuous—in brief, he is accused of being glib. That defect, if defect it is, is his principal legacy from classical psychoanalysis, in which a tendency to speak conclusively about the unconscious, the id, the ego, and so on—as though they are as solid as tables and chairs—has a long and disconcerting history.

In his willingness to look to biology for answers, however, Campbell isolated a subject that *is* as physical as a table or a chair. Unfortunately, he never crossed the abyss separating biology from psychology. Campbell went further along a somatic road to explaining myth than Jung ever did (not to mention Freud, whose physical grounding of human behavior had settled unassailably in the genitalia by 1897), but there is still lacking in his work any concrete, demonstrable relationship between the organs of the body and particular psychological states, nor is any systematic relationship of body to myth apparent. Campbell was content with making clear the metaphorical and psychological bases for the relationship. He went on to suggest that each person can use his fundamental connectedness to metaphor and archetype to create his or her own personal mythology, but the tantalizing promise of a biological approach to understanding myth was left dangling.

How then, on Campbell's view, does one "connect" to myth? Chiefly by recognizing what makes one's own self happy. The search for meaning cannot be carried out externally, only internally, in the cultivation of those states of happiness each person experiences every day. Campbell the philosopher becomes Campbell the psychiatrist, jubilantly pointing the way along which each person can heal himself of those dread symptoms of modernity: anxiety and alienation. The cure for unhappiness, Campbell says, echoing many sages and saints, is within each of us, because within each of us happiness already exists.

Campbell has been criticized for espousing a selfish hedonism, particularly by those who reflexively seek solutions to individual problems in political and social upheaval. In my opinion, his ideas are immune to such criticism. Individual human happiness cannot be reduced, even in large measure, to politics or sociology. But

Campbell does suffer from a methodological failing. His well-known prescription "Follow your bliss!" lacks utility as an explanation of mythmaking because it is so very general, so general as to open him up to the silly charge of hedonism,* the very opposite, perhaps, of what he intended by "happiness." Hedonism depends on pleasant circumstance. Happiness, on Campbell's view, is noncontingent—it depends on nothing. Noncontingent happiness Campbell calls *bliss*.

To live within an integrative "state of bliss," Campbell saw, was the very birthright of each man and woman. To do so would be to create one's own myth. In this book, however, I speculate that attaining "bliss" means following a path much less free for the choosing than anything Campbell ever proposed and certainly far less metaphorically guided. It means understanding myth, yes, but understanding it *practically* through an esoteric yet universal teaching about the body and about life in the body.

◆◆◆

The primary topic of this book is the myths of Western culture, which are divided into two groups: Indo-European (Greek, Roman, Celtic, etc.) and Egypto-Semitic (Egyptian, Judeo-Christian, Islamic). The bulk of the book is devoted to Greco-Roman and Judeo-Christian myth.

The present work, anchored in biology, looks not to psychology for guidance in approaching myth. The gap between psychology and biology is at present vast. The questions posed by psychology are not strictly within the purview of biology, and the answers provided by biology apply to no psychological categories directly.

In the psychobiology of *trance*, however, an opportunity for closing the gap presents itself. Trance is an elemental psychological state. More to the point, it is also a physiological phenomenon. And certain trance states, for example, *shamanic trance*, have profound historical and functional connections to the origins of religion worldwide. The language of the body that will unravel myth is the language of trance.

That language is spelled out in great detail in the *Yoga-Sūtra* of Patañjali, a Hindu pundit who lived about two thousand years ago. The *Yoga-Sūtra* is a manual of ancient trance craft; a direct exposition of yogic practice. Myths, however, for a variety of historical and religious reasons, are guarded descriptions of the experience of trance.

An investigation of selfhood via myth and trance must inevitably become an investigation of the nature of consciousness. Since the seventeenth century, a satisfactory theory of consciousness has been the holy grail of science. In my view, consciousness is itself Campbell's noncontingent happiness. The practical means of discovering noncontingent, a priori happiness is the true subject of myth.

Finally, the noncontingency of consciousness must somehow reveal itself as essential to matter itself, hence in scientific law. Thus, the final section of the book concerns the projection of myth into the basic paradigms of science. Science, we shall see, is ultimately a systematic description of the human organism. Myth, properly interpreted, is the key to unlocking that description. A grand synthesis of science, consciousness, and myth—by means of yoga—is the goal of this book.

◆◆◆

"Strait is the way, and narrow the gate that leads to life, and few there be that find it," Jesus said. Modern mythology has contributed the proper direction of myth: inward, into the organism. The myth is within you who reads this. So the question arises: Just *who* is you who reads this? What are the *where* and *when* of you?

What you are reading is being read with the frontal lobes of your brain, what you see, with eyes and the occipital cortex at the back of your skull. What you feel in the paper of this page

* Brendan Gill, "Face of Joseph Campbell," *New York Review of Books*, 28 September 1989, p. 16.

when you turn it is felt with the peripheral nervous system. You take those things for granted, just as you take for granted that while you ponder myth, sublime, artful, and enigmatic, your heart beats most artfully and your lungs rise and fall with the mystery of a bird in flight. Your nerves are living nerves, far more real than mere pictures in an anatomy text. Your blood is truly hot. Your skin is oiled. Your touch is soft when what you touch is soft, not when it is not. The page you touch is smooth, but the fingers you touch it with are smoother still. They can feel the smoothness of glass, of water, air, and warmth. Smoothness is somewhere in your nervous system. Texture is in the touch. Light is in the eyes. The ears are already full of sound, else you could not hear. Light, sound, texture—infinitely varied—taste and smell and pleasant thoughts crowd your body. Your sense of place and time, here and now, is your body's gift to you.

Your body is your where and when.

PART ONE

TRANCE

1

THE SOUND OF ONE HAND CLAPPING

The Zen monks of China and Japan, who have long practiced a form of Buddhism that emphasizes meditation, ask themselves the following bizarre question:

What is the sound of one hand clapping?

Buddhists call such puzzles *koāns*. It is said that they are intentionally designed to illustrate the illogicality—or at least alogicality—of existence. By definition, clapping requires two hands, but in our koān it's considered as an activity of just one. The rational mind, so current Buddhist theorizing goes, must be derailed, jarred from its familiar context in which only two hands can clap, and primed for fresh and remarkable insights into the essence of reality and so on and so forth.

Think for a moment about the sound of one hand clapping. Do you sense the eternal? Do you discern the illogic of existence? Were you jarred into a new awareness? No?

Perhaps you just haven't tried hard enough or long enough. Take a few moments more. Put down this book for five whole minutes, wave one hand in the air, and just listen . . .

Still unpersuaded? Well, all right, suppose that koāns are *not* what modern Buddhists say they are. Suppose instead that in the sixth century B.C., during the era when Gautama the Buddha himself was teaching, a koān (or its antecedents) was exactly what it appears to be—a sort of puzzle, which has an answer. *What if a koān is a riddle?*

If a koān is in fact a riddle, then like all good riddles it should provide a nice, neat payoff when solved. The answer to the koān should have the pleasing resonance of a *Eureka!*, the sudden click-of-the-tumbler feeling you get on realizing that—Of course!—a *newspaper* is black and white and read all over.

The sound of one hand clapping is just such a riddle. Yet it is a riddle whose meaning is so profound that whenever and wherever it has been understood in the past, it has generated cultural earthquakes called the births of new religions.

Jesus of Nazareth, who might be likened to a Zen master, often spoke in *parables*, which means roundabout ways of talking, deliberate evasion, riddles. Jesus even tells us why.* He speaks in parables, he says, because he does not want anyone but his disciples to understand him: "He who has ears to hear, let him hear." Which happily brings us back to the sound of one hand clapping.

There exist a few recorded instances of Zen masters witnessed in the moment of understanding this koān (or others like it). They invariably kept the answer to themselves. Some recited short, celebratory poems. But that's about it. They did not claim to have understood the illogicality of the universe, the jarring of contexts, the entry into a suprarational realm. They just went about their business.

One might suspect, of course, that, saying nothing, they understood nothing. But that would be to put too great a premium on words, something very un-Buddhist. It is left to the "unenlightened" Buddhists among us, who have written encyclopedically on the subject, to flaunt the jarring of contexts and the incomprehensibility of the koān—something that seems to have gone a bit off the deep end if a koān is simply a riddle. It's not necessary to plead the universe guilty of felonious illogic when a confession of *petite doubl'entrendre* will do. Solving a koān is a happy event, not a supernatural one.

Yet the question remains: What is the sound of one hand clapping? Simply put,

the sound of one hand clapping is the sound of your own ears.

Now, you are doubtless thinking that the answer is quite as bad as decontextualization, jarring essences, and all that rubbish. If so, you still haven't gotten the riddle. Ask yourself what actually is intended by the word "ears."

An ear is not simply that flappy thing hung out in the breeze. That thing is only a part of your ear—and not a crucial part either. No one would mistake a television antenna on a rooftop for the television itself, and just as a television set functions without an antenna, a human being can hear without that flappy thing. The real ear is inside your head. The real ear is a matched set of auditory nerves, one per ear. So the question, What does your ear sound like? is the same as asking, What does your auditory nerve sound like?

A homely comparison may help. We all know that the motor of a car makes it go. But if a car is stopped, does it follow that the motor has stopped? Obviously not. The motor may simply be idling. Only when you engage the transmission, either by clutch pedal or shift lever, does the continuing motion of the motor engage with the wheels and the car go.

Now consider a second analogy, a comparison with a television set. (It might help if you went to a television set now and turned it on.) If the television is tuned to a commercial channel, VCR, or cable jack, you see a picture.

Now do something silly.

Set the selector channel to 1 (or some other nonbroadcast band) and ask yourself: What am I looking at now?

It won't do to say *that's* not a picture. If you can see it, it's a picture. Only it's not a conventional picture. The question of what it is a picture *of* can have a variety of answers, mostly technical. But what you are looking at, on Channel 1, is the television set idling, the television set decoupled from the external world, the television set pure and simple, the thing itself. So long as electrical power is supplied to the set, or, in words that a TV repairman might use, so long as the power cord is "live," you see something on the screen, external signal or no.

We are accustomed to thinking that to listen means to listen to sounds produced by some thing outside ourselves. But the ten-billion neurons in your central nervous system (CNS) are never "off." At all times, a nonzero "electrical pressure"—a so-called resting voltage of approximately seventy millivolts within the neuron—creates a continuous tension across the

* Matthew 13:11–13.

entire cell.* Therefore, *the auditory nerve inside your head is always listening . . .*

Perhaps, if it were quiet enough, if you put down this book and listened again for the sound of one hand clapping, perhaps then you'd hear something—did already hear something—well, staticky.

It isn't a clock ticking or a breeze blowing or traffic in the street. If you hear those sounds, they're interfering. Go somewhere without clocks—or breezes—or traffic. Now try again to hear the sound of one hand clapping. Flap your hand and keep flapping your hand. That way, when you hear what the koān refers to and you simultaneously see that single flapping hand, you will, perhaps, get the joke that made the Zen master smile. If, when you read this, it happens to be the dead of winter, don't clap. Go outside. If it's quiet enough, perhaps you'll hear the "sound of snow falling," another Zen koān. Or if it's not snowing, listen to the grass growing. Or you might make up your own koān. Once you get the joke, it's not too difficult.

You need extreme quiet to hear such things because what you are listening for is very subtle, very simple, very overlookable, "a still small voice." With practice, however, it will sound as loud as you like.

So go back, be still, listen . . .

◆◆◆

Here is a useful story paraphrased from scripture.†

The wondrous Buddha, ultimate source of all koāns, we must suppose, often instructed a disciple named Ananda who was both a pest and a wee bit dim. Ananda, we're told, demanded that the Buddha explain clearly what was the true nature of reality. Noticing a large brass gong nearby and taking up a mallet, the Buddha struck the gong once and said, "Do you hear?" to his disciple. The disciple at once replied "I hear, O Sacred One." Then, as the sound of the gong slowly faded to an indistinct ringing, the Buddha once again asked "Do you hear?" The disciple replied "Divine One, I do not hear." The Buddha gave the disciple a disapproving look, then struck once more at the gong. As sound filled the air, he asked "Do you hear, Ananda?" "Yes indeed, O Lord of the Ten Regions of Space, I hear," said the disciple. But when the sound had once more subsided and the Buddha once more asked "Do you hear?" the puzzled disciple swore up and down that he did not hear at all! Again the Buddha smacked the gong, his irritation growing obvious. "Do you *hear*?" he demanded. "Yes, yes, I hear. I hear perfectly, O Perfection Itself!" the disciple shouted. As the sound faded away for the third time, the Buddha again wanted to know "Do you hear?" Scarcely able to face his master—who was the eighth avatar of Viṣṇu—the disciple whispered a meek "No." The Buddha was livid. "Oh, most foolish one," he scolded, "why do you stubbornly insist that when the gong rings you hear but when it ceases to ring you do not hear? Your hearing did not begin when the gong began to ring. Nor does it cease when the gong does not ring." And he struck the gong, which welled up a rich, brassy sound before slowly fading to—What?

Channel 1, that's what!

He who has ears to hear, let him hear!

The Buddha, in his own way, had presented Ananda with a koān, a riddle. It is the same riddle as the sound that your ears make, of one hand clapping, of snow falling.

But how is it that we can hear our auditory nerves? What would it mean even if we did? And wouldn't the sound be just *static*, random noise? Let's take those questions one at a time.

First off, don't confuse the sound of one hand clapping with an imagined sound, a sound that one invents in one's head. Such sounds are not sounds at all but thoughts. Imagined sounds are really a kind of auditory memory that one can summon up at will, like Beethoven, who remembered musical notes after going deaf. Beethoven may have heard the sound of one

* Integrating over all neurons, the total resting voltage of the CNS is therefore approximately 700,000 volts!

† From the *Surangama Sūtra*, in *A Buddhist Bible*, ed. D. Goddard (Boston, 1970), pp. 291–92.

hand clapping too, but its significance would likely have escaped him, as it has most of us.

The sound of one hand clapping is definitely not a memory. It is a real sound, though not necessarily a constant or unvarying sound. To understand how we can hear it, why in fact we cannot avoid hearing it, reflect a moment on how it is that you hear an external sound. It will help if you already know some physics and anatomy, but things will become clear as we move along.

An external sound is a pressure wave that travels through the air. The wave causes the air in contact with your eardrum alternately to pile up and thin out very rapidly (about 250 cycles per second in the case of middle C). The percussive effect of the wave causes the membrane of skin that is the eardrum to vibrate; thence, the vibration is transmitted to the middle ear, thence to the internal ear or labyrinth, and eventually to the auditory nerve. Finally, the auditory sensorium of your brain processes the signal so you can *hear* it. Along the way, the mechanical energy of the vibrating sound wave is converted into electrical pulses that travel through the nerve much as electrical signals travel along a transmission line. Your body will modulate the vibration. For example, the notes of a double bass very likely sound different to you than they do to someone else. Low pitches carry sufficient energy to vibrate the floor, your feet, your bones, your skull, and the auditory nerve itself. Your experience of sound, then, is uniquely dependent on the biophysics of your body.

Now, the point is this: *Your auditory nerves are not stimulated solely by external vibrations.*

Suppose you are in an utterly silent place. Even here, it's not quiet. Your body is itself the source of many vibrations. Some, such as heartbeat and respiration, are regular. Others, such as the mechanical vibrations that run through your body when you eat and drink, flex your muscles or talk, are irregular. By definition, a stimulation of the auditory nerve is a sound. It doesn't matter whether the stimulus originates in the eardrum or within the nerve itself.

The auditory nerve is a cranial nerve, that is, a nerve inside the skull. The cranial nerves—indeed, the encephalon in general—are primarily electromagnetic (EM) entities. In the abstract, cranial nerves are a collection of waveguides: conduits for the passage of EM waves. More concretely, sensory cranial nerves connect sense receptors with specialized regions of the cortex called *sensoria*. Thus, the optic nerves—cranial nerves are often paired—conduct signals from the retinas to the visual cortex in the occipital lobe of the cerebrum. The auditory nerves connect the eardrums to the auditory cortex in the temporal lobes. Signal conduction is generally two-way, though not over the same fibers. The sensoria act on muscles via motor roots of cranial nerves. All sensory nerves are of the nature of switches: they detect not substance but difference.* Thus, the absence of sensation cannot mean an absolute absence or nothingness, which is essentially meaningless, but only a relative absence. What is presented to a particular sensorium when its sensors detect zero difference is the sound of one hand clapping.

Each cranial nerve, indeed every neural filament, modulates every other nerve. It does so in two ways. First of all, numerous filamentary connections exist among the nerves. Second, all cranial nerves carry nonsteady currents; perforce they both broadcast and receive weak EM waves. Cranial nerves are confined in a rather narrow volume, often intertwining one about the other, which results in what is called signal "crosstalk." For example, when the optic nerve is stimulated it transmits a pulse of EM waves to the optic thalamus. Simultaneously and necessarily, it broadcasts that pulse by means of an induced wave that radiates into space and can be picked up by any conductor the wave happens to pass through, for instance, an auditory nerve. If there is an EM wave already passing through the second nerve, the induced wave will modulate it and induce a current that in turn broadcasts its own EM wave, which a third nerve can

* G. Bateson, *Mind and Nature: A Necessary Unity* (New York, 1980), p. 120–21.

pick up (along with the signal from the first), and so on, thus involving the entire encephalon.*

Nerve bundles are surrounded by a delicate, membranous sheath called the perineurium, which attenuates any EM signal incident upon it. In addition, nearly 83 percent of the gray matter and 70 percent of the white is water or gelatin, notoriously poor conductors of radiant energy. But a poor conductor is not the same thing as an insulator; a low signal is not the same thing as no signal. Our premise is that the ability to sense internal stimuli is indefinitely great, so we must assume that the sensoria are capable of detecting minute voltage changes within the nerves. Moreover, the auditory nerves are unusual among cranial nerves because they are not shielded by a protective membrane that anatomists call the neurilemma; they are thus presumably more sensitive to internal stimuli.

In an acoustically sealed environment, a person will hear two wholly internal sounds, associated respectively with the heartbeat and nervous system, and that without meditative training or inward concentration of any kind. Any stimulation, external or internal, of the auditory nerves is a sound that can be heard by the brain. Internal sound means stimulation of the auditory nerve by an internal process and does not involve the drum of the ear. Such a process need not be electromagnetic. Yours is a busy body, and many of its routine functions stimulate the auditory nerves. Every time your heart contracts, the blood it pumps collides with a right-angle turn in your aorta. The collision sets up a complex of pressure waves that reaches the skull as a vibratory resonance of the cerebral ventricles, and the brain expands or contracts slightly. Our brains are slightly *piezoelectric*, which means that under mechanical compression the static electrical energy of your brain's own structure changes into voltage-generating piezoelectric currents (currents arising from a pressure gradient) (figure 1).† Respiration has a continual and far-reaching effect on every cell of the body. Metabolism works ceaselessly: the auditory nerve is made up of cells, cells grow old and die, cells release energy and heat. Such goings-on are the very life of the body. And not to put too fine a point on it, that means the life of *your* body, *your* life. The myriad activities of your living body modulate in concert the auditory nerves, each modulation producing its own soundlet—there subliminally but there nonetheless.

But why should we limit the discussion to obvious physical stimuli such as respiration and heartbeat when there are subtler and certainly more intriguing stimuli to consider? Let us also assume that the mind is entirely physical—an old if controversial assumption. Nice distinctions between mind and matter become confused when seen from within the material seat of mind. In speaking of the physical brain then, we speak also of emotions and intellect. Emotional states are voltage changes recorded as brain waves on strip charts. Thoughts and even moral dilemmas are minute chemical and electrical processes. Your so-called lifestyle, your emotions, your moral predicament can be sensed in the physics of your brain. The auditory nerves hear those things too. And suddenly, the sound of one hand clapping has become the sound of your soul.

It won't do to say that what you hear when you hear your ears is just static. Even pure, 100 percent static should not casually be brushed aside, because that staticky noise reflects the activities and rhythms of your body; it is intimately connected to life itself.‡ Until someone somewhere sheds a bit more light on what life is and what it is not, on how it comes and goes and animates an organism, it seems premature to dismiss the sound of life as *just* static.

* The time involved is extremely short, typically measured in milliseconds.

† For a discussion of several body-brain connections, see I. Bentov, *Stalking the Wild Pendulum* (Rochester, Vt., 1988).

‡ Cf. John 1:4: "[Jesus] was life, and that life was the light of men"; light is electromagnetism.

But let's suppose, for the sake of argument, that the sound of one hand clapping is mere static. Static is a strange concept to begin with, and it gets stranger the closer you look at it. You might think it means merely the same thing as *chaos*. But the second law of thermodynamics, first formulated in the last century, places the concept of chaos at the very heart of physical science. And current theory is revealing, to everybody's amazement, that chaos is a mask for much deeper levels of organization called *nonlinear systems*.*

Static is omnipresent. Place an electrometric probe anywhere you like—in the farthest depths of outer space or ocean—and you will hear static. In 1964, Arno Penzias and Robert Wilson, radio astronomers at Bell Laboratories, discovered homogeneous background static—the so-called cosmic 3-K (three-degree kelvin) blackbody radiation—everywhere they looked in the sky (figure 2). They theorized that the ubiquitous radiation was a long-lingering aftereffect of the "Big Bang," an echo of the creation. In 1973 they received the Nobel Prize in physics for their discovery.

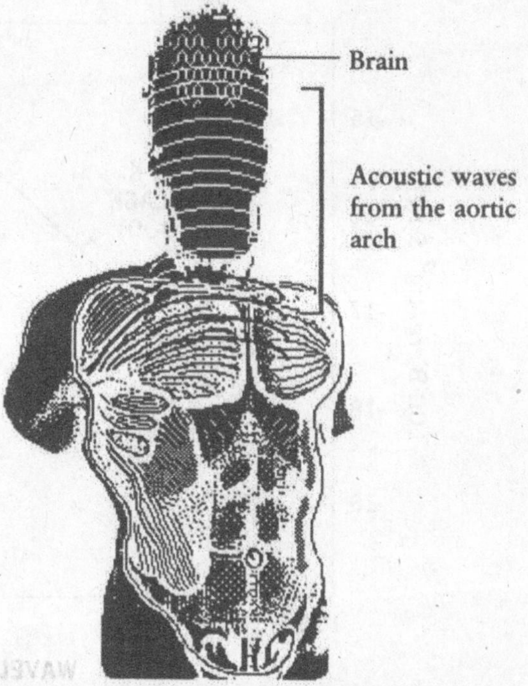

Figure 1. How the Heart Modulates the Cranial Nerves

The several wavelengths that make up the cosmic-background radiation are closely grouped in the microwave region of the EM spectrum. Specifically, they are all anywhere from about ⅛ inch to 2¾ inches long measured from one wave crest to the next. That is very close to the average length of nerves and dendritic fibers in the cranium.† As any electrical engineer will tell you, an antenna—in this case, a dendrite—will "pick up" radiation of a wavelength equal to its own length better than other radiation. It's a matter of a proper fit of signal to antenna. Thus, your auditory nerves are *already tuned* to the omnipresent microwave static.

The wavelength of 3-K static is on a human scale. Just as the English dimensions of foot, inch (< L. *uncus*, "fingernail"), and yard (< Mid. Eng. *yerde*, "staff") came into use precisely because they are natural to human beings (as opposed to giants or microbes), so does the cosmic-background radiation "fit" with the human CNS. And considering the stupendous range of wavelengths in the known electromagnetic spectrum, from mile-long amplitude-modulated (AM) radio waves to gamma rays measured in ten-trillionths of an inch, such a close a fit is a remarkable coincidence. If it is a coincidence.

The wavelength of the 3-K radiation has not significantly attenuated throughout the history of planet Earth: from the time of the primordial ooze, through fish, amphibian, mammal, and man, in other words, for more than four billion years. The same organs that are ears in man were primarily position-orienting sensors in primitive fish. In all mammals, the ears serve the dual purpose of hearing and balance. Could the 3-K radiation have played a role in modulating the evolution of the species? Could it have

* J. Gleick, *Chaos: Making a New Science* (New York, 1987).

† Dendrites are fibers that carry signals *to* neurons; axons transmit signals *from* neurons.

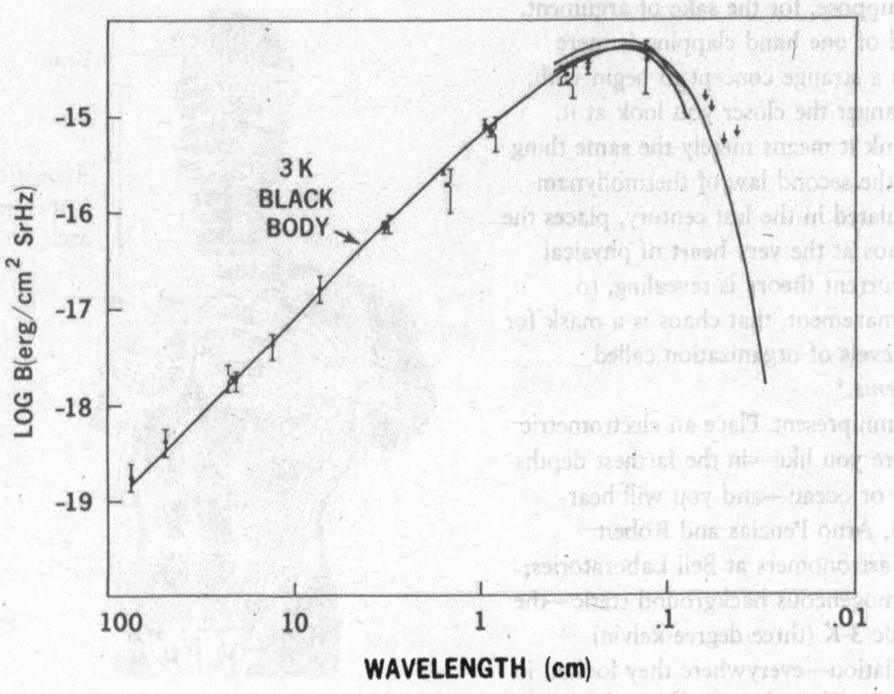

Figure 2. Three-Degree Kelvin Radiation: *Is It the "Sound of Life"?* (Robert Wilson)

guided evolution by its continual action on the position-sensing apparatus of earthbound organisms?

Static is undefinable—virtually by definition.* It correlates strongly with entropy, which is confusion by any other name; but by being both omnipresent and indefinable, static resembles nothing so much as it does the concept of *being* itself, the holy grail of classical philosophy.

◆◆◆

For three thousand years mystics have spoken about the "music of the spheres," a sound that transcends mundane sound. In the response of the human auditory nerve to the cosmic-background radiation, we have perhaps identified the music of the spheres scientifically.† The Buddha's "transcendental hearing" has been made tangible and empirical. In a semantic twist that would have delighted Parmenides (fl. 500 B.C.), the Eleatic philosopher of nothingness (μη ον), nothing *is* just static; static is nothing; not a *thing* at all, it is present everywhere, even inside the purest vacuum. Static makes nothing something!

Nature abhors a vacuum, and so too does the human intellect. Just as the cipher (0), which symbolizes nothing, revolutionized mathematics after being conceived by the ancient Hindus, so too is static a *metalogical* category having considerable implications for both physics and philosophy. To listen to the sound of one hand clapping then, is to listen to "no thing" at all—

* English "static"< Gk. *statikos,* "that which stands [around]"; the sense is of an extremely general "support" (e.g., in cognate Eng. "establish"), or it denotes an all-encompassing environment as in "status quo" and "state," something simply *there.* Cf., It. *stare* and Sp. *estar,* "to be."

† The planets too radiate in the millimeter-to-meter (approx. 1/20 inch to 1 yard) region of the EM spectrum.

or to "every thing"—and so the joke goes on and on to the last instant of recorded time.

And quite a bit longer.

◆◆◆

Both the *Ṛg Veda* and *Maitriya Upaniṣad* of the ancient Hindus, who were Indo-Europeans, tell of how the universe was created by *ṣabda brahman*, the "eternal sound" that created everything—and still inheres in everything—but is itself uncreated: "begotten, not made," as the Nicene Creed expresses it. In John 1, verse 1:

> In the beginning was a Sound, and the Sound was with God, and the Sound was God. All things were made by that Sound, and nothing not made by that Sound was made.

Is the sound of the auditory nerve that same sound? Can either sound be traced to the omnipresent static of the universe? Can you hear the three-degree blackbody radiation? Sensations of the brain itself, in the absence of external stimuli, are usually subliminal, meaning just beyond the threshold of awareness. Your awareness must be adjusted inward and amplified if you are to experience consciously your very own Channel 1. But the daily business of surviving on this planet requires that you tune your senses and your mind outward. Gross perceptual sound masks subtle internal sounds, a practical reason to meditate in quiet surroundings. An external sound often can be scaled in hundreds of volts rather than the millivolt (thousandth of a volt) and even microvolt (millionth of a volt) energies of your nervous system. It is easy to miss the exquisitely subtle inner world, just as you might not hear the warble of a wren in a foundry. You might miss the wealth of life going on inside you, not because you can't experience it, but simply because you don't know how to listen to the inner world.

Now pay close attention:

The riddles of religion describe that inner world.

◆◆◆

We have scarcely begun to scratch the surface of a body-centered approach to mythmaking. Obviously, we could ask a number of other questions modeled on

What does the auditory nerve sound like?

For example:

What do your eyes look like?

That is, what does the occipital cortex of the brain, at the back of the skull where the optic nerve terminates, look like?

Also:

What does your tongue taste like?

That is, what is the taste of the glossopharyngeal nerve, the principal sensory nerve of the tongue?

As long as we are on the subject:

What does your nose smell like?

That is, when they are not smelling flowers and food and whatnot, what do the olfactory bulbs smell like?

What about asking:

Can your skin touch itself?

Can you draw a perfect breath?

Can you tell your heart when to beat?

As it turns out, you *can* do all of the above. But first we must refine and deepen our understanding of the inner world. If we are to use the language of trance in our investigation, we need both a paradigm—a conceptual example coordinating our inner life with meditation—and a technique for realizing the paradigm. The necessary paradigm is called *proprioception*; the technique is *yoga*.

2

PROPRIOCEPTION

Proprioception is a physiologically well-defined, but incompletely understood, source of internal experience. The word is compounded from two Latin roots: *proprio*, meaning "pertaining to oneself," and *cept-*, the past participle of *capio*, a verb meaning "to take" used in many English words, for instance, *conception* and *perception*. Thus, a proprioception is a "self take," with "self" here being understood to mean not the soul, not the mind, but the organism.

In humans, the proprioceptive nervous system comprises nerves extruded by the dorsal root fibers of the spinal cord.* The proprioceptive nervous system is the neurology of bodily feeling. By means of the proprioceptive system, your body is made known to your brain. A general, visceral experience—a proprioception—can be sensed by anyone with a minimum of concentration.

Proprioception is internal touch, but in the expansive sense of proprioception we are adopting, the term applies to how you see, hear, smell, and taste your body as well. In that manner, any sensory nerve, such as an optic or auditory nerve, can be redefined as proprioceptive whenever it is internally stimulated. Often, in fact, the sense of proprioception here implied is a kind of internal touch regardless of the sense involved. At times, however, it will be useful to have recourse to the restricted, textbook definition. Fortunately, there exists in the medical terminology an accepted synonym for conventionally defined proprioception known as *stereognosis*, which in Greek means approximately the same thing as "body knowledge" or "visceral feeling."

It has been known for some time that there are really only three kinds of brain neurons: sensory neurons, motor neurons, and the neurons of the intermediate network. In the most general case,

* If you happen to be a neurophysiologist, however, you will have to modify the standard medical-dictionary meaning of *proprioception* to apply it as broadly as in what follows.

sensory neurons sense stimuli arising in an organ of sensation such as the skin, motor neurons move muscles, and intermediate-net neurons pass information back and forth between them. Strictly speaking, the vast majority of sensory neurons is not part of the CNS. Neurons of the intermediate net are far and away the most numerous. Motor neurons comprise less than 0.03 percent of the CNS, about one neuron in three thousand.

Neural fibers that transmit signals *to* neurons of the CNS are known generally as *afferents*, of which there are many varieties: single dendrites, dendritic bundles, lemniscae, and so forth. Fibers transmitting signals *from* CNS neurons are called *efferents*, of which the single axon is the most important example. Sensory neurons are grouped in long, ascending and descending *tracts*.

The distinction between sensory and motor neurons has been inherited from nineteenth-century reflex-arc physiology, superseded since then by a more dynamic view of the brain. Neurophysiologists no longer definitively separate the two functions, save at the extremes. Many areas of the brain seem to serve both purposes. Intermediate neurons link motor neurons with other motor neurons, with other intermediate neurons, and are themselves densely interconnected. A special dendrite, known as the gamma (γ) afferent, is specifically linked with signals corresponding to stereognostic changes. The reticular formation extending from the base of the hindbrain into the midbrain interconnects so many fibers from so many sources—sensory, visceral, motoric—before passing them on to the cerebral cortex, the highest level of neurological functioning, that it is beyond the present capacity of neuroanatomists to sort them all. The reticular formation is thought to provide stimuli that create a basal, steady-state awareness in the cortex (from an electrical-engineering perspective, the reticular formation is a source of static).

Perhaps the most important neural center of internal awareness and control is the hypothalamus, located in the midbrain. The hypothalamus is linked (via the thalamus, a kind of central switching station) to the organs of sensation, the cortex, the viscera, and the endocrine system—in the latter case, directly to the pituitary gland. It regulates autonomic functions such as heart rate and coordinates them with desires and emotions like sex drive and rage.

In brief then, the greatest portion of the hard wiring of the brain functions to link the nervous system *internally*. Perhaps a hundred trillion synapses (neural junctions) tie the brain together. In theory, therefore, an indenumerably vast neuroanatomical potential for internal awareness is in place.

Experimental investigations of biofeedback in humans and animals over the past thirty-five years provide sufficient grounds for assuming that control of hyperaware states occurs predictably under a variety of conditions. To cite only one example, it has been conclusively demonstrated that animals can be taught to control many bodily functions such as heart rate, temperature, blood pressure, even the release of hormones, processes that have long been thought to be wholly autonomic.*

The neuroanatomical connections of your brain are never inactive, just as the reticular formation is never silent. The apparatus of awareness—nerves, brain, and so forth—are never "off," for that would involve awareness of nothing, which, apart from being logically meaningless, is to overlook the sound of one hand clapping, the aural equivalent of nothing: Channel 1. The general principle is important enough to state aphoristically: *The nervous system is dynamic.* It never turns off. If an external signal is absent, the nervous system naturally turns upon itself with undiminished potency. In terms that a physicist would use, we can say that awareness is conserved. It never experiences nothing, unless nothing be somehow reified, as static, for example.

* L. DiCara, "Learning in the autonomic nervous system," *Scientific American* 1970 (1): 30–39; N. Miller, "Learning of visceral and glandular responses," *Science* 163 (1969): 434–45; G. Fechner, *Elements of Psychophysics*, vol. 1, trans. H. E. Adler (New York, 1966); for a thorough bibliography, see E. Green and A. Green, *Beyond Biofeedback* (New York, 1977).

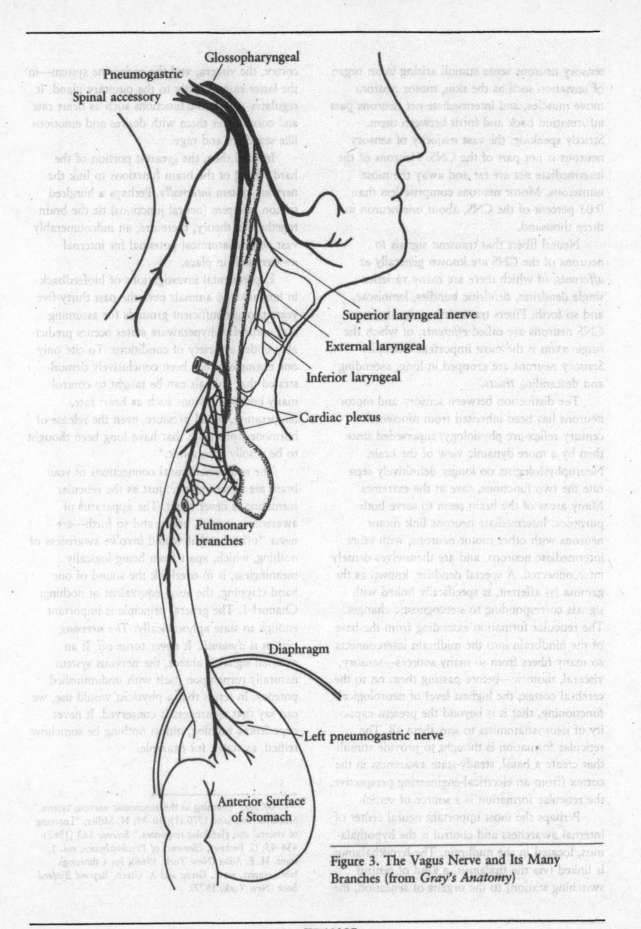

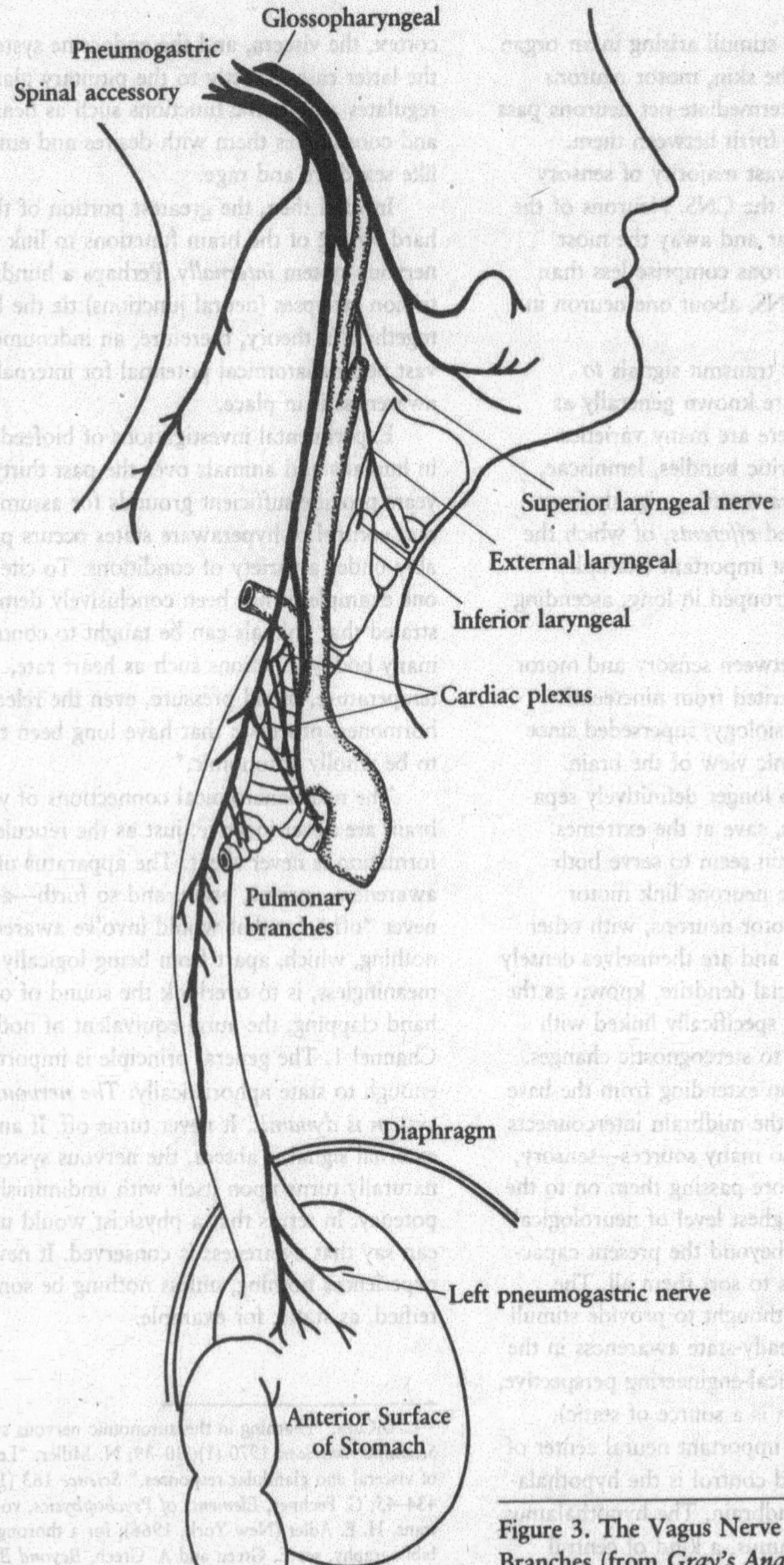

Figure 3. The Vagus Nerve and Its Many Branches (from *Gray's Anatomy*)

Only in death can we presume awareness of nothing, but because of the logical contradiction involved even in predicating such a state, it is *only* the barest presumption. To paraphrase Kant: If existence is not a predicate, neither is nonexistence. Yet a crucial distinction must be made. We are, each of us, intimately familiar with life, with consciousness. Death, however, considered as individual nonexistence, requires faith to affirm its reality, a perverse, malevolent faith, to be sure, but faith nonetheless.*

◆◆◆

The vagus nerve is the tenth cranial nerve. One of its many branches (rami) supplies nerves of sensation to the heart (figure 3). When, for instance, you feel a twinge in your heart, the sensation travels along a sensory ramus of the vagus nerve. Keeping in mind the fact of proprioception, let us look anew at the question, *Can you tell your heart when to beat?*

The Buddha once said, "Only fix your heart on one point and nothing is impossible to you."† The Buddha, we surmise, is not speaking of "fixing" the heart in some metaphorical sense but rather of literally stopping it at will. It is in a meditative context that the Buddha's remark must be interpreted.

Yet why stop the heart in the first place? What yogic aim does it serve? By now, the answer should be clear: *A heartbeat is a distraction.*

Only when the heart has voluntarily been stilled by the practice of a meditative technique is *kaivalya*, "liberation," attained.‡ In Eastern thought, liberation means salvation. Significantly, it follows on a single moment of absolute stillness within the organism.

* It is one thing to speak of a "dead body," because by it we mean no more than the absence of certain physical manifestations; it is another matter to speak of "dead awareness," to which no meaning whatsoever can be attached.

† *T'ai I Chin Hua Tsung Chih*, in: *The Secret of the Golden Flower*, trans. R. Wilhelm and C. F. Baynes, commentary by C. G. Jung (New York, 1962).

‡ *Yoga-Sūtra, Sādhana Pāda*, sutras 26 and 29, in *The Science of Yoga: Commentary on the Yoga-Sūtras of Patañjali*, 3d ed., trans. I. K. Taimni (Madras, 1968); *kaivalya* literally means "isolation."

3

SUBLIME TRANCE

Attending to the sound of one hand clapping demands *concentration*. Preferable to brow-furrowed concern, however, is a relaxed yet sincere desire to hear. We also need practice at shutting out distractions. Formal concentration is often called *meditation* and is practiced in quiet places having few distractions, where attention can be more easily focused.

When the degree of concentration becomes profound, the meditator is said to be in *trance*. Our word *trance* is derived from *transir*, an Old French word meaning "to go over"—euphemistically, "to die." In English one sometimes hears that a person has "passed away"; the original meaning of "trance" was quite similar. Trance should not be identified with hypnosis, an imprecise term for an involuntary state between waking and sleep. Meditative trance begins and ends voluntarily, and the meditator is intentionally aware of the object of his trance, namely, the focus of concentration.

No one is utterly ignorant of trance. Take, for instance, the common, everyday act of reading. Without concentration there is no comprehension of the printed word. Absent concentration, a word, a sentence, is a splotch of ink and nothing more. It has, perhaps, a "perceptual meaning": it can be seen, its shape can be distinguished from other shapes. But there is no comprehension. The act of reading without comprehension is something we are all familiar with, and usually it is associated with something called a "wandering mind," a lack of attention. It is merely a change in phraseology to equate such a state with the absence of trance. Conversely, to read is to entrance oneself.

In trance, one is not a zombie. Neither does one leave one's body, whatever that means. A *yogi*—someone trained in *yoga*, also called a *yogin* or, especially in mystic traditions, an *adept*—says that trance makes the meditator "one pointed-like." And thereby hangs the tale.

In Sanskrit, the language of yogic texts and the ancestor language of modern Hindi, the word yoga means "union," union with what Hindu sages call *brahman* or *puruṣa*.* One could not be blamed for identifying brahman with what we in the West call God; yet yoga is not a religion. Yoga can be reconciled with a comprehensive philosophy called *Sāṃkhya*. In Sāṃkhya philosophy, the supreme spirit—the puruṣa—is described first as undefinable, then—and in no particular order—as impersonal, omnipresent, all pervasive, omnipotent, eternal. Brahman-puruṣa is only defined privatively, namely, it cannot be demonstrated: it is not *this*, whatever this is; it is not *that*, whatever that is. Yet Sāṃkhya insists that it can be known, indeed, that it is obvious.

The insight of Indian philosophy, the contribution it has made to defining the human condition, is this: what can be said of brahman can be said of consciousness, and what cannot be said of brahman cannot be said of consciousness. Human consciousness, says Sāṃkhya, viewed as it were from inside out, is first of all undefinable, then impersonal, omnipresent, all-pervasive, omnipotent, eternal, not this, not that, undemonstrable, and yet all the while obvious (as obvious as knowing if you are awake or dreaming). Brahman pervades human experience. Therefore yoga: a practical method of experiencing your consciousness directly and per se, unmediated by any specifiable experience, any experience that is definable, personal, and transient, that is this, that, or the other thing. The union of yoga is therefore in the nature of a *re*union. Knowledge of brahman is the goal of yoga, but when the goal is achieved, knowledge of brahman *is* yoga. Yoga is not an "activity," and a yogi is not a hobbyist. That is not mere sanctimony or priest mongering. Yoga is no more an activity than is breathing. Breathing is definable, but it is not very personal and certainly not transient—at least not while you're alive—and certainly pervasive, potent, and obvious. Breathing is an analogy of brahman.† Logically enough, yoga takes breathing as the starting point on the road to brahman.

Yogis speak of different "yogas." Difference in yoga means difference in technique. The yogic term for technique, in the most general sense, is *kriyā*. Difference in kriyā means, perforce, difference in goals. All roads do not lead to Rome. All of yoga is not, as some believe, subsumed in mere exercise or body toning. Exercise yoga, called *haṭha* or "forced" yoga, is a collection of techniques originally intended to prepare a meditator for the demands of prolonged sitting, which is unavoidable in yoga but also rather wearisome for beginners. A dozen categories of yoga could be cited, all of them deriving from *tantra*, the vast, heterogeneous collection of Hindu spirit lore—some of it sublime, most simply superstitious—but in this book yoga means *rāja* (royal) yoga, the yoga of sublime trance, which is expounded with unsurpassed logic, subtlety, and precision in the *Yoga-Sūtra* of Patañjali (?200 B.C.–A.D. 100) and which, in varying degree, comprises all yogas.‡

Patañjali's seminal work is by far the most influential text of yoga ever written. In the same way that *Gray's Anatomy* has never been supplanted for its elegantly logical exposition of the human anatomy, the *Yoga-Sūtra* created a standard by which all other yogic treatises must be measured. Presented to the reader in the form of a string of aphorisms—the closest recognizable English analogue—the *Yoga-Sūtra* begins with simple yet incredibly compressed Sanskrit categories that are then decompressed, almost as if the book has self-inflated. What emerges from the aphorisms is trance craft, the practical science of ***sublime trance*** or ***samādhi***.

Just as important, Patañjali provides a consistent vocabulary for discussing trance. In

* *Brahman* is a term of *Vedānta*, the philosophy of the *Upaniṣads*. Puruṣa is a concept of Sāṃkhya, a nontheistic philosophical system; the two words are used interchangeably in this book. For a good discussion of the differences, see G. Feuerstein, *The Yoga-Sūtra of Patañjali* (Rochester, Vt., 1989), pp. 7–12.

† The two words have the same Indo-European root: **bhelgh-*.

‡ Tantra, yoga, and rāja yoga can be related, respectively, as family is to genus and species. The dates of Patañjali's life are imprecise because the authorship of the *Yoga-Sūtra* is disputed; two "Patañjalis," living almost three centuries apart, have been implicated. Scholarship favors a later date.

the *Yoga-Sūtra,* Patañjali dissects trance almost deductively, in a manner analogous to the step-by-step method Gray used to present anatomy. Categories are introduced one at a time and analyzed in greater and greater detail. For example, *dhāraṇā* (concentration) is but the first stage of *saṃyama,* an important catchall term summarizing the process of psychological absorption in the object of meditation. The second stage is *dhyāna* or "contemplation," which was transliterated first into the Chinese word *chan* when Buddhism spread eastward from India, then into Japanese as *zen.* (We have thus returned to the koān-type myths whence we started.) Samādhi is the third and final stage of saṃyama.*

The belief that practicing yoga makes you a sort of Hindu is a common Western prejudice. Hinduism is a loosely organized, traditional religion of India and Indonesia with which yoga coexists—but only imperfectly. To cite just one difference among many, Hindus worship more than three thousand gods and goddesses. Yoga, on the other hand, is possibly monotheistic, possibly nontheistic. One can be a perfervid atheist and still practice the most exalted forms of yoga. Words like *God, spirit,* and *soul* have a *practical* meaning in yoga. They refer to certain internal experiences that the yogi comes to recognize during his *sādhana*—his course of training. On the subject of those unfortunate dogmatic and philosophical controversies that have dominated the history of religion, the manuals of yoga are utterly silent.

In Western theology, "God," "spirit," and "soul" are primarily concepts, concepts that haunt theology. Far from being familiar in a practical sense, they are utterly unknowable, and—faute de mieux—theologians have embraced their unknowability wholeheartedly. Theology must stumble at the threshold of *praxis.* Nor is that an exclusively Western distinction. Modern Hinduism and Buddhism are agitated by endless philosophical discussion that answers to the name of theology, and yoga, as an independent, self-consistent approach to brahman, has been condemned for irreligiosity even in India.

Trance isn't Buddhism or Eastern mysticism either. It isn't antagonistic to rationality or intellect; neither is it at all alien to you. Whenever you daydream, you are in a kind of bargain-basement trance. You become "absorbed" in the object of your daydream. You are *in* trance *on* that object. You "lose touch" with your surroundings for a while; you "transit" to another reality—the world of your imagination—which seems qualitatively different from the world of the senses, the world "out there." Yoga is directly concerned with the world "in here," where you are when you read these words. By a painstaking systematization of the techniques of concentration, yogis discovered the universe within the body. Trance and the techniques for achieving sublime trance are the keys to enter that universe.

◆◆◆

The daunting notion of God as transcendent, ineffable, inconceivable, is probably of fairly recent coining, certainly within the past thirty-five hundred years. Such distancing phenomena are well known to historians of religion. Eight thousand years ago, on the other hand, our ancestors—at that time hunters and herders—did not equate divine with stupefying. In myth, divinity is so familiar, so embarrassingly human, it's often within range of contempt. The human model that a Greek god such as Zeus—who effects his will with a nod of the head—most nearly conforms to is that of shaman, the distant prototype of the god-man.

Shamanism has deep historic roots in central Asia. By the vedic Era (ca. 1000 B.C.), intentionally induced *shamanic ecstasy,* complete with initiatory rites, had long been established there.†

* *Yoga-Sūtra, Vibhūti Pāda,* sutras 1–6.

† M. Eliade, *Shamanism: Archaic Techniques of Ecstasy* (Princeton, N.J., 1964), pp. 33–66 and 375–465. Eliade's definition of a shaman comes down to his definition of *ecstasy:* the ability of the shaman to "abandon his body and undertake cosmic journeys," a far narrower definition than the one adopted here.

Ecstasy is a technical term, bound up with magical rituals far more often than it is with religion. We need not quibble over its precise meaning because ultimately it is comprehensible only within the spirit lore the shaman uses to induce his ecstasy, in other words, solely within the practical experience of the shaman himself. For our purposes, it is sufficient to recognize ecstasy as a form of samādhi that involves movement of the body, however slight.*

In yoga, ecstatic trance has been distilled into *enstasy* (sublime trance), a trance needing no fetishes—objects in which a desired power inheres—a trance from which an entire shamanic jargon, for instance, "leaving the body" or "magical flight," has been jettisoned. The transition is a consequence of the realization, over time, at once obvious and mysterious, that *all* experience occurs solely within the body. When the shaman holds his fetish, be it a spear, a ewer of water, or a tree limb, he feels first of all his own nervous system. The power or energy of the fetish is first of all apprehended within *his* neurology. Apart from that, it is the sheerest inference as to what he is feeling. Seizure of a fetish is analogous to pushing on a swing at the height of its arc, whence ensues the greatest velocity of motion. It is the proprioception that he desires to intensify at that moment with which a specific fetish, and no other, is somehow consonant.

Trance craft originated in ad hoc investigations of the "spirit world" by archaic shamans. A yoga ensued from tempering ecstatic Indo-European magical ritual with enstatic religious practices of the pre–Indo-European inhabitants of India, particularly southern India. Yoga draws whatever religious fidelity it may possess from the enstatic trance craft of the chthonic peoples. It is the ecstatic element that yoga shares with tantrism. But the tantric element is crucially important. Tantra means "that which extends [knowledge]."† In tantra, then, the *necessity* of technique, descended from fetishism, is unmistakable, and without technique there can be no yoga.

An analogy may help in understanding the origins of so curious a practice as deliberately passing into trance. Every child passes through a period of autistic and narcissistic self-awareness, fascinated by its own body. The child explores itself before it explores the world "out there." Myths are artifacts of human culture, probably of the infancy of culture, which in many ways parallels the infancy of an individual. Myth may be the inevitable by-product of *cultural autism*, meaning that the body itself becomes the central fetish and concern of culture. The petroglyphs of Australian aborigines are some of the oldest examples of primitive art in the world. A continuing theme of the earliest petroglyphs is the internal organs of the body, shown as if turned inside out, as though x-rayed; heart, lungs, kidneys, liver, and so on are clearly, almost scientifically, rendered. Given a natural environment that would not be mastered technologically for a thousand centuries, mastery of the body is not so surprising in a species as curious as ours.

The wealth of information characteristic of our own era has closed off as many doors as it has opened. We have knowledge. We do not have *gnosis*: the experience of sublime trance. Transiting to the innermost life of the organism is a function of the ability to control thinking; discursive thought is the single greatest distraction from trance. In turn, discursive thinking depends on language in the form of *voiceless speech*, what psychologists call the silent, wordlike form thoughts frequently take. The more one uses words—and we use lots of words nowadays—the more discursive our thinking gets, the more the "voice" in our head refuses to shut up. Absent an appetite for words inflamed by books, magazines, advertising, and our methods of education, the distraction of thinking is drastically reduced, and the transition to an awareness of inner life—not inner "talk"—is made accessible. Ironically, the supreme achievement of a human being may lie in his or her ability to remain absolutely quiet in mind, to not

* J. E. Kovach, "Contemplation and Movement: The Significance of Walking in Zen Meditative Practice" (Master's Thesis, UCLA, 1990) p.102.

† Eliade, *Shamanism*, p. 200.

do that which comes so easily to our species, which is to think.

Whereas it is the most natural thing in the world for us to identify with the mind and with the *I* that throughout our lives whispers to us "I am eating, I am seeing, I am John, I am Mary," on and on endlessly, archaic peoples saw "voiceless speech" as something as apart from them as what they saw with their eyes or heard with their ears. It was a mode of awareness (though they would not have put it that way) that was used and set aside and used and set aside far more readily than it is today. In paleolithic times (ca. 10,000 B.C.) there were no books, no TVs. Spoken language was less important—perhaps far less important, a lack naturally conducing to concentration and trance.

Archaic trance was the trance of intense concentration on activity rather than a distracted otherworldliness. Many activities of primitives are highly repetitive and rhythmic. When women sew garments or thresh and winnow grain, they often sit in a rhythmically moving group, often too accompanying the motion with singing and chanting. Rhythm eases labor, and rhythm can induce trance.* A trance rhythm may in fact be the most natural state of the human organism.

The archaic hunter must have had a superbly developed sensory apparatus, his eyes, ears, and nose acutely tuned to multiple stimuli. In a very real sense his survival depended on his senses. In the moment of stillness before closing with his quarry, even the breath was abated for extended—perhaps greatly extended—intervals of time. In yoga, any prolonged suspension of breathing leads naturally to a trance state. For those untrained in yoga or a similar discipline, the result is generally a swoon, a powerful, albeit uncontrolled, trance. Early "experiments" in concentration can be likened to controlled fainting spells during which the subject passes into trance but does not lose awareness of his surroundings or the capacity to act effectively. Indeed, for certain activities, his capabilities might have been enhanced.

◆◆◆

Hundreds of centuries ago, our ancestors discovered trance craft, practical meditative transitions in which all human beings can share. First-century Greek-speaking Christians called it *gnosis*, "knowledge," knowledge of the subliminal life of the body, of life below the threshold of perception. But gnosis has a history entirely antecedent to Greece and Christianity. The Hindus referred to it as yoga or tantra, the Hebrews called it wisdom, but the practices to which those terms refer are also far more ancient than either culture. We must suppose that it was systematized very gradually, and it was only over millennia that the majority of human beings lost access to the practical knowledge of the *spirit*. Even the knowledge that such a practice ever existed was lost, and today, most believers in God would probably say that death alone brings the BEATIFIC VISION. Yet the main reason for such a belief is the loss of the practical technique.

After the great Indo-European migrations from Asia to the Indian subcontinent began in about 3000 B.C., purely ecstatic Aryan rites were modified by *enstatic* chthonic religious beliefs preexisting in India. The result was the precursor to lamaism, tantrism, fakirism, and yoga, among which, for a long time, no sharp distinctions can be made.† We know little about the chthonic religion save that it occurred in the context of a highly advanced civilization known as the Indus Valley culture, which seems, on the available evidence, to have been peacefully agricultural. The arriving Indo-Europeans, on the other hand, were nomads, and by no stretch of the imagination could they be described as "civilized." If, however, as we are supposing, myth is a universal and predictable product of human awareness, even across sharply distinguished cultural groups, the common ground of spiritual practices is largely a priori and synthesis of traditions

* J. E. Kovach, "Contemplation and Movement," pp. 55–61.

† M. Eliade, *Yoga: Immortality and Freeedom*, 2d ed. (Princeton, N.J., 1969), pp. 318–59.

probably inevitable. The centrality of trance in the religion of both cultures—ecstatic in one, enstatic in the other—then served as a kind of bridge between them.

A precise, agreed-upon meaning for words like *concentration*, *contemplation*, and *trance*—as well as dozens of others—will be essential to deciphering the collection of archaic riddles called myth. So essential that, at length, we shall discover that an implicit description of yoga is at the bottom of all mythmaking.

In approaching archaic gnosis, we turn first to yoga because of its historical continuity with trance practice,* its unsurpassed clarity of presentation of its subject, and its intentional omission of explicitly religious matters, which makes its conclusions extremely general and applicable not only to shamanic practices but to the trance craft of all archaic religions. Patañjali wastes little time aestheticizing his work. There's nary a line of poetry. Indeed, every commentator on the *Yoga-Sūtra* has emphasized its mechanical, unadorned style. Patañjali himself calls his work simply an "exposition of yoga."†

Yoga is an *art*, in the old sense of the word. It is a craft. What was learned in the past was not learned "mystically."‡ Neither can faith alone lead to knowledge of the one god. Faith is a necessary but insufficient condition for gnosis. By comparison, it is far easier to learn to perform open-heart surgery by accident than to come to knowledge of the one god through good intentions alone. Surgical skill means mastery over specific, teachable techniques, including the arts of incision, suturing, the use of special tools such as scalpels and aspirators, and precise knowledge of human anatomy gained in many years of study and application. Similarly, mastery of yoga means mastery of technique. The hundreds of specific yogic techniques (kriyās) are teachable, specific, and unambiguous.

The Greek word for craft is *techne*, and as with all technology, a teacher—called a *guru*—is absolutely required in yoga, a teacher who was instructed before you, one link in the great chain of initiation into sublime trance that extends into prehistory. Moreover, the teacher must be a living teacher. The theodicy of a dead teacher like Jesus of Nazareth or Kṛṣṇa can be presented in scripture. Yet for the practical application of scripture, which, in the final analysis, is what is truly valuable in religion, a dead teacher is at best an inspiration, at worst a serious impediment, as the secular history of religion painfully demonstrates. "For the letter killeth, but the spirit giveth life."§ It is a puzzling irony that in all matters that concern us, from planting a garden to filing a tax return, we eagerly seek out a living, breathing person to show us practically what we need to know, but in the matter of knowing God, we essentially go it alone, with or without some especial book in hand, but nonetheless alone.

Patañjali was himself such a teacher, though he is long dead. The great Hindu philosopher and adept Śaṇkara (fl. ninth century A.D.), author of the *Crest Jewel of Discrimination*, the seminal document of Sāṃkhya philosophy, tells us he himself was initiated into yoga by Govinda. Neither man would countenance for a moment seeking initiation through their writings. In the *Yoga-Sūtra*, which is not so much esoteric as reticent on the subject of technique, a very great deal is left for the guru to explain to the sādhaka practically.

The most ancient figure of the teacher that has come down to us, in legend as well as fact, is the shaman. A shaman is not a priest, and the work of a shaman is often only an avocation. A shaman's special knowledge is of the spirit world. He knows strange and wonderful things. He knows, for instance, that to heal a wound you need a little piece of the weapon that caused the wound. He knows that at a certain phase of

* Ibid., pp. 311–29 and 341–58.

† Yoga-*Sūtra, Samādhi Pāda*, sutra 1.

‡ Unless by *mystical* is meant the plainly meditative sense of Gk. *myein* (μυειν): "to close up the senses." English *mystic* derives from Gk. *mystes* (μυστης, nominal of μυειν): "one who has closed [the eyes]." Cf., Matthew 13:11; Jesus describes the true gospel, revealed solely to the Apostles, as *mysteria*.

§ 2 Corinthians 3:6.

the moon embryos cannot be procreated. He knows that if he washes with water a steer has wallowed in, the water will make him like a steer: strong, stubborn, and dependable—at least for a while. He can "empty his mind" and go into trance, when he sees and hears spirits. He is mantic—he knows the future—but never in a simple-declarative way. When a member of an archaic tribe or clan felt the need to know about such things, he asked the shaman, and the basic paradigm has persisted in "primitive" cultures to this day.

A shaman knows such things as a chemist knows the formulas for making aqua regia or stannous chloride. And like most chemists he has personally discovered very little of what he knows. Much of it was taught to him by another shaman, particularly the techniques for emptying the mind to achieve ecstatic trance. Because we are placing the body at the center of our theory, a degree of genetic predisposition for "falling into trance" plays a not insignificant role. Thus, a succession of Indo-European shamans often is made up of father-to-son transmissions of shamanic lore that, in time, institutionalize extended-family groups like the archaic Eumolpids of Attica and the *cohanim* of Judaism, the tribe of Levi.

PART TWO

MYTH

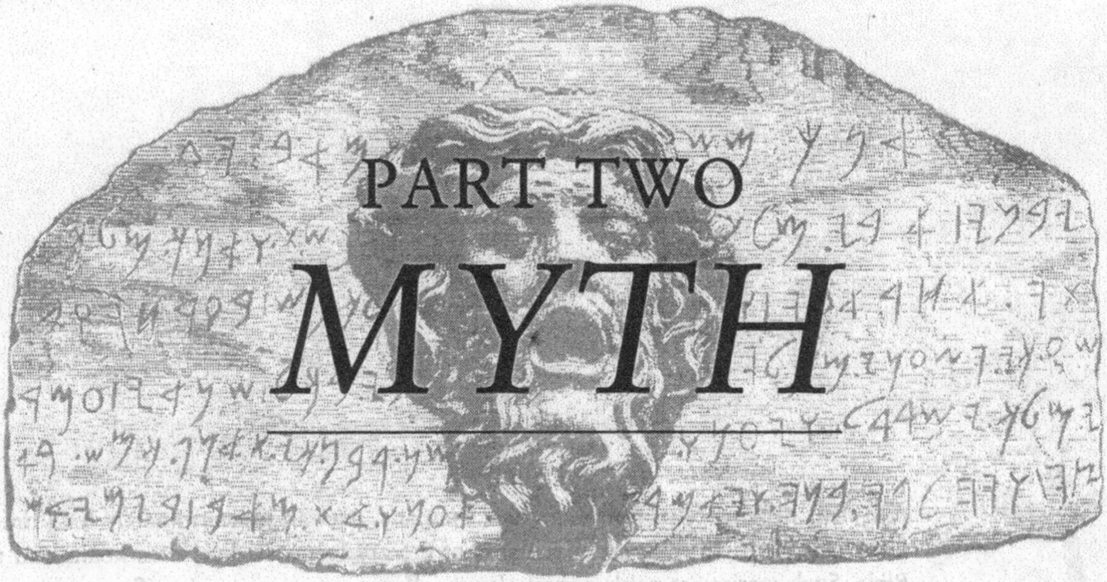

4

WHAT IS A MYTH?

From their experience of trance, archaic shamans, over an indeterminately long time, fashioned the myths that are precursors of literary forms as diverse as koāns and the Bible. Such stories are neither symbols nor allegories nor protoscientific statements. The use of metaphor and allegory—not to mention deliberate paradox—are sophisticated literary tropes that appear relatively late in cultural history, certainly not before the Antique Era. Riddles, by contrast, derive from archaic wordplay in which all people, from the most advantaged to the most primitive, take delight. And making up riddles jibes rather well with what is known about archaic modes of thought, which were concrete and expressed through tale-telling.

Myths can be likened to primitive catechisms, lessons prefatory to initiation. During initiation, the meanings of tribal legends heard by the initiates since childhood were made clear. In fact, *myths might originally have been intended for the entertainment of children.*

In plain language, myths were originally *fairy tales*, with which they've been intimately linked by scholars more than once. And adults who enjoy mythology implicitly recognize the connection. During rites of initiation, which, among the Indo-Europeans at least, was reserved for adolescent males, the practical, esoteric sense of the "fairy tale" was demonstrated by the elders of the clan in a closed conventicle.

The mythic form inevitably outgrew its original function, which was to prepare children for rites of passage that included trance craft almost, it seems, as a birthright. The Old Testament tale of Jacob and Esau, in which the latter is tricked into giving up his right as eldest to Isaac's "blessing," might mean that among the ancient Hebrews the "wisdom" passed from father to eldest male child, conformal with a right of primogeniture and, in fact, the original substance of primogeniture. Similar traditions existed in Latin, Greek, and Hindu society—all Indo-European. In general though, as society evolved, the age of initiation was postponed. Plato, an Athenian of the early fourth century B.C., taught that the ideal age to begin the practice of "wisdom" was thirty-five, when the passions of youth begin to subside.

In time, initiation ceased even to be a matter of right. When he was about to die atop Mount Nebo, Moses took Joshua apart from the rest of the Israelites: "And Joshua the son of Nun was full of the spirit of *wisdom*; for Moses had laid his hands upon him: and the *children* of Israel harkened unto him."* Jesus often refers to "the children" in this special sense, namely, the unbaptized. To enter into the KINGDOM OF GOD, which elsewhere he says lies within us, you must become as a little child, "for of such is the kingdom of God."†

Myth made its way into the canonical Christian scriptures much altered by the uninitiated, however. It is difficult to know just what is myth and what history in the Koran, for instance, a work of the seventh century A.D. The New Testament, apart from the Epistles, is probably all myth, perhaps the most sublime myth ever put into words, notwithstanding the marvelous poetry of the *Iliad*, the *Odyssey*, and portions of the Old Testament. Myth is at the core of Genesis, especially, as well as Exodus, Deuteronomy, Psalms, Proverbs, and Canticles, but also Judges, Isaiah, Micah, both books of Samuel, and Ezekiel.

◆◆◆

To discern the origins of myth, we must pierce a veil around our subject, a veil of opinions cast by philosophy, particularly Greek philosophy. Our understanding of hellenic philosophy—the philosophy of the classical period (the late fifth century B.C.), relatively late on the time horizon of Greek philosophy—unfortunately is biased in the direction of figures such as Plato and Aristotle because so little antecedent material has survived. Both men, and particularly Aristotle, are the culmination of much philosophical thinking among Greeks before their time. Greek philosophical inquiry started with the so-called presocratic philosophers, who straddle the demarcation of the archaic from the antique in history. The theories of Milesian Presocratics like Thales and Anaximenes concern themselves with questions of what was once called "natural philosophy," which is to say *science*. In the classical era Plato and Aristotle decisively turned the argument toward philosophy in the conventional sense: how human beings should live in harmony with the natural world. In brief, the Presocratics speculated about what the world was made of, the Postsocratics (Plato, Aristotle) assembled the world teleologically, in other words, toward a desired end (Gk. *telos*, "goal").

Intermediate to the Presocratics and Plato was Anaxagoras of Clyzomenæ (ca. 530–428 B.C.), who introduced into Greek philosophy what he called *nous* (< Gk. *noös*, "mind," a concept much used by later philosophers), as the organizing and directing principle of the world teleology. Only fragments of his work have survived, quoted by later writers including Aristotle, but those fragments are enough to suggest that Anaxagoras is the unsung genius of Hellenism.

We know from Plato that Socrates attended the lectures of Archelaus, Anaxagoras's pupil. Socrates objected to Anaxagoras's philosophy on the grounds that it was mechanical and ipso facto not interested in teleology,‡ which is by way of underscoring Anaxagoras's intermediate place in Greek thought. More relevant are Anaxagoras's ideas about physical sensation, in which the senses transmit messages to the nous.§ An apt image is that of a Coney Island cutout, in which the customer sticks his or her head into the cardboard body of a strongman or bathing beauty. Just so, the anaxagorean nous peers into the world through the senses, a concept of perception that is thoroughly archaic. An archaic human being, the evidence suggests, pictured

* Deuteronomy 34:9 (emphasis added).

† Luke 18:16–17.

‡ Plato, *Phædo* 98, in: *Plato: Euthyro, Apology, Crito, Phædo, Phædrus*, trans. H. N. Fowler, (Cambridge, Mass., 1911).

§ Ascribed to Anaxagoras by Theophrastus of Lesbos (d. ca. 287 B.C.), *De sensu* 38. For a thorough treatment of extant fragments, see F. M. Cleve, *The Philosophy of Anaxagoras* (New York, 1949).

himself as a spirit inhabiting and animating a body. But the nous is itself susceptible to proprioceptive scrutiny by the *psyche* or soul. Thus cognition too is externalized in archaic psychology.

Analogous to the intermediacy of Anaxagoras in Greek philosophy is the mythopoet Homer (fl. ?800 B.C.), an Ionian Greek who bridges the gap between the Archaic and Antique eras. The poetic tradition of Homer is oral, descended from ecstatic glossolalic trance states often found in shamanism. He competed for bardic honors all along the "sacred way" from Delphi to Delos, both the site of Sybilline oracles, sacred to Apollo, who prophesied while in trance.*

A distinction between body and soul is recognized by Homer, but it is an essential distinction, not one of function. The human organism as conceived by Homer differs radically from the rigorous modern view in being simultaneously material *and* spiritual. Material because concretely expressed in frequent mention of the several organs of the body. In Homer, we are given a portrayal of men to whom all experiences come as from without, not just sights and sounds but thoughts, dreams, fear, courage, the gods. Homer would not say, for instance, that Hector (a Trojan prince) "was afraid," but rather "his knees were loosened"; not "he was happy," but "he smiled." Hector is never "angry"; rather, "his heart burns within him." He cannot even die: "His limbs were loosed and his soul departed to Hades." Homeric man is simultaneously spiritual because the connectivity of his soul—or identity—to experience is not necessary to the soul's existence. In our everyday speech, we share a great deal in common with the archaic conception;† but predicate-adjective constructions like "was happy" or "is angry" are wholly modern. They betray an integrative conception of human identity that was radically foreign to the ancients and largely absent from those texts that have come down to us; and the more ancient the text (for example, the Egyptian *Book of the Dead*) the harder it is to find substantive usage. A human being in Homer is a human body: the locus of experience. Clearly, such an attitude is both a prerequisite and a spur to proprioceptive awareness, which takes for its starting point the notion of the disjunction of knower and known even as it extends to the knowledge apparatus of the knower.

Patañjali calls the ability to withdraw the mind from sensation, whatever its source, *pratyāhāra*, "abstraction." It is, he says, "an imitation by the senses of the mind by withdrawing themselves from their objects. . . . Then follows the greatest mastery over the senses."‡

We now ask: How great is "greatest"? What is the limit of proprioceptive awareness? That is the crux of the matter. How far can one go along the path of, for example, "telling" the heart when to beat? Meditation can be compared to a radical emptying of awareness. When sensations, emotions, and thoughts have been eliminated, suppresssed, or simply ignored, the awareness of the meditator turns naturally upon the "resting voltage" of the CNS (among other things). And here one might plausibly respond "So what?" The only reply is that one first must practically empty out one's own awareness to see just *what* is then revealed. Saṃyama is immersion in the object of trance to the exclusion of all else, and the result of onepointed

* The sacred way possibly was the residuum of the original route of immigration of Indo-European Hellenes into the Mediterranean from the north, through Thessaly. From there they dispersed eastward into Ionia, the Ægean littoral, and usurped the shrines of conquered chthonic races collectively known to Homer as Pelasgians. See Gladstone, *Studies on Homer and the Homeric Age*, vol. 1, pp. 200–206.

† We say "heartache" when we mean sorrow, "glad hand" for welcome, "bright eyed" for intelligent, etc. Our orthodox science, however, is wholly materialist and so dismisses the very notion of a disembodied soul as semantic confusion. The problem was noted by Kant (d. 1804), who, typically, posed the obvious yet penetrating question: If there is no soul inhabiting the body—peering out, as it were, into the world—why are the eyes shaped like focusing lenses? A television set needs no lens to process its signals into a visible image even though its stimulus to action is fundamentally the same as the optical stimulus that activates the retina, namely, an EM wave.

‡ *Yoga-Sūtra*, *Sādhana Pāda*, sutras 54–55.

immersion is *realization*. In the same way that concentration on ink inscribed upon a page leads to comprehension of meaning in words, intense concentration on the resting voltage of the CNS blossoms into spontaneous realization of the meaning that pervades one's own biology. The realization cannot be anticipated, but the testimony of religion is that it is, at a bare minimum, one of blissful satiety. This, in brief, is the "good news" of the gospels: What we seek is already ours! Its subliminal proximity, like the carrot dangled over the ass's nose, provokes the myriad aspirations of our species.

Two related items should be mentioned at once:

1. Achieving total control over one's heart requires a high degree of awareness of the body and its innermost workings.
2. Detailed awareness of the body is essential in practicing yoga.

Yogic techniques concentrate awareness. To control the heart to the point of "telling" it when to beat, a yogi's internal awareness must increase to where the entire vagus nerve can be isolated consciously. In other words, the yogi is able to single out the experience of the vagus nerve from the complex of neural sensation in his chest. Not only can the yogi experience the vagus nerve in and of itself, but by means of neurological connections to the vision area of the brain at the back of the skull, he or she can even visualize the nerve. The common ability to visualize the shape of an object with eyes closed simply by holding it indicates that the required neurological connectivity exists within us, and the topologically refined nature of that capability means that the associated neurology is dense and extensive rather than rudimentary and narrowly functional. As we have seen, the neurology of the body is far more directed at keeping the human being internally aware than externally so.

Is such a visualization a myth? And if so, what myth is it? Our answer is that it is not a single myth but refers to an entire genre of myth: SLAYING THE KRAKEN, or sea monster.

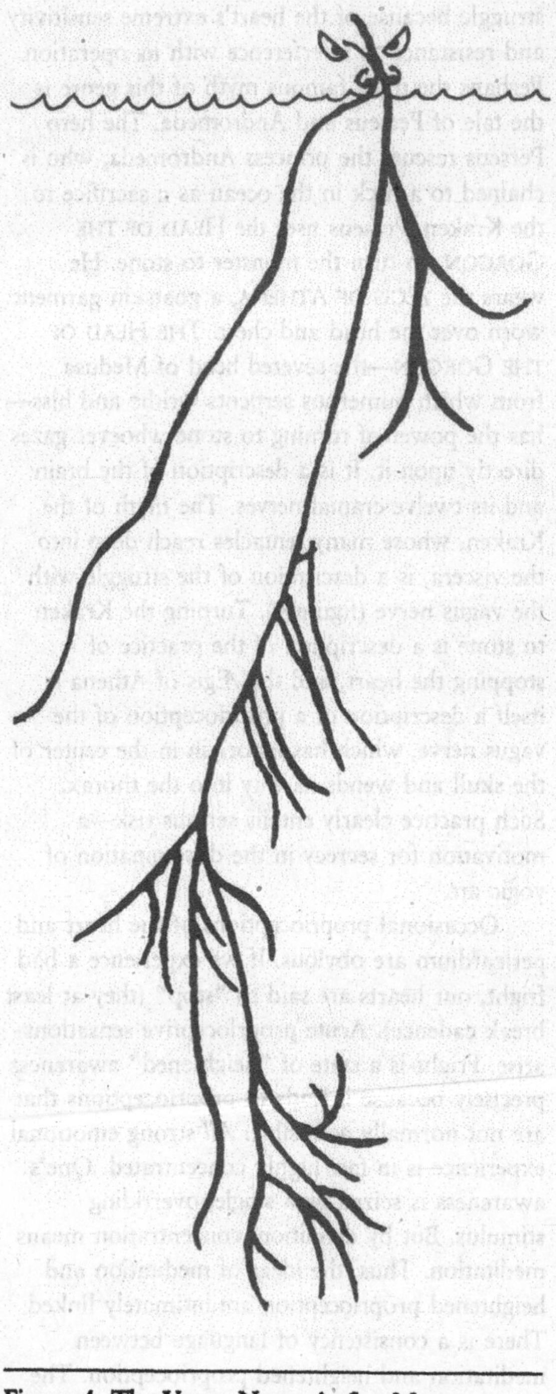

Figure 4. The Vagus Nerve As Sea Monster

Why?

While controlling his heartbeat, the yogi controls the resting voltage within the vagus nerve. The effort can fairly be described as a struggle because of the heart's extreme sensitivity and resistance to interference with its operation. Perhaps the most famous myth of this genre is the tale of Perseus and Andromeda. The hero Perseus rescues the princess Andromeda, who is chained to a rock in the ocean as a sacrifice to the Kraken. Perseus uses the HEAD OF THE GORGON to turn the monster to stone. He wears the ÆGIS OF ATHENA, a goatskin garment worn over the head and chest. THE HEAD OF THE GORGON—the severed head of Medusa from which numerous serpents writhe and hiss—has the power of turning to stone whoever gazes directly upon it. It is a description of the brain and its twelve cranial nerves. The myth of the Kraken, whose many tentacles reach deep into the viscera, is a description of the struggle with the vagus nerve (figure 4). Turning the Kraken to stone is a description of the practice of stopping the heart, and the Ægis of Athena is itself a description of a proprioception of the vagus nerve, which has its origin in the center of the skull and wends its way into the thorax. Such practice clearly entails serious risk—a motivation for secrecy in the dissemination of yogic art.

Occasional proprioceptions of the heart and pericardium are obvious. If we experience a bad fright, our hearts are said to "stop" (they at least break cadence). Acute proprioceptive sensations arise. Fright is a state of "heightened" awareness precisely because it leads to proprioceptions that are not normally accessible. *All* strong emotional experience is in fact highly concentrated. One's awareness is seized by a single, overriding stimulus. But by definition, concentration means meditation. Thus, the ideas of meditation and heightened proprioception are intimately linked. There is a consistency of language between meditation and heightened proprioception. The same words apply to both concepts. Meditation is heightened proprioception. Meditation on the vagus nerve leads to one myth, on another nerve or organ to another myth.

We can now define a myth scientifically:

Axiom I: A myth is an esoteric description of a heightened proprioception.

In the course of this book, we shall collect a number of such "axioms," the aim of which is to provide a concise summary of the hermeneutics of myth.

Not every heightened proprioception is encoded as a myth, only those describing an important "spiritual" practice. Myths were composed because they were descriptions of the primitive, mythmaking, proprioceptive consciousness from which the species has evolved and to which, by means of your nervous system, you yourself are still very much linked. A mythology based in *description* differs crucially from symbolical, allegorical, and rationalist mythologies because all such approaches seek to create a *metalanguage*, an interpretive architecture that at best parallels the meaning of myth. If, however, as we are suggesting, myths describe in detail the very organism that created them, a metalinguistic approach must fail. A description is not a metalanguage for the entity described; it is a *transcription*. Myths make use of the special knowledge of our bodies' life processes to tell us about ourselves, about who we are and whence we have come.

◆◆◆

A thorough study of myth must also examine the motivation to invent a myth. Yet the purpose that myth serves, the various *whys* of myth—which are invariably found in the context of esoteric religion—must not be confused with the *how*.

Human beings always have inquired and ever will inquire into the meaning of their existence. At times, in places, their inquiry took the shape of philosophy, sometimes exalted, sometimes skeptical, often trivial. At other times, in other places, the inquiry was religious or scientific. But long before philosophy, religion, or science, when all over the globe our species was awakening to that special, uniquely human self-awareness, an awareness of self was part of an internal awareness of the body of myth.

It is a tenet of this book that the art of entering into sublime trance (samādhi) has *not* survived in the principal religions of mankind. It is not central to modern Christianity, Judaism,

Islam, and so on; neither is it peripheral. It is simply and wholly absent from religion. It has been lost. Yet its influence can be found wherever one looks in history or in scripture. Since the work of Aldous Huxley, archaic gnosis has often been called the "perennial philosophy," a profound misnomer because in its origins it is not a philosophy but a technique having only secondary and, as always, ambiguous philosophical implications.

Revelation in the sense of a sudden, demarcating dispensation from on high is a chimera. First glimpsed, we must suppose, by archaic shamans, the inner kingdom was not revealed or even understood all at once (what in human enterprise ever is?). Analogously, twenty-four hundred years ago Archimedes worked out the laws of simple levers, inclined planes, and primitive pulleys. Then, two hundred years ago, James Watt built the steam engine, an intricate concretization of all that was known at the time about the relationship of force and motion. The one device is the lineal descendant of the others. What was the source of archimedean inspiration? Was it simple practicality? Was it curiosity? Was it idleness? We do not know. Neither are we ever likely to know conclusively what put Patañjali's shamanic forerunners on the course of study he eventually epitomized. But we do know one thing. It all began long before Archimedes was born.

Yogis don't talk much about their experiences and probably would not speak of them or understand them as decrypted myths even if they did. The era of mythmaking has ended; the texts of yoga, broadly interpreted as trance craft, long ago superseded it.

The late English novelist Christopher Isherwood, who practiced yoga devotedly, wrote a highly readable commentary on Patañjali. He titled it *How to Know God* precisely because this is what the *Yoga-Sūtra* most closely approximates in both form and content: a manual of divinity, like the manual of arms or how to fix your Volkswagen. Patañjali uses words like *God* and *soul* as if they were clearly apprehensible objects of experience. Is that to trivialize God and religion? Or is it to open up our understanding to an entirely new sense of godhood? The sense intended by myth and scripture all along: *God as experience itself*.

Myth describes, it does not symbolize. It does not allegorize or rationalize. Myth describes a systematic exploration of the human body by privileged members of archaic cultures. Myth springs from an age of universal narcissism, rooted, one must suppose, in the elemental struggle for survival. The course of evolution has placed the sources of mythopœsis in an all but irretrievable epoch. The human body, in its stubborn resistance to change, is all that we wholly share with half-savage poets unknown to Homer. That the elemental immediacy of the archaic rhapsodists is lost to us, that we have inherited their stories only as "literature," is as ironic as it is lamentable.

We must carefully distinguish myth from magic, in particular from the vast magical lore of so-called modern primitives. Myth and magic are both spirit lore. But, to borrow an analogy from grammar, magic is in the imperative mood. Magic is ad hoc, fashioned in expediency. Magic says "do this and that results." Magic is spirit manipulation. The magician knows that the "spirit world" can leverage the material world. Emotion and motion can be homologized.* Desire, in other words, can literally move matter.

In magic, desire cannot become fact without the shaman performing some action, however trivial seeming, that his desires serve hypostatically, that is, beneath the surface of things. To work his magic the shaman must fetishize his desire. He snatches up a knife, breaks a stick, chants, kills an animal and smears his limbs with blood and fat—the possibilities are as endless as they are inscrutable to someone not sharing in the hypostatic desire. Desire subtends action, and the subtensive form that results is in the nature of a technique.

Myth, by contrast, is subjunctive, suggestive, and indirect. Myth is *intentionally* mysterious.

---

* Kovach, "Contemplation and Movement," pp. 102–3; the accouterments of ecstasy are its material goals and techniques, all of which entail movement.

Something is being described in myth, something about the human body, something essential to its workings but also truly technical and beyond mere fetish: "the wisdom in the inward parts."* What is described is described obliquely. What we find, in Homer at least, is a different specimen of spirit lore from that of the *Golden Bough*. In Theocritus it is another genus altogether. The spirits are still there, the important ones apotheosized into the Olympian gods, the lesser ones demi-deified as nymphs, fauns, and satyrs. But a sacral essence has emerged, sacral because within every spirit another spirit is apprehended, if only dimly: the spirit of spirits. And with the sacred comes awe, mystery, and a seemingly unavoidable circumspection.

The sense of the sacred accompanying the transition from magic to myth introduces an entirely new cultural category into the equation: religion. Religion qua religion takes for granted not only the spirit world but, and vehemently, that the spirits are benevolent, though nonetheless fearsome—that they are in essence one *Spirit*, "one without a second," which is all-powerful, all-knowing, and propitiable. Crude distortions can be found in purely magical rituals, but trust in a benevolent Spirit is the very life of religion.

The religious impulse having taken hold, magic, along with everything else, can be valorized, divided into black magic and white magic. In broadest terms, then, white magic serves the Spirit; white magic creates myth and religion and protects the gods from ourselves and ourselves from the gods. Happiness in the Spirit displaces mere survival. Black magic is only about survival. If, however, their origins, techniques, and practices derive from the body as much as from the mind, as we are supposing, magic and religion have a great deal in common, so that to know how to practice one is to know how to practice the other. Therefore, white magic, the *protognosis* of the one god, must be kept secret.

The development of myth parallels the esoteric impulse in storytelling. From being fairy tales and childish diversions, myths came to carry a burden of meaning for adults. As the religious sense took hold, the duty to keep secret certain aspects of what had been learned of the godhead during trance established itself undislodgeably. We must confess that there is no single overriding reason why that must occur, but even so, esoterism, whatever the reasons, was fact in both the Archaic Era and antiquity.

* Job 38:36.

5

GRECO-ROMAN ESOTERISM

Myths are riddles. Or perhaps it would be more accurate to say that myths are more like riddles than they are like anything else. The urge to symbolize experience is a thoroughly modern vice. Archaic shamans used myth to *describe* the experience of trance—albeit in a veiled way. Myths are cleverly worded, culture-laden descriptions of samādhi. They may have been intended to edify those who already "had ears to hear" or entertain those who did not. In the event, the decision was left to spiritual leaders.

All over the globe, down to the present era, socioreligious rites of passage have taken place when members of a tribe reached a certain age; often that age coincides with puberty. Rites of passage were especially important to the cohesion of tribe and clan, and scrupulous vigilance ensured they were not undertaken lightly or halfheartedly. Even today, the initiatory ceremonies of many American Indian tribes of the southwestern United States are jealously guarded, as is also the case in literally hundreds of societies throughout Africa, Asia, Oceania, and Australia. To what degree the modern form of such rites preserves intact the archaic esoteric wisdom is an intriguing question, and an unanswerable one at present. But whatever else they are—or were—the initiatory rites of most "modern primitives" have remained militantly esoteric.

Myth as riddle or parable is a literary definition. It would be ridiculous to argue, however, that the priest class was an antique creative-writing class or that it spent its time making up myths as a hobby. A formally constituted priest class is strongly correlated with formal temples. The oldest extant Greek temples are votive models from Perachora dating at the earliest from only the eighth century B.C., roughly the time of the composition of the *Iliad*. (No Minoan temples have ever been found on Crete, whose fourteenth-century B.C. culture was a seminal influence on the Greeks.) We therefore suspect that such a group did not exist in the mythopoetic age of the Greeks, as is evidenced by the paucity of references to them in myth.*

* Homer does not seem to know about Greek priests or temples, only Trojan ones.

One of the many beauties of ancient mythopœsis is that it encodes its lessons within the prosaica of the world. It disguises trance using mundane images, which conform with the sublime inner journey of the hero. The contemplative life can simultaneously be an active one; concentration on breathing depends not at all on one's occupation or lack of it. To pay reverent attention to breathing while active is to practice what Kṛṣṇa, in the *Gīta*, calls *karma* yoga (< Skt. *karma*, "action"). Karma becomes *dharma* (duty)—a Buddhist adage.

The priests from the classical era on, however, whether or not they understood the esoteric significance of their myths—and we must assume that at least some of them did—were custodians of a tradition, the oldest expressible part of which, the myths themselves, antedated the priesthood's own special function. That does not imply that myths were less esoteric prior to the development of such a class, only that a priest class arose from and in harmony with the population at large—among farmers, fishermen, and warriors—and that the shaman, from whom we suppose the priest descended, originally was a working member of a working society. It is likely that trance craft was first engaged during the repetitive motions of everyday labor. The ancients may have been idol worshipers but they were certainly not idle worshipers!

Acknowledged to possess a special wisdom denied the populace at large, the priests and priestesses of antiquity were a cloistered class. Pagan temples were strictly out of bounds and were hemmed by a ring-pass-not called the *fane*—whence comes our word *profane*, literally meaning "in front of the temple" and by extension secular, worldly, and not privy to the secrets of the god. The elitism of a formal priest class is a logical outgrowth of the practicality of trance craft, at which, as with everything else in life, some individuals are better than others, in the sense that they are more devoted to actually doing it, have better concentrative powers, and so forth. The existence of a priest caste, wherever it occurs, is an infallible sign of *esoterism*, "deliberate secrecy," regardless of whether one is speaking about the pagan Mysteries of Eleusis, Christian baptism, Zoroastrianism, Hinduism, or Buddhism.

Ancient priests were not arbitrarily exclusionist. Every good reason for secrecy comes down to the practicality of meditation. Practicality means fallibility; it means sometimes getting it all wrong. Knowledge of secret rites in and of itself does not confer sanctity upon the knower. Abuses have undoubtedly occurred. New Testament accounts of the persecution of Jesus, even if not actually a myth in themselves, reflect a lethal tension between those with knowledge of secret rites but unwilling to share them and those who wished to baptize freely: "Ask and it shall be given you; seek and ye shall find; knock and the door shall be opened unto you."* Jesus compared the Pharisees to dogs in a manger. "You do not eat, neither do you suffer others to eat."

Once placed into circulation, however, individual myths have been put to exotic uses by the uninitiated in both antiquity and the present. The Latin poet Virgil, for instance, in his *Æneid*, used the homeric legends to support an imperialist conceit that Rome was the heir to Troy. Early fathers of the Church and medieval monks alike struggled to find in Apollo or Hermes a forerunner of THE CHRIST. The subject matter of art during the Renaissance was mostly myth, the bulk of which had only recently been translated from moldering manuscripts. Less than a century ago Freud took an obscure legend, that of Œdipus—which would have avoided undue notice had Sophocles not used it as the source for several wonderful plays—and put it to work as nothing less than the basis for a theory of the human mind. Speculation of that sort has gone on for millennia and doubtless will continue, but it more properly belongs to the study of cognition in general, how people hypothesize and fantasize, not how they contrived authentic myth.

The earliest Greek thinker with unmistakable esoteric earmarks was Pythagoras of Samos, who established a school of philosophy in Magna Græcia (southern Italy) in the sixth century B.C. Even in antiquity, *pythagorean* meant fanatically occult. The Pythagoreans were sworn to secrecy

* Matthew 7:7.

regarding the doctrines of the master, including a belief in reincarnation that he is said to have inherited from his master, Pherecydes. Most interesting is a fact preserved by the neoplatonic philosopher Proclus (d. A.D. 485) that Pythagoras conducted two sorts of philosophical lectures: an esoteric one to which only members of the sect were admitted, the other exoteric (not secret) for the populace at large. Herodotus, a generally reliable Greek historian of the fifth century B.C., reports that Pythagoras himself studied secret rites in Egypt, Mesopotamia, and India and that he could hear the "music of the spheres." It was Pythagoras who discovered the mathematical structure of the diatonic scale of music. He explained the harmony between notes in the scale as a function of the ratios of the wavelengths associated with each tone, similar to the principle of a tuned antenna in our earlier discussion of cosmic-background static, although it deals with acoustical rather than electromagnetic waves.

In the voluminous writings of Plato one finds a remarkable blend of mythic allegory and philosophy with esoteric overtones—for example, his famous story of the CAVE, which nowadays is interpreted nearly universally as an allegory of pure reason but more likely preserves an archaic description of the human skull. At the very end of the *Crito*, while he argues that it is far better for him to die than to escape, Socrates speaks about the "ringing in the ear of the mystic." Both Plato and Socrates, his mentor, were almost certainly initiated at Eleusis, and both were also heavily influenced by Orphism, a species of mysticism complete with secret initiation, whose origins lie in Asia Minor. Throughout the platonic dialogues, Socrates insists that there is a distinction between philosophy and "philosophy rightly understood," meaning esoterically. Apollonius Rhodius, writing of Jason and the Argonauts, tells us they sought initiation on Samothrace that "they might learn the secret rites. . . . Of these things will I speak no further . . . of them tis not right for us to sing."* A hundred examples of similar reticence regarding the various mysteries of antiquity could be cited.†

Celebrations of pagan mysteries occurred annually at Delphi, sacred to Apollo, and on the Ægean island of Delos, sacred to both Apollo and his twin sister Artemis. The most famous esoteric rites of antiquity were the Mysteries of Eleusis—also known as the Eleusinia—in honor of the goddess Demeter and her daughter, Persephone, celebrated in a sanctuary on a "sacred way" near Eleusis (long ago an independent polity but by historical times a subject state of Athens). In the very old *Homeric Hymn to Demeter*, we learn that Demeter

Showed the conduct of her rites and
Taught them all her mysteries, to
Triptolemus
And Polyxenus and Diocles also—awful
Mysteries which no one may in any way
Transgress or pry into or utter, for deep
Awe of the gods checks the voice. Happy is
He among men upon earth who has seen
these
Mysteries; but he who is uninitiate and
who
Has no part in them, never has lot of like
Good things once he is dead, down in the
Darkness and gloom.‡

The message is unambiguous and as close as archaic Greek religion gets to *soteriology* or salvation doctrine: either one knows the secret rites and is saved or one does not and is doomed. Humanity is divided into two groups, and there is no appeal from it; but what might be the meaning of "good things" is obscure save that they are likened to the experience of an initiate.

* Apollonius Rhodius, *Argonautica* 1.900–27, in *Apollonius Rhodius*, trans. E. P. Coleridge (London, 1889).

† So often, in fact, that ancient writers occasionally used the formulaic *"Silence!"* humorously, e.g., Iphigenia's attempt to befuddle Thoas in Euripides' *Iphigenia in Tauris*, in: *Euripides: Collected Works*, vol. 2, trans. W. Brynner (Chicago, 1955), 1180–84.

‡ *Homeric Hymn to Demeter*, in: *Hesiod and the Homeric Hymns*, trans. H. G. E. White (Cambridge, Mass., 1977), 470–82.

Beginning in the Bronze Age and continuing down to the fourth century A.D., Eleusis was the destination of pilgrims—men, women, even children—from all over the Mediterranean. Marcus Aurelius (d. A.D. 170), probably the noblest Roman emperor of them all, was initiated at Eleusis. The Roman poet Horace (d. 8 B.C.) cautioned that "there is a sure reward for trusty silence. I will forbid the man who has divulged the sacred rites of mystic Ceres"—the Latin equivalent of the Greek Demeter—"to abide beneath the same roof or to unmoor the fragile bark with me. Often has outraged Jupiter involved the innocent with the guilty."* Both Alcibiades, a famous Athenian admiral, and Æschylus, the tragedian, got themselves into serious difficulties—in fact, were put on trial and forced to flee from Attica—for revealing portions of the Mysteries of Eleusis. Æschylus offended the mysteries in a play, now unfortunately lost, Alcibiades in the privacy of his home (word got out, he was condemned to death in absentia, and his property was confiscated). Their auditors at once recognized the breach of secrecy, however, and condemned it, which means knowledge of the mysteries was widespread; yet, no ancient writer ever dared put on paper what was said or done that gave offense, not even Aristotle from whom we have the story.

The lack of any certain knowledge of what transpired within the sanctuary, combined with the certainty that thousands were initiated there, has given to the Eleusinia a hiding-in-plain-sight fascination for many scholars, some of whom have devoted lifetimes to solving the mystery without reaching any conclusions beyond what was obviously true to begin with, namely, that the Eleusinia were rites of the gods of the underworld and thus intimately involved with Greek conceptions of death. In this book, we shall try to open this "purloined letter."

The only other mysteries of antiquity that rival the Eleusinia, and then but dimly, were those of the Cabiri held annually on the island of Samothrace in the northern Ægean. The distinction of the Samothracian rites is that the identities of the gods in whose honor they were held is not known. They were simply called *theoi megaloi*, "the great gods." There are several important similarities between Eleusis and the Cabirian mysteries, the most important of which is that both prescribed two stages of initiation: *myesis* (lit. "closing off") and *epoptea* (gazing [up] at).† Early on, Samothrace, like most Ionian islands, became a tributary of Athens, which administered the Eleusinia, so a degree of programmatic parallel is not surprising. As with the Eleusinia, the Great Gods were chthonic gods of the underworld. Indeed, it can be said of all the greater mysteries of antiquity that they were concerned with preparing the soul of the initiate for death.

Roman religion—in general slavishly imitative of Greek—annually observed the mysteries of the Bona Dea, the Good Goddess, to which only women were admitted.‡ The Romans also celebrated the Jejunium Cereris, a festival in honor of Ceres, held in October at approximately the same time and for the same length of days as the Athenian Thesmophoria, so a typically Roman copycat rite can be inferred. Neither rite can be assigned the sanctity and awe that the Eleusinia held for the pagan world. Also, at Cumæ near Naples was the grotto of the Sybil, a woman who prophesied to petitioners while in trance. Oracular rituals are obviously esoteric and have a clear shamanic origin. Cumæ was the oldest Greek settlement in Italy, and the Romans believed that the Sybil was descended from prophetesses who dwelled in caves at the foot of the Athenian acropolis.

* Horace, *Carmina*, in: *Odes and Epodes*, trans. C. E. Bennett (Cambridge, Mass., 1927), 3.2.

† S. G. Cole, *Theoi Megaloi: The Cult of the Great Gods at Samothrace* (Leiden, 1984), pp. 23–37.

‡ Calpurnia, first wife of Julius Cæsar, attended the festival of the Bona Dea, along with many other respectable Roman matrons. Unfortunately, it was in the same year that Clodius, a patrician demagogue and libertine, also attended disguised as a woman, for what purpose can be imagined. Cæsar was so scandalized by the sacrilege that he divorced Calpurnia, although she herself had done nothing wrong, insisting that "Cæsar's wife must be above suspicion."

Esoterism was a fact of the religions of antiquity. Yet a distinction should be drawn between esoteric and esoterical. By esoteric is meant artfully intentional disguise of the true subject matter of a given myth. It requires that the mythopoet know explicitly what he is about. Esoteric means esoterism applied strictly. Esoterical, on the other hand, means that mode of treatment of myth in which the mythopoet does not know nor ever need know the true subject of his art. The esoterical poet works with material handed down through a long tradition, one with which he is thoroughly familiar but understands only implicitly. Esoterical therefore denotes a loose esoterism. Given the great age of many myths, even in the form that we have received them, we should expect that most are esoterical rather than esoteric. In a poet like Hesiod, for example, it is far from clear that he understood his subject in the strict sense. From what we know of him personally (mostly from his *Works and Days*), he seems to have been a gloomy, pessimistic misanthrope and far from "enlightened" in any sense of that much-abused word. Yet, as will be seen, his *Theogony* is one of the most marvelous works of esoterism. Homer, on the other hand, although he tells us absolutely nothing personal, seems in every line an artist with the surest and most insightful grasp of his material. His mastery of simile, of the telling poetic detail that illuminates a continent of mythic meaning in an apparent aside, convinces the reader not only that there was such a person, which is far from agreed upon by scholars, not only that he composed most, if not all, of the forty-eight books of the *Iliad* and *Odyssey*, but that he was strictly aware of what he was about. In the simple metaphor he chooses to describe the sound made by the BOW OF ODYSSEUS—"like in tone to a swallow"—over which he tarries a bare moment, a half-dozen words in a hundred thousand, he reveals with blinding clarity that he knows well whereof he sings. His skill in fashioning an overall, deep structure for his poems, as when, for example, he hangs the issue of the entire *Iliad* on Achilles' withdrawal into his tent and so propels the myth to its fatal climax almost as though the words themselves are hypnotized, is nothing short of miraculous. In brief, he gives every possible indication of creating the myth rather than merely transmitting it. A myth, like a human being, cannot be created without some spark of divinity entering the creative act. When that happens, we say the myth is the inspired word of God. Very little of what has come down to us can be so eulogized. How sobering it is to think that the greatest poet in Western culture is also the first poet of whom we have any knowledge.

Having made the distinction, we must, however, dispense with it, because in any given myth it usually is impossible to decide with what form of esoterism, strict or loose, we are dealing. A writer like Pausanias, who seems strangely detached—almost bored in fact—when on numerous occasions he introduces the material of myth into his celebrated *Description of Greece*, was initiated into the Eleusinian mysteries, and he himself tells us when he can say no more on a subject without betraying the oath of secrecy enjoined on all initiated into the "sacred rites of mystic Ceres." And as the saying goes, even Homer nodded.

Initiation is no sure benchmark of enlightenment, as Jesus tells us in the PARABLE OF THE SOWER, for much seed falls on bad ground, and there will always be some who see without seeing, neither will they understand what they hear (cf., Ecclesiastes 7:20). The distinction between esoteric and esoterical is useful only when, as in the case of a writer like Apollodorus (?first century B.C.), one gains the sure sense over the vast length of his work that much of what he includes is included only for the sake of inclusion, that although he might understand one myth, he does not understand another, and that because he does not understand, he does not know what to omit and so writes down everything he has heard or read. We are put on notice that what we are reading is not in fact authentic myth, myth as we have defined it. Call it local legend, fable, märchen, or folklore, yet it falls outside the scope of this book.

In the Introduction we reprised various mythologies from antiquity to the present. Of all such theories, the conclusion reached thus far, namely, that myth is an *esoteric description* before it is anything else, sorts most aptly with the antique approach: myth as allegory. In the waning days of antiquity, theologians like Saints Augustine and Jerome as well as Christian poets like Prudentius were reluctant to condemn wholesale the pagan classics on which they themselves had been reared. They squared their consciences with their tastes by supplying allegorical interpretations of Homer, Virgil, and many others so as to reconcile myth with scripture. We might wonder if their pious attempts, which are usually dismissed as sentimentalism, do not also indicate an understanding dimly preserved down to their epoch of the esoterical bases of paganism. Whether Prudentius understood myth in the strict or weak sense of esoterism is unclear. His own allegorizing can be interpreted in either mode. The emphasis on allegory is both unexpected and reassuring: unexpected because it runs counter to the rationalist theories that in one form or another have dominated mythology since the Enlightenment, reassuring because clearly the ancients were far closer to the sources of myth than ourselves and their opinions on the subject might all along have been accorded greater respect than has perhaps been the rule.

6

SISYPHUS AND THE STONE

Our word *spiritual* derives from the Latin word for "breath." Myth is always found in "spiritual" contexts. A paramount aim of yoga is control of breathing. Is there an esoteric connection? If so, what is it?

The Sanskrit word for the collection of techniques of breath control is *prāṇāyāma*. Manuals of yoga discuss prāṇāyāma in detail. Because both the sound and motion of breathing are a distraction to concentration, the breath must be suppressed or slowed to the point of stoppage for as long as necessary. As the lungs are brought under conscious control by the meditator, simultaneously so is the cardiovascular system. Yogis claim that when breathing ceases, *prāṇa*—loosely, oxygen—continues to circulate throughout the body in so-called subtle channels called *nādīs*. In other words, during sublime trance, life persists indefinitely without pulse or respiration. In the *Bhagavad Gīta*, prāṇāyāma is described as a method of holding the breath in the head.* In Mediterranean folklore, dolphins and porpoises were—and still are—considered to be sacred animals. They do naturally what the mystic must practice years to achieve: comfortable stoppage of breathing. A celebrated oracle of the god Apollo was located at Delphi, which means "dolphin."

When breathing is suspended, a phenomenon known to yogis as *kumbhaka*, the lungs are fully inflated and filled with air. Then, according to Patañjali, follows kaivalya.† If the breath does not stop, that is, if we exhale from the lungs, then kaivalya (liberation) does not come. Unable to control breathing, we are "bound" to the wheel of our breath. The well-known image from Buddhism of the WHEEL OF BIRTH AND DEATH is a myth of the cycle of inhalation and exhalation.

Ideally, trance occurs at the moment that the lungs and sinuses are filled with air. The effect of kumbhaka quickly spreads throughout the nervous system over nerve fibers that connect the respiratory

* *Bhagavad Gīta*, in: *The Song of God*, trans. Swami Prabhavananda and C. Isherwood (New York, 1960), p. 76.

† *Yoga-Sūtra, Kaivalya Pāda*, sutra 25.

center within the medulla oblongata at the base of the brain to the diencephalon at the front. By various techniques attention is focused on the effects of inhalation on the forebrain, which is behind your brow (where your sinuses are located). If, as we've assumed, meditation and heightened proprioception are one and the same thing, then the intricately structured diencephalon is distinctly felt during samādhi. Proprioception of the brain, especially at the instant that the breath abates, is the esoteric meaning of holding the breath in the head or "between the brows."

The process can be—and over the centuries has been—aided by numerous practical "tricks" designed to heighten proprioception of the forehead, for example, the wearing of fillets (headbands) by priests. Fillets of olive, celery, and myrtle (all more or less sacred plants) were awarded to victors in Greek athletic competitions like the Olympic and Isthmian games, which were first and foremost religious celebrations. By stimulating the touch receptors at its points of contact above the sinuses, a fillet focuses awareness there. Concentration on the experience of breath within the sinuses then turns the awareness inward. Saint Paul speaks of the "crown of victory" awarded to the disciple who perseveres, and from very ancient times Jesus, the BLESSED MOTHER, and the saints are shown in art with haloes. During prayer, Orthodox Jews to this day wear a phylactery, a long strap wrapped around the forehead and carried down to the left hand; the hand can be used to modulate the pressure of the phylactery on the brow. The same technique lay behind the widespread ancient practice of wearing religious medallions over the heart, an all-important focus for proprioception. Heracles wears the skin of the NEMEAN LION and is never shown without it in antique art; its paws are knotted over his heart. He dies because he dons the SHIRT OF NESSUS, a garment dipped in the blood of a centaur, which burns like fire and drives him to self-immolation and apotheosis. The fire is a description of thoracic proprioceptions during trance. Certain close Christian parallels can be adduced. John the Baptist wears a hair shirt, which also serves to identify him iconographically in Christian art. Traditionally thought of as a garment of penitential self-torture, the original hair shirt more likely had a practical, if somewhat extreme, meditative function. In Roman Catholicism we find the somewhat late tradition of the scapular, made of wool and slightly irritating, which touches the heart and the back and aids in focusing heightened proprioception of the thorax. In the myth of ER, Plato speaks of a mark on the hearts of the blessed.* Hinduism too is replete with bizarre practices, such as standing for days on one foot, that increase internal awareness essentially by stressing the nervous system. The widespread "spiritual" recommendation to fast periodically from food, water, or both accomplishes the same thing. When the stomach and intestines are empty, they promptly make themselves known! All such practices are futile, however, if they are not combined with breath control, which can transform the experience from gratuitous unpleasantness filled with psychological conflict, repression, and anguish to inner tranquility.

This is a very old riddle: *What rolls uphill without ever reaching the top?*

Sound familiar? It should. Sisyphus, a legendary king of Corinth, is a well-known character of Greek myth. As we have it from Hesiod, Zeus, the chief god of the Greek pantheon, has an affair with Ægina, the daughter of Asopus, a local deity of a river in the Isthmus of Corinth. Asopus learns of their affair and in a towering rage goes after the lovers. Asopus bribes the crafty Sisyphus to tell him what has happened to his child. He agrees to supply the citadel of Corinth with a never-failing spring, the fountain Pyrene, which at once bubbles up beneath the temple of Aphrodite. Foolishly, Sisyphus tells him what he wants to know. Asopus surprises Zeus, who transforms himself into a boulder and rolls uphill. Asopus gives chase, raining blows on him the while.

* *Republic* 619C, in: *The Myths of Plato*, ed. and trans. J. A. Stewart (London, 1905).

Note, boulder and river—Asopus—travel *uphill.**

Eventually, Zeus wreaks vengeance on Sisyphus by assigning him the condign task of rolling a boulder up a hillside in Hades, the Greek underworld. Sisyphus will be freed from Hades only if he can push the boulder to the top of the hill and keep it there. But Zeus, who can be nasty when provoked, rigs the business so that each time Sisyphus wrestles the stone to the summit it slips from his grasp and rolls back to the bottom. There he must start all over again—presumably for eternity.

If you haven't stopped to figure it out by now, the answer to our riddle—and the esoteric subject of the myth of SISYPHUS AND THE STONE—is *the breath.* Sisyphus is an esoteric description of respiration. Consider the following details culled from Greek myth:

- *Sisyphus's father.* In both Homer and Hesiod, Sisyphus is called *Æolides,* namely, the son of Æolus, Greek god of the winds. Æolus kept the four winds in a sack of bull's hide. The wind is an apt description of the breath, and the sack probably describes a proprioception of the lungs or at least of the chest cavity. A bull is a great-chested beast, very important in pastoral culture, and a bull's hide is an apt, ready-to-hand description of the chest. The etymology of *æolus* is unknown; it perhaps derives from very old Indo-European roots that mean to "howl" or "wail," a sound that the wind is often said to make. Both words are cognate with *bellow* and *bull.* And of course, if a man howls, he does so from deep in his chest.
- *The sibilance of Sisyphus's name.* The sound is suspiciously like that heard in the nostrils during one complete cycle of inhalation-exhalation: *siss-phus.* To discern it, close your mouth and breathe slowly, steadily, and through your nose—as a yogi would—and listen carefully.
- *Parallels with Asopus.* Asopus also races uphill with a boulder, though he never actually catches it. The image of a river quite aptly describes the flow of the breath. In Greek, *asopos* means "never silent," paralleling the endless task of Sisyphus and, again, drawing attention to the *sound* of the breath. Asopus's wife is named Metope, which comes from the Greek word for the *brow* or *forehead* (metopon). The sinuses, located behind the eyebrows at the base of the forehead, are shaped like the wings of a bird, which of course flies through the air and creates a movement of air with its wings (figure 5). When one breathes, the rhythmically moving breath penetrates the sinuses, much in the same way that a husband (Asopus) penetrates his wife (Metope) during sexual intercourse. In the Bœotian poet Theognis's version of the same myth, the summit of the hill up which Sisyphus/Asopus toils is called the brow (metopon) of the hill.
- *Sisyphus is king of Corinth.* Corinth is a Greek city located on an isthmus, a strip of land with water on two sides—often found in myth. Sisyphus founded the Isthmian games. An isthmus very likely is an esoteric description of the glabellar bone, the narrow space between the brows so significant in yoga (figure 5). The Isthmus of Corinth divides the mainland from the Greek Peloponnese, a large peninsula named after Pelops, the son of Tantalus and the grandfather of Agamemnon. Pelops or one of his descendants is involved in several prominent myths as an esoteric description of the bones of the skull.
- *Sisyphus and the narrow gate.* Sisyphus is the father of the famous homeric hero Odysseus, who also possesses a sibilant name. In Hyginus, a compiler of myth who lived in Roman times, Sisyphus

* Hyginus, *Fabularum liber* 38, in: *Hyginus,* untrans. (New York, 1976).

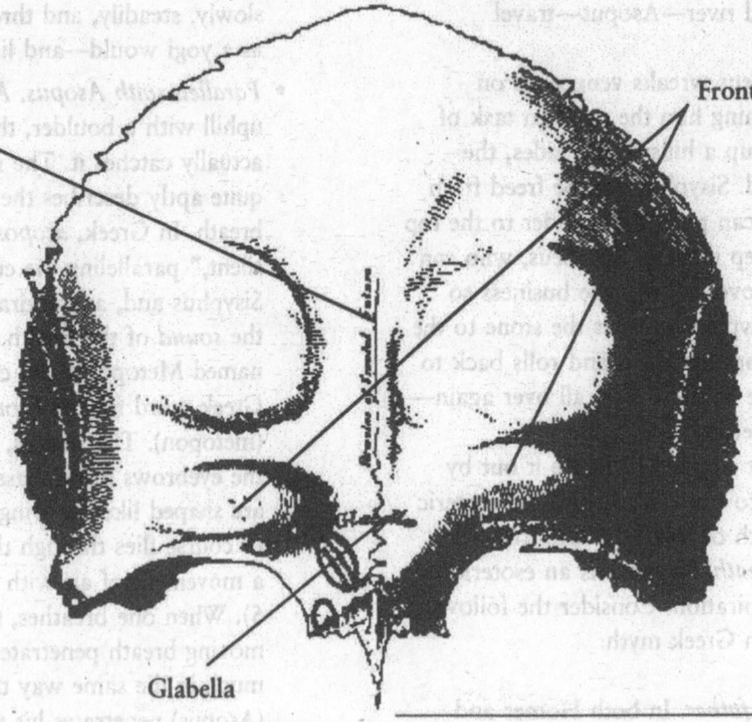

Figure 5. The Frontal Sinuses

seduces Anticlea (Odysseus's mother) in a doorway. Anticlea possibly means "keyhole" in Greek. The proprioceptive significance of doors, narrow gates, and straitened ways in general is enormous. Perhaps the most important location in the body of myth is the *frontal suture* running down the center of the forehead. (The suture is the remnant of an embryonic division in the frontal bone.) When the breath rises into the sinuses, a simultaneous proprioception of the effect of inhalation on the brain is felt as a movement of prāṇa within the cranium. The result: an "entry" of the breath into the skull. Known to yogis as the *brāhmarandhra* or "gate of Brahmā [the father god of the Hindu trinity]," the suture is marked by devout Hindus with a starlike *tilak* or by three vertical lines. Æolus lived on an island near the entrance to the Hellespont, the slender waterway connecting the Ægean Sea with the Sea of Marmara near the reputed site of Troy. It is interesting that (1) Æacus, the grandson of Asopus, built the gates of Troy, (2) Telamon, the great-grandson of Asopus, tore them down, and (3) Ajax Big, the great-great-grandson of Asopus, knocked down the Trojan prince Hector with a *boulder* in front of those same gates.

- *Sisyphus and secret rites.* In the *Nicomachæan Ethics,* Aristotle says that Æschylus was driven from Athens into permanent exile for revealing parts of the Eleusinian mysteries in his play *Sisyphus.* In one version of the myth, Sisyphus is sentenced to Hades for revealing the secrets of the gods, a reference to initiatory rites. The wily Sisyphus contrives to get out of Hades on a kind of religious technicality, and Persephone must have him sent down again. Significantly, in this version there is no mention of a boulder, yet Sisyphus manages to go up and down all the same.

The parallels between the myth of Asopus-with-boulder, on the one hand, and Sisyphus-with-boulder, on the other, imply that one myth *recapitulates* the other. In other words, they are very nearly the selfsame riddle with respect to esoteric meaning, with a boulder in both cases describing the rising breath. The Asopus riddle might take the form: *Where does a river flow uphill?* Answer: *In the* ISTHMUS OF CORINTH.

In another variant of the myth, Sisyphus is the son of Tantalus, a very disreputable character. For his many crimes, Tantalus is condemned to Hades and chained to a rock. At his feet is a cool stream. Just above his head is the bough of a fragrant apple tree laden with fruit. Whenever he stoops to drink, however, the stream dries up. When he raises his arm to pick an apple, the bough recedes. He can neither satisfy his hunger nor slake his thirst. Caught in desire, he serves his time in hell alternately bending down and reaching up without respite. Sound familiar?

In still another variant, Sisyphus is the son of Ixion, who, like his son, is punished in Hades for revealing the secrets of the gods. Ixion is tied to a rack that revolves continuously, causing him great suffering. The imagery is very similar to the Buddhist Wheel of Birth and Death, which we have already related to the respiratory cycle.

In the *Yoga-Sūtra*, Patañjali says that prāṇāyāma involves regulating the breath according to *deśa*, meaning "by place."* But "place" has to be understood in a technical sense peculiar to yoga. In his *Yoga-Bhāṣya*, perhaps the earliest commentary on the *Yoga-Sūtra*, the Hindu sage Vyāsa (seventh century A.D.) states explicitly that deśa has nothing to do with mundane geography but, rather, with location within the human body. The whole concept is quite strange to Westerners, who tend to think of the breath as the breath and leave it at that. In yoga, however, proprioception of breathing varies with the location in the body to which the yogi's attention is directed during prāṇāyāma.

Yogis have supplied names to five different "breaths": *prāṇa* for the breath in the region of the heart, *samāna* in the abdomen, *apāna* in the pelvis and legs, *udāna* in the head, and *vyāna* throughout the body. The ultimate sense of the "breaths," it should be emphasized, lies in specialized experiences of the effect of breathing within the part of the body that is the object of samādhi; the "breaths" are differentiated flows of oxygenated energy within organs or related organ groups. We might wonder, then, if the wanderings of Odysseus, son of Sisyphus, do not continue the myth of Sisyphus and the Stone throughout the esoteric "places" of the breath. The *Odyssey*, so interpreted, is then an artful attempt at describing comprehensively, and in rhythmic verse, the all-pervading experience of respiration during prāṇāyāma.

The traditional meaning of *Odysseus* is derived—very tentatively—from the Greek word for "angry" or "wrathful." But very little of the character of Odysseus as we find it in Homer makes such an etymology plausible. It is true that when he returns from Troy, he and his son slaughter the suitors who have plagued his wife, Penelope. But Homer takes such pains to make the suitors appear obnoxious and loathsome, insulting Odysseus to his face and ridiculing him in his own banquet hall, that the act of vengeance that falls swiftly and surely upon their heads cannot point to anything especially vindictive in the character of the hero. Throughout the bulk of the *Iliad* and the *Odyssey*, Odysseus is a model of prudence and good counsel, qualities not often linked to irascibility or a choleric temperament. There is but one "wrathful" man in Homer: Achilles.† When the Trojan king, Priam, wishes to ransom the body of his son Hector, whom Achilles has slain, he goes not to Achilles, who terrifies him, but to Odysseus, whose levelheadedness is famous even among the Trojans. We might instead derive Odysseus from either *hodos Sisyphos*, "wander-

* *Yoga-Sūtra, Sādhana Pāda*, sutra 50.

† The *Iliad* begins, "Sing, goddess, of the wrath of Achilles, son of Peleus."

ing Sisyphus," or the less likely but more tantalizing *ædos Sisyphou*, "song [sound?] of Sisyphus."

The RAPE OF ÆGINA, daughter of Asopus, has important parallels both in and out of Greek religion. It most prominently resembles the RAPE OF PERSEPHONE: the abduction, this time by Hades, of the daughter of Zeus and Demeter. As did Asopus, Demeter goes in search of Corē (as Persephone was known in the Eleusinian mysteries, which rites commemorated their reunion exoterically). As was Asopus, Demeter is assisted by a mortal, this time Triptolemus of Eleusis, who witnessed the rape and tells her what has happened to her child. Triptolemus is amply rewarded. Demeter, in various versions of the story, teaches him: (1) the secrets of her mysteries, (2) the art of agriculture, (3) how to fly about in a fiery winged-dragon chariot. Whatever the esoteric meaning of the DONATION OF DEMETER may be, it has the same sense for each gift. The second gift, that of agriculture, contradicts the rest of the myth because, prior to finding Persephone, Demeter's grief causes the crops to die.* Either the gift of agriculture was added on in the face of plain logic, or it describes something not precisely agricultural but *like* agriculture in some way; it implies that "the art of agriculture" is esoterically grounded, hence refers to the mysteries themselves.

When the Greek farmer plowed his fields he generally did so with oxen yoked in pairs. The yoke was passed over the neck and around the chest of the ox. In myth the back-and-forth motion of the plow through the field describes the rise and fall of the chest. Simultaneously, the breath's rhythmic contact with the "furrow" of the frontal suture (figure 5) defines the point of an esoteric plow. Finally, a yoke (cog. with Skt. *yoga*) describes breath control, during which one sits harnessed to one's spiritual duty. Greek verse originally was written back and forth on the page, one line left to right, the next right to left, and so on. The resulting form was called *boustrophedon*, "as the ox turns the plow," for obvious reasons. The pause after the word on which the verse turns (cf., L. *versus*, "a turning"), called a *cæsura*, was the point at which the rhapsodist caught his breath!

The myth of the Rape of Persephone uses timeless agricultural tasks as sources of imagery, especially as such imagery relates to the goddess Demeter, who is a specialized earth goddess entrusted with caring for the crops. An agricultural motif introduced in the Rape of Persephone is that of sowing and reaping, as fundamental to the meaning of the myth as the image of plowing, perhaps more so. From various sources, mostly Christian, we know that at a certain point in the Eleusinian mysteries the initiates were shown cut wheat and that they were required to bring with them into the sanctuary agricultural products such as seed.† The image of wheat relates to a much broader concern of Indo-European religion, namely, karma or destiny, one so important that it will require lengthy treatment later on, when we discuss the Mysteries of Eleusis in detail. Here it suffices to note that prāṇāyāma and control of one's "karma" are closely related in yoga.

Returning now to the figure of Odysseus, the above discussion is helpful in clearing up another famous story from Greek myth. Before the Achæans sailed for Troy, Agamemnon, Menelaus, and Palamedes visited Odysseus at his home to persuade him to honor the oath he'd sworn to defend Helen. They found him plowing with ox and ass yoked together, wearing an egg-shaped cap, and sowing salt as he went—in other words, feigning madness to avoid his pledge (he'd been warned by an oracle of the misfortune in store if he embarked for Troy). As he was finishing the tenth furrow they placed his son, Telemachus, in the path of the plow to test his sanity, whereupon he at once halted his strange team and gave the ruse away.‡ When Telemachus, the *son* of Odysseus, is placed in

* G. D. Mylonas, *Eleusis and the Eleusinian Mysteries* (Princeton, N.J., 1972), pp. 4–22.

† Ibid., p. 274.

‡ Hyginus, *Fabularum liber 95*. The shape of Odysseus's cap is similar to a monk's tonsure.

the furrow, the myth suggests the notion of destroying karmic seed by prāṇāyāma. Where salt is sown, nothing will grow.

As will be shown in chapter 7, if plowing with an ox describes thoracic breathing, then plowing with an ass (or a horse) stands for the nasal breath. An ass makes an unmistakable sound when it wheezes, one that is colloquially approximated by "hee-haw" but which combines an aspiration with a sort of whine.

Odysseus' use of both an ox and an ass describes the totality of respiration, lungs and nostrils functioning together. Odysseus's egg-shaped cap indicates that meditation on such a sound involves proprioception of the dome of the skull, perhaps of the meninges, the membranous tissues that encase the cerebrum. The identical proprioception is heightened by an ancient article of clothing known as a *yarmulke* (Ukr. "skullcap"), worn by some Jews while in temple, and of course Orthodox synagogues are often skull-shaped. Roman Catholic clergy wear the *pileolus*, a skullcap, the color varying according to rank. The medieval practice of tonsure, shaving away the hair on the crown of the head, accomplished the same end.

◆◆◆

In Hindu folklore, the story is told of a guru who tames an obstreperous monkey by having it shuttle up and down a pole. That is just breath control all over again. It is, as the *Gīta* puts it, to "place the mind in the breath." The art of placing the mind in the breath is the all-important technique (kriyā) of yoga.

Nearly as important in breath control is the practicality—or lack of it—in the means used to induce heightened concentration on the breath. Yoga claims that control of the breath leads to control of the mind—almost certainly via the selfsame neurological-feedback route that allows the mind to control breathing. The peaceful state issuing from regulated respiration is something we instinctively long for. Consider the habit, indulged by hundreds of millions, of smoking tobacco. Here we have a very crude breath meditation. The psychic needs that smoking satisfies are multifarious, but it is probable that smoking enhances concentration. That does not mean that smoking cigarettes is a good habit to acquire. It is an unintended technique for enhancing awareness of the breath, but one that has highly deleterious side effects. Breath control is practical. There are right and wrong ways to do it. To the extent that smoking enhances

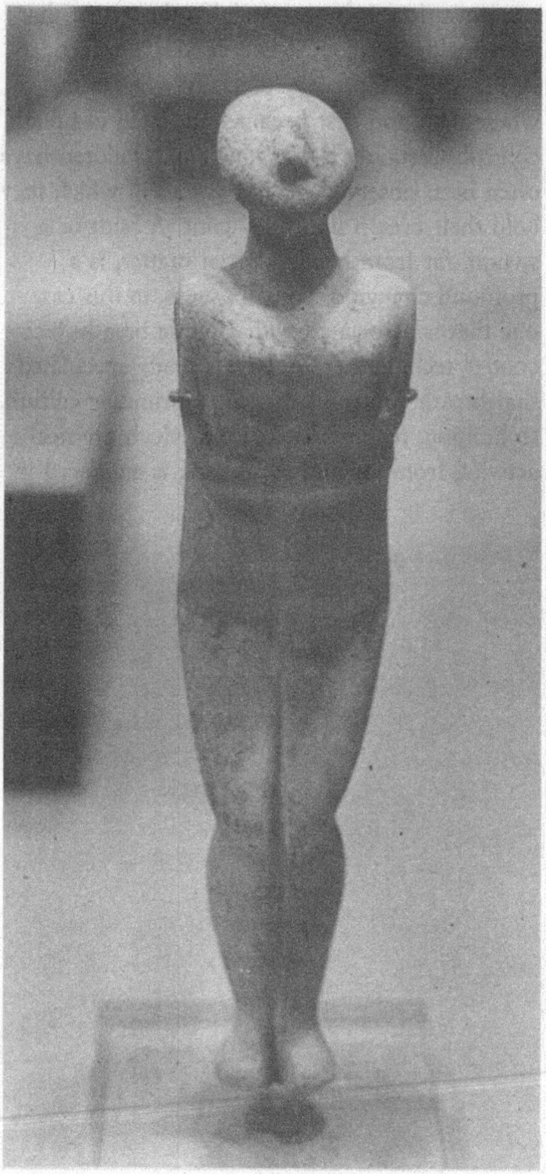

Figure 6. Female Deity, ca. 3000 B.C., from Rhodes (Metropolitan Museum, New York)

concentration, it is practical. To the extent that it harms the smoker, it is decisively impractical.

It is difficult to say precisely when and where mankind first became interested in breath control. Certainly it was long ago. Children have often been observed playing games in which they hold their breath until they faint. A faint or a swoon, far from being a trivial matter, is a profound change of consciousness, in this case one that is associated with a crude breath-control technique.* We have already speculated that breath control is related to primitive culture, to hunting, reaping, and so on. Much physical activity, from jogging to archery, is enhanced by regulated breathing. Yet overriding the benefits of respiration is the simple fact that, when all other senses have abated, it is the delicate cycle of inspiration-expiration that tethers us to the so-called world. If we are to understand that most problematic relationship, it is with respiration that we must begin.

Figure 6 is a Cycladic figurine of a mother goddess of ca. 3000 B.C., an artifact of the age when myth was science. Look at her closely. She has not eyes nor ears nor mouth. She has only a nose to indicate her face. Her entire consciousness is turned inward. She clasps her middle with all her might. She is holding her breath.

* Diogenes the Cynic (d. 323 B.C.), a disorderly Athenian philosopher, is said to have committed suicide by "retaining the breath."

7

MYTH AND ANIMALS

Anthropologia kai zoölogia: "Tales of men and animals."* Myth first emerges as stories and riddles for children. We have hypothesized that, from the first, the mythic form served an esoteric purpose: to instruct without revealing. The narrative details of a given myth drew on commonplace aspects of the specific culture. Among a great many other things, that meant animals, concerning which, even by the Stone Age, humans had accumulated a large and multidimensional fund of knowledge. Animals, and especially mammals, are susceptible to mythic appropriation because of the many affinities humans share with them, as opposed to plants, which we must assume were also well known to Stone Age peoples.

Prehistory was the age in which men first domesticated animals. The dog, the horse, cows, sheep, swine, and goats were brought under the control of humans long before there were civilizations as we understand the term. Animal husbandry was perhaps the first science, the first technology, the first art; and as is often true of a new technology, its impact on human society was enormous and transformative. Domestic animals provided food, shelter, transportation, protection, and sheer brawn. Their presence in human society was pervasive, taken for granted, and irreplaceable. One need only peruse an ancient Roman author such as Columella (fl. 25 B.C.), who wrote the *De re rustica*, an encyclopedic treatise on farming, to understand not only how inextricably animals had insinuated themselves into the affairs of men, but also in what detail, with what a wealth of understanding, they were known to their human masters.

In the long-gone age when only the dog was domesticated (10,000 B.C. at the latest), men hunted animals to survive. The hunt is perhaps the earliest collective human endeavor of which we have any sure knowledge (principally through prehistoric cave paintings, such as those at Lascaux in France, which date from around twenty-two thousand years ago). We know that early man surrounded this

* Stewart, *The Myths of Plato*, p. 6.

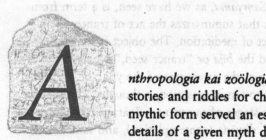

critically important activity with ritual, an essential feature of which was what Sir James Frazer has called *sympathetic magic.*

Frazer's treatment of sympathetic magic occupies fully a third of his monumental work *The Golden Bough.** The term *sympathetic* indicates that the ritual's outcome depends on establishing some likeness between the magician and the object of his magic, between the ritual and the goal of the ritual. The Lascaux cave paintings, for example, can be interpreted "sympathetically": by painting the likeness of an animal being killed, the painter-shaman, as he saw it, achieved an essential precondition for actually killing the animal and increased the likelihood of success.

Such rituals persist to this day, particularly among the nomadic Indians of the Americas, whose culture, at least when Europeans first encountered them in the sixteenth century, most nearly conformed to the prehistoric Eurasian nomads who gave us the myths of the Greeks, Celts, Persians, and Hindus. Among the Yaqui Indians of Sonora, Mexico, a strictly prescribed ritual Deer Dance is frequently performed.† The dancer is a descendant of ancient Amerindian shamans. In the reports of Jesuit missionaries, we have descriptions of the Deer Dance as it was performed in the sixteenth century. Its amalgamation into Roman Catholic ritual has left it little changed since then. As part of his costume, the deer dancer wears an actual deer's head atop his own. He wears a belt fashioned from deer hooves. He adopts a posture imitative of that of the deer and moves in rapid, staccato steps, turning this way and that suddenly, the way a deer might move when it senses the presence of a predator. He covers his eyes with a cloth so as to mimic the sensorium of the deer, which is centered in its sense of smell and hearing rather than its eyes. While he dances, the beating of a water drum suggests the deer's heartbeat; a rasp is stroked with increasing rapidity to mimic the deer's anxious breathing. Cocoon rattles wrapped around the dancer's ankles produce the sound of the deer running through the grass. The deer dancer is himself called *masu*: the deer. Throughout the rite the dancer does not speak. A typical Deer Dance lasts about fifteen minutes, and the dancer repeats the dance again and again, resting for brief periods between each set. Yet one could not describe his behavior as frenzied—frenzy would soon lead to exhaustion—only trancelike. Indeed he must, simply by virtue of continual repetition, enter into a trance, the core of which is the imagined experience of the hunted deer. The behavior of the deer dancer illustrates an important aim of sympathetic hunting magic: the attempt by the hunter to *become* the hunted.

Saṃyama, as we have seen, is a term from yoga that summarizes the act of trance on an object of meditation. The object is sometimes called the *bīja* or "trance seed," whatever occupies the awareness of the yogi, be it a thing, an emotion, a sensation, a thought. Through the three stages of saṃyama—dhāraṇā (concentration), dhyāna (contemplation), and samādhi (trance)—the meditator is brought into communion with the seed. Indeed *communion* is a very serviceable English approximation to Sanskrit *saṃyama*, as for that matter is the word *sympathy* itself, especially when the bīja is a so-called living organism.‡ *Saṃyama* is an equivalent (technical) term for what the deer dancer intends: communion with masu, the deer. In primitive shamanism we find what Frazer calls sympathetic magic. In yoga, which is the product of millennia of practical investigation of trance, we have saṃyama.

* Sir J. G. Frazer, *The Golden Bough: A Study in Magic and Religion*, 12 vols. (London, 1911–15).

† The discussion of the Yaqui Deer Dance is paraphrased from J. E. Kovach's *The Ecstatic Moment*, a work in progress.

‡ Greek συν-, from which derive Eng. prefixes *sym-* and *syn-*, descends from the same Indo-European root as Skt. *saṃ-*, all having the sense of "together with" (cf., L. prefixes *com-*, *con-*, and preposition *cum*, "with"). Sanskrit *ṃ*, called *anusvāra* by grammarians, is not a distinct character but a diacritical over the preceding vowel that nasalizes it, like the *o* in Fr. *ton* or the *a* in Port. *saõ*, which sounds something like *sum* when pronounced.

Patañjali also makes a startling claim: "By performing *Saṃyama* on the three kinds of transformations . . . knowledge of the past and future [of the object]."*

What Patañjali suggests is not far from what the deer dancer intends when he dances, his desire to merge with the deer. The object of the deer dancer's meditation is the deer. His techniques are the rhythms and accoutrements of the dance, themselves imitative of the deer. The technique of a yogi, were he interested in deer, would involve (1) thinking of nothing but a deer (dhāraṇā); (2) fixing a crystal-clear, unwavering image of a deer in his mind (dhyāna); then (3) passing into trance (samādhi)—all occurring seamlessly. That effort in turn entails an alacritous convergence on respiratory and cardiovascular control because the great discovery of yoga is that neither brain-mind, nor lungs, nor heart can be separately *fixed*. The difference between the technique of the yogi and that of a shaman such as the Yaqui deer dancer is primarily one of sophistication, even elegance. For the yogi trained in practicing communion/saṃyama, the days' long exhaustion of dancing is unnecessarily magical, theatrical, and impractical. The samādhi of saṃyama can be attained almost instantaneously. The division of yogic communion or sympathy into three phases—concentration, contemplation, and trance—is a didactic and highly artificial tool useful in training novices in yoga. In practice there is only a single experience. Call it saṃyama, as do yogis; or samādhi, as do Hindus; or Zen (a word derived from dhyāna), as do Buddhists; or prayer, as do Christian mystics; or meditation; or trance—it hardly matters.

When the deer dancer has attained communion with the deer, he knows all there is to know about the deer. In particular, he knows where to find the deer, which was the practical aim of the ritual to begin with. We have used the words "become the deer," which are somewhat misleading. The notion of *becoming* is not a true process for North American Indians, and there is certainly no intention to symbolize the deer.† Rather, becoming is instantaneous saṃyama. Saṃyama begins when the deer dancer "replaces" his head with the deer's head. In that moment, the deer is present. It is now a matter of realizing it. The realization is sympathetic magic.

To the modern mind, the whole notion of sympathetic magic smacks of telepathy and similar exotica and is more than a little outlandish. The reply to such skepticism, of course, is that the highly focused state of concentration called sublime trance is not something with which most people are explicitly familiar. What might occur to someone during preternaturally intense concentration, therefore, cannot be prejudged. Patañjali's assertion is consistent with claiming that during any experience we obtain far more information than meets the untrained eye, a fact that hypnotists exploit. Hypnosis is low-grade samādhi. What information would surface in a truly profound trance? It is a question that can only be answered *after* undergoing true samādhi, not before.

◆◆◆

Broadly speaking, yoga is defined by Patañjali, in the first verse of the *Yoga-Sūtra*, as "the inhibition of the modifications [vṛtti] of the mind [cittā]." Considered as a whole, the *Yoga-Sūtra* is a meticulously logical expansion of the terms introduced in its opening sentence: ***inhibition, modifications, mind***. When he comes to amplifying the meaning of "modifications," Patañjali is led to consider the influence of perception on concentration. It is clear from the beginning of his treatment that Patañjali does not consider perception apart from mediated perception, that is, perception without cognition, for he speaks of only five modifications: ***right knowledge, wrong knowledge, fancy, sleep***, and ***memory***. Perception falls into the categories of

* *Yoga-Sūtra, Vibhūti Pāda*, sutra 16.

† J. E. Brown, "Modes of Contemplation through Actions: North American Indians," in: *Traditional Modes of Contemplation and Action* (Tehran, 1977), p. 237.

right and wrong knowledge. Sometimes a perception is accurate; sometimes it is inaccurate. From the point of view of the yogi, however, they are equally problematic because any modification must be inhibited or suppressed.

Modifications are inhibited in two ways: (1) practice and (2) detachment.* One is objective; the other, subjective. Practice means persistent application of techniques taught by a guru, including prāṇāyāma. Detachment means lack of craving for objects "seen and unseen." Patañjali's analysis of practice and detachment is detailed but can be summed up for our present purpose as breaking the hold that the senses have on our mind's attention, the source of which is sensory pleasure and sensory pain. Clearly those concepts cannot be entirely severed from cognitive-stereognostic associations, but we can use the term *limiting case* to describe a purely sensory response of the organism, be it pleasurable or painful. Throughout this book that is what is meant by *perception* or *percept*.

The appetitive center of the brain is the hypothalamus. Through neurological interconnections too numerous to comprehend, all perceptual neurons are reciprocally linked to the hypothalamus, all, that is, except smell, which connects directly to the olfactory cortex. Thus all the senses (except smell) are directly guided by the appetites, emotional as well as physical. It is those same appetites that must be restrained in order to achieve sublime trance. In yogic parlance, the practical manifestations of appetite are summed up by the *dvaṃdvas*, "the pairs of opposites." They come down to pleasure and pain, attraction and repulsion.

Patañjali claims that attraction and repulsion are two of the great evils (kleśas) to be avoided at all costs. Equanimity is to be maintained in the face of imminent pleasure or pain, a philosophical attitude shared with Buddhists and the Stoic philosophers. The practical means of achieving detachment is to use the techniques revealed by the guru to keep one's attention ever fixed on an unvarying center of awareness within the human organism (known as the WORD OF GOD).

Disruptions to trance are instigated by specific perceptions and processed by the various sensoria in the form of desires, lusts, and passions. In an archaic culture, lacking abstractions, only the raw power of the sensation presents itself. Referring it to an animal surrogate is natural because animals embody sensory power. One of the oldest forms of storytelling was the animal fable, the best-known examples of which are the fables of Æsop, called *mythia* in Greek. Animal fables were used to convey a representative picture of human life. The persona of Æsop is probably a myth. Not only was he a mute (till the goddess Isis intervened), but he is described as being extraordinarily ugly in all his bodily parts, almost an animal himself.†

We hypothesize that the role of, say, vision during trance came to be veiled in myth under the guise of an animal. The criterion of selection was phenomenological: what was *apparently* true of a particular animal was decisive in fashioning a myth. There was no necessity for a biologically accurate understanding of animal sensoria. As prey, food source, or beasts of burden, the strengths and weaknesses of animals were keenly observed. Primitive men must have been acutely aware of how inferior to the animal kingdom they themselves were with regard to the senses. It was because of their superior sensory faculties, as well as their ubiquity in archaic cultures, that animals became so useful in sacred storytelling. The beasts might not be able to reason cognitively, but they could see, hear, smell, taste, and touch with a sensitivity and accuracy that was an awesome challenge for a primitive hunter. In other words, an animal species was first distinguished by the sense it seemed particularly to embody. To a primitive hunter, a hound *was* the sense of smell incarnate. (That an archaic hunter possessed an abstract concept of olfaction cannot be inferred.)

Among animals having excellent powers of

* *Yoga-Sūtra*, *Samādhi Pāda*, sutras 7–8, 12.

† L. W. Daly, *Æsop without Morals* (New York, 1961), pp. 16–31.

sight are birds. Thus, on our hypothesis, whenever in myth we encounter a bird such as a cormorant, a hawk, or a cock, we infer a veiled description of a proprioception of the eyes during trance. Consider the shape of the brow ridges, known to anatomists as the supraorbital arches, that define the eye sockets in a human being. They look like the outspread wings of a bird "long of wing," as Homer says. Similarly, a ram was early on identified with sight because the shape of its horns curling around the animal's eyes strongly resembles the line of the brows in the human face. Horns in general mean perception and particularly perceptual desire, colloquially referred to as "randiness." In the sign language of American Indians, the indication for "to see" is a thrusting motion with the index and third fingers of one hand—a V shape—that starts at the bridge of the nose, the place where the brows converge. Sometimes a goat is used, an animal with horns that emerge from between the eyes like a ram's. Important to the synecdoche is the fact that the horns of rams and goats are fused: they emerge from a single point. Horns are not the only criteria, however. A wolf, whose eyes glow in the dark because of the presence of a translucent film anterior to the retina, also describes vision; but a wolf, because it is a predator, describes something more: the desires of vision. A wolf was a useful theriomorphism for mythopoets, for whom the desire of the human organism for satiation was an important didactic theme.

The ears were esoterically described by the horns of a bull or cow because in bovines the ears jut out at the side of the head and emphasize the vicinity of the ears in the same way that a ram's horns emphasize the eyes. In sign language, the indication for "to hear" is a motion with the index fingers of both hands that starts at the ears and sweeps down and up, inscribing in air the shape of a bull's horns. In contrast with the horns of a ram, the horns of a bull are not fused but polar: they clearly emphasize the two sides of the head. When Odysseus, as a precaution, has himself tied to the mast of his ship while passing the ISLAND OF THE SIRENS, one of his crew leaps overboard, unable to resist the sirenic song. The Sirens are anthropomorphized hearing, and three of them have Greek names containing the Greek root *bous*, "cow" (for example, Peribœa; cf., Eng. "bovine" < L. *bos*). The crew member who leaps overboard is Butes, which means "cowherd," but his calling is given by Homer as a keeper of bees, creatures noted for the sound they make.*

Smell is most often described in Indo-European myth by a dog, particularly a hound, next by a deer, hind, or stag, finally by a bear.

For the sense of taste a lion is used because of its jaws (domesticated cats play no part in Greek myth, although they are found very occasionally in Norse and commonly in Egyptian legends), also a serpent, either because of the ceaseless action of its tongue in the case of smaller snakes or, in the case of the python, because it devours its prey whole. Indeed, to primitives, a snake must have seemed one long alimentary canal.

The sense of touch, centered in the skin, is described by a goat, which because of its occasional use to describe vision thus has an ambiguous meaning in myth, the purport of which must be inferred from context. The skin is a kind of outer garment, and the Greeks especially used goatskins for making clothing. The notion clearly survives in English *textile* < Latin *textus*, "cloth," cognate with *tactus*, "touched."

Far and away the most important bodily organ esoterically described in myth is the nose. Life, to primitives, was in the breath, and yoga can be interpreted as an attempt to experience the life energy that ceaselessly drives the diaphragm and lungs. The nose, as the external organ of respiration, is described by a horse, an

---

* With regard to the bull and hearing, we have a good example of an exception proving the rule. The Tenth Labor of Heracles relates the hero's adventures in capturing the OXEN OF THE SUN, and in book 12 of the *Odyssey*, the companions of Odysseus slaughter the same oxen. The sun would seem to indicate a myth about vision. Why then does the sun keep oxen? As it turns out, the Oxen of the Sun is very likely a pre-Indo-European myth. As important, in Homer the sun is more often described as "all hearing" than "all seeing." Gladstone, *Studies on Homer and the Homeric Age*, vol. 2, pp. 262–64.

ass, or a boar, also pigs and swine in general—all strenuous breathers.

The choice of animal depends on the culture. In Hindu myth, for example, an elephant or a goose is used as well as a horse to describe the breath. The Sanskrit word for goose is *haṃsa* (cf., Gk. *chen* and L. *anser*, "goose," and Gk. *cygnus*, "swan"), without doubt onomatopoetic, that is, it mimics, to within the failings of speech, the so-called honking sound produced by geese. Significantly *haṃsa* is also used figuratively in Sanskrit for the soul, which recalls the ancient belief, prevalent among the Greeks, that breath and soul are intimately related. The famous *Bṛhadāraṇyaka Upaniṣad* begins with a paean to the horse sacrifice. In the *Kena Upaniṣad*, the soul is likened to a horse that, rising up, takes the senses with it, just as a wild horse while escaping pulls up the ropes with which it has been staked to the earth. The context leaves no doubt that death is being described, when the life's breath departs the human form and the senses "binding" the soul to the world abandon the earthly body (Prajāpati, the Hindu Jehovah, also created the first man from earth).

The Latin word for a boar is *aper* (< *spirare*, "to breathe"; cf., *sus*,"pig"), the Greek *hys*; both words are hard breathings, hence descriptive of respiration. Verbalization of the sounds swine make is, within limits, subjective. Our own word *snort*, for example, is akin to Old English *swin* and to Old High German *Nasa*: "nose" (< L. *nasus*: "nose"). Those roots, spanning two great Indo-European linguistic families, Italic and Germanic, describe the same phenomenon: passage of air through the nostrils sounds like a sibilant whine. The sound is most apparent in strenuous breathers such as swine or donkeys. The word for donkey in Greek is *honos*, in Latin *asinus*, in Old English *assa*. In Christian myth Jesus enters Jerusalem for the last time on an ass's colt, and his disciples fill the air with *hosannas* and fan it with palm fronds, a motion and sound descriptive of respiration. The original Judaic prohibition from eating swine may not have been fundamentally a dietary matter; rather, swine were considered sacred animals.* In the third labor of Heraclès the hero slays the ERYMANTHIAN BOAR by driving it *up a mountainside* into deep snow. Running uphill into snow the boar gradually slows and eventually stops completely, allowing Heracles to capture it. Here we have a particularly poetic description of breath control: a silent, snow-covered mountainside. There is more than an echo here of Sisyphus and the Stone, yet the scene is transformed because, whereas Sisyphus fails in his labor, Heracles succeeds in attaining the transcendent peace of samādhi.

Because the nose is also the organ of smell, a separate animal becomes necessary. Hence we find the imagery of a hound, a deer, a hind, a stag, and a bear, each of which has an exceptional nose. The Yaqui Deer Dance would thus seem to have some connection to the sense of smell. Indeed, the Yaquis call the natural world—the world of the countryside where the deer live, the prelapsarian world the Yaquis inhabited before the arrival of the conquistadors and the establishment of permanent villages—the *huya aniya* or "flower world," the world before time began that might be likened to the GARDEN OF EDEN. Between sets of dancing in the deer-dance rite, a great deal of smoking goes on by both dancers and musicians. In the present day that means cigarettes, packs and packs of them. In its original form though, highly aromatic, probably psychotropic, herbs were smoked, emphasizing both functions of the nose.

Summarizing, the horns of an animal naturally describe the sensory power of the beast. Considering each sense in turn, in the case of vision, there are, at first, two optic nerves exiting from the eyes, but they fuse into one nerve (composed of one million fibers) in the optic chiasmus before continuing to the lateral geniculate body and the visual cortex at the back of the skull. In the case of hearing, the two auditory nerves never link up, but their connections to the floor of the temporal lobe are well defined. In the case of olfaction, the olfactory

* L. Schaya, *The Universal Meaning of the Caballa* (Baltimore, 1973).

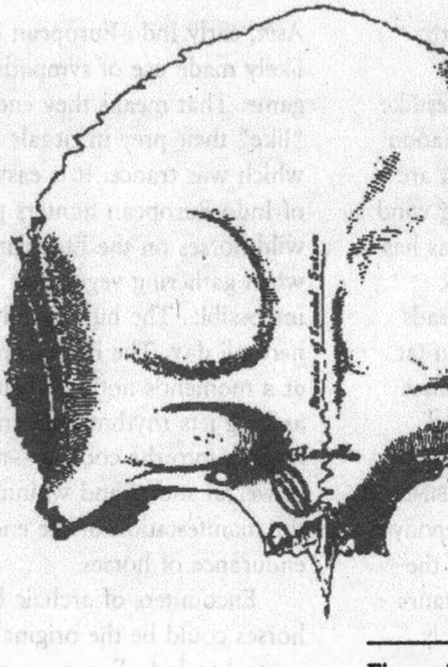

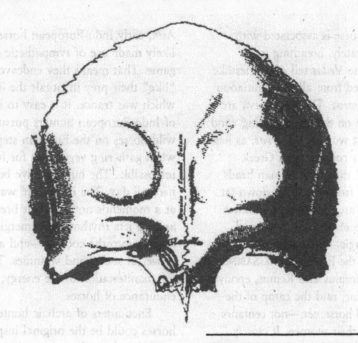

Figure 7. The Frontal Bone (from *Gray's Anatomy*)

nerves also fail to link one to the other, and their subsequent connections to the cortex are not well defined but, instead, are "lost" in a complex, upwardly ramifying collection of fibers. In the case of pure respiration, for which there is no dedicated cranial nerve, the nose extends out from the body. Turning now to the animals whose horns describe a sense, we have the ram, the bull, the stag, and the boar, respectively, for vision, hearing, smell, and respiration. The horns of a ram spring from a common point between the animal's brows. The horns of a bull do not join but thrust to the sides. The horns of a stag also do not join but, unlike a bull's horns, they are complex in configuration and reach upwards. The horns of a boar run alongside its snout.

Finally, there is what might be referred to as the sixth sense: thought, more concretely, voiceless speech. This "sense" really falls into an entirely different epistemological category from perception—namely, cognition. Voiceless speech is related to the frontal suture (figure 7), a pseudo-orifice in adults, running vertically down the center of the frontal bone of the cranium and directly in front of the frontal lobes, the higher processing centers of the brain, to which we can plausibly refer voiceless speech.

Two anatomical structures in particular merit attention: the glabella, where the frontal suture joins the bridge of the nose, and the sharply projecting nasal spine. On either side of the glabella are the frontal sinuses, shaped like the wings of a bird. The sinuses are less broad than the supraorbital arches. Hence, in myth we find them described by birds short of wing: doves, crows, and so forth, but also, because voiceless speech phenomenologically takes place inside the cranium and away from the light of the eyes, it is described by creatures of the night, for instance, an owl.* The nasal spine appears in myths as a spear or sword.

◆◆◆

Respiration is not a sense, but is intimately involved with all the senses. Especially in Indo-

* It is fashionable in New Age circles to speak of the pineal body, located well back of the frontal suture, as "the third eye," for which there is no provenance in Greek myth (a *cyclops* has one eye, not three).

European myth, the horse is associated with breath, or more accurately, breathing is described by a horse. The *Vedas* tell of a priestlike brotherhood, descended from all-male initiation cults, called the *gandharva*. The gandharva are horse-headed and ride on the "intoxicating wind [vāyu]."* The Sanskrit word *gandharvas*, as has long been suspected, is cognate with Greek *kentauroi*, "centaurs," men with human heads and torsos but equine from the waist down (at least that is how they are shown on the oldest fictile vases from Greece), who are wild and riotous yet wise in magic. One of the oldest Latin myths concerns the RAPE OF THE SABINE WOMEN, in which Romulus and Remus, eponymous founders of Rome, raid the camp of the Sabines, who are wild horsemen—not centaurs per se—and carry off their women. It closely parallels a Greek tale: the BATTLE OF THE CENTAURS AND LAPITHS, in which the centaurs, intoxicated by the *smell* of wine, go berserk and disrupt the wedding feast to which they were invited. The close etymological connection between the words *gandharva* and *centaur*, the similarity of their adventures in Greco-Roman and Hindu myth, their connection to initiation in both traditions—all indicate that we are dealing with an exceedingly old, purely Indo-European myth.†

Our Indo-European predecessors, loosely referred to as the Aryan race, on the best evidence available are thought originally to have been dwellers of the Eurasian steppes (present-day south Russia).‡ Naturally enough, in Neolithic times the broad, grassy steppes were home to immense herds of horses, and it has been surmised quite plausibly that horses were hunted for food before anyone learned how to ride them. As with the shamanic Yaqui deer dancer, whose distant ancestors also came from Asia, early Indo-European horse hunters very likely made use of sympathetic magic to find game. That means they endeavored to become "like" their prey in rituals the immediate aim of which was trance. It is easy to imagine a party of Indo-European hunters pursuing a herd of wild horses on the Eurasian steppes. It is winter, when gathering vegetation for food has become impossible. The hunters have been tracking the herd all day. The horses are wary, ready to bolt at a moment's notice. Their breaths are visible—as long jets rhythmically emerging from their nostrils into the cool air—and audible—as powerful snorts and whinnies. Their breaths are the manifestation of the energy, stamina, and endurance of horses.

Encounters of archaic hunters with wild horses could be the original inspiration of breath control in Indo-European religion. When the hunter practices sympathetic magic to capture a horse, the manner in which a horse breathes must surely inform his ritual. The hunter-shaman surely must imitate the steady, rhythmic, and powerful breathing of a horse. When breathing is made rhythmic, trance surely follows. Now, however, it is the trance of the hunter-shaman.

All over the globe the practice of a tribe or clan or subclan adopting an animal *totem* is common. The horse is the grand totem of Indo-European man. Once tamed, horses permitted the Indo-Europeans to escape the sea of grass where they seem to have originated (at least as a distinct linguistic group). And in their adoption of the horse as totem, a destiny was simultaneously selected for the entire world.

The magical imperative of a horse-hunter culture is to master the horse, to become like the horse. Thus the culture must adapt to ranging over vast distances, to the virile aggression of the stallion who fights to the death, who herds his mares together, keeping them apart from battle and reserved for copulation, who must exhaust himself, go without eating or sleeping, remaining fiercely vigilant, ever ready to lead his mares into the next valley, across the next river, over the mountains, indeed over anyone in his path, who must drive off his colts, who is, in brief, an arrogant, aloof, dominating creature sensitive to

* *Ṛg Veda*, in: *Hymns from the Rig-Veda*, trans. J. LeMee (New York, 1975), 10.126.

† G. Dumézil, *Mitra-Varuna*, trans. D. Coltman (New York, 1988), pp. 27–30.

‡ G. Childes, *The Aryans* (London, 1925), is a comprehensive analysis of the "Aryan question."

challenge, and, as Horace says of Achilles, "ever quick to anger."

Proto–Indo-European warriors—known as the Kurgan people—left Eurasia in the third millennium B.C. Within one millennium they were lording it over Europe, India, and Persia. We first meet the Indo-Europeans in history as dynastic rulers of the Mitanni, a non–Indo-European–speaking people of present day Kurdistan (northwestern Iraq). For centuries they disdained peaceful pursuits like agriculture and trade, preferring to loot and pillage. Throughout Europe and Asia the Indo-Europeans found peaceful, long-settled agrarian cultures on which to prey. Wherever we find Indo-European barrows, they are built over destroyed farmsteads and villages or on hillsides that overlook trade routes, that is, sources of plunder. Before they were conclusively identified as Indo-Europeans, archaeologists called them simply the "battle-ax folk."

When the ten-thousand-year-old agrarian "painted pottery" cultures that antedate Indo-Europeans in Europe had been destroyed, enslaved, or dispersed, the Indo-Europeans, whose ceaselessly migratory lifestyle had by then divided them again and again, inevitably turned on one another. They invaded and destroyed their long-forgotten kinsmen in wave after wave of aggressive migration. For example, the first wave of Greek-speaking Indo-Europeans into the Mediterranean were probably the Ionians. Then Achæan Greeks displaced Ionian Greeks, Dorians superseded Achæans. Centuries later, Celts—also Indo-European—pushed aside Dorians, and Celts and Dorians were displaced by Latins, the Latins by Goths, Alans, Vandals, and Lombards—in short, by Teutons. Then came the Slavs, then the Norse back-tracking into Russia. The only non–Indo-European peoples to challenge them successfully were the Huns and the Mongols, who were better horsemen. And still it wasn't over!

The next ten centuries—down to World War II—were consumed in settling how these kindred Indo-European–speaking peoples, these peoples of the horse, should live together in Europe, which has become a corral stocked with too many stallions. The Germans, French, and Italians have torn at each other since the days of Charlemagne, the English and the French since William the Conqueror. The English fought the Danes and the Dutch. The Poles battled the Lithuanians and the Russians. The French mauled the Spanish, the Spanish the English. They took their rivalries overseas, to the Americas, to Africa, Asia, and Oceania. The sailing ship was just another mounted charger, as later were the airplane and the tank (in modern military parlance, tanks are "cavalry"). Right down to the year in which these words are written, they are still ludicrously bashing one another—albeit tragically—in the benighted Balkans, these peoples of the horse.

Nowhere else on earth has witnessed such prolonged, internecine bloodletting as has Europe. And we have, for the sake of brevity, omitted the wars unleashed in the Middle East—in India, Indochina, and Indonesia—by those "Indo" Indo-European horsemen, the Persians and the Hindus, who proudly called themselves Aryans long before there were Nazis in the world.

No wonder, then, that the myths of the Greeks are stories in which war is the prevalent context, war the cultural determinant of the specifics of myth: the WALLS OF TROY, the SHIELD OF ACHILLES, the ÆGIS OF ATHENA, the BOW OF APOLLO, HERACLES' CLUB. And if not war, then hunting: the CALYDONIAN BOAR, the ERYMANTHIAN BOAR, the CERYNIAN HIND, the NEMEAN LION, the MAN-EATING MARES OF DIOMEDES. In Homer perhaps the most common epithet of an epic hero is "horse tamer," esoterically, "he who controls the breath." Narratives of mythic war and aggression, however, ultimately are at the service of describing how one achieves precisely the opposite state of consciousness from that of a warrior, that is, the profound peace of the mystic.

In Christian myth we find entirely different particulars. Instead of the WALLS OF TROY we have the CROWN OF THORNS, not the crow pecking at the eyes of the valorous dead but a dove, not Hector's "terrifying" horse-plumed helmet but a bishop's miter, not Heracles' lethal

Nessan tunic but John the Baptist's penitential hair shirt, not the battlefield but the vineyard, not THOR'S HAMMER but RUTH'S SICKLE. Yet each correspondence can, with varying precision, be shown to be two descriptions of the same bodily structure.

Greek myth also has a less belligerent side, which may be associated with a Pelasgian influence on Indo-European iconology. *Pelasgian* is an ill-defined term, much more popular in the nineteenth century than today, for the pre–Indo-European cultures of Greece and Italy. They seem to have been an agrarian people long settled in Greece, in Thessaly particularly, but also in Attica and Arcadia. Very little is known with any certainty about their religion. What is known has been inferred largely from archaic Indo-European sources such as the homeric sagas.* Nor was such influence as they exerted on the Indo-Europeans unimportant. On the contrary. We have, for instance, only a partly Greek embodiment of maternal love in Demeter's search for Persephone. Demeter is the goddess of husbandry. She also instructs Triptolemus in the "secrets" of agriculture, a Pelasgian art, and from both myths arose the Eleusinian mysteries, the holiest rites of European paganism.†

The Mysteries of Eleusis, a town in Attica, were renowned for the feelings of love and community and peace they engendered in the participants, which perhaps gives away the game because the rites of Eleusis are not mythical events, such as one finds in the *Iliad* and the *Odyssey*, but historical. The participants were not "heroes" but "hieratics"; in fact the two words may have the same etymology (Gk. *hieros*, "secret"), and likewise for "Heracles."

◆◆◆

The use of a ram to describe the eyes, a bull the ears, and so on is known to ethnologists as a *theriomorphism*, literally, "an animal shape." An animal is used narratively to describe a particular kind of experience. A further narrative step was taken when the senses were described by *anthropomorphisms*, and from those we have inherited the gods and goddesses of paganism. The temporal precedence of one descriptive form versus the other cannot be firmly established; both narrative devices date from a prehistoric age about which little can be affirmed. Frazer's exhaustive treatment of magic and religion weighs in on the side of antecedent theriomorphism. In Frazer's view, magic is virtually an atheistic art; its aims are material and practical, and the existence or nonexistence of a deity is quite irrelevant. Some material gain or advantage is anticipated by the sorcerer (shaman). Very often, as we've seen, the advantage sought is the capture of an animal. Religion, however, begins when not some sensible outcome is sought but, rather, the appeasement of an insensible god. Here we have the transition from the animal kingdom to the gods. A reverse development seems much less plausible.

One of our chief evidences for the connection between the two forms is the myth of the TWELVE SIGNS OF THE ZODIAC. *Zodiac* literally means "a circle of animals," which can be taken as presumptive evidence for the antecedence of theriomorphism. In the Chaldean zodiac used by the Greeks and Romans, a particular animal was associated with each sign, as is well known, but also with a particular part of the body. The zodiac is an invaluable collection of hundreds of archaic correlations among men, beasts, the seasons—virtually every sphere of life, and much of it is derived from augury. The zodiac is a kind of occult thesaurus, a collection of omen lore that redefines the experience of one thing in terms of the experience of another. The redefinition is sometimes obvious, sometimes not. For example, while the redefinition of the planet mars (and, by further correspondence, the god Mars) as iron is readily grasped, the redefinition of the planet venus as the herb celandine is less so. Correspondence here is almost in the nature of an equality. The alchemists of antiquity, heirs to much astrological speculation, did not

* Gladstone, *Studies on Homer and the Homeric Age*, vol. 1, pp. 100–215.

† *Homeric Hymn to Demeter*, 123.

consider the metal iron to be merely an aspect of mars but indeed as mars itself.

The ancients believed strongly in what Jung has called *synchronicity*: coincident events have coincident meanings. They were sensitive to omens, often morbidly so, and in particular to animal omens. If a Doric hunter on setting out in the morning chanced to see a wolf, a skilled predator, he anticipated good hunting. Moreover, to the hunter, the wolf was sacred to Apollo, indeed *was* Apollo in the guise of an animal. Thus the hunt and the god were knitted together meaningfully in the mind of the hunter. From our more skeptical point of view, the "truth" of the matter lies in whether the hunter did in fact have a good day, and in general we tend to suppose that the sighting of a wolf or hawk is irrelevant. Yet that is perhaps to dismiss too casually beliefs and practices having 10,000 years' experience behind them. The skilled omen reader would not look solely to the appearance of a predator for heavenly sanction but to everything in the environment that caught his attention *at that moment*. Was there a cloud passing over the sun? If so, the shadow on his path was not a good omen, for Apollo was also associated with the sun, and thus the god's affections were ambiguous. Did a raven croak? That would be a warning from Cronus. Because, apparently, the range of omens is potentially large, vaticination (omen reading) could be dismissed as unfalsifiable, hence unscientific; but also, because the number of omens is not arbitrarily large—as a practical manner, the hunter cannot notice everything in his environment *at that moment*—the truth or falsity of synchronicity ultimately rests with the skill of the vaticinator, which cannot be prejudged. His skill depends crucially on a high degree of concentration, amounting to trance. Vaticination then is a form of saṃyama, momentarily frozen awareness, as it were, of the immediate environment of the vaticinator.*

The word *zodiac* is something of a misnomer because not all zodiacal signs depict animals or at least no longer do so. Astrologers speak of bestial signs and human signs. The twelve-sign zodiac familiar to most people by way of the Greeks and Romans is derived from the Chaldeans, who seem to have taken over much of Sumerian sky lore. The Sumerians were Indo-Europeans, which suggests a connection with Persia, with India, and ultimately with the Aryan culture that systematized trance practice in the form known as yoga. The Hindu zodiac, which has only eight signs (sometimes ten), is in fact mostly animals. By the time it reached the Chaldeans, however, many of them were changed for cultural reasons.

The use of zodiacs for divinatory purposes is exceedingly old. The zodiacal sign rising in the east at the time of a person's birth is called the horoscope (< Gk. "hour sighting") and was of the nature of an omen. The idea that there is a special significance to the quarters of the heavens can almost certainly be related to the significance for primitive peoples of the *cardinal points*—north, south, east, and west—and is probably a refinement and elaboration of that belief. For our purposes, only the conclusions of astrology are an issue, not their empirical justification. Among those conclusions are redefinitions of gods and goddesses as planets and certain animals. Thus, in astrology, the war god Ares (L. Mars, "[the planet] mars personified") is associated with the zodiacal sign Aries, the Ram, and Aphrodite/Venus with Taurus, the Bull. By a form of occult transitivity, therefore, Ares becomes vision, Aphrodite hearing.

In astrology, a sign or a planet is said to "rule" a part of the body. Aries rules the eyes, Taurus the ears, Gemini the lungs, Cancer the stomach, Leo the heart, and so on. Indeed, such equations are an important clue that myth, insofar as it abounds with both deities and animals, is esoterically a description of the body. Yet even when the rulerships have been correctly identified, as they have been for millennia, a myth is curiously static, lacking both motive and rationale. The key to the myth is yoga (or something like it). The practice of yoga supplies, as a by-product, a dynamical interpretation of

* In this sense, saṃyama is synonymous with R. Heinlein's *grokking*.

myth, which is to say, an understanding of how the several parts of the body *should* be controlled during trance and why.

The third sign of the zodiac is Gemini, the Twins. In astrology Gemini rules the lungs. Therefore, in any "twin" myths, of which there are hundreds, esoteric respiration, which is to say prāṇāyāma, can be expected to play a significant role—also smell, which depends on respiration. In fact, the TWINS, considered as both myth and myth genre, is a description of just this dual function of the nose: respiration and smell.

A pattern is developing. In the first three signs of the zodiac, we have correlations with vision, hearing, and smell, leaving only the senses of touch and taste to be accounted for. The fourth zodiacal sign is Cancer, the Crab, a creature noted for its grasping claws, which can reasonably be equated with touch. The fifth sign is Leo, the Lion, or taste. The sixth sign is Virgo, the Virgin, which must then implicate the so-called sixth sense, which is voiceless speech or, more generally, thought.

The remaining six signs of the zodiac—Libra through Pisces—are problematic. Libra, like Taurus, is ruled by venus, Scorpio, like Aries, by mars. The sequence seems therefore to redefine vision, hearing, and so forth. Whereas Aries is a description of vision, Libra, the Balance, is probably a description of esoteric, that is, internal vision; Scorpio, the Scorpion, describes internal hearing; Sagittarius, the Archer (a centaur), describes internal smell; and so forth. None of the "esoteric signs" is difficult to reconcile with that hypothesis. Thus, the outline of a two-pan balance (Libra) looks like the shape of the brows with eyes closed. The shape of a scorpion's claws are polar, spread out to the sides like the horns of a bull. The horse-man of Sagittarius we have already related to the sense of smell in the myth of the Battle of the Centaurs and Lapiths.

The forms of the animal kingdom are as multifarious as the sources of myth, which are numerous even within a single culture. A useful epitome is this: Whereas several different animals can describe a single sense, they cannot describe another sense. There is a certain amount of redundancy to mythic theriomorphization. Our task now is to characterize the redundant element in myth more precisely.

8

RECAPITULATION

Anthropologists and historians have exhaustively catalogued the ways in which the traditions of different cultures both supplement and supplant one another when brought into contact. Yet even within a single culture or race, distinct groupings often occur. The Greek-speaking peoples who invaded the Mediterranean basin thirty-five hundred years ago arrived in at least three great migrations. All three groups were Indo-European, which means they probably began their westward trek on the Eurasian steppes. But it also can be inferred that long ago they were a single cultural group. As the Indo-European peoples spread out, they encountered other cultures and other myths.

The term *Indo-European* is a linguistic rather than a racial category. The racially pure Aryan who spoke the progenitor language—the Ursprache—of the Indo-Europeans no longer exists.* Language and culture, however, are intimately linked. The early Indo-Europeans were a belligerent, expansionist people. In imposing their language on the racially distinct peoples they encountered in the course of their endless migrations, they must also be expected to have imposed their culture and religion and to have accepted such trance craft as was consonant with their own.

In antiquity the similarities between, say, Greek and Hindu religion would already have been obscure, whereas the differences were more than apparent. The human body, however, is the same everywhere, and the systematic practice of trance is not an exclusively Indo-European phenomenon. On our hypothesis, much of the shamanic trance craft of the Aryans was anticipated in the trance techniques of their subject cultures. In India, where the arriving Indo-Europeans seem to have

* It was once thought that the Nordic races of Scandinavia were closest to the physical type; opinion now seems to favor the Kurds of Iraq and Turkey. Linguistically, Baltic tongues such as Lithuanian and Latvian seem closest to the posited Ursprache.

coexisted—albeit as ruling dynasts—with highly civilized indigenous peoples, the precursor(s) of yoga was long in place.*

The Greek-speaking population of Europe after the start of the Bronze Age (ca. 2200 B.C.) was far from homogeneous. We know of two successive waves of Indo-European immigration into Greece from the north and another from the east over a period of approximately fifteen hundred years. Three distinct Indo-European dialects make up what is called ancient Greek: Æolic, Doric, and Ionic. Religious integration of conqueror with conquered succeeded each invasion, with a constant reinfusion of ecstatic trance craft. Over so long a time frame the original Indo-European cultures were repeatedly and severally modified by geography and by contact with non–Indo-Europeans. The Greeks of antiquity were well aware of their differing heritages. In his *History of the Peloponnesian War*, Thucydides (d. ca. 400 B.C.) describes the indignation of the Dorian Spartans when they learn that their tributary city Platæa is besieged by Ionian Athenians. Dorian, Achæan, and Ionian Greeks clung to distinct religious practices, but their common origin in the Eurasian *Urheimat* dictated a certain amount of redundancy in the collection of legends called Greek myth.

Mythic redundancy expresses the simplicity of the trance experience itself. Concentrative techniques can be applied as one wishes. In rāja yoga, for example, the entire body is susceptible to the most refined control, but practically speaking that most often comes down to controlling the heart and breath, so myths tend to describe a limited number of things over and over, albeit with an amazing fertility of invention; and the same action/proprioception is described again and again within a single myth. The various episodes of a myth are often a stringing together of identical set pieces.

Narrative details are drawn from the culture at large and are chosen primarily for their value in assembling elements such as heroes, animals, or weapons crucial to an esoteric description of meditation. For example, when the Greeks of the post-homeric era spoke of King Menelaus of Sparta, they believed him to have been an historical figure—as he or someone like him may very well have been—who had been Agamemnon's brother, had ruled in Sparta in an identifiable region that they called Laconia, and had made war on Troy for the sake of his wife, Helen. When Homer recited his epic poems there can be no doubt that he meant that much at least. And for that very reason Menelaus—and Troy—could also serve mythic ends. Menelaus's historic and mythic "truth" are distinct categories.

In the ancient world rhetoric was systematized to a degree which has become quite irrelevant in modern communication. There were rules of imagery—many of them—known as *tropes*. An important rhetorical trope was *pleonasm*, emphasis by repetition of equivalent themes. It is perhaps the oldest and most primitive technique of prosody, reaching back to the concrete, archaic mind that finds it more expressive to list mutually identifiable phenomena rather than express the whole by a common and abstract quality. It is as common in the Bible as it is in Homer. One stripped-down example will serve to make the basic idea quite clear. In a famous scene from book 6 of the *Iliad*, Glaucus, a Lydian prince and ally of the Trojans, describes himself to the Achæan hero Diomedes by saying: "Hippolochus begat me and of him do I declare that I have sprung."† A simple, recapitulative structure informs all of ancient mythmaking.‡ The principle, insofar as it applies to myth interpretation, we define as *recapitulation*.

* In Europe, the archaeological evidence indicates that the Aryans dealt more harshly with the cultures that preceded them than they did in India, presumably because they were not much more civilized than the Aryans themselves.

† Homer, *Iliad*, trans. A. T. Murray (London, 1924), 6.206–7.

‡ Such a structure is as common in antique art and architecture as it is in literature; e.g., the entablature of the classical architectural orders describe the cranium, but so does the temple as a whole (see figures 21a–21c, p. 143).

That only the details of true myth should vary with culture is not to say there is anything at all random about the details selected. As we saw in the previous chapter, the breath is often described in myth by an animal that is a strenuous breather or by an animal with a prominent snout. Among Indo-Europeans that meant horses. In fact, the importance of horses in their myths and rituals is a hallmark of the ancient consanguinity of Hindus, Greeks, Persians, and Latins. During archaic times the horse was relatively unknown among Semitic peoples; in Semitic myth we more often find an ass or a pig describing the breath. In India we find the elephant and the swan as well as the horse. In sum, although the esoteric message of authentic myth is somewhat limited in scope, the details of a myth can vary widely depending on the particular culture under consideration. The myth can be retold a thousand different ways or readily incorporated into another tradition, all of which is especially useful in interpreting long mythic narratives.

We sum up the foregoing remarks in an axiom and its corollary:

Axiom II: The organizing principle of extended myth is recapitulation.

Corollary: The rhetorical technique of archaic myths is pleonastic.

9

THE THREE WORLDS

The many similarities among vedic, Latin, and archaic Greek culture—all of them Indo-European—have been amply demonstrated by scholars.* Chief among them is the emphasis on division into threes. In Plato's *Republic* the "ideal" society is divided into three classes: philosophers, warriors, and merchants. The same partition is found in Latin and Hindu culture, indicating an exceedingly ancient Indo-European origin, one that certainly cannot be more recent than neolithic times, when all three peoples coexisted, presumably in Eurasia.

In the *Vedas*, the god Vasiṣṭha creates the THREE WORLDS, separating heaven and hell by stretching the earth between.† That primal act of creation has several Greek counterparts, foremost being the division of the world by and among Hades, Poseidon, and Zeus, the rebellious Cronid brothers. To interpret the creation myth proprioceptively, we must divide the human body—and our experience of it—vertically into three parts: *stereognosis*, *perception*, and *cognition* (figure 8).

Redefining mythology as esoteric physiology requires a suitable frame of reference: the division of the human body into three "worlds" of distinct types of experience. Once we have established such a division, however, applying the proprioceptive hypothesis throughout the body of myth becomes systematic. The word *world* has a host of meanings important to understanding trance and its relevance to the creation of myth. In particular, the differences in trance on three regions of the nervous system are helpful in organizing authentic myth. The three regions have proper anatomical names, but in this book they are called the Three Worlds. Other, rather better-known works have called them HEAVEN, PURGATORY, and HELL. Starting with the torso, we find:

* Principally by the French ethnologist G. Dumézil, who interprets myth as ritualized socioanthropology; see his *Mitra-Varuna*, pp. 12–15, and C. S. Littleton, *The New Comparative Mythology* (Berkeley, Calif., 1973), passim; Dumézil's *Trois Fonctions* comes closest to the sense of the Three Worlds intended here.

† Ṛg *Veda* 7.86.

1. *Stereognosis*. The first world; the source of visceral proprioception or "feeling," also of proprioceptions of the sympathetic and parasympathetic systems; the body below the nostrils associated with taste (or gustation) and touch (or feeling). In myth the first world is described variously as Hell, HADES, the Infernal Regions, the PIT, and so on, also as the SEA: the "sea" of feeling. The first world is ruled by Hades but is more typically described by a female deity: Persephone, Hera, or Thetis.

2. *Perception*. The second world; principally sight, hearing, and smell, but all externally derived sensation. The region between the brow and the mouth. The second world is Purgatory. It is the site of the NARROW WAY, the SACRED GATE, an isthmus, the many perilous straits of myth. Often described as an ISLAND bounded below by the first-world sea. The second world is ruled by Poseidon or by any male deity associated with light such as Ares, Hermes, or Phœbus Apollo.

3. *Cognition*. The third world; chiefly thought, intellect, or the "sixth sense"; the head above the brow. In myth, it is known variously as Heaven, MOUNT OLYMPUS, SVARGA (Hinduism), and PARADISE (Islam and Zoroastrianism). In myth the third world is also described as a mystic SEA—the "sea" of thought—bounding the island of the second world from above. The third world is ruled by Zeus but closely associated with Athena.

Feeling is not perception, nor is perception cognition. Each realm of experience is both distinct and fundamental. First-world experience, for example, cannot be reduced convincingly to any conceivable second-world arrangement. As perceptions, one can scale *hot* and *cold* commensurately using a thermometer; as feelings, hot and cold are essentially distinct. Feeling, perception, and cognition are not convertible, one to another, à la feet to inches or years to days.

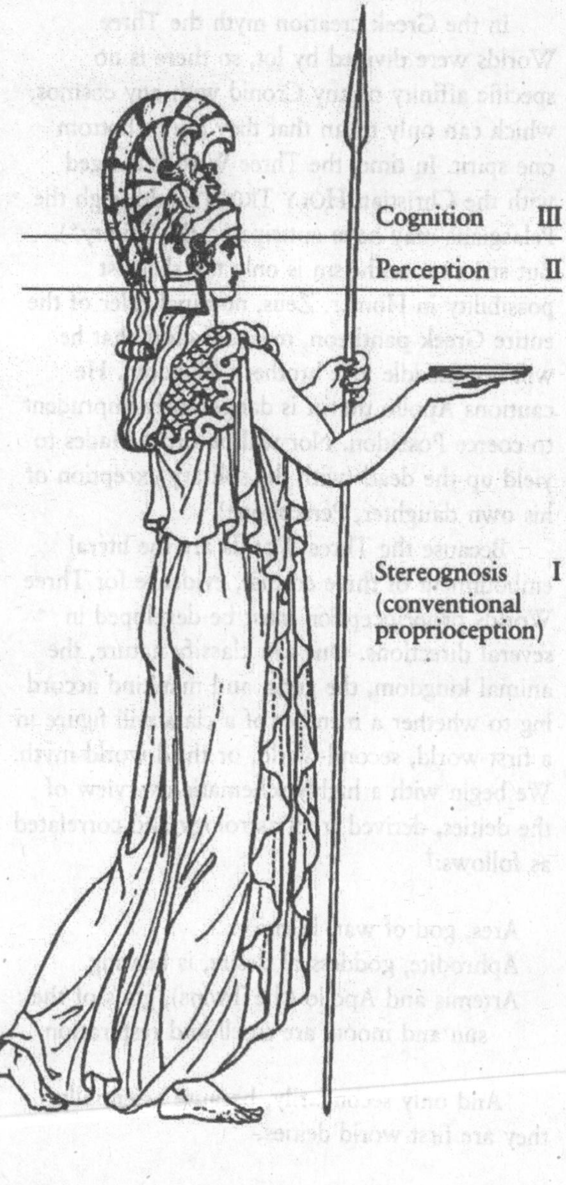

Figure 8. The Three Worlds

Cosmos (pl. *cosmœ*) is the homeric Greek word for "arrangement." By antiquity, it had come to have a much broader acceptance, that of "world." But cosmos is not necessarily the "world out there," the common modern connotation. The "world out there" is the second world, but the first world is as much an arrangement of experience as the second.

In the Greek creation myth the Three Worlds were divided by lot, so there is no specific affinity of any Cronid with any cosmos, which can only mean that they are at bottom one spirit. In time, the Three Worlds merged with the Christian HOLY TRINITY (although the Pelasgians may have anticipated the Trinity*). But strict monotheism is only the sheerest possibility in Homer. Zeus, nominal ruler of the entire Greek pantheon, makes it clear that he will not meddle in a brother's kingdom. He cautions Apollo that it is dangerously imprudent to coerce Poseidon. Nor will he order Hades to yield up the dead (with the solitary exception of his own daughter, Persephone).

Because the Three Worlds are the literal embodiment of three cosmœ, evidence for Three Worlds proprioception must be developed in several directions. One can classify nature, the animal kingdom, the gods, and mankind according to whether a member of a class will figure in a first-world, second-world, or third-world myth. We begin with a highly schematic overview of the deities, derived from astrology and correlated as follows:†

> Ares, god of war, is vision.
> Aphrodite, goddess of desire, is hearing.
> Artemis and Apollo (the Twins), gods of the sun and moon, are smell and respiration.

And only secondarily, because essentially they are first-world deities,

> Hera, goddess of the earth, is touch.
> Dionysus, god of wine, is gustation.

Let us look more closely at the Three Worlds.

* Gladstone, *Studies on Homer and the Homeric Age*, vol. 2, pp. 48–54.

† Latin equivalents are Ares = Mars, Aphrodite = Venus, Artemis = Diana, Hera = Juno; Apollo is common to both Greek and Roman myth. Greek names are preferred because Roman gods were so clearly lifted from Greek originals and because there are so many more and interesting Greek myths than Roman.

THE FIRST WORLD

The major figures of the first world are Hera, Hephæstus, Dionysus, Hades or Ædoneus, Persephone, and Thetis. In the casting of lots, Hades received dominion over the underworld. We have described the first world as having the nature of a *mystic sea*. Perhaps the oldest extant myth that describes the first world as a sea is Genesis, where the Elohist refers to the "waters . . . under the firmament."‡ Firmament here means the vault of the sky, thus, by extension, the phenomenological limits of vision. The water referred to is also the prosaic sea, which stretches from the lighted, airy portion of the universe downwards. The first-world sea is the same sea but principally in its depths, which lie out of sight, but it is also a sea in the amorphic (because essentially invisible) nature of feeling itself. Desires, appetites, and emotions are not perceptually definable. They have shapes only by weak analogy. They seem to ebb and flow, and the course of gaining meditative control of the first world is more a journey by raft than by foot.

The Greeks of Homer's day conceived the regions below the light of the sun—in other words, the interior of the earth and the depths of the sea—to be a vast, hollow cavern into which the rivers of the world emptied:

> Measureless floods of perennial rivers run under the Earth, and streams of hot and cold; . . . and great rivers of fire, and many rivers of running mud. Now all these waters are moved upward and downward by that in the Earth that swayeth like a swing. . . . There is a cavern in the Earth, which is the greatest of them all and, moreover, pierceth right through the whole Earth, whereof Homer says "Afar off, where deepest underground

‡ Genesis 1; "Elohist" is the name given by biblical scholars to the author of the first six books of the Old Testament.

> the Pit is digged," which he in other places, and many of the other poets, calls Tartarus. Now into this cavern all the rivers flow, and from it flow out again. The cause of all streams flowing out and flowing in is that this flood hath no bottom or foundation. Wherefore it swingeth and surgeth up and down and the air and wind surge with it.*

Esoterically, the ocean of feeling "hath no bottom or foundation." If we assert that our sensory apparatus precisely defines our awareness, that the sole of our foot "separates" us from the ground on which it treads, we rashly project a second-world geometry onto a first-world experience that is essentially *ageometrical*. Anyone whose foot has fallen "asleep" because of a cross-legged position on the ground can testify to how tenuous is the boundary between the organism and the world given in vision. One is tempted to say that the anesthetization of the foot is merely dysfunctional, a judgement that certainly suits the visual prejudice; but perhaps the falling asleep of the peripheral nervous system is actually removal of a neurological mask that veils a deeper connectedness between self and world.

The goddess most associated with this copious "flowing" is Hera, the wife of Zeus. The name "Hera" (< Ἥρη, more accurately transliterated as Hērē) probably derives from that of her mother Rhea [Ῥεα], "the flowing one," whom Hera almost certainly recapitulates in myth, especially as Rhea was the spouse of Cronus, whom Zeus supplanted as ruler of the gods. Moreover, Hera has a certain effective control of the sea. In the *Odyssey* she provokes storms and appears at sea usually as a vapor or a mist. She guides Agamemnon's fleet to Troy and Jason to the Bosporus. Homer tells us that Hera's chariot could travel in one stride only as far as the marine horizon, in other words, to the limits of perception, which defines the nervous-system sea.

Further encouragement for a first-world placement for Hera is that she is so frighteningly emotional. By turns adoring of her husband and volcanically jealous, Hera is frequently a vituperative scold, and she displays a certain expert brinksmanship when she wags her finger at her him. She is also occasionally scornful of Zeus's suzerainty—hysterically so when she instigates the REVOLT OF THE GODS against him. She is given to fits of unreasonable anger. Her husband accuses her of hating the Trojans so much she "would eat them" if she could, and whenever in the *Iliad* he tries to deal with Greeks and Trojans evenhandedly, Hera grows nearly apoplectic with rage. Her animal totem is the peacock, a bird of sudden, unpredictable temper.

As consort of "Father Zeus," it would be nice to equate Hera with the mother goddess of a trinity, but she can be correlated with a trinity myth only by establishing some sort of relationship between her and Gæa, Mother Earth. Melding an Indo-European trinity with the Holy Trinity presents endless problems. In the many trinities found in myth worldwide, a father god typically is the personified heaven.† In Greek myth he is Uranus. That he is a third-world god is undeniable. The child god in Greek myth is the Corē (< Gk. *korē*, "girl child"). In Judeo-Christian myth, the child god is a boy, The Christ, an intermediary between humankind and GOD THE FATHER, "which is in heaven."‡ The Christ is irremovably linked to the creation through his role as Logos,§ and the creation is the "world out there," the second world.

The Greek mother goddess, Gæa, is an earth goddess, but earth is the element that cannot be reconciled with the sea. She cannot therefore be

* Plato, *Phædo* 111C–112B, in Stewart, *The Myths of Plato*, pp. 85–87.

† In Egyptian myth, the sky is a goddess, the earth is a god, and they mate to produce Osiris; unlike the Indo-European Greeks, however, the Egyptians seem to have preferred sex in the female-superior position, to judge from their art.

‡ Matthew 5:45; see also Matthew 6:9 (Lord's Prayer), Mark 11:25, Lamentations 3:41, et al.

§ Cf., Viṣṇu, second person of *trimurti* (triune godhead), is the son of Brahmā, the Hindu father god; Viṣṇu sustains the creation in existence.

a first-world goddess, and the analogy collapses. It can be preserved only by equating Gæa with the earth *in its depths* and *out of sight* (the defining second-world sense). Homer offers some support—but only some—for the equation. Gæa is a virtual nonentity in both the *Iliad* and the *Odyssey* (Homer mentions her only three times, twice formulaically in a prayer). In her origins, Gæa is *chthonia*, "primeval earth [spirit]," which Homer denotes by ζειδωρος αρουρα (*zedoros aroyra*, "the barley-giving ground"). Curiously, Homer uses ατρυγετος* (*atrygetos*, "unharvested") as one of his favorite epithets for θαλαττα (*thalatta*, "the sea"). The root ideas of *aroyra* and *atrygetos* are intimately related in Greek, the one is in fact the inverted image of the other.† And Homer uses *eparoyros* (επαρουρος) to mean "alive." The sea is that cosmos that contains the seeds of all things, so there is no need of an earth goddess in Homer. The earth, "the wide-wayed world," is a barren place fit only for struggle and death. Ultimately, because he does not personify earth, there can be no explicit trinity in Homer. Summing up, Gæa is *not* the earth in its depths but rather just at the surface. The Greeks, as we have seen, believed the (planet) earth to be hollow and filled with rivers. Thus, it is the sea that fulfills any sense of depth in Greek myth. The earth is wholly within the second world; so too with Gæa.

That Hera is a wife goddess is as undeniable as anything in Homer can be. That she is an earth goddess is nowhere supported. That she is a mother goddess can be justified—she is the mother goddess because Zeus is the father god—but she is a very unmaternal mother, indicating again that her role as mother goddess only derives from her role as wife. Her relation to motherhood is more a happenstance of sexual heat, which she generates in good measure. The Greeks found large, round eyes particularly appealing in a woman, so it is not surprising that one of her epithets is "ox eyed." They also favored pretty arms, so she is called "golden limbed." She does not shy from using sex to gain her husband's (reluctant) approval for numerous hateful acts against the Trojans. Hera can also be placed in the first world because of her undoubted relationship to childbirth, even though, because of her husband's habitual faithlessness, most of the childbirths she concerns herself with are not her own and rarely bring out the best in her. When she interferes with the birth of Heracles—son of Zeus and Alcmene—she finally provokes Zeus to lay violent hands upon her.

After Apollo, Hera is the most problematic deity of the Greek pantheon. Often referred to as "Queen of Heaven," her claim to queenship is based solely on her being spouse to Zeus. She has no third-world attributes in myth. Nothing of reason, good counsel, or imagination—unless it be paranoia—clings to her. As we have seen, she is descriptive of several first-world affections: rage, lust, and jealousy. But there are simply too many correlations of Hera with Crete, an island, to place her once and for all in the first world. Whenever she and Zeus couple, they do so on Mount Ida on Crete, where Zeus embraces her within a cloud.‡ Moreover, her ancient seat of worship in Argos, which, as will be seen, is a second-world locale, argues against a first-world placement. What Hera seems to describe, therefore, is a general bodily warmth emanating from the first world and associated with the heart, seat of emotions, and with the genitalia. More sublimely, she is the passionate love of the father god for his creation, the ISLAND OF CRETE.

We can summarize all such marriages in a single metaphor: *fire and fuel*, an image most thoroughly developed in Vedānta.§ In every organ of the body, two very general qualities may be propriocepted: the *activity* or *energy* of that organ and, complementary to it, its *inertia* or *mass*. When, in a meditative state, the energy

* ?< α (not) + αρουργετοσ, "that from which the crop is not [yet] taken."

† Gladstone, *Studies on Homer and the Homeric Age*, vol. 1, pp. 130–32.

‡ *Iliad* 14.342ff.

§ I.e., the *Upaniṣads*; also, fire and earth, breath and food, Indra and Uma.

of the organ—meaning its own, unique form of awareness (seeing, hearing, smelling, and so on)—is focused on its mass via proprioceptions of respiration within the organ, the same "wedding" can be said to have occurred formally. The yogic term that best describes the union is *samāpattiḥ*, "fusion." Less abstractly, we have the union in every sense of *feeling* and *pleasure*, which are generalizations of second-world touch and taste. The sense of touch is ambiguous. Clearly, touch can be external, hence perceptual. That is what is meant by the "sense of touch." As has been mentioned, however, proprioception in general can be viewed as a kind of internal touching, especially when the source of experience is within the first world. The same ambiguity surfaces in the colloquial use of *touch* and *feel* as synonyms, which validates the relationship implicitly. It will be useful, however, to think of "touch" as second world and "feel" as first world. Of all the senses, taste and touch are arguably the most primitive. In our tentative classification, both are primarily first-world senses. Epistemologically the situation is far more complex. Taste is more than the sensations arising in the tongue, for which we reserve the unlovely word *gustation*. Gustation is a specialization of a more general experience, one that is diffused throughout the body. Taste *is* appetite, hence desire. Considered as the practical sense of pleasure or pain, taste is a component of all the senses. With respiration as a stimulus the meditator enjoys the eyes, the ears, and so on. Such a union is actually a reintegration, a "centering," in popular jargon, and leads to great peace.*

Hera and Zeus have a number of children—Ares, Hephæstus, and Elethyia. The latter two are closely associated with her in myth, Ares far less so. Elethyia, the goddess of parturition, is a mere cutout for Hera herself.

Hephæstus was a blacksmith and none too good-looking. Embarrassed by his ugliness, Hera flings him from Olympus. He lands in the underwater GROTTO OF THETIS, who treats him kindly, and he returns the favor by using his metalworking skills to fashion her an exquisite brooch. After returning to Olympus, he foolishly sides with his mother in a quarrel (mother and son are both first-world deities).† Taking a page from Hera's manual of child care, Zeus hurls Hephæstus from Heaven. He falls all day and lands on Lemnos in the Ægean Sea, breaks both legs, and has the breath knocked out of him. He reascends to Olympus on the back of an ass.‡

This is beginning to sound like Sisyphus, as well it should. By now his up-and-down travels between heaven and hell (Lemnos) stand out fairly well as descriptions of the rise and fall of the chest during respiration. In the *Iliad* Hephæstus is made to tell his sad tale to the assembled gods. When he is finished, Homer troubles to point out that the gods laughed as they saw Hephæstus go off, "puffing through the palace."§ His having the wind knocked out of him in Lemnos refers to the total expulsion of air from the lungs when exhalation is complete. The brooch that he makes in the underwater (first world) Grotto of Thetis likewise indicates the chest, over which brooches are generally worn, in particular, the place where the thorax joins the neck: the windpipe.

Hephæstus is a smith, hence in some way related to fire and air. His status as a smith also fixes him as a god of the first world, which is the center of warmth in the body. He is often shown on Greek pottery as holding a bellows. Like Sisyphus his name is composed solely of aspirates: *h*, *ph*, and *s*,# (in Greek, vowels don't count because the Greek alphabet originally lacked them). Hephæstus recapitulates Sisyphus,

* Oceanus and Tethys parented the Titans, hence are the ancestors of all the gods, including Zeus and Hera. In the *Iliad*, Homer describes both couples as quarrelling, i.e., disrupting samāpattiḥ.

† Zeus first turned on Hera and hung her from Olympus with two anvils attached to her feet. Anvils are proper to a smithy, so she was definitely put in her place by her husband!

‡ Apollodorus, *Bibliotheca*, in *Apollodorus: The Library*, trans. Sir J. G. Frazer (Cambridge, Mass., 1922), 1.1.23.

§ *Iliad* 1.599; Gk. *poipnyonta*, "puffing," extremely rare in Homer.

The *t* is thematic and not part of the root; in general, *tus-* and *tos-* can be dropped.

but he seems rather to emphasize the breath in the thorax and abdominal cavities, perhaps the *samāna* (diaphragmatic) breath of yoga. (It is therefore doubly interesting that one of Patañjali's more obscure sutras—*Vibhūti Pāda*, sutra 78—explicitly relates the *samāna* breath with maintaining digestive "fire.") His bellows doubtless is the diaphragm itself. His lameness is prominent in Greek art; he is always sitting down, namely, in the first world.

A meditator uses the breath as an internal stimulus of the various organs of the body, that is, as a source of proprioception. In that sense and only in that sense we may say that the breath "goes" everywhere in the body, the sense already hypothesized for Odysseus's wanderings in the *Odyssey*. As will be seen, the god who anthropomorphizes the circulation of prāṇa is Apollo. Hephæstus on the other hand describes the breath of the first world: respiration from the abdomen, up through the chest, and into the throat, reaching no higher than the sinuses before descending to the diaphragm. The image of a bellows is apt. During exhalation air leaves the lungs (the bellows), passes through the throat, and—if the mouth is shut—exits from the nose, emptying the sinuses somewhat as it does. If instead one breathes only through the mouth, the sound produced by the air in the throat is approximated by Hephæstus's name, just as that in the nostrils is described by the name Sisyphus. His marriage to Aphrodite describes the passage of the breath through the neck, the part of the anatomy for which bulls are readily appropriated as images (cf., "bull necked").* His proverbial lameness represents the impossibility of the literal breath's ascending into the cranium (third world).

Dionysus (the son of Zeus and Semele) is anthropomorphized taste. His animal totems include the panther and the serpent, theriomorphisms for taste, appetite, or both. He is traditionally known as the god of revelry and drink, in which role he is nowadays often burdened by a superficial contrast with Apollo (due principally to the work of Nietzsche). Dionysus describes proprioceptions of the thalamolimbic regions in the center of the brain as well as their neurological connections to the chest and abdomen. Dionysus is therefore a first-world god, perhaps the most important in mythology. But because taste informs every sense, he can be related to myths of the second and third worlds as well, attested to by his well-known mythic wanderlust.

On account of Hera's jealousy, the godling Dionysus is forced to wander the world. Accompanied by boisterous female acolytes, the mænads, Dionysus visits every corner of the Greek world to claim his right to receive worship as a son of Zeus. He comes eventually to Edonia, where the king, Lycurgus, treats him uncivilly and drives him from the land with a sharpened ox goad. He takes refuge in the sea and is sheltered by the sea goddess Thetis in her grotto (namely, the thorax; Thetis is the mother of Achilles, anthropomorphized diaphragmatic breathing). With her help, Dionysus returns to Edonia and incites the people to dethrone Lycurgus. Zeus punishes Lycurgus by blinding him, hence taking him out of perception and placing him under Dionysus's sway.†

The Greek word for "taste" is *hedone* (ἡδονη), similar to Edonia (an original initial *h* is often lost or gained in the evolution of a word), and the core phoneme of Edonia is *dn*, also the root of Dionysus. The Greek sense of *hedone* is far broader than literal taste, namely, gustation. It implies "delight," "pleasure," and privatively, "pain."‡ It thus corresponds to the generalized sense of taste we require to interpret Dionysus.

As often as not, Dionysus is accompanied by frenzied mænads and satyrs utterly obedient to

* The up-and-down motion of the breath in the throat suggests copulation, hence marriage. With an anthropomorphism of hearing, Aphrodite, there corresponds a theriomorphism, an image of a bull, because its horns lie in the same plane as its ears; the human throat is introduced esoterically by a theriomorphism, even though the boundary from the second into the first world is crossed.

† *Iliad* 6.130–44.

‡ Cleve, *The Philosophy of Anaxagoras*, p. 15.

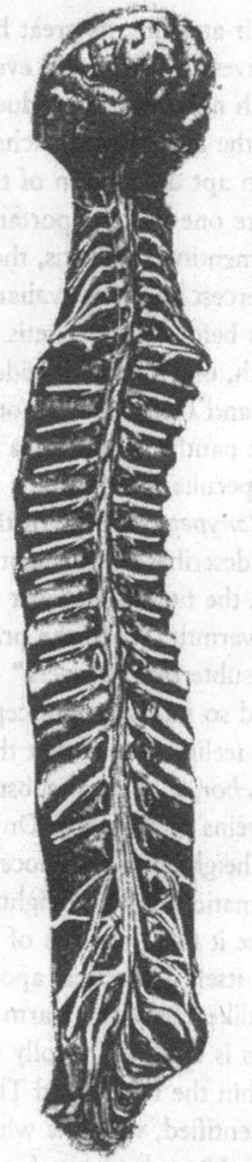

Figure 9. The Central Nervous System (THRYSUS OF DIONYSUS) (from *Gray's Anatomy*)

his will.* His singular cult fetish is the *thrysus*, a long wand with a bulbous tip, often fashioned out of a pine cone, that resembles the central nervous system from the base of the spinal cord upward through the brain stem and into the mesencephalon, which is to say, into the appetitive sensorium, and terminating near the pineal body (figure 9). The thrysus ties together Dionysus's essentially first-world nature with the limbic regions of the brain.

The underworld is called Hades (ʽΑιδες), an eponym for a god who is also called *Ædoneus* (Αιδονεος). The names are similar but derive from different roots. *Hades* means "the unseen place," whereas *Ædoneus* indicates the esoteric consanguinity of the god Hades with Edonia and Dionysus, namely, in the realm of appetite as defined above.

Hades is a bloodless figure in Homer, calm, quiet, and overshadowed by his wife, Persephone. He does not much like the sound of the horses' hooves during the battles before Troy because, pounding overhead, they disturb his repose; likewise the crack of Poseidon's trident when the god descends to battle on earth; otherwise he lacks any personal shading. His greatest act of self-assertion is to abduct his wife (Homer says nothing about it). He is repressed to the point of deviousness. He offers Theseus and Perithous chairs to sit in when they come to harrow Hell; but the chairs become part of their bodies, imprisoning them (strangely reminiscent of the loss of control over motor neurons that occurs in so-called rapid-eye-movement sleep, in which a dreaming subject cannot lift a finger to affect the "action" of the dream even if threatened). Hades is a just god, however, in no way comparable to the DEVIL, for we never see him tempting mortals. Tormenting the wicked he leaves to his father, Cronus, who lingers in Tartarus, where his sons imprisoned him.† For the most part, Hades is a distant *paterfamilias mortuum*. He presides over a cold and gloomy realm that is far from being a hell save insofar as boredom and lassitude are hellish. The souls (*idola*, "shades") who arrive there seem to be waiting for something, though it is not clear what (reincarnation perhaps). Just souls do not stay long in the underworld but are dispatched to the ELYSIAN FIELDS, sometimes known as the ISLES OF THE BLESSED. Exactly where those places are is difficult to say. They correspond to

* Euripides, *Bacchæ*, in: *Euripides: Collected Works*, trans. W. Arrowsmith, vol. 5 (Chicago, 1955).

† Poseidon approximately fills the role of Devil in Greek myth because he anthropomorphizes perceptual desire, as do Hermes and his son Pan (see below).

the Christian Heaven, which would seem to put them in the third world, and are probably outside of Hades' control, or at least they are in Homer. The Greeks did not like Hades much, as was only to be expected, but they also do not seem to have been very afraid of him. They were in terror of him only in the original sense of the word, that is, "in awe." He is a strangely metaphysical creature and not the primitively horrifying death spirit one might have expected. His most frequent epithet is "underground Zeus," meaning that he is a mere stand-in for Zeus.

The true personality of the first world is Persephone, the daughter of Zeus and his sister Demeter. Her name is spirant, so there should be a collective connection to respiration in her legends. Hades abducts her from a field of flowers on the island of Sicily, namely, the second world. The ground literally opens at her feet, and out he comes in his chariot drawn by four coal-black horses. Demeter, who recapitulates Gæa, threatens to famish the world by withholding the power of germination from everything that grows until her daughter is returned to her. An alarmed Zeus takes matters into his own hand, and on perhaps the only occasion in myth, arranges for Persephone to spend part of her time on earth, part in heaven, and part underground. This cycling motion once again describes breathing, as does her part in one version of the myth of Sisyphus, whom, as we have seen, she sends back and forth to the surface. Her close connection to the Eleusinian mysteries, which recount her abduction and restoration, suggests that she is not a description of some merely functional role of breathing, as is Hephæstus, but of an aspect of esoteric breath control. When, during the mysteries, she is ritually found, a ceremony not unlike the Greek Orthodox Easter celebration occurs. Her persistent title of the Corē, or "girl child," seems to be a reverential stand-in for her true, esoteric name, in the same way perhaps that "the Son" is a stand-in for the HOLY NAME OF JESUS, pointing in the direction of her being the residuum of a child-god savior from a pre-hellenic trinity.

Finally, Socrates' myth of Tartarus, with its billowings of air and fire, its great hollow into which all the rivers of the world eventually flood—although now they are reduced to the three rivers of the underworld, Acheron, Lethe, and Styx—is an apt description of the thoracic cavity. And here one more important homeric deity must be mentioned: Thetis, the mother of Achilles, the fiercest and most valiant of the Achæan heroes before Troy. Thetis is a sea goddess in myth, one of the Nereids, the daughters of Nereus and Doris. She is not a member of the Olympic pantheon, yet for a lowly nereid Thetis plays a peculiarly important role in myth. In her epithet *tanypeplon*, "she of the flowing robes," Thetis describes the elemental fluidity of the first world, the fluidity not just of water but of blood and warmth. When the prāṇa that energizes the "subterranean rivers" of the aorta, the carotid, and so on, is propriocepted, a distinguishable feeling results that the Greeks referred to as *ichor*, a magical substance that flowed in the veins of the gods. On our hypothesis, ichor is a heightened proprioception—hence a myth—of somatic fluidity. Heightened proprioception, because it fills the veins of the yogi with divine ichor, is itself a practical apotheosization of the yogi. Unlike Hera, the warm flow that Thetis describes is confined wholly to the first world, but within the first world Thetis and Hera can be identified, which is why, of all the Achæans whom Hera dotes on, far and away her favorite is Achilles.

◆◆◆

The first world surrounds the gestating fetus. For months before birth, a human being is aware. A fetus hears its own internal state much more easily than after its birth. More important than fetal hearing, however, is fetal touch. It is a state of true proprioceptive revery that cannot but leave a deep mark on the person. Experiences from the womb are remembered vividly during meditation on the first world; a blissful warm memory is resurrected. In proprioceptions of the navel we reexperience the flow of aliment from our mother's body, the weightless and inverted floating beyond the grip of gravity. Interiority and exteriority are dissolved and a state of placelessness—what might be called *ateriority*—emerges. Patañjali's word for placelessness is *antaraṅga*, "[an] inner limb." The aterior experience is not illusory. On the contrary, it is the essence of the inner worlds.

The reality of the fetus is almost entirely proprioceptive: the eyes, ears, nose, and mouth are plugged. To find eternal life, Jesus tells Nicodemus that one must enter into the womb a second time, that one must be "born again of water and the spirit."* By using the breath—the spirit—one reenters the fluidity of the first world, where external stimuli, a sense of space and time, cannot penetrate, where "she of the flowing robes" is queen. In the trance of the first world, one reencounters the GREAT MOTHER, the anthropomorphism of feeling.

THE SECOND WORLD

We live, each of us, within a "cone of light." The cone extends from our eyes to the horizon. Of events occurring outside that cone, defined in mathematical physics as the surface formed by causal spatiotemporal trajectories that a beam of light can follow, we can have no knowledge. Such events are acausal in that knowledge of their existence implies transmission of information at a velocity exceeding that of light. The universe outside the light cone may be infinite or finite. It may work by the same laws of physics as hold within the cone, or it may behave radically differently. We do not know.†

The sequence sea-island-sea sets off the second world as a volume of light and clarity between the amorphous, difficult-to-control experiences of the first and third worlds. An island—solidity in the midst of fluidity—is useful as a mythological locale that describes the second world, that is, the perceptual universe of stable forms and definable, relatively permanent phenomena: the world of objects and things. There is a curious paradox in such an image because the perceptual world was also considered by the ancients to be a place of illusion and suffering, illusory because its verities are only apparent, subject to birth, decay, and death. The insidiousness of the second world derives precisely from its illusion of permanence, for it is in fact an arena of ceaseless and inexorable change.‡

For obvious reasons, the second world can also be called the external world. The second world is the world of the senses, the world that distracts one from contemplation (dhyāna); as such it always has a pejorative cast in mythic narrative. The second world is the "world" in the ordinarily accepted sense of the word, for example in the phrase the "cares of the world." It is the objective world, namely, the object of most of our science.

Because an "objective" locus exists for all senses, in other words, because the organ of the sense can be *seen*, all senses can be referred to the second world, regardless of whether they are first, second, or third world under our present classification. The aesthesiology of the second world is summed up in the *provisional taxonomy*:

1. Vision dominates the "seeing is believing," nuts-and-bolts world of objective fact. Yet vision itself senses only immateriality. Light, the stimulus of vision, possesses neither weight nor mass. The organ of vision is the eye.

* John 3:3–5.

† The space formed by the light cone I am positing should not be identified with the hypothesized space lying beyond the farthest reaches of the visible universe; the one is a *subspace* of the other. The latter is a truly physical space, albeit a theoretical one at present, the extent of which depends on the age of the universe, a datum not yet conclusively given by experiment. The space surrounding the light cone is part of Minkowski space, a four-dimensional "mathematical space."

‡ Perceptually derived newtonian science relies on conservation principles for its calculations, e.g., those of mass and energy, entailing transformation of observables and continuous change (see pp. 274–75, 329–31).

2. Hearing requires the vibration of matter (air). Hearing only appears to be immaterial; it is phenomenologically immaterial. In a prescientific age the appearance of immateriality is all that matters. The organ of hearing is the ear.
3. Smell too only appears to be immaterial but actually results from a stimulation of the olfactory nerves in the nose by particles carried on the air. The organ of smell is the nose—but the nose is also the organ of respiration, a dual function that is universally described by the myth of the Twins.
4. Touch senses materiality. The organ of second-world touch is the skin.
5. Taste senses savor. The organ of second-world taste (gustation) is the tongue.

The ancient Greek word for perception was *æsthetikos*, from which comes our word *aesthetic*, "that which [pleases] the senses." Therefore, insofar as it deals with the physiology of perception, our approach to sorting out myth is aesthesiological. But it is also very much a phenomenological approach. Our word *phenomenon* comes from a Greek word meaning "to show." In archaic Greek it had roughly the same sense as our English word *shine* and described various categories of visual experience, for example, "appearance," "aspect," and "semblance."

The second world divides the first world from the third. Your daily existence is structured by the division. Awareness "roams" from one world to the next. You sometimes think, you sometimes see, you sometimes feel. You cannot, however, fail to notice the qualitative, phenomenological distinctions among feeling, perceiving, and thinking, as well as how they *seem* to be arranged vertically in your body. Phenomenologically, the appearance of a thing is the most important kind of knowledge one can have about that thing. *Phenomenology* by definition, therefore, is a word legitimately applied only to the second world. Properly speaking, a "thing" can only be a phenomenon.

In your mind's eye, "put down" this book a moment and consider the following facts. The "picture" of this book that modern science proposes is one of surprising homogeneity; at the atomic level the book looks pretty much the same from wherever you observe it. Moreover, it is mostly empty space. Chemists and physicists agree that a book is made up of atoms, which are themselves made up of protons, neutrons, and electrons. Further, it appears that the neutron is a composite of proton and electron. Further, all electrons are physically identical with respect to charge, diameter, mass, and so on, down to the umpteenth decimal place. Electrons are described mathematically by "overlapping wave functions," which means it is impossible to distinguish one electron unambiguously among the so-called clouds of electrons comprised by the paper and ink of this book. The same is true for protons and neutrons, which are all jammed into inconceivably tiny volumes, known as nuclei, separated from each other by prodigious distances relative to their diameters.

Now close your mind's eye and open your eyes of vision. Look at this book carefully. What you see is the book as *phenomenon*. How much does it conform to the book described by a physicist? Not very? Which "picture" is correct? Clearly neither is—or both are—because they serve different purposes. It is enough to recognize that there is an epistemological disjunction between cognition and perception. The disjunction indicates that the external, phenomenal world of the senses, the second world, differs qualitatively from the interior, cognitive world.

Whenever you close your eyes you take a step toward reuniting the mystic seas, a reunion that can be taken as the aim of yoga. The same idea is recapitulated in the Old Testament story of NOAH'S ARK: Noah shuts himself up inside the ark and sits out the FLOOD. According to Midrash (rabbinic commentary), the flood was brought about when an angry Yahweh (God) reunited the "waters of Tehom" that were above and below the earth*—in other words, when

* *Genesis Rabba*, in R. Graves and R. Patai, *Hebrew Myths: The Book of Genesis* (London, 1964), 253.

God reversed the act of creation. The ark is the human body, particularly, as we shall see later, the skull, and Noah is the meditator caught up in the rapture of sublime trance.

In a wholly symbolic sense, the act of opening the eyes can be equated with the act of perceiving. Then the unity of the mystic seas is disrupted. In Genesis 3:7, Adam and Eve are expelled from the Garden of Eden after "the eyes of them both were opened, and they knew that they were naked." A Greek recapitulation would be the Orphic myth of the creation of the *visible* universe, which is described as a "crack in the cosmic egg" laid by the goddess Nyx or Night (namely, black, without light). Through that crack, terrible evil entered the universe, a lesson remarkably similar to what the Elohist of Genesis teaches. Note: The second world, seemingly broad and limitless to the eye and ear, is but a crack in the infinite void described by the first and third worlds, a void that is within each one of us, for each of us "hath no bottom or foundation."

We see the disruptive, divisive character of perception again and again in myth. It lies at the heart of all ancient creation epics—for example, the myth of the TITANS, children of Gæa and Uranus, earth and sky. It is the Titan Atlas who keeps heaven off the earth.* The Titan Prometheus created man in defiance of Zeus. His wife was Pandora, who opened the box that let all the evil into the world. The box is the cranium and the opening referred to is the act of opening the eyes, the essential act of perception that "creates" the second world, the world "out there." He makes men independent of the gods by giving them the gift of fire, which he bears from Mount Olympus in a hollow stalk of fennel. A dried stalk of Cretan fennel is shaped like a three-tined pitchfork and thus is a recapitulation of the TRIDENT OF POSEIDON (see figure 25a), and the space between the brows, the fire *cakra* of tantrism. Prometheus was the son of Japetus, whose is very likely related to the Biblical Japheth, one of the sons of Noah who entered into the ark with him; the ark, which God insists must have *three* decks, is a description of the human body, particularly the skull. Prometheus suffers terribly for his assistance to mankind. Zeus chains him to a mountaintop, where each day an eagle—a bird long of wing—comes to feed on his liver. It is Heracles who frees him.†

The divisive nature of the second world is recapitulated in many sagas of struggle and warfare. In particular, the division of experience into three parts is the esoteric goad to the siege of Troy and the quarrel among three goddesses that started it all. The general sense in Greek philosophy—and by extension Greek myth—is that to perceive is a kind of defect of the soul, a defect within the "you" who experiences feeling, perception, and thought.

Fear, loathing, and scorn for sensory experience are found in Plato's dialogues and in the work of such Neoplatonists as Plotinus (d. ca. A.D. 270), whose work is thoroughly permeated with indirect references to secret knowledge or gnosis. In the *Timæus* Socrates explicitly states that "to perceive [æsthanesthein]" is to suffer. The notion is very old. Anaxagoras is quoted (by Theophrastus) as saying "Every perception whatsoever [is actually connected] with pain."‡ Lest the pain be considered symbolic or metaphoric, Theophrastus adds that "frequently when having a perception we experience pain in the manner of the perception itself, but, as says Anaxagoras, *always*."§ "With pain [μετα πωνου]" must be taken literally.

* The notion crops up everywhere on earth; e.g., Polynesians tell a tale of Tane-mahuta, god of forests, who stands on his head and with his feet pushes Rangi (heaven) off Papa (mother earth). In Egyptian myth Gep (earth) is separated from Nut (heaven) by Sho (air), the last being onomatopoetic for the nasal breath.

† Apollodorus, *Bibliotheca* 2.5.11.

‡ Theophrastus, *De sensu* 29, in: Cleve, *The Philosophy of Anaxagoras*, p. 111.

§ Ibid., 17, emphasis supplied by Cleve, p. 113. Socrates was initiated into the mysteries of Demeter at Eleusis, and we must assume that Anaxagoras was as well; initiation was so widespread in Athens as to be nearly universal. Like Socrates, Anaxagoras was driven from Athens for his esoteric teachings.

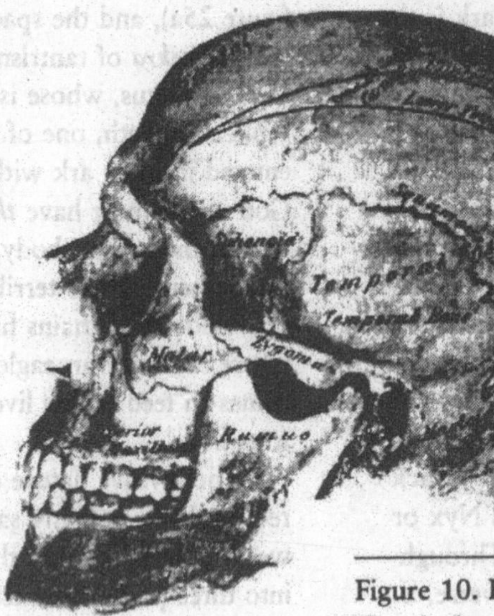

Figure 10. Bones of the Second World (from *Gray's Anatomy*)

During *any* perception—visual, auditory, olfactory, tactile, gustatory—a literal pain is present, one that can usually be sensed only in trance. On our hypothesis, the source of perceptual pain, normally only subliminal, lies in the complex structure of the numerous bones of the second world dividing the cranium from the jaw and ringing the skull roughly at the level of the eyes, ears, and nose (figure 10).*

Plato distrusted perception not simply because he believed it could yield no permanent truths but because of its seductive beauty, which can usurp the place of honor held by reason. That there is even a legitimate purpose to the creation is a real issue in Platonism. In perception the soul finds no peace, no solace, only death and suffering. Yet the extraordinary beauty of the world "out there" veils that basic truth. There is no place in Plato's ideal republic for poets, dancers, musicians—in brief, for any who rather than seeking the nearest exit as soon as possible try to make the best of things. For Plato, the problem was bound up with reincarnation. The soul returns to earth again and again to satisfy unfulfilled desires. "Best of all is never to have been born, next is to die young," wrote the poet Theognis of Megara (fl. ca. 540 B.C.).† His meaning is more esoteric than pessimistic.

The usurpatory character of undisciplined perception is the source of a great genre of myths, one so vast and well known that it would require many volumes merely to illustrate it in the corpus of myth worldwide, yet which can be summed up in the simple image of the son—perception—who rises up and kills his father—cognition. In Greek myth it is recapitulated again and again. Cronus castrates Uranus. Zeus drugs Cronus, then sets free his siblings, who have been swallowed, namely, sent down into the first world. Zeus takes Cronus's place as king in heaven, but his attitude toward the second world is much more ambivalent, as will be seen when we deal with Troy. (It is Cronus who, in Greek myth, ruled over the Age of

* In *The Journey to the West*, a Chinese epic, a Buddhist monk disciplines a chattering, misbehaving monkey by tying a tight band around its forehead. Each time the monkey acts up, the band tightens painfully until eventually the monkey heeds the monk.

† Anacreon, writing at roughly the same time, urged capitulation to the senses along the lines of eat, drink, and be merry.

Gold, the epoch of peace corresponding to the prelapsarian epoch of Judeo-Christianity.)

Zeus's ambivalence toward perception is justified. The soul must function in the world, but there is a danger: the soul may cease to discriminate between what is real and what is unreal. "The cause of that which is to be avoided is the union of the Seer [draṣṭṛ] with the Seen [dṛśyahoḥ]."* The root *dṛśt-* (see) indicates that Patañjali is speaking literally about perception, but in a more general way he describes the dilemma of puruṣa in its relationship to prakṛti.† What is real is what the yogi seeks to experience, namely, the puruṣa, the knower. What is unreal is prakṛti, the known. The quandary, the true Platonist peril, is that discrimination (Skt. *viveka*) between real and unreal might not be mastered *before* death occurs. Without having experienced the eternal before death, it will not be recognized and adored when it appears to the dying soul. That is the whole point of initiation: practice in dying.

The enmity of Zeus toward mankind is of the nature of a fundamental antagonism between, on the one hand, the first and third worlds and, on the other hand, a usurpatory second world. The second world emerges from the mystic sea, a gift of space and time in which mankind lives and breathes. But, snared by perception, men forget the gods, and from the *Upaniṣads* to the New Testament, scripture exhorts the pious to seek within themselves for happiness. "Within," on our view, must be understood literally. The second world is variously described as a vale of tears, a place of suffering, an illusion in which humanity has only a fleeting stewardship and no real home. The mythic correspondence is between the material home and the human body. In meditation one closes off the doors of the senses, to use a well-known phrase, and finds bliss in the inner world.‡ In practice, the distractions of the second world, its appetites and affinities, lie athwart the sādhaka's path. "Like a tortoise retreating into its shell," the *Upaniṣads* advise, the soul must withdraw from the world, there to wage war on desire. There is nothing easy about it, nor are there any guarantees of success.

There is something about meditation on the space between the brows that is extremely painful. The nature of the pain is describable as a cutting, a piercing, and ultimately a bursting, as of a dam, all of which, as will be seen, have to do with a singular event in the pituitary gland. There also can be no doubt that the pain is a literal one, as the disgustingly violent imagery of the homeric epics demonstrates. Warfare is an apt mythic device for describing the intially subliminal pain of perception, a pain that increases as progress is made in meditation. So many myths, from all cultures, involve warfare—hence, pain and suffering—that it is necessary to introduce it as a mythological principle: The disjunctions of perception from cognition and stereognosis are described esoterically by mythic war.

◆◆◆

"When the blast of war blows terrible in our ears, then lend the eye a terrible aspect. Let it pry through the portage of the head. Let the brow o'erwhelm it."§

Ares was the Greek god of war. The son of Zeus and Hera, in origin he is a god of Thrace, a region early populated by Greek-speaking Indo-Europeans. His war cry is deafening. He is called "brazen," "furious," "bane of mortals, blood-stained stormer of walls," and "insatiate of war," by Homer, who seems to have not much use for him. The few times he is at the center of the action, he comes off badly. A loudmouth and a braggart—albeit a handsome one—he is eager for blood; yet when he is wounded by Diomedes of Argos he flees to Mount Olympus bellowing in pain. Homer dislikes him to the point of depersonalizing him and degrades the word *Ares* into a common

* *Yoga-Sūtra, Sādhana Pāda*, sutra 17.

† Ibid., commentary.

‡ *Chāndogya Upaniṣad*, in: S. Radhakrishnan, *The Principal Upaniṣads* (London, 1953), p. 390 (all references to the *Upaniṣads* are from this work); cf., Matthew 6:5–6.

§ Shakespeare, *Henry V*, act 3, scene 1.

noun for "battle." Ares' depersonalization is perhaps on a par with that of Gæa in Homer, for whom the second world is lifeless, "full of sound and fury, signifying nothing." Perhaps his most important epithet is *andreiphontes*, "bane [lit., "slayer"] of mortals," because it demonstrates the dangers of perception—epitomized as vision—for the soul.

All in, Ares is a great disappointment because, on our hypothesis, he is an esoteric description of vision, the most important sense of the second world. The most convincing piece of evidence tying him to vision is astrology, in which Aries/Mars is the ruler of the eyes. The eye demands a male god to anthropomorphize its powers. Vision is active: the eyes seek and probe, they move in their sockets and focus. The eyes need not wait for stimuli to come to them as the passive ears await sound, the nose smell. To associate the eyes with violence is to repeat the commonest poetic imagery: the "fierce glance," the "burning gaze," eyes that "bore and pierce." The creatures of the earth most noted for acute vision are birds of prey, whose outspread wings resemble the shape of the brows. "Eagle eyed" and "hawk eyed" are proverbial. Ares' animal totems are the ram and the cock, the last almost a caricature of aggression. His color is red, of course, and he mates with Eos, the "rosy-fingered" goddess of the dawn. Occasionally mentioned is the "flashing crest" of his helmet, which perhaps describes the brows. His epithet of "brazen" gives a sense of flashing light.

He fathers nameless dragons—for example, the monster guarding the GOLDEN FLEECE—introduced only to roar and devour before being slain. When Cadmus founds Thebes, he slays one of Ares' dragons and sows the ground with its teeth. Armed assailants sprout to resist him. The same thing happens to Jason in the FIELD OF ARES (the space between the brows). Ares' children (in Homer) are Demus and Phobus ("fear" and "panic"), sheer abstractions, and yet, by the criteria of Platonism, not inferior in characterizing of what perception finally has to offer humankind. By Pyrene he is the father of Cyncnus (swan), who fought Heracles on his way to fetch the GOLDEN APPLES OF THE HESPERIDS. The apples, a gift from Gæa to Zeus and Hera, were guarded by another dragon. Heracles would have killed him, but Ares parted them with a lightning bolt.* Ares' monsters are descriptions of the great neural nexus between the eyes, where vision finds a coign of vantage on the "world out there." Monsters convey a potent symbolism: sensation run amok. In pagan art, teratomorphs (monstrous shapes) project enormous eyes and ears, long snouts, gaping mouths bristling with fangs, and talons instead of fingers.

Ares is the lover of Aphrodite, who also plays a minor role in Homer. In Hesiod, she is anthropomorphized desire, and is one of the oldest of the gods, older even than Zeus. The hesiodic tradition is less purely Greek, however, and more oriental. We have hypothesized that Aphrodite is anthropomorphized hearing, so her neglect by Homer might mean the same thing as it does for Ares: disdain for sensation. Their union describes the dominance of vision and hearing in perception. Aphrodite's husband is Hephæstus, an ugly, dwarfish god. When Hephæstus discovers Ares and Aphrodite in bed together, he captures them in a net and calls the other gods to laugh at them.† Here we see the yogic idea that the breath—Hephæstus—can be used to control the senses, for after the scandal Aphrodite lives more or less faithfully with her husband.

Aphrodite's animal totem is the bull, an esoteric description of the sense of hearing. A bull is an animal proverbial for its sexual appetites (it is known that, in women at least, music is sexually arousing). But if turning the earth with an ox-drawn plow is a description of thoracic breathing, as discussed earlier, an ambiguity results as to the esoteric meaning of an ox. In interpreting a given myth, we must judge the sense of the image from its context. For example, when Butes the Argonaut leaps overboard at the Sirens' call, the combination of his name (cowherd), his occupation (beekeeper,

* Apollodorus, *Bibliotheca* 2.5.11.

† *Odyssey* 8.267ff.

bees being distinguished for their sound), and Aphrodite's rescuing him indicates that here is a myth about hearing.* In the same myth, however, Jason plows the Field of Ares with the brazen-hooved BULLS OF HEPHÆSTUS, which is to say, breathing as the rise and fall of the chest.

Poseidon, brother of Hades and Zeus, presents a problem in his role as ruler of the second world. He is traditionally a sea god, at least as we find him in Homer. But the second world is the one experiential world that is *not* a sea. His best-known epithet in Homer is "earthshaker," for when angered he causes quakes. He uses his architectonic power to drain water from the earth rather than inundate it, as, for instance, he does at the pass of the Penæus, which carries off the water from the plains of Thessaly and which he is said to have created with a blow of his trident. It is difficult to imagine any god, and especially one as jealous of his prerogatives as Poseidon, reducing his domain in that way unless by draining Thessaly he was in fact increasing it. In myth, he is frequently called *gæaöchos*, "husband of the earth," or *hippios*, "he of the horses." He does not travel on the back of a dolphin, like his minion Triton, but drives a horse-drawn chariot and spends a good deal of his time in Ethiopia, of all places, which even the Greeks knew was not at the seaside and in fact is mountainous. He is constantly associated in myth with horses—indeed, he is variously credited with creating the horse or domesticating it—which would seem to connect him esoterically to breathing. In the *Odyssey*, when Ares, the preeminent second-world god because of his relation to vision, is taken in adultery with Aphrodite, Poseidon is the only Olympian to defend him.†

Yet by Homer's day Poseidon was explicitly portrayed as god of the sea, even though his control of the ocean is not an exclusive one. (Hera and Athena—and Zeus of course—can call up storms and tempests whenever they like.) Part of the problem undoubtedly lies in the fact that the Indo-European homeland in Russia was landlocked, so the Ursprache contained no word for "sea." Philology stratifies Indo-Europeans as follows: Before they divided, the Irano-Indian and Greco-Roman peoples were together as a single tribe no later than the pastoral stage of culture.‡ Because the Greek triad of Zeus-Poseidon-Hades derives from an extremely ancient Indo-European tradition that antedates the separation of the Greco-Romans from the Irano-Indians, Poseidon's original domain of rulership could not have been the sea. The sea-island-sea paradigm was something developed much later, after the Greeks had been in the Mediterranean basin a long time. It may also be that Poseidon's association with both sea and second world is tautological, for just as one cannot have mountains without valleys, one cannot have an island without the sea. More likely is that he is associated with the sea not in its depths, which is the first world, but at the surface among the waves, where sea breaks into foam and surf and the shape of things begins to emerge (he impregnates the nymphs Galatea, Iphimedea, and Amymone with sea spray). Sea god he may well be, yet he is still foremost a god of perception.

The Greek deity most nearly identified with the sea is Nereus, and he is not a second-world god. Nereus is the son of Pontus, "the sea," and although nominally subject to Poseidon in post-homeric myth, the two have not much in common. It seems likely that Nereus, who has his origin, as we shall see, in a third-world tradition, was substituted to fulfill the character of a true sea god—a character conspicuously lacking in Poseidon.

Poseidon's nature is violent. He has a great, almost unseemly love of sacrificial slaughter, especially of bulls, and he is child-

* *Argonautica Orphica*, 1284, in: Graves, *The Greek Myths*, vol. 2, p. 245.

† *Odyssey* 8.354–69. PASS OF THE PENÆUS describes the glabella (? *penæus* cog. with *pnoia*, Homeric "vital force," "breath").

‡ T. Mommsen, *Römische Geschichte*, bd. 1 (Leipzig, 1854), chapter 2; cited by Gladstone in *Studies on Homer and the Homeric Age*, vol. 1, p. 575.

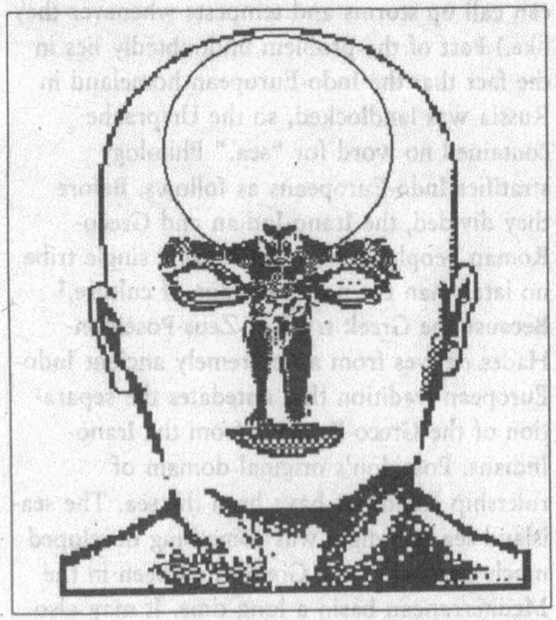

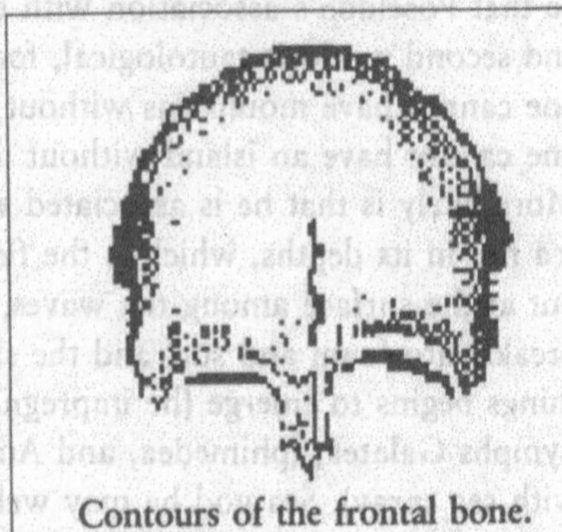

Contours of the frontal bone.

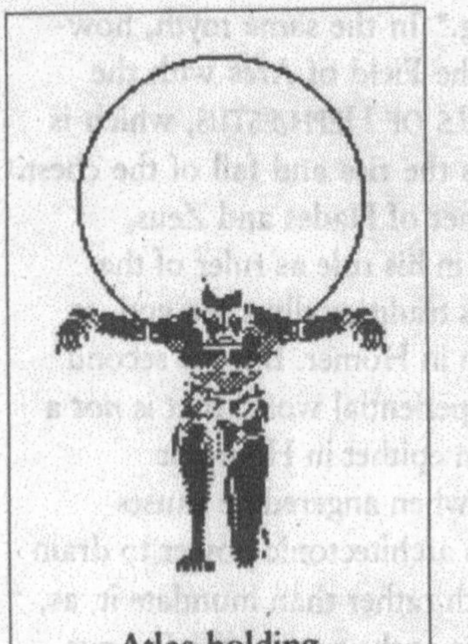

Atlas holding up the heavens

The daughters of Atlas:

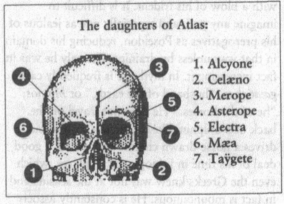

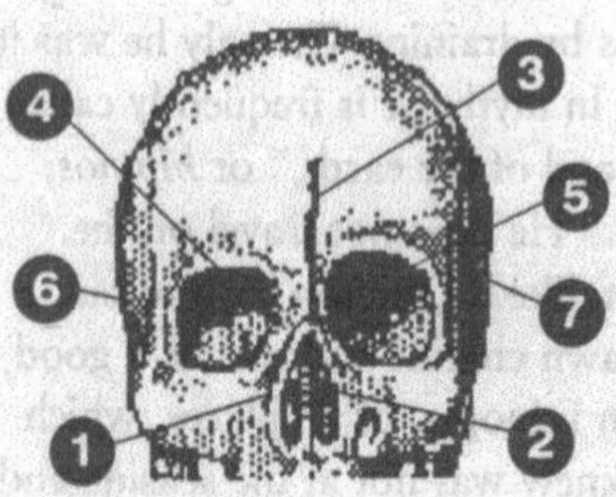

1. Alcyone
2. Celæno
3. Merope
4. Asterope
5. Electra
6. Mæa
7. Taÿgete

Figure 11. The Myth of Atlas

ishly resentful if he feels he has been slighted in that respect. His relation to animals in general fixes him in the perceptual world, for which animals are the natural impersonations of the senses. He is also the father of numerous prodigies and freaks of nature, for example, the Cyclopes, Pegasus the winged horse, the giant Antæus, the twin giants Otus and Ephialtes, and the Minotaur. The Cyclopes could well be characterized as vision incarnate, vision of a savagely unruly sort confused by desire: "The eyes of a fool are in the ends of the earth."* Poseidon has a habit of falling in lust at first sight. Where Zeus often makes at least a pretext of wooing his favorites, with Poseidon it is nearly always a case of rape. And by comparison, Poseidon's brother Hades—his unfortunate lapse in raping his niece to one side—is as chaste as a Victorian Methodist.

The bones of the second world are collec-

* Proverbs 10:24. Poseidon often journeys to the ends of the earth, i.e., Ethiopia.

tively described in Greek myth by the Titans, offspring of Gæa (Mother Earth) and Uranus (Sky). The second world lies between the first and third. The Christian Holy Trinity is in essence the same myth, with the child or SON falling between the FATHER and HOLY SPIRIT or mother. (Numerous traditions of Christianity, Judaism, and ancient Middle Eastern gnosticism associate the Holy Spirit with the female sex and the so-called feminine principle.) The operative act here is coitus. The rhythmic motion of the breath up and down in the nostrils is esoterically described by copulation between the god of the sky and the goddess of the earth. Nor is the sexual metaphor merely structural, but refers to the ecstasy of trance described by all the saints.

The Titans are notable in Greek myth—particularly in Hesiod's *Theogony* (ca. 700 B.C.)—for the numerous struggles in which they embroil themselves. The *Theogony* describes the TITANOMACHY, or war between the gods and the Titans.

Atlas, whose name means "he who suffers," is the son of the Titan Japetus. Atlas recapitulates second-world pain and describes the sequence of bones lying between the jaws (the entrance to the lower world) and the cranium, particularly those surrounding the orbits of the eyes. The bones are known by anatomists as the supraorbital arches, more colloquially as the eyebrows. The shape formed by the brows and the bridge of the nose was imagined by the ancients to be a strongman with head bent over and arms outstretched (figure 11). The frontal bone is his "burden." The central location of Atlas in the face accounts for his extraordinary importance in myth, which is out of all proportion with his role of Titan, most of whom are nonentities. He figures prominently in the sagas of Heracles and Perseus. In their entirety, Atlas and his brothers—Prometheus and Epimetheus—comprise the nasal bones, the malar, the superior maxillaries, the palate bones, the lachrymal, the vomer, and the inferior turbinated bones. Laterally these are assisted by the zygomata, the portions of the temporal bones below the squamous suture, and the occipital bone (figure 10).

The Titans are recapitulated by Otus (Gk., he who pushes up) and Ephialtes (he who leaps up), twin giants fathered upon Iphimedea by Poseidon in the spray of the sea. They stood nine fathoms (54 feet) high and struggled mightily to get into Heaven, where they vowed to rape Artemis. They describe the second world from top (heaven) to bottom (sea spray).

In a collateral Indo-European myth found in the collection of Norse sagas known as the *Elder Edda*, the gods fashion the WALLS OF MIDDLE EARTH—the place set aside for mankind—from the eyebrows of the Frost Giant Ymir. Above Middle Earth is Asgard, the home of the gods, below is Hell. A giant is the Norse equivalent of a Titan; Ymir is therefore identical to Atlas, the anthropomorphism for the bones (including the supraorbital arches) that divide the cranium from the jaw; and Middle Earth is also Troy, the epitome of the second world, as will be seen.

In effect the Titans define the second world anatomically by enclosing the apertures of perception: two eyes, ears, nostrils. The glabella or lowest portion of the frontal suture lies between the nostrils at the point where the breaths of the left and right nostrils converge and where someone meditating seeks proprioceptive "entry." The glabella, of course, is covered by muscle and skin, but if we consider it as a seventh, hidden, aperture, we arrive at the myth of ATLAS AND THE PLEIADS. Six of the seven daughters of Atlas and the ocean nymph Pleone bedded with gods and the seventh with a mortal, Sisyphus. Merope, the legendary seventh Pleiad, disappeared, supposedly because she was mortified that she alone married a mortal. The myth is quite clear that there were seven Pleiads, yet only six are charted in the constellation by astronomers. The discrepancy was noted, and commented on as such, in late antiquity. Several explanations were given for the "lost Pleiad." Some claimed that Merope was not put in the heavens with her sisters because she alone slept with a mortal or because she had accompanied her husband to Hades. None of the explanations is itself a myth but more in the line of literary criticism by educated Greeks for whom myths were venerable stories. The discrepancy is removed, however, when one realizes that the missing Pleiad is the "opening" of the frontal suture, which is literally open at birth but cannot be seen externally. And because the frontal suture is the point to which the breath in the nostrils rises, Merope is the wife of Sisyphus.

His seven daughters are at least as important in interpreting myth as Atlas himself. The daughters describe the seven orifices in the second world, establishing an important precedent: An orifice of the body is described by a *female* in myth. His daughters not only unite with important gods (Zeus, Poseidon, and Ares) but also give birth to them (Mæa is the mother of Hermes). Another daughter, Calypso, is a pivotal figure in the *Odyssey*.* Atlas's daughter Merope—meaning "bee face"—was the wife of Sisyphus, a union that can be equated with the marriage of Metope and Asopus. The Pleiads seem to have been ancient "groupies"; among them, they slept with Zeus, Poseidon, Ares, and Apollo and had children by them all (eventually, Zeus put them in the heavens as a constellation). Asterope slept with Ares—vision; it is a good guess that Asterope, whose name means "starry eyed," is herself a description of an eye socket. Alcyone slept with Poseidon, who is prominently associated with horses in myth, hence with breathing, and Alcyone's name means "jenny ass" in Greek, so we seem to be on reasonably safe ground if we see in her a description of one of the nostrils (Cæleno is the other). As for the others, Taÿgete, Mæa, and Electra slept with Zeus (Electra with Zeus and Ares), but only Mæa has much significance in myth (by default she anthropomorphizes an aural canal).

The unions of the Pleiads with the gods describe perception in the eyes (Asterope with Ares), nostrils (Alcyone with Poseidon), and ears (Taÿgete with Zeus).† The several couplings combine a piercing, outward-directed awareness with an opening in the skull.‡ Sexual imagery suits them precisely: It evokes the great pleasure that the senses give, the passionate hold that the world can have on them, and is a distant echo of the biblical Fall. For the Fall to occur, the awareness or soul must forget the inner worlds, must forsake both the HOLY MOTHER and the VIRGIN MARY and take a bride in the second world.

In the principal myths that concern him, Atlas has seven daughters, but given the many traditions that came together to form any myth and the repeated emphasis on the space between the brows, we should not expect a neat, one-to-one correspondence between all the daughters of Atlas and the orifices of the skull. When, in the *Odyssey*, Odysseus arrives at the cave of the Atlantid Calypso on the mysterious ISLAND OF OGYGIA (second world), Homer mentions that around the cave were "many birds long of wing who had their home in the sea." Birds long of wing are theriomorphisms for the eyebrows. The cave is the skull. Calypso is a daughter of Atlas, but here the seven orifices of the skull are described by the seven years Odysseus spends with her.

By Zeus, Mæa was the mother of Hermes, an important Greek god. He is in fact a description of perception in general. Not only are rams (vision) sacred to him, but he invented the *syrinx*, or pan pipes, and in his first deed he kidnapped the cows (hearing) belonging to Apollo and led them to his cave. Hermes was the father of Pan, a woodland deity associated with animals, hence with predominantly sensory experience. Indeed all sorts of animals—rams, goats, and cattle—figure in his mythic corpus. When he travels he uses winged sandals that

* Also, the Hesperids, guardians of a magical garden in the west, and the Hyads, who nursed Dionysus in a cave on Mount Nysa—all daughters of Atlas. Cf., Proverbs 9:1: "Wisdom hath builded her house, she hath hewn out her seven pillars."

† Because the theriomorphism for the passive sense of hearing is the bull, whose deity is Aphrodite, there arises the awkwardness of a goddess mating with a goddess, so mythopoets abstracted the active, male, tastelike component of hearing, which is Zeus, and made him the father of Lacedæmon, eponymous founder of Lacedæmonia (Sparta) and of a musical contest called the Charitesia in honor of the Graces (Charites). In Homer, Aphrodite is Zeus's daughter by Dione, "the goddess," namely, Zeus in his female form and probably synonymous with Hera.

‡ *Kaṭha Upaniṣad*, p. 630.

bear "him over the waves, like the cormorant, that chaseth the fishes through the . . . unharvested sea."* Homer's simile establishes Hermes in the second world. His name came to be synonymous with *cairn*, many of which were erected bearing his likeness, especially along roadways and at the entrances to private homes. A cairn is simply a pile of stones resting on the earth but supporting nothing. It is a clever representation of heaven—the insubstantial firmament which the Greeks believed was permeated with a subtle aether—and earth—the solid ground, which we may suppose has a great deal to do with the hard palate and the teeth of the upper jaw. The pile of stones that is the cairn recapitulates the separation of heaven and earth. Hermes thus recapitulates his grandfather, Atlas.

Hermes' well-known connection with roads and with communication in general—he frequently serves Zeus in the role of herald—is a reprise of the anaxagorean mind-body relationship: a ghost haunting a house. Perception links the soul to the second world. The organs of perception are metaphorical avenues of experience; alternatively they are message systems, sources of stimuli to which the ghost responds. The image of a road harmonizes with the essential spatiality of the second world, the reality in which distances are defined.

Hermes also carries a wand, the *kerykeon* (L. *caduceus*). The caduceus recapitulates the titanic pillar of the second world. Its most prominent feature is a pair of shapes: a circle below tangent to a semicircle above (figure 12). The round fullness of the circle represents the solid earth but the semicircle, like an empty bowl, is the incorporeal aether of heaven. The point of tangency is the perceptual universe, a mere crack. With his wand he "lulls the eyes of whomso he will, while others again he even wakes from out of sleep."†

Even the clothes he wears suggest the

Figure 12. Hermes with Chlamys and Petasus.

boundaries of the second world: a wide-brimmed hat, the *petasus*, and a poncho-like garment known as a *chlamys*. The effect of such a hat is to restrict the vision to a 180-degree vista directly in front of the wearer, cutting off a view of the heavens. The chlamys, on the other hand, does not so much clothe the torso as conceal it.

* *Odyssey 5.*

† *Odyssey 5.*

The function of Hermes' wand recalls another Indo-European myth, that of Māyā, mother of the Buddha. In Hindu astrology, the planet mercury (the Latin Hermes) is called *buddhi*, "mind." *Māyā* means "illusion" in Sanskrit. The manifest world is not "real" in Buddhist metaphysics because it is impermanent. Yet, if the illusion is to be dispelled, the savior (the Buddha) must be born from illusion (Māyā). The soteriology is familiar: Jesus—The Christ—must be born fully human if he is to redeem the (second) world.

Hermes is shown in Greek art leading the soul to judgment after death, in which role he is called *psychopompos*, "he who leads away the soul."* In astrology the planet mercury rules the everyday mind, the mind that is everywhere concerned with perceptual demands. The caduceus—which Hermes wields often enough in transforming men into animals—is perception itself, which lulls the soul not merely into dream sleep but into dream in the wider sense of illusion, a dream of the senses. Physiologically, the caduceus is that part of the Dionysian thrysus—the spinal cord—to which the cranial nerves of perception are connected, roughly, from the medulla to the thalamus. We might particularize Hermes further by recognizing in him a description of the thalamus, a switching center that routes signals from the sense receptors to the sensoria in the cortex. In Sāṃkhya the dream state is prefigurative of the ordinary, unenlightened condition of the human soul: it is fast asleep and dreaming. Initiation wakens it by revealing the *truth*, which is close to hand within the body. The nature of this "truth" is bound up with the esoteric meaning of the Logos or Word of God, more of which later. Under the guise of the mysterious Jacchus, Hermes is present at the Mysteries of Eleusis. Hermes describes the mind of the dying soul insofar as it has been shaped by perception into a dream state as it departs the world. The dream state, harboring as it does the hopes, fears, and desires of the expiring mind, then determines the future life of the soul. Often such lives are lived in animal bodies, hence Hermes' ability to transmogrify humans.

We next turn, briefly, to Troy and the Trojans, who are taken up in more detail later. In the *Iliad* Homer rhapsodizes at length about the fabled SIEGE OF TROY. The bones of the face are analogized in myth as a cyclopean wall, such as one finds at Mycenæ in the Argolis, in the ruins of the literal Troy in modern-day Anatolia, and the Bœotian city of Thebes, site of a famous siege described by Æschylus. The Trojans are perception rampant and their glory the glory of vision. Zeus decrees that so long as the sun shines, the Trojans will prevail over the Achæans. Therefore Hera sends the sun to set early.† In much of the *Iliad*, mythology is aesthesiology. The Trojans and their allied gods—sight, sound, and smell—are subdued by the Greeks and the gods of the first and third worlds: taste, touch, and thought. What we find, therefore, are Ares and Aphrodite more or less consistently taking the side of the Trojans against Hera and Thetis (aided by Hephæstus).

The esoteric meaning of the violence of the siege lies in literally painful experiences that arise during proprioceptions of the effects of respiration on the twelve major cranial nerves, most of which are second-world sensors. All such experiences tend to center on the frontal suture. Yogis call the frontal suture the "gate of Brahmā" because experiencing it leads to an experience of the supreme reality. "Passage" through the frontal suture is *spiritual* only, namely, by means of the breath. One attempts to propriocept one's way inside at that point using the breath as a stimulus. But why that point and no other can only be suggested for the present.‡ Behind the frontal suture is the pituitary gland, communicating with the pineal body, which is

* The jackal-headed Egyptian god Anepu (Anubis) does the same thing in the *Book of the Dead*, a manual on the art of dying.

† *Iliad* 18.209–39.

‡ In *Socrates' Dæmon*, Plutarch records that the shaman (Gk. *iatromantes*, "witch doctor") Timarchus of Cheronæa passed into trance and left his body via the frontal suture to visit the dead.

further back in the center of the brain. The pineal is attached by a stalk of nerve tissue to the base of the diencephalon. In shape, the pineal resembles a pinecone—hence, the name. For thousands of years it has figured in mystical lore. The seventeenth-century philosopher René Descartes thought it was the seat of the soul because of its central location within the skull. If the object of trance were proprioception of the pineal body—via its connection to the pituitary—at the instant that the breath stops, then the frontal suture is a reasonable place upon which to to focus.

A yogi uses breathing—and its effects—to "feel" a way into the body in much the same manner as a blind man uses a cane. When the breath rises in the nose, it strikes the bottom of the frontal suture on the glabellar bone, a metaphorical blow that is the basic image of a thousand Greek myths about war. Simultaneously the frontal sinuses fill with air and the frontal bone swells imperceptibly. Not something we pay much attention to in day-to-day affairs, proprioception of the frontal bone is intense during prāṇāyāma. When breathing slows to one or two cycles per minute, the return of a current of air to the nasal passages is emphatic and minutely observed, and the impact of the breath against the bridge of the nose is sharp, as sharp as the nasal spine that tapers to the glabellar bone (figure 7). The connection between the sharp topography of the nasal spine and the sharp pain of its proprioception is not coincidental. Touch receptors on the skin are capable of distinguishing the tips of fine calipers separated by no more than two millimeters. The neurons that distinguish closely spaced perceptual stimuli are themselves neighbors within the somatic sensory cortex (where sensations of touch are processed).* There is no a priori reason why that should be so, just as there is no a priori reason why a stimulus like the tip of a caliper that has a sharp shape should also feel sharp. Resolving the geometry of the nasal spine proprioceptively is therefore not an issue. Pressure is required to bring the sharpness of the calipers into perceptual awareness. And pressure is required proprioceptively as well, a pressure supplied by the respiratory cycle.

Figure 13a illustrates the line of sutures girding the skull. The sutures are somewhat loose and flexible at birth, but within the first year they knit together. The second world, with its six perceptual orifices (two apiece for vision, hearing, and smell), is busy with bones, fourteen in all, ranging from the large inferior maxillary bone (the mandible) to delicate lachrymal bones lining the orbits of the eyes.

Figure 13b is possibly the best-known mythic representation of the second world: the Crown of Thorns placed on Jesus' head just before the Crucifixion. In Genesis, Cain is marked on his forehead after murdering Abel; in cabala, Cain's brow is marked by a sharp horn. In the Apocalypse, Saint John mentions the "mark of the beast" several times and says that it is on the brow.

Heracles, son of Zeus by the mortal Alcmene, murdered his wife and children in a fit of rage and was sentenced by Zeus to do whatsoever King Eurystheus of Tiryns should ask of him in a year. The result was the Twelve Labors of Heracles, a cycle of related myths known to folklorists as a *saga*. By intentionally collecting myths into sagas, the mythopoets describe the systematic, step-by-step control of the organs of the body that the yogi must master. The first of the twelve labors was to slay the Nemean Lion. Eurystheus, who bore Heracles no goodwill, ordered him to kill a ravenous lion terrorizing the vicinity of Nemea near the Isthmus of Corinth. This was no ordinary lion but the enchanted offspring of Selene, the Greek moon goddess, who created it from the foam of the sea and enclosed it in an ark. Iris, the goddess of dreams, found the ark, bound it with a girdle, and transported the lion to Nemea, named for a daughter of Asopus. Heracles found the lion outside its cave but at first was unsuccessful in killing it because the lion was impervious to spear, sword, or arrow.

* W. J. H. Nauta and M. Freitag, "The Organization of the Brain," in: *The Brain*, ed. D. Flanagan (San Francisco, 1979), p. 46.

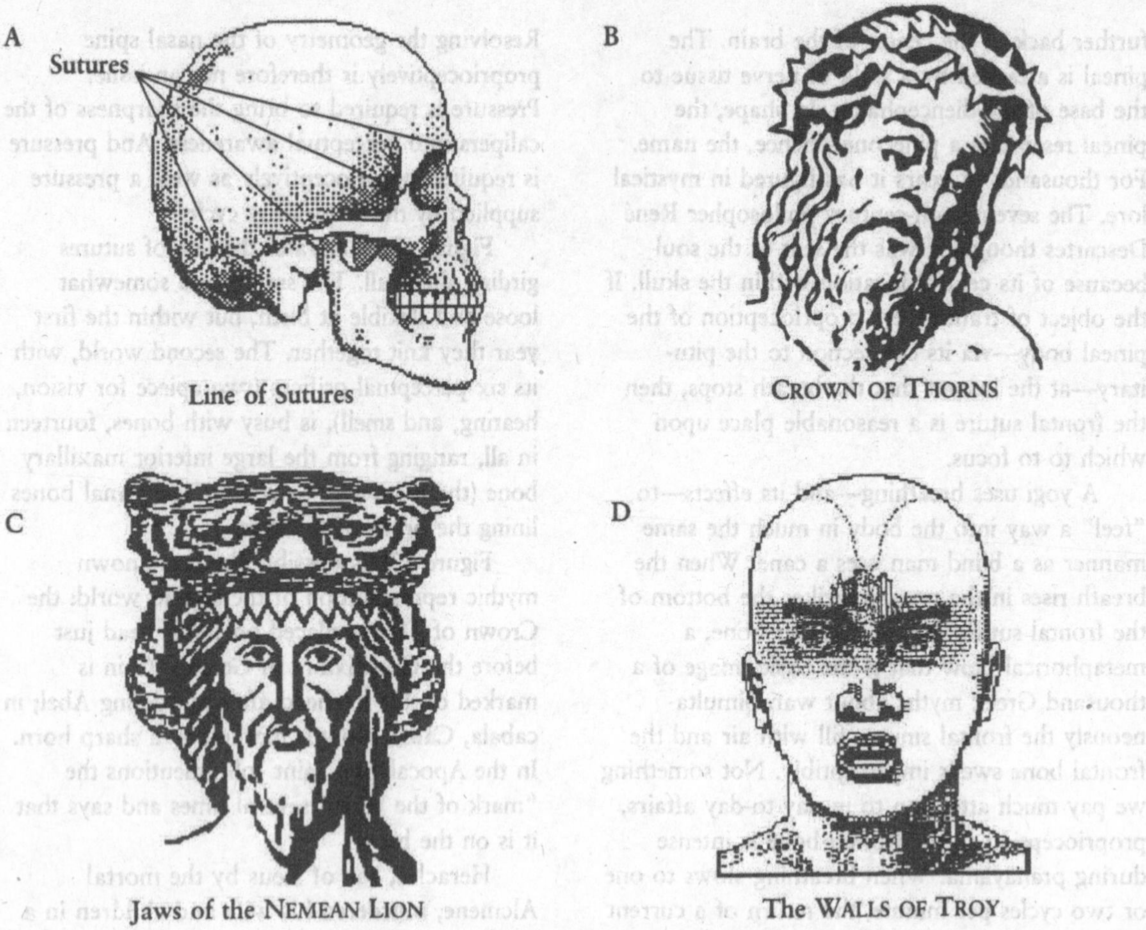

Figure 13. The Second World

With his famous olive-wood club Heracles struck the lion over the head so hard that, as Theocritus says, it made the lion's "ears ring."* He then drove it into a double-mouthed cave, blocked up one entrance, and strangled it in the other. Heracles flayed the lion using its own claws of adamant, a mythical substance of uncommon hardness. Ever afterward he wore the lion skin with the open jaws encircling his head. In antique art, the teeth of the lion often are shown biting into Heracles' forehead.

Let us look at the myth overall. Heracles strangles the lion; that is, he stops its breath. It is thus a myth about prāṇāyāma. The ringing in the ears is a heightened proprioception of the auditory nerve that naturally occurs whenever the breath is restrained. The two-mouthed cave is apparent in the gaping nasal cavities (figure 5, page 48).† Nemea, daughter of Asopus, also locates the myth in this region of the skull, as does the proximity of Nemea to Corinth. Placing the lion in an ark is yet another recapitulation of the cranium, an image of the skull during meditation similar to that found in Noah's Ark. The

* Theocritus, *Idylls*, in: *The Greek Bucoloic Poets*, trans. J. M. Edmonds, (London, 1935), 25.200–211; Euripides, *Heracles*, in: *Euripides: Collected Works*, trans. W. Arrowsmith, vol. 2 (Chicago, 1955), 153.

† Cf., *Odyssey* 13.96–112; Odysseus, after his long voyage home from Troy, comes ashore in Ithaca (in a trance) at the entrance to a two-mouthed cave.

biting of the lion's teeth into Heracles' brow is a description of the pain associated with the bones of the second world (figure 13c). So too is the girdle with which Iris bound the lion. Proprioception of the meningeal cap of the brain also is involved.

Blocking up one entrance of the cave seems to be a description of a well-known technique of kumbhaka. Your breathing alternates from nostril to nostril at roughly two-hour intervals during the course of a day.* According to tantra certain activities are favored when one nostril and not the other is in use. Yogis are extremely attuned to the cycle and make use of it in their practice. A yogi will pinch the active nostril with one finger when he wants to switch the flow of breath to the other nostril. Only in deep trance does the breath flow equally through both nostrils. Manuals of yoga describe kumbhaka and its uses in detail. Kumbhaka is considered only a preliminary technique of prāṇāyāma, so it is relevant that the Nemean Lion was the first of Heracles' labors.

◆◆◆

There are many sets of twins in myth. Perhaps the most famous are Artemis and Apollo, offspring of Zeus and Leto. Leto is one of the most enigmatic figures in Greek myth, a virtual nobody who gives birth to the greatest god in the Greek pantheon: Apollo. In the *Iliad*, Leto drives Hermes from the battlefield, but Homer tells us nothing of her origins. Hesiod makes her the daughter of the Titan Cœus.

When Leto is ready to deliver, she journeys on the south wind to the ISLAND OF ORTYGIA. Ortygia is pure myth, there being no such island in the Greek world; but nearby to Ortygia is the actual Ægean island of Delos, which at that time seemed to float here and there in the sea. Artemis is born without trouble. The parturition of her brother is another matter, however. Hera, Zeus's wife, jealous of yet another of her husband's infidelities, has placed the hapless Leto under a curse: Apollo cannot be born any place on earth where the sun shines.

Artemis is a precociously clever child. To evade Hera's curse, she instructs her mother to leap across the water to the north side of Delos and to give birth to Apollo there. Even more curiously, she selects the top of a pillar as the site of Leto's labor. On either side of the pillar grow two palm trees, and to ease her mother's labor Artemis tells Leto to pull down on a frond from each tree. In this unusual position, she gives birth to Apollo.

Our esoteric interpretation is that the myth of the Twins is a description of the dual function of the nose: respiration and olfaction. First there is the matter of their birth on an island, clearly placing them in the second world—and smell at least is a second-world sense. Second is the question of the *north* side of the island. Superficially this detail is a modestly clever way out of the dilemma posed by Hera's curse, and that of course is the traditional interpretation. In actuality though, even at the winter solstice, the sun shines on the northern side of Ægean islands—fewer hours of the day perhaps than on the eastern, western, or southern sides, but shine it certainly does. One would have to be very much farther north than the latitude of Delos for the sun not to shine there at all. The Greeks could hardly have been unaware of this fact, which alone makes the traditional interpretation suspect.

Apollo is frequently associated in myth with the Hyperboreans, a race of men who lived "north of north," and hence with Boreas, a personification of the north wind and one of the sons of Æolus. We have already met Æolus in the myth of Sisyphus and the Stone. So Apollo's connection with Boreas conforms with our interpretation of him as a description of respiration. Furthermore, the Hyperboreans are described as a people dwelling in complete darkness. Now the characteristic of the second world is that it is the world of visual experience, hence of light, hence sunlight. The inference is that Apollo describes either first- or third-world breathing. Third-world breathing would mean the breath as felt in the skull, what yoga calls the udāna breath. But for several reasons, the

* Easily verified by holding a mirrored glass beneath the nostrils.

first world is a better place to look for Apollo, in particular as the experience of prāṇa, the breath in the region of the heart, suggesting an esoteric meaning for the word *north*: downward into the chest.* Artemis, born opposite to her brother, is then related to esoteric *south*.

Prāṇa, in the present context, is a specialized use of a Sanskrit word having far broader application in yoga. Prāṇa (or *pran*) denotes a kind of vital energy, roughly equivalent to what Christians (and others, for example, occultists) call spirit and the Greeks called *pneuma*, a common term in hellenic science from the Presocratics to Aristotle. Prāṇa, in other words, is the core experience of breath. It is not exactly air or even oxygen but, almost, the heat of metabolism, which can be felt superficially as bodily warmth. We might say it is *vitality*, the *vis vitæ* (force of life) of an Epicurean like Lucretius (fl. 70 B.C.) or the subtlemost world fire of Stoics like Zeno and Cleanthes (300 B.C.). The Stoics believed that the soul was a kind of "exhalation of the blood,"† which would associate it with bodily warmth.

Other "breaths" mentioned by Patañjali—udāna, samāna, vyāna, and so on—are descriptions of specific, localized proprioceptions of prāṇa. The fact that prāṇa also has a specialized meaning, namely, the breath in the thorax, makes a good deal of sense because it is in the lungs, which surround the heart, that oxygen is transfused directly into the bloodstream, via the pulmonary artery, in the form of hemoglobin, a transfusion that can be directly experienced by performing saṃyama on the lungs. In other regions of the body the "pure" experience is more diffuse, or at least different, but at bottom all the yogic breaths are descriptions of one and the same thing: prāṇa.

Apollo was the Greek god of physical vigor and health, which ties him directly to prāṇa. His son Asclepius was the physician of the gods. In Greek myth a son is often an esoteric recapitulation of his father, especially if the son is a minor deity, as Asclepius certainly is. Particularly in the *Iliad*, Apollo or Asclepius or one of Asclepius's sons, Machaön and Podalerius, restores strength and vigor to wounded warriors and on more than one occasion brings them back from the brink of the grave.

Conversely, when Chryses, the priest of Apollo, wishes to punish Agamemnon, King of Mycenæ and leader of the Achæan host besieging Troy, he stands at the edge of the sea and calls on Apollo—"Hear me, thou of the silver bow"—to avenge him.‡ Apollo obliges by unlimbering his famous bow and shooting down Achæans in heaps, but not before he has killed all the mules and dogs in camp (mules describe respiration, dogs smell). Each man he strikes comes down with plague, and the Greeks, as the writings of Hippocrates show, believed that plague was contracted by breathing malefic vapors. That Apollo is invoked from the shore places him in the first-world sea. Also, when he is born, some traditions have the sea cover the island of Delos temporarily, placing his birth away from the rays of the sun and so evading the Heræan curse; when the sea withdraws, Delos remains fixed in one place.

Two-thirds of the nose is dedicated to olfaction, the remaining third to respiration.§ The seven nerves that supply the nose are the nasal, the anterior portion of the superior maxillary, the Vidian, the nasopalatine, Meckle's ganglion, and the right- and left-olfactory nerves. The complex innervates the nasal septum and the mucosal membranes, as well as bones and tissue too numerous to list. Connections are found with the nerves# of taste, touch, and hearing by the respiratory portion only, the two olfactories

* Since antiquity horoscopes have always been drawn with north at the bottom of a chart, east at the left.

† Marcus Aurelius, *Meditations*, trans. M. Staniforth (New York, 1964), 5.33.

‡ *Iliad* 1.39–52; Agamemnon had refused to ransom Chryses' daughter, taken at the sack of Chryse, a Cilician city allied with the Trojans.

§ Strictly speaking, the division applies only to the septum of the nose.

Usually cranial nerves or their rami, but sympathetic nerves are also involved significantly; touch nerves run to the eyeball, involving sight.

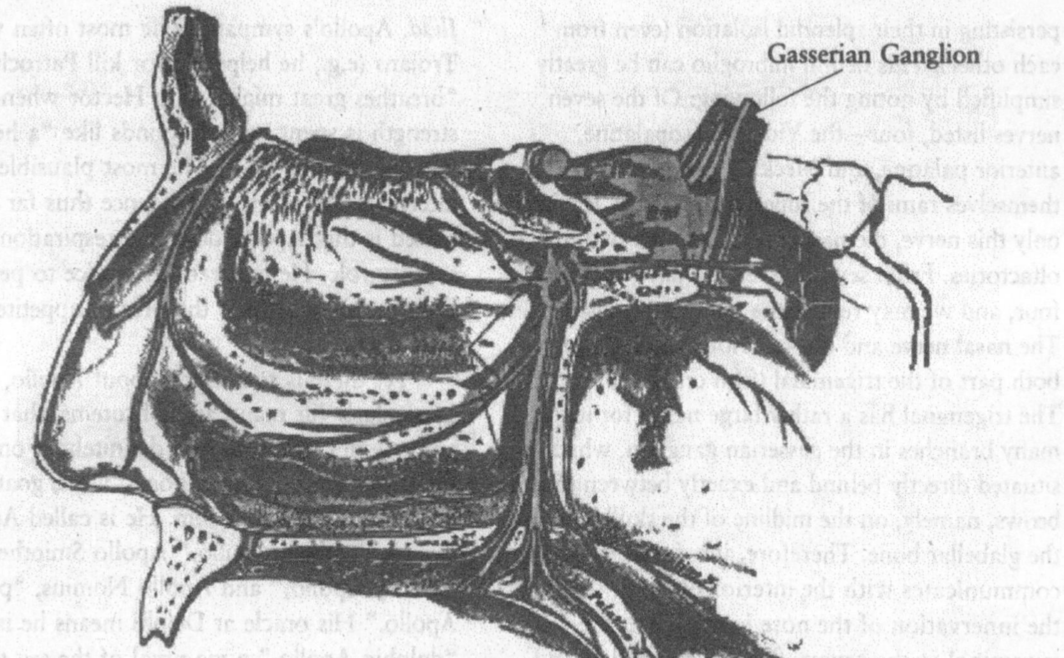

Figure 14. The Gasserian Ganglion (from *Gray's Anatomy*)

Figure 15. The BOW OF APOLLO AND ARTEMIS

persisting in their splendid isolation (even from each other). This neural imbroglio can be greatly simplified by noting the following: Of the seven nerves listed, four—the Vidian, nasopalatine, anterior palatine, and Meckle's ganglion—are themselves rami of the superior maxillary, leaving only this nerve, the nasal nerve, and the two olfactories. From seven nerves, we have arrived at four, and we may reduce the number yet again. The nasal nerve and the superior maxillary are both part of the trigeminal (fifth cranial) nerve. The trigeminal has a rather large nexus for its many branches in the gasserian ganglion, which is situated directly behind and exactly between the brows, namely, on the midline of the skull behind the glabellar bone. Therefore, insofar as it communicates with the interior of the cranium, the innervation of the nose is tripartite: the trigeminal in the center, flanked by the left and right olfactories (figure 14).

As the breath passes through the nostrils, it abrades the septum and the mucosal membranes. Because the trigeminal and the olfactory nerves are sensory fibers, delicate proprioceptions of the effects of breathing on them are possible. Those will, in the main, resolve into three "streams" of proprioception. It is precisely those streams that are described esoterically as *arrows*; the brows are the horns of the bow to which they are strung (figure 15). One of the arrows—the respiratory or trigeminal proprioception—is precisely aimed, so to speak, at the glabellar bone (namely, at the gasserian ganglion directly behind it), a jagged fissure that we have already seen gives rise to painful proprioceptions. Because a simultaneous stimulation of the olfactory nerves of the nose is unavoidable during inhalation, the proprioception will also have a tripartite character.

Once again the region between the brows takes on a crucial importance in myth interpretation. Because for all intents and purposes the breath acts constantly, proprioception of the region is likewise constant, rivaled only by the many sensations arising in the thorax.* In the *Iliad*, Apollo's sympathies lie most often with the Trojans (e.g., he helps Hector kill Patroclus). He "breathes great might" into Hector when his strength is spent, who responds like "a horse that had fed his fill."† The most plausible interpretation of all the evidence thus far presented is that Apollo describes respiration in its sensory role. He is breath in service to perception, the air that fuels the fires of appetite, the élan vital.

Yet there is something about Apollo, particularly his many animal totems, that resists any attempt to locate him definitely in one of the three worlds. Rams, boars, lions, goats, and bulls are sacrificed to him. He is called Apollo Lycius, "wolfish Apollo," Apollo Smintheus, "mousy Apollo," and Apollo Nomius, "pastoral Apollo." His oracle at Delphi means he is also "dolphin Apollo," a mammal of the sea that holds its breath, and the fact that he even has an oracle—not all that common—means he is a god of prophesy, suggesting a connection to telepathy, hence cognition. And it was at Delphi that he first achieved fame by slaying the Python after pursuing it into a hole in the ground called the *omphalos* (navel) of the world, all of which indicates a connection to the viscera; all of which can be reconciled by noting that the breath is not confined anywhere within the body.

Apollo—in bondage to Admetus for slaying a cyclops—yokes together a lion and a wild boar to help his master win the hand of Alcestis in marriage.‡ Admetus was king of Thrace, a land renowned in the *Iliad* for its horses. His name means "untamed" in Greek. In fact Admetus and the lion are descriptive of one-and-the-same proprioception: that of the chest, particularly the heart (in astrology, Leo rules the heart). Apollo and the wild boar describe the breath in the chest. The myth is a first-world depiction of the

* Meditative techniques that bring the meditator into an awareness of the brow and the thorax on a breath-by-breath, waking basis make up a branch of occult science known as *karma yoga*, to be distinguished from formal practices, known as *jñāna* yogas, of which rāja yoga is the most important example for our purposes.

† *Iliad* 15.242–70.

‡ Apollodorus, *Bibliotheca* 3.10.4.

meditative control of the heart (the lion) and the breath. Admetus's marriage to Alcestis, who is a description of touch—the Great Mother*—is an expression of the union of taste and touch, also exemplified in the pairing of Oceanus and Tethys, Zeus and Hera, and Ares and Aphrodite, among very many others. Apollo's temporary status as helot recapitulates the condemnation of Sisyphus. The breath must be broken like a wild beast before the meditative marriage (samāpattiḥ) is consummated.

Apollo's name is only debatably Greek. If it is Greek, then it appears to derive from a verb meaning "to destroy." Such a derivation squares well with the deadly effect of his bow. But Apollo and the warrior Achilles both describe first-world breathing, though they derive from different mythic traditions. Apollo is an Ionian god born on Delos, whereas Achilles is a Phthian from Thessaly. *Phthia* is an aspirate (cf., the medical term *phthisis*, "consumption," now obsolete), *Thessaly* an aspirated spirant. The Hindu god Śiva also carries the epithet "destroyer." Śiva (pronounced *shi-wuh*) is a sibilant name, which clearly relates him to breathing, and he too is famous for his magical bow (Piñāka), which plays a part in many Hindu myths, particularly in the vast collection of stories called the *Purānas*. Given that both are ancient Indo-European gods, there may well be a long-lost connection between the two.

As time went on, Apollo became somewhat dandified in Greek myth. Even in Homer he is moral and upright and incapable of the crudity of Zeus, his father, who dotes on him. By hellenic times (ca. fifth century), during the so-called age of Pericles, we find him associated, as divine patron, with poetry and music (and rather vain about his abilities, as when he flays alive the satyr Marsyas for daring to challenge him to a musical contest—and losing). The great poet Pindar of Thebes (d. ca. 438 B.C.) begins many of his odes with a prayer seeking inspiration from Apollo. For the Greeks, poetry always meant *sung* poetry, usually accompanied by a lyre. The connection of the breath in the chest, with which we are associating Apollo, and song is obvious. Apollo came eventually to embody the Greek ideal of perfected manhood: handsome, vigorous, courageous, and cultured. All such attributes, we surmise, are traceable to his original mythic function as a description of deep, regulated, diaphragmatic breathing, the source, according to Greek medicine, of health, vitality, and well-being.

There is finally the curious detail regarding Leto and the palm fronds. The image is closely related to the BOW OF APOLLO. With his bow, Apollo shoots down anyone foolish enough to anger him. In Homer he is definitely a warrior god and carries the epithet *hekaërgos*, literally, "he who works from afar," but frequently translated as "far darter" or "he who shoots from afar." Also in Homer we find descriptions of the bows used in battle, fashioned by joining together the horns of a ram. We have already noted that the brows of the eyes are described esoterically as the horns of a ram; correlation of the two images is inescapable. But the shape of the brow lines also can plausibly be likened to two palm fronds, with the trunk falling along the nose. There are two extremely ancient yogic techniques for concentrating on the space between the brows: one consists in looking up, as if at the bridge of the nose, the other in looking down, as if at the tip of the nose. Both techniques are called *trāṭaka*, "root gazing". When one looks down, into the first world, the eyes cross and the insides of the brows contract downward. This is the motion described by Leto's pulling down on the palm fronds. The inverse movement occurs in gazing up; the outsides of the brows contract downward: the movement made by the horns of the Bow of Apollo when drawn. The latter image is found in a well-known scene from the *Odyssey* in which Odysseus draws his bow and kills the suitors who have plagued his wife, Penelope, while he is away at Troy.

We now turn our attention to Artemis, the other half of the dynamic twins duo. We have already associated her with the sense of smell. As huntress, Artemis's devotion to archery was a commonplace of antique art. The animals most

* Alcestis means "strength of the home."

associated with her in myth are the hound, the deer or hind, and the bear, all of which have already been introduced as theriomorphisms of smell. In Homer she is definitely a minor goddess. In her one big scene Artemis, with Leto, nurses the wounded Trojan prince Æneas back to health in the Temple of Apollo in Troy (she doesn't even have her own temple). By bare possibility her name is related to Sanskrit *amṛtsar*, the aromatic beverage that preserved the immortality of the Hindu gods in the same way that the sacred nectar did for the Greek gods (smell and taste are strongly linked neurologically). She is also, and strangely for so militantly chaste a virgin, called on to ease the pain of childbirth. Clearly this has to do with her assistance in the birth of Apollo. Yet one cannot but wonder if the well-known technique of hyperventilation to ease delivery is not also intended.

No account of Artemis, however preliminary, can fail to mention her infatuation with the hunter Orion. In most accounts Orion is the son of Poseidon and therefore a second-world figure. In another interesting variant, Zeus and Hermes go awandering on the earth in disguise. As night falls they seek shelter at the rude hut of the elderly crofter Philemon and his wife, Baucis. Although desperately poor, Baucis and Philemon extend every courtesy to their guests without expecting recompense. When the two gods learn that the old couple is childless and, given Baucis's age, without hope of conceiving, they take pity on them. Both gods urinate on an ox hide, and from this Orion is born, hence his name (Gk. *ourianos*, "urine").* Orion grows up to become a famous hunter. One day in the forest he meets and falls in love with Artemis, who returns his passion and for the first time is tempted to forsake her virginity. She is prevented from doing so only by the deceit of her brother, Apollo. Jealous of his sister's chastity, he tricks her into killing Orion with an arrowshot.

Orion's association with foul-smelling urine is the source of his downfall. Orion is frequently associated in myth with a disreputable character named Œnopion (Wine Face), a son of the god Dionysus, who is anthropomorphized taste. The connection between taste and smell is well known. Neurologically, the olfactory nerves—uniquely among cranial nerves—do not connect directly with the hypothalamus, the center of the appetitive instincts of hunger, sex, survival. In the trance state, one senses that the olfactory nerves are heavily insulated by tubular prolongations of cephalic membranes (called the *dura* and *pia matres*) from electrochemical interactions with the nearby frontal lobes. The anterior positioning of the olfactories is unusual among cranial nerves, most of which have their origins on the floor of the fourth ventricle of the brain. Furthermore, of the cranial nerves only the fibers of the olfactories are nonmedullated, that is, are deficient in the substance of Schwann.

If, however, olfaction is neurologically isolated from the hypothalamus, how account for its appetitive qualities, its undeniable capacity to give pleasure or pain? The answer lies in the fact that the olfactories and hypothalamus are linked *indirectly* via the thalamocortical fibers (namely, nerve tracts from the thalamus into the cerebrum). Experiences of olfaction, therefore, are in large part cognitive.

Smell is strongly linked with memory, and memory is structurally complementary with voiceless speech. Cortical fibers too are nonmedullated. Only by cerebral control, then, can smell be isolated from appetite, hence from the pleasure-pain loop, which isolation, we've seen, is a prerequisite for kaivalya. The myth of Orion and Artemis describes the rupturing of the connection between foul smell and sublime smell. Artemis describes a paradisal aroma detected only when the sense of smell is turned completely on itself, that is, on the nonmedullated fibers of the brain. An intoxicating odor is mentioned frequently in yogic texts. By his increasing awareness of it, a sādhaka can gauge his progress in yoga. In reversing the FALL, the unity of the Three Worlds is restored, the CRACK IN THE COSMIC EGG is sealed, and one gradually returns to the Garden of Eden.

Britomartis, another daughter of Leto and a constant companion of Artemis, was pursued by

* Ovid, *Fasti* 5.495ff.

King Minos of Crete. To evade him she leapt into the sea from a promontory on the island of Ægina. She fell into the nets of fishermen and was rescued, but she gained the epithet *aphœa*, "she who vanished." That she recapitulates the sense of smell is extremely likely. Not only is she, as half sister, one of Artemis's favorites, but she holds the leash that restrains the hounds of the goddess. Her pursuer is the king of Crete, the single most important island in myth and in itself a description of the second world. And we have seen Ægina before in the myth of Sisyphus. It is the island to which Zeus abducts the nymph Œnone, whose name means "wine queen." Wine here is a possible recapitulation of smell, just as it is the odor of the wedding wine that inflames the centaurs into a battle with the Lapiths. Finally, Solinus tells us explicitly that Britomartis is the Cretan Artemis, also that in the Cretan dialect *britomartis* means "sweet maid,"* an etymology that may well reflect the savor of internal smell in trance. The myth therefore describes the "vanishing" of outward-vectored smell—a second-world faculty, a perception but not a vision—which too has its bounding volume, though it is much closer to the body. When external stimuli are absent—that is, when Britomartis escapes from Minos—the olfactory sensorium turns upon itself. That act is a dissolution of the second world, but it is not the permanent, irreversible dissolution of kaivalya that yoga seeks.† No one sense can be permanently isolated without the other senses.

The myth of the DIOSCURI concerns another famous set of twins: Castor and Pollux. Castor and Pollux (the latter also known as Polydeuces) were the sons of Zeus and Leda. They were as well the brothers of Helen of Troy and her twin sister Clytemnestra (the DIOSCURÆ), wife and slayer of Agamemnon.‡ In the guise of a swan Zeus seduced Leda on the same night that she slept with her husband, King Tyndareus of Sparta. The swan is possibly a description of the lateral ventricles: long, aliform cavities in the brain that surround the olfactory bulbs and are filled with a milk-white substance called the cerebrospinal fluid (figure 16, p. 102). Leda gave birth to *two* sets of twins: Helen and Pollux, who were begotten by Zeus, hence immortal, and Clytemnestra and Castor, who were the mortal children of Tyndareus.

In Greek, *castor* means "muskrat," a creature from whose glands the Greeks extracted a medicinal oil of penetrating aroma. Our "castor oil" is derived from the same word. In antiquity, the word was used interchangeably for the muskrat—a kind of beaver—and its odor, just as it is nowadays. So Castor's association with smell, as one of the Dioscuri, is plausible. Pollux was a horse tamer and a boxer, and we have already seen that the horse is a description of the breath within the nasal passages. Boxing, then, describes the battering action of the breath against the frontal bone. Both Castor and Pollux are constantly associated with horses in myth and carried the epithet *leukippides*, "the white colts."§

Pollux, as already mentioned, was immortal, Castor mortal. When Castor was about to die, his brother pled his case to Zeus and the Fates, asking that he and Castor spend alternate days in the world above ground, suggesting another meaning of the Dioscuri: the alternation of breathing between left and right nostrils. The place underground where the brothers changed places was called Therapne, "beast's breath." We have seen that yogis control alternate-nostril breathing by a technique known as kumbhaka. When, say, breath is flowing in the right nostril alone, the breath of the left nostril has gone underground, as it were, into the first world. The switch occurs at roughly two-hour intervals

* Solinus, *Polyhistory* 2.8, cited in: H. J. Rose, *A Handbook of Greek Mythology* (New York, 1959), p. 117 with n. citing A. Mommsen (1864).

† The fishermen's nets may describe the great neurological plexus that ties sensation to feeling, known to neuroanatomists as the "intermediate net." The neurology of olfaction is complex and could plausibly be described as netlike. Cf., *diktynna*, "she of the nets," a title of Cretan Artemis.

‡ *Dioscuri* and *dioscuræ* are Latinized forms of Gk. "divine lads" and "divine maids."

§ Apollodorus, *Bibliotheca* 3.11.1–2, and n. 4, in: Frazer, *Apollodorus: The Library*.

whether kumbhaka is practiced or not. In astrology, the heavenly arc transited by the sun in two hours is called a *house*. The houses are classified as masculine and feminine and are favorable to specific daily activities.

Pollux's bargain with Zeus supplies an interesting interpretation of the meaning of "a day and a night," a phrase common enough in Greco-Roman and Judeo-Christian mythology: day = inhalation (Skt. *puraka*), night = exhalation (recaka); or, more precisely, a day refers to the interval when the lungs are filled with air, a night when they are evacuated. Prāṇāyāma involves retention of breath. The goal is to lengthen the interval of retention until it can be prolonged indefinitely. The practice involves both retention, when the breath is held in the lungs, and suspension, when it is kept out of the lungs. The breath must slow down in an unstrained, unforced manner.

It is just this smooth, unhampered flow of the breath that the yogi seeks to achieve. A "catch" in the breath betrays a mind that is not at peace, a soul in a state of sin. Body, mind, and soul mutually manifest this fallen condition. Some considerable portion of this sin is acquired after birth, but there is a root sin—called ORIGINAL SIN by Christians—that inheres to the soul simply by virtue of its incarnation in a body. Hence, it is in the constrictions of the body that it can be discerned. The gasserian ganglion is at the center of the constriction, and behind it the pituitary gland. As we shall see, a catastrophic event takes place in this region of the brain when prāṇāyāma succeeds. Many Greek myths speak to this event, but PERSEUS AND THE HEAD OF MEDUSA is particularly eloquent (see frontispiece). When Perseus decapitates the Gorgon, he strikes at the second-world knot. From her blood leaps Pegasus, the WINGED HORSE: the breath is freed, and the soul springs heavenward, that is, into the cranium.

IMAGINE THE "ACT" OF MEDITATION

It is the sixth century B.C. We are in the *naos*, the inner sanctum, of an ancient Ionian temple, perhaps the shrine of Hera on Samos or that of Delian Artemis. Because we are in the naos, we are initiates, devotees of the goddess. Her cult image is before us. Candles flicker, incense burns, but we are unaware of them. With our initiate robes drawn around us, we shut them out. The walls of the naos absorb all sounds. It is as silent as a tomb.

Our attention is turned inward. We concentrate on the workings of our bodies, as we were once taught in the unspeakable mysteries of the goddess. All of our senses are alert—and the mind, especially our thoughts. Though our robes seal out light and muffle sound and smell, though our still postures neutralize touch, all these have no effect on our minds. For mind, we contemplate the breath. Full consciousness of breathing is full consciousness of bliss. Through the grace of the goddess and by absorbing the mind in the act of breathing, its relentless activity is slowed and finally stilled. Then follows an inner rapture. Utterly absorbed in the slowing flow of the breath, in a reality so pure it may be described as the spirit of the spirit, we smell roses, yea, and orange blossoms, lilies and fragrant lotuses; where there was once a universe extending to the stars, there is now a warm garden lazing in the blinding light of eternal noonday. We are become honeybees drinking nectar in the womb of a lilac. *Yes!* That is the experience we strive for. The scent of lilac is the goddess Artemis, *is* the Blessed Virgin.

Because meditation is practical, our experience of it is its own measure. It is furthered and hindered by our strengths and weaknesses. In other words, it is *moral*, as are all our works. We call upon the goddess from a place of darkness, or why else would we call on her at all?

Because meditation is practical we start out small. We make mistakes. We are not always in the garden. Cares and worries, doubts, lack of discipline, and sensual longings distract us. But we have the testimony of the hierophantess, the priestess who revealed the mysteries to us: persist and gain the peace of Elysium.

So we try again to experience the goddess. We long for her fragrance. We've been there forever, it seems. We have done what we had to do to have our moment with her. We didn't always understand it. We did it and learned by the doing. We learned that some things we did hindered us and some did not. Anger hindered us, disrupted our concentration. Greed hindered us. And lust. Are those good things? We don't know. Are they bad? We think so, but it's not really an issue with us. We seek the goddess. There is nothing else. As our practice is perfected our minds steady. We experience subtle changes. The concentration on our olfactories tints the inner sea blue. It brightens somewhat. The nearer we are to the goddess, the more that is so, the subtler the fragrance we detect, the bluer the sea—until all is bathed in a clear azure. If asked, we would no longer describe ourselves as being in the sea. We are in the sky above a desert or in the mountains. We are in a heavenly garden and our goddess is nigh, clothed in deep blue.

The two olfactory bulbs, situated behind the frontal bone and its tightly closed suture, are approximately within the third world. More than any other sense, olfaction participates directly in cognitive processes. Artemis and Athena derive their mythological virginities primarily from the proximity of the faculties associated with them—smell and voiceless speech, respectively—to the frontal bone (figure 5, page 48, and figure 7, page 59).

THE THIRD WORLD

The third world is also a mystic sea: the sky as sea. It is the sky in its imperceivable heights, just as the first world is the ocean in its imperceivable depths. The two mystic seas are united in one sea, but the union is *not* the mystic union that is the goal of trance craft. Rather, it is a union of imperceivables in the center of which is the perceivable. The visible universe is surrounded by a perceptual void. The location of the entrance to Hades, namely, the first world, is not at all clear in myth. Often it is a subterranean passage, the way that Heracles, Theseus, and Odysseus take to Harrow Hell. Other times it is in the west, at the horizon, boundary of the second world. West is the direction of the setting sun, where the light disappears. It is the limit of vision of the world "out there," the place to which Hera's chariot carries her in a single stride.* To go straight down in the body is to exit from the second world as well; it is the personal limit of perception. Thus, the two entrances to Hades are reconcilable.

Within the individual human organism too there is a perceptual void. We see, think, and feel simultaneously; yet the experiential loci of vision, thought, and feeling do not intersect in the same way, for example, as a volume of water intersects identically with the volume of a vessel into which it is poured. As concepts the voids of thought and feeling "surrounding" each of us can be said to intersect, but only metaphorically. As an experience, however, the unity of the first and third worlds is a given, described in myth by the STREAM OF OCEAN that surrounds the known world. The Stream of Ocean is the seamlessness of experience, the "flow" of awareness. All the gods and goddesses are ultimately descendants of Oceanus and Tethys,† who anthropomorphize the first world–third world unity. Yet the goal of trance still is to dissolve the second world and thus eliminate all the worlds, for the first and third worlds come into being only in the creation of the second world. In other words, the ancient cosmogonies are tautologies. The goads to dissolution are the quarrels of Zeus and Hera and Oceanus and Tethys in Homer. Homer also tells us that if one could pile three mountains one atop the other, the distance to heaven would be bridged.‡

You have been asked to "imagine meditation." Before reading the next section, it will be useful for you not to imagine but actually to meditate. Stop reading. Put aside this book. Sit awhile, in a comfortable position, with your eyes closed and the room completely darkened.

* The boundary of the Minkowski space cone.

† *Iliad* 14.201ff.

‡ *Odyssey* 11.315.

"Observe" the darkness for half an hour at least before returning to the light. . . .

◆◆◆

You have now "seen," perhaps, that the darkness of meditation is far from a uniform shade of black. Rather, it is permeated by twinklings of light, momentary flashes, scintillations, and, yes, the tiniest whirlpools, all of which are doubtless related to the functioning of the optic and ophthalmic nerves. In Greek folklore the poet Homer, who immortalized the phrase "WINE-DARK SEA," was said to be blind. But was he? Is the ancient allegation of his blindness a myth? Is it a clever description of proprioceptive sight?

Just as the ear is never deaf, so too the eye is never blind. Even to the blind.* To equate vision with perceptual seeing is an error analogous to the one made by Ananda when he claimed no longer to hear absent the sound of the gong. When you closed your eyes, a black curtain took the place of the second world. You looked but you did not "see," at least not as you are accustomed to. As time passed, your mind steadied. You "saw" that the curtain is not devoid of color. There was a soft, nearly subliminal glow throughout. The black curtain was not precisely black, more a deep indigo, a violet, because when your eyes were closed—in fact, whenever there is very little ambient light—the pigment rhodopsin† in the rods of your eyes gave to the darkness a deep violet color—the color of wine, within which you seemed to be submerged. Thus, sitting in that darkness, you sat within Homer's fabled "Wine-Dark Sea," όινοπε πoντός.

The Greek root of *œnope*, usually translated as "wine dark," is *œnops*, itself compounded of *œnos* (wine) and *ops*, which literally means "eye"; our word "optic" comes from it. We've already seen the root *ops* in myth in the proper name Metope, which is derived from the Greek word for forehead, *metapon*, literally "among the eyes." Thus, wine-dark really means *wine-eyed*. When Boll and Kühne—German biologists who in the nineteenth century named the pigment giving an indigo cast to darkness—combined *ops* with *rhodo*‡ (Greek for "deep red") to coin *rhodopsin*, they unwittingly duplicated the imagery of the *Odyssey* of twenty-seven centuries before!

The similarity is not just a pleasant irony or beguiling coincidence but demonstrates the fundamentally descriptive purposes of archaic narrative: in naming rhodopsin, Boll and Kühne almost certainly intended no more than to describe its technical function in acclimating to darkness. So too with ancient mythopoets. Homeric myth is poetical in its exoteric form. Its esoteric agenda, however, is to describe. But myth is descriptive in an even more specific sense—after all, poetry too describes reality in a general way. Myth describes its subject *technically*, in the sense of Boll and Kühne.

An ancient kōan illustrates proprioceptive vision in exactly the same way that the "sound of one hand clapping" describes proprioceptive hearing: *What is the face of your parents before you were born?*

Before birth, your eyes are closed. There is no perception. The face of your parents is your own face is the face of Caesar's wife is the face of the man in the moon—It's all the same. It's what a blindman sees, what Homer saw: the Wine-Dark Sea. The WINE-DARK SEA is the third world, the waters that are "above the firmament."

◆◆◆

The third world is the natural place to look for Zeus, Greek god of the sky. Zeus, the eldest Cronid brother, is the all-powerful father god of the Greek pantheon. His name is cognate with Sanskrit *Dyaus*, the vedic sky god. Initially, it seems, Zeus was the day sky itself. The word *day* is probably related to Dyaus and had the

* Cf., the miracles in which Jesus gives sight to the blind.

† Rhodopsin, also known as *visual purple*, is essential in adjusting to night vision.

‡ In Apollodorus, a Rhode is mentioned as the daughter of Poseidon, god of the sea.

sense that "wild blue yonder" has in English.*

Zeus's father, Cronus, ate his children as they were born. Zeus was the youngest, and by the time of his birth, his mother, Rhea, had had enough. She handed Cronus a stone wrapped in a blanket, which was eaten in Zeus's place, and she sent Zeus off to Mount Dictys to be raised by the she-goat Amalthea and a swarm of bees. When he was old enough, he dethroned his father and freed his brothers and sisters, who had all the while been growing in Cronus's innards, and established the classical Olympian pantheon with himself as titular head.

For all his grandeur, however, when it comes to conventionally religious behavior, Zeus is something of an embarrassment, rather like a Borgia pope is to Catholics. He worries and frets over his pleasures. He endlessly concerns himself with questions of status, with sheep and cattle. He demands his share—as do his worshipers, it bears remembering. He's also an incorrigible adulterer, and he dotes on his many bastards, among them a goodly number of Greek heroes such as Perseus and Heracles. His marriage to Hera, chief goddess of the first world, is the union of the mystic seas. But he is constantly cheating on his wife with mortals—second-world experience—and he nearly always abducts his favorite of the moment to an island, namely, to the second world. He takes Ægina, daughter of Asopus, to the island of Œnone. He takes Mæa to Crete. Leto, mother of Apollo and Artemis, flees to Delos. The list is long. Zeus and Hera quarrel throughout the TROJAN WAR. They are reconciled only after the city falls, when, esoterically, the distinctions among the worlds are dissolved in trance.

In sum, Zeus is as lustful and greedy, as vengeful and petty as the most "fallen" of mortals, and his humanity betrays his origin within the human form. Neither is he atypical as Greek deities go. He differs from the "lesser" gods and goddesses and from men mainly in his power to transform desire into fact, and even that has its limits. The only clear reason for the preeminence of Zeus among the gods seems to be his persistent mythological connection with *fate*, which he does not so much determine as subserve. During the *Iliad* he uses a balance scale weighted with Greek and Trojan tokens to sense the direction in which the fates of the opposing sides are tending. He then acts to further the desired outcome. No other Olympian has access to such knowledge. It was common among the Greeks to swear oaths by Zeus and the Fates, a trio of grim sisters whom the Greeks called the *Moiræ*.

Moiræ is a word used by Anaxagoras in his theory of the composition of the universe. Anaxagoras's cosmology is based on two concepts: *æther* (αιθηρ) and *ær* (αερα), the one being rarified, warm, bright, and dry, the other dense, cold, dark, and moist. Æther and ær are elemental qualities but are themselves made up of moiræ: "particles." The moiræ are infinite in number. All three words—æther, ær, and moiræ—are used by Anaxagoras in connection with *sperma* (σπερμα), "seed."

Although æther and ær make up everything in the world, they are most obviously components of the sky, for which both are synonyms in Greek literature. Zeus's ability to "read fate" would then seem to be related to his consanguinity with the moiræ of the sky elements, contemplation of which gives knowledge of the "seeds" of all things, their burgeoning, evolution, and ultimate fruition. On our hypothesis, Zeus is a description of a proprioception of the highest processing center of the brain: the neocortex ("highest" in the neurophysiological sense, i.e., the CNS hierarchy).

Zeus's animal totem is the eagle, a bird long of wing, which would seem to put Zeus in the second world. But the eagle was also the highest-soaring bird known to the ancients. It soars so high as to disappear; thus an eagle is an apt description of the third world in its heights.

When one day Zeus comes down with a splitting headache, he asks Hephæstus to cleave his brow with an ax. Out jumps Athena, the virgin goddess of wisdom. Athena is an esoteric description of voiceless speech, which seems to

* A. B. Cook, *Zeus: A Study in Ancient Religion*, vol. 1 (Cambridge, 1914), pp. 1–8.

be located behind the brow whence she emerged. In myth, particularly in Homer, she often whispers to the heroes from behind, grasping them by the hair to make her presence known, which emphasizes her rearward position in the skull.* She is often a mere presence in scenes from mythology, for example, on the battlefield before Troy, but she is usually invisible, and she is almost never shown without her visored helmet in Greek art, emphasizing the cranium.

The sixth sign of the ancient zodiac was Virgo, the Virgin. In ancient astrology the sign was associated with Athena, the most aggressively chaste goddess in myth. Her temple in Athens is called the Parthenon, from Greek *parthene*, usually translated as "virgin." She bears the epithet *parthenopæa* in myth. But by now we should be alerted to the root "ops" in a mythic proper name. Parthenopæa means "virgin faced." Furthermore, the astrological sign of Virgo was known as *Ophincus* to the Greeks, which means "the furrow." And with that bit of ancient sky lore, we can tie all the descriptions together in one package.

The furrow in question is none other than the frontal suture. To describe the vagina as a furrow is to use an extremely ancient image. Our word *husband* once meant "tiller of the earth" as well as a married man. Myth analogizes the rhythmic motion of the breath in the sinuses to the motion of the penis and the vagina. Before and immediately after birth, the frontal bone is in two parts. Within the first year, it knits together along the frontal suture, the spot from whence Athena leapt. Hence it is a "tight" furrow, hence *virgin*. One only need look at a skull, something with which the warlike Greeks were doubtless quite familiar, to comprehend the imagery.

The Athens of myth is as an esoteric description of the third world and is a recapitulation of Athena herself. Cranaus (Gk. *cranaos*, "rocky") was king in Athens before Erichthonius. Our word *cranium* is derived from Greek *chranos*, "helmet." Bone is disguised as rock or iron again and again in myth. Athena's helmet is yet another recapitulation of the brow, the place where, esoterically, Hephæstus strikes his ax, the place where the breath touches the frontal suture. Also, the proximity of the aliform (wing-shaped) frontal sinuses to the frontal suture is certainly relevant to the well-known connection in Christian myth of the Virgin Mary and the Holy Spirit, who in the guise of a dove begets on her the Word of God (The Christ) (figure 5). In that regard, the martyred Saint Ignatius of Antioch (d. ca. A.D. 100), who almost certainly had gnosis, says "Mary's virginity was hidden from the prince of this world . . . brought to pass in the deep silence of God." The frontal suture is hidden from *sight*: "the prince of this [second] world."† The "silence of God" refers to the sound of one hand clapping or Word. As we have seen, the frontal sinuses suggest the wings of an owl, a creature of darkness; the owl is a totem of Athena.‡

The rhythmical swelling of the frontal bone (figure 16) with the breath is like a sail taking the breeze, and Athena is often associated with warships in Greek myth. Regattas were held in her honor during the games of the *Panathenaeca*, though they are otherwise unusual in ancient Greek athletic competition. In the famous myth of Jason and the Argonauts, the heroes sail off in search of the GOLDEN FLEECE in a ship designed by Athena herself. Part of the mainmast was hewn from the WHISPERING OAK OF DODONA, a shrine in mainland Greece. During the voyage the oak whispered advice (in a woman's voice) to Jason, leader of the Argonauts. The mainmast supports the sail, of course, and the whole idea recapitulates voiceless speech, Athena herself. Athena is also Odysseus's protectress on his long voyage from Troy to Ithaca.

In Homer, Hephæstus is the son of Zeus

* *Iliad* 1.195–200.

† Ignatius of Antioch, *Epistle to the Ephesians*, in: *Early Christian Writings: The Apostolic Fathers*, trans. M. Staniforth, rev. ed. A. Louth (London, 1987), 19.1–2 see also n. 16 at p. 68.

‡ Athena's chariot is pulled by short-winged owls in Greek art.

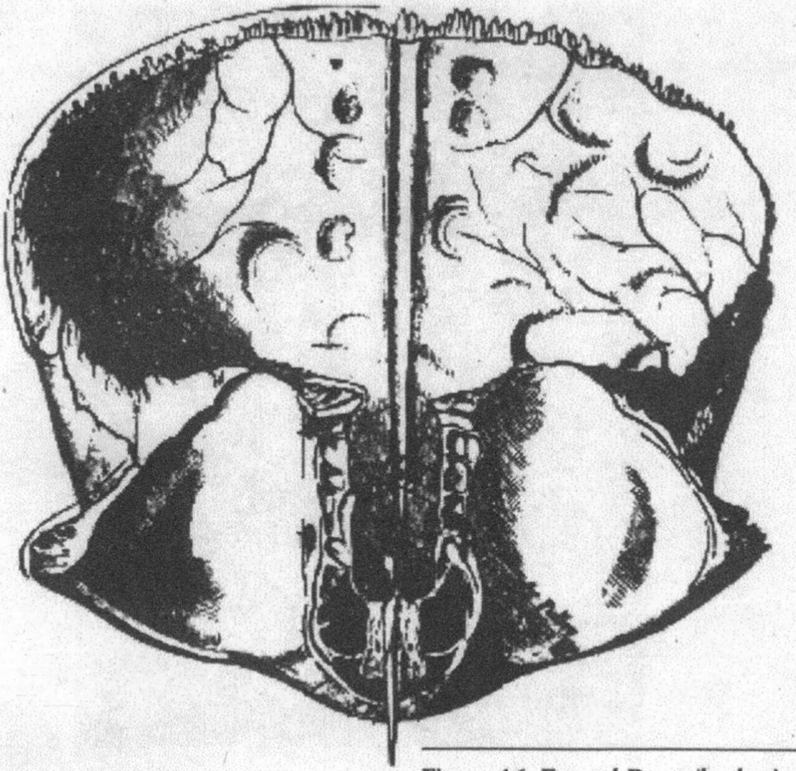

Figure 16. Frontal Bone (back view) (from *Gray's Anatomy*)

and Hera; in Hesiod, of Hera alone, a sort of virgin-birth counterpart to Athena. His association with Athena derives from the fact, well known to yogis, that thought and breath are intimately connected and must be reciprocally controlled. Every drawn breath "inflames" first the perceptual processing centers (sensoria) of the brain and second, probably indirectly, the cognitive centers. The usual result is an increase in the rate of respiration, in other words, a positive-feedback loop and a cycle that the yogi must break into at the root if he is to control it. The god associated with control of the cycle in its deepest neurophysiological workings is not Hephæstus, whose context is primarily the sheer mechanics of diaphragmatic breathing, but Apollo.

Not only does Hephæstus cut Athena from her father's brow, but egged on by Poseidon, one day he actually tries to rape her. He succeeds only in ejaculating onto her knee (namely, where one bends to reach below). Properly horrified, Athena cleanses herself with a bit of wool and tosses it from Olympus. It fertilizes Gæa, and in due course Erichthonius, a wee snake-man, is born. Athena affectionately tucks him into her helmet, and eventually he becomes king of Athens. A description of breath as a serpent is common in yoga. Most likely it has to do with the similarity of the hiss of a serpent to the sound of the breath in the nostrils. Egyptian art shows a serpent emerging from the brow of pharaoh (figure 17). It is such a common icon in Egyptian art that there is a name for it: the *uræus*. Both Plato and Herodotus believed that the Greeks got their myths from Egypt, so it's possible the Egyptians gave the uræus to the Greeks in the form of Erichthonius.

The blow from Hephæstus's ax that releases Athena from her father's brow is a description of the breath striking the bottom of the frontal suture. It is also Hephæstus's ejaculation. The

Figure 17. Head of a Pharaoh with Uræus (note also the wings of a bird, which describe the frontal sinuses)(Alinari/Art Resource, New York)

imagery of ejaculation is mysteriously apt because when the breath stops at the top of the inhalation-exhalation cycle, a cataclysmic experience ensues involving a rush of hormonal output from the pituitary gland. The experience is very much *like* an outflow of fluid—in reality pulsed neurological energy—descending from the cerebrum and "liberating" the yogi from the bonds of karma. We shall have more to say regarding this pituitary catastrophe later. Thus the two directions that myths concerned with this region take: love and war. Athena is frequently shown in Greek art holding a spear, and a cult statue of her brandishing a spear, called the Palladium (< Gk. *pallo*, "she who brandishes"), figures prominently in the *Iliad*. The spear is a description of the spikelike nasal spine at the bottom of the glabellar bone (figure 16).

Of war, no more for the moment. Of love, Zeus and Hera are the mythic paradigm. The second world is their couch of love high atop Mount Ida on Crete, wrapped in a cloud that Helius the sun cannot penetrate.* It is a trysting place, between the realms of each. The esoteric meaning, at least in Homer, is that love and sex, desire and meaning, are wholly internal experiences that can sanctify the external world but are not of its essence. Just as a flower, a growing thing seen with the eyes and smelled with the nose, with petals rustling in the breeze, derives its life from roots unseen within the earth and from moisture borne invisibly from the sky, so too the second world bodies forth the imperceptible essence of the mystic sea.

* *Iliad* 14.344.

THREE-WORLD TRANCE

One of the most confusing words in English—whether used in philosophy or biology—is *mind*. We tend to make it synonymous with intellect or cognition, and there are practical reasons to tolerate such a view. In Sāṃkhya and Vedānta, however, the word for mind is *cittā*, the "stuff" of consciousness; yet the stuff of consciousness is *not* consciousness. In this book, the working definition of mind is *a posteriori consciousness*, which comes down to saying that mind is internal experience. Consciousness alone is absolutely a priori, as are its metaphysical equivalents: God, brahman, puruṣa, existence. That means there is no logically necessary epistemology of consciousness. When, however, one experiences anything, the provisional interiority of experience requires that the *content* of awareness be awareness of some organ of the body. That content is a posteriori because consciousness is its necessary antecedent. That internal content is *mind*. All experience is ultimately an internal matter: "In the mind is sight and hearing; all else is deaf and blind."* Yet vis à vis perception, mind is a priori. Indeed, Hindu philosophy can be thought of as a comprehensive rationalization of perception, a facing down of the epistemological implications that the void surrounding perception has for the human organism. What is the *place* of that organism in the cosmœ if the cosmœ themselves—taken as an epistemological unity—are not logically a "place"?

Patañjali includes as objects of contemplation phenomena that to a modern way of thinking are not properly things at all: emotions, thoughts, conceptual processes. Patañjali can do that because in the archaic tradition out of which yoga emerged such experiences were identified with proprioceptions of specific structures within the organism. It was only much later that they were generalized into experiences of the mind. In our expanded sense of proprioception, emotions can be redefined as proprioceptions of the first world, of the heart and stomach primarily; individual thoughts and conceptual processes are proprioceptions of the third world. Western philosophy, however, because of its identification of the individual self with a body-mind locus, sees fit to extend the use of the words *object* and *thing* only to elements of the second world, namely, perceptions, even going so far as to explain (or attempt to explain) thoughts and emotions in terms of physical laws derived solely through the perceptions.† Scrutinized by a twentieth-century radical-empiricist philosopher, whom we might call a *perceptualist*, such terms are labeled (libeled?) as examples of *epiphenomenalism*, quaint relics of a misguided and foolishly metaphysical phase of human knowledge. By a severe reductionism then, the perceptualist spares science a number of thorny paradoxes.‡

Whether that is anything more than a trivialization or begging of the question is as yet unresolved. Regardless of whether one calls them "contents"—as does Patañjali§—or phenomena or epiphenomena, thoughts and emotions and processes are capable not only of being experienced but also of being exhaustively experienced, of being examined, of being meditated upon, by an archaic consciousness convinced that such things are as external to it as the moon and stars.

Patañjali begins the *Yoga-Sūtra* with a concise definition: *Yoga is the inhibition of the modifications of the mind.* The word used for "modification" is *vṛtti*, literally "whirlpool."#

Go outside and look up at the sun (with eyes closed of course). Immediately, the visual field (as biologists call it) is bright, golden, but

* Epicharmus of Cos (d. ca. 443 B.C.); quoted by Plutarch, *Moralia*; in: *Moral Essays*, trans. R. Warner (London, 1971), p. 102.

† "Explain" is patently perceptual in origin (< L. *explanere*, "to flatten").

‡ J. R. Smythies, "Aspects of Consciousness," in: *Beyond Reductionism: The Alpbach Symposium*, ed. A. Koestler and J. R. Smythies (Boston, 1969), pp. 233–45.

§ Sanskrit *pratyaya*, "[any] content of consciousness, not necessarily a bīja," often translated as "object."

\# *Yoga-Sūtra, Samādhi Pāda*, sutra 2.

scarcely uniform. It is filled with myriad eddies, often multicolored. The medium in which the eddies appear is known as cittā in yoga, which translates roughly as "mind" in the verse quoted above. The purport of the sutra, therefore, is that the yogi is expected to inhibit the eddies. (The Sanskrit word for "inhibition" is *nirodha*.) The eddies cannot be eliminated, but their rapid proliferation and transformation into mental imagery must be suppressed. Anyone who has tried to stop his mind from wandering can appreciate the difficulty, and that is to deal with the vṛtti *after* they have coalesced in the formation of gross images, not directly in their intangible, elusive, and evanescent polymorphism. Looking at those countless whirlpools, you can perhaps understand the aptness of the "sea" in describing the inner world and the "voyage" such mastery entails, an imagery at the heart of a myth like Jason and the Argonauts.

Patañjali, as we have seen, summarizes the meditative process in the term saṃyama, which has three parts:

1. Concentration [dhāraṇā] is the confining of the mind within a limited area.
2. Uninterrupted flow of the mind towards the object is contemplation [dhyāna].
3. Contemplation when there is only consciousness of the object *and not of the self* is trance [samādhi].*

In his exposition, Patañjali makes use of the concept of a modification (vṛtti) to describe anything that roils the mind. Closely related is his concept of the *kleśas*, "afflictions," pernicious contents of the mind (pratyaya), which interfere with absorption in the meditative seed. Kleśas are subtle contents of consciousness, for instance, anxiety, neurological dysfunction, literal neuropaths, whose practical effect is to block the samādhi on which a yogi is intent. But when the "modifications are nearly gone, absorption in one another of thinker, thinking, and thought, occurs as in the case of a clear jewel on a colored surface."†

The nature of the metaphor is quite unexpected in an "exposition" that is remarkably unadorned in style, and its use strongly suggests that Patañjali is here attempting to describe a literal experience, something he himself has observed, and is not grappling with the poetry of some inscrutably ponderous "truth." What he in fact seems to be saying is that, in concentrating sight-cum-cognition (mind), saṃyama occurs simultaneously with an extraordinary change in the visual quality of the seed: it becomes transparent. Everything that can be known about the bīja is then known, past and future.

Patañjali himself sees nothing unusual in all of this. Yoga is a science, and he is merely reporting observations made by him and others on the effects of sustained concentration. The clinical detachment he maintains throughout is nowhere better illustrated than by the following sutra:

> The condition of the mind in which the object [pratyaya] that subsides [in the cognitive-perceptual field] ever remains the same as the object that rises is called the transformation of focus.‡

The sense of focus here referred to is called *ekagrāta pariṇāma* and is not necessarily visual; meditation can occur with the eyes closed. Because of the dynamic nature of every faculty, however, vision is a component of every experience, and parameters that apply to it like focus and clarity are always present in consciousness (over nerve tracts connecting the visual centers in the occipital cortex with the rest of the nervous system). Patañjali's system applies to all bījas, gross or subtle. It applies to so-called internal experiences—stereognosis and cognition—as well as external perception.

Meditation on a gross internal object, for

* *Yoga-Sūtra, Vibhūti Pāda*, sutras 1–3, emphases added.

† Ibid., *Samādhi Pāda*, sutra 41.

‡ Ibid., *Vibhūti Pāda*, sutra 12.

instance the encephalon, can lead to trance accompanied by properties of *flow*, *transparency*, and *focus* of experience. Such images, culled from the sutras, are suggestive of two principles: clarity and water. They are not descriptions unique to Patañjali. They may be found in the *Vedas* and the *Upaniṣads*, where brahman is described as "light in water." What the *Yoga-Sûtra* teaches us is that it is a description that applies to anything that is concentrated on to sufficient depth and is an inevitable part of the process of saṃyama. Concomitantly, it sheds light on such descriptions in the Indian scriptures, suggesting that they are something more than poetic sentiment in the face of the sublime.

We shall now attempt to illustrate saṃyama in a myth. The myth concerns Menelaus, king of Sparta and brother of King Agamemnon of Mycenæ. Menelaus is a third-world figure—and not simply because he is here associated with Athena—but the conclusions are applicable to all three worlds. It is because the third world is mind explicitly, whereas the first and second worlds are mind implicitly, that a third-world myth is particularly illustrative of saṃyama. When Menelaus departed Troy after the sack of Ilium, he neglected to appease the goddess Athena, who in retaliation sent a storm to drive him off course. After years of wandering he limped into Pharos, a port on the Nile delta, at the head of five ships.

There he meets the nymph Eydothea, who counsels him to seek out and capture her father, Proteus, the proverbial Old Man of the Sea, who alone can tell Menelaus what he needs to know to get home. (At the time Menelaus is still ignorant of his offense to Athena.) He and three companions go down to the sea. On the beach where Proteus comes to sleep among his sea lions, they lay in wait, disguising themselves with stinking sealskins. After Proteus arrives and goes to sleep, Menelaus throws off his skin and seizes the wily sea god, who has magical powers that allow him to change his appearance at will, becoming successively a lion, a snake, a leopard, a boar, running water, and a flowering tree. Menelaus has been warned, however, and refuses to let go through all of those transmogrifications. Finally Proteus calms down, resumes his natural shape, and begins to prophesy.*

That the above is a distant Greek counterpart to Patañjali's discussion of saṃyama seems likely. Not only does Menelaus succeed in controlling the wild oscillations of the mind, here impersonated by a sea god, but he is instructed practically in how to do this by Eydothea, a figure whose very name suggests meditation ("image goddess") and who, as Proteus's daughter, can be reliably identified with the god himself. Greek *eide* is familiar to readers of Plato as his word for the immutable and eternal Forms, derived from a verb that means "to see." It is therefore suggestive of the unchanging, of something motionless, which is just the effect that Patañjali describes as the end of saṃyama: a steady, transparent image, like a "clear jewel on a colored surface." Moreover, the goddess who provoked the entire episode, Athena, is the esoteric representation of voiceless speech, of thought. The storm she sends is a recapitulation of the struggle with Proteus; it is the mind that is storm-tossed, the mind—here described by Menelaus—that is as cluttered with uncontrolled thoughts as the sea is with waves. Finally, Menelaus's arrival in Egypt with five ships involves the senses—sight, hearing, smell, touch, and taste—in the meditative act. Menelaus gains the knowledge that he seeks, just as the yogi, with all his faculties marshalled, by performing saṃyama gains "knowledge of the past and future."†

Eydothea performs one other service for Menelaus and his three companions.‡ When they complain of the stench on the beach and balk at drawing the repulsive hides over themselves, she anoints their nostrils with ambrosia, the sweetly scented food of the gods. The image of a

---

* *Odyssey* 4.351ff.

† *Yoga-Sûtra, Vibhûti Pâda*, sutra 16; Menelaus, in fact, does learn the past (Agamemnon's murder) and the future (he will get home safely to Sparta).

‡ With Menelaus, the four elements: fire, earth, air, and water. Menelaus is a description of air.

fragrant garden, so common in myth, describes a deep meditative state, one that involves the breath's action on olfactories that have been purified by yogic practice.

The myth of Menelaus and Proteus describes a state of liberated peace to which cognition (Menelaus) attains when its myriad modifications (Proteus) have been smoothed out. It is significant that Menelaus, virtually alone among the heroes, returns home (with the beautiful Helen), raises a family, and lives to a ripe and happy old age.*

The immediate aim of saṃyama is knowledge. After successfully training his awareness, Patañjali claims, a yogi derives complete knowledge of the meditative seed by performing saṃyama on it. For example, by performing saṃyama on the sounds of a songbird, the yogi can understand the feelings of the bird and why it made that particular sound and not another. The yogi would then know if the bird is hungry or frightened or sexually aroused. His understanding will then have been expressed verbally, of course, but the form of knowledge that allowed understanding—saṃyama—is more of the nature of an intense intuition brought on by the yogi's utter control of his nervous system.

Both yoga and Buddhism would be one in describing logic—an essentially third-world capability—as the practice of saṃyama upon a set of propositions that serve as seeds. Geometry, for example, is axiomatic, that is, all of its conclusions come from postulates that are not rigorously derivable. For close to twenty-five centuries geometers have regarded Euclid's first postulate that "through two points a straight line can be drawn" as self-evident. Occasionally the words "plausible" or "reasonable" are used. Yet it is at least possible that what Euclid calls "self-evident" is more or less the same thing that Patañjali calls the end result of saṃyama. The argument that the straight-line postulate is demonstrable is spurious. A mathematical line is not capable of being drawn with compass and ruler. Moreover, modern relativity theory has cast serious doubts on even the perceptual reality of euclidean space. Euclidean planarity is *not* scientifically demonstrable.

Patañjali might argue that such basic logical tools as the aristotelian syllogism, contradiction, contraposition, and hence entire logicomathematical arguments are the results of saṃyama, are apprehended within a momentary state of deep trance. Samādhi denotes an experience of indeterminate intensity. Some trances are deeper than others, and a yogi learns how to deepen them at will. Analogously, mathematical ability can be considerably developed in a given individual. From the point of view of yoga such a development means that the subject's ability to concentrate on purely cognitive pratyaya (which strictly speaking can then be called bījas), namely, discrete symbols and propositions, has improved. Yet concentrative powers can be extended to levels far exceeding the requirements of symbolic logic.

In the *Ṛg Veda* the *muni* (the Vedic Era yogi) is said to dwell in the two seas.† Exoterically the bodies of water intended are the Bay of Bengal and the Arabian Sea. Yet what can it mean that the muni "dwells" in those seas? On our view it is a way of describing the intermingling of stereognosis and cognition with perception. India itself, a long and tapering peninsula, divides the two seas as the second world separates the first and third. When trance overtakes the yogi, the waves of the one lap against the other, drowning him in the Vedantic "ocean of bliss."

We summarize our analysis of the Three Worlds in one axiom:

Axiom III: There are three categories of myth: esoteric descriptions of the first, second, and third worlds during heightened proprioception.

* Proteus tells Menelaus that he is destined for Elysium, the Greek paradise.

† *Ṛg Veda* 10.136.5.

10

THE NUMBER OF THE BEAST

Anyone who has read ancient myth, regardless of its source, cannot have failed to notice the frequent recurrence of certain numbers. The most common mythic number is three, followed by seven, five, six, and nine. Three is found in the myths of the Hindus in Asia, the Greeks and Italo-Celtic peoples of Europe, even the Maya of Central America. Five is relatively more important in Greek and Hindu myth, seven and twelve in Semitic and Egyptian religion. Nine occurs in Greek, Hindu, and Buddhist storytelling.

The number three, we hypothesize, refers to the Three Worlds. Thus, in Greek myth we have the trinity of Hades, Poseidon, and Zeus. Quirinus/Pluto, Mars, and Jupiter fill the same roles in Roman myth. In Norse myth Hel, Thor, and Odin (or Wotan) rule over Hell, Middle Earth, and Heaven, respectively. In Hinduism are Śiva, Brahmā, and Viṣṇu. In Christianity we find Father, Son, and Holy Ghost, although the triad, coming as it does from a non–Indo-European source, presents certain problems vis-à-vis the Three Worlds hypothesis; it is, perhaps, related to the archaic hellenic or pre-hellenic "trinity": Zeus, Apollo, and Leto. Æschylus attributed the invention of number to Prometheus and considered it the greatest discovery he bequeathed to mankind.* In creating man, Prometheus created the Three Worlds, the primordial introduction of enumeration following upon the "one without a second" of Sāṃkhya.

In the myth of Atlas and the Pleiads, the number seven was identified with the number of the orifices of the skull: two eyes, two ears, two nostrils, and the frontal suture. After Troy, perhaps the most significant location in Greek myth is the Bœotian city of Thebes. Both Troy and Thebes are "seven-gated" in myth. Seven also figures prominently in both the Old and New testaments. In the Apocalypse especially, seven is found again and again. In Genesis too, seven is the organizing number of the myth. It is in the well-known Judaic *menorah*, a temple object described in the Bible, that the meaning of this numerology is most quickly grasped. A menorah is a seven-branched candelabrum.

* *Prometheus vinctus*, trans. H. W. Smyth (Cambridge, Mass., 1922), 5.468.

Over the course of the Festival of Lights (Chanukah), a new candle is lit each evening until all seven are burning. Finally, on the last day of Chanukah, an eighth candle is lit.* In conformity with the proprioceptive hypothesis, six of the seven flames of the menorah describe the second-world orifices of the skull: two eyes, ears, and nostrils. The candle flames are descriptive of the appetitive nature of the senses, the desire that can be felt in meditation.† Each orifice can be anthropomorphized by a deity (called in Judaism a *demiurge*) to whom that orifice is sacred. The mouth is the orifice of the sense of taste. So the seventh candle is the *mouth*—not the frontal suture. When perception is inhibited by various meditative techniques, awareness turns inward; the seven flames are "extinguished."‡ The eighth candle is the frontal suture. There is something special about the eighth candle, and Merope (the frontal suture) is special among the Seven Pleiads.

Five is the number of the senses: vision, hearing, smell, taste, and touch. It is not too surprising, therefore, to find the number cropping up in tales of war and conflict—tales of the second world—for example, the five Pandāva brothers and their bitter opponents (also their cousins) the five Kaurāvas, who figure prominently in the Hindu epic *Mahābhārata*.

The sixth sign of the zodiac is Virgo, a reference to Athena, who is anthropomorphized voiceless speech. To the Pythagoreans, six was the first perfect number; namely, the sum of its factors (other than 6) equals the product:

$$3 + 2 + 1 = 3 \times 2 \times 1 = 6$$

Thought is a sixth sense, on our hypothesis. Whenever in myth we encounter a numerology based on five, we are dealing with a description of the meditative control of the perceptual senses, on six with control of voiceless speech (the ordinary mind) as well, a distinction of great utility in myth interpretation.

The esoteric meaning of nine seems to derive from Pythagorean sources and rests on its being equal to three threes. Because human gestation requires nine months, nine has the sense of bodily completion. In the *Iliad* Helen is wooed by nine Achæan chieftains. To avoid trouble, Helen's father, Tyndareus, lays down the condition that all nine swear to defend against any usurper the man chosen to be her husband, a pact that leads straight to the Tojan War after Helen's abduction by Paris. Helen, we hypothesize, is a description of the soul. Her nine suitors must then describe the entire body, the organs of which vie for the soul's attentions.

When the Greeks decide that someone must fight Hector man to man, Nestor places the tokens of nine chieftains into the helmet of Agamemnon and casts the lot. Out jumps the lot of Ajax Big. The nine lots were those of Diomedes, Ajax Big, Ajax Little, Idomeneus, Meriones of Crete, Eurypylus of Ormenius, Thoas of Ætolia, Odysseus, and Agamemnon himself. In males—and the *Iliad*, at least exoterically, is about fighting men—there are nine openings in the body: eyes, ears, nostrils, mouth, urethra, and anus.§ The warriors cannot, however, be placed in a one-to-one correspondence with the nine apertures of the male body. Individual myths are not put together quite so systematically but accrue over a long period of time—perhaps centuries—and the numerology of a myth is distinct from its characters. We expect to see duplication, redundancy, with the emphasis depending on the meditative processes described. The eyes, ears, and nose are, relatively speaking, more involved in meditation than the openings of the lower world, and even within the second world a hierarchy exists, the nose and eyes being more prominent than the ears in the bulk of ancient myth. The lack of precise

* Exoterically there are eight candles because after the recapture of the Temple, the single-day's supply of holy oil that remained burned (miraculously) for eight days. Nine-branched menorahs also are used.

† Propriocepted to varying degrees in different organs.

‡ An echo of Buddhist *nirvāṇa*, loosely, "liberation" but in its etymology having the sense of a "flame snuffed out" for lack of air.

§ Cf., *Śvetāśvatara Upaniṣad* 3.18.

univalency between the numerology of a myth and its characters will crop up again and again.

The Christian myth of the NINE CHOIRS OF ANGELS is an illustration of nine as bodily completion contrasted with spiritual completion. Although exalted, the angels yet fall short of the perfection of the deity. Noteworthy is Lucifer, of the ninth and highest choir of angels, the archangels, who fell from grace before the CREATION OF THE WORLD. The esoteric sense of nine is less obviously descriptive, however, and more symbolic. Because nine indicates the failure to achieve perfection, we must exclude the pseudoörifice of the frontal suture; we are left with nine orifices in the male body, ten in the female.

Polydigit numerals like 10, 12, 50, 70, and so on are frequently cited in myth. During the homeric era (prior to seventh century B.C.) the Greeks had not yet arrived at the use of the cipher (0). In a base-ten number system such as that used by the Greeks, it is quite possible (although computationally awkward) to have a concept of an aggregate of fifty things without simultaneously having a concept of the cipher. It will be a whittled-down concept from the point of view of its mathematical utility; but it will still convey the sense of the number five, namely, five sets of ten. In a proprioceptive, which is to say, in a preperceptual awareness, it is probably not possible to have a concept of nullity—utilitarian or otherwise—because notions of *on* and *off*, so readily analogized perceptually by simply opening and closing the eyes, will not occur in an awareness that is primarily internally oriented.

Polydigits such as 50 can be reduced to single-digit numerals by a numerological technique that is as simple as it is ancient. One simply adds the digits until one reaches a single-digit sum. For example, 12 ▪ 1 + 2 = 3; 50 ▪ 5 + 0 = 5; 70 ▪ 7 + 0 = 7.* The 3003 gods of the Hindu pantheon then become 3003 ▪ 3 + 0 + 0 + 3 = 6 (the five senses plus voiceless speech, the "sixth sense").

Promethus, who created man, was punished for 30,000 (▪ 3) years by Zeus. The figure suggests that Prometheus was responsible for placing in the human form all three cosmœ: stereognosis, perception, and cognition.†

In Genesis 11: "And Terah lived seventy years and begat Abram [Abraham]." In verse 32, we read "the days of Terah were two hundred and five years." In myth, a son often recapitulates his father, which is to say, he replaces him esoterically in the narrative of long myths, and especially so in the case of a figure as significant as Abraham. Is it just a coincidence then that 70 ▪ 7 + 0 = 7 and 205 ▪ 2 + 0 + 5 = 7? After the birth of Abraham, Terah ceases to be a significant figure in the Old Testament; Abraham has replaced him. As with ancient Greek, Hebrew uses the capital letters of the alphabet as numerals. Greek *alpha* (A) and Hebrew *aleph* (א) are the first letters of their alphabets and are used for the numeral *1*, and so on. Cabalism, the explicitly esoteric side of Judaism, makes extensive use of letter-numeral correspondences in interpreting Old Testament verses, especially proper names.

In the *Iliad* the Trojan king Priam has fifty sons. Homer tells us that within the palace of Priam "were fifty chambers of polished stone, built each hard by the other; therein the sons of Priam were wont to sleep."‡ Fifty reduces to five, the number of the senses, and Troy is the mythic battlefield where the hero struggles to control sensory disruptions of trance. Of his fifty sons, only nineteen were by Hecuba, the rest by concubines; 19 ▪ 1 + 9 = 10 ▪ 1 + 0 = 1, almost certainly Hector. By using fifty rather than five, Homer—or the tradition he drew on—maintained the esoteric meaning of five while allowing himself narrative freedom. The Trojan War

* We define the symbol ▪ to mean "numerologically equal to." A century ago students studying arithmetic were taught an algorithm called *casting out nines* to shorten multiplication and long division. To work, the algorithm makes implicit use of archaic numerology.

† Æschylus, *Fragmenta*, presumably from *Prometheus solutus*; the source is Hyginus, *Astronomia* 2.15, who in *Fabularum liber* 54, also gives the figure of 30 ▪ 3 years (in: Frazer, *Apollodorus: The Library*, n. 2, p. 228).

‡ *Iliad* 6.242–46.

lasted ten blood-drenched years. Throughout that time Achæan heroes like Achilles slew Trojan princes left and right. A meager supply of five such princes would have been exhausted in the first book! As it happens, all Priam's sons save one, the young Polydorus, had been killed by the time Troy fell to the Greeks; while a captive, he too was murdered.

Pairs of five also are common in myth, for example, five brothers and five sisters. Such a device allows for narrative flexibility while keeping the numerological emphasis on the number five. These are not myths about the number ten therefore. Similarly for pairs of threes or pairs of sevens, for example, NIOBE AND HER CHILDREN, slain by the Bow of Apollo (assisted by Artemis). The esoteric meaning is the dual nature of every sense, its taste-touch nature, so such pairings will always be equally divided into male (taste or appetite) and female (touch or visceral sensation) figures.

Finally, there is the well-known 666, the so-called number of the great beast.* Numerologically, 666 ≡ 6 + 6 + 6 = 18 ≡ 9: the body as it falls short of perfection.

The most dedicated practitioners of Greek numerology were the Pythagoreans, who mingled sophisticated number theory with mysticism. The Pythagoreans are said to have discovered irrational numbers, namely, numbers that cannot be represented as the ratio of two integers. The discovery so horrified them that they drowned the man responsible for it and swore their membership never to reveal the existence of "surds," as they referred to the irrationals. Still more disconcerting was their realization that there are many such numbers. The modern mathematical theory of the so-called real numbers has proved that the number of surds is uncountably infinite.†

Pythagoras was enormously influential as both a philosopher and a mathematician. It is of interest to note that his philosophical master (guru?) was Hermodamas, a man said to be a descendant of Homer, so there is perhaps a distant connection between the numerology of the *Iliad* and *Odyssey* and Pythagorean numerology.‡

* Apocalypse 13.18.

† A common example of a surd is the decimal 1.414 . . . = $\sqrt{2}$, where the ellipsis indicates an infinite decimal expansion in which any finite sequence of digits never repeats itself.

‡ Diogenes Laërtius, *Peri biōn dogmatōn*, in *Diogenes Laertius*, vol. 2, trans. R. D. Hicks (London, 1925).

11

THE MANTRAS OF MYTH

There is a famous anecdote concerning the Buddha and an obstreperous disciple who wearied him with questions, the thrust of which was: Why does the soul transmigrate? The Buddha—as was his habit—answered with a story.

Once there was a traveler who journeyed far from home. As night fell, he entered a lonely wood, full of wild beasts and highwaymen. A robber was lurking there, who wounded the traveler with an arrow and stole his purse, then left him to die. A second traveler chanced by, heard the groans of the first, and rushed to comfort him. In order to bandage the wound and stanch the flow of blood, he reached at once to withdraw the deadly arrow. Before he could, however, the fallen traveler seized him by the wrist, asking: "Are you a surgeon? I will let none but a Brahman heal me." Most fortunately for him, the second traveler was indeed a physician skilled at treating arrow wounds. "Yes," he said, "in truth, I am a Brahman and a surgeon." Again he reached for the arrow, but the wounded man gripped him even more tightly. "Thanks be to the lord!" he exclaimed, "who protects honest travelers and has delivered me. But tell me—quickly, for I am close to swooning—Did you see who it was that struck me down? My soul burns to know the villain's name." The surgeon was perplexed. Time was running out. "I know not the robber's name," he said patiently, "I but saw him ride away." He would have withdrawn the arrow immediately then, but still the wounded man prevented it, beseeching him: "His caste then! You must know from his garb to which caste he belongs." The surgeon let go the arrow and scratched his beard. After a moment he said: "He was a Kśatriya [warrior]," then reached for the arrow. But the wounded man was unwilling to have it removed before he learned: "What was the color of his horse?" "Black," said the surgeon in dismay—

Here the Buddha broke off his story. Turning to his importunate disciple, he asked: "Tell me, O Wisest, what will happen to the traveler who was wounded?" The disciple thought about it, then said: "Surely he will die." "Indeed," said the Buddha. "And so will you, long before I can explain why you have incarnated in this wretched world."

The point of the Buddha's story is obvious: Do what must be done without troubling why. There is an immediacy to archaic thinking, an attitude that is tightly directed at the stimuli of the present and not much mediated by words. It is not philosophical but phenomenological, not interested in questions that can be characterized as explicitly weighty or profound. It would be a serious mistake to approach myth as explanatory of the universe in any sense that overabstracts or idealizes individual experience. For Patañjali, both the world (prakṛti) and the self (puruṣa) that experiences the world are prosaically real.*

At the same time we must be wary of belittling archaic experience. We must search for the empirical stimuli most meaningful to it. Yet how can we gauge meaning for a consciousness seemingly so remote from our own? To what can we appeal besides our own age's preoccupation with theory to interpret it for us? What do we share with archaic consciousness? Better, what have we retained of it in our own thinking?

Fortunately, language connects each one of us to the individuals of the past. The words we use and the way in which we use them—in other words, their sounds and syntax—are literal artifacts of archaic thinking. No analysis of mythmaking is complete that fails to include its tonal, morphemic, and syntactical properties. We have already outlined one aspect of the latter: the structure (syntax) of authentic myths is pleonastic, that is, repetitive. Such a syntax has a natural analogue in the practice of *mantra*: a sound repeated again and again so as to induce trance. The repetition is either vocal or mental, either with the voice or through voiceless speech.

Everything that we know about primitive worship suggests this natural structure, from the intimate connections among dancing, chanting, and the earliest recorded rituals (for example, the *Vedas* or the Egyptian *Book of the Dead*) to the well-defined meters of ancient literature. Repetition of idea, repetitive syntax, and mantra are aboriginally united in myth, and the more ancient the myth the more that is true.

◆◆◆

The use of mantras is common in yoga. At a certain point in their sādhana, yogis are taught to meditate on them. Mantras represent an intermediate stage in the mastery of both mind and body that is the practical aim of yoga. A mantra is yet another example of a bīja or seed, an object of contemplation. Other bījas are *yantras* (patterned icons on which the yogi focuses his mind), fire (for example, the flame of a candle), even portraits of saints. In the general approach to yoga adopted by Patañjali in his *Yoga-Sūtra*, anything at all can serve as a seed for meditation.†

In mantra meditation, the faculty of voiceless speech (Athena) is used to repeat the mantra again and again until a state of samādhi is reached (the act of repetition is called *japa* in yoga). Mantra meditation uses *smṛti* (memory) essentially. The sādhaka continually remembers a word given to him by the guru. Different mantras result in different trance states (samādhis), with a difference in the knowledge realized through saṃyama. When trance is attained, the yogi is said to merge with the mantric seed and to become one with it.

The breath provides a subtle internal sensation that produces sound on which the meditator can concentrate. For example, the rise and fall of pressure in the cranium due to inhalation stimulates the eyeballs and hence the ophthalmic branch of the trigeminal (fifth cranial) nerve, the primary touch receptor of the eye. At the same time, respiration stimulates sight in the optic nerve by its action on the retina and on the nerve itself. The meditator thus can sense ocular structures; he can both feel and see them. The act of concentration, it is plausible to assume, requires a specific distribution of electromagnetic energy in the encephalon and, in the case of meditation on the eyes, one that is unique to those organs. By means of complicated inductive processes, the concentrative act modu-

* *Yoga-Sūtra, Kaivalya Pāda*, sutra 16.

† *Yoga-Sūtra, Vibhūti Pāda*, sutras 1–48.

lates the auditory nerve, and a unique internal sound, one associated with the eyes, results. A similar process can be prescribed for every organ of the body, resulting in a set of distinguishable *phons*, which we define here as internal sounds and which can be used to map the nervous system.

Heracles' eleventh labor was to fetch the Golden Apples of the Hesperids, kept in a sacred garden far to the west of Greece and beyond the PILLARS OF HERACLES, a recapitulation of the Titans Japetus and Themis, who describe the bones of the nose. The garden was walled in and protected by an immortal dragon with "a hundred heads . . . which spoke with many and diverse sorts of voices."* The myth obviously involves the sense of taste because of the apples; yet the dragon with diverse voices clearly introduces internal sound. Internal for several reasons: the wall over which Heracles must shoot his arrows, the streams of breath in the nose; the dragon's name, Ladon (father of Metope [Gk. "brow"], who figures in the myth of Sisyphus and the stone); and the "hundred heads," which simply means that the myth concerns the head (100 = 1). The diverse voices describe a multitude of internal sounds heard by a sādhaka during *lāya yoga*, the yoga of internal sound. Initially they are cacophonous, but as the sādhaka gains mastery over his body and achieves inner tranquility, the sounds can be sorted out using the breath.

Homer mentions writing only once, in the *Iliad*,† where he describes the message Bellerophon delivers to Jobates as made up of "deadly signs." In an archaic mentality, we speculate, an alphabet is a collection of magical formulas, above all of mantras. Bellerophon rides the winged horse Pegasus. The horse is the breath, and his wings indicate that the breath can penetrate into the cranium as a movement of prāṇā synchronous with the felt rhythm of respiration and continuous with it; hence the connection of Bellerophon with writing, a cognitive art. The Hellenes—as the ancient Greeks are properly called—borrowed their alphabet from the Phoenicians. Their own popular histories ascribe the invention of writing to the mythic king Cadmus, a figure who migrated to Thebes from Canaan. The Phœnician alphabet, like the Hebrew, was a consonantal syllabary, which means it originally lacked vowels. The names of most Greek mythological figures are derived from words that are not Greek.‡

As an example consider the proper name *Menelaus*, actually two word-particles joined together (dispensing for the moment with Latinate transliterations), *mene* + *laos*. The second particle is a modifier of the first and may be omitted from the discussion, leaving the root *mene*. Noting that the root contains vowels lacking in the aboriginal Greek tongue, we subtract them to get *mn*, a phoneme readily identified within a host of Indo-European words, all of which have the connotation *mind*: *mens* (L.) and *manas* (Skt.), both of which mean "mind," *mimnaomæ* (Gk.), "remember," *meinen* (Ger.), "think," from which we derive English "mean" and "mind." And of course mantra is derived directly from *manas*.

A word about the letter *n* is necessary. Nine, as we saw, is the number of the beast, the body as a whole, and the phonics of nine are illustrative of the relationship between sound and meaning in myth. The symbolic meaning of nine is material completion, expressed in all Indo-European roots for the integer by the phoneme *n*—often in the all-important first (acrophonic) position—significator, as will be seen, of the third and highest world: for example, *novus* (L.), *ennea* (Gk.), *nava* (Skt.), *neun* (Ger.).

The question naturally arises: Why the phoneme *mn*? What is the reason for its persistence through thousands of years of cultural and geographical evolution? To answer the question fully we will have to come up with a convincing Indo-European meaning for what we call

* Apollodorus, *Bibliotheca* 2.5.11.

† *Iliad* 6.153–97.

‡ J. M. Allegro, *The Sacred Mushroom and the Cross* (New York, 1971), pp. 5–6.

"mind." That is well-nigh impossible to do in a manner that agrees with every way that we ourselves use the word, from "Mind your manners!" to "Mind over matter." Yet our aim is not as ambitious as that. The central question here is the relation of mantra to myth.

Sanskrit roots are particularly useful because it is the language in which Patañjali wrote. The phoneme *m* (= *im*) is also the core of the Sanskrit *smṛ*, "memory."* That this is a cognate to *manas* is as undeniable as the relationship between the meanings of the words *mind* and *memory*. The phonemes *m* and *n*—similar in that both involve a humming or twanging sound produced in the nose—also occur frequently in Indo-European–derived words that have the general meaning of "into" or "in." For instance, Greek *en*, *endo*; Latin *in*; German *in*, *an*; and English *im-* and *in-*, as in "impress" and "impose," all of which suggests that the connection that exists between the meanings of *mind* and *memory* is the same that exists between a substance and a mark made in that substance. We also know that Patañjali saw mind as composed of a literal "stuff," which he called cittā: "Yoga is the inhibition of the modifications of the mind."†

The word *impression* is illustrative. Not only is it in English and the Romance tongues synonymous with *memory*, as, for instance, when we speak of our impression of what happened in the past, but it is so in precisely the lockean way we are suggesting that *smṛ* relates to *manas*, the tabula rasa. Mind (manas) is the collection of all the marks (smṛti) that it has received through experience. More accurate than *smṛti* is *saṃskāra*, "impressions," which are left in cittā by experience. To the Indo-Iranians, mind was conceived as something akin to photographic paper and a memory as that which is recorded in or upon it. We speak of individuals with "photographic memories," describe dreams in terms of their "imagery," as we do literature, the supremely mental art form. Recent discoveries in what is called *neuronal selection* take a far more dynamic, process-oriented approach to mental experience, but such theories do not recognize anything like cittā as playing a role in consciousness. It is difficult to say at present how they might eventually be reconciled with yoga.‡

But still the question remains: Why *mn*? It is obvious that simply listing every instance of it in the various Indo-European languages will not yield an answer. If, however, we approach the problem proprioceptively, with emphasis on the sense of hearing, a solution naturally suggests itself: "(When these) modifications are nearly gone, absorption in one another of thinker, thinking, and thought, occurs as in the case of a clear jewel on a colored surface." Patañjali here singles out what happens visually when trance takes place. He is giving aspiring yogis a signpost, as it were, to guide their meditations.

What occurs in the auditory field when the yogi passes into deep trance? The nervous system is dynamic, not static. We have thresholds of response—the sensitivities of the various sensory organs shield us from an enormous number of stimuli—but we can define meditation as a means of continually lowering such thresholds, especially when they involve proprioceptions. Hence, the auditory field cannot be "empty" during trance, if only because a suitably trained meditator hears the impingement of atmospheric molecules on the eardrum, a phenomenon that is virtually continuous, albeit incredibly subtle.

The crucial question is how *low* can the threshold be set? Patañjali, as we've seen, claims that the yogi's awareness can compass even the atoms; that means the atoms of his own body. Before dismissing too quickly a claim to such power, we should keep in mind that neurophysiologists have already demonstrated that the human CNS can discern the impact of a single photon (a quantum of light) on the retina. The behavior of large assemblages of molecules—and

* Unless noted otherwise, phonemes are pronounced acute: *m* is read as "im," *n* as "in," *mn* as "min," etc.

† *Yoga-Sūtra*, *Samādhi Pāda*, sutra 2.

‡ G. M. Edelman, ***Bright Air, Brilliant Fire: On the Matter of the Mind*** (New York, 1992).

with 100 billion neurons the brain is large enough to qualify—is called *chaotic* by physicists. The chaotic behavior of the molecules of the CNS modulates the auditory nerves to produce what we have called the sound of life (i.e., the sound of one hand clapping). Now, we ask, what happens when the auditory nerves are stimulated by a chaotic *external* source, specifically the atmosphere when no conventional sound wave disturbs it? Can the auditory sensorium *represent* such a stimulus the way it can a single tone like high C? It seems unlikely. What is likely is that when the external stimuli are sufficiently random (i.e., are chaotic) the auditory sensorium cannot *represent* them except by substituting, as it were, its own sound—the sound of one hand clapping—which is of the nature of a subliminal hum. We give to the chaotic external stimulus the suggestive name *oceanic experience.* There are an infinity of such chaotic phenomenal *sets.* The CNS reverts to its own self-sound whenever presented with an instance of the oceanic experience. Clearly the argument can be extended to the reaction to chaotic sets by CNS sensoria: visual, olfactory, and so on, but oceanic experiences in the visual and auditory cortexes are the most common. A visual oceanic experience of course is the ocean itself, the wave-tossed sea. Or the sky. Or clouds. The connection to the mystic seas is clear, but the epistemological questions raised are less so, and we shall return to them when we take up the Nereids later. For now it is important to keep in mind that the epistemological boundaries between organism and the world are far more indistinct than is naively supposed.

We stipulate that the name Menelaus is mantric, and more generally we stipulate that *all* myths having the phoneme *mn* emphasized in the names of its central characters esoterically describe the third world: cognition but especially the neocortex. Examples of the correlation of mythic *mn* or *n* with the third world are not hard to find. Athens is a place name eponymously derived from Athena, voiceless speech or thought. The leader of the Athenian contingent before Troy was King Menestheus. On the one occasion in which Homer mentions Menestheus (other than in passing), he places him in the company of Nestor, the son of Neleus. The sage Mentor has become synonymous with wisdom and intelligent advice.

What then must be the nature of the phon from which the mantric name Menelaus is derived? The phoneme *mn* indicates that it is of the nature of a hum or a ringing. In the *Yoga-Sūtra*, Patañjali says of the supreme deity Īśvara (pronounced *eesh-wuh-ruh*) that "his mantra is *Oṃ*."* The Sanskrit word used by Patañjali, here loosely rendered as "Oṃ," is *praṇāva,* literally "a hum," like a bee might make. Recall the infant Zeus, god of the third world, nurtured by bees, and Merope, the wife of Sisyphus, whose name means "Bee Face" in Greek and may refer to what yogis call the *cin lāya*, an internal sound said to be like that made by a bee. In chanting the praṇāva, the *ṃ* sound—essentially a nasalization of Sanskrit o†—is held in the larynx and nose and allowed to vibrate there as long as possible, dying out slowly and blending with the silence, then repeated immediately. A meditative drone results that approximates the subtle internal humming with which the yogi desires communion (saṃyama). One concentrates on the space between the eyes and notes any changes in internal sound (lāya). Given the centrality of the brows in myth on the one hand and the sacrality of Oṃ in Buddhism, Hinduism, and yoga on the other, whatever sounds the name Merope and the praṇāva are meant to describe could be one and the same sound. The goal of the technique is practical. By familiarizing the external ear with a simulacrum, meditation on the internal phon is facilitated.

Much of Indian music is concerned with creatively evoking the "primordial" vibration. Indian instruments, for the most part, use open tuning. A note is selected to be sounded repetitively, around which melody and rhythm are

* *Yoga-Sūtra, Samādhi Pāda,* sutra 27. Sanskrit *ṃ* is sounded like velar *n* (ṅ), drawing attention yet again to the sound of the breath in the nose.

† The Sanskrit character transliterated as *o* is actually a dipthong that can more accurately be rendered by *au*; hence one often sees Àum instead of Oṃ in English.

constructed. Techniques such as chanting and drone-based harmonies, found worldwide, serve two functions: rite and practice. They are a form of worship and meditation simultaneously. Because they make use of perceptual sounds, they are basically preparatory to and imitative of an internal phonic rapture experienced in external silence.

Patañjali's explicit association of the praṇāva (Oṃ) and the supreme deity Īśvara, whom two sutras before he has called omniscient, also establishes *ṃ* as a cranial phon. Īśvara represents what we in the monotheistic West would call God, whose abode is Heaven. The Christian Father God is derived in part from the Hebrew Jehovah, with whom it is reasonable to equate Īśvara. Like Jehovah, Īśvara is omnipresent as well as omniscient; equally clear is his father-god status. Īśvara is thus also related to the Greek Zeus or the Latin Jupiter. The internal experience Īśvara describes is found in every organ of the body, more pertinently in proprioceptions of the gods and goddesses that describe those organs: Agñi (fire), Vāyu (air), Indra (thunder), and so on, just as Zeus is present in Ares, Apollo, and Dionysus.* In an archaic consciousness, that is what *omniscience* and *omnipresence* mean practically: God partakes in every experience. He is "the ear of the ear, the mind of the mind, the sound, indeed, of sound, the breath of the breath, the eye of the eye."† The distinction made between "ear" and "sound" is the difference between a phon and an external sound. The hum of Īśvara pervades the entire body. To paraphrase Saint Paul: "In his sound we all live and breathe and he is never very far from us."

Because Īśvara is a father god, he is a personal god. In Vedānta there is a being subtler than any god, roughly corresponding to the Hebraic *En Soph*, the Islamic *Allah*, the Christian *God*, the Egyptian *Nut*, the Greek *Uranus*, and the Amerindian *Manitou*, all of which can be related esoterically. The *Upaniṣads* refer to this ineffable and wholly impersonal essence about which nothing can be said, only known, as *brahman*. Hindu scriptures are at pains to make brahman the source of all the gods. The concept of the Ineffable One achieved a rather sophisticated development in Indian philosophy.‡ Patañjali belongs to this later era, but the meditative discipline of which he treats extends back much further in time, to an archaic consciousness of internal sound in which Īśvara is an aspect of brahman and contained within it in the same way that the mantra *Oṃ* is found within the word *brahman*.

That a mantra is only derived from a phon implies an important difference between the two: A mantra is a word; a phon is not a word. By "a word" we mean a *verbal sound*, that is, a sound that can always be articulated with lips, tongue, larynx, hard palate, and so on—something *speakable*. A phon, on the other hand, is a *proprioceptive sound*, unambiguously discernible to someone in samādhi yet not readily captured, as it were, by configurations of voice and far less so in combinations of letters, which serve a different faculty from audition altogether: cognition. A mantra is only a verbal approximation of a phon and is subject to variability—often extreme variability—of verbal and scribal expression.

As an example consider the sound produced by striking a sheet of brass. It is conceivable that different observers hearing this same sound will use different—but almost certainly similar—words in speaking or writing about it: *clang, bang, twang*, and so on. The actual sound issuing from the brass depends on several factors—how hard the brass was struck, the thickness of the sheet, and so forth—yet a uniformity of diction still results. Which verbalization—*clang, bang, whang*—is correct? The answer of course is none. The squeal of metal, the crack of glass, the screech of tires, indeed the overwhelming majority of sounds heard every

* Somatically, fire = warmth, air = breath, and thunder = vibration.

† *Kena Upaniṣad.*

‡ See Saṅkara, *The Crest Jewel of Discrimination*, trans. Swami Prabhavananda and C. Isherwood (Hollywood, Calif., 1947).

day cannot be precisely expressed in words. In one sense they cannot be expressed at all but can only be suggested because the gulf between hearing and touching, namely, tactile shaping of the mouth, is qualitative rather than quantitative. A mantra, in other words, derives onomatopoetically from the propriocepted phon.

TABLE 1
PHONETIC CORRESPONDENCES AMONG INDO-EUROPEAN LANGUAGES

	INDO-EUROPEAN	SANSKRIT	GREEK	LATIN	GERMANIC
1.	g	j	γ	g	k
2.	d	d	δ	d	t
3.	b	b	β	b	p
4.	k	ch	κ	c	h
5.	p	p	π	p	f
6.	gh	h	χ	h	g
7.	dh	dh	θ	f	d
8.	bh	bh	φ	f	b
9.	gh	gh	φ, χ, θ	gu	gw

TABLE 2
PHONETIC CORRESPONDENCES BETWEEN LATIN AND GERMANIC

	LATIN	GERMANIC
1.	v	w
2.	p	v
3.	c	g
4.	j	y

Etymological transformations can assist in organizing mantras. In the evolution of Sanskrit, Greek, Latin, and Germanic (English) from hypothesized Indo-European root phonemes, the correspondences in table 1 and table 2 occur regularly.* (These correspondences have been codified as Grimm's law, after the nineteenth-century philologist.) The correspondences are cited not solely to demonstrate that mantras occurring in myth involve similar relationships from language to language—they undoubtedly do—but also to provide a philological data bank of possible variant expressions for the same phon. In other words, given that a mantra is only an approximation of an ineffable internal sound, the above examples show different ways in which the identical phon might be mantrically rendered within a given language.

For instance, in Greek mythology Leda is the mother of the Dioscuri, a famous set of twins, and Leto is the mother of Artemis and Apollo, also twins. Both women's names have been translated as meaning "stone" (< Gk. *lithos*). It is almost certain that the names spring from a common mythic source. If we assume that a particular proprioception lies behind the two names, then their similarity can be explained as the inexactitude of expressing a phon verbally. The core of the proprioception sounds like the phoneme *t* or the phoneme *d*; it is actually neither, but line 2 in table 1 shows that those phonemes are reasonable outcomes of attempting to put the underlying phon into words.

Other correspondences useful in myth analysis should be listed. Very important are *l* for *r* (and vice versa), *v* for *b*, and *th* for both *t* and *d*. The aspirates *h* and *s* present a special case, both having much to do with the way one breathes a particular consonant when pronouncing it. *H* is generally treated as a vowel and, very often, *v* as well. The given transmutations have to do with the tonal qualities of the language involved and even, perhaps, with differences in racial genotypes that manifest as differences in aural and auditory constitution from people to people.

Use of a mantra requires that the meditator continuously repeat it, either aloud or mentally using voiceless speech, until a state of trance is reached. What happens in the perceptual-cognitive continuum during prolonged repetition of a symbol is crucial. For instance, if the mantra used is the first half of the name Menelaus, we of course get the following string

* *Harper's Dictionary of Classical Literature and Antiquities*, ed. H. T. Peck (New York, 1965), pp. 750–52.

of thoughts in the mind of the meditator: *mene mene mene mene* ad infinitum. But if that goes on long enough it is identical to *neme neme neme neme* or *emen emen emen emen* or even *enem enem enem enem*. All four mantras—*mene*, *neme*, *emen*, and *enem*—lead to the same trance state. (To grasp this fully one must simply try it.) Furthermore, although *mene* is composed of only two consonants—albeit closely compounded—the same effect is observed regardless of how many there are. Again, using the full spelling of Menelaus, *sans* vowels, and running the letters together so as more accurately to portray what happens in meditation, we get *mnlmnlmnlmnlmnlmnl* ad infinitum, equivalent to *nlmnlmnmlmnlmnlnlm* and *lmnlmnlmnlmnlmnlmn* and even to the permutations *mlnmlnmlnmlnmlnmln*, *nmlnmlnmlnmlnmlnml*, and *lnmlnmlnmlnmlnmlnm*. Because a mantra is only an approximation to begin with, the order of the consonants is indifferent to the samādhi achieved. It is trance on the phon it expresses that is important. If—as seems reasonable—we assume that the operation of the central nervous system and the internal sounds generated by it vary little from race to race, then our phonic analysis can be expanded across cultural lines.

Proteus is not alone in Greek myth in being gifted with prophetic powers. It is a trait he shares with all the gods and goddesses of the sea. Chief among them—if we leave out Poseidon—is Nereus, like Proteus titled the Old Man of the Sea. What is the importance of the differences in the various names? We could explain it as a result of two separate traditions, but that merely defers the question. Nereus's name suggests that he is a third-world god. In analyzing Menelaus's esoteric meaning we concluded that the phoneme *mn* describes the phonic quality of the mental world. But we also saw that the phoneme *m*, part of the praṇāva, is derived from a proprioception of the body's hum, of what might be called its homeostatic, minute-to-minute vibration, one that is neither exclusive to nor emphasized within the third world. It is the phoneme *n* that singles out cognition. If we reduce *Nereus* in the way that we did *Menelaus*, we end up with the phoneme *nr*.* How does the phoneme *r* modulate the third-world meaning of Nereus?

Several factors must be considered. First, an *r* often springs up between two vowels, making it easier to pronounce the sequence. Philologists call that *intervocalic r*. In Nereus, it falls between epsilon (short *e*) and eta (long *e*), in which case there is good reason to interpret the *r* as intervocalic. But we know that not all instances of *r* are intervocalic even when the letter falls between two vowels. Sanskrit preserves the distinction by using two characters: *r* (semivocalic *r*) and *ṛ* (vocalic *r*), the latter pronounced like the *r* in *interest*, a word often elided in pronounciation to something like "intrist." Vocalic *r* can be understood as "intrinsic" *r*. Semivocalic *r*, save when it falls acrophonically, can always be suspected of being intervocalic.

Second, on the basis of philological evidence,† vocalic *r* is traceable to extremely old Indo-European roots for words connoting origin, creation, growth, bringing forth, and emerging. The English word that perhaps best represents the type is the verb *arise*. We see it also in the zodiacal sign Aries, the ram, the first sign and in gnostic symbolism the creative spark from which the world sprang. The sun enters Aries at the spring equinox, very near to the Hebrew Pesach and the Christian Easter. Christ himself is the LAMB OF GOD, but he is also THE WORD, the secret sound of the creation, of which "nothing that was not made was made."

There is a third possibility. If mantras emphasizing *m* are onomatopoetically derived from a hum that is experienced proprioceptively, then mantras emphasizing *r* might derive from an internal *roar*, from a phon that sounds like such a noise. In Hindu myth, the god Rudra (Howler), vedic predecessor of Śiva, rules over wild beasts, animals that must have impressed archaic societies with their roars.‡ The connec-

* To refer to the procedure for eliminating vowels from proper nouns, I use the word *reduce*.

† Allegro, *The Sacred Mushroom and the Cross*, pp. 4, 210–11.

‡ Greek *therion*, "beast," reduces to aspirated *r*.

tion between *r* and *l* is important. The latter sound is at the root of the Greek and Latin words for lion. If we reduce the Latin *leo,* we isolate the phoneme *l.* That allows us to place many myths that concern wild beasts into a proprioceptive framework, namely, appetite or first world. For instance, in a myth we have already seen, Heracles slays the Nemean Lion. Heracles is the Greek sādhaka, the aspiring yogi, who attains to an important trance state by performing saṃyama on a phon which resembles a howl or a roar. We might also mention the Old Testament FURNACE OF BAAL, the roaring flames of Hell and Sheol (both of which reduce to *l*), and the fact that Apollo is known as "the Destroyer" but is the god of creative fire as well.

Possibly then, Nereus (nr) means "source of *n.*" Or if *r* is intervocalic it reduces to *n.* If *m* is a hum and *r* a roar, then *n* can best be described as a whine. It is from that neurophysiological whining that the Greek word *noös* (mind) derives. Menelaus's duel with Proteus/Nereus means that the yogi, in taming the mind, becomes like the mind, indistinguishable from it, as a clear jewel is one with the surface on which it rests. He merges with the sound of the mind.

Nereus, whose name is typically translated to mean "the wet one," has an obvious etymological relationship to the Greek words *neniptæ* (wash), *neus* (ship), and *næad* (water nymph). On Doris, the daughter of Oceanus and Tethys, he sired the fifty Nereids, one of whom, Thetis, was the mother of Achilles. Among them, Nereus and his daughters describe the mind and the five senses.

None of the above illuminates the connection between the archetypal element water and the phoneme *n.* For help here we appeal to Nereus's other name, Proteus, which literally means "the first one" and refers to the same quality of water as does Homer when he calls Nereus *halios geron,* "the ancient one of the sea." Water was the primordial element in the earliest cosmologies of the Presocratics—for example, that of Thales— whose work predates Anaxagoras's more systematic cosmology. He called water the *arche* of all creation; it came first, hence Proteus's name. Thales is an extremely shadowy figure, who represents the seventh-century B.C. transition from stereognosis to perception as primary mode of awareness. Thales is reported to have claimed that he had achieved apotheosis, and is remembered for his absent-mindedness (he once fell into a well, as though in a trance). Prior to Thales are only Homer and Hesiod and semimythical shamans like Epimenides of Crete. Although Thales' *arche* is a literal liquid, a rather different sort of liquid was posited by Heraclitus of Ephesus (fl. sixth century B.C.), who described the universe as the state of multiform flux of a light, ethereal fire guided in its evolution by the divine Logos or Word. The concept was extremely difficult to grasp, even to the ancients (who dubbed Heraclitus "the unintelligible one"). Plato took Heraclitus's Logos and wedded it to anaxagorean nous. It is in the union of such ideas—flux, word (sound), and reason—that we might glimpse the connection between flowing water, the cranial phoneme *n,* and mind; and in Homer that all comes down to making the third world a mystic sea.

Philosophers such as Thales, Heraclitus, and Plato are examples of men striving to generalize proprioceptively derived concepts, such as flux, to the world at large. Proteus, on the other hand, derives from a wholly mythical tradition, one that is archaic and narcissistic. He is descriptive of the meditative attempt to control the visceral and cognitive stimuli that are comprised within the meditative sea and that constantly interrupt concentration.

Nereus's father was Pontus, "the sea," whose name occurs in the well-known homeric *œnope ponton,* "Wine-Dark Sea," and it is natural that Homer, an Ionian Greek, would draw his imagery from his environment. Ionia is a civilization dwelling literally in the midst of the sea. From the earliest times fishing and seafaring have been carried on here. There is no aspect of life on these shores and in these islands that has not been shaped by the sea. No wonder it occurs so often in Homer, who lived in Ionia all his life: the unharvested, the endless, the Wine-Dark Sea. The entire *Odyssey* takes place amid the waves and on "sea-girt Ithaca."

Vineyards are as endemic to Ionia as seafaring. Islands such as Lesbos and Chios were renowned for providing the finest wines in the Mediterranean. More important is the Greek word for wine, *œnos*, which reduces simply to *n*. The sound, as we have seen, derives from a phonic whine proprioceptcd during deep trance on the cerebral cortex. Any agent capable of affecting the physiology of the higher brain presumably will also affect the nature of this whine. Alcohol is such a substance, one of the few that can penetrate the blood-brain barrier enough to alter behavior significantly. We hypothesize that the striking similarity between the Greek word *œnos* and third-world mantras derives from very ancient proprioceptive experiences of the cerebrum during states of intoxication. The use of alcoholic beverages reaches far into prehistory. Its effects on internal hearing could have been noted by many, and its role in the development of religion by heightening proprioception might be significant. The same can be inferred of any intoxicant, for example, the mead of the Bible or the hemp used in the Orient. Intoxicants like wine make their user/abuser more aware of the basal whine of the cerebrospinal system, hence their *n*-like names.*

Yoga, at least in the exposition of Patañjali, explicitly rules out the use of drugs and aims at achieving so-called transcendental states of consciousness without them. Drugs may reveal an ongoing, profound, and blissful experience of life, but they do not create that experience nor can they prolong its revelation without an inevitable debilitation of the body. Certain recent theories, particularly of Biblical exegesis, that locate the religious impulse in the use of drugs, including alcohol, are therefore highly suspect insofar as they insist upon a continual rather than exploratory and initially adventitious use of drugs for heightening internal awareness.† The use of drugs cannot be central to any but the most primitive religions and their myths because eventually they must defeat their own purpose.

The epithet "wine dark" is an ingeniously compact description of the meditative sea. It tells us that it is a sea of sights and sounds or, in proprioceptive terms, of photons and phons, if we define a photon as a proprioceptive experience of the visual centers of the brain. Both faculties are compassed in the single word *wine*, which articulates tone in two ways: color and pitch. With some license we may say that "wine dark" means the same thing as *whine dark*.

In the *Odyssey*, Odysseus is thrown from his wrecked ship into the sea and is at the point of death when

> a great stream of sea water gushed up through his mouth and nostrils. So he lay *without breath* or speech, *swooning*, such terrible weariness came upon him. But when now *his breath returned* and *his spirit came to him again*, he loosed from off him the veil of the goddess [Ino], and let it fall into the salt-flowing river. And the great wave bare it back down the stream, and lightly Ino caught it in her hands.‡

The stopping of his breath and the passage of Odysseus into trance (swoon) are central to this incident. It is by holding on to Ino's veil that the sea is calmed. Ino's name—which reduces to *n*—speaks to the point eloquently: she is the meditative whine, absorption in which brings the state of profound peace that Homer so movingly evokes in the ensuing lines of the *Odyssey*. She is the unexpected ascent into trance, heralded only by a high-pitched whine such as an epileptic hears just before a seizure. Ino was the daughter of Cadmus, king of Thebes, who brought the alphabet to Greece. ("Seven-gated" Thebes is the only Greek city of mythic stature comparable to Troy. It was besieged by Heracles

---

* Cf., Hindi *bhang*, "hemp," which, because of the plosive nature of *b*, reduces to *ng*, the phoneme at the base of our own "ring."

† Allegro, *The Sacred Mushroom and the Cross*, passim; the stalk and bolus of a mushroom, like the thyrsus, resemble the brain plus spinal cord.

‡ *Odyssey* 12, in: *Homer: The Odyssey*, trans. S. H. Butcher and A. Lang (New York, 1950), pp. 80–85, emphasis added.

and six other heroes, thus relating it to the apertures of the skull.)

The Greek word for "violet" is *ion*, which also reduces to *n*. It describes a color that is not so much a pale purple as an indigo, close to but not identical with black. The wines of Ionia were called *melœ*: "black." In the jargon of physics a true blackbody—an object that absorbs all light impinging its surface—is never actually found in nature. Instead, what one finds is only an approximation in which the "black" object is radiating in the indigo region of the spectrum, the two shades being practically indistinguishable to a casual scrutiny. To the archaic eye, however, it is possible that the violet shadings were striking. In such an awareness our black never exists as a color.* We see this in many of the Indo-European–derived words for night, which contain the "purple phon" *n*: *nox* (L.), *Nacht* (Ger.), and *nyx* (Gk.). Related and worth mentioning are *nidrā* and *nilaḥ*, Sanskrit for "sleep" and "indigo"; *somnus* and *niger*, Latin for "dream" and "black"; and *kyanos*, the clearly related Greek word for "blue." The practice has persisted in India to the present day of writing sacred verse in fulgurant letters of silver upon indigo paper, an esoteric description of the Word (ṣabda) propriocepted during trance as brilliant light within the darkness of the Wine-Dark Sea.

Finally, there is the moral supremacy of purple in the ancient world. *Assumere purpuream*, "to wear purple," meant "to become Caesar" to the Romans, and even earlier violet had been worn by Greeks who considered themselves noble enough. In Catholic rite, purple is the holiest color after white. Bishops wear a purple cap that covers only the cranium. In antiquity purple dyes were obtained from juice pressed from seashells of the genus *Murex*, rounding out almost poetically the intimate symbolism that exists among color, sound, and the Wine-Dark Sea.

◆◆◆

Thetis, daughter of Nereus, is far the most eminent of the fifty Nereids. Both Zeus and his brother Poseidon desired her, and it was Thetis who rescued Zeus by fetching the hundred-handed giant Briaræus when all the Olympians save Hestia revolted. It was Thetis who received the great gods Dionysus and Hephæstus after they'd been cast into the sea. It was Thetis' wedding that all twelve deities attended. Above all, it was Thetis who was the mother of Achilles, mightiest of the Achæan warriors before Troy.

Because she is a sea goddess Thetis possesses the same power to change shape as Nereus. By seizing her and maintaining his grip throughout the struggle, a hero could win her for his own. But the Moiræ (the Fates) had decreed that any son of Thetis would outstrip his sire, and none of the gods was courageous enough to try her virtue. It fell to Peleus of Ægina to win her. Heeding the advice of Chiron, a centaur, he stole into her submarine grotto and concealed himself behind a variegated bush. Thetis arrived on the back of a dolphin, as befits a true Nereid, lay down, and fell asleep (as did Proteus on the beach at Pharos). Peleus had no easier a time of it than Menelaus. Thetis transformed herself successively into an inferno, water, a lion, a serpent, and finally a cuttlefish that squirted him with sepia ink. His passion proved more tenacious than her trans-mogrificatory range, however, and she submitted to his embrace.†

In Patañjali's description of saṃyama—absorption in one another of thinker, thinking, and thought—the word used to mean "absorption" is *samāpattiḥ*, "fusion." Both words lend themselves readily to sexual imagery. There is something about saṃyama that is erotic, then, attested by the frequency with which such imagery crops up in myth. Christianity gives us the parable of the BRIDE AND THE BRIDEGROOM, in which Christ himself is the groom and we are his intendeds.‡ A little too pat perhaps, though we see a lingering archaic sexual response to trance in a parallel myth: CHRIST AND HIS

* W. J. Verdenius, *Parmenides: Some Comments on His Poem* (Groningen, Netherlands, 1942), pp. 6–7.

† Ovid, *Metamorphoses*, in: *Ovid: Metamorphose*, trans. F. J. Miller (Cambridge, 1968), 11.221; most mythopoets make Zeus the sire of Achilles.

‡ Matthew 25:1–13.

CHURCH. In Catholic dogma the Church is the mystical bride of Christ, but proprioceptively it is almost certain that references to churches, temples, mosques, and so on are esoteric descriptions of the human body. Meditation on a subtle, vibratory energy—denoted by the Word of God—that pervades the entire body is pleasurable, focused, and leads to great peace throughout the nervous system, all of which the imagery of coitus comprehends.

The yogic word for "transformation" is *pariṇāma*, transformation as *change of consciousness*, a phrase with a long—not entirely salutary—history in philosophy, biology, psychology, and more recently anthropology. It has come to have something of the dramatic about it. The meaning of "transformation" in yoga, however, is prosaically technical. Patañjali recognizes three transformations useful for describing the evolution into trance summed up by the term *saṃyama*. First is *nirodha pariṇāma*, meaning "restraint transformation" and characterizing dhāraṇā, the experience of restraining attention to one thing (Skt. *nirodha* has the sense of "nothingness" or "vacantness"; i.e., dhāraṇā is more a matter of repeatedly *not* paying attention to many things than it is attending to one thing). The end of nirodha pariṇāma is dhyāna, the experience of contemplating the one thing remaining after the many are ignored. Once dhyāna is attained, that one thing may yet alter in appearance in subtle ways, so *samādhi pariṇāma*, "trance transformation," begins, bearing the yogi toward samādhi. Finally, there occurs an abrupt, discontinuous change comprehended by the term *ekāgrāta pariṇāma*, "one-pointedness transformation," in which not only is there an experience of just one thing, but there is just one, unchanging experience of just one thing:

> The condition in the mind in which the "object" (in the mind) which subsides is always exactly similar to the "object" which rises . . . is called *Ekāgrāta Pariṇāma*.*

That Patañjali, who is scrupulously economical with words, feels it necessary even to introduce the term *pariṇāma* is significant.† Call it change of consciousness, transformation, heightened concentration, or even realization—there is a homely experience attendant to successful concentration, the practical effect of which is intuition or, better, comprehension.

The phonic properties of the myth of Peleus and Thetis are different from those found in the myth of Menelaus and Proteus. Peleus's name reduces to *pl*, Thetis's to *tht*.‡ The phoneme *p* is a plosive, produced by a precise parting of the lips during exhalation and not involving the vocal cords at all. We may safely treat it as a vowel, that is, a way of breathing. Peleus then reduces to simply *l*, a phoneme, as we have already mentioned, that has affinities with the root *r*, which describes a proprioceptive roar. The commonest description of it is a lion, a description of the first-world sense of taste in particular and of the appetitive nature of the senses in general. A lion indicates warmth and active energy, located most clearly in the heart and bloodstream ("lionhearted" is an ancient metaphor).

Thetis's name presents complications. It is actually a polyphoneme: *th-t*. The first particle (th) is an aspirate. The second (t) at first appears to have no easy interpretation. The first half of Thetis's name describes the breath in the lungs (first world); the most important organ of the lower world being the heart, we hypothesize that the *th* in the goddess's name describes the beat of the heart. To describe the sound that the heart makes in beating as a *thud* is a commonplace; the correspondence between *t* and *d* noted in table 1 supports our conclusion. Thus, the WEDDING OF PELEUS AND THETIS appears to describe meditative control of the heart and lungs (Thetis) by means of deep concentration on a mantra that expresses a dull roar (Peleus).

* * *

* *Yoga-Sūtra*, *Vibhūti Pāda*, sutra 12.

† The entire *Yoga-Sūtra* could easily be accommodated in a pamphlet-sized book.

‡ I retain the aspirate (h) because the Greeks used the single letter θ (theta) to write *th* in "Thetis."

Controlling the heart to the point of stopping and starting it at will is required if the yogi is to achieve undistracted contemplation.* Myths in which the phonemes *t* and *d* are prominent (along with *l*) describe meditation on the heart.

The Wedding of Peleus and Thetis, celebrated on Mount Pelion with all the gods and goddesses in attendance, is a recapitulation of Peleus's seizure of Thetis. At the wedding feast, the 12 (= 3) thrones erected for the Olympians describe the active awareness of all the faculties of the body during meditation. The imagery of a throne describes the fixing of each sense in space and time, the holding of the senses and the mind (dhāraṇā) to a single meditative seed.

All the trance states we have described are examples of *sabīja samādhi*, "trance with seed." Sabīja samādhi is an integrated experience. It is artificial to imagine it as having distinct parts, for example, seeing, hearing, and so on. There occurs a general, ineffable proprioception that, nevertheless and after the fact, may be approximately described in terms of the individual faculties of awareness. The myths of Menelaus and Proteus and the Wedding of Peleus and Thetis do not describe experiences occurring separately. In practice, the protean mind is calmed simultaneously with heart and lungs, for it would be ridiculous to assume that a state of concentration sublime enough to fix the heart could include a mind going at a full gallop. All of the senses and the mind attended Thetis's wedding in the cave of the centaur Chiron on Mount Pelion. Sight was present as the wedding torch raised on high, hearing in the songs of the Muses, taste as Ganymedes with his ewer of nectar, smell in the centaurs throwing darts of sweet-scented fir, touch as Hera, thought as Athena. Zeus himself gives the bride away.† He must have been smirking because, as Euripides knew, Zeus was Achilles' real father. A union between the first and third worlds is therefore at the bottom of the myth. Cuckolded Peleus is Achilles father only insofar as Achilles recapitulates him.

The presence of Zeus, ruler of the third-world sea, "lord of the dark cloud" in which the controlling destiny of the organism is somehow contained, speaks to the fatedness of the wedding. It is Achilles who is to bring upon Troy the destruction that the Moiræ have decreed. The FALL OF TROY means the unity of cognition and stereognosis, so Eris, goddess of strife and a mere cutout for Ares as noisome perception, is "disinvited" by the gods. In resentment she sends in her place the APPLE OF DISCORD, which leads to a quarrel among Hera, Aphrodite, and Athena and ultimately to the TROJAN WAR.

◆◆◆

Proteus/Nereus and Thetis are drawn, respectively, from the third and first worlds. Both are deities of the sea. The first world too is a mythic sea; but it is not the Wine-Dark Sea. That is the mental realm, the waters above the firmament. The third-world sea has its own color (violet), its own mantra (n), and its own goddess (Athena). So too in *Peleus* is the key to the lower world. His name in Greek means "muddy," something dark and dim. The root *pl* is found in our own word "black" (note the correspondence of *b* and *p* in table 1) and in the Latin *flagare* and the Greek *phlegein* (the correspondence of *p* and *f*), both of which mean "to burn," an etymology based in combustion that produces black smoke. Photons (light) discerned during proprioception of the lower world are approximately described as "soot colored."

Tartarus is the infernal region of Hades, in other contexts called the Pit, Sheol, or the LOWEST CIRCLE OF HELL. *Tartarus* reduces to *tt* or simply *t* (d). The same phoneme occurs in "dark" and in Sanskrit *tamas* (dark), where the *m* is intervocalic and not part of the root. By the correspondence of *r* and *l*, *dr* becomes *dl*, the root of "dull," a word that better than most describes the first world. The rhythms of the underworld are ponderous, sluggish. The contractions of peristalsis, the thud of the heart, the swelling of the lungs, occur at a snail's pace

* Wilhelm, *The Secret of the Golden Flower*, pp. 21–65, is an excellent treatise on Chinese heart-centered meditational techniques.

† Euripides, *Iphigenia in Aulis*, in: *Euripides: Collected Works*, trans. W. Arrowsmith, vol. 4 (Chicago, 1955), 703ff., 1036ff.

compared to the nervous system's action, which manifests as a high-pitched whine. Rather, the first world is a sea of slow rumblings and yields a composite phon best described as a dull roar. The letters *d*, *l*, and *r* turn up regularly in first-world myth, even more regularly in myths dealing with Apollo, two of the more famous being Apollo's slaying of the DELPHIC PYTHON in the deep crevice that the Greeks called the navel of the world,* and the slaying of Tityus, a giant, whom he imprisoned in Tartarus for attempting to rape Leto. In general, *r* is unimportant save acrophonically.

What is the core mantra of the second world, the creation? We have noted that the figure most intimately associated with the creation is The Christ. He is also described in scripture as the Word. Greek for Word is *Logos*, which reduces to *lg*, whereas *Christ* reduces to *chr*; but *l* and *r* are interchangeable, leaving the phonemes *rg* (logos) and *ch* = *kh* (Christ). Appealing to lines 1, 4, and 12 of table 1, we rewrite both as *kr*, or yet more simply—as *k*.

The choice looks promising if only because *k* is ubiquitous in myths of every stripe, but it is so far unassigned to any of the three worlds. Many Indo-European–derived words containing *k* (or its obvious correspondences) have the meaning "to create": *creare* (L.), *fingere* (L.), *facere* (L.), *gruowan* (Gmc.), *genesis* (Gk.), *kṛ* (Skt.), and our own *make*. The Greek mother goddess who creates the second world is Gæa (k). In Hinduism the world is created by desire, *kāma*. Cognate are *karma* and *kleśa* (action and pain), the two "modifications [vṛtti]" that Patañjali explicitly describes as interfering with saṃyama, and *kriyā* (deed), the word for yogic technique.† *Karma* and *kleśa* possibly are connected with an extremely old Sanskrit word for fire, *arka*,‡ and with the word *saṃskara*, which in meaning approximates English "sin." Thus in Greek we find *arche*, "first [thing]," described by Heraclitus as a "fiery flow." Recalling the analysis of Menelaus's name, we have the word *mark*, "[something] created in the mind." Also given in Greek are *ergon* (work) and *kineo* (move). For giving men fire—perception—Zeus chained Prometheus to Mount Caucasus, where his liver was daily torn at by an eagle. *Caucasus* reduces to *kk*, and the sense of pain intended is *gruesome* (cog. with Ger. *grau*, "horrid"; cf., L. *carcer*, "jail," which reduces to *krk* and suggests the notion of the second world as *locus pœnæ* or Purgatory). Prometheus placed the fire in the dried stalk of a fennel plant, one of several ways that paleolithic humans may have preserved precious fire. By a kind of metonymy the fire and its container at length came to have the same name in the Ursprache: **rk*, whence comes English *ark*.

In the *Timæus*, Plato refers to a fire located behind the eyeballs that gave to them the power of sight. Eventually, the bones of the second world that surround the "fire" of the eyes were collectively described as an esoteric ark. Arks are common enough in Indo-European myth. The Greek Eve was called Pandora. She was fashioned by Hephæstus as a nasty gift for Prometheus (Foresight), who wisely declined, although his brother, Epimetheus (Hindsight), foolishly took her to wife. Pandora opened her celebrated ark and so loosed every imaginable evil on the world, yet another image for the CRACK IN THE COSMIC EGG. The image of an ark is older even than that of the Titans.§

The connection of the phon *k* with fire is naively apparent: a fire crackles. Yet a fire is also a chaotic phenomenon and so can be described as a visual and auditory oceanic experience. We hypothesize that proprioception of the visual and auditory cortexes while meditating on the light and sound of a literal fire, as must often have happened around archaic campfires (and still does), leads to an awareness

* The DELPHIC PYTHON is possibly the colon; colonic contractions also must be controlled.

† *Yoga-Sūtra*, *Kaivalya Pāda*, sutra 30, and *Samādhi Pāda*, sutra 24.

‡ *Bṛhadāraṇyaka Upaniṣad*, p. 151; cf., Skt. *agñi*, "fire," and *Ṛg* Veda, the *Veda* concerned with hymns to the fire spirit and burnt offerings.

§ In Roman myth, the sun, which defines the second world by its light, was called simply "the Titan," as though there was no need to mention any other.

of the sound of the visual cortex—when isolated from the sound of the auditory cortex—that is approximated by a *crackling* or a *clicking*. (The auditory cortex, we have seen, when isolated from the visual cortex, produces a much more high-pitched sound.) At the phenomenal level, however, the *k* phon *appears* to describe the internal sound of a medial horizontal section of the brain, that is, of the second world.

In Greek myth the three judges of the underworld were Rhadamanthys, Æacus, and Minos. Minos certainly seems to derive from a third-world phon; Rhadamanthys has strong first-world overtones; that leaves *Æacus* = *k*, for the second world. Æacus built the Scæan Gate at Troy.

Finally, Vedānta recognizes three major castes or social groupings: *brahman*, *kśatriya*, and *vaiśya*; the second caste (kshtr), corresponding to the second world, is that of the warriors.* (Brahman, the most reverenced caste, corresponds to the third world, and vaiśya—lit. "herders"—to the first.)

Examples could be provided at length and in a variety of related contexts, but we sum up by saying that the phoneme *k* describes the creative, moving, active power that brought forth the second world and sustains its existence. The English word that best describes sensory pleasure is *orgasm*, from Greek *orgia* = *rk*. Also important is *work*, cognate with Greek *ergon* = *rk* (terminal *n* in Greek is inflectional) and German *werken*, which is related to the root *wrch-*, denoting what is naively real, namely, perceived (cf., Ger. *wirklich*, "real"). On the testimony of Genesis, the necessity to work to sustain (second world) life is the direct result of the Fall and the expulsion of Adam and Eve from the Garden of Eden. Note that *Eden* reduces to *dn*, the root of Dionysus, Edonia, and so on; the myth centers on tasting forbidden fruit. Jehovah's last words to them on their way out were "In the sweat of thy face shalt thou eat bread."† But the Hebrew could just as well be translated "brow" as "face."

Proprioceptions of the organs of perception bring simultaneous awareness of a phon that is approximated by *k* whether or not the organ is functioning externally. Because sight is the dominant sense of the second world, it is not surprising to find *k* prominent in words such as Sanskrit *cakśus* (eye), Latin *oculus* (eye), and Greek *derkesthæ* (see). The monster Argus (rk), whose name derives from a Greek word meaning "bright," was called *panoptes* (all seeing), had one hundred eyes, and was the offspring of Agenor (kn). Ares mates with Aglauros (kr), which is also the name of a daughter of Cecrops, legendary first king of Athens. Aglaura opened the box with the snake-man Erichthonius inside. Erichthonius, you will recall, was born to Athena as a result of her rape by Hephæstus, esoterically the rhythmic motion of the breath against the glabellar bone between the eyes, the heart of the second world. Erichthonius means "red-earth man" in Greek." Red is the color of Ares. Athena is third world. Hephæstus is first world. We have a trinity myth with the name of the child god related to the god of vision. Aglaura was turned to stone (bone) for opening the box, which seems to recapitulate the myth of PANDORA'S BOX, a second-world creation myth comparable to the Fall.

Lykios, "wolfish," is an epithet of Apollo. Wolves are theriomorphs for vision. The epithet has something to do with the neurological connections of breathing to seeing. The flow of air in the nostrils greatly stimulates the trigeminal nerve, which also innervates the eyes. The connection surfaces again in the myth of Odysseus. Odysseus, closely associated with myths concerning respiration, has Autolycus—Lone Wolf—for a grandfather.

In the *Iliad* the phoneme *k*, or its correspondences, is prominent in words denoting piercing, stabbing, breaking, and the like. The homeric word for "kill"—invariably by sword or spear—is *kteino*.‡ The same root occurs in English

* The most reverenced class of the ancient Roman tribes, after the *flamens*, were the *luperceres*, "wolf tribe" (< L. *lupus*, "wolf"), who ranked above the *quirites*.

† Genesis 3:19.

‡ Homer's verb is *apokteino*; *apo-* is a prefix.

break, *crunch*, and *crack*. Bearing in mind that the meditator's task is to gain a proprioceptive entry to the cranium via the frontal suture, then Greek *kleis*, "bolt of a door," is revelatory. Related too are Latin *clavus*, "key," and English *key*. Perhaps the most influential myth in which *k* figures is the CRUCIFIXION. *Crucifixion* derives from Latin *crucificere*, "to fix to a cross" (< L. *crux*), an esoteric description of the shape formed by the planes of the eyes and nose.

We have tentatively arranged the mantras occurring in myth in table 3. Very roughly, they describe the following phons: first world—a dull roar; second world—a clicking; third world—a whine. The above ascriptions will be augmented as we proceed.

TABLE 3
MANTRAS
OF THE THREE WORLDS

FIRST WORLD	SECOND WORLD	THIRD WORLD
t, th	*k, kh*	*n*
d, dh	*g, gh*	*r*
l	*ch*	*m*
m	*m*	*m*

Another axiom is needed:

Axiom IV: The proper nouns of authentic myth are of two kinds: (a) mantras derived from phons and (b) words descriptive of meditation.

12

SACRED GEOGRAPHY

Quid tibi visa Chios, Bullati, notaque Lesbos,
quid concinna Samos, quid Croesi regia Sardis,
Zmyrna quid et Colophon? maiora minorave fama,
cunctane prae Campo et Tiberino flumine sordent?

(What did you think of Chios, my Bullatius, and of
famous Lesbos? What of charming Samos? What of
Sardis, royal home of Crœsus? What of Smyrna
and Colophon? Whether above or below their fame?
Do they all seem poor beside the Campus and Tiber's steam?)

Horace, *Epistulæ* 1.11, "To Bullatius," 1–4

S*ic scripsit Horatius.*

Eight hundred years after the end of the Archaic Era, the lure of the Greek past still tugged at the Roman imagination. Myth and geography were especially intertwined. To an educated Roman such as Horace the islands of the Ægean and the cities of Asia Minor were rich with mythical allusions. Chios was reputed to be the island on which Homer had been born; and the Argonauts stopped there on their way to fetch the Golden Fleece. Hera herself was born in Samos. And in Colophon, Calchas, the blind prophet of the Achæans before Troy, ended his days.

In those eight hundred years the race had entered the Antique Era. In all probability the ancient myths were as enigmatic to Horace as they are to us. Mysteries, for example those of Eleusis, were still celebrated and even continued into the third century A.D., but they had by then become largely secular events, related only by ritual to their shamanic origins. Moreover, Horace wrote when a new myth, that of The Christ, was coming out of the East, the fervor of whose disciples would topple utterly the hoary deities he worshiped.

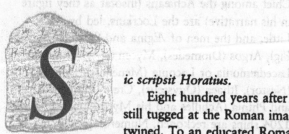

Judeo-Christian myth too is enriched by a large number of sacred place-names: Eden and the Land of Nod, Sinai and Horeb, Zion, Jericho, Nazareth and Bethlehem. Some are identifiable on a map, some are not. Cartography, however, is largely irrelevant. Proper nouns in authentic myth are mantrically derived or are descriptions of meditation. The question is: To what organs of the body do such places refer? Where exactly are Bethlehem and the Sea of Galilee?

It is reasonable to believe that propriocepted sounds—phons—do not, in the main, differentiate a Semitic human body from an Indo-European one, so we are free to conduct our analysis with either corpus of myth. We can then correlate the two so long as we keep in mind the philological characteristics of the particular language, Greek or Hebrew.

Our aim is to correlate proprioception with place. In Greek myth the association of place with myth is fixed and inviolable. Mount Ida is the preserve of Zeus and Hera, Rhodes of Helius, and, of course, Athens of Athena. In the *Iliad* each warrior's home is meticulously accounted for. Agamemnon is king in the Argolis, Menelaus in Laconia. There could be no confusion in this; just so, there should be no doubt that the phonics of these place names have a distinct proprioceptive significance. In like manner we can treat other topographical features that figure prominently in myth: rivers, springs, lakes, isthmi, and—perhaps most important of all—mountain peaks. Many of the male deities of the Greeks were born in caves on the sides of mountains, and several heroes were born or reared or, as with Achilles, educated on a mountain.

Esoterically, a mountain describes the human body seated in meditation, which then assumes the shape of a triangle, that is, a peaked shape. The Buddhists describe the body in meditation as MOUNT MERU. The equivalent to Mount Meru in Greek myth is MOUNT OLYMPUS. The top of the skull is always the apex of the mythical mountain, but the corpus of myth uses the image of a mountain to describe other parts of the body also important in meditation, for example, the root of the nose (MOUNT ATLAS) and the pectorals (MOUNT PELION).

Rivers, lakes, and springs describe the "wet" areas of the body: veins and arteries, intestines, the cerebral ventricles, all of which are, to one degree or another, objects of meditative control. Examples in myth are the river Alpheus, which Heracles diverted to cleanse the AUGEAN STABLES (i.e., purification of the sense of hearing); the rivers Styx, Acheron, Lethe, and Nepenthe that gird Hades; the pool Pegæ into which Hylas the Argonaut disappeared; and the STYMPHALIAN MARSHES, where Heracles slew the razor-winged birds sacred to Ares.

Of particular interest are the isthmi, the straits and narrows, the defiles that recur in myth. They describe the frontal suture and its lower portion, the glabellar bone, the region where the breath is "bottled up" on its way into the brain. Chief among many are the Straits of Messina, where Odysseus passed between the monster Scylla and the whirlpool Charybdis; the isthmus at Pharos, where Menelaus tricked Proteus; and at Corinth, where Sisyphus was king.

◆◆◆

In his famous catalogue of the ships, Homer lists the contingents of the army before Troy. Chief among the Achæans (insofar as they figure in his narrative) are the Locrians, led by Ajax Little, and the men of Ægina and Salamis (Ajax Big), Argos (Diomedes), Mycenæ (Agamemnon), Lacedæmonia or Laconia (Menelaus), Pylus (Nestor), Ithaca (Odysseus), Crete (Idomeneus), and Phthia (Achilles and his Myrmidons). In all, 1204 ships are reckoned. Numerologically, 1204 = 1 + 2 + 0 + 4 = 7. Moreover, the contingents are frequently expressed in groups of 50 ships (50 = 5).*

The significance of seven has already been discussed. It describes the number of apertures in the skull and is thus closely linked with the second world. That makes eminent good sense

* *Iliad* 2.494–877; other figures are given, e.g., 1186, but they all reduce to 7.

because the war with Troy is primarily a second-world myth. The Achæans describe the forces exerted during meditation to turn the senses inward and to hold them there until internal concentration (proprioception) is achieved. The total number of ships, numerologically reduced, correlates perfectly with the number of apertures that must be controlled. That they come in groups of fifty recapitulates the overall sensory goal of each member state of the expedition.

The mantric phon associated with the second world is approximated verbally by any word that sounds like a click. The core phoneme here is *k*, also *kr/rk*. The commonest homeric noun for the Greeks besieging Troy is Achæans (kh), who can be taken en masse to describe all the senses.* Examining Homer's list, the first place-name that fits this criterion is that of the Locrians (reduces to *lkr* = *rkr* = *rk*), led by Ajax Little, a man described by Homer as excelling all the Achæans in the use of the spear.† The imagery of a spear is sharp, thrusting, and painful. Next—passing over for the moment Ajax Big of Ægina—comes the fierce warrior Diomedes of Argos (reduces to *rg* = *rk*), after Achilles the Achæan chieftan most feared by the Trojans, who is the kinsman of Glaucus of Lycia, as Homer troubles to point out in a lengthy digression.‡ *Glaucus* reduces to *glk* = *krk* = *kr* and *Lycia* to *rk*. *Lykios* means "wolf," the theriomorphism for vision, and the Lycians are allied with the second-world Trojans in the *Iliad*.

Superficially, Menelaus's homeland of Lacedæmonia would appear to satisfy the phonic properties of the second world. If it is divided into its constituent roots we get *lake* and *daemonia*, which reduce, respectively, to *lk* = *rk* and *dmn*, the first of which is a second-world phoneme. For the reasons already discussed, however, Menelaus is of the third world. We therefore appeal to the other category of mythic proper noun: words descriptive of meditation. The literal meaning of Lacedæmonia is "lake-demon land." The word *demon* is derived from a Greek root meaning "force." Assuming that it described an energy felt in the cerebrum, what or where was its "lake"?

Within the brain matter are a collection of hollow spaces, called ventricles, which are filled with a milky fluid (the cerebrospinal fluid). There are five such, at varying elevations along the brain stem, ranging from the lateral ventricles tucked directly beneath the cerebrum to the fifth ventricle just above the medulla at the base of the brain (figure 18). The cerebrospinal fluid passes from one to the other through various foramina (passageways), in much the same way that the waters of the American Great Lakes drain from Superior to Ontario on their way to the Saint Lawrence (the spinal column). It is probably to at least one of the ventricles that the descriptive word Lacedæmonia applies, most likely to the two lateral ventricles because of their proximity to the third world.

The example of Menelaus and Lacedæmonia illustrates the relationship between terrestrial and sacred geography. In the same catalogue of the heroes, Homer generally appends terse descriptions of their homelands to the warriors' names. He calls the home of Menelaus "ravined Laconia,"§ as might be expected in an esoteric description of the channels that connect the cerebral ventricles, and indeed the wrinkled, furrowed topography of the cerebrum with its fossæ and sulci is also suggested The actual geographical region of the Peloponnese known as Laconia does possess numerous water-bearing gullies and ravines. Yet it is not those per se that interest the archaic mythmaker so much as their utility in fashioning an esoteric description.

Next on our list of probable second-world phonic place-names is Crete (krt), whose Achæan contingent was led by King Idomeneus, also a "famous spearman" according to Homer. He is noteworthy for his armor, which included boar's tusks on his helmet and a figure of a cock on his shield. Both animals are sacred to Ares,

* Homer never uses Achæan as a singular noun. It is always "the Achæans."

† *Iliad* 2.494–877.

‡ Ibid. 6.119.

§ *Iliad* 2.582.

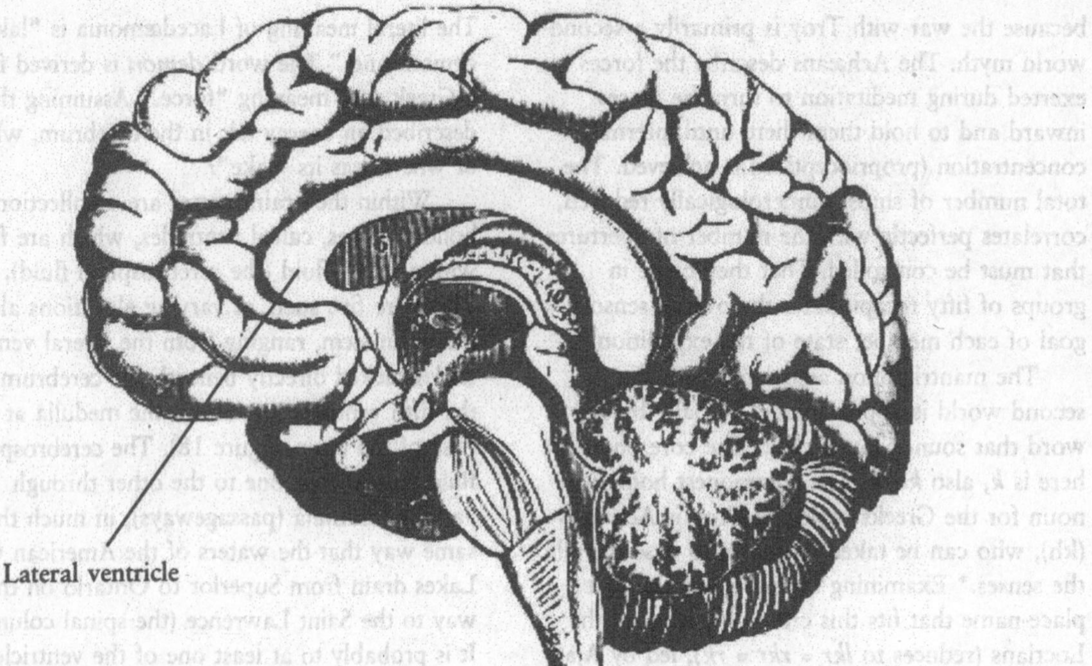

Figure 18. Lateral Ventricles of the Cerebrum (from *Gray's Anatomy*)

the preeminent second-world deity. Crete is the island most clearly associated with the second world throughout the corpus of Greek myth. Idomeneus also has the singular if little known honor of being co-commander with Agamemnon of the entire expedition.

The remaining chieftains require special consideration, either because the place-names associated with them deviate from the phonic structure of the second world or because they require an elaboration of their histories to make the connection clearer or, as with Nestor of Pylos, because we are dealing with another phonic set altogether.

Ajax's homeland is Ægina: *gn* = *kn*. If *n* is derived from a third-world phon and *k* from a second, what does *kn* describe? A phon is a propriocepted sound associated with a particular region of the body; but there exists a certain amount of variance to its localizability as well as a degree of overlap. The transition from the second to the third world is accompanied by a transition in the phonics of meditation as well. The phoneme *kn*, therefore, will be associated with a coronal cross-section through the upper portion of the second world and, equivalently, the lower part of the third. By a similar line of reasoning, the phoneme *kl* or *kt* will arise in the upper portion of the first world (the lower half of the second world) because, as we have already concluded, *l* and *t* are derived from the first world.

In the myth of Sisyphus and the Stone, Sisyphus travels up and down from Tartarus (lower first world) to Corinth (upper second). Sisyphus betrayed—therefore knew—the secret of how to find Ægina, the daughter of Asopus and Metope. But Ægina is the upper second world (kn). That means she is found just above the brows, at precisely the level of the olfactory

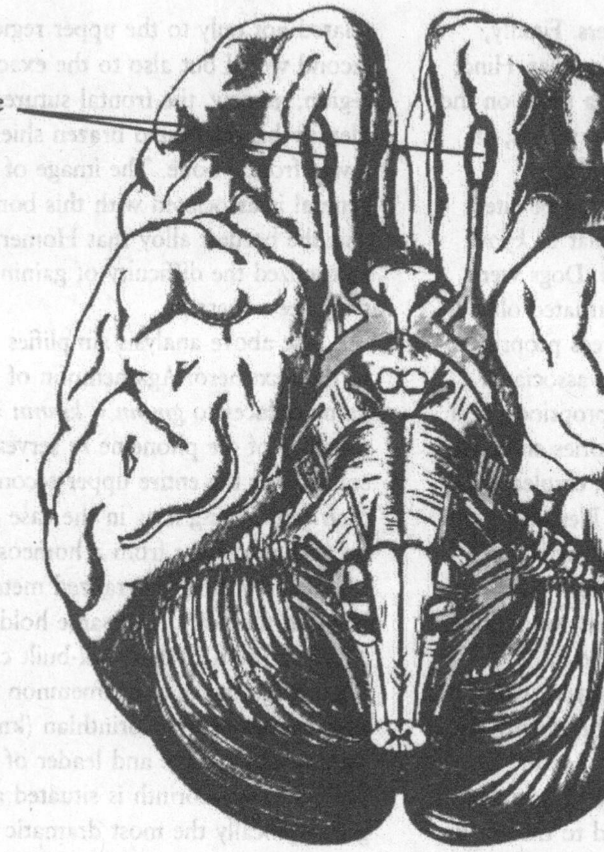

Figure 19. Olfactory Nerves (from *Gray's Anatomy*)

bulbs (figure 19). How to find Ægina is simply how to find the way into the proprioceptive garden. In fact, *kn* is the defining olfactory phon. Both Ægina and the Greek word for "dog" (*kyon*; cf., L. *canis*) reduce to *kn*, and *centaur* ≡ *knt*. The dog is sacred to Artemis and noted for its well-developed sense of smell. The centaurs were apt to riot if they smelled wine and were already half equine. Because smell and respiration are so intimately connected, it is no surprise that Sisyphus knows the secret. Metope (Gk. "forehead"), Ægina's mother, was the daughter of the serpent Ladon. A monster of the same name appears in Heracles' eleventh labor—retrieving the Golden Apples of the Hesperids—whom the hero slays with an arrow shot over the wall of a sacred garden in the west. A serpent's hiss is onomatopœsis for the breath, and we have seen the arrow imagery in the BOW OF APPOLLO (Heracles' bow was a gift from Appollo). Also related are the names Hyacinthus (knt) and Narcissus (nrk), both strongly aspirated. The former, a favorite of Apollo, was struck by a discus aimed at his head by Zephyrus, the west wind. Like Menelaus, he was a Laconian, namely, from the third world. Narcissus was a beautiful boy changed into a flower at his death. When she was abducted by Hades, Persephone was bending down to sniff a narcissus on Mount Nysa (*ns* = *sn* ≡ *hosannah*). Persephone, as already noted, is a description of respiration. Ægina, as it turns out, actually does lie between Athens (third world) and Argos (second) on a map (see figure 20 on p. 141), a fact not lost on ancient mythmakers. Finally, there is Heracles' pursuit of the Cerynian Hind, sacred to Artemis. Cerynia (kn) is a town on the south shore of the Gulf of Corinth, that is, at the second-world–third-world boundary.

Visual expressions of *kn* also can be cited. Greek *kyanos*, "blue," is very similar to *kyon*, "dog," and likewise reduces to *kn*. Dogs were "the blue ones" because dogs incarnated olfaction in archaic mythopœsis. Whereas proprioception of the cerebrum as a whole is associated with a violet photon, heightened proprioception of the frontal lobes and the olfactories embedded within them produces a clear blue, cerulean inner light. In Christian myth the Blessed Virgin is always garbed in blue. In Greek myth Poseidon is often styled *kyanochaite*, "blue flowing," and linked to smell by his well-known association with horses. Athena, the most cerebral of Olympians and the goddess who prompts Odysseus's rescue from the stormy sea by "putting a thought" into him,* has the epithet *glaukopis*, "grayish-blue eyed," singling out a color (glaukos) often applied to the sea in Homer.

Summarizing, concentrating one's inner awareness on the cerebrum leads to an experience of a whine or a ringing. As the locus of concentration moves downward, a click is discerned (along with a painful sensation) within the whine. Continuing, the ringing abates and only the click is propriocepted. Continuing, the click dies off, and a howl and a thud are experienced superposed against a faint hum (m) as the first world is meditated upon. (It must be emphasized that the entire process focuses on proprioceptions of the effects of breathing on each locus of concentration.) The sequence is thus *n* → *kn* → *k* → *kl* (kt) → *l* (t).

Homer refers to Ajax Big as a citizen of Salamis, a tiny island between Ægina and Attica with a very sibilant name. It was in the narrow Straits of Salamis that the Athenians carried off their greatest victory when they destroyed the Persian fleet in the fifth century B.C. Ajax can be related not only to the upper region of the second world but also to the exact center of that region, namely, the frontal suture. We can identify his celebrated brazen shield with the lower frontal bone. The image of bronze in general is associated with this bone because it was the hardest alloy that Homer knew of and epitomized the difficulty of gaining proprioceptive access there.†

The above analysis simplifies our treatment of the next hero: Agamemnon of Mycenæ. His name reduces to *gmmn* = *kmmn* = *kmn*. The presence of the phoneme *m* serves to diffuse the sound over the entire upper second world rather than centralizing it as in the case of Ægina, because *m* derives from a homeostatic hum associated with a generalized metabolic well-being in the body. The same holds true for Mycenæ (mkn), "that well-built citadel."‡ It is often forgotten that Agamemnon was the commander of the Corinthian (kn) levies as well as king of Mycenæ and leader of the expedition against Troy. Corinth is situated at what is geographically the most dramatic spot on the Peloponnese: the isthmus to the mainland. The phonic structure of Corinth, *krnt*, is very close to Indo-European roots that connote tightness or narrowness (e.g., L. *angustiæ* [nkt], "defile" or "narrow way," cognate to L. *angere*, "strangle," and Eng. *anxiety*). Indeed, the common Latin prefix *con-* (kn) carries the sense of *kn* into a multitude of contexts: *contract*, *congeal*, *concentric*, *conjunct*, and so on, the general meaning of which seems to be convergence to a point.§ (Clytemnestra murders her husband by pulling a nightshirt down over his face while she strikes with an ax.# In other words, Agamemnon dies "choked off" in darkness and out of the second world.) Yet *Corinth* is thought by Greek scholars not to be a Greek word, namely, not Indo-

* *Odyssey* 5.

† The Greek word for bronze is *chalkis* (*chlk* = *klk* = *kl* = *kr*); the glitter of the second world is implied.

‡ *Iliad* 2.569.

§ Cf., Gk. *kai* and L. enclitic *-que*, "and," the sense of joining together, a *conjunction*.

\# Æschylus, *Agamemnon*, trans. H. W. Smyth (Cambridge, Mass., 1926), 1381–83.

European. Therefore, on our hypothesis, its resemblance to Indo-European roots can be supposed to express a universal biophysics of the human body. In any case, that such words have their ultimate roots in second-world phons means the influence of proprioception on the development of language must have been considerable.

Agamemnon was not simply king of Mycenæ but was for the Achæans a kind of king over all. The word *crown*, from which *king* is derived, reduces to *kn*. A crown is worn with its lower rim touching the brow at the boundary of the second and third worlds, precisely the region assigned to olfaction and the phoneme *kn*. The CROWN OF GLORY, spoken of by the prophets and apostles—especially important in Paul—describes a proprioception of the second-to-third-world boundary *after* the meditative struggle has been won, namely, after kaivalya is attained.* The Crown of Thorns, on the other hand, describes the same struggle *before* attaining kaivalya. Troy itself is described by Achilles as "a sacred headband [kredemnon]" to be won or lost.† Heracles frees Prometheus by taking his bow and shooting the eagle that tears at Prometheus's liver. He then wreathes his brow with olive leaves.‡ Curiously, the word used by Apollodorus for "wreath" is *desmos* (δεσμος), "fetter." It is barely possible that we have a scribal error for *anadesme* (αναδεσμη), "chaplet," but not at all likely—the word is used only for a woman's garment. Moreover, the ancients had an odd custom of wearing crowns in memorial of Prometheus's bondage on Mount Caucasus.§

The meditative significance of the crown suggests that king and hierophant are closely connected. We know that to be true for the Indo-Europeans.# Certainly, the Egyptian pharaoh was both, and he is distinguished in art by the Double Crown of Upper and Lower Egypt. The king in other words might originally have been a shaman or priest who had attained liberation and whose crown was the outward, esoteric mark of his status.

Nestor of Pylus is a third-world figure. Pylus is in the Peloponnese, the esoteric cranium, and on the evidence of Homer's catalogue would seem to have been a vassal state to Menelaus's Lacedæmonia. When the Greeks decide that someone must fight Hector man to man, it is the third-world sage Nestor who places the tokens of nine chieftains into the helmet of Agamemnon (kmn) and casts the lot.

The esoteric location of Ithaca, homeland of Odysseus, is the practical goal of yoga, which is to enter into the cranium via the breath, and we must postpone the discussion for the moment. We turn next to Diomedes, king of Argos. Argos reduces to *rk*, and after "Achæans" Homer uses "Argives" most often to describe the besieging Greeks. Diomedes, like Ajax Big, is always at the center of the fighting before Troy. He is also noted for his shield and his bronze armor, which in the middle of the conflict he exchanges for the golden armor of Glaucus, a Lycian and a Trojan ally. Bronze is the metal of Ares, gold of Apollo. Diomedes also is a particular favorite of Athena, who assists him in wounding Ares when the god enters the fray on the side of the Trojans. Like Ajax, Diomedes relates to the frontal bone, but unlike Ajax, who perishes by falling on his sword in a sheepfold, Diomedes returns safely to Argos. His exchange of armor with Glaucus—an exchange of bronze for gold that became a proverb in antiquity—describes the transformation of perception that results from the destruction of Troy. When Glaucus dons the armor of bronze, it is a prescription for the fallen state of perception.

We now take up the other key concept involved in locating Ithaca, that is, the idea of

* Isaiah 28:5; 2 Timothy 4:8; James 1:12; 1 Peter 5:4; and Apocalypse 2:10. Also known as a halo < Gk. *halos*, "threshing floor," a circular path followed by oxen in threshing out grain.

† *Iliad* 16.100.

‡ Apollodorus, *Bibliotheca* 2.5.11; Athenæus, *Depnosophistæ*, trans. C. B. Gulick (Cambridge, Mass., 1957), 15.472.

§ Apollodorus, ibid., n. 3.

\# Dumézil, *Mitra-Varuna*, pp. 21–24.

the west, one of four cardinal points of the compass, all of which have esoteric significance. At all times and in all places primitive peoples have systematically divided the circle of the horizon according to characteristics that are simultaneously cosmological and psychological. Thus, for example, the Amerindian Poncas placed the entrance to their encampments on the west; the Zunis associated various colors with the directions; the Aztecs linked the directions with animals and the seasons.* As for the Greeks, we know that in virtually every instance they sited their temples so as to face the east and identified the points of the compass with certain gods and goddesses, for instance, Apollo with the north. Christians on the other hand face their cathedrals and basilicas toward the west. Palestine is bounded on the west by the Mediterranean Sea, on the east by desert. Esoteric water is the element of stereognosis and cognition, earth and air of perception. Thus, for Semitic cultures—Babylonian, Hebrew, and Assyrian—west is associated with the inner worlds, east with the external world. Conversely, the topography of Thessaly and Thrace, where the earliest Greek-speaking Indo-Europeans settled, has the Ægean to the south and east and dry, mountainous land to the west; so east and south become associated with internal experience, west with perception. But the most important reason for the 180-degree turnabout is that Christian churches were meant to be experienced from the inside, Greek temples solely from the outside, therefore the design of the one must be reversed relative to the other just as, where driving on the right is prohibited, cars are designed with the steering wheel on the right.

A recurrent theme in Greek mythology is that of the winds. The north wind was Boreas, the south Notus, and the west Zephyrus. (The east wind is conspicuously absent from myth.) These were kept in an ox-hide sack by the god Æolus. The symbolism of an ox has two esoteric applications: first to the ears because of the disposition of its horns, and second to the neck and chest where the yoke is fastened in plowing. Because plowing is an image of respiration—wind—the ox-hide sack describes the chest, specifically the lungs. Æolus, because his name reduces to *l*, is a first-world god.

The question now is how to orient our esoteric compass within the human body in a manner consistent with the winds of myth. Boreas is perhaps the most often mentioned of the three. His father was the monster Typhæus (reduces to *tph*), whom Zeus imprisoned in the underworld, and his grandfather was Tartarus, the personification of Hell in Greek myth. Boreas's name is derived from a Greek word meaning "to devour," also indicating the first world as his place of origin. Therefore, with reference to the body, north must mean straight down. When Apollo pursues the chthonic python, he chases it first to the north, then down into the omphalos.

Immediately a seeming contradiction arises: How do we reconcile the fact that the thorax is the source of warmth in the body with the plain knowledge that to journey northward from Greece leads to colder and colder climes? The answer can only be that since the thorax is located in the middle of the torso it cannot be considered to be very far north in an esoteric sense. The stomach and bowels are therefore the northern extremes of the body, and their digestive functions support the Greek meaning of *Boreas* (devourer) quite well. Also, to say that the north wind of myth is an esoteric description of the breath in the lower torso makes good sense because in yoga one breathes diaphragmatically, that is, one allows the stomach to distend fully to accommodate the motion of the diaphragm during respiration. The technique enhances the smooth, unforced rhythmicity that someone meditating strives to propriocept fully and gives the sensation that the breath rises from the gut.

The relative coldness of the lower alimentary canal correlates with our designation of the first world as the realm of the Great Mother. Greek cosmology made use of four archetypes: *fire*, *earth*, *air*, and *water*, of which earth and water

* J. Lindsay, *Origins of Astrology* (New York, 1971), pp. 20–21.

were thought to be feminine principles. Earth and water esoterically symbolize the fleshiness and liquidity of the bowels, and Aristotle himself calls them the "cold qualities" of the universe.* It is also worth recalling that in Christian myth the lowest circle of Hell is a kingdom of ice.†

Other evidence that the first world corresponds to mythic north comes from numerous legends of the god Apollo. Two ancient shrines especially are connected with his worship: Delos, the place of his birth, and Delphi, the spot where he descended into the omphalos to slay a python (the alimentary canal) sacred to the Great Mother. Both place-names have strong first-world phonic properties. Delphi was the scene of the Stepteria, a festival held in Apollo's honor, during which a great processional to the north occurred. Herodotus informs us that offerings were sent from the north to Delos by a mythical people known as the Hyperboreans, a fabulous tribe that has intrigued scholars of myth since antiquity; all manner of speculation has been expended in explaining who they were and what they were intended to describe.

In Greek *hyperborean* means "dwelling above the north." Traditionally that has been taken to mean "beyond the north" or "north of north," which is puzzling because Apollo is a fire god and would seem to have little to do with so frigid a locale. The enigma disappears, however, if we take Hyperborean to mean what its literal translation—above the north—suggests esoterically: above the bowels or in the chest. Part of the confusion arises of course because of a naïve association of north with up; but sacred geography inverts this wholly arbitrary relationship, quite logically too, because the ancient mythmakers thereby kept in coincidence the cold regions of the globe and body.

The association of Apollo with both the first world (Delos/Delphi) and the second (by means of his very ancient epithet *lykios*, "wolfish," i.e., vision) implies a neurophysiological connection between the heart and lungs and the eyes. The *Upaniṣads* testify to such a connection, as we have seen. The neurological connection is the vagal system—the ninth, tenth, and portions of the seventh and eleventh cranial nerves.‡ The complex provides sensory and motor roots for the heart, lungs, nose, eyes, and tongue (figure 3). The duality of apollonian fire in the heart and eyes and apollonian air in the lungs is superficial. The aristotelian elements fire, earth, air, and water, are divided by male and female gender. Air and fire are both male elements, and Apollo was the classical ideal of masculinity.

Apollo's name, which has traditionally been derived from the Greek word for "destroy," *apollymæ*, describes a first-world sound: a howl produced by rhythmically expelling air from the lungs via the throat and mouth. We may expect that in its original—hypothetical—Indo-European form it was approximated by a sound like "wow wow." Our English surname Powell is illustrative. The BOW OF APOLLO DESTROYER describes the flow of breath felt as a rhythmic battering against the base of the frontal bone—similar to Pollux, the boxer twin of the Dioscuri, and of course Achilles; although in Achilles we have more the sense of piercing the frontal bone with the SPEAR OF PELEUS, a gift from the centaur Chiron, given at the wedding on Mount Pelion to Peleus, who in turn gave it to Achilles on his departure for Troy. The sharp thrust of the Spear of Peleus describes the same experience as the arrow shot from the BOW OF APOLLO ARCHER (it might in fact be a more ancient simile, antedating the use of the bow by Indo-Europeans).§ We have a constellation of myths involving the phonemes *l* and *pl*: Apollo, Pollux, Peleus, Pelion. What links them is the direction

* Aristotle, *Metaphysics*, in: *The Philosophy of Aristotle*, ed. R. Bambrough, trans. J. L. Creed and A. E. Wardman (New York, 1963), pp. 41–47.

† See, e.g., Dante's *Inferno*.

‡ There are also connections to the trigeminal (fifth cranial) nerve.

§ Apollo is Śiva, the third member of the vedic trinity, who is is also known as "the destroyer," is an archer, and possesses a sibilant name. Śiva is a development of the vedic Rudra—Howler—whose name suggests a first-world roar.

north. Peleus was king in Phthia, to the north of the Peloponnese.* Mount Pelion is in the north as well. When the sons of Alœus wanted to get into heaven, they piled Mount Pelion on top of Mount Ossa. Ossa describes respiration. Machaön and Podalirius, sons of Asclepius, are from the extreme north of Greece. Thus, within reason, we have established mythic north as down with respect to the body.

Consistency requires that south be up, that is, the third world. First, Pelion is south of Ossa. By placing Pelion atop Ossa, the Alœdes were going from north to south in assailing heaven. When Odysseus washes ashore in Ithaca at the entrance of a two-mouthed cave (the nasal cavities), Homer tells us that one entrance led northward to the infernal regions, the other south to the abode of the gods. The Greek personification of the south wind was Notus, which reduces to *n*.† The etymology of Notus is *notios*, "wet," apparently because in the Ægean the south wind brings rain in autumn. But of course rain falls from above, and Homer himself specifically associates Notus with "the clouds of father Zeus,"‡ the preeminent third-world god. The idea of wetness evokes the third-world sea, and there can be little doubt that Notus is cognate with Nereus, the Old Man of the Sea.

In the myth of Sisyphus and the Stone, we referred to the Peloponnese as an esoteric description of the entire skull, not just the bones of the face that comprise the second world. Pelops is a curious figure frequently associated with bones in myth. His father, the wicked Tantalus, cuts Pelops up and feeds him to the gods and goddesses at a dinner party on Mount Sipylus. Pelops is then put back together bone by bone, and life is breathed into him. Demeter gives him an immortal shoulder bone made of ivory (namely, the color of bone). He kills Stymphalus, a rival king, tears him apart, and scatters his bones. Pelops's son Atreus, father of Agamemnon and Menelaus, kills his three nephews and feeds them to Thyestes, his brother. After the unwitting Thyestes eats his fill, Atreus shows him the skulls of his children, which touches off a blood feud extending over three generations. Pelops's sister Niobe is turned to stone. The Greek soothsayers tell Agamemnon that Troy cannot be captured until the bones of Pelops are brought to Troy, and Odysseus is sent to get them. Bones bones bones.

Pelops had twenty-two children. Twenty-two bones make up the skull: fourteen facial and eight cranial. Pelops himself named the Peloponnese, which means the "island of Pelops." It is the heart of classical Greece, extending south from the Isthmus of Corinth. It was in the Isthmus of Corinth that Pelops won a kingdom and a wife, Hippodæmia, in a chariot race. He arranged for the chariot of King Œnomæus of Pisa to come apart and entangle him. Given that horses denote breathing, we again seem to be considering an esoteric description of kumbhaka, and especially because the race takes place in Corinth, the narrow space between the eyes, where Sisyphus was king. Also, *Hippodæmia* means "horsetamer" in Greek. The race followed the course of the river Alpheus, a curious river in Greek mythology because it was said to flow for the most part underground, namely, in the first world where the breath arises, emerging in Sicily, an island, namely, the second world. The Peloponnese is bounded on the north by the Gulf of Corinth. The southern Peloponnese is Laconia, the kingdom of Menelaus bounded by the Ionian Sea.

We have two choices for aligning an east-west axis within the body: either from back to front (dorsal-ventral) or front to back (ventral-dorsal). With respect to the head these become posterior-anterior and anterior-posterior. For a variety of reasons, now to be discussed, we choose the former arrangement. First of all is the persistent occurrence in Greek myth of a sacred garden to the west, for example, the Garden of the Hesperids. References to gardens are esoteric descriptions of the sense of smell, which func-

* *Achilles* = *chl* = *kl*, *k* referring to his piercing function.

† The ending *-tos* (> *tus*), like *-tor* in Nestor, indicates gender and facilitates pronunciation in Greek, so *n* (or *ns*) is the root.

‡ *Iliad* 2.145.

tions through the nose and the olfactories, both located at the extreme front of the cranium. The Greeks personified the west wind by Zephyrus, a name that—like Sisyphus—suggests the sound of the breath in the nostrils. Sisyphus's citadel within Corinth was called Ephyre (cf., *zephyra*), also onomatopoetic for the breath in the nostrils and perhaps related to the fountain of Pyrene, which gushed up beneath the temple of Aphrodite.*

The Greek noun for all things western is *hesperœ*, also quite sibilant. By classical times authors such as Horace often referred to Italy as Hesperia, because it lay to the west of Greece.† The Hesperids were named for their mother Hesperia, the daughter of Hesperus, the Evening Star;‡ but they were also Atlantids, that is, daughters of Atlas, fixing them with even greater certainty near the space between the brows. When Heracles comes after the sacred apples, of which they are guardians, he needs the assistance of Atlas in finding their secret grove. Atlas, it may be remembered, was at that time preoccupied with holding up the heavens, to which appalling task Zeus had sentenced him for his part in the revolt of the Titans (yet another image of suffering and bondage related to the second world). Heracles reluctantly agrees to shoulder his burden while Atlas leaves to fetch the apples. As might have been predicted, the Titan is not eager to take up the firmament again and offers to bring the fruit to Eurystheus (the tyrant at whose behest Heracles performed the labor). Fortunately for Heracles, Atlas is as dull-witted as he is strong. He foolishly consents to resume his post when Heracles complains that he simply has to have a pad for his aching shoulders and will return as soon as he's found one. Atlas never sees him again. It is natural to assume that the pad is placed at the back of Heracles' neck; the spot that corresponds to the interorbital space in our physiognomic interpretation of Atlas. Again, the myth singles out the brows as a locus of pain, a fate that Heracles, a yogi, evades.

The celebrated Pillars of Heracles (the Straits of Gibraltar) flanked the passage to the western ocean (the Atlantic) and lay close to the Atlas Mountains. The pillars therefore describe the bones that make up the glabella and may be reasonably equated with Atlas himself. The identification of the Straits of Gibraltar with the site of Atlas's labors is of fairly recent origin. Homer understood Atlas to stand far out in the ocean and was closer to the aboriginal meaning of the Titan, which is a personification of the sea-girt second world.[5] We might also mention the Saronic Gulf, the expanse of blue water west of Athens and toward the Bay of Eleusis where each would-be initiate into the Eleusinia washed a sacrificial pig. Saronic reduces to *srn*, hence can be related to many Indo-European words for swine (sn), theriomorphized nasal breathing.

We can now take up the case of Odysseus, ruler of Ithaca, which lies to the west of Greece. In the catalogue of the ships Homer describes Odysseus as the leader of the "proud Cephallenians." The name is clearly derived from the Greek word *kephale*, "head," particularly the brain. Mantrically, it is an aspiration (pha) of the phoneme *k* (the *l* is intervocalic). Geographically, Cephallenia is a group of islands—only one of which is Ithaca—off the western coast of Greece. Yet Homer himself never says that Ithaca is an island. Rather, Ithaca is the end of the world, never-never land. Ithaca is the goal of Odysseus once Troy has fallen. Like Cephallenia, Ithaca is the state of consciousness in which breath has transformed perception by dissolving it in the PRIMEVAL SEA. Ithaca is where Odysseus is from—the breath

* There are many *ephyrœ* in Homer, e.g., *Iliad* 2.658, 6.152–53; *Odyssey* 1.251, 259. See also Gladstone, *Studies on Homer and the Homeric Age*, vol. 1, pp. 505–21, for *ephyre* as related to a walled citadel. The etymology carried over to Latin *porta* = *pr (t* intervocalic), "doorway."

† *Hesperos*, ? cog. with L. *spirare*, "to breathe," and *sperare*, "to hope."

‡ Either Venus or Mercury, depending on which precedes the sun in the ecliptic on a given day.

5 Atlas is also the name of a mountain in Arcadia, which reduces to *rk*, a second-world mantra; the oldest legends concerning Atlas are Arcadian.

starts in the esoteric west—but save for narrative consistency, Ithaca is not really where Odysseus is going. For Homer that goal overwhelmingly is Odysseus's wife, Penelope, and his marriage bed. Ithaca is therefore an island by default, because once Troy has fallen, the barrier between the breath and the cranium is gone. Prāṇā flows freely throughout the organism. The sādhaka has entered the inner world and the journey is now within a wholly watery cosmos.

If west is the front of the cranium, consistency requires that east be the back of the cranium. Because the mechanics of breathing through the nose entail an inhalation of air into the nostrils (Zephyrus, the wind from the west), thence upward to the frontal sinus and downward into the lungs (Notus, the wind from the south), followed by an exhalation that is, substantially, an up-and-down-and-out motion (Boreas–Notus), but does not involve a motion either to or from the back of the skull (east), the lack of myths concerning the east wind (known as Eurus) is explained.

Greek temples were nearly always sited so as to face the east (a prominent exception is the north-facing Temple of Apollo at Bassæ, the direction associated with Apollo). Nor was anyone allowed inside the temple except the priest. Putting together the siting of the temple and its fane—the proscribed interior—the direction indicates the existence at the back of the skull of an internal light analogized by the sun, which rises in the east. Yogis call the light *mūrdha jyotiṣi*. In Greek myth its best-known expression is the Golden Fleece, which Jason brought back from Colchis, a land far to the east of Greece. Jason began his journey in the north, in the Thessalian city of Jolcus, a first-world locale, namely, from where the breath rises toward the cranium. The back of the cranium contains the visual cortex. Given that the brain is predominantly electromagnetic in its functioning, it is not surprising that it can be propriocepted as intense optical radiation, namely, as literal light.

Troy too is east of Greece. The Trojan expedition embarked from Aulis, a first-world place name. In the *Odyssey*, Menelaus takes a roundabout way home: his course brings him to Egypt, namely, into the south, the third-world compass point, and his homeland of Laconia is in the extreme south of the Peloponnese. The area between Laconia and Thessaly contains Argos, Mycenæ, and Corinth. All are second-world place names. According to the homeric catalogue, the Corinthian littoral was within the dominions of Agamemnon.

We now have a complete esoteric compass correlating the posture of the human body with the cardinal points of the horizon (figure 20). Furthermore, we've indicated in a general way how to go about understanding straits and isthmi, mountains and lakes, islands and seas, as they occur in authentic myth.

◆◆◆

Reviewing the work thus far we can collect several statements that serve as axioms in an aboriginal interpretation of mythology:

I. A myth is an esoteric description of a heightened proprioception.

II. The structure of authentic myth is pleonastic.

III. There are three categories of myth: esoteric descriptions of the first, second, and third worlds during meditation.

IV. The proper nouns of authentic myth are of two kinds: (a) mantras derived from the phons and (b) words descriptive of the practice of meditation.

We can now interpret myth without recourse to new first principles.

No axiom is concerned with philosophical, ethical, or religious questions. Myths did not arise from a need to supply answers to such questions. Their origins are so remote from us in time that we must put aside customary and compulsive intellectualizing if we are to understand them, and we must especially avoid glibly equating mythology to symbology. The theory of myth as a description of heightened proprioception follows from an ability—admittedly hypo-

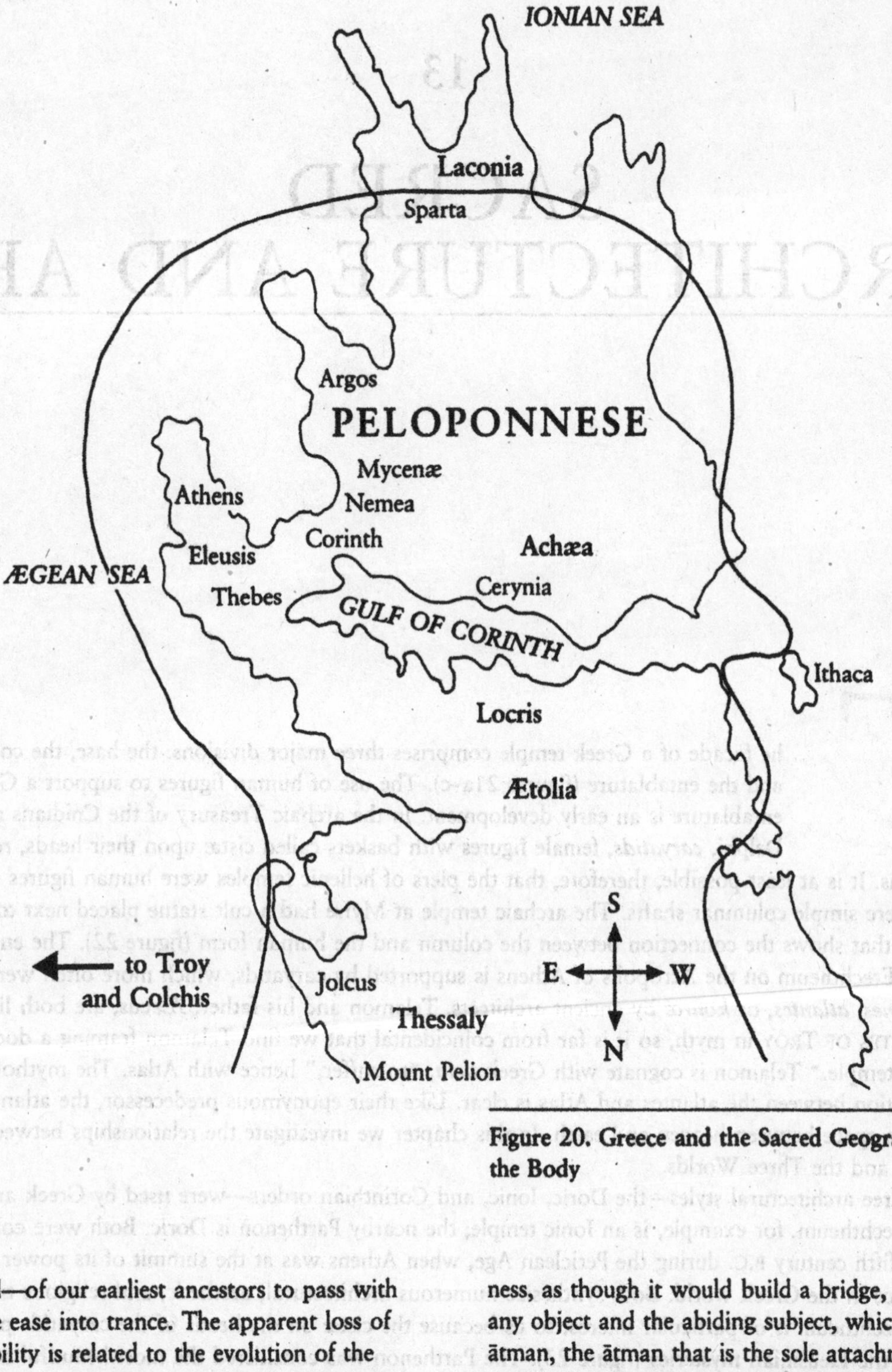

Figure 20. Greece and the Sacred Geography of the Body

thetical—of our earliest ancestors to pass with relative ease into trance. The apparent loss of that ability is related to the evolution of the human nervous system, one that has led to an increasing reliance on the cortex—the seat of intellect—for a filtered experience of the world.

Yoga is a form of Know Nothingness: "know no thing-ness." It seeks to throw awareness, as though it would build a bridge, between any object and the abiding subject, which is the ātman, the ātman that is the sole attachment of the heart; and all of that would be philosophizing par excellence were it not for the ability of yoga's technical wisdom to reify intellect, bring it to life, and supply an experience for every idea—unto God itself.

13

SACRED ARCHITECTURE AND ART

The facade of a Greek temple comprises three major divisions: the base, the column, and the entablature (figures 21a–c). The use of human figures to support a Greek entablature is an early development. In the archaic Treasury of the Cnidians at Delphi, *caryatids*, female figures with baskets called cistæ upon their heads, replace columns. It is at least possible, therefore, that the piers of hellenic temples were human figures before they were simple columnar shafts. The archaic temple at Myræ had a cult statue placed next to the facade that shows the connection between the column and the human form (figure 22). The entablature of the Erechtheum on the Acropolis of Athens is supported by caryatids, which more often were called *telamones*, *atlantes*, or *kouræ* by ancient architects. Telamon and his father, Æacus, are both linked to the GATES OF TROY in myth, so it is far from coincidental that we find Telamon framing a door into a Greek temple.* Telamon is cognate with Greek *tlein*, "to suffer," hence with Atlas. The mythological connection between the atlantes and Atlas is clear. Like their eponymous predecessor, the atlantes create a space between heaven and earth. In this chapter we investigate the relationships between the temple and the Three Worlds.

Three architectural styles—the Doric, Ionic, and Corinthian orders—were used by Greek architects. The Erechtheum, for example, is an Ionic temple; the nearby Parthenon is Doric. Both were completed in the fifth century B.C. during the Periclean Age, when Athens was at the summit of its power and influence in the Greek world. Both synthesize numerous architectural, aesthetic, and religious traditions. The Erechtheum is of particular interest to us because the cistæ on the heads of the caryatids played a role in the Eleusinian mysteries (figure 23). The Parthenon was considered the most beautiful building of antiquity and Doric the most dignified of the orders. Doric is also the oldest of the orders.

The vocabulary of Greek architecture is filled with words that denote parts of the body, correla-

* According to Hyginus, Telamon's grandfather, Sisyphus, mated with Anticlea in a doorway to father Odysseus.

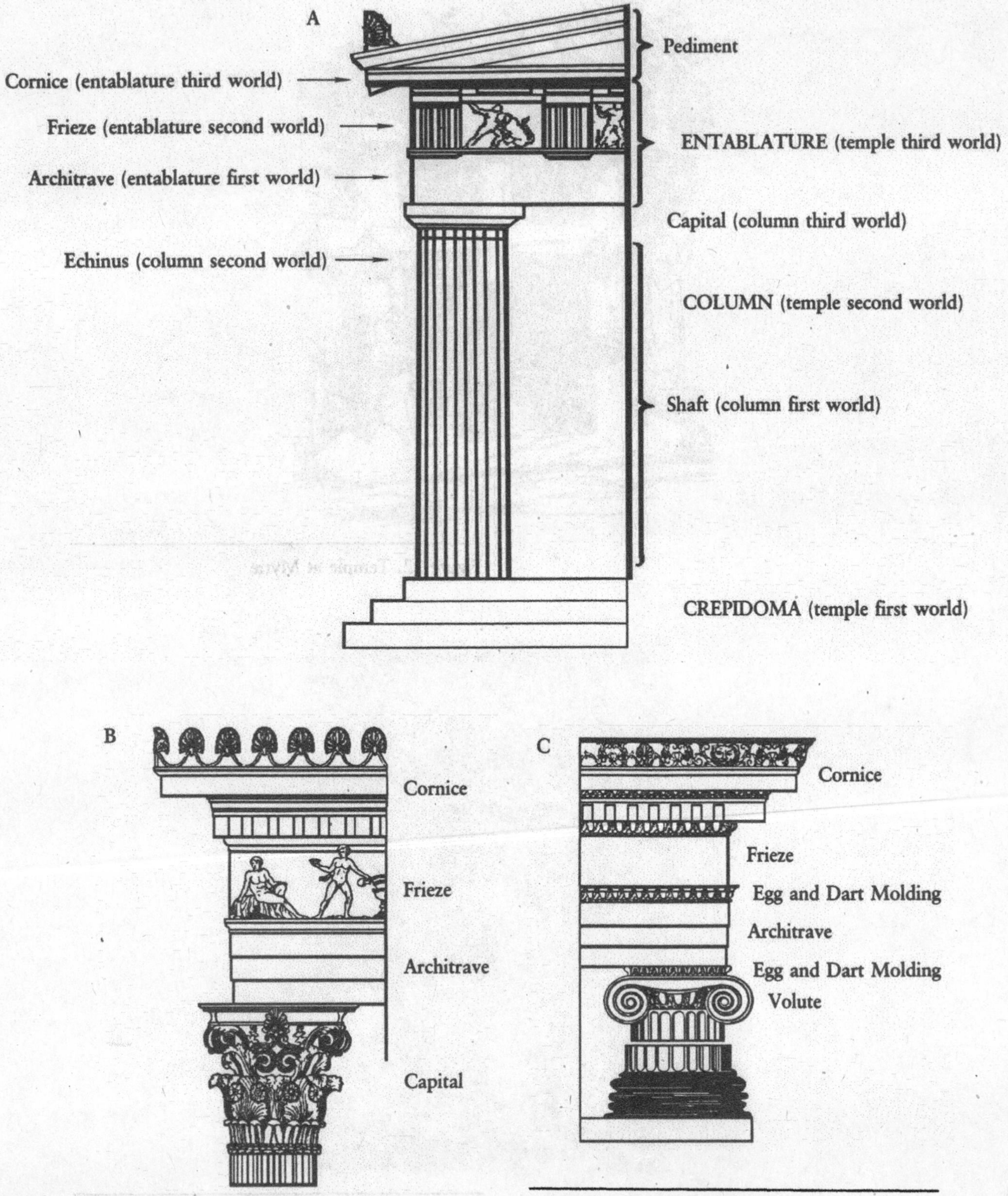

Figure 21. Classical Orders (A) Doric, (B) Corinthian, (C) Ionic.

Figure 22. Temple at Myræ

Figure 23. Caryatid of the Lesser Propylæa, Eleusis (with cistæ)

tions that by themselves might be ascribed to mere simile. Yet we know that the human figure above all other forms obsessed Greek artists, architects included. On the proprioceptive hypothesis, Greek architecture in general—and purely religious buildings in particular—might be expected to continue the obsession by depicting the Three Worlds. One of the beauties of a trabeated Greek temple is the ingenuity with which it repeatedly incorporates the theme of the division into threes. Not only does the facade have three parts, but so do the individual columns: shaft, necking, and capital, and the entablature: architrave or lintel, frieze, and cornice. The capital of a column has three parts: the necking (echinus), the molding, and the plinth; the temple always sat on three steps called the *crepidoma*; and so on, in Chinese-box fashion, down to the design of the moldings, a generic term for the stonework that divides the facade of a Greek temple into its several parts.

The compelling image of the temple is the skull. The columns create the spatiality of the second world, a place of light and air. What we see, when we stand well back and take in a Greek temple as a whole, the way it was meant to be seen, is a massive stone pediment separated from a massive stone base by a columnar group that is permeated with air and light. The contrivance is so accomplished that pediment and entablature seem to float in space. The Doric columns of the Parthenon are ever so slightly swollen; the several cylindrical drums that together make the shaft are of unequal diameters, and the resulting curve is close to hyperbolic (figure 24a). The technique, known as *entasis*, effectively animates the stone, which bulges with an all but biological dynamism in the same way that a man whose chest is inflated projects vitality. Greek sculpture was always done with the chest of the subject swollen with air. Entasis is the equivalent theme in architecture.

There is no plausible architectural theory that accounts for entasis, even though its use was both ancient and widespread. Entasis was used in the archaic period of hellenic architecture, and precedents can be found in Mycenæan designs (e.g., in the candelabrum of the *megaron*, "great hall," at Phæstus). The Mycenæans—or Achæans—were predecessor hegemonists in Greece to the Dorians and have close historical connections to the Minoan culture on Crete. The Cretans, who may or may not have been Greek but who contributed enormously to Greek culture, used columns that tapered from the top down (figure 24b), which correlates still more closely with an interpretation of the columns as the thorax swollen with air. The Cretans were heavily influenced by the Egyptians, and numerous motifs of Greek architecture can be shown to have Egyptian parallels, particularly the design of the all-important columnar capitals. As with all the elements of Greek architecture, entasis was not meant to be appreciated in isolation. Very nearly imperceptible, wholly subtle, it contributes decisively to the airy, floating quality of the overall facade. The temple showing the greatest entasis is the Temple of Apollo near Miletus, where, significantly, it is confined to the upper two-thirds of the shaft. Apollo, as the god of physical vigor, is the deity most clearly related to the circulation of élan vital or prāṇā within the body, particularly in the chest. His name, as we have seen, can be related to numerous words having the sense of "swollen" or "filled [with air]": *phallus*, *bellows*, *blow*, *inflate*, *hollow*, *bull*, *howl*; the list is long.

Several other recurring themes in Greek temple design continue to puzzle the experts. First, the entablature is so heavy, so massive, that it defies common sense to describe it as functional. Also, as technique improved and Doric temples grew larger, the number of steps leading up to the peristyle—the "wall" of columns surrounding a temple—was not increased; rather, the rise and tread of the crepidoma were increased (resulting in some very big steps!). Even the triglyphs (figure 25), so prominent in the Doric order, are a mystery. Yet they can be understood at once as renderings in stone of the same three cranial nerves: trigeminal, left olfactory, and right olfactory, that we have seen in the myth of the Bow of Apollo. And right below the triglyphs in the Ionic order is a rendering of that very bow in the shape of the volutes, which of course look just like eyes.

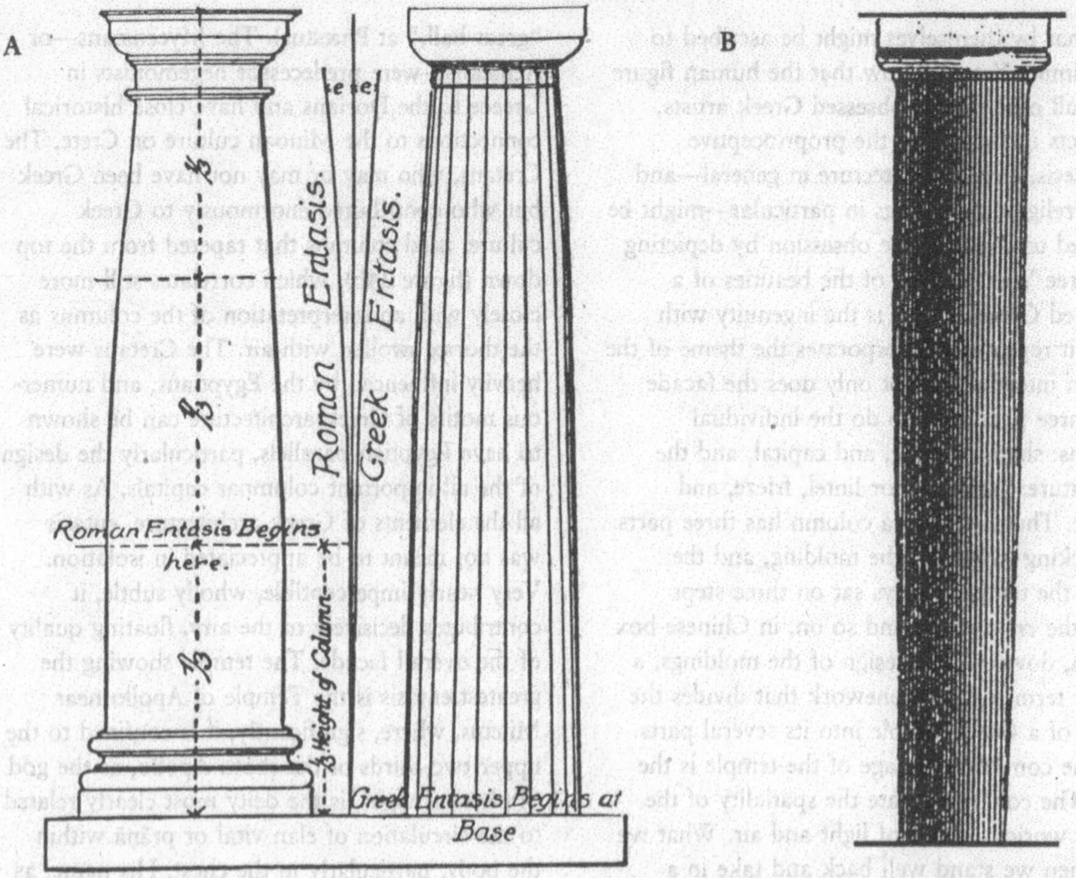

Figure 24. (A) Entasis of a Doric Column, (B) Minoan Column from the Temple at Cnossos on Crete

Architects have tried without much success to resolve the problematic elements of the classical orders, chiefly by deriving them from hypothetical wooden prototypes long since vanished. Yet if a building is first made of wood and then redone in stone, the volume above the architrave should decrease, not increase, if only because the effort required to raise an equivalent volume of stone and keep it there is enormous compared to wood. Clearly the Greeks wanted those massive architraves, friezes, and entablatures for reasons having nothing to do with practicality.*

The entablature recapitulates the Three Worlds. The architrave, the base of the entablature, is the first world, the frieze is the second world, the cornice is the third. Classical friezes—the second world, the domain of men, of recognizable shapes and images—were often figuratively sculpted. The iconography of the friezes is invariably of struggle and warfare, very frequently involving horses. Favorites are the Battle of the Centaurs and Lapiths,† the GIGANTOMACHY (the war between the Olympian gods and goddesses and chthonic giants), and Bellerophon and Pegasus; two of those myths

* The architrave is especially important because it bears the weight of the entablature (third world) and so fulfills the role of Atlas. The architectural treatment of lintels, even in private homes, is therefore always significant.

† The Ionic frieze within the peristyle of the Parthenon is so decorated, the Parthenon being Athena's temple.

emphasize the horse and the third Heracles and his bow. The Ionic style, as noted, goes so far as to render the Greek bow itself in the volutes of the capitals (figure 21c).*

In the place of a figuratively sculpted frieze, the Doric style of the Parthenon alternates triglyphs with bare stone blocks called *metopes*. In the very place where we speculate that the space between the eyes is being described, the architectectural nomenclature uses the Greek word for "forehead" that proved so significant in the myth of Sisyphus and the Stone. The metopes of Ionic temples were decorated with ox skulls (bucrania), a practice that is almost certainly archaic and demonstrates that the equation of metope with a forehead was made very early and was not metaphorical.

In the column, considered as an integral three-world design, the base together with columnar shaft is the first world, the capital is the third, and the capital is divided from the shaft by an incised annular groove called the *echinus*, "hedgehog," another prickly image at the point where the column is narrowest—and a very odd one, because a columnar echinus does not resemble a hedgehog in the slightest. The echinus represents the point of tangency on the caduceus of Hermes and so describes the second world: it is a mere crack in the stonework. In the Ionic order the echinus is molded into an alternating series of eggs and darts, the sharp imagery of the dart paralleling that of the echinus as well as describing the nasal spine. This region of the column also corresponds to the interorbital space or Field of Ares, which is linked with the sowing of karmic seed and the Crack in the Cosmic Egg.

In antiquity and before, the Acropolis of a Greek settlement was a fortified peak where the residents took refuge in time of war. The Acropolis is the top of the second world; above it is only sky. So in a sense we are back at the frontal bone, the bone of the forehead. The Athenian Acropolis is crowned by the diadem of the Parthenon, the temple of Virginal Athena. Athena and Poseidon once competed for the affection of the Athenians. Athena gave them the olive tree. Poseidon struck the rock of the Acropolis with his trident to create the horse. The TRIDENT OF POSEIDON is a description of the same three nerves that were considered in the myth of the Bow of Apollo, and once more we have an image of piercing, lancing, and the like associated with the second world (figure 25).† The triglyphs of the Doric frieze recapitulate the trident. The cistæ borne by the caryatids are decorated with three sheafs of wheat that strongly resemble a trident, and the same motif—some form of trifurcation—appears again and again in the decorations of friezes, capitals, and moldings of all three orders. Athena won the contest, however; the city was named for her and the Parthenon built in her honor. Athens and no other city is called "violet crowned" in Greek literature, deep violet being the defining color of the third world.

Greek pottery is most often divided into three bands. In figures 26–28 the relationship of the three regions to a temple column and the human figure is explicit. The bottom and top bands most often are decorated with peaceful scenes of animals grazing contentedly or with festoons of vines and garlands (especially the top) or with abstract patterns, whereas the middle band, more often than not, shows scenes of war and death. The interpretation of such scenes is obvious. The flowers and grapes describe the delightful internal "garden" that meditation on the breath uncovers; the abstract patterns correspond to the nonfigurative photons experienced during proprioception of the visual centers of the brain: patterns, colors, and so forth. The oldest Greek pottery is called "geometric" by archaeologists because it eschews figurative designs entirely (figure 27).‡ The practice survives in the Greek maeander, a wandering pattern incised on the abaci of Ionic

* Archaic pottery shows the Titans with large round eyes that look like miniature volutes.

† Acropolis: "city peak"; also, *akro* = *akr* = *ark* = *arg* = *Argo*.

‡ Cf., Islamic religious art: its horror of figurative representation, its intricate arabesques and filigrees.

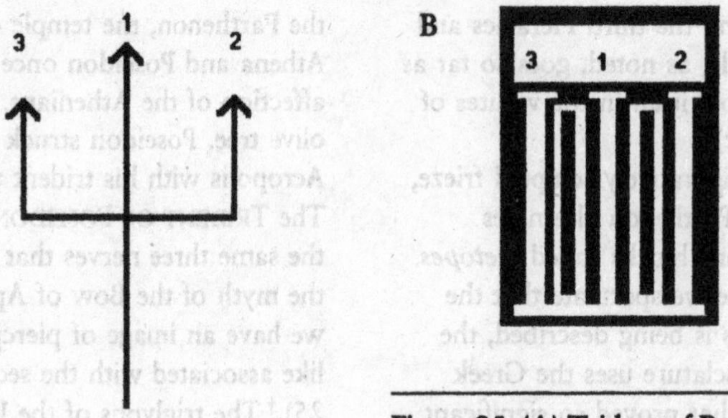

Figure 25. (A) Trident of Poseidon, (B) Metopic Triglyphs. 1) Trigeminal, 2) Left Olfactory, 3) Right Olfactory

capitals, which is to say, on the part of the capital that recapitulates the third world. Figure 28 is a transitional piece, geometric everywhere but in the middle band, which shows a line of armed men. The drawing is rudimentary, but the shape of the Mycenæan shields they hold, scalloped at the sides, resembles the shape of the interorbital space—the space between the eyes. The SHIELD OF AJAX, the nonpareil Mycenæan warrior, merits several lines of Homer's *Iliad* and can be related to the same space.*

A source of controversy is the degree to which the classical *sectio aurea*, "golden section," was used in designing temples. The Greek architect who designed the Parthenon (with Callicrates) and several other famous temples (e.g., the Temple of Apollo at Bassæ) was Ictinus (fl. 420 B.C.). Ictinus worked long after the time of Pythagoras, who is responsible for the mystification of numbers. The golden section, we are told, was used by Plato (who called it simply "the section") as a means of demonstrating metaphysical arguments geometrically, and Plato probably received it from a pythagorean source.† It can be defined in the following manner. If one divides a straight line into two coterminous parts such that the ratio of the length of the larger part to the length of the smaller part (the mean ratio) equals the ratio of the length of the original straight line to the length of the larger part (the extreme ratio), we have a golden or "divine" section (also known as the extreme and mean ratio). The Greeks believed strongly that a rectangle constructed on the basis of such a section was *objectively* the most pleasing to the eye.

The Greeks made use of dynamic symmetry; that is, the lengths of the sides of rectangles for instance were not commensurable and involved the square roots of numbers like 5, 3, and 2, all of whose roots are irrational numbers. The use of such numbers, which arise because the Greeks are interested in the ratios not of line segments but of *areas*—quadratic as opposed to linear ratios—contributes a tension to the proportions of Greek temples that is absent in Roman architecture, where the ratios are strictly rational: two to one, three to one, and so forth. Thus, the interiors of Roman temples can easily be laid out in squares or parts of squares, contributing to a static, settled sense of proportion. The same is never true of Greek temples, which always have—for want of a better way of putting it—something left over. The "something left over" works to drive the design dynamically, as if striving to incorporate the "something" organically, which comes down to constant recapitulation of the root-five propor-

* The only other shields to receive such treatment by the bard are those of Hector, Diomedes, and Achilles, the last at great length. All three have a special relationship to the interorbital space.

† J. Hambidge, *The Parthenon and Other Greek Temples: Their Dynamic Symmetry* (New Haven, Conn., 1924), p. 1 and n.

Figure 26. Amphora with Three Worlds

tion. Each part of the temple reflects the other parts and, indeed, continues almost as if it were in creative motion. The facade or elevation of the Parthenon can be related by means of root-five proportioning to the floor plan of the temple and vice versa, and both can be related to the intercolumnar distances that proportion the spatial relatedness of the facade.*

The facade of the Parthenon has a "square root of five" plan, which incorporates the golden section automatically. The number that expresses the overall ratio is $\sqrt{5} = 2.236\ldots$, where the three dots indicate an infinite string of numbers any finite selection from which never repeats (i.e., a surd). The ratio of the base of the rectangle to a side is approximately 2.236:1 (so that when squared to get an area, the ratio 5:1 results). Starting with $\sqrt{5}$, one proceeds by a process of subdivision to the true golden section, in which the ratio is 1.618, that is,

$$1.618 = \frac{(\sqrt{5} + 1)}{2}.$$

But 1.618 is very close to the numerical value of the ratio of the width to the height of a *facial rectangle* containing the organs of the second world, namely, from ear to ear and from the nostrils to the tops of the eyebrows (figure 29a), the Greek facial ideal.

It is an unanswered question as to why, if our hypothesis is correct, the root-five proportions of the second world lead to an objectively superior aesthetics, as Plato sincerely believed they did. To answer that would require an understanding of the functional relationship between the proportions of the skeletal anatomy of the face and its neurophysiology, something never seriously attempted. In brief, it means that what is most beautiful to us is our own nervous system, with which all "external" beauty must

* Ibid., pp. 1–47. The process can be likened to approaching a limit in the calculus.

Figure 27. Attic Pottery (geometric period)

Figure 28. Mycenæan Shield and the Second World on an Attic Amphora. (Metropolitan Museum, New York)

accord. When one gazes at a Greek temple one is gazing at a phenomenon that mirrors—as much as it is given to achieve in stone—the epistemology of the one who gazes. It is as though one has inserted a key into a lock and turned it, a hand into a glove that fits. The second world has been configured by the architect so as to resonate with the nervous system of the gazer: brow merges with entablature, body cleaves to stylobate, eyes and ears and breath complete the space between. The psychosomatic confluence of knower with known is the aesthetic substratum of ancient art and architecture.

The space within which each column is centered, the so-called intercolumnar rectangle, is *not* a root-five rectangle but a 0.618 rectangle, and 0.618 can be related simply to the arithmetic inverse of a root-five rectangle (i.e., 0.618 = 1.618 – 1), namely, one stood on its side. There are six such rectangles *wholly* enclosed within the facade—the six Titans who support the heavens—and two that overlap the space to the right and left of the facade. But that is the region we are ascribing to the ears. The phenomenology of the ears is just this: there exists *no* spatial boundary to right and left, but rather an acoustical boundary only, which is nonspatial and indistinct. Moreover, it is those same overlapping spaces that are the "something left over" (figure 29b).*

The facade of the Parthenon describes the second world overall. The defining root-five proportion of the facade is recapitulated again and again in the parts. In particular, the architrave over the columns is based on a 5:1 areal proportion. The Parthenon is an especial embodiment of the facial rectangle because it is steeply pedimented. Temples lacking a pediment are generally too broad relative to their height to give a golden section.

The Parthenon is often said to be the crowning achievement of antique art. Unfortunately, the temple has been ravaged by war and ignorance, especially during the war the Greeks fought in the 1820s for independence from Ottoman Turkey. We have virtually no colored artifacts from the Parthenon. From the existing remains, however, archaeologists infer that the triglyphs were painted a dark blue. The triglyphs corresponded to the second world–third world transit that the breath makes from the nostrils to the olfactories, one that centers on the metopic suture (figure 25b, p. 148). This deep-blue portal is the gateway to the sea. In *Iphigenia in Tauris* Orestes, son of Agamemnon, enters the temple of Artemis by climbing up the column and going through an opening in the metope. Later, the chorus chants "Dim wine-dark rock, where sea flows into Wine-Dark Sea."† Once again, deep blue is Artemis' color and the color of olfaction.

Our interpretation sheds light on a puzzling interpolation in another manuscript of Euripides. In his *Orestes* the chorus, whose duties include announcing the entrances of dr*amatis personae,* alerts the audience that a Phrygian is about to enter through the door of the palace at center stage. When the Phrygian comes out, however,

* The Hindus used root-five rectangles in designing altars (Hambidge, *Parthenon and Other Greek Temples*, p. xvi). In the *Upaniṣads* the ears sense the quarters of space, as in Buddhism. Patañjali, in his discussion of the senses, relates hearing to aether: void. The dynamic symmetry of Greek architecture and the phenomenology of hearing are congruent: the "something left over" is the infinite decimal string of a surd. A surd describes the incommensurability of space and sound; i.e., sound has no length, though it does have an explicit temporal dimension that can be likened to a length. Time and space are necessarily involved in all perceptual measurement—as sight and sound, they define the bulk of the second world—but time is only implicitly involved in current real-number theory (J. W. R. Dedekind [d. 1916] resolved the topology of the real numbers by placing them in one-to-one correspondence with the points of a straight line, a purely visual phenomenon; using "cuts," he managed to include surds, which he analogized as "holes" in the line). The conclusion I draw is that rational numbers are visual, surds (< L. *surdus*, "deaf," i.e., incommunicado) auditory. Surds are unavoidable short of purging the nervous system of the hearing faculty or, alternatively, redefining real-number topology by cuts on a line *and* temporal intervals. Zeno of Elea (school of Parmenides) exploited the difficulty by revealing paradoxes of motion that arise from the infinite divisibility of the number line. Relativity has shown the paradox can be removed only by introducing Minkowski space (see note p. 177). See A. P. Ushenko, *The Philosophy of Relativity* (London, 1937), pp. 242–50.

† Euripides, *Iphigenia in Tauris*, 109ff., 390.

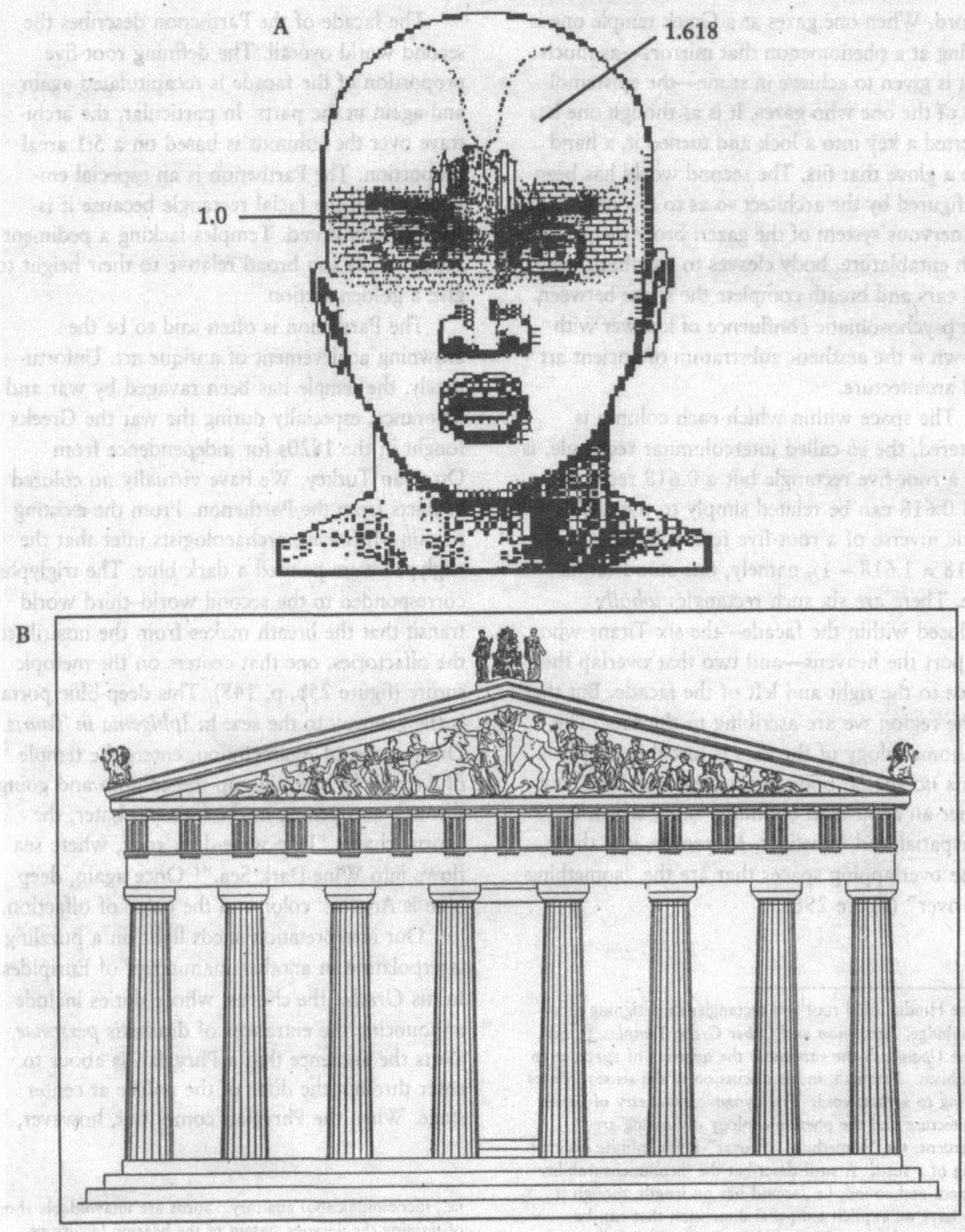

Figure 29. (A) *Sectio Aurea* with Elevation of Parthenon Superimposed, (B) Inverted Root-Five Rectangles of the Facade. In (B), rectangles overlap sides of the temple (numbers indicate relative lengths, in any system of units, of the sides of a root-five rectangle)

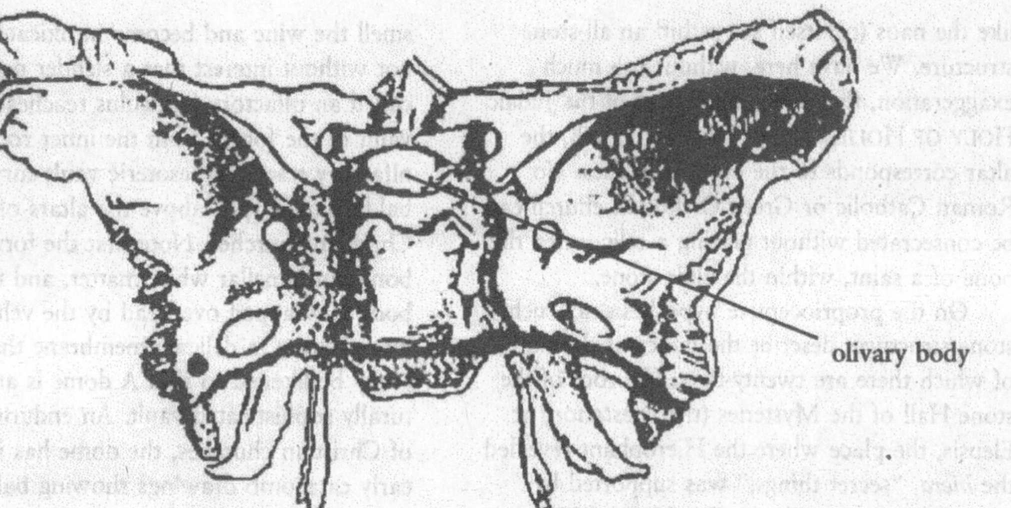

Figure 30. Sphenoid Bone with Olivary Body (from *Gray's Anatomy*)

he claims he has jumped into the action from the "Doric triglyphs." Clearly the chorus's stage direction is an interpolation after Euripides. The scholium in the margin of the manuscript, descended from Alexandrine commentary of the third century B.C., duly notes the discrepancy but explains that it was considered too dangerous for the actor to jump. The obvious question is why the contradictory lines remain in place, literally side by side, when it would have been easy simply to delete the Phrygian's lines (certainly easier than making him jump!). Because the chorus must announce from where the actor enters, the conclusion can only be that the entrance from the metope was so important it could not be emended. The audience had to suspend disbelief, common enough in the drama, to reconcile the actor's health with an apparently essential detail of the story.*

The playwright in both cases is Euripides. The themes of the plays are intimately related: one deals with Iphigenia, the other with her brother. If there is an esoteric sense to the triglyphs of the columns in one play, the same sense can be affirmed in the other. Phrygia is the location of Troy, which can be related to the second world, hence to the capitals of the columns, and the Phrygian in question is part Helen's Trojan retinue. Finally, Tauris is on the shores of the Black Sea. Phrygia borders the Hellespont, the western entrance to the Black Sea. That the Phrygian leaps from the building recapitulates the wrong-headed, outwardly directed awareness that Troy always describes in Greek myth.

The use of stone is itself important. A Greek temple—once one had passed through the peristyle—was essentially a large room (cella) with walls of stone inside of which was another, smaller, room of stone called the *naos*. In the naos of the Parthenon was the famous statue of Athena by Phidias (d. ca. 420 B.C.). Stone has properties that directly assist meditation. It effectively muffles sound, but more importantly it absorbs ambient electromagnetic radiation. Contemplation of the whine (n) of the nervous system, an internal electromagnetic phenomenon, is greatly enhanced within an all-stone structure

* Euripides, *Orestes*, 1366–89. The interpolation is discussed in L. D. Reynolds and N. G. Wilson, *Scribes and Scholars*, 3d ed. (Oxford, 1991), p. 15; the authors, a trifle bewildered, conclude that "something is wrong with the passage."

like the naos (n), itself set within an all-stone structure. We have here, without too much exaggeration, the Greek equivalent of the Judaic HOLY OF HOLIES. In a Christian church, the altar corresponds to the Holy of Holies. No Roman Catholic or Greek Orthodox church can be consecrated without placing a relic, often the bone of a saint, within the altar stone.

On the proprioceptive hypothesis, all such stone structures describe the bones of the skull, of which there are twenty-two. The roof of the stone Hall of the Mysteries (the *telesterion*) at Eleusis, the place where the Hierophant revealed the *hiera*, "secret things," was supported by twenty-two Ionic pillars.* The Holy of Holies might therefore describe some location deep within the brain. There are two major candidates: the pituitary gland and the pineal body; both have long been associated with mystical practice in Hinduism.

The pituitary body lies within a deep depression of the wing-shaped sphenoid bone called the sella turcica (figure 18). In front of the sella turcica is the olivary body, shaped, as its name suggests, like an olive (figure 30). The entire complex is behind the gasserian ganglion, hence between the eyes and on the line of the frontal suture. Recall Athena's gift of the olive tree to the Athenians in her contest with Poseidon.

The pineal body is located under the fornix—Latin for "vault"—a structure of the midbrain described in anatomy texts as having four *pillars*. Both the fornix and the pineal body are closely hemmed in from above by the optic thalamus. *Thalamus* means "wedding chamber" in Greek, and we have seen that *saṃyama* can be translated as "communion," *yoga* as "union" or "junction," both of which comport well with the image of a wedding. The aroma of wine figures prominently in Greek wedding myths—especially the Wedding of Peleus and Thetis and the Battle of the Centaurs and Lapiths, the latter episode provoked when the centaurs (horse men) smell the wine and become intoxicated—so it is not without interest that a slender nerve fiber called an olfactory fasciculus reaches under the vault of the fornix from the inner root of the olfactory tract. The esoteric vault survives in silk baldachins draped above the altars of early Christian churches. Note that the fornix is not bone but lamellar white matter, and the pineal body is wrapped overhead by the velum interpositum, a delicate membrane that could easily be likened to silk. A dome is an architecturally sophisticated vault. An enduring element of Christian churches, the dome has its origins in early catacomb drawings showing baldachin-like canopies attached to four wooden staffs and placed over the heads of The Christ or the Holy Family.† A splendid example is Bernini's great bronze baldachin over the high altar of Saint Peter's and directly under the dome of the cathedral. Because the earliest churches were domeless basilicas, the evolution of the dome may be explained as a vast elaboration of the altar canopies. The dome of the church above its cruciform floor plan recapitulates the baldachin that shelters the altar crucifix, and both designs describe the cranium above the cross formed by the brows and the frontal suture. Gothic cathedrals are the culmination of traditions of church building going back to the earliest basilicas and can be appreciated fully only from within the nave. Medieval master builders achieved an articulated, luminous architecture that hypnotized the senses and hurled them like shot arrows from the rose window on the facade, fulgurating like the ājñā cakra it describes in stained glass, to the altar, above which is a dome.

At Eleusis, site of the holiest mysteries of antiquity, maidens carried the hiera in cylindrical chests called cistæ; the same are shown on the heads of the caryatids on the Stoa of the Maidens of the Erechtheum. The decorations on the cistæ are similar in many respects to the decorations on Ionic and Corinthian capitals, particu-

* Mylonas, *Eleusis and the Eleusinian Mysteries*, p. 82; the telesterion was designed by Ictinus.

† E. B. Smith, *The Dome: A Study in the History of Ideas* (Princeton, N.J., 1950).

A

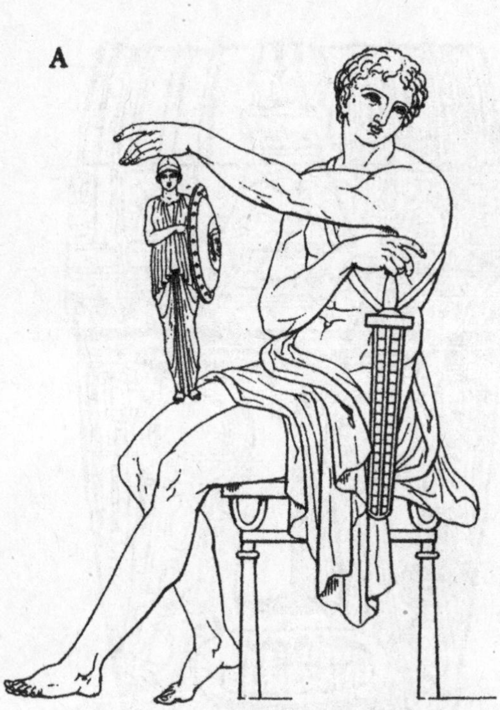

B

Figure 31. (A) Gemstone with Diomedes and Athena, (B) Egyptian Wall Painting

larly in the use of trifurcated wheat stalks and rosettes (figure 21b). A literal contiguity exists between the cistus and the head, an example of a *principle of contiguity*: the cistus *is* the head. Ignatius of Antioch, in aid of scorning the gaudy religious parades of pagans, exhorts Ephesian Christians that "you are all pilgrims in the same great procession, bearing your God and your shrine and your Christ and your sacred treasures *on your shoulders*,"* in other words, their heads. Ephesus in Asia Minor was the site of the largest temple of antiquity, the temple of Artemis. There survives a fearsome Asiatic icon known as the Ephesian Artemis, a statue of the goddess unlike any other, notable for the citadel of stone on the crown of the head, and certainly familiar to Ignatius, who could count on his readers to sift the esoteric sense of his words.† It is unclear whether Ignatius, in contrasting pagan ceremony with Christian meditation on the skull, was aware of the esoteric meaning of the pagan cistæ; his tone is not encouraging.

Contiguity is another form of recapitulation. It is probably an extremely old iconological

* Ignatius of Antioch, *Epistle to the Ephesians* 9.5, emphasis added.

† Ibid., n. 6 at p. 67. Replicas of the statue were carried in processionals.

principle because it is so simple. Figure 32a is an ancient carved gemstone showing the Achæan warrior Diomedes of Argos. Diomedes is particularly favored in the *Iliad* by Athena. Indeed, he fights in her place when Zeus forbids the Olympians to engage in combat for either the Achæans or Trojans. On his knee is a small figure of Athena holding her shield. In his hand is a sword. By contiguity the pictorial elements of Diomedes, the Shield of Athena, and the sword are all identifiable. Diomedes is the sword, but his chest is obviously inflated, so the sword is the breath. The Shield of Athena describes the frontal bone. Therefore the gemstone is itself a myth, a description of the piercing of the frontal bone by the breath told by the simple device of contiguity.

◆◆◆

With the Minoan civilization on Crete as mediator, Egypt exerted a strong influence on Greek art. During most of its history, Egypt was a theocracy. The spiritual and temporal power exercised by Pharaoh infinitely surpassed anything the mere popes of the Middle Ages would claim. Religion in Egypt reached into every corner of life, not surprising in a culture that even as late as the fifth century B.C. was relatively continuous with its archaic origins because of geographical isolation. In a well-known remark, the historian Herodotus claimed that the Greek gods were descendants of Egyptian prototypes. Jean-François Champollion's (d. 1832) translation of the Rosetta Stone in the early nineteenth century unlocked the many Egyptian papyri that for millennia were as silent as the Sphinx. His translation showed that the religion of Egypt probably did not influence the substance of Greek religion as much as Herodotus claimed, but there can be no doubt that it strongly influenced its form: a formal priest class, temples, and art. The subject is vast and we can do no more than note the fact.

Egyptian religious art is far more complicated than Greek. We see in it evidence of contiguity as an organizing principle (figures 31a and b), testifying to its extreme antiquity. Contiguity, therefore, can be likened to a visual

Figure 32. Mayan War God

pleonasm. The flower pressed to the nose of the princess *is* the nose of the princess, which is to say, it is the internal nose or rhinencephalon that is being propriocepted. The sun disk atop the queen's head *is* the light inside her head. An Egyptian artist typically painted his human figures with a larger portion of the whites of the eyes showing beneath the pupils than is usual, which suggests the technique of root gazing so central in the myth of the Bow of Apollo.

As a final illustration of the global use of the skull in sacred art, figure 32 shows a war mask of Teohuetlan, the supreme deity of Central American Indians such as the Mayas and Aztecs. All the motifs of the Greek entablature are in evidence, from the strong brow line to the tiny face in the center of the forehead.

14

THE SIEGE OF TROY

The second world is but a crack in the proprioceptive universe. The eyes, nose, and ears push apart the waters of Chaos. The most comprehensive myth to describe the result of the primordial separation is the *Iliad*. The *Iliad* takes place in the tenth and final year of the siege of Troy, and the events described occur over the course of fifty days, from the time that Achilles withdraws into his tent by the sea until the night he emerges to kill Hector in front of the Scæan Gate.

Troy has no connection to the sea. Homer tells us that when Paris wished to fetch Helen, he had a ship especially built for the purpose.* The only danger facing Troy comes from the sea. On the other hand, Troy is much associated with the eight rivers of Phrygia (rk). The rivers describe the eight cranial nerves over which external sensation reaches the brain. Scamander is by far the most important of the rivers in Troyland. It was the river along which the Trojans grazed their horses, so it can best be equated with the trigeminal nerve, the nerve that senses the flow of breath in the nostrils. The headwaters of the Scamander were two sacred fountains, describing the source of the trigeminal on the floor of the third and fourth ventricles of the brain.

The antecedent cause of the war was the JUDGMENT OF PARIS. The only goddess not invited to the Wedding of Peleus and Thetis was Eris, ruler of strife and discord. To avenge the slight, she comes to the party in disguise and tosses a golden apple—the Apple of Discord—into the midst of the reveling. Inscribed "To the Fairest," it immediately provokes a quarrel among Hera, Aphrodite, and Athena as to whom the cryptic compliment refers. To settle the matter they seek out the herdsman Alexander—in reality, Paris, son of King Priam and Prince of Troy—on the slopes of Mount Gargarus in the Troäd (the vicinity of Troy). Alexander has gained a reputation for honesty, and the three goddesses ask him to arbitrate their dispute. Each tempts him with what is uniquely hers to give. Hera offers riches, Athena

* *Iliad* 5.61–63.

wisdom, and Aphrodite the most beautiful woman in the world for his wife. Paris must of course choose Aphrodite; as a prince of Troy he himself recapitulates the second world. The Judgment of Paris eventually leads to his elopement with Helen, Menelaus's wife, and to the Trojan War. In that titanic struggle Hera and Athena remember Paris's choice and are implacably hostile to the Trojans. Aphrodite on the other hand sides with Priam and his fifty sons.

Why did Helen choose Paris? The wife of Menelaus and the daughter of Zeus and Leda, Helen was born from an egg. Her birth therefore recapitulates the Fall—or at least its possibility.* Helen is the nearest thing in Homer to an esoteric anthropomorphism of the human soul, radiantly beautiful but subject to desire for sensory pleasure. Helen elopes with Paris while her husband Menelaus is away on Crete.† Because Menelaus is third world, we have a moral. The mind's absence from its true nature and wandering within the senses—Crete—is the precondition of the Fall. Helen is never very happy about her choice. The soul, which is beautiful in its own nature, cannot be fooled for long when it unites with the transient beauties of perception. Like Ares, Homer tells us, Paris is exceedingly handsome, yet over the course of the siege Helen comes to hold him in little more than contempt.‡ Although not exactly a coward—Paris is an archer of no mean accomplishment and his name means "fighter" in Greek—he is an uxorious and self-indulgent sort, content to dally in the boudoir until his wife's taunts drive him into battle. His prowess with a bow relates him to the brows and to the bones of the second world in general. Paris particularly describes the orbits of the eyes, as does Mount Gargarus (krk). His elder brother Hector tells him he should wear a "coat of stone" for all the troubles he has brought on his homeland.§

Paris's abduction of Helen (reduces to *ln*) describes the rupture that the second world causes between the first world (Helen) and the third (Menelaus). As anthropomorphized soul, therefore, Helen is like the presocratic *hegemonicon*: the soul considered as ruler of the body and seated, according to Anaximenes, on a throne within the heart. Trance establishes a smooth connection between the heart and lungs and the central nervous system. A reciprocity of action mediated by the vagus nerve is established between mind and body, calming both; the harmonies of respiration and pulse are introduced to the cerebrum, which then reacts to slow the lungs and heart, which further react to still the mind, and so forth. A negative-feedback situation arises that slowly damps out all three functions and leads to the anaractic state Patañjali calls kaivalya.#

◆◆◆

The natural rhythmic approach to reuniting Helen with Menelaus is blocked by the WALLS OF TROY behind which Paris hides his stolen bride. The Walls of Troy are the fourteen bones of the face.** The main gate—called the Scæan Gate in the *Iliad*—is the glabellar bone. The cranium comprises eight bones. With the fourteen bones of the face, there are twenty-two skull bones in all. Is it merely a coincidence that twenty-two is the number of the children of Pelops? His name contains the root *ops*.†† Pelops

* When Night laid the Cosmic Egg, it broke open to create the second world and release pain and pleasure, the twin evils of sensuous experience, into the universe. Related too is the myth of Eurynome, the first goddess, who divided the sea from the sky. She created the serpent Ophion from the north wind. Ophion grew lustful and mated with her, and by and by Eurynome laid an egg around which the serpent coiled itself seven times. The pressure cracked the egg and the creation appeared. The myth is probably Pelasgian, but we see in it the seven orifices of the second world—each coil cracked the egg once—as well as the notion that desire (lust) drives the creation. In the Japanese creation myth, the sun goddess Amaterasu emerges from a cave; a mirror (the second world) is held to her eyes and a bawdy dance performed.

† Cf., *Cyprian Epic*, a hymn to Aphrodite of great antiquity, cited in Gladstone, *Studies on Homer and the Homeric Age*, vol. 2, p. 194; the *Cyprian Epic* is part of a collection of hymns to the gods known as the Epic Cycle.

‡ *Iliad* 6.352.

§ Ibid. 3.57.

\# *Yoga-Sūtra, Kaivalya Pāda*, sutras 31–34.

** 14 = 5, the numerology of Troy.

†† *Pelops*: "muddy face."

was the grandfather of Agamemnon, who led the Greeks to Troy, and of his brother King Menelaus of Sparta.

The building of the Walls of Troy was the result of a quarrel among the Olympians. For their part in the Revolt of the Gods, Zeus indentured Poseidon and Apollo to King Laomedon of Troy. With the help of the mortal Æacus, they built the wall surrounding the city. Laomedon refused to pay Poseidon for his work and gained the eternal enmity of the god for his city. The Revolt of the Gods is therefore a recapitulation of the Fall, and Laomedon's treachery, of which there is more than one occurrence, shows yet again the mistrust with which the mythopoets viewed perception. Zeus, however, is not eager to see Troy destroyed—perception is necessary to the fate of the organism—but he is bound by the Moiræ, who have decreed that Troy must fall. Poseidon is ordered from the fray by Zeus when he too ardently assails the Trojans. Lord of the second world and one of the sons of Cronus, Poseidon is keenly aware that the Three Worlds were divided by lot and that his subordinate role is not one of essence.* He acts to reassert the dominion of the Cronids over Troy. His anger is hot and furious but also in the nature of a father's toward a wayward son. Because he built the Walls of Troy, he has the right to tear them down. His differences with his brother over the fate of the city is a matter of when, not if, Troy should fall. The decree of the Moiræ that Troy should crumble to dust is no more and no less than their decree that each of us must die. Our eyes will someday lose their sight, our ears their sound, and all our other senses will depart with them. Poseidon's rulership of perception speaks to the illusory nature of the "world out there." The second world is an island, but like Atlantis it is an island that *must* sink beneath the waves.† That is the natural order that the deceit of Laomedon seeks most unnaturally to evade. The result, as the Buddha tells us, is grievous suffering.

The walls were impregnable to assault save where Æacus had worked: the Scæan Gate, on the west, where a wild fig tree grew (the gasserian ganglion or possibly the olivary body).‡ Æacus was the great-grandson of Atlas, the grandson of Asopus, and the father of Telamon. When Heracles too was cheated by Laomedon, he, his many sons, and other heroes, Telamon among them, besieged the city. Telamon breached the Gates of Troy, literally tearing stone from stone to get inside, though he did not dare enter the city ahead of Heracles and so faked a stumble at the gates. His stumbling and the collapse of the gate are recapitulative. Telamon was of the generation of heroes who preceded the heroes of the homeric sagas. His son was Ajax Big, often called Telamonian Ajax by Homer and a towering figure in the *Iliad*. By far the largest in stature of the Achæans, he is remarkable for his imperturbability in combat, indomitable courage, and fabulous strength. When everyone else is on the edge of panic, it is Ajax who rallies them and holds the Trojans at bay.

As descendants of Atlas, both Ajax and his father Telamon can reasonably be related to the bones of the face that lie between the forehead and jaw, namely, the second world, a relationship nowhere better illustrated than in the bloody episode involving the counterwall the Greeks erect to protect their ships from the Trojans' furious assault. Some of the most vivid scenes of the epic occur at or near this structure. It is Ajax who, along with his kinsman Teucer, the best archer among the Achæans according to Homer, posts himself at its gate—Ajax covering Teucer with his shield—and around whom the terrified Achæans rally. Hector, the eldest son of Priam and Hecuba, leads the assault on the gate of the Achæan wall. He tosses a boulder at Teucer and breaks his bowstring. Also present at the gate are

* *Iliad* 15.184–99.

† Atlantis < *Atlas*; the inundation of the city describes the collapse of the second world.

‡ The efforts of Apollo and Poseidon were indestructible (Pindar, *Pythian Odes* 8.39–46, and Apollodorus, *Bibliotheca* 1.205–7; see also *Iliad* 6.434).

the Lapiths, famous for their battle with the centaurs and in the *Iliad* part of the Achæan host. It is they who stem the tide at the critical moment.* Exoterically, the wall around the ships is an ingenious plotting device, which fills out Homer's narrative with stirring scenes of valor, adds variety to the story, but departs not at all from the esoteric significance of the *Iliad*: the savage struggle to break down the walls of the second world, and again we find a fabulous bow—a recapitulation of the Bow of Apollo—close by the gate of perception. After Troy falls to the Achæans, Poseidon and Apollo tear down the wall around the ships. For nine days they direct the floods of eight rivers against it, and Zeus sends torrential rain. On the tenth day, the wall collapses, "dissolves into the salt sea."† It was in the tenth year of the siege that Troy fell. The parallels between the Walls of Troy and the WALL AROUND THE ACHÆAN SHIPS are too numerous to ascribe to chance. They are the same walls, and the dissolution of the Achæan wall in the sea is a recapitulation of the Fall of Troy.

The fighting of the *Iliad* surges back and forth between the Trojan and Achæan walls. The climactic battles of the war before the city falls are fought in darkness or near darkness. By decree of Zeus, however, the Trojans prevail when the sun is high—as is meet for anthropomorphisms of vision. The image of the sun at noon fixes a timeless moment:

> When the sun had reached midheaven, then verily the Father lifted on high his golden scales, and set therein two fates [kere] of grievous death, one for the horse-taming Trojans, and one for the brazen-coated Achæans; then he grasped the balance by the midst and raised it, and down sank the doom of the Achæans. . . . Then himself he thundered aloud from Ida, and sent a blazing flash amid the host.‡

* *Iliad* 8.320–25; 12.127–36, 180–81, 290–91.

† Ibid. 12.17–32.

‡ Ibid. 8.68–76.

The golden scales of Zeus are Libra, the Balance of astrology, which, we have seen, is an esoteric description of the pattern formed by the brows, the nose, and the closed eyes, the eyes in meditation. The motion of the scales is the same motion as that of the Bow of Apollo. The result is a blinding flash of light. During root gazing, a yogi gazes straight up (at the *ājñā cakra*), towards the noon position of the sun, in order to propriocept internal light. The use of the word *kere* for the "fates of grievous death" introduces the central phon of the second world: *k*. The Ker was the Greek "angel of death," who separated the soul of a fallen warrior from his senses. All of the fighting between the walls is but this single moment of death: when the sun reaches the meridian and karma is incinerated.

◆◆◆

As with the Achæan and Trojan walls, there is no fundamental difference between the Trojans and the Achæans. The former and most of the latter are second-world figures, which is why, though victorious, many of the Greeks come to miserable ends. Ajax, who is often paired with Hector before a gate or entry way, kills himself with the sword given him by Hector at the end of their famous duel. The only Achæan chieftains to escape are Menelaus and Nestor (third world) and Odysseus. Diomedes and Idomeneus return home, but only to find that like Clytemnestra, the wife of King Agamemnon, their spouses have been faithless. The infidelity of the Achæan wives is a recapitulation of the abduction of Helen by the second world and the destiny of all the chieftains who represent it. Diomedes is eventually driven out of Argos and settles in Italy, as does Idomeneus. Agamemnon, of course, perishes at the hands of Clytemnestra and her lover Ægisthus on the night of his return to Mycenæ. Clytemnestra is sister to Helen and one of the Dioscuræ.

The epic is ambivalent as regards the outcome of the war. The Trojans are not evil because their citadel is destroyed, nor are the Greeks justified in destroying it. In their warfare (namely, during second-world trance), the heroes are tumbled together, twined one round the other in life and death, chaotically and savagely. To divide the second-world energies into two camps is a clever storytelling device, and one that almost certainly was inspired by an actual siege on the plains of Phrygia.

Agamemnon leads the Greek expedition. If there is a word to describe him, it is *imperious.* He appears in the poem as the one hero whose fame derives principally not from anything he does—indeed, he frequently behaves infamously—but from who he is. Agamemnon leads the Achæans into war in the belief that he will gain glory for himself. The destruction of Troy is incidental to the gratification of his desire for fame and booty. He becomes, therefore, a pawn of fate, for which the city's fall serves a higher purpose. The reasons for his preeminence are never explicitly set down by Homer, who seems to take it for granted, and it has been speculated that it derives from the historical importance of Mycenæ prior to the fourteenth century B.C. Yet we cannot explain every aspect of his homeric personality on that basis.[*]

Agamemnon's name carries a strong third-world phonic structure. The second half of it reduces to *mn*, suggesting that to control the senses (k) demands control of the mind (mn). In Homer, we see Agamemnon's mental connections chiefly in his dreams. To begin the vindication of Achilles, who has been wronged by Agamemnon, Zeus sends the king *oulos oneiros*, "a bad dream."[†] The dream deludes him into believing that Troy is his for the taking. Agamemnon's hubris leads to a horrible defeat on the field of battle and his humiliating embassy to Achilles. Significantly, the dream takes the form of Nestor, a third-world figure, who is not a warrior but an old man, and who functions in both homeric poems as something like an "armchair general."

Who then is Agamemnon? Is he not himself the bad dream, the illusion that leads the soul into the world of the senses, where pleasures begin and end and inevitably become pain? Says Homer: "[The quarrel began] when at the first there *parted* in strife Agamemnon of Atreus's line, king of men, and goodly Achilles."[‡] The focus of their dispute was the girl Briseis, who had been awarded to Achilles after the sack of the city of Thebe, a Trojan satellite. In the same engagement Agamemnon took Chryseis, the daughter of Apollo's priest, Chryse, who prays to the god to restore his child. Apollo promptly sets about slaughtering Achæans, but not before he has shot all of their mules and dogs with his arrows; the former are associated with respiration, the latter with smell. Calchas the fortune-teller interprets the omens, and Agamemnon is compelled to give up Chryseis. He then takes Briseis from Achilles out of sheer malice.

Chryseis (*chr = kr*) is the second world and Agamemnon cannot have her to keep; that is, after all, the overriding message of the *Iliad*. And yet Briseis does not belong to him either. She is a first-world figure (*br = r = l*), the domain of Achilles, Thetis's son, also indicated in the phonic properties of Thebe (tb). When Agamemnon realizes that he cannot stop Hector from destroying the Achæan ships without Achilles, he sends the girl back (and much besides), but is spurned by the proud son of Peleus.

When Thetis learns of her son's humiliation, she begs Zeus, who owes her an immense favor,[§] to tip the scales towards the Trojans. For his part, Achilles sits out the conflict and ignores Agamemnon's bribes, brought by Odysseus, to return to the field of battle. Because Odysseus and Achilles both describe the breath, the esoteric meaning of the EMBASSY OF ODYSSEUS is analogous to setting a thief to catch a thief.

* There exists no certifiably historical proof of Agamemnon's kingship other than in myth, most of it deriving from Homer. Whether there actually was or was not such a ruler is unimportant here; the *Iliad* is not primarily a historical record.

† Ibid. 2.6; *oulos*, "bad," has no moral connotation in Homer; rather, it means ill-omened.

‡ Ibid. 1.4–6, emphasis added. Agamemnon < ?[*h*]*ekamnemon*, "emerging from memory"; we infer an archaic connection to Hermes because both are conduits for messages from Zeus. Agamemnon is descended from Atlas, Hermes' grandfather.

§ She sided with him during the Revolt of the Gods, when he was chained in Tartarus at the instigation of Hera. Tartarus is the first world, so Thetis is the one to assist him.

Achilles spends all of his time *in his tent*, literally out of sight, that is, out of the second world and in the first. His companion Patroclus is ardent for battle and prevails on Achilles to lend Patroclus his armor, in which guise he terrorizes the Trojans until Hector kills him and strips the armor from his body. After the death of Patroclus, Thetis goes to Hephæstus and tells him to fashion new armor for her son. Mindful of his debt to her for taking him in when he was thrown from Olympus, Hephæstus forges a brilliant suit of armor—the description of the shield takes up two hundred lines. Achilles, overwhelmed with grief at the death of his friend, relents from his grudge with Agamemnon. He dons his new armor and returns to the fray, driving the Trojans back within their walls.

The cousin of Ajax Big, Achilles too is the great-great-grandson of Asopus, the river god who recapitulates Sisyphus. He is also the grandson of Æacus. The inescapable conclusion is that he is a mythic variant on Hephæstus, the breath driven up by the diaphragm to impinge against the frontal suture. More specifically, Achilles describes the very slow, steady, and forceful form of respiration that results when the breath flows in both nostrils simultaneously, which occurs only in profound trance. Achilles thrusts at the Walls of Troy again and again with his spear, eventually piercing the frontal suture. In front of the Scæan Gate, he slays Hector. The *Iliad* ends with the funeral of the Trojan prince consecrated by his father.

Achilles is wholly of the first world and describes the assault on the city from below. The assault from above, the third world, is described by Menelaus and Nestor, but far more indirectly. Menelaus we have already discussed. He too fights a duel—with Paris, driving him from the field in shame. Nestor is a description of cognition. He can be relied on for sage advice, stirring exhortation—generally through an appeal to history (memory)—and pleas for unity. It was Nestor who advised the Achæans to build a wall around their ships, and it was Nestor who settled the tricky question of who would face Hector alone. He has a third-world name (reduces to *ntr*) and so does his father, Neleus (*nl* = *nr*). We learn a good deal of his youthful exploits (most of it from his own lips), for example, how he aided the Lapiths in their famous battle with the centaurs. Nestor is of the third world, the Lapiths of the first, and the centaurs of the upper second.* The Lapiths are victorious. The tale recapitulates the alliances of the *Iliad*: mind, heart, and lungs versus the senses or, alternatively, cognition and stereognosis contra perception.

Nestor also tells of a war between the Pylians and Arcadians for the city Pheæ. Certain details from that little-known conflict suggest it too is a recapitulation of the Trojan War. The Pylian king Arethous is killed and his armor taken by Lycurgus, who gives it to his kinsman Ereuthalion, leader of the Arcadians. Nestor challenges Ereuthalion to combat and aided by Athena slays him.† Similarly, in the *Iliad*, Achilles gives his armor to his kinsman Patroclus, who enters the fray as a ringer for Achilles. Lycurgus can be related to Lycaön, a Trojan prince.‡ Both names contain *lykos*, the Greek word for wolf, and so are related to vision.§ On the one hand we have Nestor, a third-world figure, aided by Athena, also third world; on the other Achilles, first world, is assisted by Thetis, a first-world goddess.

Patroclus is the son of Menœtius (mn). Patroclus (Gk., "glory of the father") is not mantric but descriptive of third world meditation, as we infer from the following story in Philostratus. The shade of Achilles appears to Apollonius of Tyana and tells him that, after

* Nestor calls them "monsters of the mountains"; see *Iliad* 1.

† Ibid., 7.124–60.

‡ Gladstone, *Studies on Homer and the Homeric Age*, vol. 1, p. 233; the Lycians are allies of Troy.

§ The wolf is a particularly ferocious predator. The animal is thus a good description not simply of vision but of outwardly directed, desire-driven vision. Glaucus of Lycia is also involved in an exchange of armor, which describes the inversion of perception. Significantly, although several Trojans bear wolflike names, not one of the hundreds of Achæans mentioned by Homer does.

their deaths, his (Achilles) ashes and those of Patroclus were mingled in a single golden urn.* The deep love Patroclus and Achilles share recapitulates in a general way the first world-third world alliance necessary to destroy the second world. But something far more specific to meditative technique is described here: the mingling of the ashes, Achilles adds, "[means] we are as one." The reference is to closely guarded yogic techniques for "placing the breath in the head" or "fixing the breath in the space between the brows," the arklike place where first and third worlds meet, the "golden urn." The mind (Patroclus), here reduced to cognition severed from the breath, cannot alone suppress perception (Hector). Clad in "golden armor," however, Achilles pierces the walls of the city, the role of Hephæstus in making the armor again indicating that the armor describes some prepotent technique of prāṇāyāma that inverts perception, that is, turns it inward. The imagery of the father in Patroclus's name is another correlation of a father god with the third world.

While Nestor is busy advising the Achæans, Antenor counsels the Trojans, significant because Antenor's name also reduces to *nt* and because during the war he urges Priam, the Trojan king, to give back Helen and sue for peace. Antenor is one of the few male Trojans to escape death when at last the Greeks take the city. Another is the celebrated Virgilian hero Æneas, who is portrayed in the *Iliad* as also desirous of striking a bargain with the Achæans to end the war. Both men have strong third-world names.

The final Achæan chieftain of note is Diomedes of Argos. In sacred geography Argos lies dead center in the second world, not far from the Isthmus of Corinth. Diomedes, son of Tydeus, is a favorite of Athena and Hera, both in the *Iliad* and in Greek art. He is the sole anthropomorphization in whom both the first and third worlds unite against Troy. Accompanied by Odysseus, Diomedes enters Troy on a midnight foray. As anthropomorphized respiration, Odysseus can penetrate the skull. Diomedes is a descendant of Bellerophon, who tamed Pegasus, the Winged Horse; therefore Diomedes too can penetrate the cranium as did his ancestor.† The chieftains undertake their adventure at night—namely, in third-world darkness—to recover the Palladium, a cult statue of Athena brandishing a spear, fallen from heaven in the long ago. The Palladium was kept in the citadel of Troy, the most sacred structure in the city. Soothsayers told the Greeks that Troy could not be captured so long as the Palladium remained in the citadel. Odysseus and Diomedes manage to remove it, thus fulfilling the demands of prophesy. Esoterically, the capture of Troy entails meditative control of voiceless speech, thus the capture of Athena in the guise of the Palladium.

◆◆◆

Hector is the most valiant of the Trojans. Until the return of Achilles, he almost singlehandedly thwarts an Achæan victory. His name sums up his esoteric meaning: *'Εκτωρ*, "prop." He describes the crossbar with which one secures a door from the inside. Hector is often found in the *Iliad* defending the Scæan Gate or attacking the gate in the Achæan wall. When at last Achilles faces Hector, the latter runs three times around the Walls of Troy, searching for an open gate, an image that quite deftly associates him with a description of the walls. After Hector's death at the hands of Achilles, Priam comes to ransom his body. The king must pass through not one but two sets of gates to reach the corpse. The first leads through the Achæan wall, the second into Achilles' hut, closed with a bar of fir so cumbersome that only Achilles among mortals can open the door unaided. In both instances, it is Hermes who slides back the bar for the old king. Hermes is perception in general, so it is interesting that he tells Priam that he

* Philostratus, *Life of Apollonius of Tyana*, in: *Philostratus*, vol. 1, trans. F. C. Conybeare (New York, 1917), 4.16; Apollonius was a famous magus of antiquity who, pagans later polemicized, was comparable to Christ in spiritual power. Philostratus (fl. A.D. 217) remarks that Apollonius "practiced the *true* wisdom . . . and interviewed the Brahmans of India" (ibid., 1.2, emphasis added).

† *Iliad* 5.385–90.

(Hermes) may not enter Achilles' hut, the first world and the place to which Achilles retreats after his quarrel with Agamemnon.*

In a famous duel with Hector, Ajax Big comes close to ending the war all by himself. Unlike his father, he does not break into Troy; rather, he hurls a boulder at Hector, knocking him down. Though the combat is ended by the heralds before either man is killed, it is conceded by both Achæans and Trojans that Hector has had the worst of it.† Ajax's victory, because it involves knocking down Hector, is a recapitulation of the Fall of Troy, identical to the destruction of the city's walls. If Hector's contest with Ajax (also with Teucer) recapitulates Telamon's tearing open the gates of Troy, then the death of Hector is the proper esoteric ending of the myth. Hector blocks the breath from entering the frontal fissure at the glabella, namely, by propping up the Scæan Gate (analogously, he describes the brow of the hill toward which Sisyphus labors to bring the stone). The several images are linked by Æacus, who built the gate, to Asopus, his grandfather, ultimately to Sisyphus, the breath recapitulated by Asopus. Here is an intricate sequence of recapitulations of the impact of the breath/boulder on the glabella/Scæan Gate/Hector/prop and the collapse of the latter when the former stops. Homer mentions the fall of the city only once, when he describes the destruction of the wall of the Achæans by Apollo and Poseidon (who built the Walls of Troy). The death of Hector is the end of the *Iliad*. So far as Homer is consulted, it was the end of the whole bloody business. In the *Iliad* there is no TROJAN HORSE. The Trojan Horse is mentioned in the *Odyssey*, also in Virgil's *Æneid*. Frantic to end the protracted siege and return home to his wife, Odysseus suggests a ruse: The Greeks must build a wooden horse and leave it by the Scæan Gate. An armed party led by Odysseus conceals itself inside the horse. Although warned not to by the prophet Laocoön, the Trojans bring the horse within the walls, which leads to the capture of the city.‡

By various ways and with varying success, the Achæans return to their homes, at which point Homer shifts focus to the figure of Odysseus. With Troy destroyed, he enters the Primeval Sea and begins the journey to Ithaca. It will be ten more years before he is safely arrived there.

◆◆◆

Odysseus of Ithaca is a class unto himself in Homer. The *Odyssey* takes place on the sea, but the proprioceptive odyssey is far from over. The obstacle to reunion with his wife is no longer perception in its grossly external manifestations, which are the orifices of the second world, but is far more subtle. On his way to Ithaca, Odysseus must extirpate the neurological roots of perception and what might cautiously be described as its psychology rather than its physiognomy. Hence, his principal opponent after leaving Troy is Poseidon, who sends numerous storms to drive him off course. In entering the inner world, the sādhaka has left behind the mask of sensation. He must now meet perception face to face.

* Ibid. 24.440–65. Fir is highly scented. At the Wedding of Peleus and Thetis, the centaurs throw darts of fir. Priam is a king—he wears a crown, and we have seen already the connection between a crown and olfaction, the upper second world.

† *Iliad* 7.66–132.

‡ An intriguing postscript to the *Iliad* suggests that Helen eloped with Paris only as far as Egypt—namely, the south, the third world—where a miraculous switch occurred. An ethereal double (eidolon) was substituted for the real Helen by Proteus, who is connected in several myths to Menelaus and the third world. Paris then went on to Troy with ectoplasmic Helen. After the Fall of Troy, Menelaus retrieved his wife (*Fragmenta* 26, Stesichorus [b. 632 B.C.]; see Rose, *A Handbook of Greek Mythology*, p. 232). The entire war was fought for the sake of an illusion! There is an echo here of an obscure sutra of Patañjali: "The mind can enter another's body on relaxation of the cause of bondage and from knowledge of passages" (*Vibhūti Pāda*, sutra 39 with commentary). Associated with this power, or *siddhī*, is the yogi's ability to create artificial bodies, called *nirmāṇakāya* and used to burn up karma. Sāṃkhya maintains that the involvement of puruṣa with prakṛti is illusory, mere dream; kaivalya is the experience of waking up from the dream. By using an artificial body, the yogi avoids contamination by prakṛti. Thus, the Trojan War could be interpreted as the struggle by the Trojans *not* to awaken from the dream and to hold on to their ectoplasmic Helen.

In book 5 of the *Odyssey* Homer tells of Odysseus's sojourn with the nymph Calypso, the daughter of Atlas, on the mysterious Island of Ogygia. Odysseus arrives there alone, the last of his crew having perished at sea as a result of yet another offended god, Hyperion the Titan, on whose cattle they have foolishly dined. The destruction of the crew, following the sacrilege, bears a distant resemblance to the biblical story of Adam's expulsion from Eden after feeding on the forbidden fruit of the TREE OF THE KNOWLEDGE OF GOOD AND EVIL, as well as to Persephone's eating of the pomegranate seeds that Hades cunningly offered her to keep her in the underworld. In all three cases the ingestion of a certain food led to bondage: Adam's to toil and suffering, Persephone's to Hell, and Odysseus's to Calypso. Pleasure leads to pain. Indulgence in the senses (second world) necessitates suffering in the senses. This principle, often loosely referred to as karma, is common in Indian philosophy, where it is closely linked to the concept of metempsychosis or transmigration of the soul.

Ogygia is a second-world locale because it reduces to *gg* = *kk* = *k*, and Calypso is equally clearly a second-world goddess (her father is Atlas), so Odysseus's imprisonment can be understood as his entrapment by the illusory power of the senses. Calypso's name is both mantric and descriptive; not only does it reduce to *kl*, but it means "veiler" or "enchantress," and Homer makes much of the fact that while Odysseus is with her he indulges in lots of sexual activity. Her name also contains the root for the Greek word *kalon*, "beauty"; it is likely that in her deeper origins she derives from the radiant beauty of sunlight and by extension from the phonic properties of vision itself. In other words, proprioception of the eyes and the visual centers of the brain, for instance, the optic nerve, the optic thalamus, and the occipital cortex,* is associated with a golden light *and* an internal sound that approximates a clicking: *kl*. Crickets were sacred to Apollo, who among other things is a god of golden light bearing the epithet *nomios*, "he of the meadows"—places where, on a hot summer's day, the noise of insects is abundantly evident, often deafeningly so, providing a concrete auditory label to a common pastoral scene, one especially meaningful to the primitive shepherds among whom myths first arose.

If we appeal to the Greek meaning of *Calypso*—Veiler or Concealer—and combine it with her second-world status, we see that the following verse (from the *Īśa Upaniṣad*) is a wonderful summary of book 5 of the *Odyssey*:

> The face of truth is covered with a golden disk. Unveil it, O Pusan, so that I who love the truth may see it.†

Calypso is the outer golden sheath, entrancing, exquisitely beautiful, like the sun, yet only the beginning of the proprioceptive journey that the breath (Odysseus) makes on its way to the truth. The outer, veiling sheath Patañjali calls the "covering of light"—*prakāśavaraṇa*—which must be pierced by the yogi.‡ The covering of light can be interpreted as a description of (1) perception in general, (2) the body as percept, namely, the body seen with the eyes, and (3) the brain, perceived during autopsy but propriocepted as intense electromagnetism (light) during trance. It is a "covering" because no percept can directly convey the self-awareness of what is perceived. Awareness in another can only be inferred during perception, including a perception of one's own image in a mirror; the image of the brain "discovered" in an anatomy book is the epistemic equivalent of an image in a glass. The self-awareness or experience of an organism is known interiorly by stereognosis and cognition, which are epistemologically coequal with perception (à la Hades, Poseidon, and

* Structures lying in the same horizontal cranial section as the eyes, hence all in the second world. Cf., Old Skt. *arka*, "fire," for the origin of Calypso's name.

† *Īśa Upaniṣad* 15.

‡ *Yoga-Sūtra*, *Vibhūti Pāda*, sutra 44.

Zeus) and cannot be reduced to it.* Interiority is thus "covered" during perception. The covering is removed during samādhi when, with the dissolution of perception, the categories of interior and exterior are as empty of meaning as they are in a dream. In the myth we are considering, Troy is itself the covering of light that must be pierced, and Homer often uses the word *xanthos*, "fiery yellow" or "glowing," to describe the Trojans (Xanthus is an alternative homeric name for the Scamander, the principal river—cranial nerve—of the Troäd).

Odysseus's stay with Calypso (in some accounts for as much as seven years) recapitulates the Trojan War, the struggle to separate Helen (the soul) from Paris (the second world). She is therefore the equivalent of Aphrodite, whose birth in the spray of the sea off Cythera describes the second world,† which begins where the breath enters the nostrils, just above the dark ocean of the first world and below the ocean of the third. It is surely significant that Cythera is a large island that divides two seas: the Ionian and the Ægean, *n* and *k*.

Homer tells us that Odysseus grew miserable as the years wore on, that Athena, who describes his ultimate third-world goal, persuaded Zeus to set him free, and that Zeus at once sent Hermes to order Odysseus's release. The choice of Hermes is apt. He is the son of Mæa, a Pleiad, one of the daughters of Atlas and a second-world goddess. Homer relates the god's arrival on Ogygia in the following passage:

> But when he had now reached that far-off isle, he went forth from the sea of *violet blue* to get him up into the land, till he came to a great cave, wherein dwelt the nymph of the braided tresses [Calypso]: and he found her within. And on the hearth there was a great fire burning, and from afar through the isle was smelt the fragrance of cleft cedar blazing, and of sandalwood. And the nymph within was singing with a sweet voice as she fared to and fro before the loom, and wove with a shuttle of gold. And round about the cave there was a wood blossoming, alder and poplar and sweet-smelling cypress. And therein roosted birds long of wing, owls, and falcons and chattering sea crows, which have their business in the waters.‡

Homer is concerned with enumerating the pleasures afforded to each sense by Calypso's home. Hermes has left the sea of "violet blue" and entered a glittering earthly paradise where "even a deathless god who came thither might wonder at the sight and be glad at heart." The chattering of the sea crows and other birds long of wing are especially pertinent. Homer distinguishes between the scents of cedar and sandalwood wafted "from afar" and those of the cypress, alders, and poplar that surround the cave. Calypso's island is within the neurology of the second world, so it is possible that Homer's distancing of the odors of cedar and sandalwood means that they arise in proprioceptions of other areas of the brain. In the Old Testament we find numerous references to the smell of cedar, all of which suggest its sacred character. When Solomon built his celebrated temple he fashioned the altar (on which the ARK OF THE COVENANT rested) out of cedar.§ When one smells cedar, what is actually being smelled? Because odors, like all experiences, are sensations created within the olfactory sensorium, the answer to our question must be that one senses a particular arrangement of the sensorium. If the odor of cedar is descriptive of the third world, then the olfactory trance of the meditator must be very deep and one-pointed to allow him to detect it. We are not arguing what might be called the naïve-solipsist position. Cedar trees do exist and their leaves and bark do emit distinct odors, but

* In psychology this covalency is expressed in a well-known conundrum: "How can the brain be in the head when the head is in the brain?"

† Hesiod, *Theogony*, in: *Hesiod and Theognis*, trans. D. Wender (London, 1973), 188–200.

‡ *Odyssey* 5.28–36, emphasis added.

§ Song of Solomon 1:17, 5:15, 8:9; 1 Kings 6:10, 15–18.

the chemicals given off by the cedar are in some special way congruent with purely internal olfaction, with the resting voltage of the olfactory bulbs. The congruency does not have to be an identity. Just as for internal sound the mantras expressed as words are merely onomatopoetic approximations, so too with internal odors. The olfactory cortex smells *like* cedar, at least on the report of the Old Testament. That another mythic tradition should describe it differently is probably as inevitable as the fact that cedars do not grow everywhere. As for sandalwood, it too is derived from a resinous substance extracted from the bark of a tree (*Santalum album*) and may well involve olfactory processes similar to those necessary for the perception of cedar.

Alders, poplars, and cypresses, on the other hand, have in common the imagery of death (second world). Alders were sacred to Cronus, Zeus's father, whom the Olympian gods overthrew and who has come down to us in the figure of the GRIM REAPER, an image of cutting suggestive of the second world. The poplar (or aspen) was planted by Hades in the Elysian Fields as a memorial to his mistress, the nymph Leuce; on his way back from Tartarus, Heracles wove for himself a wreath of its leaves.* Cypress trees have been planted at the gates of cemeteries and beside graves since antiquity.

To Homer, Calypso is "she of the braided tresses," which can be interpreted either as a description of the manner in which several cranial nerves† are entwined one about the other behind the eyes or, equivalently, as yet another image for the tight, painful band of proprioceptive sensations that gird the skull at the level of the second world, also known in myth as the GIRDLE OF VENUS. A loom weaves together diverse strands analogous to the way that the senses bind the soul to the world. Patañjali says that to pierce the covering of light brings one in contact with *mahā-videhā*, literally, "great knowledge" but derived from the same Indo-European root as Greek *idein* and Latin *vidēre*, "to see." Mahā-videhā is beyond *buddhi*, "intellect," also the Sanskrit word for the planet mercury.‡ The Greek word for the rod used to drive home the threads of the warp and woof and make them firm is *kerkis*, from which comes *kerkyon*, Hermes' wand, with which he deludes the minds of mortals, but here the image concerns tying the mind to the world "out there." The wand is what applies the "covering of light" to the eyes. Relevant too is the passage in the *Odyssey* that describes Penelope's unraveling of the burial shroud of Laërtes (Odysseus's supposititious father) to dupe the wooers who plague her in her husband's absence.§ It refers to the meditative peace that follows proprioception of the third world (Penelope).# Homer gives the epithet "she of the braided tresses" to one other figure in the *Odyssey*: Circe, who lives on an island, is a witch, and whose name reduces to *kr*.

The events of the *Iliad* elapse over fifty days, and five is the number of perception. The events of the Odyssey, although they contain lengthy recollections by Odysseus of his ten-year voyage home, require but forty days. Though he is not precisely localizable in the body (to which his wanderings in the *Odyssey* amply testify), he does have a destination: his home in Ithaca, summed up by the images of his marriage bed and his wife, Penelope. Her name suggests the third world; in other words, the breath must reach the cerebrum. The climactic scene of the *Odyssey* is Odysseus's destruction of the fifty suitors with a fabulous bow that only he can bend. To prove the bow, he first shoots an arrow through the holes in twelve (■ 3) ax heads set in a row. Homer expends many words

* Virgil, *Æneid*, in: *Virgil's Works*, trans. J. S. Mackail (New York, 1934), 8.276–78.

† The optic, trigeminal, and abducent, to mention only three.

‡ *Yoga-Sūtra*, *Vibhūti Pāda*, sutra 44 with commentary, pp. 350–51.

§ *Odyssey* 19.148ff.; Athena is the goddess of weaving, e.g., in the myth of ARACHNE'S WEB.

\# Cf., the Gordian Knot, which Alexander the Great cut in twain; the tradition behind the knot was that to unravel it entitled Alexander to rulership of the (second) world. *Gordian* reduces to *krt*.

describing how Odysseus seals off the great stone *megaron*—his banquet hall—in preparation for the grisly slaughter, in which he is aided by his son, Telemachus, and the swineherd Eumæus.* The bow we have seen in the myths of Apollo and Artemis. The narrow passage through the ax heads is the frontal suture. The suitors, who revel, drink, and in general consume the contents of Odysseus's storehouse, are the senses, which must be sealed off in the skull—a "hall of bone"—if they are to be suppressed. And at the moment of maximum drama, Homer pauses to describe in a near-perfect simile the sound that fills the room when Odysseus plucks the bowstring: "It sang sweetly beneath his touch, like to a swallow in tone,"† the anaractic hum of the nervous system heard as the ascent into trance begins. The entire episode recapitulates the destruction of Troy.

We can now grasp the esoteric meaning of Telemachus (Gk. "final battle" or Armageddon). Had Odysseus not turned aside the plow when Palamedes placed the infant Telemachus in the furrow, his karma would have been destroyed while still only a seedling and the suffering at Troy averted.

◆◆◆

In the *Upaniṣads*, the soul "rises up" and all the senses attempt to follow it. In the same way, the Greeks must follow Helen to Ilium to win her back, and the Trojans contend with them to keep her. Disguised as a Wooden Horse and led by Odysseus, the Greeks enter the Walls of Troy and tear them down. The two endings to the war are united in yoga. Hector falls. The Greeks secret themselves in a horse; the horse is breath. "Put your mind in your breath and you will conquer," Kṛṣṇa advises Arjuna on the battlefield of the *Mahābhārata*, another Indo-European epic from the same era. Kṛṣṇa, one of whose many titles is *balyogeśvar*, "master of yoga," is Arjuna's charioteer. He drives the horses. If the meditator merges his awareness with an awareness of his breath, he can "slip through" the frontal suture and reunite the mystic seas, tear down the Walls of Troy, reconcile Odysseus with Penelope, Zeus with Hera, and Helen with Menelaus. The precondition is that Achilles must pierce the frontal bone.

Quite clearly, no one—yogi, saint, or mystic—literally cracks open the frontal bone and lives to tell the tale. Left out of the equation is the effect of prāṇāyāma sensed, not at the frontal suture, which is merely the practical seed (bīja) of the trance, not even at the gasserian ganglion lying directly behind it, but penultimately at the pituitary gland, a stalklike appendage of the hypothalamus on the sagittal midline of the brain that controls the endocrine system.

The pituitary gland has been called the "master" gland inasmuch as it controls the overall development of the body by the outputting of a powerful hormone. It is in fact identical to the *ājñā cakra*, "fire wheel," of tantrism, a center of "spiritual" energy. On our hypothesis, the ājñā cakra—as with all the seven cakras—is not an organ of the so-called etheric body (Skt. *manomaya kośa*), astral body (vijñānamaya kośa), or of any other "transphysical" *kośa* (body), but is an apt image for proprioception of the pituitary body, which is certainly physical.‡ *Cakra* means "wheel" in Sanskrit. A proprioception of the pituitary gland feels like a whirl of neural energy, and certainly the use of rosettes on the mouldings of Ionic capitals is consonant with such a description (figure 21c). The Hindus speak of the cakras as like flowers, perhaps best rendered by the motifs of Corinthian capitals (figure 21b). The entry into the sublime trance of kaivalya is accompanied by a singular event in the pituitary gland that affects the pineal body. The relationship of the pineal body to the pituitary gland, indeed to the endocrine system as a whole, is far from clear. To judge from its apparent

* *Odyssey* 21–22. See also *Odyssey* 15.100–129.

† Ibid., 21.411.

‡ The word *kośa* appears nowhere in the *Yoga-Sūtra*. The introduction of metaphysical "vehicles" into many discussions of yoga, chiefly as a result of the influence of H. P. Blavatsky (d. 1891) and her Theosophical Society, is unfortunate and the result of ignorance of the heightened, yet absolutely physical, awareness into which trance leads the sādhaka.

activity only, it might as well be dormant. Given its prominence in tantrism, however, it is even more important than the pituitary.

The event that triggers the *pituitary catastrophe*, as we might define it, begins as a unique reaction to an olfactory-gustatory proprioception mediated by the olfactory fasciculus (and related to myths like the LAST SUPPER that precede a cataclysmic, world-altering Crucifixion).* When awareness becomes concentrated on the pituitary, we hypothesize, there *sometimes* follows a sudden, cataclysmic outflow of pituitary hormone that then energizes the dormant pineal body. The release of the hormone is proprioceptively as a tearing, a rending, the blow of an ax—any of a thousand such images in fact—quite literally painful and dangerous, as anyone who has had an epileptic convulsion can testify. (On our hypothesis, epilepsy is involuntary trance.†) The degree of danger is directly related to the preparation of the sādhaka through *aṣṭaṅga* yoga.‡ If the yogi has prepared himself under the tutelage of a guru, the danger is eliminated. The preparations involve purification of the body and control of the passions—rage, anger, lust—because of the interference of hormones such as adrenalin, thyroid, and testosterone with pituitary hormone. Again the paramountcy of praxis is to be stressed. Ethics—or morality—is secondary. The seven deadly sins (pride, anger, lust, gluttony, envy, sloth, and covetousness) are deadly in a most literal sense: the hormones associated with the emotions are fatal during the pituitary catastrophe. Control of sexual passion, for example, must not become an end in itself; control of testosterone *is* such an end. Yet this control is not in the nature of a *repression*, which always has pernicious psychological effects that "backfire" on the organism, but is a practical diminution of endocrinal output. None of this is to say that the moral results of controlling the seven deadly sins, that is, harmony, sobriety, continence, and so on, are unimportant or undesirable, only that in its "fallen" incarnated condition the organism cannot successfully achieve them without first extirpating the endocrinal kleśas that engender sin. As Jesus says "Seek ye the kingdom of God and all these things shall be *added* unto you."§

Nothing about archaic Indo-European culture suggests that control of the passions was highly valued. It was only after a long epoch of civilization during which the warlike Indo-Europeans absorbed the values of subject peoples that what might be called their ethical situation improved. Nevertheless, even without preparation, the citadel of the pituitary can still be forced, so to speak, the basic trope of the Trojan War, indeed of most archaic Indo-European myth.

The pituitary catastrophe demarcates the emergence of a completely new stage of the organism. Moreover, as with several important endocrinal events, it is irreversible. It can no more be reversed than puberty can. Once kaivalya is attained, there is no going back to the dream of the senses. The yogi proprioceives the impact of his ever-slowing breath against the glabellar bone until the breath stops, and "in the twinkling of an eye," as Saint Paul says, the perceptual crack dissolves and the prelapsarian unity of experience is restored. The entire *Iliad* hangs upon the sublime moment when the breath, in the guise of Achilles in his tent, emerges to pierce the cranium in a world-shattering blow that electrifies every neuron in his brain and brings the yogi into the presence of God. Troy has fallen, never to rise again.

* Cf., Matthew 27:50–51: "Jesus . . . yielded up the ghost. And, behold, the veil of the temple was rent in twain from the top to the bottom; and the earth did quake, and the rocks rent." See also *Ṛg Veda* 3.32.12, in which Indra strikes the sky dragon Ṛta with his club, touching off a downpour, and Apocalypse 16:1–9: seven angels pour out seven poison-filled vials on the world at the SECOND COMING.

† The Greeks, as with other ancient peoples, considered epilepsy to be a divine gift rather than a disease. The drugs used to control it, the hydantoins, are sweet-smelling organic compounds ($C_3H_4N_2O_2$). On the present view, epilepsy is related to a pituitary disorder.

‡ See p. 208.

§ Luke 12:31; cf., Matthew 13:12: "For whomsoever hath, to him shall be given." The context of both verses, and others like them, is initiation into the mysteries of the KINGDOM OF HEAVEN.

15

THE CRACK IN THE COSMIC EGG

Chaos was first of all, but next appeared
Broad-bosomed Earth, sure-standing place for all
The gods who live on snowy Olympus' peak,
And misty Tartarus, in a recess
Of broad-pathed earth, and Love, most beautiful
Of all the deathless gods. He makes men weak.

Hesiod, *Theogony*, 116–21.

This passage, one of the most famous in the literature of antiquity, is Hesiod's account of the creation of the world. Hesiod wrote in the eighth century B.C. and may have been a younger contemporary of Homer. We might well expect to find esoteric meaning in his verses, especially in his proper names: Chaos, Gæa (earth), Olympus, Tartarus, Eros (love). Hesiod called his poem a *theogony*, literally, "gods' birth," an account of their origins. To the extent possible in an archaic poem, it is a serious statement concerning two central mysteries: being and nothingness.*

The introduction is the trickiest part of any cosmogony, for obviously it must beg the origin of the prime existent. "Chaos," Hesiod confidently asserts, "was first." The word Hesiod uses to explain Chaos's presence is *geneto*, "was born," implying an antecedent mother at least, but Hesiod avoids any characterization whatsoever of that reality. Neither the vedantic brahman nor the Christian Logos can properly be said to have been "born." Phonically, *geneto* is equivalent to Greek *kinethe*, "moved"; each reduces to *kn*, an upper-second-world phon.† Thus, instead of a myth about *on*, "absolute being,"

* The *Theogony* was enormously influential. All later cosmogonies incorporate it in whole or in part, including those of Plato and Aristotle.

† The endings *-the* and *-to*, appended to *kine* and *gene*, are grammatical and can be left out of the analysis.

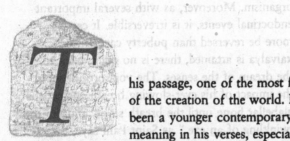

Hesiod is here describing the creation of *kinesis*, "motion"; in Greek the particle *kin-* connotes the restless phenomenality of the second world. Instead of saying "Chaos was," the sense in Genesis, he says "Chaos moved," and everything that is was created.

On our hypothesis the *Theogony* takes for its esoteric subject the origins of perception and is only collaterally an explanation of the literal heaven and earth. Because of the characteristically Greek tendency to fashion macrocosmic-microcosmic equivalencies, the *Theogony* could be and was applied to the external world. Esoterically, however, it describes the phenomenality of opening one's eyes, of waking, when the dark and trancelike unity of the cosmœ is sundered by movement-filled perceptions of the second world.

Absent the second world, there is but one world, not three. In line 116 the appearance of Mother Earth creates simultaneously a floor for Heaven (Mount Olympus) and a roof for Hell (Tartarus). The space between is the second world. In Hesiod's own words: Gæa (k) divides ***niphoëntos Olympou*** (snowy Olympus) from Tartarus (tr). *Niphoëntos*, an adjective, derives from ***niphas***, "snow," which reduces to ***n***. Again we find the top-to-bottom sequence ***n–k–t*** as the organizing phonics of the myth. The argument has partial support in Homer, who always describes Olympus as ***aganniphos***, "snowy peaked." The salient fact here is not that the summit of Olympus is snowcapped—at nearly ten thousand feet it could hardly avoid it—but that the Greeks, along with the Latins (nix) and Germans (Snee), use words whose core phoneme is *n* to express our word "snow." Hesiod lived and worked in Bœotia, where snow is a rarity, except as it is visible on the tops of mountains throughout the year; but snow is a near-perfect description of the transition from the manifest to the unmanifest, from matter to æther, earth to sky.

Mount Ida is a peak in Phrygia (actually a chain of peaks), which the gods of the *Iliad* visit whenever they wish to observe the action at Troy (particularly true of Hera). The implication, at least in Homer, is that unless they descend from snowy Olympus to Ida they cannot *see* the conflict. According to the geographer Strabo (d. A.D. 22), Troy was settled by one-third of the population of the island of Crete.* When they arrived in Phrygia, the Cretans renamed a nearby chain of mountains after Cretan Ida—in some myths the birthplace of Zeus—which at over eight thousand feet is often snowcapped. The two Mount Idas should not be thought of as different mountains in myth, however. Mount Ida is never described as "snowcapped," but often as "wooded," teeming with animal life and vegetation, and flowing with cool streams—a sufficient description of the fertile second world, seat of genesis, change, and becoming, including life and death. The movement of the gods from Olympus to Ida parallels the transition from cognition or stereognosis to perception. Crete, as the paradigm of the second world, is the place within which vision operates, a notion consonant with the tradition that makes Cretans the ancestral Trojans.†

Hesiod's next foray (after a summary of the effects of Eros on men and gods) in three lines recapitulates all of the above:

> *From Chaos came black Night and*
> *Erebus.*
> *And Night in turn gave birth to Day*
> *and Space*
> *Whom she conceived in love to*
> *Erebus.*‡

Hesiod is at pains to provide the Olympians with a "sure-standing place," a "[secure] resting place." The etymology of *Olympus*, though not a settled question, is interesting. One suggestion is that *Olympus* is compounded of *lyma* and

* Strabo, *Geographica*, vol. 6, trans. H. L. Jones (Cambridge, Mass., 1929), 13.1.48.

† Zeus alone has no need to leave Olympus because he is "far seeing." Yet he sometimes prefers to sojourn on Phrygian Gargarus (krk), a royal box whence he keeps tabs on the visible world. Mount Gargarus, site of the Judgment of Paris, is the highest peak in the Idæan chain.

‡ Hesiod, *Theogony*, 12–120.

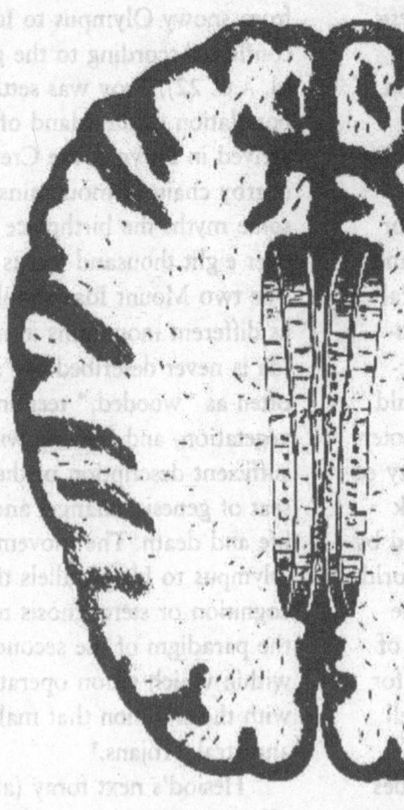

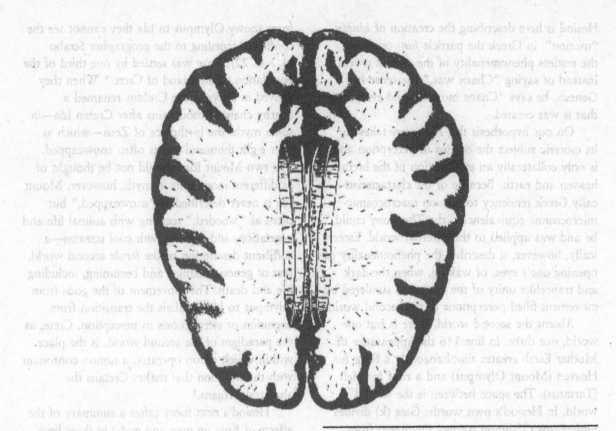

Figure 33: The FEET OF THE LORD (from *Gray's Anatomy*)

pous, "pure foot," conforming to Hesiod's description of the earth as a sort of footstool for heaven up from which rise the "blessed gods." Echoes of the idea can be found in every major religion of the world, which suggests a proprioceptive origin. If one surgically makes a horizontal section of the cranium at the level of the corpus callosum, the pattern formed by the convolutions of the brain resembles two human feet (figure 33). The same pattern has given rise to a variety of symbols subsumed under the myth of the FEET OF THE LORD. The five senses are the five toes of the divine foot.

We've already seen that the capitals of Greek temple columns are recapitulations of the second world. Of the three major classical orders the Corinthian was the last to be used in temples. A distinctive feature of Corinthian capitals is the representation of acanthus leaves around the optiform volutes (figure 21b). A comparison of an acanthus leaf with the cross section of figure 33 reveals strong similarities. Moreover, the acanthus plant derives its name from the Greek word *akantha*, "bear flower," presumably because its leaves resemble the footprints of that animal. The bear was sacred to Artemis, anthropomorphized smell, and is one of the few quadrupeds capable of standing comfortably erect, a talent it frequently uses to reach beehives suspended from the boughs of trees. With both hind feet planted firmly in the earth, it strains to pluck the sweet-scented honey that its nose tells it is just above, hidden in the buzz and hum of the hive—an apt image of the yogi seated in meditation attempting to propriocept the olfactory bulbs. The earth on which the bear stands describes the second world, the level of the corpus callosum; the hum of the bees describes the third world, site of the olfactories.

The well-known yogic technique called

khecarīmudrā consists of stretching the tongue to the back of the throat, literally probing for an afferent nerve(s) carrying sensations of smell along the inner root of the olfactory tract. The tongue must be stretched so far back in the throat that yogis will sometimes cut the muscles at the base of the tongue, although that is not strictly necessary. When taut, the tongue will taste its own neurology at the same time it touches the olfactory tract (through the skin). In practice, the tongue moves suddenly and surely to a point behind the uvula, almost like a snake striking.* The motion of the tongue closes a switch, so to speak, allowing an intense proprioception of a rod-shaped structure of the nervous system comprising the spinal cord, vagus nerve, glossopharyngeal nerve, and a bulbous portion of the mesencephalon that includes the hypothalamus and pituitary gland. The structure is described in myth as the Dionysian wand or thrysus. The inner bottoms of Greek drinking bowls frequently depict Dionysus biting his tongue. The Gorgon's Head also appears on the Ægis of Athena with her tongue between her teeth (see frontispiece). We might also mention the olivewood CLUB OF HERACLES, which he uses to stun the Nemean Lion. The olive was the single most important ingredient of ancient Greek cookery, hence associated with gustation. The Club of Heracles (and the vedic Indra) can therefore be identified with the stretched tongue.

Yogis use khecarīmudrā to assist in stopping the breath and call the sensation of tasting the tongue itself "eating the cow,"† which might seem sacrilegious because eating the flesh of cows is tabu in Hinduism, the nominal religion of most yogis. Yet for that very reason the sacral aim of the technique is underscored. A marked parallel can be drawn with the Christian sacrament of the eucharist, in which the sacred body and blood of The Christ are consumed. The Hindu deity most evocative of The Christ is Kṛṣṇa, an avatar of Viṣṇu, second person of the Hindu trinity. The prohibition on eating cow flesh in Hinduism derives from the affectionate relationship between cows and Kṛṣṇa. Just as Jesus is imagined to be a shepherd in Christian iconology, Kṛṣṇa is a cowherd in the *Purānas*, a collection of devotional stories dating from the ninth century A.D. Kṛṣṇa's commonest appellation is Hindi *Govinda*, figuratively "cowherd" but, more precisely, from Sanskrit *govid*, "cow sensation," with a collateral sense of "[cow] fragrance." The pituitary catastrophe can be touched off by an olfactory-gustatory stimulus, hence the close-at-heels connection of Christ's institution of the eucharist at the Last Supper on Maundy Thursday and his death on Good Friday. Before Zeus and Hera embrace on Crete, a coition that describes the union of the first and third worls, Hera prepares her seduction by sending Hypnus (Sleep) to the top of a *fir* to make Zeus drowsy, that is, entrance him‡ The bough on which Hypnus perches is an olfactory nerve. During the funeral of Hector at the end of the *Illiad,* wine is poured out on the ground, something that occurred after every Greek ritual sacrifice of an animal (perception). Finally, Orestes' rescue of Iphigenia is his penance for matricide (he murdered Clytemnestra to avenge her betrayal of Agamemnon). To achieve purification Orestes enters the temple of Artemis—anthropomorphic olfaction—via a metope and retrieves her image; nor is violence absent from the myth: his boon companion, Pylades, does not survive the adventure.

Yogis speak also of the *soma* fluid that drips into the back of the throat from the crown cakra in the skull and can be tasted with the stretched tongue during khecarīmudrā when the breath stops. The Last Supper, then, is an esoteric description of khecarīmudrā, with the body and blood of Christ describing proprioceptions of the the tongue, teeth, and palate when the soma fluid is sensed with the tip of the tongue, a configuration esoterically described as the HOLY GRAIL. The proprioception referred to

* Cf., *kuṇḍalinī*, the divine serpent that tantric yoga seeks to arouse; in Egyptian art we find the uraeus emerging from between the brows and figurines bearing a scorpion, poised to strike, atop the skull.

† Elaide, *Yoga: Immortality and Freedom.* p. 247.

‡ *Illiad* 14.23lff.

is extraordinarily difficult to attain and depends critically on the purification of the body beforehand. Coming as it does immediately before the eschatological catastrophe, the search for the Holy Grail requires an especial sancitity in Parsifal and Galahad, who are Christian sādhakas. The closest Greek parallel is Ganymedes, Priam's granduncle, who was abducted by Zeus to Mount Olympus to be cupbearer to the gods, that is, to serve the sacred nectar and ambrosia. *Abduction* conveys the rapture of trance, and, with a little goodwill, the un-Greek notion of personal salvation—Ganymedes was deified by Zeus. To recompense King Tros of Troy (Priam's great-grandfather) for the loss of his son, Zeus gave him a pair of matchless stud horses. From them two stallions were bred for Æneas. When Diomedes wounds Æneas, the horses become his. During the struggle for the horses, the archer Pandarus, Æneas's boon companion, is killed thusly: "So spake [Diomedes] and hurled [his spear]; and Athena guided the spear *upon his nose beside the eye*, and it *pierced through his white teeth*. So the stubborn bronze *shore off his tongue at the root*."* That Pandanus is an archer is not unimportant: the streams of breath in the nostrils are the shafts of the mythic bow. Diomedes then drives the horses to the ships, that is, into the third-world sea. What Zeus gave, Zeus took back, as must happen where Troy is concerned.

King Priam of Troy was given the name Podarces (Bear Foot) at birth. But when Heracles sacked Troy to punish King Laomedon—Priam's father—for not honoring the agreement laid down for the rescue of Hesione, he slew all of Laomedon's five sons except Priam,† but allowed Hesione (Priam's sister) to ransom him with a golden veil worn around her forehead. Hesione describes a respiration-induced proprioception of the horizontal section of the skull containing the sutures that join the cranium to the bones of the face. Podarces was then renamed Priam, which means "he who was redeemed."

Priam is king of Troy, so he can be equated with the second world. He had two wives, Arisbe and Hecuba, plus numerous concubines. It is surely no coincidence that he had fifty sons, namely, the five senses—nor that Arisbe was the daughter of Merope (Bee Face), a woman of the same name as the wife of Sisyphus, nor that Hecuba was the daughter of Metope, a woman of the same name as the wife of Asopus.‡ The fact that a golden veil wrapped about the forehead (metopon) was the price of his redemption needs no further explanation. We have already mentioned how Achilles describes Troy itself as a "headband."

Of course there is more significance to the divine feet than the shape of the encephalon. To be ever aware of the proprioceptual pressure exerted by the feet, to be always at the Feet of the Lord, is bound to affect the symbolism that a meditator might use in fashioning a myth. Placing oneself at the feet of another is an admission of weakness and of dependence on the other. It asks for mercy, bespeaks humility. Anger, greed, and vice are necessarily at odds with such a posture and with the feelings that accompany it. In short, it is an image that conforms in many respects with the ethical structure of every major religious system having its origins in antiquity.

One exception is the ethos of the Greeks themselves. Their myths are full of fiery heroes who place small value on humility, for whom mercy is a sign of weakness. So long as the characters of Greek myth treat only one another barbarously they are relatively free of divine interference;§ but when they flout the gods their doom is sealed. The most illustrative example—as well as the most famous—is Œdipus, a tragic king of Thebes. What is not often considered is

* *Iliad* 5.244–96, emphasis added; the spear is the tongue, the two stallions describe the olfactory nerves.

† Apollodorus, *Bibliotheca* 3.12.3–5.

‡ Ibid. Alternative mothers are mentioned for Hecuba by Apollodorus. The question "who was Hecuba's mother?" was a popular one in late antiquity, e.g., Suetonius, *Tiberius* 70.

§ There are exceptions; the *Eumenides* (Furies), for instance, punish crimes against one's kin.

the meaning of his name—"swollen foot"—which was given to him by the shepherd who rescued him after his father, Laius, had Œdipus's feet pierced with a nail and exposed him on Mount Cytheron. The piercing and binding recall not only the Crucifixion but the sharp and painful proprioceptions of the second world (Cytheron). His adoption by a shepherd (on the side of a mountain) recapitulates the image because the second world is equivalent to a collection of horned animals such as rams, bulls, and stags.

Œdipus's mother was Jocaste, a woman with a lower-second-world name (*j* = *i* = *ya*, thus *Jocaste* reduces to *kt*). Her marriage to King Laius (l), Œdipus's father, was not made in heaven. The Delphic Oracle tells Laius that any child born to Jocaste will kill its father. Laius, encountering the adult Œdipus many years later in the defile between Delphi (dl) and Daulis (dl), becomes tangled in the reins of his chariot and is dragged to his death. Jocaste hangs herself. Œdipus blinds himself with a pin.

The oracle foretells the destruction of the father by the son, a prediction common enough in myth, which esoterically restates the usurpation of awareness by perception. This is just the condition that yoga is meant to undo. Thus, prāṇāyāma—Laius dragged to his death by his horses—subdues perception, described by the strangulation of Jocaste. The return to internal unity is described by the blinding of Œdipus, after which, on the advice of the blind seer Tiresias, he abdicates the throne and dies at Colonus in the domain of Athens, the third world. It should be obvious that Tiresias and Œdipus are one and the same. Œdipus's impious marriage to Jocaste (kt) obviously supplants his father (Laius = *l*) and is yet another instance of the usurpation of experience by perception.

We can now end our analysis of Mount Olympus, dwelling place of gods and goddesses. The foot of Olympus rests on the second world. Its peak is in heaven. Olympus is the dome of the skull and extends from the frontoparietal to the parietoöccipital fissure. It is the *pure foot,* the "seat of the deathless gods that standeth fast forever. Not by winds is it shaken, nor ever wet with rain."*

Hesiod next relates at length the story of the Titans. Their name is perhaps related to *tlein,* "to strain," a derivation that makes good sense because Atlas, who belongs to a later generation of Titans, struggles to hold heaven off of earth. Judging by where in his narrative Hesiod chose to introduce them, that is, after Gæa has brought forth the mountains and valleys of the world, it is clear that the Titans are second-world deities. Their names—in the order that Hesiod gives them—are Oceanus, Cœus, Creus, Japetus, Hyperion, and "last, after these . . . crooked-scheming Cronus."† The care that Hesiod takes to set off Cronus from the other male Titans is noteworthy. Not only does he state explicitly that Cronus emerged last from Mother Earth, he even lists him after the females, who are born immediately following Hyperion. Their names are Thea, Rhea, Themis, Mnemosyne, Tethys, and Phœbe. Because they are the consorts of the male Titans—Tethys with Oceanus, Phœbe with Cœus, Mnemosyne with Creus, Themis with Japetus, Thea with Hyperion, and Rhea with Cronus—they need not be considered separately. It is highly significant, however, that in six Titaness names, comprising fourteen syllables, the letter *k* does not appear once. Conversely, in the six names and sixteen syllables of the male Titans *k* occurs four times, three of them at the initial letter of the name.

Oceanus (kn), Cœus (k), Creus (kr), and Cronus (krn) are second-world figures. Japetus presents difficulties; but the fact that he mates with "lovely ankled" Clymene, daughter of Oceanus, to produce Atlas and his brothers provides him with strong second-world connections. His name reduces to *pt*. The suffix *-tus* is a standard Greco-Latin inflection for masculine gender, so we may reasonably shorten *pt* to *p*, a

* *Odyssey 6*. Cf., Kṛṣṇa's description of ātman (which is brahman): "Not wounded by weapons, not burned by fire, not dried by the wind, not wetted by water," *Bhagavad Gītā*, in *The Song of God*, p. 37.

† *Theogony*, 140–41.

plosive. This connects him to the breath. He is Atlas's father, and we have identified Atlas with the bridge of the nose. It is possible that he corresponds to the Old Testament figure of Japheth, one of the sons of Noah (n), who entered into Noah's Ark during the biblical flood.*

Hyperion's name cannot be exclusively mantric. Translated it means "he who is above the violet," which would seem to place him in the third world. How then can he be a Titan? There are six Titans, a number that relates their birth to an esoteric description of the five senses *and* voiceless speech. The Titans describe the bones of the second world, but at least a portion of the frontal bone—the HELMET OF ATHENA—must be included, introducing the third world. Hyperion describes that connection. He is a stand-in for Uranus. As evidence there is his union with Thea, on whom he begets Helius (Sun), Selene (Moon), and Eos (Dawn). The "lights" of the three worlds, Helius, Eos, and Selene recapitulate the births of the Titans themselves from Uranus and Gæa (Thea, like all Titanesses, is an earth goddess) and maintain the basic theogonic structure. The primordial coupling of Heaven and Earth is repeated dozens of times, woven over, around, and through itself, filling Hesiod's narrative with primitive sex and unending parturition: one becomes two becomes three. Important and logical distinctions exist among the various matings, however. Whereas the union of Uranus and Gæa produces the five senses plus cognition (voiceless speech), their union under the guise of Hyperion and Thea produces the variation of one primary experience, to wit, sight, throughout the three worlds.

Helius, the light of the first world through his well-known connection with Apollo, underscores again the neurological connection between the heart and eyes via the vagus nerve. Proprioceptively, the rising and setting of the sun are, as a limiting case, equivalent to activation and deactivation of the visual circuitry of the brain. The eyeballs, occipital cortex, and optic thalamus turn on, then off. Helius' home is below the eastern horizon, in a cup that floats in the sea.† It is possible that the cup is a description of the human heart, for which simile there exists ample poetical amplification down through the centuries. Thus, when Helius each morning drives his chariot heavenward, heralded by his sister Eos, he describes the onset of visual perception.

Hinduism credits a limited expression of selfhood known as *jivātma*, said to dwell in the heart. Jivātma has clear affinities with what psychologists call the ego. Equally clear is its relationship to the Presocratic hegemonicon, which dwells in the heart. Therefore, the everyday personal experience of identity must be tied to the heart. Such a configuration is not apparent: apparently, the personal self is located within the skull. The foundation for the belief, then, can only be proprioceptive. In a heart-centered consciousness, the eyes are like periscopes. The wake-sleep cycle, in which the jivātma enters and leaves the eyes, corresponds to the day-night rhythm of the sun. And if our previous interpretation of the Dioscuri, Castor and Pollux, is to be retained, the same alternation must occur, albeit less drastically, with each cycle of inhalation and exhalation.

The on-off cycle of perception is an embodiment at the grossest level of a much deeper process occurring in all three modes of awareness. Consider the following verse of Patañjali: "The process, corresponding to moments which become apprehensible at the final end of transformation . . . , is *Kramaḥ*."‡ The transformation (pariṇāma) to which Patañjali alludes involves three fundamental modes of existence recognized by Hinduism: the *guṇas*. The guṇas comprise every experience in a mixture of inertia, sensation, and spirit. Rāja yoga aims at bringing the three principles into equilibrium so that the cyclic evolution of the meditator's awareness through the guṇas comes to an end.

* Genesis 7:13.

† Athenæus, *Depnosophistæ*, 11.469.

‡ *Yoga-Sūtra, Kaivalya Pāda*, sutra 33.

In the normal, uncontrolled course of the cycle, says Patañjali, the result of imbalance in the guṇas is an "apprehensible" moment: an instant of conscious time. For second-world experience it is equivalent to perceptual time or, more simply, to *change*. The perceptual sensoria are constantly switching—flickering?—on and off, only seeming to be continuous because of the dynamic background of proprioception. Proprioception is also switching on and off, but at a much more rapid rate. The sequence of transformation is called *kramaḥ* by Patañjali. *Kramaḥ* (krm) has a second-world phonic structure, which suggests that the actual process is prominent in trance as a literal crackling-cum-hum. The word means "sequence" in Sanskrit—at least that is the way it is usually translated. We see in it the basic phoneme of creation, *kr*, suggesting that "growth" or "progression" is closer to its original sense.

In the final analysis the *Theogony* treats of the identical creational process. Each instance of experience has, as its original impulse, an experience of kramaḥ. Not the sun but desire, not the moon but imagination, not the dawn but sight, are being rhapsodized. Hence a "theogony": how it is that sight, hearing, smell, taste, and touch are born, maintained, and transformed in the nervous system.

Eos has the well-known epithet *rhododaktylos*, "rosy fingered." Red is associated with both Ares and the second world. She is a feminine representation of perceptual desire. The name Eos is almost certainly derived from Greek *phos*, "light." Under her Latin name, Aurora, however, her connection to Ares is much clearer. Apollodorus explicitly places Eos in Ares' bed, for which sin Aphrodite cursed her with an insatiable longing for mortals (she beds down with more than a few).* Loving Eos can be a catastrophe. Tithonus, son of Laomedon and prince of Troy, mated with her. Eos obtained immortality for him but neglected to confer eternal youth. As Tithonus aged he shrank to imperceptibility, becoming at last nothing but a voice shut in a chamber. We have already seen Laomedon's connection with the Fall. (The Fall of Troy starts with his treachery.) The myth of Eos and Tithonus suggests voiceless speech, with his crypt being the esoteric cranium. In the Garden of Eden, Satan is a whispering serpent, and Tithonus was the father of Memnon (mn), king of Ethiopia. The moral? When cognition weds perception, there will be hell to pay.†

Eos's recapitulative function assists the narrative line of the *Theogony*. Because Hesiod begins at the beginning, introducing the classical Olympians only after he has told the history of their forebears, he must use other deities to represent the senses until their anthropomor-phizations arrive. Ares does not appear until line 921, so Hesiod has earlier introduced Eos to act his part, and Cœus before Eos, and Day before Cœus.

Selene, the moon, is third-world light, primarily, we must assume, because of the blue to indigo (n) shades typically seen on moonlit nights, perceptible colors that approximate the imperceptible luminosity of the upper world. Selene was the mother of the Nemean Lion, a cave-dwelling monster slain by Heracles in his first labor. She wove the lion from the foam of the sea. Selene reduces to *n*—the *l* is intervocalic—and the proper noun Nemea has third-world phonics. Because the Nemean Lion is Heracles' first obstacle on the road to his apotheosis, it must describe some practical difficulty in attaining third-world trance, in stilling the shifting currents of the mind. Its foamy origins indicate, however, that it straddles the second world, a location we see in the exoteric placement of its jaws in sculpture: where the dome of the skull joins the bones of the face. Figure 13c tells us vividly that the bite of those jaws is real enough in the trance state.‡

* Apollodorus, *Bibliotheca* 1.4.4.

† *Homeric Hymn to Aphrodite*, 218ff., in: H. G. E. White, *Hesiod and the Homeric Hymns*; see also *Odyssey* 5.1 and *Iliad* 20.237. Ethiopia is where Poseidon goes when he leaves the second world. *Tithonus* means "grasshopper," an adroit image for the mind that flits from lust to lust.

‡ The third-world Nemean Lion, an Indo-European myth, should be distinguished from the first-world Chaldean Lion of astrology; the controlling phonics of the myth is *nm* = *mn* in *Nemea*. Selene is also called Mene.

With the birth of Cronus, "most terrible of sons . . . who was his vigorous father's enemy,"* Hesiod reaches a crucial point in the narrative: the CASTRATION OF URANUS. Uranus is castrated because he buried in the earth six of his more monstrous sons: the three Cyclopes and the three Hecatonchires, the "hundred-handed ones." Uranus hated them "from the first," though Hesiod never really says why. Her husband's cruelty angers Gæa, fair to bursting with further hideous progeny and quite uncomfortable. (Hesiod relates that she "groaned.") Turning in sorrow to her Titan sons, she pleads for their help and gives to "crooked Cronus" a saw-toothed scimitar of adamant:

Great Heaven came, and with him
brought the night.
Longing for love, he lay around the
Earth,
Spreading out fully. But the hidden
boy [Cronus]
Stretched forth his left hand; in his
right he took
The great long jagged sickle; eagerly
He harvested his father's genitals
And threw them off behind.†

Thence Cronus, the youngest Titan, becomes ruler over all. The Titans then emerge from underground to separate heaven and earth. Once again, perception has usurped the throne of the cosmœ.

The seed of Uranus fell into Mother Earth and, in a year's time, the Eumenides, Giants, and Meliæ (ash tree nymphs) were born. And after them, Cytherean Aphrodite and her companion (often her son) Eros and "comely Desire [Himeros]." Hesiod never describes explicitly the freeing of the Hecatonchires and Cyclopes, for whose sakes Mother Earth inspired her son to patricide. We conclude, therefore, that the births following Uranus's castration recapitulate their release, and especially when Uranus's burying of his sons echoes the fall of his seed into the earth.

The myth can be correlated with the Œdipus legend, in which a second-world son overthrows a first-world sire and usurps the throne. In the *Theogony*, however, the conflict is between the second and third worlds (at least in the passage we are considering). The mother in both tales has a strong second-world name (*Gæa = k*). In both myths there is a reference to something "swollen"; in one case it is Œdipus's foot, in the other Gæa's procreative innards, from which the senses (led by Cronus) are trying to escape. The grasping, externally directed appetites of the body are what is meant by the three hundred arms of the Hecatonchires. The Cyclopes with their three huge eyes set in the middle of their foreheads, defiling the spot sacred to Athena Parthenopæa, represent uncontrolled sensory desire in its most distilled form—vision.‡

The six monsters recapitulate the six male Titans, but in ways that imply a degeneration of the Titans' primarily passive behavior—they simply maintain the space within which perception works—into a rapaciously active, self-asserting, bestial "life force." Note Hesiod's own description of the Cyclopes, "insolent Brontes and Steropes . . . proud-souled Arges," and of the Hecatonchires, "Cottus and Gyes and Briaræus. Insolent children." Cronus frees them with a sundering blow, one that dethrones Uranus at the same time that it severs the unity of the worlds. Again, note Hesiod's words: "Longing for love, [Uranus] lay around the Earth/ Spreading out fully." Uranus brings the night and attempts to shut off the "openings" to the second world, but does not see Cronus, "in a hiding place . . . [in] his hands the saw-toothed scimitar."§ Why hidden? Because, as *Cronus* (kn) indicates, he describes the upper-second world, the region of the olfactories, which is within his father's realm and from where his act takes on an odor of treachery. Small wonder he is known as "crooked scheming."

Uranus's unhappy fate draws a curtain on

* *Theogony*, 137–39.

† *Theogony*, 177–82.

‡ Ibid., 146: "Energy and craft[iness] were in their works."

§ Ibid., 175.

the first portion of Hesiod's epic. He has told of the creation of the world and Cronus's enthronement. Esoterically his subject is the act of perception, his moral the ardent propensity of perception to dominate experience, to become identified with the substance of reality. In sum, Hesiod has described the Fall: the freeing of Desire, as Aphrodite, from her heavenly abode, Uranus. That her release is the direct result of harvesting cosmic seed suggests an archaic connection of Greek myth to yogic philosophy and karma.

◆◆◆

First from Chaos came Mother Earth, the broad, fecund, and relatively undifferentiated locus of the second world; to those qualities may be added hardness and sharpness. Second, Hesiod told of the emergence of Day and Space, introducing into the second world qualities of openness and clarity. Third came the Vault of Heaven, which serves to demarcate the upper boundary of the second world (the hard earth is itself the lower bound, and Uranus is only defined relative to Gæa). Fourth to appear were the Titans, who support the heavens and rigidly finalize the space carved out for perception. Fifth came the Hecatonchires, the Cyclopes, the Giants, Meliæ, Love, and Desire, each sprung from cosmic seed (karma), burgeoning forth to fill the crack in the worlds, providing—for want of a better word—a psychology of perception that is determinedly external, ignorant of heavenly realms, willful, egocentric, and woefully ensnared in the demands of pleasure and pain (kleśas). Cronus is now king in the earth:

And Night bore frightful Doom and
the black Ker,
And Death, and Sleep, and the whole
tribe of Dreams.
Again, although she slept with none of
the gods,
Dark Night gave birth to Blame and
sad Distress,
And the Hesperides, who, out beyond
The famous streams of Oceanus, tend
The lovely golden apples, and their
trees.
She bore the Destinies and ruthless
Fates,
Goddesses who track down the sins of
men
And gods, and never cease from awful
rage
Until they give the sinner punishment.
Then deadly Night gave birth to
Nemesis,
That pain to gods and men, and then
she bore
Deceit and Love, sad Age, and strong-
willed Strife.
And hateful Strife gave birth to
wretched Work,
Forgetfulness, and Famine, tearful Pains,
Battles and Fights, Murders, Killings of
men,
Quarrels and Lies and Stories and
Disputes,
And Lawlessness and Ruin, both
allied,
And Oath, who brings most grief to
men on earth
When anyone swears falsely, knowing
*it.**

Hesiod has plunged the world headlong into the sphere of *karma*, which must be discussed in some detail before returning to the narrative of the *Theogony*.

◆◆◆

Karma. No concept of Hindu philosophy is so vexatious—unless it be brahman, which is admittedly undefinable. It is difficult to prise the meaning of karma out of the Sanskrit. Translated literally, *karma* means "action." In its etymology it is cognate with English *go*. Karma is immanent in and formative of all experiences that are appetitively motivated. For example, that all creatures must eat, drink, and reproduce is the result of karma; but so are ego needs for

* *Theogony*, 211–32; the list comprises the fifth manifestation of the world.

fame and recognition. Karma covers actions in all three worlds. Karma is the psychological dynamo of activity. We want and so we work, need and so strive. Karma is the unavoidable burden of *doing something* with which sentient beings are laden. But karma is also basic neurophysiology. We open an eye and are compelled to see. We cannot normally avoid hearing or feeling or thinking or respiring—the point of the myth of Sisyphus and the Stone. "All is awhirl," said Lucretius.

Imagine the human genome. Imagine 200 thousand coiled springs tamped down into a sphere half the diameter of the period at the end of this sentence. The gene is compressed desire. And the universe that evolved the gene—not by coincidence—is ceaselessly, relentlessly in motion from the galaxies to the quarks, and ourselves along for the ride whether we like it or not. So naturally we have come to like it. Never mind the goals, we prefer goal-directed activity in and for itself. Goals become abstracted into values, values symbolized by money. Far from being grossly material, money is a great advance in human culture because it is the constant visible significator for the experience of value. Value must here be understood as a core experience of the organism, even more concretely, as a proprioception of the appetitive sensorium per se, isolated from any external stimulus (*decathected* in Freudian terms). That this core experience almost inevitably becomes associated with material objects, when it is called desire, is the result of ignorance, according to Patañjali, of confusing the knower with the known. Desire must be turned on itself. Yet because we do not know desire in and of itself, the desire we share with rotating galaxies and vibrating atoms, the relentless activity of the world, must become mechanical, and ourselves grow desperate.

The Hindus long ago asked themselves the question: What is the alternative to doing? What occurs when sight and sound, taste, smell, and touch are extinguished, along with thought? What is left to awareness then? Our (Western) reply, of course, is nothing. One dies, and that is an end to it. We equate life with perceptual life or with perceptual life modulated by thought and emotion, which are mere grace notes, demihemiquavers in the universal cacophony, superfluous doodles. Over and against this caricature of true life, Sāṃkhya asks, What if within each and every one of us there vibrates an a priori experience? What, asks Vedānta, is known in dreamless sleep, when perception and cognition cease? What are we—each one of us—experiencing then? Do we disappear, as it were? Or is there a fundamental reality that we encounter yet fail to remember? Is there a life beneath—below? deeper than?—what we normally call life?

Yet all such questions are moot where karma is unchallenged.

Karma is destiny in action. It is the series of acts that engages the soul between birth and death, what the soul was meant to do in this life. Karma implies a multiplicity of paths to a single goal. The most practical, least abstract, and irreducible manifestation of that goal is breathing. The number of breaths drawn in the course of a life is karmically predetermined. Physiologically that means that the endocrine system must be genetically programmed to allow a maximum number of inhalation-exhalation cycles. The only sure-fire way to prolong life is to slow down respiration. By implication, to stop the breath is to live forever! That does not mean that the body or any part of it endures forever, only that in trance something else, something that is "not this, not that" remains.

Karma is not sin, though sin is always karmic. The karma that is not sin is called *dharma*, "duty" (especially by Buddhists). Hindus do not call their religion "Hinduism" but *sanātana dharma*, "eternal duty," suggesting that religion too is *compelled* action. The karma that *is* sin is summed up in the term *kleśa*, "affliction." Patañjali mentions kleśas frequently and cites five particularly invidious examples: "The lack of awareness of Reality, the sense of egoism or 'I am-ness,' attractions and repulsions towards objects and the strong desire for life are the great afflictions [kleśas] . . . in life."*

* *Yoga-Sūtra, Sādhana Pāda*, sutra 3.

Each kleśa is a description of a particular, isolatable pattern of energy in the body; concerning them, Patañjali says further: "Their active modifications are to be suppressed by meditation."* Prāṇāyāma and cardiovascular control operate pari passu with mental control. Hence the suppression of kleśas is measured by the degree to which those same rhythms respond to the will of the meditator.

The last three kleśas mentioned by Patañjali are "attraction" or *rāga*, "repulsion" or *dveśa*, and the "wish to live" or *abhiniveśa*. All are related to the pleasure-pain status of an organism, which in turn is correlated with breath rhythm, heart rate, and mental poise. Chemically, breath, heart, and mental functions can be correlated with the ebb and flow in the nervous system of monoamines such as noradrenaline and serotonin (via the bloodstream). Although a great deal of data has been accumulated, a coherent theory of how heart, lungs, and encephalon are coordinated through neurochemistry has yet to emerge.† From the point of view of yoga, however, the emotional states accompanying attraction and repulsion are proprioceptively grounded experiences of somatic patterns—including monoamine output—that manifest as fluctuations in the cardiovascular, respiratory, and nervous systems.

Whether one labels the fluctuations as basically instinctual or learned is immaterial; they are all kleśas. Yoga makes the claim that by working directly on the fluctuations, the underlying kleśic patterns can be altered—even suppressed indefinitely. Thus, in the teeth of a charging bull, a meditating matador's heart rate might not skip a beat; an escaped convict—suitably trained—might not even respond to the enticements of a streetwalker. Because of the demonstrable connections between heart, lungs, and mind, the mental states in these examples must also be neutral, calm. To the degree that this is true, yoga claims that the matador and the convict are free of dveśa and rāga.

Yoga therefore has superficial affinities with behavioral psychology; both work on the symptoms—perceptual observables—of psychological states.‡ They differ strongly insofar as yoga's millennia-long study of the trance state has given it the capacity to alter the symptoms of anxiety voluntarily, with a subtlety and directness quite lacking in present behavioral techniques, which are essentially coercive. Furthermore, yoga has no a priori interest in rendering an organism adaptable to its "environment," a term that, used behaviorally, is synonymous with the second world. In yoga, pleasure or adaptivity is as much an obstacle as pain or maladaptivity, and *environment* includes cognitive and proprioceptive stimuli as well as perceptual. As a concession to behaviorism, we might say that because yoga allows such refined observations of the first and third worlds it has in fact perceptualized them (rather than slandered them as "epiphenomena"). We must also admit that for the same reason perceptions are internal states of the organism, something as obviously true as it is irrelevant absent heightened proprioceptive capacity.

Neurologically the relation of perception to kleśas is illustrated by the myriad connecting fibers among the senses, the cerebrum, and the spinal cord. External stimuli are routed by the thalamus, eventually affecting the brain and the ganglia of the torso. The second world, therefore, has a superficial resemblance to a nexus of the first and third. We've mentioned the constrictive and painful nature of proprioceptions arising there—for example, the structural convergence on the frontal suture—all of which define the second world as a *junction* (kn) both neurologically and experientially, a concrescence of nerve, tissue, and bone that is intimately related to a meditator's experience of kleśas.

In going from the first to the third worlds a tactile proprioceptive progression occurs. Initially there is the watery, relatively cool and dark

* Ibid., sutra 11.

† B. Katz, *Nerve, Muscle, and Synapse* (New York, 1966).

‡ For radical behaviorists the words *mind, self, emotion,* etc., have either severely limited meanings or no meaning whatsoever.

"sea" in the abdomen, warming somewhat in the thorax. The fluidity of the first world is heightened by the rhythms of respiration and blood flow. Passing through the throat, which shares the flow of breath with the lungs, we arrive at the second world proper, and an abrupt change occurs. The teeth, hard palate, and bones of the face are rigidly in place. Sharp sensations are felt where the nasal breath touches the bridge of the nose; the eyes are warm; a tight band circles the skull. We have emerged from the sea onto dry land, Mother Earth, the islands of Ogygia, Crete, and Cythera, Troy, the Isthmus of Corinth, and the WALLS OF JERICHO—the imagery is endless. Then another discontinuity. We are at the bottom of another "sea," that of the mental world: wine dark, electric, flowing with imagery and inhabited by a thin, ghostly voice. Our sequence then is from water to earth to water or, simplifying it even more, from soft proprioceptions to hard to soft.

The hard, earthen aspect of the second world lends itself to a metaphor from agriculture: the sowing of seed, an extension of mythic imagery in which the breath is a plow, for example the myths of Odysseus and Telemachus and Jason and the brazen-hooved Bulls of Hephæstus. What is the seed that is sown in the plow's path? Patañjali:

> The reservoir of *Karmas* which are rooted in *Kleśas* brings all kinds of experiences in the present and future lives.
>
> As long as the root is there it must ripen and result in lives of different class, length and experience.
>
> They [experiences] have joy or sorrow for their fruit according as their cause is virtue or vice.*

The seed is experience itself, not a good experience or a bad experience, but experience per se. The goodness and badness of the experience are merely categories of seed. Furthermore, just as a true seed, planted in earth, puts forth roots to maintain itself, so too does an experience establish a pattern and an imprint in the nervous system, however slight, which Patañjali refers to as a kleśa. The grasping function of a root and the constrictive nature of second-world proprioceptions correspond metaphorically. If, say, an experience is repeated, the initial kleśa, or imprint, will modulate the organism's reaction. More repetition means increased modulation. Analogously, the more a true root is nourished the deeper it gets rooted.

Kleśas, then, are memories, not simply cognitive memories, but a generalized, heterodynamic stability throughout the body. Mnemonic behavior is not confined to so-called animate objects. Both mechanics and electrodynamics recognize states of matter and energy showing preferred directions, frequencies, boundaries, and other parameters, clearly selected—to use the most neutral word that comes to mind—because of their similarities to prior states.

One of the aims of yoga is to meditatively undo any and all conditioned responses that exist within the nervous system. Yoga aims at breaking the hold that even so-called unconditioned or autonomic responses have on the organism. Yoga's chief tool in accomplishing these goals is the effect of breathing on the relevant neurophysiological structure, be it a nerve, collection of neurons, or ganglion. The repetitive nature of respiration is important here because it was by repetition that the kleśas took root; only a repetitive method can eradicate them. The use of especially chosen mantras is therefore a natural approach to altering behavior.

Proprioception tends to project, as it were, all three cosmœ into the same experiential plane. If the eye is acting externally it cannot be acting proprioceptively. To speak of kleśas as proprioceptions of the imprints made on the nervous system by perceptual stimuli is to speak about nothing at all. Thought is redefined as a proprioception of the cerebrum. Emotion is a proprioception of the heart (first world). Essentially,

* *Yoga-Sūtra*, *Sādhana Pāda*, sutras 12–14.

then, honoring behaviorism in the breach, we are dephenomenalizing perception in the same way that behaviorism phenomenalizes cognition–stereognosis. *All* experience is a configuration of the nervous system, which is wholly internal. The teleology of myth is the exclusion of perception from awareness and the return of the soul to a profound unity, summed up in the myth of the Primeval Sea. There is something alien about the second world, something perilous—yet there is something divine as well: Ares is a god; so is Hermes. Aphrodite is a goddess. To what extent are they sacred? To what extent profane?

If we decide not to conflate the Three Worlds, we must still recognize that purely proprioceptive experiences enter into the commonest of perceptions, for example, the well-known phenomenon of seeing tiny, almost transparent globules whenever we look at a large, monotone object such as the sky. Because the globules have something to do with the state of the retina, they are internal, yet it can be argued that they are actually external because they involve density variations at the surface of the eye. As the plane of interaction for all objects regardless of distance from the subject, the retinal surface can be thought of as external to that subject. But even so, there seems to be a qualitative difference in our experience of those globules, particularly discovered as an inability to attach a distance to—to measure, say in inches—the spatiality of the experience of the globules. We might, perhaps, remove the ambiguity by describing the globules as *transitional* visual entities possessing both a perceptual and a proprioceptive quality.

More nearly proprioceptive are aspects of experience related to subjective variation in the reactions of different observers to the same stimulus. One person calls green what another sees as blue. One may hear an A-flat tonic in a score, another an E. The question is not whether one or none of those judgments is correct (a line of inquiry that sooner or later must issue in nonsense) but rather how to order the variations proprioceptively. Such idiosyncratic variations relate to the structure of perception rather than to its meaning, to its form and not its content. They represent the practical way that perceptions are composed within a given nervous system.

Pitch, timbre, rhythm, harmony, and melody differentiate auditory stimuli. Each parameter comprehends an indefinite number of subparameters. Timbre, or tone color, means that a pitch played on tuba sounds different from the same pitch played on a saxophone. Perceiving the distinction implies awareness of two dissimilar distributions of aurally engaged neurological energy. The difference might be slight, as, for example, when a given pitch is played first on an alto saxophone and then on a tenor. Yet it is the minute alterations in perception that presently have the greatest interest for us. Out of them we can assemble a structural description of a particular sense. The elements of such a *sensory declension* will be fundamental qualities of all experiences that involve a particular sensorium; more significantly they will be associated (at least in theory) with fundamental circuits in the brain; and it is through those circuits that a transition to proprioception from perception is made.

As is well known to art historians, the impressionists were profoundly affected in their approach to painting by the invention of the camera (ca. 1840). In examining photographs and the techniques of photography they were forçed to see for perhaps the first time the means by which images are constructed with elementary variations in the intensity of light. The grainy mosaic of a photograph provided the impressionists with theretofore hidden insight for introducing light into paintings in a *structural* way. The impressionists were scientific; to paint impressionistically required discipline and observation. It is possible to see in their works just what aspects of light interested them: mistiness (Corot and Monet), shimmer (Monet, Pissaro, Renoir), contrast (Manet and Degas), color (Monet, Renoir, Degas), and reflection (all of the above save perhaps Manet). Ultimately their preoccupation with formal structure inspired still more radical attempts to understand and manipulate the components of a painting (e.g., cubism) and an inevitable leap into *abstrac-*

tion: the attempt to paint the third world.

Parameters like mistiness, shimmer, and so on make up the phenomenal declension of vision. They are instances, cases, of visual perception that apply unequally to all experiences. They are not exhaustive nor free of redundancy and ambiguity nor of meanings not exclusively visual in their range of application. They are simply obvious choices, for which alternatives exist.

Similar declensions exist for the other senses. Touch, for example, can be parsed in terms of smoothness, rigidity, tremor, warmth, and texture. Hearing shares several parameters with vision: tone, clarity, shimmer, harmony (akin to contrast), echo (akin to reflection), and composition. By introducing variables that relate to temporality or intensity, each case of the declension can be refined even further, for example, rapid shimmer, deep tonality, high contrast. When anthropomorphized, such experiences—which are not wholly internal or external—are of only secondary importance in myth because they have to do with multifarious shadings of primary sensoria. We have entered the realm of the demons as opposed to that of the gods.

◆◆◆

Greek myth abounds with *dæmones*, male and female. Dryads, næads, satyrs, and telchines figure in a great many legends, among which the tales of Marsyas the Satyr, who challenged Apollo to a flute-playing contest, and Eurydice the Dryad, beloved of Orpheus, are prominent examples (especially in antique art). As part of the harsh Christian reaction to polytheism, all were hellish creatures, though there is no such sense in paganism. Socrates frequently mystifies his interlocutors by referring to his *dæmone*, "familiar genie," who mysteriously communicates with him. The minor deities, so confusing in their abundance, point a long and wraithlike finger into a stereognostic age, an era when the gods and goddesses of the Greeks were all mere demons.* Only after millennia of primitive animism, during which the resident demon of every rock and tree, mountain and forest, river and lake, was accorded due reverence—only then, slowly and with numerous local variants, did the classical Olympians emerge. As the various species of god and demon were esoterically systematized, the projection of inner (proprioceptive) reality onto external phenomena became more perfect and close fitting, so that by the eighth century B.C. Hesiod could write of "thirty thousand immortal demons who dwell on Mother Earth, guardians of mortal men."†

Recall the horrors that follow the enthronement of Cronus:

> *Battles and Fights, Murders, Killings of*
> *men,*
> *Quarrels and Lies and Stories and*
> *Disputes,*
> *And Lawlessness and Ruin, both*
> *allied,*
> *And Oath, who brings most grief to*
> *men on earth*
> *When anyone swears falsely, knowing*
> *it.*

Things couldn't be much worse. But then:

> *And Pontus's firstborn child was*
> *Nereus,*
> *The honest one, the truthful. . . .*
> *And he is gentle and remembers Right,*
> *And knows the arts of Mercy and the*
> *Law.*‡

Nereus and Doris parented the fifty "passing lovely" Nereids. In twenty melodic lines Hesiod tells us their names, many of which caress the ear: Lysianassa, Ploto, Amphitrite, Eudora, Galena, Cymothoë, Halimede, Pherusa, Dynamene, Galatea, Hippothoë, Cymodoce, Cymatolege, Pontoporæa, Thetis, and Psamathe.§

* H. J. Rose, *Religion in Greece and Rome* (New York, 1959), p. 109.

† Hesiod, *Works and Days*, 252–53; 30,000 = 3: the Three Worlds, the totality of experience.

‡ Hesiod, *Theogony*, 233–36.

§ Ibid., 242–62; different—though very similar—Nereid lists appear in the extant mss. of Hesiod.

The Nereids are the "most beloved of goddesses. . . . Rosy-armed . . . trim-ankled. . . . Laughter-loving. . . . Perfect to look at," and so forth. Appearing in the hour of deepest dread, the delightful Nereids are not only a palliative to the hideous progeny of Night, they are also positively redemptive of the second world, of the creation. Because the Nereids represent a mingling of the three worlds, are the presence in perception of proprioceptive qualities emergent from the mystic sea, they intimate the possibility of cleansing by water. Like the filamentary spray off the ocean's waves, implied in so many of their names, the Nereids tether our sensory world and its unpleasantness to a neurological abyss. They tell us that perception cannot occur without the participation of deeply fundamental configurations of the organism, structures so basic that they are easily overlooked but that become accessible in trance. By concentrating on the milk-white light of Galatea, on the shimmer of Pherusa, on Glauconome's laughter, on scented Halimede, on the ichoric streams of Thetis, perception is fleetingly sacralized, and the mystic sea foreshadowed. "I can call spirits from the vasty deep" boasts Owen Glendower. If he could—and they do come!—they would be the Nereids, conjured from the unfathomable depths of his own nervous system.

It is hardly surprising then—given their parents—that the names of the Nereids describe various aspects of the sea. Thus Ploto means "floater," Cymothoë translates as "wild wave," Cymodoce and Cymatolege as, respectively, "wave taker" and "wave calmer," Pontoporæa as "sailor," and Psamathe as "the sandy one." Still others, though not so obviously neritic, are evocative enough: "the speedy one" (Pherusa), "the potent one" (Dynamene), "the milky one" (Galatea), and "wild mare" (Hippothoë). The syllabification of Nereid names is nicely suited to Hesiod's dactylic hexameters. Nonetheless, the names suggest an intermingling of water and light. In fact, they seem to describe the transient experiences congruent with the cases of our sensory declensions. Doris (d) and Nereus (n) bracket the human organism, from stem to stern as it were. Their offspring, then, are the host of biological energies encountered between the two extremes.

There are fifty Nereids, so they describe the second world and its five senses primarily and only secondarily the first and third worlds. Again, Hesiod "creates" the middle world, rather than all three worlds; the first and third are defined only in relation to the second and disappear into the unity of trance once perception is curtailed. The birth of the Nereids is Hesiod's sixth and most intriguing recapitulative theogony.

◆◆◆

To achieve a reversal of theogony requires an ability to annihilate perception at the moment when perceptual stimuli have their greatest hold on one's desires. Proprioception of the inner sea must therefore be the reinforcing experience nonpareil, the most satisfying response to any and all stimuli, in behavioral terms, that an organism can receive. Our logic comes inevitably to the proprioceptive hypothesis: *The organism is accessible to its own awareness* ad minutias. Only if the hypothesis is granted can we include the state of the organism in both the stimulus and response to an event. The organism itself is the essential component of reinforcement. Pleasure and pain, the two pillars of behavioral psychology, are first and foremost configurations of the organism. Trance isolates the pleasure-pain configurations, eliminating the need for a perceptual event to trigger them. Yet yoga claims much more than this. It claims to have discovered configurations related to profound well-being, to peace, truth, bliss, and to *satcitanand*: "Truth, the consciousness of bliss." That is no vague concept of bliss, no philosophical truth, but an accessible configuration of the organism.

Returning to myth, then, in particular to the myth of the Primeval Sea, we are reminded of the second verse of Genesis: "And the earth was without form, and void; and darkness was upon the face of the deep. And the Spirit of God moved upon the face of the waters."

The creation proceeds from a motion, a wave in the sea. Hence, in order to reverse the creation, the wave must be calmed. The ripples of perception must be smoothed, along with their associated memories and emotions. Meditation achieves this quiet state by stages. Through a variety of techniques it integrates and harmonizes the heterogeneous motions of the second world with the rhythms of the body.*

If, however, reversal is not achieved, Genesis gives a sequence of events leading to the creation and habitation, the indwelling, of the second world by consciousness. By the fifth day "every living creature that moveth, which the waters brought forth abundantly," has appeared. We are told of "whales" and "winged fowl,"† transitional forms of awareness. The whale inhabits the lower sea; the winged fowl "swim" in the upper. The crucial fact here is that these are breathing species, creatures with lungs. This links them unavoidably to the second world, to which they return of necessity for air or rest. It subtly adumbrates the connection between breath and karma. The manifestation of the world is empowered by the need for the soul to breathe, a demand incarnated in our very metabolism, which requires oxygen to burn food. The heat thrown off in the process is a perceptualization of our desires, our pangs for the things of the senses.

On the sixth day man appeared, and from him woman—but also the "beast of the earth after his kind" and everything that "creepeth upon the earth." Then, in a passage that makes clear the esoteric nature of the book of Genesis, we read:

> And God said, Behold, I have given you every herb bearing seed, which is upon the face of all the earth, and every tree, in the which is the fruit of a tree yielding seed; to you it shall be for meat.‡

In light of what Patañjali has written concerning the sowing of karmic seed, we can interpret the verse as meaning that the second world comes into existence to provide an arena wherein the soul can work off its karmic debt, accumulated in previous incarnations. In yoga that is known as "burning up" karma, for which several kriyās were discovered, particularly root-gazing at the fire cakra.§

The Roman Catholic practice of placing ashes on the brow at the beginning of Lent describes this wholly internal conflagration, which accompanies the pituitary catastrophe. As with the decapitation of the Gorgon, an irreversible change takes place in the functioning of the gasserian ganglion. The constriction of the second-world nervous system is cleared out by fire and sword in the imagery of myth. It is worth recalling that Perseus was conceived in a blinding shower of gold that descended on his mother Danaë, yet another esoteric recapitulation of the catastrophe. Danaë was then shut up in an ark by her father Acrisius (kr) and the ark cast into the sea. Given the recapitulative structure of myth, all of these episodes—the shower of gold, the shutting up in an ark, and the decapitation of the Gorgon—are mutually identifiable and occur simultaneously.

The events of Genesis are partitioned by the phrase "And the evening and the morning were the first [second, etc.] day." Hesiod never explicitly identifies a theogony with a day, but to do so is a natural metaphor springing from the concept of kramaḥ, the sequence of dawnings (mornings) that lead to a perceptible instant of conscious time. The appearance of humans on the sixth day parallels the birth of the Nereids in Hesiod. Prior to the biblical sixth day is the creation of myriad conscious entities. All are expressions of appetitive potentials (saṃskaras) within the Primeval Sea and all are inferior to human awareness. God gives to Adam and Eve "dominion over the fish of the sea, and over the fowl of the air, and over every living thing that moveth upon the earth"—a pithy summary of the Three Worlds. Hesiod paints what precedes the arrival of the Nereids in bleaker and more

* *Yoga-Sūtra, Sādhana Pāda*, sutras 30–55. See also Kovach, "Contemplation in Movement," p. 78.

† Genesis 1.21.

‡ Ibid., 1:29.

§ *Yoga-Sūtra, Sādhana Pāda*, sutras 10–11 with commentary.

baleful colors. His fifth theogony fills the world with all the evils of earthly existence, incorporating the idea of the Fall into the theogony itself, a catastrophe the Elohist postpones for a few chapters.

In the famous poem of Hesiod's old age, known as the *Works and Days*, he catalogues the activities of daily life according to favorable and unfavorable days for their accomplishment:

> *Fifth days [of the month] are harsh*
> *and frightening; take care.*
> *They say that on a fifth, the Furies*
> *helped*
> *Strife to bring forth dread Horcus*
> [Oath], *whom she bore*
> *To bring a punishment to perjurers.**

Horcus appeared in the fifth theogony; in fact, his appearance concluded it. The parallel is all the more striking because it comes from the selfsame author of the two poems. And even if the Hesiod of the *Theogony* and the Hesiod of *Works and Days* were not the same man, the convergence of the two traditions on Horcus and the number five cannot plausibly be ascribed to sheer coincidence.

The phonics of the dreaded Horcus reduce to *kr*, similar to karma (krm). He was midwived by the Furies (Erinyes, also called the *Eumenides*, "the kindly ones," an apotropaic euphemism), creatures associated with crime and retribution. Hesiod's fifth creation begins with the birth of the Ker (kr), a vicious death goddess known to Homer, and ends with that of Horcus. All life's ills are compassed by that dolorous sound. Hesiod laments that he was born into the "fifth race" of humans created by "Far-seeing Zeus. . . . This is a race of iron," whose sad lot it is to "work and grieve unceasingly [by day]; by night, they waste away and die."†

The proprioceptive interest of the Nereids is their permeation of all three worlds, their interweaving of proprioceptive and cognitive experiences with perceptual ones. But that is the role humanity fulfilled in the creation:

> Let us make man in our image.‡

> For thou has made [man] a little lower
> than the angels, and hast crowned him
> with glory and honor.§

Are not the Nereids of myth angels? Do they not represent the immanence of the divine in the creation? We are dealing here with the sixth day of the Bible and the sixth theogony of Hesiod. Six is the number of cognition, of reason, the faculty that graces our species; and the Nereids, as their name indicates, are the daughters of Nereus, the Old Man of the Sea, the god of remembrance and cognition.

The sixth day of the week is Friday, and in astrology Friday is under the rulership of the planet venus (Aphrodite). Aphrodite's birth amidst the waves of the sea seems, then, to establish a connection with the Nereids. The foam of the sea is an esoteric description of the mingling of proprioception with perception. Hesiodic Aphrodite is anthropomorphized desire, so what we have is the birth of desire, but also, because the following day, Saturday, is the Sabbath, the day on which all work (rk) must cease, we have a prelude to prāṇāyāma. The Sabbath describes the stoppage of the breath and the great peace that follows the death of desire. Holy Saturday is the only complete day in the Crucifixion myth in which Jesus lay in the tomb. It is no great liberty to conflate Golgotha, "the place of the skull," where Jesus died, with the tomb in which he was shut up before rising in glory on Easter Sunday. The tomb is the esoteric cranium.

The fifth sign of the zodiac is Leo, the Lion, a theriomorphism for the sense of taste, more generally for appetite. It is followed by the sixth

* *Works and Days*, 802–4. Cf., Laomedon, fifth king of Troy, whose treachery provoked the gods.

† Ibid., 169–78; in alchemy, iron is linked with Mars, a second-world god.

‡ Genesis 1:26.

§ Psalms 8:5.

sign, Virgo, the Virgin, an image that also evokes the Nereids, nubile sweetness and light, the pursuit of whom is arduous for mortal men, as is amply testified to in the myth of Peleus and Thetis. In astrological lore Virgo is ruled by the planet mercury, which is interpreted in the casting of horoscopes as an indicator of rationality. With Virgo we must also associate the goddess Athena, the most revered virgin of myth and the source of wise counsel throughout the Homeric epics. The Virgin stands sixth, as a mental counterpoise to and a culmination of the lower faculties sequenced by the first five signs: the Ram (sight), the Bull (hearing), the Twins (smell and respiration), the Crab (touch), and the Lion (taste).

We can outline a recapitulation of the creation myths in the zodiacal progression. Aries, for example, is said to be a fire sign by astrologers. It is therefore a source of light. And because the zodiac is arranged cyclically, the twelfth and last sign, Pisces (the Fish), eventually precedes the first, Aries. Hence it is consistent to say that the primordial light of Aries emerges from the primeval sea of Pisces, a water sign:

> And the Spirit of God moved upon the face of the waters. And God said, Let there be light: and there was light.

After Aries comes theriomorphized hearing—Taurus, an earth sign:

> And God said . . . let the dry land appear: and it was so. And God called the dry land Earth.

After Taurus comes Gemini, an air sign associated with smell as one of the esoteric Twins:

> And God said, Let the earth bring forth grass, the herb yielding seed, and the fruit tree yielding fruit . . . and it was so.

Herbs and fruiting trees, of course, are particularly noted for their fragrance.

With Gemini, the third sign of the zodiac, the three principal sense modalities of the second world are complete. The fourth sign, Cancer, a water sign, is touch, and it bounds the creation from below with the second primeval sea, as Pisces bounded it from above. Astrologically the ruler of Cancer is the moon:

> And God said, Let there be lights in the firmament. . . . the greater light to rule the day, and the lesser light to rule the night.

The ruler of the fifth sign, Leo, is the sun. Leo is a fire sign, the second after Aries. We have returned, via the zodiac, to the light of the first world, to Helius and Apollo (both of which reduce to *l*, as does Leo) and to the mystic connection, encountered before, between the eyes (Aries) and the heart (Leo).

Genesis introduces the senses a day at a time (save that touch and taste are both introduced on the fourth day). On the fifth day the animal bodies that incarnate the senses appear. The Fall comes later, after man and woman have been created. In the *Theogony* man and woman are absent in the flesh, but the template of the Three Worlds is in place. The emergence of that template is itself the Fall:

> Let us make man in our image.*

The enigmatic plural form, appearing in a scripture that is the first great testament to monotheism, testifies as well to the triune nature of experience. Cognition, perception, and stereognosis—They are the "we" who are implied. Beyond them is something deeper still. Call it Chaos, brahman, puruṣa, or pure consciousness itself. It has neither beginning nor end. Having no attributes, it cannot be discussed. We must leave it in the eternal silence that is its essence—and ours.

* Genesis 1:2–16.

16

DREAM, DEATH, BIRTH

If both the *Theogony* and Genesis describe the manifestation of second-world awareness, the question arises: Why does the process commence in the first place? We have already supplied a tentative answer: The soul incarnates in order to perceive, in particular, in order to breathe. But that is only what Aristotle (d. 322 B.C.) might have called the *final cause* of manifestation, its end. Consciousness creates for itself, as it were, eyes, ears, and nose, piercing the primordial seas perceptually and supplying Aristotle's *material cause*, the substance or substances through which the process is reified. Antecedent is the *efficient cause*, which means the source of the processional energy, especially the energy of movement.

Aristotle's philosophy was the culmination of a long development in Greek thought. Before Aristotle, before Plato, before Socrates, philosophers such as Parmenides, Thales, and Heraclitus first used proprioceptively derived essences (fire, earth, air, and water) to order the so-called natural world. In the teachings of Socrates, moreover, we encounter perhaps the first attempt to use the same categories in the service of explaining humankind's place in the natural world. Thus, by a circuitous route, the analysis returned to the place from which it started: the human form.

Aristotle too sheds light on the manner in which originally proprioceptive experiences were transformed into cognitive systems, eventually into what we call science. During the transformation, the concept of motion underwent a profound change. The Greek word for motion is *kinesis*, which connoted much more than locomotion (phora). For Aristotle it meant the entire process of becoming. Thus, in manufacture, not only were the various motions of the craftsman in fashioning a tool or other article part of kinesis but also the uses to which the finished products were put as well as the idea in the craftsman's mind that engendered the act of production.

Manifested reality—the creation—for the Greeks was permeated by the trinity of *ousia, dynamia*, and *energea*. Translated, they mean, respectively, "being," "potency," and "becoming." Kinesis clearly belongs to the third category; but to describe a phenomenon fully, Greek philosophers sought always to involve the other two concepts in their analyses.

The most persistent question of natural philosophy for the past twenty-five hundred years has been the identification of the fundamental element—or elements—of which the universe is made. For the physicists of the seventeenth century it was primarily *matter*. For those of the fifth century B.C., it was primarily form (eidos). Our word *matter* is derived from Latin *materia*—ultimately from *mater*, "mother [earth]"—but the Greek word for matter was *hyle*, which reduces to *l*. *Eidos*, or form, reduces to *t*. Both are first-world phons; the knowledge of matter comes directly from the sense of touch. For us, however, matter is dead; for the Greeks it was vital. The Greek conception, older and more narcissistic, expresses each human being's first and most lasting acquaintance with the sense of touch as internal, first within the womb, then within sensoria that process acute and demanding emotions: anger, lust, and hunger. Primitive Greek science, struggling to emerge from the chaotic arena of proprioception, animated matter with all sorts of wishes, tendencies, and proclivities, for example, the "yearning" in heavy objects to unite with the center of the cosmos, or the "desire" of the stars to move in circles, notions that were popular with Greek astronomers and not finally laid to rest until the publication of Johannes Kepler's *Astronomia nova* in the seventeenth century.* The struggle, we hypothesize, corresponds to functional changes in human neurophysiology that impelled an increasingly perception-centered awareness. We can even place a date on when the transition from the Stereognostic Age to the Perceptual Age was irreversible: the seventh century B.C., the time of the presocratic philosophers.

A more sophisticated animism informs the concept of *pneuma*, "vital force," which the Stoics applied indifferently to living and nonliving things. In fact, the ancients made no clear-cut division into what nowadays we would call organic and inorganic matter.† Pneuma was attributed especially to fiery—even explosive—phenomena, a correlation that can be traced to proprioceptions of warmth in the thorax and genitalia. Similar too was the Stoic belief in the hegemonicon, the directing energy of the soul (psyche), which responded to sensation and which they judged to be located in the heart.‡

There is something in Plato's doctrine of eternal Forms that is evocative of touch. There is the intimation of a mold, into which a subtle tactile experience is poured, a hypotangible reality (the same idea evolved into the kantian *categories*). And even though *eidos* (form) is derived from Greek *idein*, "to see," it would be tendentious to argue that Plato ever intended his Forms to be visualizable. In fact the verb *idein* is so old and has such a wealth of meanings that we might wonder if its first-world phonic structure doesn't derive from an epoch of neurological development when sight and touch were vastly more interconnected than they were even in the homeric era.§

Aristotle's usage of form is more dynamic than Plato's. Every process has a potential (dynamis) to evolve, to work itself out along formal lines, to reach what can be described as a fruition, an *entelechea*: "striving toward an end." Aristotle's fourth and formal cause denotes an essential principle of any process, one that both precedes the process and requires its evolution, which "informs" it. *Ousia* applies most directly to the formal cause. Ousia is the core of physical existence, indeed of all experience. While the process or entity is evolving, its ousia is properly described as kinesis. To limit the extreme generality of the concept of ousia so as to make it useful in describing nature, Aristotle introduced the notion of *physis* to signify the ousia of living processes.

Aristotle was not needlessly multiplying

* Kepler wasn't free of anthropomorphisms, as his ascription of a kind of "laziness" to the planets shows.

† J. Lindsay, *Blast Power and Ballistics: Concepts of Force & Energy in the Ancient World* (New York, 1974), p. 156.

‡ Ibid., p. 192.

§ Homer uses the word in at least thirteen different ways. Connections between sight and touch would have been more functional than organic, because there is no evidence to suggest major evolutionary changes in the human nervous system within a time frame that compasses the development of language.

categories. Rather, he strove to make a subtle distinction, absolutely necessary to his way of thinking, which was closer to archaic awareness than is our own. He refused to collapse manifest reality into a perceptual prison—indeed, he could not even consider such an option. His introduction of physis was his main concession to perceptualization. Physis provided Aristotle with a superficial subject—in the bare grammatical sense of that word—one that was not mechanical-perceptual but nonetheless could be extended by analogy into mechanics (though that was at most a secondary aim). For Aristotle there were no legitimate subjects save ousia, the underlying reality (hypokemenon) of existence; and physis was ousia.

Aristotelian physis denoted the formative principle in every living organism, the plan or gene. Every state of being—physical or mental—to which the entity attained was both restrained and impelled by its physis. If we are to go beyond glittering generalities, in other words, if we are to raise hellenic science above puffy speculation, we must return somehow to the proprioceptive roots of natural philosophy. Two ideas will be useful:

- Philosophical categories were originally religious categories.
- The oldest religious categories expressed in words are mantras.

A comparison between the way that, say, Homer uses certain words, for instance, *thymos*, *dynamis*, *eidos*, and the uses to which the earliest Greek thinkers such as Empedocles, Heraclitus, and, in time, Plato and Zeno put those terms shows a continuous and ever ramifying development of the original archaic concepts. *Physis* and *ousia* each reduce to *s*, a phoneme associated with respiration. It would be difficult to select a theme of Greek philosophy that had a greater influence on their various systems than breathing, not to mention so wide a currency. From the time of the Hippocratics in the sixth century B.C., down to the Neoplatonists of the Christian era, the Greeks displayed amazing ingenuity in the wealth of meanings, analogies, and inferences they drew from respiration while formulating a philosophy of nature. Anaximenes, a Presocratic, believed that air was the primary material of the creation: "Just as our souls, which are made of air, hold us together, so does breath and air encompass the world."* The world itself breathes. The word that Anaximenes used for "soul" is *psyche*; "breath" is *pneuma*. Both are found in Homer,† as well as in the writings of the Stoics. *Psyche* is a spirant.‡ *Pneuma* is not, but it also carried a somewhat different meaning in presocratic philosophy: force. The implication is that there is *a force in the breath*, an energy that powers it.

The distinction between the sound that the breath makes in the nostrils (s) and the power behind that sound (pnm) is important. The sound of the breath is a manifestation of the force of breathing. We have postulated a need for the soul to breathe as the motive of incarnation. Carrying our reasoning one step further, we identify pneuma with this force: the necessity to respire. Of the four types of causes, the formal and final causes are the important ones. Moreover, they are homologous. "Panta rhea," said Heraclitus: All is flow, cohesive and teleological process, in which the beginnings of things anticipate their ends. Ousia-physis and pneuma are united in the same way that the sound of the breath is inseparable from breathing. And because ousia, according to Aristotle, is the formal cause of existence, that which engenders and directs evolution, pneuma is the final cause of manifestation.

We are close to the idea of a seed, a karma or a kleśa, from which everything else follows as a matter of course. Physis is intimately related to plant life in both Homer and Aristotle. In book 3 of the *Physics* Aristotle states explicitly that "physis is *arche*," meaning "first [principle]" or "formal cause." Arche was not an ancillary

* Quoted by Ætius, 1.3–4; in: E. Zeller, *Outlines of the History of Greek Philosophy* (Cleveland, 1965), p. 46.

† Homeric pneuma is *pnoie*.

‡ In the *Iliad* we often find *de psychen kapyssen*, "to breathe."

concept, not a product of some byway of Greek thought, but was in continual use by the philosophers of antiquity. Aristotle inherited the concept from Plato, who had made it synonymous with the transcendent Forms themselves. Heraclitus used it to mean both the "beginning" and the "end [telos]" of things. In Homer it means "beginning" and "old"; the last sense survives in English "archaeology." The sense of arche is not simply tacked on to the meaning of physis; rather, it places the term in the widest possible philosophical context known to Aristotle. *Arche* reduces to aspirated *k*, the sound of incarnation. It is the archæ, the seeds of karma, that guide the evolution of all things, living and nonliving. Considered statically, the seeds are ousia; dynamically they are *energea* in kinesis: essence incarnated as movement.

The Greeks believed the soul to be composed of air, the vehicle of breath. Naturally enough, air was associated with heaven—also (from air's subtlety and fineness, which render it capable of supporting mental experience) with *noös*, "intellect." Hence the soul, in its own essence, which is awareness, is capable of understanding and guided in its evolution by *pronœa*, "providence." The Greeks in general and Aristotle in particular believed movement to be a "propensity" of the soul (also of air); compelled by pneuma, the soul *must* move if it is to achieve its destiny.

Does the above discussion explain why the soul incarnates in the first place? If by "explain" we intend a reason or reasons that fix once and for all the cause of psychic evolution, the answer is no. To the Greeks all cause was relative.* The underlying ousia, constantly changing its appearance—That was what mattered. To isolate a single cause of manifestation would be to deal with phenomena mechanically—a methodology having small attraction for the Greek natural philosophers because, in proprioceptive terms, it sunders the unity of the worlds. Of all possible paradigms, the human body supplied the model of unity. For just as the breath, driven up and down by pneuma, can be described as continuously flowing between the two internal seas of the body, stimulating and animating the organs of perception, so too perceptual reality in general can be defined as a condition of agitated energy *between* mind and matter: ὑλε ↔ κινησις ↔ νοος (*hyle* ↔ *kinesis* ↔ *noös*), what we shall call *the dynamic template of the universe.*

The visible cosmos is only a locus of disequilibrium within the totality, a sphere of light and space through which pneuma passes, the airy soul carried with it. But this passage of the soul into kinesis is just incarnation (***kinesis* = *genesis***). Hence, the embodied soul can find no rest. Sooner or later the visible cosmos must change completely from whatever stage in which the soul happens to find it. The second world, in short, must perish. There is nothing so natural as death.

If we may be so bold as to speak for Aristotle, we venture the claim that his chief grievance with modern science, were he miraculously to reappear in our midst and be schooled in its practice, would be that it ignores the trifaceted nature of reality, makes no attempt to reflect the ultimate division in its equations and calculations, but attempts rather to compress all three worlds into the second world, to which, for a priori reasons alone, it ascribes final validity.

The Greeks, and particularly Aristotle, although familiar with the principles of what we would call mechanics, placed no great importance on the subject in isolation from teleological factors. It was not until the seminal work of Roger Bacon (d. ca. 1294)—well into what might be called the age of perceptual science—that purely mechanical phenomena came to be considered worthy of scrutiny in and of their own right and without regard to a priori reasoning about what was and was not "proper" behavior for material systems. Whereas a sense of propriety is cognitive and emotive, mechanics is preeminently perceptual. It relies on concepts derived from analogies with the senses: hearing, to some extent seeing, above all on balancing, which is a form of touching. Hence mechanics requires experiment crucially, procedures apprehended immediately in perception.

* With the exception of Aristotle's first cause, the "unmoved mover."

Because of its perceptual biases, the scientific outlook treats individual subjects as having absolute validity. Science makes subjects into objects and grants them independence from any nonobjective whole; but to do so it must also grant to objects irreducible properties: mass, length, charge, and others. All else becomes, ugh, metaphysics.

Under the right conditions the aboriginal state of consciousness could be experienced anew. And yet historically that does not occur. Functionally our senses have grown increasingly divorced from each other with the passage of time. Perception has become fragmented, its unity elusive, even uncomfortable. The average *phenomenal locus* of experience has risen in the spinal column. More and more we have become absorbed in our minds.

It is inevitable, however, that perceptualism run its appointed course in the development of the nervous system and science return to a metaphysical outlook. The evolution of a concept of *energy*, for example, to the stage of technique where the hamiltonian (energy) function is central to physics, is a revival of the idea of a changeless, conserved substratum of reality so dear to Aristotle's heart. Humanity is entering into a Cognitive Age when "oceanic" concepts, modified in light of what has been learned during the last twenty-seven hundred years, once more dominate scientific thinking.

◆◆◆

Whatever reason the soul has for incarnating, it is to be found in the seeds, the archæ, already dormant in the mystic seas:

> *And Night bore frightful Doom and the black Ker,*
> *And Death and Sleep, and the whole tribe of Dreams.*
> *Again,* although she slept with none of the gods,
> *Dark Night gave birth to Blame and sad Distress.**

* Hesiod, *Theogony*, 211–14, emphasis added.

Night is Nyx, which reduces to *nk*. The aboriginal darkness she describes is reminiscent of the Sufic notion that the ultimate reality is not white light but black light. Her parthenogeneses produced all the ills of the world. From her own dark womb they emerged. The only god with whom she mates is Erebus, in Hesiod's second theogony.† Erebus, whose name means "that which is covered," in other words, "darkness," is simply another variation on Night herself. So we again have parthenogenesis. Before Nyx was Chaos, that which moved and in so doing precipitated the creation. Within Nyx, then, there must already have been the seeds of corporeality.‡ Her very name reinforces the presumption: *k* veiled by *n*. The final question is how did the seeds come to be lodged in her womb.

Our model for natural philosophy is organic. Because they are seeds, which ripen into likenesses of themselves, experiential seeds must be other experiences. In parmenidean terms: "From being only being, from nonbeing only nonbeing." From experience only experience, never nonexperience. An experiencing process can only become another experiencing process, never a nonexperiencing process. In extremis, it is a kind of sleep: "And Death and Sleep, and the whole tribe of Dreams," a marvelous line that is worth rendering in the original: *"kai Thanaton, teke d'hypnon, etikte de phylon Oneiron."* The sequence of *n*s in the proper nouns—a well-considered trope called parachresis—fairly jumps off the page. The sequence they describe is deep within us. From death, which is *thanatos* (*n*, an unpronounceable sound, not an unimaginable nothingness) comes sleep, *hypnos* (*n*, the anaractic whine of the third world), and from sleep comes the tribe of dreams, *oneiræ* (*n*, the transmogrifications of cognition). Death. Sleep. Dream. The soul redescends into matter. The dream becomes reality, a locus of experience governed by the "ruthless, avenging Fates," whose birth Hesiod records four lines

† The episode parallels Genesis 1:5; the emergence of Nyx from Chaos is at least contemporaneous with Gæa's creation.

‡ Nyx is a fecund aspect of Chaos.

later. When the soul leaves the body, pneuma—now better described as *logos*—creates a new visible cosmos patterned on the death dream.

The Hindus claim that at the moment of death, the soul withdraws into the heart, its telos. Leaving the body, the dreaming soul falls into a deep sleep, called death, which is to say, it hears thanatos (n), then it sleeps, then it dreams. The sequence is unbounded. Birth succeeds death and death succeeds birth. Between is dream, an illusion that grips the soul fatally, which carries into rebirth the traces of its oneiric fantasy: transiency, impermanence, instability, in a word, kinesis (kn). The seed is sown anew.

Plato referred to the process we are describing as *metempsychosis*, "transmigration of the soul." It was central to his philosophy and particularly prominent in one of his most important dialogues, the *Phædo*, where Socrates, about to die, takes leave of his disciples (including Plato) and describes the afterlife. Pythagoras too taught metempsychosis and according to Empedocles could recall twenty of his previous incarnations. It was an essential part of the orphic mysteries, an Eastern-influenced species of hellenistic mysticism. Ovid's *Metamorphoses* preserves many variants of the doctrine in literary form. There are clear indications of it in Homer—not so clear in early Christianity (when it was exoterically understood as the resurrection of the dead) except among gnostic sects. Yet for reasons not absolutely clear, it disappeared as an acceptable belief of Western religion.

It may be time to reinstate it.

For here is the answer to our final question: The soul incarnates because it has disincarnated—if that is not too unlovely a word. *It is born because it has died.* Because, moreover, of the way it has died: through sleep, through dream. *It must die because it has been born.* Each person must pay the price of birth. Kinesis must reach telos, *tl*, the stage in the respiratory cycle when the air has left the lungs, the chest emptied and sunk.* Just as assuredly kinesis must then come to arche. Finally, from telos, via arche, kinesis is reborn, the stage of breath when the lungs are expanding, the air flowing in the nares, stimulating the eyes, the ears, all the senses and the mind. The aspiration of perception is described phonically by *kh*,† the root of *arche*, also part of *Achilles*, who hides in his tent, his mother's undersea grotto, with his Myrmidons (mrt) before rising to assault the Walls of Troy.

In occult science the soul cannot die; namely, by its nature it must always be conscious of *something*. Yet it cannot cease reincarnating until the reservoir of karmas is exhausted and that something is (full awareness of) the ātman. Then, according to yoga, the cycle of birth and death is broken and kaivalya attained. A practical struggle to control the birth-death cycle has guided the ethical structure of all religions with proprioceptive origins, which is to say, every major religion of the world, from animism to Judeo-Christianity. The assertion must be justified of course. But it is so fundamental to religious formation that we may do so most directly if we take it to be an axiom and investigate deductively how it is true:

Axiom V: The ethical component of an archaic mythicoreligious system derives from the attempt to control reincarnation.

We can describe religion, as did Frazer, as the gradual investing of myth with overt ethical significance. The narrative structure of myth may—and usually does—persist as a religion develops, but it will become increasingly allegorical. Allegory is watered-down esoterica. Allegory alone cannot sustain religious belief. The vacuum is inevitably filled by a morality, which, we hasten to add, has been there all along but now assumes an importance by omission, as it were, of proprioception.

Before continuing, however, further instances of the reincarnational themes of mythology must be demonstrated.

* Cf., *Ætolia* = *tl*, the proper name applied to Greece *north* of the Gulf of Corinth, the first world of sacred geography.

† The Greek letter for this sound is χ (chi), which is the shape of a cross, the nexus being the second world; the image of a nail driven there was used by Christianity.

17

THE MYSTERIES OF ELEUSIS

Demeter is a goddess not much involved in legend. Her Latin name is Ceres, which reduces to *kr*, and she is the guardian of the arts of agriculture. She is almost certainly a Greek elaboration of a Pelasgian earth goddess. The lessons in husbandry she gave to Triptolemus are an esoteric reference to the sowing of experiential seed. We can therefore expect her to be intimately involved in myths dealing with reincarnation if, in fact, any exist. The story of Erysichthus and the Oak of Demeter is a likely candidate.

Erysichthus, a son of Myrmidon, lived in Thessaly with his only daughter, Mæstra. He lacked wood for the construction of his banquet hall. Though warned not to by the goddess herself, he cut down an oak sacred to Demeter. At once he was consumed by a ravenous appetite. Nothing could satiate it, though he ate night and day. He grew thin and weak, unable to provide for himself, and took to selling his magical daughter, Mæstra, for a livelihood. Mæstra, as it happened, possessed the power of assuming various animal shapes, a gift from Poseidon. After a while she would desert her new owner and return to Erysichthus, who would then sell her under another form, there being, presumably, no end to them.*

As his misfortunes suggest, Erysichthus's dilemma is representative of the woes that follow unbridled indulgence in the senses, particularly that of taste. Sensory desires, then, are the seeds sown by Erysichthus, which is why the symbolism of a child is so appropriate. When Erysichthus chops down Demeter's oak he reaps the punishment for his sins. The sense of taste links him to the first world, as do the facts that his father was Myrmidon and his homeland Thessaly. In several important respects, he is a corrupt variation on Achilles, who also was a Thessalian (from Phthia) and led the Myrmidons to Troy. Erysichthus is sometimes called Æthon, which means "blazing" or "fiery"; Achilles is likened by Homer to a "devouring conflagration." When Achilles, as the personification of meditative breathing

* *Bulfinch's Mythology*, ed. E. Fuller (New York, 1962), pp. 138–41.

arising in the chest, hurls himself at the Walls of Troy (represented by Hector) and knocks them down, we are reminded of the meaning of Erysichthus's name: "earth tearer." Achilles has no magical daughter (though he does have a son, Neoptolemus), and so the comparison ends.

Metaphorically it is not unusual to speak of the soul as being "wed" to this or that type of experience. The myth of the WEDDING OF PSYCHE AND AMOR is a famous example. The gender of the Greek word *psyche* is feminine; Erysichthus' child is a female. Mæstra's transformations describe different incarnations of the soul through which it gratifies different desires, presented in the myth as theriomorphisms: a horse (respiration), ox (hearing), bird (sight), and stag (smell). It is through Poseidon's intervention that Mæstra is allowed to change her shape. Poseidon is not only ardent perception but also the "lord of horses." His role in the myth emphasizes that it is the impulse to breathe, to animate the senses by means of the breath, that guides metempsychosis.

In another myth Demeter has an uncharacteristically passionate dalliance with Jasion the Cretan. She lay with him in a thrice-plowed field and and gave birth to *Plutus,* "wealth." As is obvious from his name, Jasion is the breath. The THRICE-PLOWED FIELD is the space between the brows, the same region of the cranium represented on Doric temple friezes by a triglyph.* The esoteric sense of Plutus is debatable. His name of course relates him to Pluto, the Latin Hades. He seems to symbolize the deadly—yet ample—harvest of experience that results when karmic seed is sown by means of the breath, what Christianity calls "sinning in spirit." At the Judgment of Paris, Hera offers Paris wealth, so perhaps the meaning of Plutus comes down to the sense of touch, by which material goods are directly possessed.

The only other myth—easily her most important legend because it is linked with the founding of the Eleusinian mysteries—in which Demeter plays a significant role is the Rape of Persephone. The Mysteries of Eleusis were the holiest rites of the pagan world. What we now seek to understand is how much of the reverence accorded the Eleusinia is a consequence of practical instruction afforded the initiates in techniques for controlling reincarnation.

Concerning the great antiquity of the Eleusinian mysteries there can be no argument. Modern scholarship places the date of their origin in the second half of the fifteenth century B.C., when Erechtheus was king in Athens.† We know that by the eighth century B.C., an era of great social disquiet in Greece, a large earthen terrace had been constructed, and that the trouble and expense involved in building it could only have been justified by the existence of a popular cult of great antiquity.‡ It is likely that the Eleusinia were a Greek incorporation of Pelasgian rites of the dead. The earliest written account of any substance is the *Homeric Hymn to Demeter* (author unknown):

And rich-crowned Demeter . . . made fruit to
Spring up from the rich lands, so that
The whole wide earth was laden with leaves
And flowers. Then she went, and to the
Kings who deal justice, Triptolemus and
Diocles, the horse-driver, and to doughty
Eumolpus and Celeus, leader of the people,
She showed the conduct of her rites and
Taught them all her mysteries, to Triptolemus

* Jasion's Cretan origin places the myth in the second world. Diodorus Siculus makes Jasion a Titan, also second world.

† Mylonas, *Eleusis and the Eleusinian Mysteries*, p. 14.

‡ "Hymn to Demeter," in: *The Homeric Hymns*, 2d ed., T. W. Allen, W. R. Halliday, and E. E. Sikes, eds. (Oxford, 1936), p. 111.

And Polyxenus and Diocles also—awful
Mysteries which no one may in any way
Transgress or pry into or utter, for deep
Awe of the gods checks the voice.
Happy is
He among men upon earth who has seen these
Mysteries; but he who is uninitiate and who
Has no part in them, never has lot of like
Good things once he is dead, down in the
*Darkness and gloom.**

The injunction to secrecy was absolute. At the beginning of the secret part of the ceremonies, the herald of the Eleusinian cult, the Hieroceryx, presiding over a solemn congregation of the *mystæ* (those to be initiated), administered an oath of silence to all present.† A breach was punishable by death—which does not mean that it never happened. Æschylus nearly perished of indiscretion. Other famous entrants into the *telesterion*, the "hall of the mysteries" (< Gk. *telos*, "goal" or "finis"), include Socrates, Plato, Aristotle (very probably), Pausanias, and Alcibiades. Plutarch was an initiate. So were Sophocles, Euripedes, and Aristophanes, and among famous Romans, Cicero, Horace, and the emperor Hadrian. The time frame of the list, which could easily be lengthened by dozens of names, is several centuries, from Sophocles at the beginning of the fifth century B.C. to Plutarch (fl. A.D. 100); and even further, for we know that the Emperor Marcus Aurelius and his roguish son Commodus were initiated towards the end of the second century A.D. If we add the period of time extending back to the supposed establishment of Demeter's cult at Eleusis, we come up with something over sixteen hundred years. Even granting that the Greater Mysteries were celebrated but once a year—in the autumn—the number of people who passed through the portals of the telesterion during that time must have been enormous.

Nor would it be correct to give the impression that only the illustrious or the learned were candidates for initiation. True to the Athenian spirit, the Eleusinia were open to all: men, women, children, even slaves (with the exception of the earliest epoch of the cult, when non-Greeks were barred). Nevertheless, the polity of Eleusis was a satellite of Athens, and the mysteries were, in a real sense, the responsibility of the Athenians.

Because the compelling myth of the Eleusinian rites was the abduction of Persephone (Demeter's daughter) by Hades (t), the mysteries were essentially a first-world myth or, at least, a first-and-second-world myth and complementary with the Rape of Ægina, in which myth Ægina is forcibly taken by Zeus to the isle of Œnone, namely, the third world. Persephone is never addressed by name in the mysteries, only as the Corē (< Gk. *koure*, "the maid"), which reduces to *kr*, bringing out not only her second-world origins but also her role as the personification of cosmic seed: the child that grows between the first world of the mother and the third world of the father. Her father is Zeus, which presents no difficulties; but we have already speculated that her mother, Demeter, is a second-world goddess.

It would be nice if the name Demeter derived from *meter*, "mother," as at first glance it would seem to. But the word *Demeter* is probably not Greek. If it is a Greek word, it may derive from *gedera*, "peninsula" or "isthmus."‡ Very old citadel cults of Demeter existed at Thebes and Megara, both of which lie in the medial plane of sacred geography and quite near to the Corinthian isthmus.§ A citadel is a fortress, the defining myth of which is the Walls of Troy. Of all the gods and goddesses in the Greek pantheon, the one most often shown in

* *Homeric Hymn to Demeter*, 470–82, in: H. W. E. White, *Hesiod and the Homeric Hymns.*

† Possibly the same *diathematos*, "oath," was extracted from the mystæ of the Cabiri on Samothrace; see Cole, *Theoi Megaloi: The Cult of the Great Gods*, pp. 36–37.

‡ "Hymn to Demeter," in: Allen et al., *The Homeric Hymns*, p. 115; Stephanus of Byzantium is cited for the etymology of *Demeter*.

§ Ibid., p. 124, n. 4. Thebes = Troy.

art wearing a literal crown—as opposed to laurel wreathes, ivy garlands, helmets, and so on—is Demeter. The crown, we have noted, denotes the second-third world boundary, adding to the confusion. Finally, Homer seems unaware that there is any connection whatsoever between Demeter and Persephone. The latter is merely the wife of Hades in his poems.

A way out of the dilemma would be to posit that Demeter links the first and second worlds in the same way that a stalk joins the roots of a plant to its seed-bearing blossom, a metaphor particularly suited to her by virtue of Demeter's explicit agricultural connections in myth. Demeter is the earth both in its depths and at the surface. Demeter thus describes what might colloquially be referred to as the "desires of the heart."

How does the heart come to bear the marks of karma? And how, through meditation, can the "marks" (saṃskāras) be erased? Yoga interprets the health of the heart—or lack of it—as the manifestation of the soul's desires. In the *Gītā*, Kṛṣṇa refers to the literal heart in a person and describes how the practice of yoga can physically alter it:

Yoga purifies
The man of meditation,
Bringing him soon to brahman.
When the heart is made pure by that
yoga,
When the body is obedient,
When the senses are mastered,
When man knows that his ātman
Is the ātman in all creatures,
Then let him act,
*Untainted by action.**

Elsewhere Kṛṣṇa says:

Not hoping, not lusting,
Bridling body and mind,
He calls nothing his own:
He acts and earns no evil. . . .
When the bonds are broken
His illumined heart
Beats in brahman.†

We might add:

My heart is fixed, O God, my heart is fixed: I will sing and give praise.‡

The Sanskrit word for "heart" is *hṛdaḥ*, which (applying Grimm's law) becomes *kardia* in Greek, *Herz* in German, and *cor* in Latin. The purification of the heart is the purging from it of *krt*, the melting of it into *brmn*, a blissful high-pitched hum that can be propriocepted in the thorax. Taken literally it means a neurological transformation of the heart, an alteration not of the nerves, their number and placement (such is an impossibility), but of the manner in which they function. Yet short of performing autopsies on the hearts of deceased yogis,§ it is impossible to verify such an inference. If our hypothesis were correct, such experiments should reveal a marked lack of necrosis in the cardiac tissue, a smoothness in the muscles, an absence of arterial occlusions. All those symptoms would attest to the purging of karmas which is the aim of yoga.

The Greater Mysteries (Eleusinia) were preceded in the spring by the Lesser Mysteries (Antheria)—primarily lustral and prefatory to the Eleusinia—which included a bath in the river Ilissus (ls). Anyone guilty of homicide or sacrilege had to participate in the Antheria. The Antheria have been persistently neglected by scholars of the mysteries. Because they involved a ritual bath, however, a supposition can be made that they were the first, crucial initiation, the *myesis*, "closing off the senses," which was accomplished by lowering the *mystes* into water.

* *Bhagavad Gītā*, in Prabhavananda and Isherwood, *The Song of God*, p. 57.

† Ibid., pp. 52–53.

‡ Psalms 57:7. Cf., Jeremiah 4:4: "Be circumcised in your hearts"; the heart is *cut* by yoga, a literal pain is felt when the karmas are removed.

§ Whether unfortunate or no, yoga; prescribes immediate cremation.

It would have been his or her first experience of the inner world. Otherwise we are at a loss to explain why, even before they have reached Eleusis, the participants are already called "mystæ." The Eleusinia would then be a further stage of initiation.*

On the day before the Eleusinian celebration proper began, certain revered objects known as the *hiera* of Demeter, whose exact nature is unknown—and the source of endless speculation on which we hope to shed some light—were taken by the Eleusinian priesthood to Athens from the *anactoron*, a cavelike holy of holies within the telesterion. When the processional arrived in Athens, the hiera were brought at once to a special sanctuary below the Acropolis known as the Eleusinion. An honorary messenger, the *phæthyntes* of Eleusis, was then sent up to the Parthenon to herald the arrival of Demeter in Athens.

The time set aside for the actual celebration was nine days, from the fifteenth to the twenty-third of the month of Bœdromion in the Greek calendar or roughly from the autumnal equinox to the first of October in ours. The timing marks the mysteries as a harvest festival and supports the hypothesis that they were bound up with ideas of karma, fate, and metempsychosis. The first four days were spent entirely at Athens and were given over to a curious combination of revelry and lustration.

On the first day, the *archon-basileus* of Athens, who functions throughout the celebration as a sort of master of ceremonies, summoned the people to the *agora* (the marketplace). It is fitting that a festival that depicts the freeing of the soul from karma should begin among the merchants, where what matters is that what is owed is paid and what is paid is owed. *Agora* reduces to *kr*, the second world, the arena of karma, the space between the seas of birth and death. The assembling of the multitude there announces that the mystæ approach the goddess as sinners.

The second day was known as the *elasis*. At the shout of "To the sea, O Mystæ!"† those citizens who desired initiation and who met a few not-very-stringent requirements‡ betook themselves to the shore for a purificatory bath. Each carried a sacrificial pig. The pig, as we've seen, is a theriomorphism for the breath. Pigs were sacred to Apollo and at Eleusis, in Demeter's own precincts, pigs were sacrificed at the time the telesterion was erected.§

When the mystæ ritually washed themselves, their pigs under their arms, they did so in the Saronic Gulf, the expanse of blue water west of Athens and toward the Bay of Eleusis, an arm of the Ægean. *Saronic* reduces to *sn* and is the first of several proper names associated with the mysteries that have a phonic structure suggesting respiration. Most important is Eleusis itself, located on a bay of the same name and overlooking the narrows at Salamis (slm), where the ebb and flow of currents is strong and perhaps mimes the flow of breath into the frontal sinus.# *Elasis* derives from a word meaning to cleanse. Like *Eleusis*, *elasis* reduces to *ls*, what might be called the clear sound of the purified breath, also the root of the Greek verb *lythein*, "to loosen," the word used in the manumission of slaves.** Prāṇāyāma entails more than control of the breath; it also means cleansing by and of the breath, because it is in the breath that the effects of karma are manifested. To undo kleśas, the breath must be purified by making it steady and smooth.

The pigs were sacrificed at the end of the second day—the Greeks marked the turn of the day at sundown, so the pigs were actually killed on the third day—foreshadowing the events of the next day, when a general sacrifice on behalf

* Greek words used again and again in the Eleusinian literature: *myesis* is the first stage of initiation; *mystes* means one who has undergone myesis; *mystæ* is plural for *mystes*.

† *Halade mystæ!*

‡ E.g., not committing a homicide within the past year.

§ Mylonas, *Eleusis and the Eleusinian Mysteries*, n. 125, p. 249.

Indeed, the trickiness of the current allowed the Athenians to devastate the Persian armada of 480 B.C.

** In describing Heracles' freeing of Prometheus from Mount Caucusus (= karma), the verb Apollodorus uses is *eleuse*, "set loose"; cf., Elysium, the Greek paradise.

of the whole city of Athens took place. The significance of a sacrifice on the third day indicates that it is the second world that is being immolated: the second world comprises three principal avenues of experience, the last of which (to follow the exoteric order of the zodiac) is smell or breath.* The rite is akin to the Latin Suovetaurilia celebrated at the end of May, in the third month of the Julian calendar, when the sacred *ager romanus*, the "Roman field," was purified by burnt offerings of a ram, a bull, and a boar.

The fourth day was known as the Asclepæa, in honor of the god Asclepius, the source of healing power in Greek myth. Apollo was the father of Asclepius, whose presence in the mysteries reflects the rejuvenative power of the breath: its ability to undo kleśas, the root of which, *kls*, is found in the god's name. His retinue included the goddess Hygea (health), an aspiration of *k*, and Jaso (s) (healing). Homer mentions two sons, Machaön and Podalirius, surgeons both, who repair the wounds of Achæan heroes throughout the *Iliad*. In the tradition behind the mysteries, Asclepius arrived too late from his shrine at Epidaurus to take part in the general sacrifice and so, for his benefit, it was reenacted on the fourth day. The Asclepæa was a comparatively late addition to the ritual of Eleusis; the worship of Asclepius at Athens was not introduced until Periclean times (ca. 420 B.C.). To interpret it proprioceptively is thus a cautious matter. We can expect that, whatever aboriginal meaning attaches to Asclepius, it will be found at Eleusis in a less than clear-cut form.†

The question remains: For what reasons did Asclepius come to be associated with the fourth day of the mysteries? We must first take into account rites occurring on that day in the historical epoch prior to his formal inclusion in the celebration. All the evidence suggests that it was a day of rest. The mystæ were required to remain at home while latecomers to the festival were ritually cleansed.

The presiding magistrate of the fourth day was not the archon-basileus of Athens but the *archon-eponymus*. A shadowy official, the archon-eponymus oversaw the *patria*, rites related to the ancestral religion of the city.‡ The whole idea of ancestry must be evaluated from an esoteric perspective. The word itself simply means "what has gone before" (< L. *antecedere*). Ancestors are a part of the procreative chain, therefore are efficient causes. It is not too speculative to suppose that symbolically they represent the sources of karmic seed, the archæ. Ancestor worship is extremely important in primitive religious practice of our own era. Just as the Olympians of Greece were often frantically involved in the affairs of mortals, the spirits of ancestors take an active part in the lives of modern primitives, approving, disapproving, making known their wishes through omens such as dreams and the behavior of animals. A belief in metempsychosis is also common among primitives, though in a much more truncated form than is found, say, among Hindus. Often, for example, it is believed that this or that person's soul has gone into an animal body or into a plant (a tree is a not unusual destination) but has then returned to the original human body after a while. Or else it is thought that, although it is true for some, reincarnation is not always the case at death. Paradise exists. So does Hell.§ But in all instances there is another life somewhere.

Belief in an ancestral spirit, which lived with the tribe in corporeal form and now lives with it spiritually, accords with reincarnation. The heart of animism—the sole recognizable religion

* Breath = swine = Apollo, one of the Twins or Gemini, the third sign of the Chaldean zodiac; the hesiodic connection of a mythic day to a sign of the zodiac has already been discussed.

† Also true of Dionysus, a latecomer to the Greek pantheon, yet one who is frequently mentioned in the secondary literature as having a connection to the Eleusinia. The connection can only be that he is a first-world god.

‡ Mylonas, *Eleusis and the Eleusinian Mysteries*, p. 251.

§ Hinduism also recognizes an incorporeal afterlife short of kaivalya; their heaven is called *svarga* and defines an intermediate—probably oneiric—state between death and rebirth, which always follows.

among most primitives—is that soul or awareness may dwell anywhere. There is a soul in the human body of course; but there is one in a dog too. There is a spirit in a house, in a tool, in a grove of trees, even in stones. The flux of consciousness is multiform. In such religions the ancestors are very much alive and ever among their offspring. The continuity of an individual with his past, including his ancestors, is intimately bound up with his own identity. We hypothesize that ancestor worship is a vestige of the doctrine of metempsychosis: An ancestor is a description of a previous life of the soul.

The ritual sacrifices of the fourth day, centered around the figure of Asclepius, describe the extirpation of the deeper karmas within the soul, those deriving from forgotten lifetimes symbolized by the ancestors. It was not until long after homeric times that the idea of blood guilt, that is, the belief that the onus of an individual's deeds rested not only with the individual but with his or her heirs, was supplanted by a standard of justice that limited itself to the perpetrator of a crime. Vengeance could be wreaked and recompense given down all the generations of the Greek *œkos*, a word meaning "household," the collection of kin, retainers, and slaves living under the same roof.*

The fourth sign of the ancient zodiac is Cancer, a water sign ruled by the moon. Astrologically Cancer is the sign of the Great Mother, the chthonic goddess who held sway in prehellenic (Pelasgian) religion and before the arrival of the Olympians. Each zodiacal sign exercises a kind of sovereignty over particular aspects of life. Cancer is associated with the home, mother, nurturing, and the like; but it is also explicitly linked to memory and more importantly to ancestry, to the origins of body and soul.† We have speculated that the mystæ had already been initiated into prāṇāyāma at the Antheria. If so, they were ordered to stay at home on the fourth day to practice what they had learned. It was a foreshadowing of what was to come when the celebration returned to Eleusis, when, via the breath, they would descend into the first world, find the Corē who had been forced to wed Hades, and restore her to her mother.

The compulsion of rape is a recapitulation of the stone that repeatedly forces Sisyphus back down into Tartarus: the necessity to respire that results in reincarnation. Persephone was not then free of the underworld (any more than yoga is an absolute dispensation from exhalation). Because Persephone ate the five seeds of a pomegranate Hades cleverly offered her, Zeus, after consulting the Moiræ, decided that she must live with Hades for one third of the year. The pomegranate is an esoteric description of the heart itself (a cross section of the heart resembles a cross section of a pomegranate, which is full of blood-red seeds).‡ The rest of the year Persephone lived with her mother and father: a third with Demeter and a third with Zeus.

The fifth day of the mysteries was known as *pompe*, which literally means a departure, the leaving of the second world. Crowned with myrtle (Gk. *myron*), the mystæ were led by the *ephebes* of Athens through the Dipylon Gate in a brilliant processonal back to Eleusis, some fourteen miles away. Dipylon Gate means the "double gate," possibly a veiled reference to the nostrils. It was oriented to the northwest, the direction of Eleusis but also, in sacred geography, the directions associated with respiration and the lower world. The whole procession was led by a donkey.§

* M. I. Finley, *The World of Odysseus* (New York, 1976), pp. 74–113. Cf., Exodus 20:5: "I the Lord thy God am a jealous God, visiting the iniquity of the fathers upon the children unto the third and fourth generation of them that hate me."

† The moon was Selene, a third-world goddess and so linked to memory. Cancer, the Crab, is perceptual touch, but originally the fourth sign was *procyon*, "the swallow," a bird that feathers its nest in the eaves of houses, often above the lintel of a doorway; lintels describe the brow line.

‡ The cult statue of Hera at Argos—after Samos, her most sacred shrine—shows her holding a pomegranate. Hera is the preeminent first-world goddess. The fruit in the Garden of Eden that leads to the Fall is likely the heart as well.

§ Aristophanes, *Frogs*, 159; cited in: Mylonas, *Eleusis and the Eleusinian Mysteries*, p. 252.

What is known of the pompe squares with an esoteric interpretation in which the mystæ are symbolically following the breath into the first world. But not the breath alone: The procession was led by a priest known as the Jacchagogus, so called because he was entrusted with the care of the statue of Jacchus, a mysterious god associated with the Eleusinia. His temple was known as the Jacchion, hard by the Dipylon Gate. The statue of Jacchus was crowned with myrtle and a torch, placed in a carriage drawn by an ass, and led the procession all the way to Eleusis. *Jacchus* (kh) is an aspiration of *k*. Once the mystæ arrived at Eleusis, Jacchus's role in the celebration came to an end,* though all along the Sacred Way hymns were sung to him. The Athenians believed that the benevolence of Jacchus contributed to the defeat of the Persians at the Battle of Salamis, in the narrows leading into the Saronic Gulf that we've already associated with the flow of the breath.† More important is that Jacchus suggests Hermes, the psychopomp, who leads the soul to judgment in Hades. Hermes describes the *death dream,* the cognitive-emotive condition of the dying soul. It is precisely the death dream that must be overcome; thus, once the pompe has arrived at Eleusis, Jacchus must go.

Early in the Mysteries of the Cabiri on Samothrace, the initiates poured libations into a pit within the temenos but outside the telesterion.‡ There was also a well at Eleusis called the *callichoron*, the well of "the lovely dance." It was at the callichoron well that Demeter rested when she arrived in Eleusis looking for Persephone, but its role in the Eleusinia is not known. Because it is outside the telesterion, it might have been the place where an extinguishing of torches occurred.

Behind the Jacchagogus were the *panageis*, "all holy [priestesses of Demeter]," bearing the hiera upon their heads. Next came the officials of Attica: the archon-basileus and others. Bringing up the rear were the mystæ themselves, each carrying a sacred wand made from myrtle boughs and known as a *bacchos* or thrysus, which we have already identified with the spinal cord plus midbrain. (The Romans took the name Bacchus—their Dionysus—from the wands.)

The procession moved slowly into the nearby hills, passing a sacred fig tree. A wild fig tree also marked the Scæan Gate, the Gate of Troy built by Æacus. Eleusis is on the water, so at some point the procession had to begin its descent to the sea. That occurred, appropriately enough, in a defile where stood the Sanctuary of Apollo, the god who perhaps more than any other points the way to first-world respiration. His shrine was sited there, according to legend, on instructions from the Delphic oracle, which prophesied that sacrifice should be made to Apollo at the place where a galley should be seen running on dry land. No such miracle was observed, as it happened, but two devotees, Chalcinus and Dion, saw a snake hastening into its hole at the foot of Mount Pœcilon; deciding that was omen enough, they built a temple on the spot. The snake is a theriomorphism for the first world and was sacred to Dionysus(= Dion). The image of a galley with its rhythmically moving oars is a not unnatural description of respiration.§ The eager substitution of a snake omen for a galley is therefore not surprising.

The next landmark of any prominence that the mystæ passed was a shrine to Aphrodite, very close to the seashore. Aphrodite is the principal goddess of the second world and synonymous with the pleasures of the senses. The intersection of the Sacred Way with her shrine recapitulates the departure from the second world that the pompe describes. The siting of her temple, virtually on the beach, suggests Aphrodite's birth in the foam just above the waves.

The pompe then moved immediately to the coast and followed it closely to where the road is squeezed between the Bay of Eleusis and the Rhetian Lakes. At that point it was necessary for the mystæ to cross a narrow bridge that was

* Mylonas, *Eleusis and the Eleusinian Mysteries*, p. 257.

† Ibid., p. 255.

‡ Cole, *Theoi Megaloi: The Cult of the Great Gods of Samothrace*, p. 31.

§ Central to the myth of Jason and the Argonauts.

deliberately kept to a width of under five feet to prevent wheeled vehicles from crossing.* An obvious surmise is that the precaution heightens the symbolism of the narrow suture between the frontal sinuses, where the breath turns downward on its way to the lungs. A curious ceremony known as the *krokosis* (< Crocus, the legendary first dweller in the territory) occurred when the initiates crossed. A saffron-colored ribbon was tied around the right hand and the left leg of each. Saffron is a second-world color associated with Eos (Dawn). *Krokosis* reduces to *kr*, a second-world phon. The binding of the initiates suggests the same constrictive proprioception that the bridge describes.

What, then, is the meaning of the crossing of another bridge over the river Cephisus, which the mystæ reached just before entering Eleusis? Is it a recapitulation? Does it describe another phase of the inner journey? Or does it mean nothing in particular? After all, the mystæ had to get into Eleusis somehow. The last alternative is unlikely because the crossing of the Cephisus was also marked by a special ceremony. As the initiates passed silently over the bridge, men with covered heads hurled insults at the notables among them. The jibes were intended to humble the mystæ; in other words they were apotropaic formulas, akin to "knocking on wood" in function. There is also the phonics of *Cephisus* to account for. Applying Grimm's law gives the etymology *kephisus* < *khephisus* < *hephisus*, similar to *Hephæstus*, first-world breathing.† From the bridge, the procession entered the temenos, the sanctuary of Demeter and the Corē. The sixth day of the mysteries, the *teletē*, was about to begin.

The teletē, as the name suggests, was the final goal of the initiates. Everything known about the Eleusinia up until the time the mystæ arrived in the temenos, whether from literary sources or artifacts, can be accepted as more or less factual because the mysteries themselves had not yet begun. The mystæ were still in the dark, so to speak, regarding what was to come. As to what happened after the time of entry into the temenos around sundown on the fifth day, not only is testimony scanty, confused, and contradictory, but it is for the most part pure inference or—what is worse—supposition and especially subject to esoteric interpretation. Pagan initiates were absolutely enjoined from discussing the mysteries. We have deliberately reticent testimony from Pindar (*Fragmenta* 102: "Happy is he who, having seen those rites, goes below the hollow earth"), Sophocles (*Fragmenta* 719: "Thrice happy are those mortals, who, having seen those rites, descend to Hades"), and Aristotle (*Art of Rhetoric* 48: "They suffered [initiation], not because they needed to learn anything, but to feel the soul"); indirect references in Aristophanes' *Frogs*, Euripides' *Heracles*, and Æschylus's *Iphigenia* and *Sisyphus* (the latter not extant and not sufficiently indirect, for the play almost got him torn limb from limb until he took refuge on the altar of Dionysus); mere asides from worldly pagans such as Athenæus (fl. A.D. 200) and Pausanias (d. ca. A.D. 176) and Neoplatonists such as Porphyry (b. A.D. 233) and Proclus; extensive commentary in Plutarch (d. ca. A.D. 120); and a

* Mylonas, *Eleusis and the Eleusinian Mysteries*, pp. 255–56; it was later widened.

† The Cephisus was also the site of the temple of Themis, the Titaness and spouse of Japetus, both of whom are anthropomorphisms of the bones of the nose. *Themis* = *th* (*m* is intervocalic); she is much associated with Theseus (th) in myth. In certain authors it is Themis who preordains the Fall of Troy, drawing attention yet again to the esoteric connection between the breath and fate: the breath animates sensory desire but also, through prāṇāyāma, destroys desire (karma). Themis also figures in the myth of Deucalion, a Phthian and the Greek Noah. Deucalion was the son of Prometheus, who warned him of the coming Flood when Deucalion visited his father on Mount Caucasus. After the deluge Themis instructed Deucalion to throw stones over his shoulder, whence men sprang up from the ground to repopulate the earth. The motion of the stones suggests the myth of Sisyphus: the breath is esoterically described as a stone to be moved about during prāṇāyāma. There is also a subtle use of contiguity. Deucalion throws stones over his shoulder; yet what is "over his shoulder" is just his shrouded head. As with Sisyphus the breath is being raised into the cranium. Although we have no explicit reference to the breath as a plow here, the myth seems clearly related to that of Jason, who plows the Field of Ares—the space between the eyes—to create armed assailants: anthropomorphisms of kleśas.

crucially important remark in Themistius of Paphlagonia (d. ca. A.D. 388). The only literary sources that have the temerity to suggest actual occurrences within the teletē are early Christian writers, whose primary aim was to discredit and even to ridicule the Eleusinia, among them Clement of Alexandria (b. A.D. 150), the African deacon Tertullian (fl. A.D. 197), the Roman presbyter Hippolytus (fl. A.D. 250), and Bishop Asterius of Amasea in Asia Minor (fl. A.D. 400).*

That granted, we know that the ceremony of the *kernophoria*, "the carrying of the *kernœ*," commenced on the night of the teletē. Kernœ was the name given to the sacred vessels brought to Eleusis by the mystæ, who now broke the partial fast imposed on them when the Eleusinia began. (Fasting, we have already noted, aids proprioception; when the alimentary canal is evacuated, unmediated visceral sensation ensues.) Their breakfast commemorated Demeter's drinking of the *kykeon*—water mixed with barley and mint—when, in the myth, she arrived at Eleusis in search of Persephone. But the kernophoria may have had an esoteric meaning as well. Athenæus tells us that "after [the kernophoria], the priest celebrates the mysteries, removes the objects from the *thalame*, and gives them to those who have *borne the kernos aloft*" (emphasis added). *Thalamus* means "wedding chamber" and not coincidentally is also the name of an important structure within the mesencephalon associated with sensual appetite, hence taste. But no sooner has Athenæus said the preceding than he feels a need to qualify it: "And he who has carried them—*that means he who has borne aloft the kernos*—tastes these things" (emphasis added).† What is the point of his periphrasis save perhaps to hint at a special meaning for "borne the kernos aloft"? The haṭha yogic technique of khecarīmudrā makes the tongue of the sādhaka supple enough to stretch far back into the throat to touch the skin above and behind the uvula with the aim of tasting the *soma* liquid. In and of itself khecarīmudrā is no more than a stretching exercise, one of many in the haṭha regimen. Combined with the practices of rāja yoga, and only within rāja yoga, it can be fully exploited to heighten proprioception of what lies above the uvula within the brain: the pineal body and, above the pineal, the thalamus. During the Mass the moment that the chalice is presented to the communicant is called the anaphora (Gk. "lifting up"). We have already identified the liturgical chalice (Holy Grail) with the stretched tongue and locked teeth of khecarimudrā; thus Christian anaphora and pagan kernophoria are esoterically equivalent.

After the kernophoria, the mystæ donned special robes brought with them to the mysteries. Again, the robes, like every other aspect of the teletē, must be carefully scrutinized. The hierophant is known to have worn special robes. Plutarch tells us that Alcibiades was condemned for "mimicking the mysteries and showing them forth to his companions in his house, wearing a robe such as the hierophant wears when he shows the sacred secrets to the initiates." The robes of the mystæ, like everything else having to do with esoteric practice, must have had a practical function. Capacious garments with many folds have long been associated with a priest class, from the *peplœ* of the hieratic maidens who carried the cistæ, down to the chasubles of Roman Catholic priests and the cowls of medieval monks. A peplus is a gown of many folds frequently rendered on statues unearthed within the temenos of Eleusis. A

* Clement, *Protrepticon* 2.12–19, in: *Clement of Alexandria*, trans. G. W. Buttersworth (London, 1968); Tertullian, *Ad naturam* 2.39; Hippolytus, *Refutatio omnium hæresium* 5.8.164, in: J. P. Migne, *Patrologia*, vol. 6 (Paris, 1846), p. 3150; Asterius, *Homilia in sanctissimos martyres*, in ibid., 60.324B; Athenæus, *Depnosophistæ* 9.56; Pausanias 1.37, in: *Pausanias: Description of Greece*, trans. W. H. S. Jones (London, 1921); Porphyry, *De abstinentia* 4.16; Proclus, *Timæus*, 293; Plutarch, *Moralia: De profecta in virtute*, and *Parallel Lives: Alcibiades*, 19–22, and *Themistocles*, 15; Themistius, *De anima*, fragment preserved by Stobæus (fl. fifth century A.D.) and quoted by Mylonas in: *Eleusis and the Eleusinian Mysteries*, p. 264.

† Mylonas, *Eleusis and the Eleusinian Mysteries*, p. 271; Athenæus quotes the Stoic philosopher Polemo (d. ca. 270 B.C.), the teacher of Zeno of Elea.

monk uses his cowl to cover his head while praying. The priest pulls the chasuble over his head at the most solemn moment of the Mass (rather, he used to before the liturgical "reforms" of the Second Vatican Council, which shows only that whatever esoteric function the chasuble once had, it is no longer understood in this century).

On two famous pieces of antique art, the Lovatelli Urn (figure 34a) and the Torre Nova Sarcophagus (figure 34b)—both made in Italy by Roman artisans of the third century A.D. but long associated with the Eleusinia by iconographers—Heracles (who is the Greek sādhaka), clearly identified by the lion skin he holds, is prepared by stages for initiation. Most interesting for our present purpose are the representations of Heracles seated with head and face completely covered by a stole.

On the Lovatelli Urn a priestess stands behind him holding a winnowing fan over his head. There are two possible interpretations: respiration and vision. A winnowing fan, of course, is used to fan the air in separating wheat from chaff. The image might be wholly symbolic: the separation of the initiated from the uninitiated. But it might also be an esoteric representation of the breath (as with the palm fronds in the myth of JESUS ENTERING JERUSALEM). The winnowing fan also introduces an image of the threshing floor. Otus and Ephialtes, the *Alœdes*, "sons of the threshing floor," were two gigantic offspring of Poseidon who made war on the gods.* The threshing floor might refer to the winnowing that takes place there. Or it might describe the air filled with golden particles of wheat, hence internal light. The Alœdes piled Mount Pelion on top of Mount Ossa to force a way into Mount Olympus and were prevented only by a wilier than was usual Artemis. In the form of a doe, she got them to cast their javelins into each other. Pelion we have already identified with the pectoral muscles of the chest; Ossa strongly suggests breathing. Artemis Cervina (i.e., "the doe") is smell, and the javelins describe the same experience as the arrows of the Bow of Artemis: the streams of breath directed at the frontal suture. A subtle internal fragrance heralds the onset of the pituitary catastrophe, during which the usurpation of experience by perception (The Alœdes) is defeated.

Otus and Ephialtes once imprisoned Ares in a bronze vessel until he nearly expired.† Again note that Heracles' face is covered, closing off the light of the second world. The seated Heracles places his bare feet on the fleece of a ram, the theriomorphism for vision. The bronze vessel, which, incidentally, they hide in the house of their stepmother, Eribœa (Gk. "many cows"), is the bones of the second world (the ark)—bronze being selected by Homer because in a myth about vision, shining bronze serves particularly well as an esoteric description.‡

In the next (clockwise) scene on the Lovatelli Urn and the Torre Nova Sarcophagus, we see Heracles being purified by ritual sacrifice.§ The urn shows him sacrificing a pig. Both the urn and sarcophagus show a priest holding a disc with three poppy stalks while pouring water from a jug—onto a fire on the Torre Nova Sarcophagus, a pig on the Lovatelli Urn. The

* *Odyssey* 11.305–20. C.f., Ruth's seduction of Boaz on the threshing floor of Bethlehem; their grandson Jesse(s) was David's father, a line that led to Joseph and Jesus (Ruth 3–4).

† *Iliad* 5.385–90. Poseidon is the ruler of the second world, and Ares is vision. His imprisonment (unto death) describes curtailment of perceptual vision, after which, because of the dynamic nature of experience, internal vision must ensue. Ares cannot really die so he is rescued by Hermes, i.e., perception.

‡ The Greek word for threshing floor is *halos* (> Eng. "halo"), the connection being the circular path trod out by the oxen (Eribœa, also a second-world figure). The myth recalls the GOLDEN VEIL OF HESIONE, breath used to propriocept the osseous "crown" of the second world (see p. 174), and Danaë and the Shower of Gold. When Themis tells Deucalion to toss stones over his shoulder, she also tells him to cover his head with a shroud (see note, p. 203). Coming right after Deucalion has emerged from the ark, the shroud recapitulates the closing off of the senses in order to "purify" them that the voyage in the ark describes.

§ Roman art often reads right to left, so the scene may be prior in the mysteries to that of the seated Heracles.

A

B

Figure 34. Detail of (A) Lovatelli Urn, (B) Torre Nova Sarcophagus three poppy stalks, like the three stalks of wheat on the cistæ, describe the tripartite innervation of the nose: trigeminal nerve plus the left and right olfactory nerves. By the principle of contiguity the water flowing from the jug and the three poppy stalks describes the same internal experience: the flow of breath, which must stop because the pig is sacrificed and the fire is extinguished, a pleonastic trope if ever there was one.

Taken as a whole—the use of special garments by monks and priests, the Lovatelli Urn, and the Torre Nova Sarcophagus—the above remarks can be interpreted to show that the esoteric function of a hieratic robe was to block from view techniques performed by the mystes to enhance concentration on internal light while controlling breathing. The indictment of a certain Andocides says only that "this man, wearing the robe and imitating the hierophant, *showed* the hiera to the uninitiated." How then, we must wonder, can the hiera be literal things, cult objects, as is generally supposed, if, as the presentment of the jury suggests, all it takes to reveal them is to wear a priestly robe? Can we possibly imagine that Andocides removed a sacred cistus, within which the hiera must have been locked in some way, from the temenos? That he broke open the lock? Such is inconceivable. In his defense, Andocides tells the judges of the Areopagus "*you have seen* the hiera of the goddesses so that you must punish the impious but save those who committed no injustice"*—enormous effrontery had he done anything so outrageous as to steal a cistus.

The precaution of wearing robes was necessary even inside the telesterion because not everyone admitted was privy to everything revealed. The initiates had to be given special permission to approach the *adyton*, loosely, "the holy of holies," the inner sanctuary or naos of a Greek temple, which at Eleusis probably was the anactoron. Until each mystes was individually initiated, he or she was still being proved by the hierophant and his assistants. Also, there were occasional interlopers. Livy tells us that two youths wandered into the temenos, wholly by accident it seems, only to be condemned and executed. Ælian reports that a certain Epicurean (a member of a philosophical sect antagonistic to the mysteries) entered the adyton without permission and died, presumably from retributive sickness. Another man, according to the same author, climbed up to see into the telesterion but fell and was killed.† Before the Ictinian telesterion was built, the celebration was held in the open air, which would have made the robes absolutely necessary.‡ We might also recall how Socrates at the end of the *Phædo* pulls his bedclothes over his face in the presence of his disciples when he dies. Precautions taken in yoga include the locking of doors into the room where initiation takes place, an oath administered by the guru, and the distribution to the sādhakas of sheets or blankets to conceal the body during meditation.

At the end of the celebration of the teletē of the Eleusinia, a day was set aside for the special ceremony of the *epoptea*, "the gazing up [at]," in which especially selected mystæ who had been initiated at Eleusis in the previous year were taken aside and given advanced instruction. The ceremony of the epoptea is reminiscent of Christian confirmation, described in the New Testament as another, higher baptism.§ The epoptea was the highest stage of initiation at both Eleusis and Samothrace. Indeed, it may

* Andocides and his accusers are quoted in *Eleusis and the Eleusinian Mysteries*, p. 297 (emphases are Mylonas's). Alcibiades was condemned merely for wearing "a robe like the hierophant wears when he shows the sacred secrets" (Plutarch). Clement of Alexandria, who almost certainly was initiated into the true mysteries of The Christ, believed or wanted his readers to believe—so intent is he on discrediting the Eleusinia—that the hiera were "things," and silly things at that; but he doth protest too much, raising a suspicion that he knew the hiera were *not* things and the Eleusinia *not* a species absolutely apart from Christian baptism.

† Mylonas, *Eleusis and the Eleusinian Mysteries*, pp. 225–26.

‡ "Hymn to Demeter," Allen et al., *The Homeric Hymns*, p. 111; there was no telesterion, only a temenos, prior to the seventh century B.C., the period before Athens incorporated Eleusis.

§ John 1:33.

have been the main reason for the Eleusinia as opposed to the Antheria. The preparatory Antheria can be be likened to instruction in what Patañjali calls *aṣṭaṅga yoga*, "the yoga of eight parts," really only a part of rāja yoga.* Sexual abstinence (brahmacārya), fasting, training in posture (the *āsanas* of haṭha yoga), dedication to nonviolence (ahiṃsa) and truthfulness (satya), freedom from covetousness (aparigraha) are part and parcel of yogic discipline; but they are always secondary.† Any attempt to pursue these behaviors for a priori, namely, purely moral reasons, must fail from the point of view of yoga because it serves to substitute for perfect concentration yet another value or attachment in the yogi's consciousness. Implicit here is the reasonable belief that one will concentrate on what one values most highly. Attachments are invidious to spiritual progress because in the day-to-day awareness that a yogi must work with they interrupt the flow of saṃyama and make imperfect one's knowledge of the breath and the subtle biological energy that impels it.

The sheer practical problems of initiation en masse warrant discussion. The hierophant and his deacons prepared the mystæ first by fasting, which heightens internal awareness and second, it seems, by dancing. The sacred dances of the Eleusinia, of which frequent mention is made by ancient authors, were definitely not orgiastic revels but probably of a sort known as line dances or circle dances. Their practical purpose too was to enhance proprioception by prolonged, measured, and rhythmic motion. The sacred dance was likely choreographed by the "all holy" priestesses of Demeter, who are shown leading processionals on sculptural artifacts found at Eleusis. Supposing the dance to be led by a priestess, the cardiovascular rhythms of the mystæ would become entrained with hers;‡ and given that she was a full initiate, pulse and respiration will be slowed sufficiently for instruction to be effective. Then the torches would be extinguished in the callichoron well, the mystæ seated, and the initial initiations begun. If the mystæ were instructed in groups of a hundred or so, as might be inferred from the size of the telesterion, the use of dancing could significantly shorten the ritual.

That the preparatory yoga—summed up by Patañjali in the compound word *yama-niyama*, "restraint and observance"—is far more stringent than what was expected of Greek mystæ is not surprising. Most of the Eleusinia was in the nature of a mass initiation (similar to the mass baptisms mentioned in Acts 4), and we know only a few requirements for admission to the teletē, nothing whatsoever regarding credentials for those admitted to the epoptea, save that they had already to have seen the teletē; therefore—a reasonable inference—the criteria must have been more demanding.[5] Mastery of prāṇāyāma, namely, what was learned in the water baptism, is a prerequisite for the "vision [khyāti] of the self," the epoptea.

Those mystæ admitted to the epoptea were called *epoptæ*, literally, "those who gazed up [at]" or "those who beheld," suggesting that the rite included an important kriyā known to yogis as "root gazing," in which the eyes are focused upward at the bridge of the nose. We have already seen the technique esoterically described in the myth of the BIRTH OF APPOLLO and in the battle before Troy. Tantric yoga calls the all-important spot just above the bridge of the nose the "fire wheel" (ājñā) cakra). The Christian sacrament of confirmation descends from the rite of "baptism by fire" instituted by Christ and referring to a higher—or at least a distinct—baptism than the water baptism. By steadfast attention to ājñā cakra, the sādhaka beholds mūrdha jyotiṣi, "cranial light."

◆◆◆

What was the archaic purpose of the Mysteries of Eleusis? Was it the attempt to

* *Yoga-Sūtra, Sādhana Pāda*, sutra 28.

† Cf., lust, anger, pride, sloth, envy, greed, and gluttony, the seven deadly sins of Catholicism.

‡ Kovach, "Contemplation in Movement," pp. 76–7, 87–91.

5 Mylonas, *Eleusis and the Eleusinian Mysteries*, pp. 258–61.

control metempsychosis? That might be the sense of the *Hymn to Demeter*:

Awe of the gods checks the voice. Happy is
He among men upon earth who has seen these
Mysteries; but he who is uninitiate and who
Has no part in them, never has lot of like
Good things once he is dead, down in the
Darkness and gloom.

Heracles is the paragon of the initiate in Greek myth. Not only does he himself achieve apotheosis—by self-immolation—but he wrestles with death to save the entombed Alcestis, wife of Admetus, after she has voluntarily died in her husband's place. When Heracles presents Alcestis to the redeemed Admetus, she is strangely silent. Heracles explains that she is not yet purified, and that three more "dawns" must pass before she is finally free of death. The myth is strongly reminiscent of Jesus' caution to Mary Magdalene, at dawn of his third day in the sepulcher, that she may not touch him,* and especially because both Jesus and Alcestis have made the ultimate sacrifice on behalf of others. Whatever spiritual condition John and Euripides refer to is a deep secret.†

Alcestis would thus seem to be a recapitulation of Persephone. In Greek her name means "strength of the home," which is to say the *pnuema* that drives the breath and animates the body, temple of the soul. Heracles further advises Admetus (verse 1149) that "it is not lawful for you to hear her voice." Now The Christ is also the Word—on our view an ultra-high frequency sound—so perhaps the esoteric sense of *noli me tangere*, "touch me not," is that Mary "cannot [yet] hear" Jesus in his divine nature: the Word of God. There is a crucial division between the proprioceptions Jesus and Mary describe esoterically. The several parallels, including the sex inversions (Alcestis → Jesus, Admetus → the Magdalene), underscore our contention that resurrection is a wholly internal and spiritual event, not a literal one, and that the Holy Sepulcher is the human body. Euripedes' tale is not only much older that John's, but it derives from an entirely different esoteric tradition; so the lack of a universal savior—a wholly exoteric dogma—in the Greek myth is not surprising. Apollodorus has Persephone free Alcestis, sending her back to the surface as she did Sisyphus.‡ As with Persephone, the Alcestis myth is essentially Pelasgian; a wife dying for her husband is the only indisputably Indo-European element in the story (cf., Hindu rite of suttee).

In the *Theogony* we saw that the sequence of birth and death is at the core of the myth of the BIRTH OF THE GODS. The moment of death is a moment of passing into a dream from which one wakes as a different creature. The challenge that the mysteries present is how to control what one dreams, indeed how to remain awake in the face of the arrival of the Ker, the horrifying death goddess who savagely separates the soul from the body. The Ker is no less than a projection of the mind of the dying man, but that is scarcely something that can be appreciated in the hour of death, much less coped with. In confronting the Ker, the soul recoils into dream and from that moment the opportunity for liberation is lost, for whatsoever a man meditate on in life, so shall he meditate in death. The terror of death is thrust upon the dying man in the form of the stoppage of his breath, a moment of sheer panic. *That* is the critical

* Euripedes, *Alcestis*, 1141–47; Heracles advises that Alcestis "is still consecrated to the gods below"; John 20:17: "Jesus saith unto [Mary], Touch me not; for I am not yet ascended to my Father." Only John provides these words during the episode outside the Holy Selpucher; significant because, of the four canonical gospels, John's is the most cryptically mystical and esoteric in both style and content.

† In 1 Corinthians 15:51–2: "Behold, I show you a mystery; We shall not all sleep, but we shall all be changed. In a moment, in the twinkling of an eye . . . for the trumpet shall sound, and the dead shall be raised incorruptible, and we shall all be changed"; resurrection depends on hearing a mystical sound (cf., Matthew 24:31, Apocalypse 1:10).

‡ *Bibliotheca* 1.9.15.

moment. Although it is largely anecdotal, the testimony of so-called near-death victims—especially near death by drowning—is unanimous that once the terror passes a tranquil, euphoric interlude ensues, followed by a brilliant white light, "the vision of the self." The expiring soul is granted a momentary vision of itself as though in a mirror—the true self that is brahman—toward which it must maintain a steadfast concentration amounting to adoration.

What the Eleusinia taught, then, was that the stoppage of breath is not the end of anything. One need only face the experience once—with equanimity, faith, and, as important, with expert training—to learn that the breath will rise again. The Corē will return from the netherworld. During the *dromena*, "that which is enacted," the mystæ, we are told, searched for the missing Persephone, calling out her name. Each time her name was called, the hierophant struck a special gong* the sound of which can readily be imagined, the ringing sound of death itself, thanatos. Yet that is the same sound that one must hearken to if the panic of the death dream is to be avoided. Again, in the testimony of near-death victims, the vision of light gives way to visions of deceased friends and dear relatives who calm and reassure the victim. But those visions, having superseded khyāti, are themselves the insidious heralds of a dream. It is already too late. The samādhi of the death dream is taking hold, and there is reason to believe it will soon become a nightmare. Near-death victims, for some reason, began to breathe again. Had the death dream deepened, they would have died. They were spared the inevitable confrontation with demons—the vision of the jivātma—the ego. As a proprioceptive state of the soul, ego death is itself a myth. It is the DREAM OF THE SEVEN DEADLY SINS. Only after he withstood the hideous demon Māra did the Buddha attain nirvāṇa beneath the BO TREE (the CNS). Can the phonic resemblance of Sanskrit *māra* to Hebrew *mara*, "Mary," be coincidental? Both women appear to a savior just before his "resurection" and both must be avoided at all cost. Sanskrit *māra* shows strong ablaut (Skt. *vṛddhi guṇa*) of vocalic *r* (ṛ), strongly suggesting that the original phoneme was intrinsic, not intervocalic.† The distiction is crucial: the *r* in Māra and Mary is descriptive of a phon. At the moment of death, amidst a cacaphony of internal sound generated by the death throes, a literal *murmur* or basal *rumble* is heard rising steadily from the first world. It must be ignored, i.e., must not become the bīja of the ensuing death dream. The sādhaka (or expiring soul) ignores (dhāraṇā) the first-world murmur and concentrates (dhyāna) on the whine of the Logos. The goal is samādhi, liberation from karma, and cessation of birth and death. Neither the Magdalene and the Word (Jesus) nor the Budd and Māra may *touch*; nor can Admetus *see* Alcestis while she is "consecrated to the gods below." Aesthesiological distinctions collapse during what Patañjali calls *asaṃprajñāta samādhi.*

At the climactic moment of the dromena, we are told, the hierophant opened the doors to the *plutonion*, no more than a rocky hole in the earth, and led forth the lost—now found—Persephone. The breath has returned from the the realm of Hades (Pluto). Recall that Hades, driving a quadriga of four black stallions, emerged suddenly from a rent in the earth and seized Persephone in the moment she inhaled a flower, the precursor to the pituitary catastrophe. Breath, fragrance, and death have merged into a single prepotent mythic image. Persephone's return from Hades is the triumph over death that Sisyphus fails to achieve but that mastery of prāṇāyāma makes possible: the indefinite suspension of breathing. Note also, an abduction to Hades is followed by a resurrection from Hades. The parallel with Christ's death and resurrection is *breathtakingly* close. The Corē is the daughter of the Goddess. Jesus is the Son of God. On the

* Apollodorus, *Fragmenta* 36, cited in: Mylonas, *Eleusis and the Eleusinian Mysteries*, p. 264.

† ?**mṛya*, cog. with *mṛta*, p.p. of *mṛ* "die"; cf., Russ. *mir*, "deep earth," Eng. *mortal*, and Skt. *hṛdaḥ*, "heart." The Hebrew character set is a consonantal syllabary: *mara* = *mr*.

cross, "they filled a sponge with vinegar, and put it upon hyssop and put it to his mouth. When Jesus therefore had received the vinegar, he said, It is finished, and he bowed his head and gave up the ghost,"* a gustatory precursor.

The Corē must spend one third of the year with Hades, one third on earth with Demeter, one third on Olympus with her father Zeus. The *Apostles Creed* confesses that Jesus Christ, God's only begotten son

> was conceived by the Holy Ghost, born of the Virgin Mary, suffered under Pontius Pilate, was crucified, died, and was buried. He descended into hell, [1] but on the third day, he rose again from the dead [2]. He ascended into heaven [3] to be seated at the right hand of the Father, from whence he shall come to judge the living and the dead.

The lesson is this: The breathless trance duplicates the death trance. Like the Buddha, Jesus as human being, in his human nature, or *physis,* must face the demons of Hell (in his divine nature or ousia, however, The Christ is eternally free). What is learned during prāṇāyāma can be remembered at the moment of actual death. Prāṇāyāma is not a technique for avoiding death, which cannot be avoided if birth has not also been avoided, but simply, in the words of Paul, of enduring it and taking away its "sting."† The mysteries are a practical exercise in dying.

The praxis of prāṇāyāma shows that when the breath stops a brilliant inner light appears, one on which the dying soul must perform saṃyama, else dream ensues. Thus, the mysteries must have both revealed that same light and showed the mystes how to see that light whenever he wished, else how might he come to adore it?

But evidently purification is necessary before divine light can be revealed. *There are real physical dangers entailed in the practice of yoga.* An epileptic suffers a kind of uncontrolled trance. Typically his eyes roll up, he hears a high-pitched ringing, his jaws lock, he smells unusual odors, his tongue automatically rolls back toward the roof of his mouth, his limbs thrash about. The correspondence with the techniques of yogic meditation on light, sound, smell, taste, and touch is virtually one to one. Yoga, then, is a species of controlled epilepsy.‡

The tale of Semele, a mortal and the mother of Dionysus, is cautionary. Ignoring his warning, she insisted on beholding Zeus in all his panoply and was burned to a crisp by lightning (except for Dionysus, in her womb at the time). Because Semele is the mother of the anthropomorphism of taste, her fate seems bound up with the riotous and debauched appetites implied by the word *dionysian.* The soul unpurged of karmas and kleśas risks much at the hour of death.§ In myth Zeus wields the lightning bolt, and we have already seen how the pituitary catastrophe can be described as a cataclysmic stroke from above (the third world). The ancients believed that anyone struck by lightning (and especially one who survived it) was henceforth of divine status. This reverence extended even to places struck by lightning. The Romans erected a monument called a *bidental,* "two fanged," on such a spot, suggesting the sense of being bitten and, esoterically, the locked jaws of the epileptic. It is hardly farfetched to describe a grand mal seizure as like a stroke of lightning.

Anxiety is the symptom of transient kleśas

* John 20:29–30; the hyssop bush was used by the Hebrews to sprinkle lamb's blood on the lintels of doorways at the first Passover (Exodus 12:22).

† 1 Corinthians 15:55.

‡ There exists a rare form of sudden death, to which women are more susceptible than men, in which the person dies as the result of a single inhalation of a flower.

§ Semele (cog. with *Selene*) is the moon. In astrology, the moon, by its rulership of Cancer (memory, origins, but also final fate) is the planet whose horoscopic placement indicates the karmic status of the organism, its aggregate credits and debits, both of which are comprised in the word *sin.* Dionysus's rescue by Hermes Psychopompus indicates that desires survive death to lead the soul into its next life; Dionysus does in fact bring Semele out of Tartarus, and she is renamed (Apollodorus, *Bibliotheca* 3.4–5).

sown from day to day.* Electroconvulsive therapy (ECT) dramatically relieves depression and anxiety, both of which are symptoms of kleśas, but it is a medical mystery why it works. Each kleśa leaves a trace in the physical body—the covering of light—particularly in the nerves behind the brows, including the corpus callosum on which ECT is believed to act. By meditation—and apparently by passage of electrical current—kleśas can be erased. During ECT, however, a gag is used to prevent the tongue from rolling back and completing the yogic circuit that purges the kleśas, so the effect is usually short-lived.

Our hypothesis, then, is that regardless of trauma, *death is initiated by the endocrine system.* Nor can it be stressed enough that the death undergone by the mystes and conventional death are nearly equivalent experiences. The former is voluntary and reversible, the latter involuntary and irreversible (epilepsy is involuntary but reversible). Something like the pituitary catastrophe occurs in death, the severity of which depends on the degree of prior preparation for it.† Praxis inoculates against the catastrophe by exposing the sādhaka to the endrocrinal efflux at a pace carefully controlled by his guru, which is perhaps the most persuasive argument for the necessity of esoterism: the argument from physical survival. Similarly, the older one is at the time of death, the less the amount of pernicious hormones (testosterone, estrogen, adrenalin, etc.) in the bloodstream,‡ the more likely that death will be peaceful even without initiation and praxis. Moreover, at any age the catastrophe is mitigated indirectly simply by having avoided the seven deadly sins while alive. Hinduism recommends observance of the four *āśramāḥ*, "stages of life" (lit., "hermitages"), the last of which requires the elderly householder to leave his or her family and possessions for a life of ascetism in the forest. Having survived to old age, the householder takes advantage of bodily changes wrought by climacteric or menopause to prepare for death; initiation is often undertaken at the time.

Regardless of initiation, living a moral life means dying a moral death. If, on the other hand, one has throughly indulged the seven deadly sins, regularly flooding his or her body with endocrinal intoxicants, then regardless of initiation, the catastrophe will be severe, and the stunned soul, driven from maintaining the vision of the self into a dream of the senses, will be hard put indeed to recover its equanimity before it is too late.§ Supposing the sin to be anger, as the simple soldier William advises Prince Hal on the eve of Agincourt, "there are few die well that die in a battle; for how can they charitably dispose of anything, when blood is their argument?"# How can anyone, dying in a fit of murderous rage, undergo an emotional volte-face in the few moments remaining to him? Is it not far more likely that Demus and Phobus—panic and fear—twin sons of Mars, will complete their father's bloody work, overcome the dying man, and lead him into who knows what nightmare. A "charitable disposition" at the hour of death, achieved through faith (virtuousness), good works (yogic praxis), or both, is the goal of life.

In the *Upaniṣads* we read that "there are a hundred-and-one arteries of the heart. Only one of them passes up to the *sahasrāra* [the crown of the head]. Going up by it, one goes to immortality."** Other yogic texts speak of 72,000 (■ 9) channels leading from the heart. Themistius tells us that the way to Hades is not straight but has

* Yogis refer to transient karma as *kriyamaṇa* (lit., "mental work"). Often sown and reaped in a single day, kriyamaṇas arise in the hopes and fears of quotidian life (see *Yoga-Sūtra, Vibhūti Pāda,* sutra 23 plus commentary pp. 320–22).

† Implying that a physician can revive a dying person by timely injection of hormonal antagonists.

‡ Pernicious because they interfere with equanimity. The ancient physiocracy of the four *cardinal humors* (blood, phlegm, choler, and melancholer) affecting temperament may derive from proprioceptions of the output of the endocrine glands.

§ "Stunned" is to be taken literally: "O death, where is thy sting?. . . The sting of death is sin; and the strength of sin is the law" (1 Corinthians 15:55–6), i.e., *lex talionis* or law of karma. The outflow of hormones sends the organism into clinical shock.

Henry V, act 4, scene 1.

** *Chāndogya Upaniṣad* 6.16.

many "branchings and forkings." In Plato's *Phædrus*:

> Now the place which is above the Heaven no poet here hath ever praised. . . . which hath no color and no shape, and hand cannot touch [it] . . . is comprehended only by . . . Reason [nous]. . . . beholding *again* that which is, [the Soul] is satisfied, and the sight of That which is true feedeth it. . . . The Soul, then, having beheld these and also other things . . . and having eaten of this feast, sinketh down again into the inward part of this heaven and cometh home into her House. And when she is come the Charioteer maketh the Horses to stand at the manger, and casteth ambrosia before them, and thereafter giveth them nectar to drink. . . . This is the life of the Gods. . . . other souls . . . strive after that which is above, but are not able to reach up to it . . . and depart uninitiated, not having seen That which is. . . . but when a Soul, having seen these things *aforetime*, is now not able to follow . . . being overtaken by some evil chance, and filled with forgetfulness and wickedness, . . . then the law is that she shall not be planted in the body of any beast in the first generation. . . . For unto Man's shape no soul attaineth which never beheld the truth. . . . The man, therefore, who . . . is always a partaker in the perfect mysteries, he alone becometh verily perfect.*

This is pure Orphism. "Having seen those things," the soul does not forget, is the basis of Plato's famous theory of *anamnesis*, "recollection." Anamnesis does not mean, as is often inferred, simply a recollection in this life of what was learned in previous lives. Far more important to Socrates, anamnesis is the ability of the soul to recollect what was shown in the mysteries while undergoing the ascent into the final dream, the death dream, the dream that Hermes the Psychopomp describes:

> This is the myth, when a man has breathed his last, the spirit to whom each was allotted in life proceeds to conduct him to a *certain place. . . . There that befalls which must befall*; and having abided there *for the due span of time* they are brought back hither by another guide, and so they continue for many circuits of time.†

Socrates adds that the soul is fledged, it has wings (a reference to its airy nature), and it must soar toward the Truth above. "Other souls are not able to make it": the myth of Icarus and Dædalus. It must leave the body by the channel—be it nerve or vein—that runs to the crown of the head, for which ascent it must have practiced. It must already know how to propriocept that subtle channel. The Orphics also held that the body was a tomb, in which the soul is punished. Like a locked door of a prison cell, the body serves to keep the soul from evading punishment, at the same time, the body protects the soul. The unprepared soul, never having "seen those things," on leaving the body encounters the pure vibrating Word of God, a sound that begins at the highest frequency of the death whine. Like a perfect servant, the Logos creates a reality that is congruent to the condition of the soul, be it man, beast, or insect. "In my father's house are many mansions. I go to prepare a place for you."‡ Initiation is the key that opens the door to the Logos in safety. Plato also speaks of the bifurcation of the roads, one leading to Elysium, the heavenly fields, the other to Tartarus, the abyss beneath the earth.§ In the myth of Er he says that the parting of the ways is triple: one

* Plato, *Phædrus* 247C–249D, in Stewart, *The Myths of Plato*, pp. 313–17, emphasis added.

† Plato, *Phædo* 107E, quoted in: Mylonas, *Eleusis and the Eleusinian Mysteries*, n. on p. 268, emphasis added.

‡ John 14:2

§ Plato, *Gorgias* 524A, in: Stewart, *The Myths of Plato*, p. 118.

way to heaven, one way to Hades, the other to Lethe, the River of Forgetfulness (before rebirth, the soul must forget its previous lifetimes).* The Orphics speak of souls lost in the "mud" of Hades (Peleus < Gk. *pelas*, "mud" or "darkness"). Finally, Themistius explicitly compares the experience of the mystæ to that of the expiring soul (emphasis added):

> The [dying] soul has the same experience as those who are being initiated into the great mysteries . . . at first one wanders and wearily hurries to and fro, and journeys with suspicion through the dark as one uninitiated: *then comes all the terrors* before the final initiation, shuddering, trembling, sweating, amazement: then one is *struck with marvelous light, one is received into pure regions and meadows, with voices and dances and the majesty of holy sounds and shapes*: among these he who has fulfilled initiation wanders free, and released and bearing his *crown* joins in the divine communion, and consorts with pure and holy men, beholding those who live here uninitiated, an uncleansed horde, trodden under foot of him and huddled together in *mud and fog, abiding in their miseries through fear of death and mistrust of the blessings there.*"

Verbum sap sat!†

The crescendo to which the teletē was building was the revelation of the hiera. The hierophant, standing in the anactoron, "within a blazing light," opened the cistæ and showed them to the mystæ, at which point the teletē was concluded so far as the mystæ were concerned.

Every word of it must be interpreted esoterically. The esoteric cistus, we have already speculated, is the skull of the mystes. Opening the cistus, then, would be the revelation of the inner sounds, smells, and lights. That would seem to trespass on the rites of the epoptea, but we must remember that our literary sources for what went on at the Eleusinia are extremely confused. It is probable that many of the events described are conflations. Thus, the moment when the hierophant appears in the opened door of the anactoron could very well be an esoteric reference to the epoptea. And the same applies to references to a sudden opening of the *opæon*, an aperture in the "ceiling" that admitted light into the telesterion. After all, so far as is known, the only people who expressed themselves on the subject of the Eleusinia were individuals who had never been initiated. Alternatively, there may have been some purely ritualistic display of opening a literal cistus and taking something out in *anticipation* of the epoptea—in other words, esoterica within esoterica.

The Eleusinia gave hope to tens of thousands in the ancient world. If, at some unknown date, the line of succession to the office of hierophant was somehow broken, the legitimacy of initiation compromised, and the sixteen-hundred-year-old celebration of Demeter and the Corē ended, it is no worse than what happened to Christianity and Judaism. More likely, however, is the gradual supplanting of the Mysteries of Eleusis by the Christian mysteries. The reasons for the transition are outside the scope of this book. They involve a shift in ethics and mores, neither of which is ever universal or absolute but only in fashion. The morality of the Eleusinia was the morality of paganism, and by the period of the Late Empire it was a corrupted morality. If the Christian mysteries offered no less than the Eleusinia, as we are supposing, then, *non cæteris paribus*, its appeal to morality and ethical conduct must inevitably have prevailed.

Initiation is no guarantee of piety or devotion. Most seed will fall on bad ground. A

* Plato, *Republic* 614C, in: Stewart, *The Myths of Plato*, p. 135, plus commentary pp. 130–32. Conversely, if the death dream is resisted, the soul recalls all of its previous lives in attaining kaivalya, as happened to the Buddha under the Bo Tree.

† The source of this ancient proverb—"A word to the wise is sufficient"—may in fact be initiation into the divine "word" (verbum).

person can undergo initiation and be utterly unchanged by it, a consequence of the practicality of initiation. It is the individual application of what is taught in the mysteries, the daily, hourly, and moment-to-moment praxis of what was learned, that provides salvation—merely learning the techniques is woefully insufficient.

Therefore the great gurus have always been careful to whom they revealed the "holy, unspeakable things." If a man, dissatisfied with his country, goes to a new country, he can still achieve earthly happiness. If his spouse displeases him, he can remarry. If he leaves one religion for another, it is of no consequence, for the fundamentals of religious belief are never too dissimilar. But if he leaves the truth, where will he go?

18

JASON AND THE ARGONAUTS

To claim his rightful place as heir to the Kingdom of Jolcus, the hero Jason must retrieve the Golden Fleece from Colchis, an enchanted land that lies far to the east of Greece. The way to Colchis, which lies beyond Pontus (the Black Sea), is blocked by the CYÆNEAN ROCKS, which move about in the Bosporus; in other versions of the myth they are known as the Clashing Rocks (Gk. *symplegades*) because they slam shut and crush ships trying to pass through.

Jason has learned the whereabouts of the prophet Phineas, who knows how to pass the Clashing Rocks safely. Phineas betrayed the secrets of the gods, for which Zeus blinded him and subjected him to the torments of three winged demons called Harpies. Jason and his crew drive off the Harpies, and a grateful Phineus tells him that to traverse the Clashing Rocks he must release a bird as the rocks part and row through immediately after it. The helmsman of the Argo is a blindman, Tiphys of Siphas, summoned to the crew of the Argo by Athena. With the help of Athena, who holds apart the rocks and shoves the Argo through, Tiphys manages to steer the ship into the Black Sea, though the bird (a dove) has its tail feathers cropped by the rocks and the Argo loses its stern. That night they beach their ship on Thynia, a desert isle, where they see Apollo with his bow, wreathed in his golden, flowing hair. They build an altar, chant a hymn to Apollo, and sacrifice a goat.* The next day they sail to Colchis. After many adventures, they retrieve the fleece and return safely to Jolcus.

Jason journeys to the LAND OF COLCHIS with fifty companions called the Argonauts.† Fifty describes the five senses, a division that the Greeks themselves are credited with inventing. The fifty Argonauts traveling to Colchis describe an inward journey into trance, a withdrawal of the senses from

* Apollonius Rhodius, *Argonautica* 2.285–345, 574–688; Apollodorus, *Bibliotheca* 1.9.22. Cf., Euripides, *Iphigenia in Tauris*, 241ff., 1403–407; aided by Athena, Orestes sails through the Symplegades to rescue his twin from the temple of Artemis.

† There were actually forty-nine Argonauts; Jason was the fiftieth.

the world. Their purification takes place in the Argo, the esoteric cranium.

Meditation clearly involves mind as well as body, yet the numerology of five appears to limit the myth to the sensory realm. Thought—a sixth faculty—appears to be excluded, an omission that allows us to prove the rule. From the myth we learn that Athena—anthropomorphized voiceless speech—advised Jason to hew a bough from the Whispering Oak of Dodona, an ancient Epirote oracle sacred to Zeus and held in great reverence by the Greeks, and to fasten it to the Argo's mast; whence it conveniently guides him to the Golden Fleece.* Clearly, we have here a myth that describes voiceless speech: Athena herself.† Far from being left behind, thought directs the five senses in this myth.

Foremost among the Argonauts is Heracles, who does not complete the journey, leaving the expedition in Mysia to follow his companion Hylas. Noteworthy too is Orpheus, the celebrated Thracian bard who describes esoteric hearing. He leads the Argonauts in chanting, and it is Orpheus who speaks to Apollo when they have passed into the Wine-Dark Sea.

The fathers and kinsmen of prominent Homeric heroes are also aboard: Telamon (father of Ajax Big) and Peleus (father of Achilles), who are the sons of Æacus, Menœtius (father of Patroclus), and Periclymenus (brother of Nestor), who can change his shape at will. Worth mentioning are Coronus (the son and therefore the recapitulation of Cæneus the Lapith, who fought the centaurs; because he was invulnerable they suffocated him, his soul escaping in the form of a bird)‡ and Castor and Pollux, the Dioscuri, esoteric descriptions of alternate-nostril breathing.

In the course of the journey a vain and boastful Heracles challenges the rest of the crew to a rowing-endurance contest. The rhythmic motion of an oar is an apt description of the breath, one especially suited to the seafaring Greeks; it also complements the imagery of a sail. As it turns out, it is Heracles and Jason who hold out longest before shifting their oars (Heracles' oar snaps); but significantly the last two to fade before these are none other than Castor and Pollux. In the same moment that Heracles' oar breaks, Jason swoons.§ The sequence, then, is the Dioscuri leave off rowing—in other words, alternate-nostril breathing ceases—Heracles, the Greek equivalent of a yogic aspirant or sādhaka, breaks his oar, and simultaneously Jason passes into a swoon, which is nothing if not samādhi. Because Jason and Heracles leave off rowing at the same time, they must be equivalent elements of the myth. The snapping of the oar suggests the onset of the pituitary catastrophe.

The Argo comes ashore, and Heracles goes into the forest for wood to replace his broken oar. He manhandles an entire pine tree, roots and all, ripping it from the ground; the sense here is that of destroying karmas during the pituitary catastrophe. A pine, like all conifers, is sweetly scented, providing the olfactory precursor. "Meanwhile," as Apollonius says, Hylas, Heracles' devoted companion, has gone to fetch water for Heracles and Telamon and is pulled by næads (water nymphs) into the pool of Pegæ nearby. Hylas's sudden disappearance into the pool suggests the reunification of the Three Worlds in the mystic sea when prāṇāyāma succeeds and the breath stops. "Meanwhile" indicates the death of Hylas is simultaneous with Heracles uprooting the pine. We have a recapitulation of the Fall of Troy, hence Telamon's connection to the story (Telamon tears open the Gate of Troy when he and the Heraclidæ [sons of Heracles] besiege the city). When Heracles learns of Hylas's fate, he is inconsolable and refuses to rejoin the Argo's company. They sail

* Some versions place Dodona in Thessaly rather than Epirus. *Thessaly* is an aspirated spirant, *Epirus* a plosive.

† For the ancient practice of duplicating an important deity by a person, animal, or object associated in myth with that deity, see Rose, *A Handbook of Greek Mythology*, pp. 117–19.

‡ Ovid, *Metamorphoses*, trans. M. M. Innes (London, 1955), 12.515–37.

§ *Argonautica Orphica*, 646ff.

off to Colchis without him.* Heracles is a sādhaka—like Ananda, he habitually gets into trouble—so his presence is no longer needed once the goal of yoga, that is, entry into the Wine-Dark Sea, has been attained. Jason is now on his own.

Finally, we must consider Phineas and the vision of Apollo on the island of Thynia. Phineas's blindness means that he is already "looking" inward. Blindness is frequently associated with psychic powers in Greek myth. The blind seer Calchas advised the Greeks at the siege of Troy. Odysseus, on his way home from Troy, consulted the blind prophet Tiresias. Œdipus became a sage after blinding himself. The blind Tiphys is described as a "prophet" by Apollonius. Phineas could not have betrayed the secrets of the gods, that is, the rites of initiation, had he not known those secrets himself.

Near the beginning of the voyage, the Argonauts stopped at Samothrace to be initiated into the Mysteries of the Cabiri.† Samothrace is the island of Electra, the daughter of Atlas who mated with Zeus and Ares (the two gods together in a myth describe something like "heavenly vision"). Apollonius tells us that the Argonauts sought initiation that "they might learn the secret rites . . . and so might fare safely over the chilling sea. Of these things will I speak no further . . . of them 'tis not right for us to sing."‡

Once the Argonauts have passed the Cyænean Rocks, night falls, and they encounter a luminous Apollo, to whom they chant "Ever be thy locks unshorn." Seen within the darkness of the third world, Apollo's hair is the Golden Fleece recapitulated. The word for "chant" used by Apollonius is *molpē*, which in Greek means a rhythmic motion. Rather than the frontal suture, the Apollonian light is now the bīja.

Patañjali speaks of the light (jyoti) at the back of the head,§ which he describes as the "vision of perfected beings." In the moment of maximum dilation of the frontal suture, maximum stress occurs at the rear of the skull (i.e., 180 degrees away). The stress is propriocepted over the cerebellum, the center of balance. Above the cerebellum is the occipital cortex, the visual sensorium. The cerebellum is in fact a sort of rudder—here at the stern of the second-world ark (the Argo). The loss of the dove's tail feathers and the Argo's stern as the Argonauts pass the Clashing Rocks describe the proprioception of occipital stress and thus an ascent into trance, into a state of consciousness that is dizzying, disorienting, and often terrifying. The assistance of Athena in holding open the Clashing Rocks and the immediate appearance of Apollo with his bow recapitulate the frontal suture and the eyes. All this occurs on the isle of Thynia, "the flowing land." The sādhaka is still within the stream of the breath, but now it is the breath propriocepted *within* the cranium. The blindness of Phineas, the assistance of the Virgin, the Bow of Apollo, the image of a golden ram's fleece—all converge on this one point: Jason and the Argonauts is a myth about internal vision, involving both root gazing and breath control.

In his chant before the ALTAR OF APOLLO, the great optical chiasmus, Orpheus praises Leto, Apollo's mother, as the only creature with a right to touch Apollo's golden hair. Leto, as has been noted, is so important in Homer and Hesiod, yet so unimportant in all later authors, as to be nearly inexplicable.# As the oldest mythopoets of any substance, their inclusion of Leto in the pantheon of the Hellenes is one of the few threads between Greek myth and the archaic matriarchy the Indo-Europeans inherited

* Apollonius Rhodius, *Argonautica* 1.1160ff; Theocritus, *Idylls*, in: *The Greek Bucolic Poets*, 13.30–45.

† In some versions only Orpheus is initiated. Orpheus then founded the orphic mysteries, underscoring again the person-to-person form of initiation. Only he who has been initiated can initiate.

‡ Apollonius Rhodius, *Argonautica* 1.900–927; the entire *Argonautica* is a recapitulation of two dozen lines! Odysseus was also initiated at Samothrace on his voyage home from Troy.

§ *Yoga-Sūtra, Vibhūti Pāda*, sutra 33.

Gladstone, *Studies on Homer and the Homeric Age*, vol. 2, pp. 147–55. I refer to the *Homeric Hymns*, of which Hesiod is said to be the author.

from the Pelasgians. Leto is the darkness of the third world. During *samādhi mūrdha jyotiṣi*, the trance of cranial proprioceptive light, light is mantled in darkness, like a child held in its mother's arms, like an embryo, like the Argonaut's vision of golden Apollo in the darkness.* This quiet realm of darkness—the place that flows—this "wine-dark" circumambience proprioceptual posterior to the dove-winged frontal sinuses, is the Virgin Mother.

◆◆◆

We have seen that the frontal suture, the lower portion of which terminates between the brows, is a region of enormous significance in practical mythmaking. Within the brows themselves are hollows known as the frontal sinuses; during trance, they can be felt and visualized as the outspread wings of a bird (see figure 5). During inhalation they fill with air, during exhalation they empty.

The structures of the body that respond directly to the rhythms of breathing are not just the obvious lungs and sinuses. Respiration takes place from birth, when the entire skeleton—and the frontal suture in particular—is rather more pliant than in the mature adult. The rib cage, for example, allows expansion and contraction of the lungs. We reach adulthood with a pervasive accommodation by the entire body to the demands of perhaps its most basic function. An archaic awareness, with its element of autism, inevitably becomes fascinated by respiration. All yogic breathing practices descend from a proprioceptive awareness in which every nuance of inhalation-exhalation is sensible.

Breathing can be described as an applied sinusoidal mechanical stress on the body that comprises both shear and strain components. The stress acts critically at the location of a skeletal suture. Polymeric materials like bone acquire a *memory* when stressed repeatedly. The line of a suture develops a sensitivity to mechanical forces that temper it by their continuous action.

One such phenomenon is the expansion and contraction of the frontal bone. This fan-shaped process may be sensed by means of its own fibers, which act as nerves of extremely high capacitance.† The more profound the state of meditative absorption, the more perfect is the awareness of the bone. What is felt, then, is the rhythmic opening and closing of the frontal suture as the sinuses first swell with air, then empty. Of course, in perceptual terms, dilations of the cranium are virtually nil; but the proprioceptive nervous system is distinguished from the perceptual precisely in its ability to detect virtual stimuli. Patañjali: "His [the yogi's] mastery extends from the finest atom to the greatest infinity."‡

Because of the touchlike aspect of every faculty, proprioceptive experiences of imperceptible distances, which is to say of cognitive lengths, are possible via thalamocortical fibers. Using a technique of rāja yoga, a yogi discerns the jagged interface between the halves of the frontal bone (figure 35). In a very ancient esoteric representation, the juncture of the segments of the frontal bone is described as a *vagina dentata*. The virtual motion of cranial bones from front to rear occurs along the line of sutures that girds the head. Among those sutures are the squamous and lambdoid fissures. Such a movement (known as a slip stress) is proprioccepted at the beginning of sādhana as a painful cutting sensation heightened by the presence of the wormian bones, which line the sutures from birth. Painful or not, that is the place from which the sādhaka must begin the inward journey.

He approaches the obstacle practically. By

* Parmenides, *Fragmenta* 9.3: "Everything is full of light together with darkness," in: Verdenius, *Parmenides: Some Comments on His Poems*. Dark and light are dynamically related, scaling each other reciprocally over the length of the spectrum. *Dark*, meaning phenomenal proprioceptive darkness, not scientific *black*, is not equivalent to absence of proprioceptive light.

† The frontal bone itself is poorly innervated; very proximate though are several cranial nerves, each acutely sensitive.

‡ *Yoga-Sūtra, Samādhi Pāda*, sutra 40.

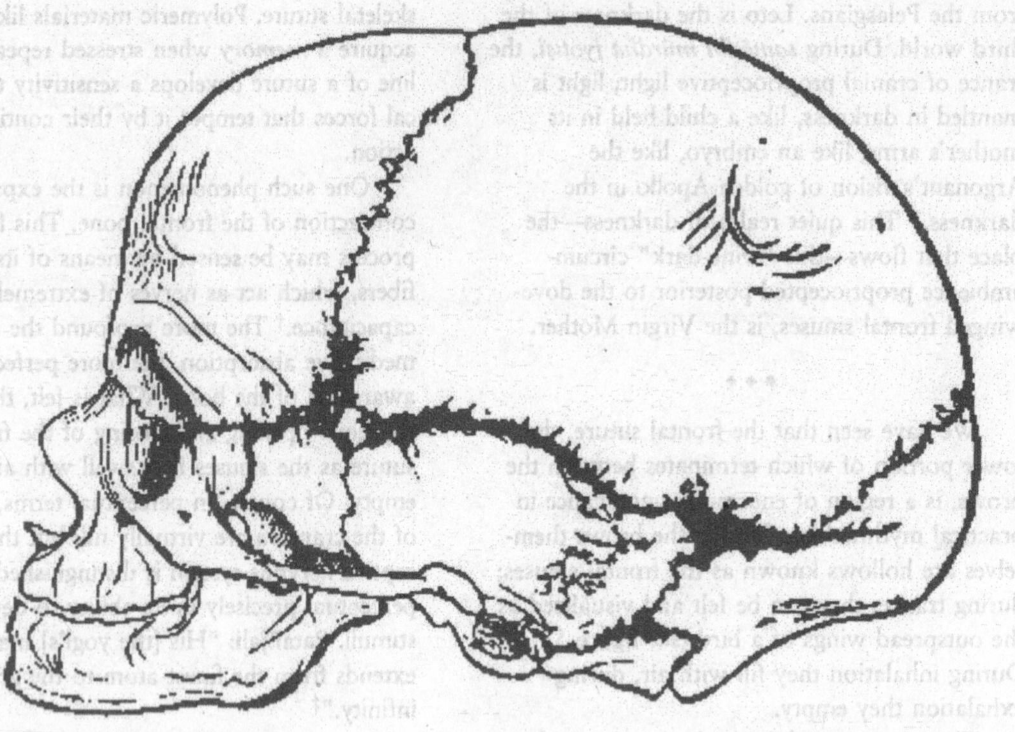

Figure 35. Structure of Frontal Bone with Wormian Bones (from *Gray's Anatomy*)

instruction in the techniques of meditation, he learns that it may be breached by means of the breath, which momentarily dilates the suture a few dozen microns.* He concentrates on the dilation. Perhaps he sits in meditation for hours at a time.† As the trance deepens, he becomes more aware of subtle, rhythmic changes. With each breath, he feels the outward swelling of the frontal bone more distinctly—it's like a sail taking the breeze—and his breaths become less frequent, allowing him time to concentrate completely on the line of the suture while it is "open." Beyond it he sees a light—a proprioception of the optic nerves at the place where they decussate to form the optical chiasmus.

The sinuses are reservoirs of breath that flank the frontal suture. The breath flows during prāṇāyāma, but ever so slowly. As breath seeps out of the sinuses, it is simultaneously propriocepted as a movement of prāṇā throughout the cranium. The breath has not actually entered the skull, rather the motion of the breath *feels* continuous into the sinuses—where it is momentarily bottled up—thence throughout the cranium. In Christian myth, that the frontal suture is not literally ruptured accounts for the venerable, if illogical, tradition that Mary was a virgin, before, during, and after her insemination by the Holy Ghost. Her insemination was truly spiritual, that is, by the breath.

* * *

The Greek alphabet is derived from a Phœnician prototype lacking vowels. The same is true for both Hebrew and Sanskrit. Sanskrit, for example, has no character for solitary *a*, only characters for *ta*, *ka*, *ma*, and so forth (basically the characters for *t*, *k*, and *m* with

* One micron (μ) = 10^{-6} meter; so 20 $\mu \sim 0.01$ inch.

† Not at all unusual; formal practice (sādhana) normally occurs twice a day for several hours at a time.

diacriticals attached). Philologists call such languages *consonantal syllabaries*. In Sanskrit, Hebrew, and Greek, vowels first appear as shadings on the pronunciation of consonants. They indicate how air is expelled from the mouth during pronunciation. Only when specific characters for vowels are written does one have a true alphabet.

The proper noun *Jason* is a Late Latin transliteration of the Greek Ιασων. There is no *J* in the Greek alphabet. Correctly transliterated from the Greek, Jason is written *Iason* and pronounced *ya-sun*.* The terminal *-on* in *Iason* merely indicates masculine gender and is not part of the root. In its origins then, the name Jason was probably something like *Ias* (Ιασ). Discounting the vowels, we arrive at a single phoneme: sibilant *s*. It is quite possible, however—in fact, because of the surviving doubled-vowel form *ia*, it is very probable—that the initial syllable (i) of Ias was aspirated, namely, pronounced as if written with *h* prefixed, called the *spiritus asper*, "hard breathing," and indicated in Greek orthography by a raised, inverted comma, to give ῾Ιασ, transliterated as *Hias*.

As a spoken language evolves, and especially before the ability to write has become widespread, loss of initial aspiration is predictable and conforms to Grimm's law, which requires that the pronunciation of a sound move forward in the mouth.† It is equivalent to dropping an aitch in Cockney English. That seems to be what happened in the case of Jason. If we supply the aspiration, we can dispense with the *a*, giving *His*.‡ The initial *h* was probably voiced, namely pronounced as in "hit" rather than "inherit." The upshot is something pronounced like English *Hiss*. *Jason* is thus an onomatopœtic rendering of respiration, not entirely surprising in a son of Æson (s), grandnephew of Sisyphus, and great-grandson of Æolus, god of the wind.

During deep meditation, one breathes through both nostrils simultaneously. It is only when Jason lays down his oar that the rowing contest ends. Thus, Jason seems to describe deep meditative breathing such as occurs prior to stoppage of the breath altogether. Meditation on the breath is a healing process. The Greek god of healing, an attendant to Asclepius, was Jaso.

What, then, does our analysis imply about the esoteric origins of the proper name Jesus (< Gk. *Iesous*, pronounced *yea-soos*), son of *Joseph* of the tribe of *Jesse*? In the next chapter, we take up the question in detail.

* Throughout this book, initial *J* is written where, in almost all cases, *I* is meant, e.g., Jocaste and Jesus; the practice has a long history, and I have decided not to emend it for sentimental reasons.

† E.g., $g \rightarrow k \rightarrow ch$; $v \rightarrow p \rightarrow b$; and $ia = ya \rightarrow j$; so Iason → Jason.

‡ Ancient texts also give *Ieson* for the name of the hero, supporting the choice of a shorter vowel.

19

JUDEO-CHRISTIAN ESOTERISM

In the early Church, the communion rail was a barrier to the *catechumens*, those who, professing faith in Christ Jesus but not yet baptized, were being prepared for baptism. Only if you had already been initiated into the mysteries of The Christ were you permitted beyond the rail. The same barrier, called an *iconostasis*, survives somewhat more prominently in Orthodox churches; when closed, it completely hides the altar. In old Anglo-Saxon churches it was called the rood screen. The plain intention of such devices is to hide the priests at the altar, often during the most solemn parts of the Mass. Until the liturgical "reforms" of this century, the priest kept his back to the congregation and even pulled his vestments over his head while consecrating the host.*

The models for Christian esoterism are the parables of Jesus. A parable means a roundabout way of discussing something. A parable is therefore a Christian myth. Jesus specifically links parables to the mysteries when, in explaininging the Parable of the Sower, he tells his apostles "it is given unto you to know the mysteries of the kingdom of heaven, but to them it is not given. . . . Therefore speak I to them in parables: because they seeing see not: and hearing they hear not, neither do they understand."† The problem, it would appear, is that even when shown the mysteries of the inner kingdom, many do not recognize them for what they are. Initiation is a gift not to be wasted. In Matthew 7:6: "Give not that which is holy unto the dogs. Neither cast ye your pearls before swine, lest they trample them under their feet, and turn again and rend you." Again, in Matthew 7:14: "Strait is the gate, and narrow is the way that leadeth unto life, and few there be that find it." Ignatius of Antioch, writing to

* Cf., Plato; at the end of the *Phædo,* having drunk the hemlock, Socrates pulls the bedclothes over his face just before he dies.

† Matthew 13:11–13; cf., Matthew 13:34: "Jesus spake unto the multitude [the unbaptized] in parables; and without a parable spake he not unto them"; Mark 4:34: "And when they [Jesus and his disciples] were alone, he expounded all things."

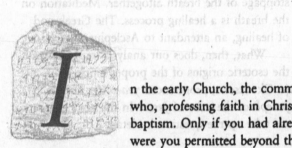

his fellow Christians as he was being led to martyrdom, likewise uses the image of "the gateway, through which we are escorted by Death into the presence of God. You are initiates of the same mysteries."* But many catechumens might have been baptized only in the symbolic sense practiced today, namely with a sprinkling of water or momentary immersion or anointing of the forehead with oil. Their understanding had first to be prepared.

Alexandria in Egypt was an important center of early Christianity and a veritable seething cauldron of gnostic sects for three centuries. One of the local Christian panjandra was Clement (died before A.D. 220), and to judge solely from his surviving writings, he had almost certainly received the true baptism. Clement presided over a school of sacred learning in Alexandria about which little is known. Eusebius of Cæsarea mentions the school as being in existence in his time (fourth century A.D.) and adds "*we have heard* that it is managed by men powerful in their learning and zeal for divine things,"† suggesting that he did not know explicitly what went on within its precincts. Clement himself in his *Stromateis* tells us that he searched for salvation until finally, in Palestine, he found a man (one of five, he claims) who could reveal to him the true meaning of the gospels. The man was Pantænus, rector of the school of sacred learning before Clement. Pantænus was a disciple of Polycarp, who was a close disciple of Saint John the Evangelist, who was baptized by Christ himself. Eusebius tells us that Pantænus had traveled to India and that "he orally and in writing expounded the treasures of the divine doctrine." During Easter week, Clement held closed baptisms to which only certain parishioners were admitted. In the treatise *What Rich Man Can Be Saved?* Clement seems to be especially inviting wealthy Alexandrine Greeks to the "greater mysteries," as he referred to them. In his *Exhortation to the Greeks* Clement says "We, who have become disciples of God, have entered into the really true wisdom, which leaders of philosophy only hinted at, but which the disciples of the Christ have . . . comprehended."‡

Great efforts were made not only to keep the mysteries secret but also to keep secret the mysteries, namely, not to divulge that there were even secrets to be kept. Clement's *Stromateis* is explicitly about "Christian gnosis" but without giving anything away on paper. Nonetheless, a truly remarkable letter of about A.D. 200 from Clement to someone called Theodore (otherwise unknown) has survived. In it Clement castigates Carpocrates, founder of a heretical Christian sect in the early second century.§ Carpocrates taught that Satan freed from his control only those who did his bidding unhesitatingly. More to the point are the rumors circulating in antiquity that the Carpocratians had somehow got hold of a *secret gospel* by Saint Mark, the companion and scribe of Saint Peter himself. The passage of primary interest to us in Clement's letter reads as follows:

> Of what they say about the divinely inspired gospel of Mark, some is altogether false, and other things, even if they contain some truth, are mingled with fabrications, and so falsified that as in the proverb even the salt loses its flavor. Now during Peter's time at Rome, Mark wrote what the Lord had done, not, however, baldly stating all of it, nor hinting at the secrets, but selecting what he thought would help increase the faith of the catechumens. After Peter's martyrdom, however, Mark came to Alexandria, bringing his own notes and those of Peter, from which he added to his earlier book things suited to progress toward gnosis, and so he composed a more spiritual gospel. . . . But he still did not make known the

* Ignatius of Antioch, *Epistle to the Ephesians* 12.2–3.

† Eusebius, *Ecclesiastica Historia*, vol. 1, trans. K. Lake (Cambridge, Mass., 1980), 5.10.1, emphasis added.

‡ Clement of Alexandria, *Protrepticon* 11.87, in: Buttersworth, *Clement of Alexandria*.

§ Clement is actually attacking the followers of Carpocrates, who was deceased by the time of the letter.

unutterable things, neither the hierophantic teaching of the Lord. . . . He also added certain aphorisms that, as mystagogue, he knew would lead the hearers into the innermost sanctuary of that truth hidden by seven veils. . . . He remanded his work to the church in Alexandria, where it is carefully guarded and read only by those being initiated into the greater mysteries.*

Both "mystagogue" and "hierophant" refer to an instructor in mysteries or holy secrets.† Clement often speaks of Christ as the "Hierophant," calling to mind Paul's remarks, in Hebrews 5:5–6, that Jesus is of the line of Melchizedek, a high-priest-like figure from Genesis. Clement then gives Theodore patently shocking advice:

> Never give way to the Carpocratians. Never even concede that the secret gospel is from Mark but deny it on oath. For that reason does Solomon say to us "To a fool, speak folly."‡

The necessity for secrecy was so intense that it approved subornation of perjury and transgression of the fifth commandment: "Thou shalt not bear false witness."

The part of the canonical Bible that Clement's letter most invokes is 1 Corinthians 2:6–10:

> Howbeit we speak wisdom among them that are perfect: yet not the wisdom of this world, nor of the princes of this world, that come to nought. But we speak the wisdom of God in a mystery, the hidden wisdom, which God ordained before the world unto our glory: Which none of the princes of this world knew: for had they known, they would not have crucified the Lord of glory. But as it is written, *Eye hath not seen, nor ear heard, neither have entered into the heart of man,* the things God hath prepared for them that love him [emphasis added; see also Ephesians 3:1–9].

Internal evidence from elsewhere in Clement's letter allows us to reconstruct its context. Theodore, it seems, had recently submitted a sort of report to Clement concerning the Carpocratians and the unwholesome uses to which they were putting the secret gospel: salvation lay in sinning with a will! But Theodore was evidently still a little curious about the gospel, which evidently even he had not read, and sought guidance from his bishop. In his choleric reply, Clement says that carpocratian doctrine is "polluted . . . . shameless . . . blasphemous and carnal." He says that by "deceitful art" the Carpocratians have pried a copy of the gospel from a "presbyter of the church in Alexandria"—Clement's own church! (The doctrinal scandal to one side, that possibly is why Clement was so irked.)

Mark's "canonical" gospel is believed, on stylistic grounds, to be the oldest book in the New Testament, probably dating from around A.D. 75. In the opinion of most scholars, the canonical Gospels of Matthew and Luke are expansions on canonical Mark. The three books make up the so-called synoptic Gospels because of their many narrative and stylistic similarities. Scholars suspect that the synoptic Gospels derive from a single, lost manuscript sometimes referred to as Q. It would make sense if secret Mark were Q or a very early version of it. Passages briefly quoted by Clement fall in canonical Mark 10:13–46, which deals, among other matters, with one of Clement's favorite themes: how will the rich man be saved? There is a curious narrative gap in canonical verse 46: "And they came to Jericho: and as he went out of Jericho with his disciples . . ." So what happened at

* See M. Smith, *Clement of Alexandria and a Secret Gospel of Mark* (Cambridge, Mass., 1973), for the Greek text.

† Greek *mystagogos*, "he who leads [one] to the mysteries," and *hierophantos*, "he who reveals what is secret."

‡ M. Smith, *The Secret Gospel: The Discovery and Interpretation of the Secret Gospel According to Mark* (New York,1973), p. 16; cf., Proverbs 23:9.

Jericho? Secret Mark, according to Clement, fills in the gap with an episode involving a notorious woman called Salome. Clement also says that before canonical Mark 10:32, secret Mark tells of a strange nocturnal interlude between a rich—also naked—young man raised from the dead (Lazarus?), and Jesus, who "taught him the mystery of the kingdom of God."* Needless to say there's nothing remotely like that in canonical Mark.

Thus, it looks as though canonical Mark might actually be a condensation of secret Mark. Canonical Mark, with its "things suited to progress toward gnosis," might have been especially intended for those not yet admitted to the greater mysteries. It is known that Matthew and Luke were intended for Christians in Syria and Asia Minor, and because neither explicitly mentions the greater mysteries, that can only mean Syriac and Asian catechumens. The assumption of an esoteric core to Christianity makes sense out of a confusing proliferation of gospels. The traditional author of the fourth gospel is John the Evangelist, one of the original TWELVE APOSTLES. But the Gospel According to John has long been recognized as descended through a tradition entirely different from the synoptic gospels. It holds an intermediate position between the esoteric and exoteric gospels of Mark. It is identifiably more gnostic than canonical Mark, Matthew, or Luke, yet presumably less so than secret Mark. It seems more suited to the well-known gnostic tastes of Egyptian catechumens during the second century.

From the beginning of the present account, we have claimed objective superiority for an approach to myth based in esoteric practice rather than in symbolism or philosophy. The schismatic condition of the early church from the first century to the orthodox consolidation five hundred years later is starkly illustrative. The maddening number of heretics, apostates, and schismatics of every conceivable doctrinal hue that mangles early church history is much simpler to understand now. Schismatism *must* arise when an exoteric majority tries to make intellectual sense of the canonical gospels without practical experience of gnosis, rather like the wrong-headed testimony of the blind men who each touched a different part of the elephant before describing the beast.

In early fifth-century Egypt a controversy raged along esoteric-exoteric Christian lines. Of course at that time the dispute was not characterized quite that way. Rather, it was seen as a struggle between orthodoxy† and heterodoxy. *Orthodox* quite simply meant exoteric. *Heterodox* on the other hand could mean everything from the true and authentic mysteries to wackiness like Carpocratianism.

The list of heresies, as they are now known, is mind-boggling. And for the most part the divisions among the sects revolved around the meaning of the INCARNATION: How can a human being also be a divine being? This quarrel was unresolvable exoterically. Or rather, it could be resolved only by the sword, which is pointedly exoteric and suffers not at all from interpretive ambiguity. The real problem was that the myth of the Incarnation had too many answers. Some, Arianism for instance, were possibly profound answers. Some were merely interesting or clever. All were largely irrelevant. The version that eventually won out is summed up in the Athanasian Creed: "I believe in God, the Father Almighty, and in Jesus Christ his only begotten Son, who was conceived by the Holy Ghost, born of the Virgin Mary, suffered under Pontius Pilate, was crucified, died, and was buried [and so forth]."‡ Be assured that every participle, noun, and preposition of it was scrutinized to exhaustion.

Polemical debate was the order of the day. Orthodoxy taught that Jesus of Nazareth had two *natures* but one *personality*. The Monophysites

* Smith, *The Secret Gospel*, p. 16; it's likely that this was the verse the Carpocratians were tricking out salaciously.

† "Orthodoxy" in the present context has little to do with the present Orthodox churches of the East.

‡ Athanasius (d. A.D. 373) was a doctor of the Eastern Church and bishop of Alexandria. A bitter—and successful—opponent of Arianism, it is debatable whether he had been initiated into the true mysteries.

said he had but one nature, and that was divine though his body might be human. The Docetists, astral projectionists of their day, thought Jesus was superlatively divine but in an ectoplasmic body that only "appeared" human. The Marcionites, with truly stunning common sense, said that between good and bad was a state that was not all good and not all bad (an inkling of the Three Worlds?). Some sects, particularly the "gnostic" ones, went off on wonderfully arcane tangents. The Pelagians maintained that original sin was a hoax, the Carpocratians that the church founded by Jesus and the Twelve Apostles was in reality a homoerotic mutual admiration society, the Montanists that, say what you like about Jesus Christ and the incarnation of the Son of God, a certain Montanus, bishop of Phrygia, had incarnated the Holy Ghost!

The most far-reaching quarrel in the early Church was that between the orthodox and the Arians, the entire dispute hanging improbably on a single letter, *iota*, truly a distinction without a difference.* One could go on and on. In the ninth century, in a schismatic death rattle, Greek-speaking Christians led by Photius, patriarch of Constantinople, broke with the Roman church en masse because he would not respect the pretensions of Nicholas I to primacy.† Once the original baptism was lost, the authority of the papacy, which originally rested on an ultimate veto power over initiation pragmatically vested in Peter and his successors (Matthew 16:19), could no longer be sustained.

"Gnostics" such as Carpocrates and Marcion can be explained as failures of esoterism at the first level: *There is a secret to be kept*, a secret that is otherwise known as the myth of the Incarnation. At the second level—*The secret is . . .* —esoterism failed not at all; the essence of the mysteries—knowledge of the God within the human body—remained unrevealed, and while controversy raged the true mysteries went begging.

The secret gospel of Mark survives only in a few fragments quoted in the letter to Theodore. It is virtually certain Clement never meant for other eyes to see the letter, and its accidental recovery in Palestine (in 1958) was a blessed opportunity to peek behind the scenes of the early church in Egypt. But what happened to secret Mark? From Clement's letter we know it could be found in Alexandria at least until the end of the second century. Where did it go from there? The upshot of the doctrinal civil war in Egypt was the triumph of the exoteric faction. The orthodox deacon Cyril (later Saint Cyril, Doctor of the Church) gained the see of Alexandria and in 391 connived at a fire in the great library, a collection of 530 thousand papyrus rolls amassed since the days of Aristotle. The secret gospel, a summary of it, or references to it might have been destroyed in the holocaust.

Far more may have been lost in that catastrophe than the secret gospel of Mark, however. Cyril knew very well what he was about, because also up in smoke went irreplaceable works by both pagan authors and exponents of rival mystery religions, books that might have indicated curious and wholly disturbing similarities between Christianity and non-Christian mystery cults. In light of then recent history, it was a catastrophic prospect. Persian Mithraism was very popular in the Roman army until well into the fifth century A.D. Sundry mystery cults had gained a following among educated Greeks and Romans, the very people with whom the early church sought to ingratiate itself.‡ The

* *Iota* = Gk. ι = Eng. *i*; the dispute hinged on whether the prefix *όμο* or *όμοι* best expressed an inexpressible Incarnation. Arius (d. 336) was a priest of Alexandria who denied that the Son was either equal or consubstantial (όμο) with the Father. His teachings were condemned at Nicæa in 325; in the meantime, however, several powerful barbarian tribes had been mischievously converted to Christianity by arian bishops—notably the Goths, who were instrumental in destroying the Western Roman Empire. As a result Arianism persisted in the Gothic kingdoms in Gaul and Iberia down to the seventh century.

† The final break came in the eleventh century, in a showdown between Patriarch Michael Cerularius and Hildebrand (Pope Gregory VII).

‡ Noteworthy were the cults of Isis and Thracian Orpheus; in the first century A.D. they were as "hip" as est and scientology are today.

status of the church was yet uncertain, it being not a century since the edict of the emperor Galerius had legitimized Christianity.

From the orthodox perspective, it was the most natural thing in the world to lump all gnostics together. By the fifth century, gnosis had ceased to mean knowledge of "the innermost sanctuary," as it had in the time of Clement two centuries before. Usually it meant no more than "occult" in the worst sense: irrational, mantic, obscurantist for the sake of obscurity. Those with ears to hear were already a vanishing species. Orthodoxy had triumphed, and Cyril may have acted in the diabolically sincere belief that by burning the "heretical" books he was merely tidying up after the great doctrinal mess. After all, he is almost certainly innocent of any suspicion that he knew what the books meant. Still, one is moved to tears at the thought of such riches destroyed in the service of ignorance.

The dates of Clement's life supply a clue as to how the greater mysteries were lost to the West. Clement lived and died just before the final mass persecutions of Christians during the third century, when, it is possible, the majority if not all of those initiated into the true mysteries perished. Given the opinions of Jesus himself on the matter, there may never have been many of them to begin with.* The Galerian edict of 311, which placed the empire on the side of tolerance of Christianity, though not approval of it, points out that the Christians had reacted to earlier persecutions by either going to their deaths or, in a species of dumb insolence, becoming mute with respect to both the pagan gods *and* their own god. The former group of Christians may have included all or most of those who had received the esoteric baptism. Saint Cyprian (d. 258), martyr and bishop of Carthage, stresses, however, that persecution alone, even unto death, is insufficient for salvation: "He who is without the Church cannot be a martyr. He cannot reach the kingdom of heaven. . . . This shall not be a crown of faith."† That seems hardhearted, even cruel, unless we keep in mind that Christian baptism, like initiation at Eleusis, was especially concerned with practical instruction in the art of dying. This goes a long way toward explaining the eagerness, even enthusiasm, for martyrdom by early Christians like Ignatius of Antioch and Polycarp. They embraced the opportunity to put into practice what they had learned from initiation: how to die.

In perhaps the final, lingering irony neither Clement nor Origen (d. ca. A.D. 254), who in many respects resembles Clement, were ever beatified, much less canonized, by the Church. The exclusion of Clement, who in all probability was one of the few Christians of the third century to know firsthand the true baptism instituted by Jesus of Nazareth, demonstrates how powerfully the Church turned against Gnosticism and anyone with the slightest interest in the subject.‡

If there were survivors, they may eventually have migrated to the Albigensian colony in Provence. The history of the Church in southern France can be traced to Irenæus, a gnostic bishop from the East who founded a Christian community at Lyons in the late second century.§ Tradition tells us that Irenæus (d. 220) was baptized by Polycarp (d. 169), bishop of Smyrna and martyr. Polycarp had been baptized by John the Evangelist, who lived long and died around A.D. 100. (It

* In Matthew 16:19, Jesus to Simon Peter: "I will give unto thee the keys to the kingdom. And whatsoever thou shalt bind on earth, shall be bound in heaven; whatsoever thou shalt loose on earth shall be loosed in heaven," and in Matthew 22:14: "For many are called but few chosen." Both verses clearly indicate an intention on the part of the founder of Christianity to exclude people from Christian mysteries.

† Cyprian, *Unity of the Church*, in: J. H. Robinson, *Readings in European History*, vol. 1 (Boston, 1904), p. 21; for edict of Galerius and *Codex Theodosiana* versus heresy, ibid., pp. 22–7.

‡ Clement's eclecticism has relegated him to the position of a philosopher who merely "prepared the way for a fuller exposition of Christian teaching"! See Buttersworth, *Clement of Alexandria*, pp. xii–xiv, plus note on inside-rear jacket flap.

§ Irenæus too mentions the Carpocratians as possessing "secret sayings [Gk. *logia*]" of Jesus.

is vitally important to trace such connections back to the Apostles or their immediate successors if we are to understand the path of propagation of the true mysteries, not to mention their disappearance from Western Europe.) The Albigensians were strictly celibate. Growth in the sect had to come through conversions, which were few and far between. In the thirteenth century, this curious sect was exterminated to the last man, woman, and child (in a crusade provoked by the medieval pope Innocent III) precisely because the Albigensians practiced "occult heresies" not found in the exoteric *magisterium* or official teaching of the Church.

A second likely candidate for repository of the mysteries is the Celtic Church of the Britsh Isles. Christianity had reached Britain by the middle of the second century. In the fifth century Christianized Rome permanently withdrew its legions and exposed the island to invasion and conquest by pagan Angles, Saxons, and Jutes from Germany. Christian Britons were hunted down, and many fled to the mountain valleys of Wales, into the West Country, or across the Irish Sea. Ireland had never been part of Roman Britain, though according to legend saints Patrick and Brigid had converted the island to Christianity at the behest of Pope Celestine (d. 432). After subduing Britain, and in the process dividing it into seven petty kingdoms, the Anglo-Saxons did not bother to invade Ireland as well. Thus, assuming that Patrick (d. ca. 461) had knowledge of the true baptism, the Celtic Church, neither challenged nor threatened in Ireland, may have preserved the gnosis. Several clues that such was the case can be found in the work of the English priest Bede (d. 735).*

In the late sixth century Pope Gregory the Great sent Saint Augustine of Canterbury to return Britain to the faith. Augustine and his followers soon encountered remnants of the early Celtic Church, which either had never been wholly absent or had filtered back into Britain from Ireland or both. The Celts were an Indo-European people, closer kin to the Latins than to the Greeks but clearly distinct from both. Where Christian esoterism is a jumble of Egypto-Semitic sacerdotalism and Platonism, the Celtic Church, isolated during the Roman era and the Anglo-Saxon ascendancy, evolved a mythology that mingled Christian with Indo-European esoterism in unusual ways, for example, attributing the founding of Glastonbury Abbey to Joseph of Arimathea of all people. Also worthy of note among a vast corpus of myth are the Arthurian cycle (a duodecesimal myth) and the exploits of Mac Óc and Fionn mac Cumail. So fertile is Celto-Christian myth that one begins to understand it by assuming an early, self-conscious understanding of the proprioceptive bases of myth, which is to say, strict esoterism. That could only have come about in a well-regulated monasticism safe from scrutiny by the uninitiated. And indeed, the Celtic Church rediscovered by Augustine was essentially monastic. In all likelihood it had been that way since the earliest days of Christianity in Britain.

It is too often forgotten that monasticism, some form of which is always closely brigaded with initiatory rites, came to the West largely *from* the West, that is, from Ireland (though adapted to the Rule of Saint Benedict, an Italian). The Celtic bishops, unlike their Gallic and Italian counterparts, had no administrative duties, such being assigned to the office of abbot.† A Celtic bishop led an entirely cloistered existence and was in charge of spiritual matters only, which we interpret as instruction in meditation or *prayer*. The "reforms" of Augustine and his successors exactly reversed the roles of abbot and bishop, not to further prayer in the esoteric sense—nothing in Bede suggests that Augustine (or Bede) was an initiate—but to assert the primacy of the archbishop of Canterbury throughout Britain. Evidence for the original form lingers, however, in the peculiarly English use of *minster*, "monastery," which is always attached to an episcopal see, for example, Westminster and Yorkminster.

* Bede, *A History of the English Church and People*, trans. L. Shirley-Price, rev. ed. R. E. Latham (London, 1968).

† Ibid., 3.4, plus note p. 342.

The office of bishop was instituted in Christianity to provide a legitimate, diocesan authority for baptism; disputes could be resolved by the archbishop or if necessary by Rome. In the Catholic and Anglican churches, the right to administer the higher sacraments (confirmation and holy orders) is still reserved to a bishop, and within a diocese a priest exercises his *faculties* as priest at the pleasure of the local bishop. This is a fact of utmost importance because the injunction to secrecy was absolute, no matter the circumstances.* A bishop was powerless outside of his own province. If the faculty of baptism were granted to clergy only on a case-by-case basis, the untimely death of a single archbishop could end the line of legitimate transmission throughout an entire (Theodosian) diocese within one generation. The death of a pope could end it everywhere in Christendom. Yet because, from earliest times, the Church was esoteric–exoteric in both membership and structure, the institutional church could conceivably continue *sans raison d'être*. And the earlier in Church history such a death might occur, the more far-reaching its effects. Absent a faculty to initiate, the last of the truly baptized would take the secret to his or her grave. Pope Clement I (fl. A.D. 100), the fourth bishop of Rome from Peter, indicates that the potential for such a misfortune was early acknowledged, for the Apostles appointed elders (presbyters) of the church "and then went on to add an instruction that if these should fall asleep [die], other *accredited persons* should succeed them."†

Regarding the Celtic Church, our scenario depends on whether Saint Patrick was an initiate. We know that in 441 he received the *pallium* from Pope Leo the Great (d. 461). The pallium was a special robe, a head covering in fact, given only to archbishops. Bede records Boniface V instructing Archbishop Justus to don the pallium only "when you are celebrating the Holy Mysteries."‡ (We have already noted the practical function of stoles in the Eleusinia.) It is difficult to know who if any among those prelates acted from unvarnished knowledge of esoteric praxis rather than reverence for mere ceremony. Up until Saint Silverius (d. 537), all the popes save two were canonized, which might indicate something (Paul often uses the word *saint* to mean "one who has been baptized"). The sixth century was a time of great turmoil, when Arian Ostrogothic kings ruled in Italy and persecuted Catholics. We might tentatively locate the final esoteric-exoteric watershed in approximately A.D. 550, at least in the West. Coincidentally, that was the time when the emperor Justinian in Constantinople reasserted imperial authority over the city of Rome. Spiritual power might also have been removed to the East, only to die out there at some later date. The situation is extraordinarily complicated, however. Already in the codices of Theodosius II of A.D. 438, we discover secular authority promulgating and enforcing laws that harshly discriminate against heretics and non-Christians, one sect of which, the Manichaeans, the forerunners of the Albigensians in Provence, is singled out for particularly severe treatment. If the Albigensians, via the Manichaeans, had preserved the authentic gnosis as we have suggested, then the Theodosian Code would seem to indicate the ascendency of exoterism in the East by the early fifth century.

As to when the mysteries were lost in Britain, we can only speculate. In five books Bede never once mentions Saint Patrick or his commission to convert Ireland, so we can surmise that the mysteries vanished before Bede's time and probably before the death of Augustine in 605. Like the good Christians that they were, the Celtic bishops submitted to the ecclesiastical authority of Rome at the Synod of Whitby

* Save in the case of someone unbaptized and in imminent danger of dying, in which case the transmission of gnosis ends anyway. Also, because initiation is practical not inscrutably mystical, once the kriyās have been revealed, they cannot very well be *un*revealed. This accounts for the tradition that a baptism is valid when the faculties of the priest have been revoked by his bishop or even if the priest has been defrocked.

† Clement I, *First Epistle to the Corinthians* 44.1-2, in: Staniforth, *Early Christian Writings: The Apostolic Fathers*, emphasis added.

‡ Bede, *A History of the English Church and People* 2.8.

(664). They had taken Jesus' advice and rendered obedience to the new caesar in Rome, who wielded the magisterium in name only. In any case, by the thirteenth century the exoteric magisterium was all that was left for the vast majority of European Christians.

Christian initiation was not completed in a single ritual but revealed in stages, which also contributed to a winnowing of the gnostic faithful. Thus, John the Baptist "baptized with water," whereas Jesus "baptized in holy fire." In Acts 8:14–17, many in Samaria were baptized only "in the name of the Lord Jesus" before Peter and John arrived to "[lay] hands on them [and] they received the Holy Ghost," as if the laying on of hands were a privileged rite, one involving a literal *manipulation* of the initiate. In rāja yoga a guru puts his hands upon the sādhaka not for any symbolic reason, as in the Catholic or Anglican rite of confirmation, but to show practically how to meditate.* As is the case with yogic *updeśa* (initiation) down to the present, the true Christian baptism was given strictly by person-to-person instruction. That does not mean exclusively oral instruction; for example, in India, more often than not a guru simply demonstrates yogic techniques. Roman Catholic teaching has always insisted that only a priest can bestow the sacraments (baptism, confirmation, extreme unction, etc.).

In canon law the magisterium of the Church has always meant scriptural *and* extrascriptural instruction. The two are referred to by Catholic theologians as "scripture and tradition." The Church always fiercely defended the doctrinal importance of *tradition,* "that which has been given across [generations]." Indeed, a fiery disagreement over the relative importance of scripture and tradition was at the heart of the Protestant Reformation in the sixteenth century. The insistence on tradition or extrascriptural teaching can be traced back to the early Church. Indeed, one cannot adequately account for the historical emergence of a hierarchical church without predicating the belief among Christians in a special competency that priests and bishops (and deacons) possessed but lay brethren did not. When the Protestant churches eliminated the doctrinal importance of tradition, trusting all to "scripture and reason," as Martin Luther said, the hierarchical church was doomed.

It was a hollow controversy, because by the time of the Reformation the true mysteries were utterly unknown to the so-called universal Church. Had it been otherwise, had some secret inner *camera* of the Roman church actually preserved the esoteric baptism for fifteen centuries, such knowledge would certainly have been invoked (if not revealed) by Catholic polemicists like Johann Eck, who engaged in several no-holds-barred debates with Luther. The Diet of Worms of 1521, which formally anathematized Martin Luther, makes no mention of anything remotely resembling esoteric practice. It reaffirmed the doctrinal importance of tradition, but by then tradition had come to mean the voluminous collection of papal encyclicals and bulls, the decrees of synods and general councils, and the adherence to numerous pious practices such as the veneration of the saints and the Blessed Virgin. The necessity of a priest class was to be defined solely in terms of an inscrutable descent of an inscrutable Holy Spirit during the ceremony of ordination. It is still defined essentially that way.

If, however, *priest* originally meant someone initiated into esoteric practice, then Catholicism has at least managed to maintain until the present the original person-to-person external *form* of initiation. Baptism, the taking of the eucharist, confirmation—to this day they are distinct sacraments, but traces only of the stages of initiation into the mysteries of The Christ. Other, lingering institutions of esoterism from the early Church are cloisters, confessionals,

* The avowedly mystical intentions of the Greek Orthodox Church are so manifold as to make it impractical to go into them at this time. The entire Orthodox liturgy is described as a *mystagogy*, namely, an instruction in the mysteries; and "the mysteries" is what Orthodox priests call the seven sacraments of Roman Catholicism. The sole extant copy of Clement's letter to Theodore was found in the ancient Orthodox monastery of Hagia Sabba in Palestine. See also Eliade, *Yoga: Immortality and Freedom*, pp. 63–65, for a discussion of *hesychastic* breath control in the Orthodox Church down to at least the eighteenth century.

monasteries, and monastic orders in general with their vows of silence and their emphasis on solitude.*

The central dogmas of the Roman church are said to be *mysteries*, a word that originally meant "to plug up the eyes, ears, and mouth," in other words, to turn the senses inward in the manner of the legendary three monkeys who neither see nor hear nor speak evil. The grand, glittering ritual of the Mass—especially the High Mass—which is a myth in itself, a sort of play acting, subtly veils the sanctification of the five senses that occurs when they are turned inward. When the celebrant of the Mass holds aloft the brilliant white host, when the acolytes ring the Sanctus bells and shake the perfumed censer—all beneath the stone (bone?) dome above the altar, all suggesting something of the inner experience—then are the senses purified. The SACRIFICE OF THE MASS is a sacrifice† of the senses, a reorientation of the eyes, ears, and nose from their normally outward foci to a single internal experience.

The vast number of gnostic texts await esoteric interpretation. Christ's remark, in the apocryphal Gospel According to Thomas, that "the sign of the Father in [a disciple] is a movement and a rest" is an echo of the central role of respiration in the Christian mysteries: respiration acts more continually than the heart; a steady undulation throughout the body with two important pauses per cycle—at maximum and minimum inhalation. Thomas's gospel is a small part of the *Nag-Hammadi Library*, a collection of gnostic texts written in Coptic and discovered in the Egyptian desert in 1949. After eighteen centuries, many papyri from the library were severely deteriorated, although Thomas survived relatively intact. Only recently has a complete translation become available.‡

The Gospel According to Thomas is not one of the so-called canonical books of the New Testament, but it sheds valuable light on first- to second-century A.D. gnostic practice, which seems to have included breath control. The question of what is or is not a "canonical" text depends of course on how one interprets the purpose of Christ's ministry. If one believes, as do the majority of Christians, that there was no authentic *esoteric* magisterium, namely, one deriving from Jesus, in the early Church, then one can dispense with Thomas and many other "apocryphal" books, which is what Archbishop Cyril did when he ordered all noncanonical texts destroyed. If, on the other hand and as is presupposed throughout this book, one affirms that an esoteric teaching not only existed but was Jesus Christ's *essential* magisterium, then a gnostic text like Thomas must be considered on an equal footing with the canonical Gospels. Moreover, neither canonical nor noncanonical texts reveal the esoteric teaching explicitly. The esoteric magisterium is neither doctrinal nor confessional. Not one dogma of Christianity—not the Trinity, not the Resurrection, not the Incarnation, not even the necessity of a personal redeemer such as Jesus of Nazareth—touches it.

Each mystery is itself a myth—or, as Jesus said, a parable—a deliberate obfuscation intended to divide the faithful who are ready for baptism from those not yet ready, as was done literally at the dismissal of the catechumens during the Mass (< L. *missa*, "dismissal"). Such doctrines are "true" insofar as they buttress esoteric practice, presumably because experience showed that the questioning mind of one newly baptized often needed doctrinal reassurance. For those reasons, then, it is a matter of mere preference which scriptural tradition is of greatest value for understanding early Christianity; but because gnostic texts at least hint at the existence of an esoteric magisterium, they must be ceded pride of place.

Evidence for Judaic esoterism is plentiful. From antiquity through the Middle Ages, rabbis wrote voluminously on mystic practices. Israel ben Eliezer, known as the Ba'al Shem Tov, an eighteenth-century Lithuanian Jewish mystic and

* If the true mysteries had survived anywhere, it would have been within the monastic orders; but Luther was himself an Augustinian monk, and he had no difficulty in doing away with monasticism entirely.

† From L. *sacrificere*, "to make holy."

‡ *The Nag-Hammadi Library*, 3d ed., ed. R. Smith (San Francisco, 1988).

founder of Hasidism, knew the ancient mystic tradition called *hekalot* or "halls." *Hekala* was a way of inducing trance by recitation of certain secret Hebrew words so as to ascend to (the halls of) heaven. The practice is similar to mantric meditation. Judaism also preserved many rites, places, and personages of a distinctly esoteric odor down to hellenstic times, for example, the much-documented community of Essenes (also militantly celibate) at Qumran near the Dead Sea and the practices in the temple during the high holidays. There is also the cabala, something of an embarrassment to modern, liberal Jews, but which in rabbinical tradition is the esoteric form of the Mishnah, the orally communicated wisdom imparted to Moses on Mount Sinai at the time he received the Torah or nonsecret wisdom. Presumably, it was the same "wisdom" later imparted by Moses to Joshua on Mount Nebo.

The coming of divine revelation atop a mountain is common enough in Judeo-Christian myth, for example, in the TRANSFIGURATION and Crucifixion.* It has numerous counterparts in Greek, Hindu, and Buddhist legend. In almost all cases, we suspect, "mountain" equals "human being sitting in meditation," when the body assumes roughly a triangular shape. A mountaintop is a skull, and somewhere within the skull is Clement's "inner sanctuary."

* Jesus was crucified on the MOUNT OF CALVARY; *calvarius* < L. *calvus*, "a skull" (Aramaic *golgotha*).

20

THE MYTH OF THE CHRIST

Here is another riddle: What is not far from every one of us? In it, we live and move and have our being.*

Is the correct answer the sound of one hand clapping? A sound we can never elude for as long as we live? The above paraphrase is from Paul's sermon to the Stoics and Epicureans in the Areopagus at Athens. Clearly, his teaching is something more complicated—although not necessarily more profound—than a koān. It is about "living and moving and being." We are talking about an elaborate, extended myth called the New Testament.

Throughout the New Testament, we find a constant refrain of "the name of God," "the name of the Lord," "the name of Jesus." The Gospel of John speaks almost continuously of the Word of God or the Name of God.

Neither is the issue confined to the New Testament. The Old Testament is even more stuffed with references to the Name of God or Word of the Lord. One can open up the Old Testament virtually at random and find them. In fact, there is not a single revelation of God to man in the entire Bible—starting with the Torah and continuing all the way through the Hagiography, the Greater Prophets, and the Minor Prophets, all the way to Malachi—that is not also accompanied by a revelation of God's ineffable Name. Christians claim such references are scriptural precursors of Jesus of Nazareth, which is to say, prophesies. Orthodox Jews, however, might argue that whereas The Christ is indeed the Word of God, Jesus of Nazareth was not The Christ.†

Nor is the issue confined to the Bible. In the *Hymn of Cleanthes*, a prayer of the Stoics, we read "Lord of the manifold name, eternal and everlasting is thy power! . . . To call upon thy name is meet

* Cf., Acts 17:28.

† Greek *christos*, "anointed," is a direct translation of Heb. *mashiach* > Eng. *Messiah*.

and right for mortal kind."* Greek philosophy of every stripe, from the presocratic Heraclitus (fl. sixth century B.C.), on through Plato and the zealous Neoplatonist Plotinus, continuing—and especially—with the gnostics, seeks to explain, analyze, and interpret the *logos*, "word," in its relation to man and the cosmos.

Neither is the Word of God a Western concoction. In Hinduism we have the Name of Kṛṣṇa and the Name of Rāma, in Buddhism the Name of Amitābha (Amida in Japan) and the practice of ***nembutsu***, in Islam the Name of Allah. In so-called primitive religions of the present era the practice of calling on a secret name for aid, protection, and even salvation is so widespread as to be universal. The myth of the Word of God is essential, in fact, to all ancient religions. It is *the* core myth, the mystery—above all others—that must be plumbed.

◆◆◆

Hindu scriptures speak of a "sound of God [ṣabda brahman]" or *vāc* (Skt. "word"; cog. with Eng. "voice") that created the universe and still pervades it, so fine that "a knife cannot cut it," "water cannot wet it"; although "moving, it moves not." Thus, the Word of God, whatever it is, is equivalent to brahman, whatever that is.

Knowledge of brahman, or puruṣa, is the goal of yoga. Puruṣa is the limit of internal awareness because it is awareness itself. The stages a yogi passes through on his way to knowing puruṣa are the subject of the last *pāda* (book) of the *Yoga-Sūtra*. His argument is far from clear and thus can only be summarized here. Briefly, the puruṣa—the yogi's true self, the sole knower in the universe—must be disentangled from prakṛti, all that can be known of the universe apart from puruṣa. The prerequisite for the disengagement of puruṣa from prakṛti is a return of equilibrium among the three guṇas, the modes of existence. When the guṇas have been equilibrated, the puruṣa can know only itself. At that point all karmas and kleśas are extinguished and kaivalya is achieved, never to be reversed. The puruṣa cannot be revealed all at once, however. It is first demonstrated by the guru as an internal light, an internal sound and so on, on which the sādhaka meditates. The puruṣa, paradoxically, is itself the experience on which the yogi must perform saṃyama to attain kaivalya. As we have seen, the yogi seeks to control his body because without internal stillness he will not "hear" the sacred Word, which guides him; although once heard, it can never again be missed:†

> And thine ears shall hear a word behind thee, saying, This is the way, walk ye in it, when ye turn to the right hand, and when ye turn to the left.‡

The techniques of rāja yoga are directed at experiencing the sacred Word. All else is either preparatory or irrelevant.

Although a philosophical system in the Western sense is not part of yoga, many yogis adhere to the philosophy of Sāṃkhya. According to Sāṃkhya, cittā (the stuff of consciousness) is antecedent to everything else in the universe. One can no more create consciousness than create existence; neither concept, properly understood, is a predicate. Consciousness proceeds from nothing. In Indian philosophy ṣabda brahman, the Sound of God, is consciousness itself. It created everything in the universe and inheres in everything. It is both individual consciousness (ātman) and universal consciousness (brahman). Imagine a lantern covered by a shroud perforated by an infinite number of tiny slits. The light burning at the center of the lantern is brahman, each ray of light emerging from a slit is ātman. Therefore, the ***Upaniṣads*** say, "ātman is brahman." It is an analogy similar to the Coney Island-cutout analogy that describes archaic attitudes on the relation of

* Cleanthes (d. ca. 220 B.C.) was a disciple of Zeno the Stoic and succeeded him as head of his school in Athens. The translation is from Staniforth, *Marcus Aurelius: The Meditations*, p. 29.

† The Hindus make the puruṣa identical with the god Kṛṣṇa, who plays a flute, a reference to a particular internal sound (lāya) heard in meditation.

‡ Isaiah 30:21.

body to soul. Brahman-puruṣa "peers" into the manifest universe (the creation) through an infinite set of eyes, it hears through an infinite set of ears, it thinks with an infinite number of minds, of which your eyes and ears and mind are but instances. Each instance is ātman or soul. Yet it is only an analogy, for the *Upaniṣads* are at pains to stress that neither ātman nor brahman has attributes such as color, sound, or intelligence. Nothing positive can be said of them, only *neti neti*: "not this, not that."

The same cautions apply to *consciousness* as a (highly controversial) term of Western philosophy. Radical empiricists deny the term any meaning whatsoever, but then empiricism only accepts positive statements as meaningful, so there is a certain amount of question begging in its assertions. Empiricism is a philosophy that derives directly from the procedures of scientific verification. If, however, science is trapped in a "prison of light," that is, if it arbitrarily makes perception the touchstone of truth, then of course positivism results because positivism and perceptualism are really one and the same thing. Later we shall discuss the role of consciousness in philosophy, particularly Greek philosophy, in more detail. For now we appeal only to the phenomenological understanding of the term. Consciousness is something each of us understands even though we cannot define it positively.

In the early Church, the antecedent nature of consciousness was expressed by saying that the Word of God was "begotten, not made," that it "proceeded directly from the Father." Furthermore, "all things were made by him [the Word of God]; and without him was not anything made that was made." The Father, then, is the nothingness of brahman. The Word is the connection of the Father with his creation. The Father "has revealed himself in His Son Jesus Christ, Word of His own from *silence* proceeding."*

Judeo-Christian religion begins with ABRAHAM THE PARIARCH. Abraham was born Abram, the son of Terah of Ur, a city in Chaldea. (Chaldea, in the heart of Mesopotamia, was a nation subject to many external influences, including the religious practices of the Indo-Europeans in Persia and India.) After God made his covenant with Abram, he renamed him *Abraham,* "father of nations." The similarity between his name and *brahman* might be a linguistic coincidence, but it could also be a clue to the origin of the myth of the Father in Christianity. To "sleep in the bosom of Abraham" is proverbial in Judaism and Christianity, a happy estate strongly evoking the "peace of brahman," in Vedānta the supreme goal of each man. The Father is a recapitulation of Abraham the Patriarch.†

What of the Son? In John especially, Jesus, the Son of God, is the Word of God. In the Apocalypse he tells us "the Word is the Name of God." The angel Gabriel, in announcing the coming of The Christ into the world, tells Joseph and Mary, "Thou shalt call his name Jesus: for he shall save his people from their sins."‡

> Be it known unto you all, and to all the people of Israel, that by the name of Jesus Christ of Nazareth, whom ye crucified, whom God raised from the dead, even by him doth this man stand here whole. . . . Neither is there salvation in any other: for there is none other name under heaven given among men, whereby we must be saved."§

There would seem to be a great deal at stake in correctly identifying the Name of God. What then is that "name" that preserves us from sin?

On the Christian view we are asked to believe it all comes down to J-E-S-U-S, a name found nowhere in the Old Testament, much less the *Gītā*, the *Upaniṣads*, the Buddhist *sūtras*, or

* Ignatius of Antioch, *Epistle to the Magnesians* 8.4, in: Staniforth, *Early Christian Writings: The Apostolic Fathers.*

† Abraham's son was Isaac. Like Jesus, Isaac (< Heb. *Issachar*) is a sibilant name. That the son of Father Abraham and the Father's son should be similarly named is not surprising, nor that Isaac's mother was Sarah.

‡ Matthew 1:21; Luke 1:31.

§ Acts 4:10–12.

the Taoist texts. Now the implausibility of this, to say the very least, is not the main objection to the Christian interpretation of the Name of God. Plausibility is not really an issue in matters religious: "I believe just because it *is* absurd," said Tertullian. The problem is that such an interpretation, taken in the context of all Christian beliefs concerning the Name and the Word, is hopelessly confused and contradictory. For not only is Jesus the Word, but also the Bible is the Word, and although we might conceive of a spiritual Jesus creating the universe, it is quite another matter to imagine a primeval volume of the Bible—from Genesis to the Apocalypse—out among the stars with hammer and nails, busily making everything that was made and not making those things that were not made. If Isaiah and Ezekiel and John and a dozen others tell us that "the word of the Lord came upon me," are we then to imagine that the vision that invariably succeeds those words follows upon a very heavy book dropping on their heads? Granted it is a caricature, still, it is a caricature not belied by the confusing use of the terms "word of God," "Jesus the Christ," "Bible," and "Torah" by Christians and Jews.

Much of the problem is semantical. The traditional interpretation of *onoma Iesou*, "[the] name of Jesus," uncritically assumes that "name" and "Jesus" are appositive, whereas in Greek the relationship is as likely a possessive genitive: "the name [that belongs to] Jesus." If, however, *Jesus* is onomatopoetic of breath, *onoma Iesou* is a cunningly esoteric usage of the Greek descriptive genitive: "the *Jesus-y* name." In neither case does "the name of Jesus" mean "the name, Jesus," nor does it reveal the secret name, any more than writing "the name of my father" reveals my father's name.

Several of the sacraments of Roman Catholicism are essentially rituals of *naming* or *renaming*. In baptism the catechumen receives an exoteric name. In the early Church that was always the name of the godfather, which could be feminized in the case of a female catechumen; for example Antonius bestows the name Antonia. The same is true for confirmation, where the candidate takes the name of a patron saint. In matrimony the bride takes the name of her husband, which conforms to the imagery of the soul—regardless of its current sex of incarnation—as the Bride of Christ. The Christ is the Word of God, so, esoterically the catechumen receives the Name of God during authentic initiation. This act of renaming is extremely old and persists in the initiatory rites of passage of "modern primitives." More pertinent here is the case of Joshua, initiated by Moses on Mount Nebo. Before that event Joshua was named *Oshea ben Nun*, "Oshea, son of Nun." Afterwards he received the name Yehoshua, identical to *Jesus*, and again, because Jesus is the Word of God incarnate, Oshea has esoterically received the Name of God from Moses. Saint Barnabas, one of the companions of Paul who has left us an "apocryphal" gospel, refers to Joshua as "Joshua ben Nave."* In both cases—*Nun* and *Nave*—the exoteric name reduces to *n* (as does *Nebo*), the essential third-world phon. It appears therefore that in Judeo-Christian myth the "Heaven of the Father" is identifiable with the third world. Joshua is the Semitic Achilles, who leads the Hebrew assault on the walled citadels of Canaan (kn). His renaming recapitulates the consanguinity of Achilles and Patroclus, son of Menœtius.

In Hebrew the literal name of Jesus derives from *yehoshua*, a word that originally meant "breath" but also has the sense of "protection" and "peaceful." In other words, it describes trance on the breath. So when the Angel of the Annunciation, a recapitulation of the Holy Spirit, tells Mary "thou shalt call his name Jesus: for he shall save his people from their sins," a double entendre results between a literal sound, that of the breath, and the approximation of that sound, *Yehoshua* (transliterated in the Vulgate as *Jesus*). The Name of God is hiding in plain sight, as it were. Ineffable it may be, it has here become effable.

Ineffable, of course, means that the Name of God *cannot* be spoken—not *should not* be

* Barnabas, *The Epistle of Barnabas* 12, in: Staniforth, *Early Christian Writings: The Apostolic Fathers.*

spoken—in the same way that an internal sound cannot be spoken but only rendered approximately in words as a mantra. In the Old Testament, the mantra used most often for the Name of God is *Shem*—also one of the sons of Noah—from which derives *Semites*, figuratively, "the people of the sacred sound in the breath." In the New Testament, the mantra is Ιησους (Iesous), "Jesus."

Jesus enters Jerusalem on Palm Sunday "riding upon an ass's colt" while the crowds shout "Hosannah! Blessed is the King of Israel that cometh in the name of the Lord."* *Hosannah* (sn) is another onomatopoesis for the sound of the breath, specifically, the harshly nasal sound produced by an ass (cf., L. *asinus*, "an ass's colt"). The waving of the palm fronds describes the rhythmic motion of air during respiration. Jesus' entry into Jerusalem—the Mountain of Zion (*zn* = *sn*)—describes the sussurating movement of the breath within the frontal suture, the esoteric gateway to the cranium or Heaven. The early Christians made use of an ass's head to represent The Christ during their secret rites.† The Old Testament, too, frequently introduces asses into narrative. The ability to control the wind is often attributed to saints (for example, Peter, Paul, and John) and could mean roughly the same thing as mastery of prāṇāyāma in yoga. Jesus calms the winds from the deck of a ship.‡

Jewish mystical sects like the Essenes lived in desert monasteries having large cisterns. The archaeological evidence shows that the volume of water that could be held in their cisterns—for example, at Qumran—far exceeded the needs of the community for drinking water. Because stone cisterns are troublesome to build—and expensive—there must have been a compelling reason for making them so large. We know that they were used for ablutions (ritual washings), which played a curiously large role in Essene religious practice.§ But even granting that cleanliness is nigh unto godliness, the Essene cisterns were outsize. If, however, initiates were lowered into a full cistern to a depth of several meters, they not only would be compelled to hold their breath but, because of water pressure, also would hear numerous internal sounds that are variations on the sound of one hand clapping.

Christian mystics shared with the Essenes the ritual of baptism by water, often called the "baptism of John [the Baptist]" or "baptism in the name of the Lord Jesus." The Carpocratians made much of the fact that in the secret gospel of Mark the rich young man visited Jesus "naked." Clement, however, in his letter to Theodore, pointed out that what secret Mark says is "wearing a sheet over his naked body."# If prolonged immersion was the actual technique for baptism into "the kingdom of God," then the young man's costume, far from being licentious, was eminently practical. The purpose of water baptism in Christianity was not a symbolic washing away of sin in the Blood of the Lamb but a practical introduction to internal awareness. The aim of the water baptism was roughly similar to that of the sensory-deprivation tanks used in experimental psychology today, save that a "sense dep" tank fails of the most important esoteric purpose: stopping the breath. The Blood of the Lamb describes, not the water baptism, but the baptism in "fire and holy spirit" that only Jesus was competent to perform.**

By virtue of his sibilant name, Jesus, like Jason, was originally a description of deep, meditative breathing. But more than that, like

* John 12:12–14.

† Tertullian, *Apology* 16.1–2, Minucius Felix, *Octavius* 9.3, in: *Tertullian: Apologia and De Spectaculis* (trans. T. R. Glover) and *Minucius Felix* (trans. G. H. Rendall) (Cambridge, Mass., 1977).

‡ Matthew 8.23–26. Cf., Euripides, *Iphigenia in Tauris*, 1477–81; Poseidon calms a storm-tossed sea to speed Orestes and Iphigenia (the Twins) to Athens, the third world.

§ Principally from the writings of Josephus (d. ?A.D. 100) and Philo of Alexandria (d. ?A.D. 50).

\# Smith, *The Secret Gospel*, p. 17.

** Latin *agnus*, "lamb," < *ignis*, "fire," cog. with Skt. *agñi*, "fire." A lamb is hornless and so theriomorphizes internal sight. The horned ram, a fire sign, theriomorphizes external sight.

Apollo, Jesus is an anthropomorphization of a vital energy common to every faculty: prāṇa, propriocepted within sight and sound, taste and touch, thought and smell. So important was Apollo in the religious opinion of antiquity that the early Christians likened him to The Christ in their attempts to proselytize among pagan Greeks. As Dolphinish Apollo his connection to forced restraint of the breath by immersion in water—the technique by which the Word was first revealed to Christian catechumens—is implicit, but the comparison was facilitated by Apollo's role as anthropomorphized prāṇa. The Presocratics, we have seen, posited the existence of an energy they called pneuma, which drives the world in its evolution. More importantly, pneuma is the energy that drives the breath.[*] This energy, revealed by respiration, Plato called Logos, or Word.

With Apollo necessarily comes Artemis, who is recapitulated—albeit crossculturally—in the myth of the BELOVED DISCIPLE. James and John are brothers and are the Christian equivalents of the Twins. Jesus named them *Boanerges*, literally, "children of thunder." In Greek myth Castor and Pollux (the Dioscuri) are the sons of heavenly Zeus, whose most common epithet (after Cronides) is "thunderer," but they are also, as we have noted, the sons of earthly Tyndareus, whose name is virtually a homonym for "thunder." John is described in the New Testament as a beardless youth, the Apostle "whom Jesus loved, who had lain close to his breast at the seder."[†] Jesus' especial love for John, then, is an estoteric description of the intimate relationship between breath and olfaction. Compared with the twinship of Apollo and Artemis, John (Heb. *Jokannan* = *kn* = *Canaan*, LAND OF MILK AND HONEY, taste and smell; cf., *Cæna*, where Jesus turned water into wine) can be compared to Artemis, the feminine aspect of the nasal function, that is, smell. Without pushing the comparison too far though, we can use the traditional effeminacy of John to understand him as the feminine side of the brain—the right brain—and, because the olfactories do not cross (decussate), he describes both the right breath and the right sense of smell.[‡] If John is smell, then the Apostle James must be a recapitulation of the breath. After Peter, he is the most highly regarded of the Twelve Apostles. When Peter leaves the Holy Land, it is James who takes charge of the Church in Jerusalem, the city whose name means "peace" but also contains the root *shem*, the Holy Name.

Peter (< Gk. *petra*, "rock") was given his name by Jesus himself. Because the equivalence of rock with bone is so widespread in myth, Peter, we surmise, is a description of the cranium. The other apostles—like the Argonauts who accompanied Jason—are the remaining senses and the mind.[§] In his moving apostrophe to the Father at the end of John's gospel, Jesus speaks of the Apostles as those whom God gave him out of the world, whom he has kept safe, and who have themselves kept the Word. He begs the Father to sanctify them in the truth—"Father, Thy Word is truth"—before sending them back into the world.[#]

◆◆◆

Thus far, we have confined our attention to the Word as the force that drives the breath. During trance, when the attention of the yogi is riveted within the cranium, proprioception of the

[*] Greek *pneuma* derives from the same Indo-European root as Skt. *prāṇa*.

[†] John 21:20.

[‡] In the earliest Christian art, John is invariably placed on Jesus' right hand. According to tradition, John was bishop of Ephesus, where the great temple of Artemis was located.

[§] *Argo* and *ark* are almost certainly the same: *rg* = *rk*. Whereas Jason traveled with the Fifty Argonauts and Jesus with the Twelve Apostles (12 ■ 3), Noah had only three sons, whom he took inside the ark with him (by divine fiat the ark was constructed with three floors). Jason, Jesus, and Noah are all prominently associated with a dove. In Judeo-Christian myth, however, the emphasis on prāṇā yāma is much more evident. Noah's eldest son was Japheth, almost certainly identifiable with the Titan Japetus, the prosaic breath of the second world. The other sons were Shem and Ham, who describe inner breaths. And of course *Noah* reduces to *n*, the anaractic whine of the cranium heard at the onset of the pituitary catastrophe: the Flood.

[#] John 17:6–19. In the Ark of the Covenant were kept AARON'S ROD (= caduceus) and the show bread, or *manna*, which fell from Heaven.

twelve cranial nerves is intense. The Old Testament myth describing the cranium is Noah's Ark. The Hebrew word for ark is *aron*, "a closet." (It was Aaron, brother of Moses, who had the right to touch the ARK OF THE COVENANT without harm coming to him.) English *ark* is derived from Latin *arcanum*, "a chest," which has come to mean "hidden," as in *arcane*. Hebrew *aron* and English *ark* are essentially describing the same thing: the cranium. Jesus tells his disciples to "go into your closets [aronim] and pray in secret." In other words, go within the cranium and meditate. Within the skull, the focus of meditation is the prāṇa flowing within the cranial nerves, but focus on prāṇa can best be achieved after mastery of prāṇāyāma, when the breath has stopped or slowed considerably. The awareness of the meditator *contracts* after the suspension of breathing, both literally and metaphorically zeroing in on a vanishing point within the skull that lies near the pineal body—vanishing because one is dissolving the second world, dissolving perception. Yet the means for doing so is precisely perception, perception turned in on itself: "If therefore thine eye be single, thy whole body shall be full of light."* The approach to the vanishing point, where the presence of the divine Word is experienced simultaneously within all the senses, is esoterically described in the myth of the CROSS OF CALVARY. The nexus of the Cross of Calvary, that same vanishing point, is where the head of The Christ rested. *Christ* is written with an initial *X* (Gk. *chi*).

Contraction of perception means contraction of the senses, all of which must become one-pointed. For the sense of taste, the technique is khecarīmudrā, the stretching of the tongue into the cava of the throat. Aaron carried a staff, reminiscent of the Dionysian thrysus, a description of the spinal cord plus nerves leading into the mesencephalon that includes the glossopharyngeal nerve, the nerve of the tongue. His ability to touch the Ark of the Covenant describes khecarīmudrā. If a sādhaka has not been properly prepared, khecarīmudrā combined with prāṇāyāma is certainly perilous and might provoke a cataleptic fit. Aaron is the cause of much suffering to the Jews because he instigates worship of the GOLDEN CALF—leading to riotous eating, drinking, and debauchery—while Moses is away on Mount Horeb.† It is interesting that Moses must ascend and descend the mountain three times before receiving the Decalogue on stone tablets, paralleling Sisyphus and the Stone. When Aaron turns to his idol, it is a description of the tongue withdrawn from khecarīmudrā and directed toward the grosser, exoteric sensation of taste.

The Golden Calf was made from melted-down earrings, from "the earrings which are in your ears," Aaron tells the Hebrews, so their refashioning into a calf is a recapitulation of hearing, but now it is perceptual hearing. By contrast, Mount Sinai (sn) describes immersion in the cleansing sound of the breath in the skull and is essentially the same mantra as hosannah (sn). It is where Moses sees God in the form of a bush that burns without being consumed, his samādhi mūrdha jyotiṣi. The color of the BURNING BUSH is somehow *like* the color of the exoteric calf, which heightens the sacrilege and is one of the reasons why Moses is so incensed on his return. Gold and silver belong to God.‡ The color of the internal Burning Bush is not compared to the colors of gold and silver because they are valuable, rather they are valuable because they are like the color of the Burning Bush. The two most perfect examples of antique sculpture were the chryselephantine statues of Zeus at Olympia and Athena in the Parthenon.§ *Chryselephantine* is a term used to describe a technique in which the sculptor covers carved

* Matthew 6:22.

† Exodus 32:1–7; Horeb is the name of a chain of mountains, of which Sinai is the tallest, in the Wilderness of Sin.

‡ Ezekiel 16:17: "Thou hast . . . taken *my* gold and *my* silver and made them into idols," says God.

§ We do not know what happened to the Athena Parthenos; the Phidian Zeus was so beautiful even the Christians could not bring themselves to destroy it. Brought by the Christian emperor Theodosius the Great (d. A.D. 395) to Constantinople, it was destroyed in a fire in 475.

stone with gold and ivory. It is another attempt at approximating the silvery gold light radiating from the thrones of Zeus and Athena in the third world. So too is the image of the Golden Fleece. If one chooses a snow-white sheep's pelt to dye the color of gold, the result is a silvery gold. No combination of words can adequately describe mūrdha jyotiṣi, just as no word adequately reproduces internal sound. Only an approximation is possible, but it is an approximation born of something actually seen rather than a symbol of something imagined. One imagines Jesus, importuned by the unbaptized to describe heaven. He looks around at the landscape of Judea and says: "Look now, the kingdom of God is like to a tawny grain of mustard seed, which grows into that great bush right there, the one with the golden flowers that the birds nest in. Look you, it's there! I have seen the light of heaven, and I tell you it's *like that mustard bush*."*

And then: "Who among you would like to see that light? I tell you truly, I shall not show it to just anybody. It's for your own good. You must be pure of heart to see God and live to talk about it":†

> Thou shalt not take the name of the Lord thy God in vain: for the Lord will not hold him guiltless that taketh his name in vain.‡

After an initiatory water baptism in which the Name of God is "taken" by the catechumen, a period of purification is necessary before further initiation. The sequence recalls the division into mystæ and epoptæ at the Eleusinia, a division into those who were ready "to gaze at [epoptein]" mūrdha jyotiṣi and those not yet purified. In Roman Catholicism and Anglicanism, that means postponement of the sacrament of confirmation: baptism in holy fire. Because the practical basis of baptism is lost, however, with only a husk of symbolic rite surviving, the purification that should precede confirmation has been reduced to delaying the sacrament until the confirmee is older (and presumably wiser). In the *Doctrina Apostolorum*, a very early document on the "two Ways [didache]" of living—one good, one evil—the faithful are warned that "No one is to eat or drink of your Eucharist but those who have been baptized in the Name of the Lord; for the Lord's own saying applies here, 'Give not that which is holy unto dogs.'"§ Again, the eucharist is linked with a caveat of purification.

Eleusinian epoptea, Christian confirmation, and yogic root gazing have essentially the same aim: the vanishing of perception in intensely focused cranial trance. In Christian myth baptism in holy fire contributes another limb to the Cross of Calvary, that of concentrated vision, as khecarīmudrā contributes concentrated taste. Because it involves focusing on the space between the brows, root gazing singles out for especial attention passages in scripture referring to lintels. Recall Exodus, where at the first Passover the Jews daub the blood of a ram over the lintel of their doorways to ward off the ANGEL OF DEATH. As we saw in the myth of Sisyphus and the Stone, the mythic significance of doorways and lintels is their usefulness in describing the frontal suture and brow line. In the Old Testament we find the image of the VALLEY OF DEATH, the same painful proprioception focused this time on the "valley" of the frontal suture vis-à-vis the "mountains" of the metopic eminences (figure 7). Yet again, the RED SEA (red is Ares' color, the god of war), in parting for the Israelites, describes the dilation of that suture: "The waters returned and covered the chariots and the horsemen and all the hosts of Pharaoh,"# essentially the dissolution of the second world in the Primeval Sea when the breath stops (the inundation of the horses).

In the New Testament we find the three

* Cf., Matthew 13:31.

† Cf., Matthew 5:8 and 13:13.

‡ Deuteronomy 5:11.

§ *Didache* 9.8, in: Staniforth, *Early Christian Writings: The Apostolic Fathers.*

\# Exodus 14:28.

crosses of the Mount of Calvary (L. "skull") on which the Crucifixion takes place. At the Transfiguration, Jesus takes Peter, James, and John onto a mountain where they have a vision (trance) of Jesus and the prophets bathed in a blinding white light. In the New Testament, John the Baptist, crying "Behold the Lamb of God. . . . I saw the Spirit descending from heaven like a dove," is the first to bring the future apostles John and Andrew to Jesus for initiation. Jesus then asks "What seek ye? They said unto him, Rabbi, which is to say, being interpreted, Master [guru?], where dwellest thou? He saith unto them, Come and see. They came and saw where he dwelt, and abode with him." Then, solely after seeing Jesus' "dwelling," Andrew is converted and "findeth his own brother Simon [Peter], and saith unto him, We have found the Messias." Soon they bring others, and Jesus says (to Nathanael) "Ye shall see heaven open."* Lamb, dove, and heaven are closely linked in an initiation ceremony.

In the Bible the phrase "to lift up the eyes to heaven" occurs frequently; a hundred occurrences of it could be cited. It easily translates into Greek as *epoptein*. Thus, it is the same technique (root gazing) that describes Leto's grasping of the palm boughs at the Birth of Apollo. "To lift up" or "to raise" one's eyes toward heaven—the third world—always initiates a biblical verse in which the narrator—for example, Daniel or Ezekiel or Jeremiah or Isaiah—undergoes a vision. In Genesis, Abraham, on the point of sacrificing Isaac, is prompted by Jehovah to spare his son: "And Abraham lifted up his eyes, and looked, and behold behind him a ram caught in a thicket by his *horns*."† Whereat he sacrificed the ram instead. The words "lifted up his eyes" and "behold behind him," seemingly contradictory, can be reconciled if one interprets "behind" to mean back into the cranium, namely, within the organism (cf., "behind" in Isaiah 30:21). A "thicket" is a description of the gasserian ganglion. The image of a ram caught in a thicket is widespread in the Middle East and appears in Babylonian statuary of the third millenium B.C., indicating that the probable origin of the myth is in the East. David slays the giant Goliath (klt) with a sling, the stone striking the Philistine in the forehead; and is sent into the fray by his father Jesse, the esoteric breath.‡ The frame of a sling is Y-shaped, like the brows. The bending of the sling, the palm boughs, and the bow formed by the supraorbital arches are one and the same kriyā. David is further linked with the intraorbital space in the DEATH OF ABSALOM, David's renegade son, who, while riding upon a mule, is caught by his hair in the boughs of an oak and strangled between "the heaven and the earth; and the mule that was under him went away."§ David has seated himself "between two gates" and appointed a watchman to await news of Absalom:

> And the watchman went up to the roof over the gate unto the wall, *and lifted up his eyes*, and looked.#

Seated thus, David learns of the death of his son. We have here an Old Testament description of prāṇāyāma (especially in the mule, theriomorphized breathing, that runs from beneath its rider and leaves him to strangle).

In the New Testament the disciple Stephen was one of seven deacons appointed by the Apostles especially to minister to the faithful: "And when the Apostles had prayed, they laid

* John 1:32–51. Cf., John 10:2: "But he that entereth in by the door is the shepherd of the sheep."

† Genesis 22:13, emphasis added.

‡ 1 Samuel 17:15-49; significantly, Jesse sends David into battle directly from a sheepcote. Cf., Kṛṣṇa and the milkmaids (gopis) who carry jars of yogurt on their heads. Kṛṣṇa breaks the jars with a slingshot and the yogurt drips down onto the foreheads of the gopis, who extend their tongues to lick at it. A much more pleasant image, the breaking of the jar nevertheless recapitulates the pituitary catastrophe (yogurt is sour, like the vinegar presented to Jesus on the Cross). By contiguity, the jar on the head of a gopi *is* the head of the gopi.

§ 2 Samuel 18:9. The ram caught in a thicket is recapitulated in Absalom caught by his hair.

Ibid., 24, emphasis added.

their hands on [the seven]." Stephen reproaches the Jewish Sanhedrin (a priestly council) for delivering Christ to the Romans for crucifixion. The Jews do not at first react, but "he, being full of the Holy Ghost, looked up steadfastly into heaven and . . . said 'Behold, I see the heavens opened, and the Son of man standing on the right hand of God.'" At which they stone him to death. Stephen's trance is movingly described: "All that sat in the council . . . saw his face as it had been the face of an angel."*

Saint Stephen was not only the first martyr of the Church, but he is also said to have performed "wonders and miracles" like Jesus.† The question now presents itself: Is his death a historical record or a myth? Is it a recapitulation of the Crucifixion itself, with stones rather than a crown of thorns used to describe the death of perception that occurs when the awareness is entirely focused on the space between the brows?

"What I have done, you can do."

◆◆◆

Nothing we have said thus far requires that Jesus be an entirely unhistorical figure. Jesus of Nazareth can be likened to a guru, one of the greatest gurus the world has known. Because of the earth-shaking effect of his teachings, he must have been what the Hindus call a *satguru*, a guru plenipotentiary, who brings into the world the "ocean of grace," the drops of which he bestows—or withholds—on whomever he wishes. Grace is a concept to which no known conceptual categories apply. When a devout Christian, Buddhist, Muslim, or Hindu speaks of grace, he is always changing the subject, referring to that which cannot really be discussed yet somehow must be discussed. In this book, the emphasis has been on praxis, the means by which salvation can be attained. But there is a real danger of misconstruing yoga as something mechanical, even arrogantly so, in its assertion that it can "teach" salvation. Nothing could be further from the truth. Any human endeavor, whether it be the attempt to raise a child, write a book, or, yes, know God, cannot succeed without faith and devotion. Patañjali specifically lists absolute faith in Īśvara as one of the preconditions for success in "inhibiting the modifications of the mind" that the yogi strives to achieve (others are chastity—or at least continence—dispassion, and industry).‡ Praxis, yes, but always "God willing, with God's grace."

Grace is not opposed to praxis. It is not a complement to praxis. Even more so, it is not earned by nor does it follow necessarily upon praxis, neither does it precede praxis. Devoted praxis is praxis accompanied by what Roman Catholic theology calls *actual grace*, the grace of acting without sinning.

Action is a perilous thing, for every action is a potential snare: in the response of the actor to his action, one of the kleśas—attraction, repulsion, fear of death, or ego—to which all human beings are inclined, might be reinforced. The reservoir of karmas is infinitely deep:

> The sin of Judah is written with a pen of iron, and with the point of a diamond: it is graven upon the table of their heart.§

The soul is always a hair's breadth from falling out of grace regardless of its actions, for any action can be pharasaical, "a whited sepulchre" that apparently conforms to the Law yet is performed without true piety. "For God knoweth the secrets of the heart":#

* Acts 6:3–15 and 7:55–58; Jesus, Son of Man, is also Lamb of God, conceived on 25 March (Feast of the Annunciation), when the sun is entering the zodiacal sign Aries, the Ram.

† Acts 6:8. The miracles of Jesus, his apostles, and the prophets have numerous parallels in the *siddhīs* (perfections) of yoga, e.g., diasappearing into thin air, mind reading, clairvoyance, and clairaudience. All depend on manipulation of prāṇa. The interested reader is referred to *Yoga-Sūtra, Vibhūti Pāda*, sutras 16–37. Siddhīs are acquired as a by-product of advanced yoga. Patañjali's well-considered opinion (sutra 38) is that zeal for yogic power per se is a fatal "obstacle" to kaivalya.

‡ *Yoga-Sūtra, Samādhi Pāda*, sutra 20.

§ Jeremiah 17:1.

\# Psalms 44:21.

Who can say, I have made my heart clean,
I am pure from sin?*

That judgment is left to God.

The state of actual grace is its own verification. Ultimately, the doubts and worries over the fidelity and piety of one's actions are themselves manifestations of ego (asmitā), the only cure for which is grace. Ultimately, the soul must weary of scrutinizing its motives. Its desire to know the truth must displace every other concern: "Thou shalt have none other gods before me."† "Before me" means other affections that distract from constant remembrance of the Holy Name; one shows devotion practically and from moment to moment. Baptism gives to the catechumen a specific experience upon which to concentrate throughout the vicissitudes of the day.

If grace is everything and praxis nothing, can salvation come without baptism? Yoga recognizes the capability for passing into trance seemingly without effort or training. Spontaneous trance states are known as *jadasamādhis* and are mentioned by yogic texts (along with the trance-inducing properties of drugs—including, presumably, alcohol and cannabis). Yoga holds that jadasamādhis are frankly gratuitous—possibly arising from what we would call individual genetic mutations—unteachable, hence impractical. Ultimately, yogis would say, an individual's ability to pass into trance without effort or training is a result of past-life experiences.‡

Patañjali claims that extreme devotion—*bhakti*—to God (Īśvara) can induce spontaneous samādhi in an individual. Immediately the sixteenth-century Spanish Christian mystic Saint Teresa of Avila comes to mind. Teresa was a devout Reformed Carmelite nun who according to witnesses and her own testimony would pass into rapturous states while praying to an image of Jesus. During those episodes she would fall into a swoon, losing all consciousness of her surroundings. A "swoon," of course, is a colloquial expression for trance; losing all consciousness of her surroundings save the icon of Jesus is ekagrāta pariṇāma; the icon is the seed (bīja) of her trance (samādhi).

No extant document indicates that Teresa was ever trained in formal meditative practice, although that is perhaps not apposite. Long before her time, certainly by the Middle Ages, Roman Catholicism plainly recognized the special nature of mystical prayer or *meditatio*. Scholastic theologians divided meditatio into three parts: *consideratio*, in which the person praying selects an exclusive object of prayer—the Trinity, say—followed by *contemplatio*, in which he concentrates his mind solely on the holy Trinity, culminating in *raptus*: mystical communion with the trinity of Father, Son, and Holy Ghost.§ Not coincidentally, the three stages of meditatio exactly parallel the three stages of saṃyama.

Also interesting are Saint Teresa's attempts at describing raptus. It was, she reported, like being "pierced through the heart with an arrow." In our discussion of the myth of the Kraken (sea monster) we speculated that meditation on the vagus nerve is necessary to control the heart and, *pari passu*, the breath and mind of the yogi, and that such meditation is not without risk, is possibly even lethal.

The case of Saint Teresa can be explained as an occasion of bhakti: extreme devotion to God. Yoga, it should be stressed, sees bhakti as a sacred gift of Īśvara. If one has the gift of bhakti, one is truly blessed and has no need of rāja yoga, meditation, prayer, or anything else to achieve kaivalya, the technical yogic term for what Christians call salvation, Buddhists nirvāṇa or *satori* (Zen Buddhism), and Hindus *mokśa*.

* Proverbs 20:9.

† Deuteronomy 5:7.

‡ *Yoga-Sūtra, Samādhi Pāda*, sutra 19; Patañjali refers to anyone possessing such abilities either as a *videha* or a *prakṛtilaya*.

§ Taimni, *The Science of Yoga*, p. 123; *raptus* = past participle of L. *rapēre*, "to snatch," from which Eng. *rape*; *raptus* = "snatched", a description of the suddenness of the transformation in awareness (samādhi pariṇāma); the sensuality of Teresa's description of her swoons has been much commented on, predictably enough by Freudians (see also Bernini's seventeenth-century sculpture of the saint in trance, undeniably gorgeous but also markedly prurient).

The problem—if problem it is—presented by bhakti is that it falls outside the scope of texts like the *Yoga-Sūtra*, indeed outside the scope of rational discussion entirely. A yogi understands bhakti as a sacred gift granted to an individual soul who has been struggling for many incarnations to achieve salvation, and for that reason it is unteachable. Bhakti may be the fruit of previous, albeit forgotten, mastery of technique.

For most of us (and Teresa of Avila might well have been an exception) virtue is insufficient. "His name *through faith in his name* hath made this man strong," says Paul.* But the esoteric meaning of "his name" is the core mystery, most sacred and profound, revealed to the catechumen by a priest to whom it was previously revealed, in other words, to the sādhaka by the guru who was himself once a sādhaka. All the faith in the world will not bring the revelation of the Holy Name unaided. And once revealed: "Whoso looketh into the perfect law of liberty, and continueth therein, *he being not a forgetful hearer, but a doer of the work*, this man shall be blessed in his deed."† The antipathy between faith and practice vanishes in a yogic context because yoga does not distinguish between moral and practical virtue.‡ One practices yoga with absoulte faith in the efficacy of the kriyās revealed by the guru.

In yogic philosophy, which is exoteric and to be unambiguously severed from yogic practice, the human body has been especially designed by brahman as a vehicle for communion with brahman. The creature can know the Creator, face to face as it were, as Jacob did, when he climbed the ladder (the body) to heaven and was renamed Israel, "He who struggled with God," and lived to tell the tale. The Christian corollary is Paul's remark, already quoted, that the "hidden wisdom" he imparts is "what God ordained before the world *for our glory*" (emphasis added), namely, before the creation of the human form described in Genesis. The "glory" to which Paul refers is the BEATIFIC VISION.§

Admittedly, the notion of every man and woman not only becoming God, but actually being God incarnate, is blasphemous to Western ears. Yet consider, no Christian would be willing to say what God *is*. Is this not equivalent to being unable to say what God *is not*? The issue of whether or not a human being is divine—and what that might mean—is therefore an open one. The resolution of the problem lies in understanding the practical basis of "God realization," in understanding that God realization is just this: It is something one *realizes*, internally, with no necessarily external manifestations. It does not mean *doing* anything.

During initiation, the guru reveals to the sādhaka the ṣabda brahman (Word) that impels his heart and lungs and tells him or her that "this is God; meditate on it till you *realize* it." Realize here means perform saṃyama and pass into samādhi with this Word as bīja. The sādahka must have faith in that practical instruction. Perhaps the closest Christian parallel are the words *Ecce agnus dei*, "Behold the lamb of God," spoken by the celebrant at the elevation of the host during the Mass. Those words have survived from the protocol of the secret baptism of the early Church. They describe the moment of revelation of the Word as internal light. "Lamb," of course, indicates the space between the brows (L. *agnus* cog. with Skt. *agñi*, "fire"). We do well to meditate on their meaning.

Ignorant of their esoteric purposes, we take our myths more or less literally. It is the overtly theatrical (not to mention melodramatic) notions of divinity embodied in those myths and inherited by the religions of the West that interfere with understanding the wisdom of self-perfection to which they call each of us. Perhaps the most

* Acts 3:16, emphasis added.

† James 1:25, emphasis added.

‡ An unfortunate distinction having a long history in Western philosophy and going back in some cases to misinterpretations of Plato (see, e.g., *Gorgias*, passim); several mischievous dualisms—Manichaeanism and Docetism—have been the result.

§ Cf., Paul's words with John 20:46: "Not that any man hath seen the Father, save he which is of God, he hath seen the Father."

perfect summation of that practical wisdom are the sacred texts of yoga.

There is a great mercy implied here, namely, that one does not have to be a born saint, which is to say, have access to inscrutable spiritual power, to come to gnosis. One need only be embodied in human form. Of course one also must have humility sufficient to recognize that salvation, whatever it means, requires assistance beyond the strengths of one's own ego. One must seek out a master and ask humbly, just as that master humbly asked his or her master, and so on back to an age when salvation myths were first elaborated and before. Yet of all the virtues humility, it seems, is ever in short supply, save, perhaps, among children, which possibly is why Jesus lays such emphasis on coming to him "as a little child," without guile or pretense to knowledge.

In two well-known incidents from the gospels Mary Magdalene washes the feet of Christ, once with her tears and again with precious, sweet-smelling ointments; the latter occasion establishes a connection between her esoteric meaning and the olfactories.* Both times she humbly dries his feet with her hair. Here is the Christian myth of the Feet of the Lord. When Jesus is crucified, it is Mary Magdalene, John, and Mary the mother of Jesus who take up their station at the FOOT OF THE CROSS. We might also note that if we combine the imagery of the third-world sea with that of the Feet of the Lord, we arrive at the myth of Christ's WALK UPON THE WATERS.†

◆◆◆

The Christ arrived in the world in Bethlehem, Hebrew for "house of bread," describing the internal "communion" of the senses. Wise men came from the East, led by a star that hovered over the stable where the Christ Child lay in a manger wrapped in swaddling clothes. They presented gifts of frankincense, gold, and myrrh. Shepherds watching over their flocks by night were led to the stable by a heavenly host singing God's praise.‡ Inside the stable the father, a humble carpenter, and his young wife, still a virgin somehow, kept their vigil surrounded by a sheep, an ox, and an ass. All is silence bathed in golden light from the star.

The BIRTH OF THE CHRIST is a description of an experience of initiation into the mysteries. A theriomorphism for each sense is present except for smell, described by the GIFT OF THE MAGI. The Virgin Mary is the anthropomorphization of voiceless speech and the third-world sea. A favorite scene of Christian art is that of Mary, Jesus, and Saint Anne, the mother of Mary. Mary holds the infant, and Saint Anne, standing behind, embraces both. Anne, the grandmother, describes the third-world whine that envelops the sādhaka during meditation and within which the Virgin Mary is immaculately conceived. The carpenter, Joseph, is a recapitulation of the breath; the nails he drives foreshadow the nails of the Crucifixion. JOSEPH'S HAMMER is the Semitic parallel to the Spear of Achilles. Jesus too will be a carpenter, rhythmically driving nails.

The myth of The Christ is the central myth of Western civilization, the cynosure around which our culture circulates, although at times and of late it is increasingly averting its gaze. The Christ is an anthropomorphism of the Word, the subtlemost, omnipresent vibratory energy that permeates the cosmos and rotates the galaxies and the atoms alike. The "good news" of the Gospels is that although galaxy and atom are essentially remote from ourselves, our bodies are not. If that Word vibrates in everything that is, as John declares, then it vibrates within each of us. In the sacrament of baptism the catechumen is shown, in a miraculously simple manner that beggars the convoluted didactics of dogmatic theology, how to maintain constant awareness of the living Christ, The Christ that is life itself. At the moment of baptism, however, the profundity of what is revealed to the cat-

* John 12:3–5; Luke 10:37–48.

† Matthew 14:22–26.

‡ Matthew 2:9; Luke 2:8–14.

echumen is often not immediately apprehended. One must realize it by faithful attention until that moment arrives when the initiate is snatched up into the "third heaven," as Paul describes it, "caught up into paradise and hearing unspeakable words, which it is not lawful for a man to utter."* Yet all along, the initiate is contemplating the *same* experience. What is shown in baptism cannot be different than what is realized finally in the Beatific Vision toward which baptism is directed. "I am the Alpha and the Omega," the Christ declares at the close of the New Testament, "the beginning and the end, the first and the last."†

* Corinthians 12:2–4. Paul was initiated by Ananias, an event esoterically described as a vision on the road to Damascus (Acts 9:1–18).

† Apocalypse 22:13. On our view, the Apocalypse is a long, lurid description of the death dream. We might call it a Christian Book of the Dead, but a more apt parallel would be to Buddha's demon-beset enlightenment under the Bo Tree.

21

SIN AND SALVATION

The Christ is the Logos of Plato, the hellenic philosopher perhaps most concerned with ethical matters, with the question of personal salvation. The pagan god most akin to The Christ is Apollo. Apollo is far and away the most beloved son of Zeus. His birth on Delos is closely associated with that of the Virgin, his sister Artemis. His mother, Leto, is directed by Athena to Delos floating in the sea. After Apollo is born, Delos becomes fixed in place, as do the the Clashing Rocks after Jason has passed through. When Christ dies on the cross, the veil of the second temple is rent asunder, never to be mended again. There is something about the wanderings of Leto before she can give birth that is reminiscent of the search for an inn by Mary and Joseph. In the Christian tradition, however, the character of the myth is vastly altered by influences from the Orient. The question of salvation is raised explicitly, something for which it would be very difficult to find a hellenic religious counterpart. Greek religion was concerned almost exclusively with propitiating the Olympian gods, often through ritual sacrifice. A priest class was late in developing—certainly after 800 B.C.—and distinguished only by its competence to perform ritual sacrifice. Often the only qualification was to be born into one of a very few families in each hellenic community. Explicit moralizing was the self-appointed responsibility of sages like Socrates. What we call religion, the Greeks would call philosophy. There is no mystery here. The true mystery is not how far apart the Greek and Christian myths are, but how close.

A sense of moral urgency is not unique to Christianity. Buddhism at one time was zealously evangelical and spread rapidly throughout the East, converting Tibet, Japan, and Korea. Comprehensive spiritual systems do not, in general, lay claim to such disparate cultures without asserting some importunate morality, which must be such as to scale formidable barriers of language and geography.

Clearly, Christianity exercises an imperative, proselytizing judgment on non-Christian religions, both doctrinally and pastorally. It was born in the Middle East, yet it reached adulthood in Northern and Southern European cults, Protestantism and Catholicism, or what could be described as a Germanic and a Greco-Roman variant. In Palestine, it is a minority religion, supplanted long ago by an even more evangelical sect: Islam.

The difference between much of the Old Testament and much of the New lies in the difference between war and peace, not in what they teach esoterically. When Paul says "Know ye not that ye are the temple of God?"* he but repeats Ezekiel: "My tabernacle also shall be with them: yea, I will be their God, and they shall be my people. And the heathen shall know that I the Lord do sanctify Israel, when my sanctuary shall be in the midst of them for evermore."†

What accounts for the difference is the relative cultural status of the people who created the myths. The *Iliad*, for example, as a completed, oral poem, dates from what is rightly referred to as the Dark Age of Greece (ca. 1000–700 B.C.), the turbulent centuries after the collapse of Mycenæan hegemony. The Old Testament goes back to a time when the Hebrews variously contended with Canaanites, Babylonians, Assyrians, and Persians for sovereignty in Israel. Christian myth, on the other hand, arose during the two-hundred-year *pax romana* (ca. 20 B.C.–A.D. 180), a period of political stability and relative peace in the eastern Mediterranean.

The *pax romana*, insofar as it influenced morals, undermined the warlike attitudes behind the ethical structure of the myths. It was no longer necessary to equate virtue with virility in such an obvious fashion. In short, the image of the hero as a religious figure underwent a vast change. Religion became civilized at the same rate as its practitioners, esoteric and exoteric together. Still, the division is not an absolute one. Christianity produced the myth of the Crucifixion in wondrously bloody detail, and much of Hebrew myth is a long string of slaughters, massacres, and enslavements.

The LAND OF ISRAEL is itself the human body, and the myth of the TWELVE TRIBES OF ISRAEL is a cabalistic, hence esoteric, description of the parts of the body, of which the myth of the Twelve Apostles is a lineal Judaic descendant. Both are related to the myths of the Twelve Signs of the Zodiac and the Twelve Labors of Heracles. It is at least possible that all duodecimal myths derive from descriptions of meditative control of the twelve cranial nerves.‡

The Christian churches insist on the historical Jesus' being the only "true" master, yet the gospels tell us that he himself sent the Apostles out to baptize, leaving it up to them who should be "saved." It was Peter, not Jesus, who decided that non-Jews (gentiles) should also hear the Word of God and be baptized in the Name of Jesus.

Peter's decision can be interpreted as consistent with claims for the spiritual primacy of Jesus worldwide. Peter, as the Roman church characterizes his role, was the vicar of Christ, and the popes claim to be the vicars of Christ to this day. But putting to one side the many reasons to doubt the plausibility of Jesus' uniqueness—his relatively late appearance in the history of human religions, many of which differ little with regard to moral teaching from Christianity; the existence of religious traditions antedating Christianity that predict the coming of great teachers besides their own, the existence of teachers such as Muhammad who appear *after* Jesus in history; the pernicious theological chauvinism instigated by the claim to primacy—ignoring for the moment all those objections and a host of others, it is worth pointing out that the meanings of phrases like "the Word" and "the Name" have an ancient esoteric context in religions besides Christianity.

Jesus himself is often somewhat lackadaisical in his attitude to scripture: "Ye have not his word *abiding in you*. . . . Search the Scriptures, for in them ye *think* ye have eternal life: and they are they which testify of me. And ye will not come to me, that ye might have life."§ Here is Paul on the same tack: "Forasmuch as ye are manifestly declared to be the epistle of Christ

* 1 Corinthians 3:16, 2 Corinthians 6:16.

† Ezekiel 37:27–28.

‡ Alternatively, 12 = 1 + 2 = 3, a recapitulation of the Three Worlds, the totality of experience.

§ John 5:38–40, emphases added.

ministered by us, written not with ink, but with the Spirit of the living God; not in tables of stone, but in the fleshy tables of the heart. . . . For the letter killeth, but the spirit giveth life."* The lesson seems clear enough: Scripture is a testament to something that happened long ago. It is not itself what happened any more than a review of a play is the play. And what of value can a review communicate where the action—like the death of Agamemnon or of Rosenkrantz and Guildenstern—takes place offstage?

Paul speaks of the "church" as the "bride of Christ." But what, we ask, is that church, that bride, apart from the human body made fecund by the Holy Spirit? This then is the meaning of the Incarnation: not that one human body alone was divine, but that all men are divine simply by being embodied. "What I have done, you can do." When asked who he is, Jesus never claims to be the "Son of God"; rather, he claims to be the "Son of Man." That mysterious phrase, the meaning which has deviled theologians for two thousand years, is Jesus' way of underscoring the *biological* basis of his divinity, a biology, the Church has always taught, that was completely human. At the end of his gospel, the Apostle Luke tells us, speaking of the faithful, that "They returned to Jerusalem and were always in the temple blessing God." What could this temple be, in which one *always* prayerfully abides, save the body? Blessing means prayer, profound awareness of one's life, one's breath. Blessing is yoga, a word meaning "union" in Sanskrit and cognate with Greek *zeugma*, "a yoke." During meditation, the lungs are felt within the chest like a harness worn by a horse. We do not breathe by means of them so much as a mysterious, rhythmic energy breathes through us. "My yoke is easy, and my burden is light."†

◆◆◆

What happens if knowledge of the WORD OF GOD is not attained in this life? On some interpretations of the New Testament, one is punished—more or less catastrophically. In Protestantism, one goes straight to Hell. In Catholicism one has the option of going straight to Hell or to the MOUNT OF PURGATORY, an afterlife halfway house from which, following an indeterminate epoch of purgation, the purified soul proceeds to Heaven. In any event, there is no return of the soul to earth.

Doctrines that posit the return of the soul to earth under certain conditions are reincarnational. Hinduism and Buddhism are examples, although the Buddhist position is much harder to conceptualize because it explicitly rules out the existence of a soul. But reincarnation was for the first few centuries of the Christian era an accepted belief among Christians, though it never became dogma. It was not until the Council of Nicaea in A.D. 325 that a belief in reincarnation was formally condemned as heresy. That date, as we have seen, likely falls *after* the knowledge of the true baptism was lost by the orthodox church. If reincarnation as a belief is somehow tied into the purposes of the mysteries, then a conciliar condemnation, however august, presided over by however many popes, archbishops, and deacons, cannot be accepted as conforming to the true mystic practice instituted by Jesus of Nazareth, assuming for the moment, there was such an historical person.

The belief in reincarnation was most common among gnostic Christians. Moreover, it was an essential part of their belief. Early Christians esoterically called the necessity of death original sin and reincarnation the resurrection of the dead. From an Eastern perspective the resurrection of the dead is an estate no less fatal spiritually than original sin; indeed, it is the obverse of it. Christianity is quite properly described as a redemptive religion. The senses are turned inward in meditation. Practically, that means that they are stimulated by the action of breathing alone. They are said to be centered in themselves, in their true nature, which is the WORD OF GOD. The connection, once established, is irreversible and from then on the meditator knows practically how to maintain it: "He who finds his life will lose it, and he who

* 2 Corinthians 3:3, 6.

† Matthew 11:30.

loses his life for my sake will find it."[*]

And Paul: "Thou fool, that which thou sowest is not quickened, except it die."[†]

But Jesus is the breath. So one who removes consciousness voluntarily from the life of the world and places it on the *life* revealed in the breath, or even beyond the breath, is one who is saved. Saved from what? From karma. Jesus is quite emphatic in his likening of the world to a prison into which one is sentenced until the "uttermost farthing" is paid.[‡]

Recall the famous biblical verse "For I the Lord thy God am a jealous God, visiting the iniquity of the fathers upon the children unto the third and fourth generation of them that hate me."[§] The seeming hardheartedness of these words is dramatically altered if we decide that "fathers" here means the previous incarnations of the children.

Again reading in Ezekiel we find: "Behold, all souls are mine; as the soul of the father, so also the soul of the son is mine: the soul that sinneth, it shall die."[#] Here we find the ideas of father, son, and sin tightly knitted together. Ezekiel goes on to describe a curious relationship between a father's deeds and those of his son, which is too lengthy to quote here entire but which may be conveniently divided into four parts. In verses 5–9 we are told that if a man "be just . . . he shall surely live." (What separates these phrases is a typically biblical example of pleonasm setting forth the ways that a man is "just," for example, if he "hath [not] defiled his neighbor's wife . . . hath not oppressed any . . . hath covered the naked," and so on and so forth.) If that same man

> beget a son that is a robber, a shedder of blood, [etc.] . . . he [the son] shall surely die; his blood shall be upon him[self]." . .

And if "he [the son] beget a son, that

> seeth all his father's sins which he hath done, and considereth, and doeth not such like . . . he shall not die for the iniquity of his father, he shall surely live. . . Yet say ye, Why? doth not the son bear the iniquity of the father? [an apparent allusion to Exodus, to which Ezekiel immediately replies:] When the son hath done that which is lawful and right . . . he shall surely live. . . . he shall not die. (10–21)

Finally, Ezekiel drops entirely the theme of father and son and addresses himself to the general idea of the righteous as opposed to the wicked:

> All his transgressions that he hath committed, *they shall not be mentioned unto him*: [emphasis added] in his righteousness that he hath done he shall live. Have I any pleasure at all that the wicked should die? saith the Lord God: and not that he should turn from his ways, and live? But when the righteous turneth away from his righteousness, and committeth iniquity . . . shall he live? All his righteousness that he hath done shall not be mentioned . . . and in his sin that he hath sinned . . . he shall die . . . Yet saith the house of Israel, The way of the Lord is not equal. O house of Israel, are not my [the Lord's] ways equal? are not your ways unequal? . . . why will ye die, O house of Israel? For I have no pleasure in the death of him that dieth, saith the Lord God: Wherefore turn yourselves, and live ye. (22–32)

The complexity of the verses—the transition from father to son to grandson to an impersonal self subject to judgment—should not obscure the fact that it is the experiential (karmic) lineage of but a single soul that is being described. Ezekiel's introduction of a generalized state of righteousness or of wickedness, which he clearly applies to a single human self, is a recapitulation of the metempsychoses of the soul, moving from good to evil lifetimes, that he has esoterically described as the descent from father to son.

* Matthew 10:39.

† 1 Corinthians 15:36.

‡ Matthew 5:25, Luke 12:57–59.

§ Exodus 20:5.

Ezekiel 18:4.

The contradiction with Exodus is only apparent, since there Moses is warning of what will befall the soul if it persists in its evil ways: the worship of "graven images" and the like, whereas the whole thrust of Ezekiel 18 is that the soul must turn from wickedness and embrace that "which is lawful and right." His transgressions then will "not be mentioned unto him," which is to say his sins will be requited, evil will have been paid for with good.

That we have here an all but equivalent doctrine to the Hindu law of karma should be self-evident. It explains the rather obvious symmetries found in Ezekiel 18, as well as why the prophet has bothered to even bring up the entire subject of collective guilt in the first place. Outside of a reincarnational framework there is no reason to link a son's misdeeds with his father's good deeds and vice versa. That we are here dealing with a Judaic text, which nowhere explicitly mentions metempsychosis, is not apposite. Like all ancient scriptures, the Old Testament is permeated through and through with esoterism. In cabala, references to reincarnation are not hard to find.* There it is called the doctrine of *gilgul enshamot*, literally, "the rolling of the souls,"† similar to the myth of the Wheel of Birth and Death found in Mahāyāna Buddhism, still more suggestive of Socrates' description of the rise and fall of reincarnating souls in the *Phædrus*. Hebrew *shem* is "breath," so *gilgul enshamot* also means "the rolling of the breaths." The metaphor can be correlated with the notion of the cyclical motion of pneuma, driving the psyche through the Three Worlds as it incarnates and disincarnates.

But there is obviously more to Ezekiel's argument than meets the eye. Why, one asks, does a "good" father reincarnate as a "bad" son? And why then does the "bad" son take birth as a "good" grandson? It would seem, on the face of it, that the ways of God *are* "unequal."

Well, no. According to yogic philosophy, just such a sequence of births is not only possible but likely. The karmic debt accumulated by a soul during countless lifetimes cannot be requited in a single incarnation simply by the performance of good deeds. Certain karmas are "deeper" than others, and sooner or later even the just will be tempted to succumb to the deep-seated desires they embody, necessitating yet another birth.‡

One way out of the dilemma—perhaps the only way—is to have the karmas undone en masse, which corresponds to a fundamental alteration of the nervous system, so that the kleśas are "burned up" completely. In part that requires the interposition of sanctifying grace in the experience of the soul. Christian dogma refers to such a divine intervention as the Forgiveness of Sin. Under the proper circumstances the soul does not have to pay for its sins.

Consider the significance of Ezekiel's phrase "O house of Israel," an esoteric reference to the human body. The famous Twelve Tribes of Israel are the various energies in the body that are objects of meditative control:

> The hand of the Lord was upon me, and carried me out in the spirit of the Lord, and set me down in the midst of the valley which was full of bones. . . . And he said unto me, Son of man, can these bones live? . . . Thus saith the Lord God unto these bones; Behold, I will cause breath to enter into you, and ye shall live. And I will lay sinews upon you, and will bring up flesh upon you, and cover you with skin, and put breath in you, and ye shall live. . . . there was a noise, and behold a shaking, and the bones came together. . . the sinews and the flesh came up upon them, and the skin covered them above. . . . and the breath came into them, and they lived. . . Then he said unto me, Son of man, these bones are the whole house of Israel. . . . Behold, O my people, I will

* Schaya, *The Universal Meaning of the Cabbalah*, pp. 86 and 114.

† Hebrew *sham*, "soul," contains the root phoneme *sh*, linking it to respiration and air as in Greek.

‡ *Yoga-Sūtra, Kaivalya Pāda*, sutras 2–10.

open your graves, and cause you to come up out of your graves, and bring you into the land of Israel. . . . Behold, I will take the children of Israel from among the heathen, whither they be gone, and will gather them on every side, and bring them into their own land.*

It is difficult to know where to begin in these verses, since they are pregnant with esoteric meaning at every turn. We note at once that the act of rebirth proceeds from a "noise" (Heb. *kol*, literally, "a sound") and a "shaking" (*ra-ash*, "a loud noise"), in other words, a motion which, as we've seen, seems to be the sine qua non of ancient cosmogonies. True motion is only a percept. The act of incarnation and the act of creation are equivalent. Again the second world is in emphasis. The fact that Ezekiel's vision takes place in a valley of dry bones (earth) makes this clear. The image of a gully in the earth is an apt description of the bones of the second world, which contains numerous irregularities of contour where the organs of perception are situated. In the beginning of the *Theogony*, immediately following the birth of Gæa, we read of the creation of "mountain clefts" wherein live nymphs and such like.† And, of course, where are valleys there too are mountains, which is why the second world is thick with peaks such as Mount Atlas, Mount Cyllene (birthplace of Hermes), and Mount Gargarus (where Paris rendered the famous verdict that provoked Hera and Athena so). But of all the depressions in the physiognomy of the cranium the most important is the one between the eyes, where the frontal suture is knitted into the spine of the nose. Esoterically it is most likely that while meditating there Ezekiel passed into trance.

Noteworthy too are Ezekiel's words "The hand of the Lord . . . carried me out in the spirit of the Lord, and set me down in the midst of the valley." The implication is of a sudden rapture and abandonment of the corporeal world. In short, it describes a meditative trance state. Indeed, virtually every chapter in the book of Ezekiel begins "And the word of the Lord came unto me," whence follows a vision of some sort, a divine message delivered by the mysterious "word of the Lord."

Finally there is Ezekiel's use of the phrase "among the heathen" in verse 21. The Hebrew is *goyim*, which literally means "the nations," in the sense of a tribe or clan, and is rendered in the Latin Vulgate by *gentiles*, "[those] born," birth signifying the Fall. We recognize the root phoneme *k* in both words, which is appropriate to the interpretation we have brought to the verses. The Lord's declaration that he will "take the children of Israel from among the heathen, whither they be gone," might mean that the souls of his elect will be brought into human bodies, "will [be] save[d] . . . out of all their dwelling places, wherein they have sinned. . . . Moreover I will make a covenant of peace with them . . . and will set my sanctuary in the midst of them for evermore."‡ Might those other "dwelling places," esoterically interpreted, mean nonhuman incarnations, savage beasts, fish, and fowl? There is nothing in the doctrine of metempsychosis to gainsay that interpretation. Animal bodies serve as vehicles of soul in which karma may be reaped but not sown, where the senses are utterly in control and life is an endless round of eating, mating, sleeping, and, nearly always, violent death. There is no peace there, only ceaseless craving, prowling, hunting; all is kinesis, relentless genesis, pain.

Recall too the dream of Saint Peter in the Acts of the Apostles, where he learns that the gospel, God's word, is to be preached to the gentiles:

> Peter went up upon the housetop to pray about the sixth hour: And he became very hungry, and would have eaten: but

* Ezekiel 37:1–21.

† *Theogony*, 130.

‡ Ezekiel 37:23–26.

> while they [the soldiers sent to fetch him] made ready, he fell into a trance, And saw heaven opened, and a certain vessel descending unto him. . . . Wherein were all manner of four-footed beasts of the earth, and wild beasts, and creeping things, and fowls of the air. And there came a voice to him, Rise Peter; kill and eat.*

Here we find the gentiles, those who are not the children of Israel, likened to wild animals. And can it be a coincidence that the soldiers who have come for Peter were sent by the centurion Cornelius (krn), whose name derives from the Latin *corneolus*, "horned," or that, when his trance overtakes him, Peter is seized by the pangs of appetite, or that he sleeps on the "housetop," the third world and the natural source of dreams, or that six is the number of cognition?

Yet it is not necessary to draw so extreme a conclusion. It is not required that the esoteric meaning of the gentiles be equivalent to bestial incarnations—though that may be part of the truth—only that "the gentiles" describe human beings who behave like animals. For does not Ezekiel say: "out of all their dwelling places, wherein they have sinned"? An animal cannot sin; it may only reap the consequences of prior human incarnations, existences that ended in a dream of the senses. The House of Israel is not just any human body. It is that of an initiate, of one who has learned the sacred "word of the Lord," who does not worship graven images, which is to say, the pleasures of the second world. The myth of the CHOSEN PEOPLE has little to do esoterically with the Hebrews of history, save that it was among their priests that it was first promulgated, one of the many images they chose to veil the experience of the soul in meditation. That means that a Jew, a true child of Israel, is any person who has been initiated into the mysteries of the "kingdom of God," who has been shown practically the way into the inner sanctuary, the lost garden: cedar-scented, perfumed "with myrrh, aloes, and cinnamon," who has touched the peace that "passeth understanding."

◆◆◆

The Crucifixion is a violent myth. When the breath stops and the pituitary catastrophe is triggered, a dangerous moment ensues before the peace of kaivalya is attained. The imagery of the *Iliad* is strangely reminiscent of the imagery of the death and resurrection of The Christ: "For he [Jesus] is our peace, who hath made both one, and hath broken down the *middle wall of partition* between [dividing] us. . . . Having abolished in his *flesh* the enmity, even the law of commandments contained in ordinances; for to make in himself of twain one new man, so making peace."† The words "commandments contained in ordinances" seem to refer to a primeval division of the world, a division that is bound up with "the hidden wisdom which God ordained before the world."‡ for "[Wisdom, the Word personified] hath builded her house, she hath hewn out her seven pillars. She hath killed her beasts."§ "Wisdom crieth at the gates, at the entry of the city, at the coming in at the doors. . . . When he [God] gave to the sea his decree, that the water should not pass his commandment: when he appointed the foundations of the earth: Then I [Wisdom] was by him, as one brought up with him. . . . blessed are they that keep my ways. Hear instruction, and be wise, and refuse it not. Blessed is the man that heareth me, watching daily at my gates, waiting at the posts of my doors."# Waiting for what? For entry into that place that was "east of the garden of Eden," where God had stationed the

* Acts 10:9–13.

† Ephesians 2:14–15, emphasis added.

‡ 1 Corinthians 2:7.

§ Proverbs 9:1–2; "killed her beasts," i.e., theriomorphism for purged perception.

\# Proverbs 8:3–34.

"cherubim and a flaming sword which turned every way to keep the way of the tree of life."* The sword again illustrates the danger of passing into trance unprepared.

Then follows a meditative stillness and paradisal sense of well-being that is the end of all spiritual practice. All fears and anxieties vanish. The self is established in its true nature. Then one knows that "peace of God which passeth all understanding. . . . Those things, which ye have both learned, and received, and heard, and seen in me, do: and the God of peace shall be with you"† after "having made peace through the blood of the cross."‡ The Crucifixion is the same myth as the Fall of Troy, is in fact the same as the myth of the Flood found in Genesis 7. The biophysical event that coordinates the myths across cultures is the pituitary catastrophe, variously described as a rupture of the temple (Crucifixion), breaking into a citadel (Troy), and a cataclysmic downpour (Flood, Holy Grail, Kṛṣṇa and the Gopis).

The life of Samson, a judge of Israel at the time the Hebrews are under the heel of the Philistines, has many affinities with the life of The Christ. Samson's father was Manoah (mn). His mother—name unknown—is barren, but an angel appears to her to announce that she will conceive a son, a Nazarite, which means that "no razor shall come on his head." Manoah confronts the angel and asks his name. The angel replies "Why askest thou thus after my name, seeing it is secret?" When grown, Samson slays a lion and he kills one thousand Philistines with the jawbone of an ass. The hair of his head is braided with seven locks, which the harlot Delilah shears, causing him to lose his prodigious strength, whereat she binds him with "seven green withes which had not been dried," the cranial nerves. The green of the withes indicates the activity, the life force, of the nerves as conduits of perception but simultaneously as bindings to the second world. Indeed, the significance of hair throughout the Samson myth is directly related to the great density of nerves in the cranium, for which hair serves as an esoteric description. In proprioception of the cranium, the hairs of the head and the nerves of the scalp are not practically distinguishable. Samson's being a Nazarite (= *nz* = *Zion*, third-world buzzing or ringing) speaks to the same experience as does Jesus of Nazareth. By contiguity, hair and nerves are one and the same. The Philistines take Samson to Gaza (*kz* = perception) and blind him, then cast him into a prison house where he turns a grinding wheel fettered like an ox. They bring him from there into their temple and mock him. When Samson pushes apart the pillars of the Philistine temple, the roof collapses on three thousand Philistines while they are banqueting, paralleling the Last Supper that precedes the Crucifixion.§ Internal taste and smell are again preliminary experiences to the pituitary catastrophe.

Paul compares the exertions of Samson to the parting of the Red Sea, the first Passover, and the destruction of Jericho.# In the collapse of the Walls of Jericho, the stimulus appears in the auditory nerves: Joshua tells the Israelites to blow their horns for seven days. The destruction of the second world is perceptual death, but that coincides with what most understand as death, when the world "out there" vanishes. Likewise the blast of a trumpet signals the SECOND COMING of Christ:

> And then shall appear the sign of the Son of man in heaven: and then shall all the tribes of the earth mourn, and they shall see the Son of man coming in the clouds

* Cf., the Clashing Rocks in Jason and the Argonauts, which move about to block the way to the Golden Fleece, and the Inuit legend of Giviok, who paddles a magic kayak through the channel between two icebergs, though they move to block him. Esoteric east in Judeo-Christian myth is the same as west in Indo-European myth, i.e., in the direction that the eyes normally look. The Tabernacle of the Temple was entered from the east, and the gatekeepers were priests, sons of Kore (kr) (1 Chronicles 9:18–19). In Ezekiel 11, the wicked are punished at the eastern gate, the interorbital space where karma is immolated during trance.

† Philippians 4:7–9.

‡ Colossians 1:20.

§ Judges 13:1–17, 15:13–17, 16:4–31. Samson carries the Gates of Gaza to a hilltop (16:3): root gazing.

Hebrews 11:28–32.

of heaven with power and great glory. And he shall send his angels with a great sound of a trumpet.*

If the Birth of Christ—the First Coming—is baptism into the mysteries—including the water baptism and confirmation—then the Second Coming is the individual death, the death of each one of us, when the Logos appears to the expiring soul. As with the Eleusinia the Christian mysteries were an attempt to control the death trance. Those faithful who have their attention fixed on the third world—heaven—at the moment of drawing their last breath will be gathered up: "And they shall gather together his elect from the four winds, from one end of heaven to another. . . . But of that day and hour knoweth no man, no not the angels of heaven, but my Father only."† No one knows the hour of death. In Greek myth, that is decided by the Moiræ and known only to Father Zeus; in Christian monotheistic myth it is the "Father only." The Evangelist next explicitly compares the Second Coming to the Flood:

> Verily, I say unto you, *This generation shall not pass, till all these things be fulfilled.* Heaven and earth shall pass away, but my *words* shall not pass away. . . . But as the days of Noah were, so also shall the coming of the son of Man be. For as in the days that were before the flood they were *eating and drinking,* marrying and giving in marriage, until the day that Noah entered into the ark, And they knew not until the flood came, and took them all away; so shall also the coming of the Son of man be. Then shall two be in the field, the one taken, and the other left. Two women shall be grinding at the mill; the one shall be taken, and the other left.‡

Verse 34 has been the source of enormous confusion and consternation throughout Christendom. How can the generation of the Apostles have "passed away" and the Second Coming not have occurred? When it was realized that Jesus would not return even by the time John died,§ the date of the eschatological catastrophe was repeatedly postponed until, when A.D. 1000 came and went without the Second Coming for which people all over Europe had prepared themselves, it ceased to be a preoccupation in Roman Catholicism. By the seventeenth century, however, the Protestant churches had revived the notion, and every generation since has been pleased to indulge the fantasy that it is privileged to live in the "time of the last days." The irony is that the statement is as true now as when Jesus defined it: "This generation shall not pass away until I come." When Jesus comes *is* the passing away of each member of a generation. Also in verse 34, "my words shall not pass away" is possibly a scribal error for "my word shall not pass away." When heaven and earth are gone, only the Word shall remain, "as it was in the beginning, is now, and ever shall be through all ages of ages."#

The necessity of constant attention to what was taught in the mysteries, lest at the moment of death one be caught unready, also is stressed:

> For yourselves know perfectly that the day of the Lord so cometh as a thief in the night. For when they shall say Peace and safety; then sudden destruction cometh upon them, *as travail upon a woman with child;* and they shall not escape. But ye, brethren, are not in darkness, that that day should not overtake you as a thief. . . . Therefore let us not sleep, as others do; but let us watch and be sober. *For they that sleep sleep in the night; and they that be drunken are drunken in the night.***

* Matthew 24:30–31.

† Ibid., 31–36.

‡ Ibid., 34–41, emphasis added.

§ John 21:22, Jesus speaking of John: "he [shall] tarry till I come."

Concluding words of the Doxology.

** 1 Thessalonians 5:2–7, emphasis added.

Or, as a Hindi proverb puts it: "Do not let your horses run all day and expect to call them in with a whistle at night."

> Watch therefore: for ye know not what hour your Lord doth come. But know this, that if the goodman of the house had known in what watch the thief would come, he would have watched, and would not have suffered his house to be broken up. Therefore be ye also ready: for in such an hour as ye think not the Son of man cometh.*

Night and death, not unnaturally, are equated. The "day of the Lord" is the coming of the divine light at the moment of death. The image of the woman with child refers to the soul. A female in most myths, and especially in Christian myth, which likens it to a Bride of Christ, the soul carries the seeds of karma that will lead to rebirth. To "watch" means simply to meditate, to call constantly upon the Name of the Lord, the core technique of the water baptism.

The Eleusinian return of the Core is the Second Coming. The writings of the Greek philosophers concerning the travails of the dying soul as it searches for the way to Elysium here apply equally. In Christian myth, however, the myth is much more animated by the force of karma and retribution, by the wages of sin. Jesus' death on the Cross describes the "burning up" of karma during the pituitary catastrophe. Before purgation the brow is marked with the "number of the beast"; afterwards "they shall see his face, and his name shall be in their foreheads."† At the moment of death the dying soul huddles, as it were, within the breath, like the archer Teucer beneath the shield of Ajax Big amidst the slaughter at the Gates of Troy, while the Word of God absorbs, or takes into itself, the reservoir of karmas waiting to wash over the disembodied soul and launch it into the next dream. The soul must be watchful—not prone to sleeping, hence to dreaming—for the Word of God is the perfect servant—"I go to *prepare* a place for you"—and will fashion whatever reality the expiring soul truly desires, though its desires be imperfectly known even to itself.

Jesus of Nazareth was a man who received initiation into the archaic "wisdom" and passed through death unscathed. In so doing, he realized his identity with The Christ. The eternal Word within him that brought him safely into the Kingdom of God was nothing essentially apart from his own dear Self. He then taught others how to do what he had done. He was not the first human being to attain the Crown of Life, the Heavenly Jerusalem, nor the last. But Jesus of Nazareth's conquest of death is part of *our* heritage. In the words of Saint Ignatius (echoing Paul):

> We . . . have since attained to a new hope . . . and now order [our] lives by the Lord's Day instead (the day when life first dawned for us thanks to Him and His death. That death, though some deny it, is the very mystery which has moved us to become believers, and endure tribulation to prove ourselves pupils of Jesus Christ, our sole Teacher).‡

◆◆◆

In Hindu folklore, Jānaka, the king of Rājasthan and a master of yoga, died of fever. His years of spiritual practice had rid him of all desires (vāsānas) save two. As his soul departed, he dreamed not solely of the Lord, who satisfies all desire, but of the waters of a cold clear lake in Kashmir and of the fruit of a particular apple tree. Immediately, he was reborn as a pike that swam in the waters of the lake for three years. When the fish had died, the soul that animated it, the soul of Jānaka, was reborn as a worm that bored through those same sweet apples for a hundred lifetimes till it had eaten its fill. At last the soul, having slaked its desires, was reborn a man who attained kaivalya and godhood.

* Matthew 24: 42–47.

† Apocalypse 13:16–18, 22:4.

‡ Ignatius of Antioch, *Epistle to the Magnesians* 9.1ff.

Eschatology, the study of the "last days," is at bottom thanatology. The supreme eschatological irony is that what we fear most is precisely the opportunity for eternal happiness. The moment of death is the moment of "return" to the infinite void that is our true self. There is little sense in trying to characterize the nature of that transcendental life offered by a compassionate God to each expiring human soul. Death is the last for which the first was made. It finishes and perfects us. To fear and shun death is perverse. Alternatively, what we suppose we want most ardently—earthly life—is precisely the ailment that is tormenting us. Unable to seize the opportunity that death presents, we truly are damned to eternal fire. Unslaked and unslakable desires drive us from birth to birth in a cycle of incarnations that is infinite. If we no longer credit an eternal "lake of fire," something we neither know nor understand, perhaps we *can* tremble at the prospect of eternal and unrequited yearning, worry, doubt, anxiety, loss, bereavement, shame, and terror—which we know all too well—and reckon accordingly.

The Hindus have a saying. There are three evils in life: not getting what you want, getting what you don't want, and getting what you want. How many times must we possess food and sex and the so-called beauties of this world—art, music, poetry, and so forth—before we realize there is no peace in any of them? How many families must we raise, how many careers pursue? How much success and failure, reward and punishment, do we need? We are not suggesting puritanism here, only pragmatism. Each of us has been man and woman and beast of burden countless times, and that we might not forget it, our very brow has been formed in the shape of a yoke. We plod under the goad of the senses like oxen, not reckoning where we have been or whither we are going, "like water willy-nilly flowing." The soul that expires thirsting for wealth, be sure that soul will attain wealth. And if that same soul uses that same wealth, not to ease its journey to the truth, but rather to attain still greater wealth, to protect and defend it as a dog would a bone—a bone tossed to by its master withal—that soul hazards rebirth in direst poverty or as a dog with many bones to snarl and grasp at. For the last shall be first and the first shall be last.

Neither is wealth a barrier to enlightenment. Once there was a seeker of truth named Sukhya Das who searched all of India to find that satguru who could reveal to him the reason he was born. In time he heard of King Jānaka, who knew the truth and could expound the inner meaning of the Vedas. So Sukhya Das journeyed to Jānaka's kingdom, and coming to the palace where Jānaka lived he was admitted to his presence. Sukhya Das looked around him and saw the great wealth that surrounded the king. In his soul an ember of envy burned, and he spurned the king, thinking "this rich man can teach me nothing." He was about to go away when Jānaka, who had divined his thoughts, asked that Sukhya Das share just one meal with him, to which Sukhya Das reluctantly agreed. They were seated at the sumptuous dinner table, and delicacies were brought forth one after another and laid upon gold plate. Sukhya Das happened to look up and saw a sharpened sword suspended by a silken thread above his head. He feared for his life and could not take his mind from the sword. When the meal was finished, Jānaka asked him whether he had enjoyed it. Sukhya Das replied that he did not know. He had been so distracted by the sword above his head that he had not tasted a mouthful. Jānaka smiled. "Just so," he said. "Neither do I taste of my wealth, for my mind is ever fixed on the Word of God that is uttered in my heart." Then Sukhya Das understood and was initiated by Jānaka and learned the truth.

This world we live in is itself the very Mount of Purgatory. While here we must either pay for our sins or have them forgiven. *Tertium non datur*. None of us is justified. The sequences of births and deaths that leads each to this life, this time, this day and hour, is hopelessly convolved. We can never sort it out, never make the balance come out right. Each event of our lives, whether for good or ill, is a check drawn on an account we can never examine, for most of it has been forgotten. Incarnation means forgetfulness. In dying, we either escape to the eternal or drink deeply at the Lethean spring. This is the greatest mercy imaginable: we could not bear the knowledge of where we have been, what we have seen, what we have done to others, and what has been done to us by others. Yet, though forgotten explicitly, our past perseveres *implicitly* in what Patañali calls our *vāsānas*, "tendencies," a term that comprises karmas and kleśas both. The world is most practically understood as mysterious, rather than rational, a mystery synonymous with amnesia, which we cannot pierce, save through personal enlightenment, any more than we can simply decide to remember what we have forgotten.

Yet just because the ocean of karmas has been forgotten does not mean it cannot still sweep over us. Waves of so-called fortune, good or ill, buffet us from moment to moment. There is no mystery here, *nor is there injustice in this world*. That is a hard lesson, and for most of us an all but unlearnable one. The sense of ego—asmitā—that has led us into Purgatory is ever resentful of the restrictions entailed by its own free choice and ignorant of the ocean of karmas, the myriad credits and debits, that circumvail its every action. If we look just to the present, we are like bookkeepers who balance their ledgers with the dollars column covered, content that the pennies add up exactly. If we look just to the present life, we will at best be mystified, at worst resentful. Jesus speaks to that resentment in the parable of the vineyard: those who came to work early in the day received the penny; those who came late received the penny. "What is that to you?" Jesus seems to say to those who are angered by apparent inequity.

And anger comes all too easily. Why has this happened to me? Why did that happen to him? I don't deserve *this*. I deserve *that*. That anger is directed at anything but ourselves. We raise a clenched fist in defiance of the universe while forgetting that the supreme being is not different from our own dear self. There is a saying: when a pickpocket meets a saint all he sees are the saint's pockets. A covetous soul sees pockets everywhere and what is in them and wonders furiously why it is not in *his* pocket. If wealth is given or withheld, we have given or withheld it. If illness comes we have sent it. The Logos within has created a universe for each of us that matches perfectly the universe of want that clouds our soul. It created sun and moon. It can easily create misfortune or good luck. It is perfectly honest, perfectly patient. It knows what is best, what is necessary, what should not be evaded. You cannot fool it because it is you.

The only way out of this mess is forgiveness. When asked how often we must forgive our transgressors, Jesus says "seven times seven times." If thy enemy strike thee on thy cheek, turn to him the other cheek. And if he take your shirt, do not deny him your cloak. Jesus but echoes Socrates, who declared that it is far better to have evil done to oneself than to inflict evil on another. In absorbing evil, even unto death, we can be sure we are clearing the balance sheet. In inflicting evil, we may very well be ensuring another birth for ourself, another life in which to ensure yet another life, and who can say where the death dream will lead him, in what body he will awaken? Who can control his dreams?

In dreams begin responsibilities, yes, but also much more. The oneiric state is atemporal and aspatial. From the standpoint of the second world, it is completely "internal." In dreams we participate in the creative power of the Logos, a power that cannot be known plenipotently until the moment of death. Internal creates external. Thought fathers deed. No one would dispute the metaphorical truth of this; but we are suggesting something far more radical. The influence we exert over the world need not work solely through the efforts of our hands or through the tools we fashion with those hands. It can come unmediated, but only after puruṣa has extricated itself from prakṛti.

The shaman recognizes this power to create "reality" in dreams and has many techniques for harnessing it. The aborigine in Australia will watch his dogs as they sleep. If a dog moves its legs as though running, the aborigine believes that the dog has dreamed of capturing prey, and he will take that dog hunting in the morning. The action of the dog is not simply an omen, but evidence for a future reality that the dog is creating. And because the mind of the dog presumably is less complicated than our own, because when it comes to catching prey canines are focused, ardent, and intent—all the ingredients of saṃyama—that very singleness of purpose gives the aborigine confidence in the dream of the dog.* For most of us, however, the oneiric state is so confused, so rife with ambiguity, contradiction, and conflicting impulses, that little use can be made of this power. At the moment of death, however, the Logos that is our own dear self "comes in great power and glory" and whatever dream we dream while expiring—in *all* its complication, conflict, and ambiguity—will come to pass in our next life.

In forgiving our enemy seven times seven times we acknowledge our fallen state, but at the same time we gain forgiveness for ourselves. Forgiveness cannot be feigned: never let your left hand know what your right hand is doing, the essence of Zen. Only true love can blind us to our own intentions. As a physiological state of the organism, love is itself the evidence of forgiveness of sin. It indicates a literal alteration of the organism. It is a feeling that floats above the ocean of karmas. It is dear to us precisely because it is the intimation of a life outside retribution and reward. Love is a state of sanctifying grace. To live in love is to put all sense of right and wrong out of mind. When Mary Magdalene washes the feet of Jesus with her tears, he tells those who watch—and who would interfere—"Verily, the love she feels means her sins have already been forgiven." The tears we shed, whether in love or in sorrow, descend from the corners of our eyes, from the space between our brows. They are the figure of a spiritual poetics that mark our bodies. In the same way that the yoke that marks our status as beasts of burden is visible in the shape of our brows, the tears we shed embody the dissolution of karmas, the forgiveness of sins. They are tokens of the Flood itself, the cataclysm that forgave sin, cleansed the earth, and led Noah into a promised land, as well of the Apocalypse†—the pituitary catastrophe—when God shall "wipe away our tears." They are the sweat of our brows to which expulsion from the garden condemned us, the same brows that bead with perspiration when we are afraid and that worry and concern permanently furrow.

* R. Lawlor, *Voices of the First Day* (Rochester, Vt., 1992), pp. 37–38.

Faith is necessary, however, faith in our own dear self, which is compassion itself. Vastly more karmas have been forgiven us than are held against us. Because we are in such a morass, the Lord is ever merciful and willing to forget if only *we* are willing to forget. Without faith we are always a hair's breadth from falling into the dream of the senses. Only if from moment to moment a clear choice is present, a place—that is not a place—to occupy our devoted attention, can we avoid the dream. For all our talents the message of gnosis is that what we *must* do is simply to draw a perfect breath—and especially when it is our last. Nothing more is expected. If salvation depends on any talent, however slight, then salvation is for an elite.

Once there was a seeker of truth named Ananda. Through grace Ananda had found a satguru, who had initiated him into knowledge of brahman and had even made Ananda his companion. One day the satguru decided to test Ananda. "Take this bucket," he said, "and fetch me water." Ananda, eager to please the Lord incarnate, went down to the river. There he happened upon a lovely young woman who also was drawing water. At that moment the guru gave permission to the demons to tempt Ananda, who was immediately filled with lust for the young woman. He pursued her to her home, she begging all the while to be left unmolested. Her husband was waiting for her to return, and when he saw what Ananda was up to he intervened to protect his wife. But Ananda, by now completely a prisoner of lust, assaulted the husband, threw him to the ground, and was choking the life out of him when the guru bid the demons go. At once Ananda awoke from the

† *Apocalypse* < Gk. *apokalyptein*, "to unveil," i.e., to remove the covering of light (cf., Calypso).

spell and found himself with his hands around the husband's throat. Horrified at what he was doing, he rushed back to the guru, prostrated himself, and begged to be punished in expiation of his sin. The guru stroked his beard a moment, then said, "Anandaji, where is my water?" So Ananda went and fetched water, which is what he was supposed to be doing all along. The lesson of course is that forgiveness is the rule rather than the exception in the universe at large, and it is one's duty to forgive oneself as much as to forgive others. "If you see virtue, rejoice," says Patañjali, "if vice, remain indifferent." And especially when the viciousness is one's own. Only in detachment can vice be overcome. Desperation is the "unforgivable sin because it destroys the sine qua non of forgiveness: the humility to ask for it."

If the early Christians suppressed metempsychosis as a doctrine of the Church, it may well have been because they recognized that it is a doctrine susceptible to heinous abuse. If we believe only that each of us reaps what was sown, callousness and indifference to suffering can easily overtake us, as the uses to which the Hindu caste system are put amply demonstrate in the present, chattel slavery in the past. The only recourse is compassion—Judge not lest ye be judged. Love thy neighbor as thyself—Because none is justified, none may judge. When you point a finger, *three* fingers point back at you (bodily poetics once again). One must have faith that there is no injustice in this world, *yet one must also act as if that does not matter.* Another hard lesson.

The differences between the Old and New Testaments are largely a matter of emphasis and derive from an historical necessity to reconcile the sinner with the Law (Heb. *torah*). In reality there was no conflict between the Law and personal salvation, because the Law, from the days of Moses, had always two parts, exoteric and esoteric, written and oral, which were meant to function in tandem. By Jesus' day, however, the esoteric oral tradition had become the property of the *cohanim*, the priesthood. At the high holidays, the high priest revealed the "unspeakable Name" to only one or two select individuals within the Holy of Holies.* We speculate that John the Baptist had been one of the elite few and that he in turn initiated Jesus of Nazareth in defiance of the temple hierarchy, a defiance that cost him his head and launched Jesus on an inevitable collision course with the Sanhedrin. Although they could not say so openly, preferring to let the Pharisees debate Jesus in public, the cohanim knew well what was at stake: control of the secret wisdom, the essence of the Law handed down historically since the days of Moses and mythically, in works putatively written by Moses, since Abraham.

After his baptism, the situation that Jesus faced was similar to that encountered by the Buddha 600 years earlier. Judaism and Hinduism, as a practical matter, had capitulated to sacerdotalism and the lex talionis. "Fear ye the Lord," a phrase that appears in one guise or another again and again in the Old Testament, is rare in the New. Canonical regulation of behavior, for which Deuteronomy and Leviticus served as paradigms (much of which, we suspect, had originally an esoteric meaning), had overwhelmed Judaism. In India the rigidities of the caste system had made the Brahmans sole arbiters of a bewildering polytheism deriving from the devotional rituals of the Vedas and *Brāhmaṇas* but having little to do with their esoteric purport. The Buddha's reaction was to desacralize the myriad rituals of Hinduism, essentially by ignoring them, and to refuse in principle even to discuss theology. His efforts were bent toward amending present behavior but always, we hypothesize, in accordance with an esoteric praxis. Because by his day belief in reincarnation was so firmly and so openly established in India, he could not renounce it exoterically, as could the Christians in Palestine. Instead, cognizant of the dangers, he drastically modified it and left extremely vague what was reincarnated, an attitude that survives in modern Buddhist notions of the subject.

* This extreme exclusivity heightens the probability that when in A.D. 70 the Romans sacked Jerusalem, leveled the Second Temple, and slaughtered the priests, the esoteric wisdom was extinguished in orthodox Judaism.

Jesus too focused exoterically on compassion as a way around the prescripts of the Law, especially in his sharp disagreements with the Sadducees, a sect that reduced Judaism to lawyerly formalism. As with the Buddha, Jesus displays an impatience, amounting at times almost to exasperation, with religious legalism. On our view, Jesus' arguments depended on an understanding of the futility of personal justification solely through adherence to the Law in the present incarnation of the person. There was simply too much indebtedness from previous lifetimes to be reckoned. His urgent prescription was to sweep it all under the rug of compassion, to see it as water over the dam, to wipe the slate clean and begin anew. Baptism into an esoteric praxis could accelerate the forgiveness of sin. For the unbaptized, patience (< L. *pati*, "to suffer") was the virtue to be cultivated.

Neither should we look to our secular institutions to provide the Kingdom of God. Individuals are saved, not institutions. Absent a policy of saved individuals, there is no salvation of their institutions, which must always and can only represent the aggregate moral complexion of their members. The structure of our institutions, from the marketplace to the legislature to the military, necessarily conforms to the impersonal cause-consequence behavior of the second world, to its kinetic ruthlessness. If you would play solely by its rules, be prepared for the worst. It is as mechanical as a coiling, recoiling spring. Fortune and misfortune are not simply twins: they are identical twins. Rome fell because Rome rose. One dies because one is born. There is no illusion but another overtake it. The Buddhist version of the Golden Rule indicates a way out of the clutches of this *machina infernalis*: "Not by hatred is hatred requited, but by love is hatred requited." As a behavioral canon the Buddha's words thwart our basic instincts. Yet that is precisely their virtue, for to say that the instinct to strike back has justice to recommend it is like saying that when a sash weight falls and a window rises justice has been satisfied rather than the laws of mechanics. The system of weights and window is not a closed system; the energy that drives it has been paid for elsewhere in the universe, in another time, at another place. That is called grace.

No institution devised by humankind in 10,000 years has complacently rationalized forgiveness. Yet every institution has contrived certain roles for individuals—judge, govenor, magistrate—who are expected to exercise compassion and to set aside the strict demands of law as the situation presents itself to his or her *individual* conscience. Grace cannot be rationalized, however, and usually we must render to Cæsar what is Cæsar's. The world would simply cease to funtion otherwise, for good or for ill. Whatever the Logos purposed in creating the world—can it be anarchy?

Politics and religion are strange bedmates. When Jesus drives the usurers from the temple, he is first and foremost cleansing the temple: the human body. The action described is spiritual and esoteric, not political. Second, *licit Jovi non licit bovi*. It was Jesus of Nathareth—not just anyone—who acted so. Save yourself—as he did—before worrying about the malefactors of this world, who, like the poor, are always with us and in fact *are* us. We should not rush to take up arms, and anger is always the last, never the first, resort. We place ourselves in great spiritual peril whenever we set out willfully to right the wrongs of the world.

Politics is first of all political economy. The world is a machine truly hell-bent on its own devices, mechanically meting out rewards and punishments. We cannot change it essentially. We can, however, escape its claims to our allegiance by fixing our attention, indeed our every drawn breath, on the eternal within us. Be in the world but not of it. And besides, we have it on the best authority that no evil deed goes unpunished: "Vengeance is mine. I shall requite," saith the Lord. The mills of the Gods grind slowly, but they grind exceeding small.* Leave it to them. Be content with righting the wrongs that life presents us from moment to moment, including and foremost among them

* Cf., Luke 16:17: "It is easier for heaven and earth to pass, than one tittle of the law to fail."

our own. The evil of the day is sufficient unto itself. We have opportunities aplenty to mend our life in concert with those immediately around us. The sweep of history is too grand a canvas for most of us to pose against. By refusing to be the sword of justice we increase the sum of goodness and mercy in the world, but we also avert that same sword from our own necks.

History has shown all too often how easily envy, hatred, and resentment masquerade as the pursuit of justice on a grand scale, and there is always a grave danger of confusing the personal with the political. Democratic institutions, whatever their failings, are laudable because they block too facile a connection between the personality of a monarch, tyrant, or generalissimo and the reins of power, a power that does not simply corrupt but corrupts *further*, that degrades that which was fallen to begin with. In his personality Hitler was an antisemite, Mao an anti-intellectual, Stalin a paranoiac. Their works we know. It is no small wonder of our age that so-called revolutionaries who exercise not the slightest control over their private passions and deformities, nor worry much that they don't, would with blithe hubris turn our institutions topsy-turvy to lay violent hands upon an elusive justice. Instead, let us seek *first* the Kingdom of Heaven, and all good things will be added. To him who has, more will be given. To him who has not, even what he thinks he has will be taken away.

22

MYTH:

The Historical Foundation of Western Learning

Œdipus, mighty master of my fatherland,
We have come as supplicants to yours altars. . . .
For the land is blasted!
Blasted in the bud the country's crops;
Blasted the cattle in our fields;
Blasted the seed in the barren wombs of women.
The god of fire and fever has brought this deadly plague.
Swooped and struck the city.
And so dark Hades abounds in groans and lamentation.
Neither I, nor these children here,
Consider that you are a god, Œdipus,
But we do count you first among men:
Skilled in human affairs,
But also in the dealings with the gods.
For you came to this city of Thebes,
And delivered us from the bloody tribute
Paid to that savage songstress.
You rid us of the Sphinx.

Sophocles, *Œdipus Rex**

History is beguiling. So much so that the Greeks personified it as a woman—Clio—who inspired poets to sing her glories. As the eldest of the nine Muses, daughters of Zeus and Mnemosyne, Clio holds a special significance for us. Because of the recapitulative structure of authentic myth, the interpretation of the other Muses must somehow proceed from her true mean-

* Trans. C. R. Walker (New York, 1966), pp. 4–5.

ing. Phonically her name reduces to *kl*, which is strongly second world. Her connection with history derives from the seedlike nature of this phon. Clio is the beginning of things, the germ planted in the second world that blossoms into perception.

We might go so far as to claim that Clio is the only Muse, her sisters descriptions merely of the various ways in which her burgeoning is experienced. But such an assertion risks overgeneralizing her meaning in myth, where she is an unimportant figure. It would be more to the point to describe Clio and her sisters as representations of a particular perceptual state known as *beauty*. The Greek word for beauty is *kalon*, a root we have already encountered in the myth of Calypso and the Island of Ogygia, wherein Calypso embodies a blinding radiance associated with the neurophysiology of the second world. We recognize it too in our English words *golden* and *glory*. The Muses (the Camenæ in Latin) describe an indwelling of heavenly glory in the external world. More concretely, they refer to experiences in which the third world (Zeus and Mnemosyne) is neurologically mingled with the second, in which cognition modulates perception amelioratively.*

An extreme example of this intermingling—extreme in the sense that it is far removed from a mythopoetic impulse—is the writing of history, wherein the poetic gift is applied to chronicling the past. Perhaps the most famous worshipers at Clio's altar were Thucydides and Herodotus. Both men, it should be stressed, made no clear-cut distinction between history and myth. Though often viewing the "facts" of myth skeptically, they both took for granted the historicity of the Trojan War, for example, or Heracles' vendetta against Thebes, and much else besides that we would consider the sheerest legend.

Herodotus is often called the "father of history," and it would be a comparatively easy matter to demonstrate, as has been done,† his influence on subsequent historiography, from Strabo and Polybius to Machiavelli, Guicciardini, and Winckelmann, down into our own era. His influence goes far beyond a mere listing of names and dates, but extends unavoidably to an outlook, a set of prescriptive values, a sense of historical meaning-in-the-large that is mythically derived. In the Genealogies of Herodotus's Ionian predecessor, Hecatæus of Lesbos (fl. 500 B.C.), the organic connnection between ancient history and myth is still more evident.

To illustrate the point consider the case of Alexander of Macedon, popularly known as Alexander the Great. We know from a number of sources‡ that toward the end of his short life Alexander believed (or at least pretended to believe) that he was a god and that he began to expect divine honors from his soldiers, who, being good Greeks, were not of one mind in according him so exalted a status (as the Conspiracy of Hermolaus proves). In his defense let it be said that he had a good deal of encouragement from myth. For had not Heracles, the mightiest warrior of them all, ascended to Olympus and become a god? And what of Orpheus, who according to legend was worshiped while still alive? And if Greek tradition alone were insufficient to license self-apotheosis, there were bushels of myths among his eastern subjects, sagas and legends aplenty, to justify even the wildest dreams of ego.

Over the centuries Alexander's career has been variously received. Arrian praised him highly, when he did not excuse him. Plutarch was less fulsome, though still approving. Seneca and Lucan thought him a villain, an inspiration for the truly revolting excesses of Caligula and Nero. During the Renaissance he was praised by Bacon and Montaigne, lampooned by Rabelais, censured by Erasmus. In the seventeenth century he was an exhortatory figure for aristocratic Frenchmen, such as the Seigneur de Saint-Évremond, but an object of reproach for Restoration Britons like Nathaniel Lee and Sir William Temple. And by the middle of the eighteenth

* Thus similar to nereids.

† W. Dilthey, *Gesammelte Werke*, bd. 8 (Stuttgart, 1926), part 2, pp. 163–71.

‡ Principally Arrian's *Anabasis Alexandri*.

century, at the dawn of the Enlightenment, he had reached what was perhaps the nadir of informed historical regard for his character and accomplishments.*

Now it is quite true that many and probably most of these opinions do not focus explicitly on Alexander's claims to divinity. To some he was a model of heroic aloofness, a creature lifted from pettiness and vulgarity by a noble and, yes, even a godlike temperament. To others he was merely a rapacious despot who was never so happy as when he was pillaging or wreaking havoc among his cultural betters. But it would be as impossible to remove the awareness of Alexander's megalomania from these varying judgments on his character as it would be to isolate the question of Christ's divinity from the consensus of opinion that has grown up around him. And in both cases, it is irrefutable that the claim to a transcendent identity derives from myth.†

Consider too the tale of Œdipus. When, in the passage cited above, the Theban elder says: "Neither I, nor these children here, consider that you are a god, Œdipus," he is raising a possibility that has absolutely no counterpart outside myth: the god-man. It is interesting that Sophocles even alludes to it, for nowhere in antique literature is it suggested that Œdipus is divine. But what is perhaps more interesting still are the uses to which the myth has been put in our own time. The so-called science of psychoanalysis has elevated the woebegone figure of Œdipus from a protagonist to a paradigm, from a major character in a minor myth—which almost certainly would not have achieved the notoriety it did had not Sophocles trained his genius upon it—to the key to unlocking personality.

A natural question arises: How valid are the concepts of psychoanalysis in light of proprioceptive theory? Does psychoanalysis *explain* myth in the accepted sense of the word? The answer, of course, is no, it does not. A theory of mythmaking in general is not a primary nor even a secondary aim of psychoanalysis, although it is often assumed to be useful in interpreting the symbolism of individual myths. Instead, psychoanalysis endeavors to expose so-called subconscious needs that underlie human behavior, of which myth and religion are only a part, albeit a significant part. And in fact it would not be out of order to say that orthodox analysis tends to view all religion as a collective obsessional neurosis.‡ That being granted, we conclude that a psychoanalytic approach to myth is antagonistic to a proprioceptive one. The proprioceptive hypothesis is a statement about yoga, a précis of yogic science, and at no time has yoga ever even suggested that religion is neurotically grounded. Rather the opposite, in fact.

Nowhere is the antagonism more in evidence than in the interpretation of the Œdipal myth itself. For psychoanalysis the story of Œdipus of Thebes is not simply another myth. It is *the* myth, *the* symbolic construct with overriding centrality in human cultural etiology. Analysis does not so much interpret this myth as axiomatize it. The question of psychoanalysis's validity, therefore, comes down to the question of the validity of the mythic primacy of the Œdipal legend.§ Yet we have seen again and again that the subject matter of true myth is very narrow, that one myth is communicating the selfsame message as another, even though the symbols selected from myth to myth for illustrating that core meaning may and in fact do vary enormously. In the case of Œdipus we must agree with psychoanalysis that the central symbolism involves a family: father (Laius), mother (Jocaste), and child (Œdipus). But we have also examined myths in which that particular symbolism is either lacking or is of only secondary and adventitious importance, for example, that of Jason and the Argonauts. Yet even if we select a myth containing those symbols, we at once notice pronounced discrepancies between the

* G. C. Brauer, Jr., "Alexander in England: the conqueror's reputation," *Classical Journal* 76, no. 1 (1980): 34–47; in fairness, Alexander did go on to inspire Bonaparte and Hitler.

† If, for the moment, we conflate religion and myth.

‡ Freud used these very words to describe religion in his famous essay *Totem und Tabu*.

§ Here we are assessing psychoanalytic theory, not therapy.

way they are used in that myth and their role in the tale of Œdipus.

Take, for example, a myth that we have already correlated with that of Œdipus: the RANSOM OF PRIAM. Because of the etymologies of *Œdipus* (Swollen Foot) and *Podarces* (Bear Foot), the name that Priam was given at birth, and because of the interpretation of the image of a foot at which we previously arrived, namely, that it is a reasonable description of the cross-section of the brain at the level of the corpus callosum and not a symbol, we were led to equate Œdipus with Priam. Furthermore, because the names of the fathers of both Œdipus and Priam, respectively, Laius and Laomedon, are both first-world phons, we may also equate them. Thus far it would seem that the psychoanalytic and proprioceptive approaches to the myths are in harmony or at least do not contradict each other. When, however, we come to the feminine symbolism pertinent to these myths, the women whom Œdipus and Priam married and on whom they fathered children (respectively, Jocaste and Hecuba), a serious functional divergence is evident: Jocaste is Œdipus's natural mother, whereas Hecuba bears no blood relationship at all to Priam (being, in one version, the daughter of King Cisseus of Thrace). The discrepancy is the more noteworthy when we consider certain remarkable parallels between these women. To begin with, each has a strong lower-second-world name,* each comes to a pitiable end, and each is involved in an act of blinding: Œdipus puts out his own eyes when he learns of the incestuous nature of his marriage, and Hecuba blinds Polymnestor, king of Thrace, because he slew her last surviving son, Polydorus. In both cases the acts were carried out with brooch pins.†

Given the crucial importance of the incest theme in psychoanalytic theory, the problem presented by, on the one hand, Œdipus's illicit mating with Jocaste and, on the other, Priam's perfectly legitimate marriage to Hecuba, is paramount. Either the myths are not equivalent (isomorphic), in which case the proprioceptive approach is false, or they are equivalent, in which case it is psychoanalysis that has erred. If we say that the myths are not equivalent then we must also say that the host of parallels listed above are sheer coincidence or that some third hypothesis is necessary to account for them. Because it is the nature of a systematic approach to data to minimize hypotheses rather than to introduce them ad hoc, we are understandably reluctant to resort to a new hypothesis now, especially when, taken in their entirety and analyzed proprioceptively, there is no fundamental inconsistency between these myths. Proprioceptively the blood relationship between Œdipus and Jocaste, as well as the lack of one between Priam and Hecuba, is not crucial. Rather, what is crucial are the neurological connections between the first and lower-second worlds that these characters collectively describe. The meaning of the myth of Œdipus and Laius is the usurpation of experience by perception, a theme with which all myths about sons who overthrow or kill their sires concern themselves.

It may very well be that every child, between the ages of three and six, experiences and then represses intensely erotic longings for the parent of the opposite sex. And it may also be true that these desires are inextricably bound up with the child's psychological development. But if it is true, it has little, perhaps nothing, to do with the myths of Œdipus and Electra as they have come down to us.

And here the strengths of psychoanalysis must be considered apart from its shortcomings. The disorder with which analysts have had the greatest success is hysteria; and the elimination of hysterical symptoms sometimes seems to be correlated with recollection by the analysand (the person in analysis) of painful, nearly forgotten memories. The exact origin of those memories is a matter of some consequence in the theory behind psychoanalysis. When the first patients to be analyzed revealed a horde of repressed memories that were overtly sexual in content,

* Hecuba = Hecate, *kt*, as with Jocaste; see R. Graves, *The Greek Myths*, vol. 2, rev. ed. (London, 1960), pp. 341–43.

† The rarity of blinding with a pin in myth underscores the discrepancy even further.

Freud at first believed that they arose from literal childhood-seduction experiences, something he found quite disturbing. It was only in trying to account for this scandalous epidemic of incestuous pathology that he was led to posit an "Œdipus complex," which transferred the sphere of explanation for the memories from parental actions to the inchoate sexual fantasies of the child. The validity of his generalization is still a matter of dispute. It is possible that actual incest occurred more often than Freud's Victorian sensibilities could tolerate. But it does not seem likely that he was wrong in every case or even in a significant number of cases. And his subjects must have been remembering something. The question, of course, is *What?*

A possible, though admittedly controversial, answer is provided in the Hindu idea of reincarnation. Patañjali:

> By performing Saṃyama on the three kinds of transformations, knowledge of past and future.
>
> By direct perceptions of the impressions, knowledge of the previous birth.*

The impressions of which Patañjali writes are called saṃskāras, a word we have seen several times now that reduces to *skr* (after eliminating the Sanskrit prefix), similar to English *mark*. It is plausible to translate it by our word *sin*, in the sense that a sin is a mark or stain upon the soul (psyche). Saṃskāras are explicitly related to karmas and kleśas, which may be conceptualized as modifications made in the nervous system—as well as other places, for example, the cardiovascular system—by repeated behavioral patterns.† What Patañjali seems to be suggesting is that, just as a kleśas can be understood to be a "perceptual memory," so too certain saṃskāras may be interpretable as *protocognitive memories*. They are both a priori and formative, in the sense of a template, of the cognitive apparatus of the incarnated soul. They are impressions arising from experiences in previous lifetimes that the organism still holds and that can be scrutinized only in the trance state. But what can a scrutiny of a memory mean if not, in some sense, a remembering?

It should be obvious that the "direct perceptions" alluded to by Patañjali are not everyday occurrences; but for that matter neither is hypnosis, which is the context in which the analysand often recalls repressed memories. And in fact hypnosis *is* a sort of low-grade trance. By inducing hypnosis in the patient the analyst simulates a trance state, which is just the psychological milieu wherein, according to Patañjali, "knowledge of the previous birth" is possible. This being granted, we may be able to clarify Freud's difficulties with regard to the literalness of the incestuous events: They both did and did not happen. They did happen, but in a previous existence; they did not happen to the child, but are real memories nonetheless.‡

Current psychoanalysis rarely makes use of hypnosis save in the most intractable cases. Other, more practical techniques have been evolved, almost all of which also originated with Freud himself. One of these is often called free association. But here again the similarities with trance are significant. Free association can be likened to a state of revery that borders on trance—if not at times becoming identical to it. The seeds of the trance are particular and highly complex implications of words spoken by the analysand. If we add the setting in which the rigorous analysis takes place, namely, in utter quiet (the analyst rarely speaks), supine, often with eyes closed and usually facing away from the analyst, we have all the ingredients necessary for trance: an object of meditation, a technique for meditation, and a meditator, all in a medita-

* *Yoga-Sūtra*, *Vibhūti Pāda*, sutras 16, 18.

† To the extent that the repetitions are involuntary they conform with our idea of sin.

‡ The "real memories" are not necessarily incestuous in origin, though they *are* sexual; incest is merely the most obvious form, given the presuppositions of psychoanalysis, in which to express them. Underlying the entire argument is the distinction between cognitive and perceptual events, i.e., third- and second-world experiences.

tive setting. A yogi, examining the situation, would not find it remarkable that saṃskāras deriving from previous lifetimes are thereby revived—though, given the powerful techniques for inducing trance that yogis typically employ, he might find it crude.

The analyst is a witness to the trance. And because the analysand is communicating with "deeper" levels of selfhood, namely, is communicating with his or her self, he or she may communicate with the analyst, who becomes a sort of scribe of the analysand's own personal meditation, who writes it all down and mulls over it, interprets it. But what is "it" if not a myth? *A myth is an esoteric description of a heightened proprioception* (Axiom I). The analysand is experiencing just such a heightened proprioception of the cerebrum (third world). And the esoteric element is supplied by the analysand's ignorance of the true meaning of the seed: "the previous birth." Hence the transcribed meditation is a kind of unintentional myth, but a myth all the same.

To pursue the case of psychoanalysis any further would be a digression from our theme, which is the influence and relevance of myth in our own culture. We have briefly traced this influence in two areas: historiography and psychology. We've seen that in the former case myth is at the foundation of historical writing, while in the latter it has been not only formative of a certain school of psychology, namely, psychoanalysis, but can allow for a reinterpretation of analytic technique (albeit at the cost of introducing a radically un-Western idea: reincarnation). To extend the range of this influence is not difficult.

In art, for example, a clear line may be traced from antiquity to the present (if we consider the ways medieval art was influenced by Byzantine art). To do justice to pagan mythic themes was considered a primary goal of many Renaissance painters, for instance, Masaccio, Titian, and Veronese, who in turn influenced seventeenth-century artists such as Poussin and the academic styles of the eighteenth and nineteenth centuries. And of course, until the seventeenth century, the vast bulk of Western art was devoted to themes drawn from Judeo-Christian myth.

In architecture the picture is clearer still, since so many ancient buildings survived the Middle Ages. Both Alberti and Palladio drew on these moldering examples for their own aesthetic ideas, as well as on the recently rediscovered writings of Vitruvius. And the impact of those men on later architects is well nigh incalculable.

Music poses special problems. The word itself is derived from Greek *mousa,* "muse." Scholars have identified several chromatic scales used in antiquity, among them the æolian and lydian. The connection to Greek poetry, most of which in its origins was prosodic, is significant. Classical Indo-European languages are noted for their elaborate metrical forms. Spoken Sanskrit early incorporated musical pitch into recitations of the Vedas. Anyone who has listened to such a recitation can attest to the all-encompassing drone, produced solely with the voice, that envelops the ears. Sanskrit has four different characters for *n*: velar, retroflex, alveolar, and palatal; moreover, the diacritcal anusvāra nasalizes all thirteen Sanskrit vowels and should also be included. Indian music makes use of a drone, which mimes the subliminal hum of the nervous system. Instruments such as the sitār, vīnā, and oud produce otherworldly, "trippy," even psychedelic sounds that inspired pop musicians in the second half of this century. Music was explicitly likened to a drug. Perhaps the greatest revolution in culture in this or any other century was the electrical amplification of music (ca. 1930), which brought into the foreground of attention sounds that mimicked the internal whine of the nervous system.

With literature we are on perhaps the soundest ground from which to assert myth's formative preeminence in Western culture. Homer was the paradigm even in antiquity. We need only cite the example of Virgil, self-styled worshiper of Homer, and his tremendous influence on all subsequent literature. With his supposed foreshadowing of Christ in his *Fourth Eclogue* and his popularity with later Christian writers, such as Jerome and Augustine, Virgil binds together the literature of antiquity and the

Middle Ages in a coherent lineage. And in so doing, he reaches through both the Renaissance and the Enlightenment to our own time.

Because of limitations of space and because it has been more than adequately treated elsewhere, we have neglected in this summary to include the influence of such philosophers as Plato, Aristotle, and Plotinus, as well as the whole corpus of Judeo-Christian scripture, all of which, we have posited, are related to mythic, which is to say, proprioceptive ideas. It is therefore no exaggeration to state that, of all the identifiable sources of Western learning, myth is historically the most potent.

There is, however, one area of modern life that we have thus far avoided: science. We have done so not because a case for the influence of myth cannot be made. We established the *primæ facies* for such a view in our discussion of aristotelian *energea*. We concluded that proprioceptively derived concepts were present in Aristotle's reasoning even if he did not explicitly acknowledge them. And there we left the matter, because to push our argument any farther in time than the fifth century B.C. would have been premature.

In considering the development of modern science we may not appeal to mythic sources quite so obviously. Whereas with Aristotle and the Presocratics it might have been permissible to reason from Homer's use of words like *psyche*, *pneuma*, and *dynamis* to their application by the earliest Greek physicists, when we come to thinkers such as Galileo, Bacon, and Newton—not to mention those who come after—we must admit that such an approach is useless and probably misleading. Rather, what we now set out to accomplish is a demonstration of how the physiology of the human body, particularly its neurophysiology, has irremovably contributed to scientific theory, if only because body and brain are, in the last analysis, all one has to work with in so theorizing. We have but one, limited, example of such an irremovable neurophysiological influence: rigorous psychoanalysis. There, the somewhat fortuitous presence of the trance state dictated the course of therapeutic technique. We shall try to push our analysis into more clearly scientific domains—mechanics and electrodynamics and from there as far as quantum electrodynamics, perhaps the most successful scientific theory there is.

PART THREE

SCIENCE

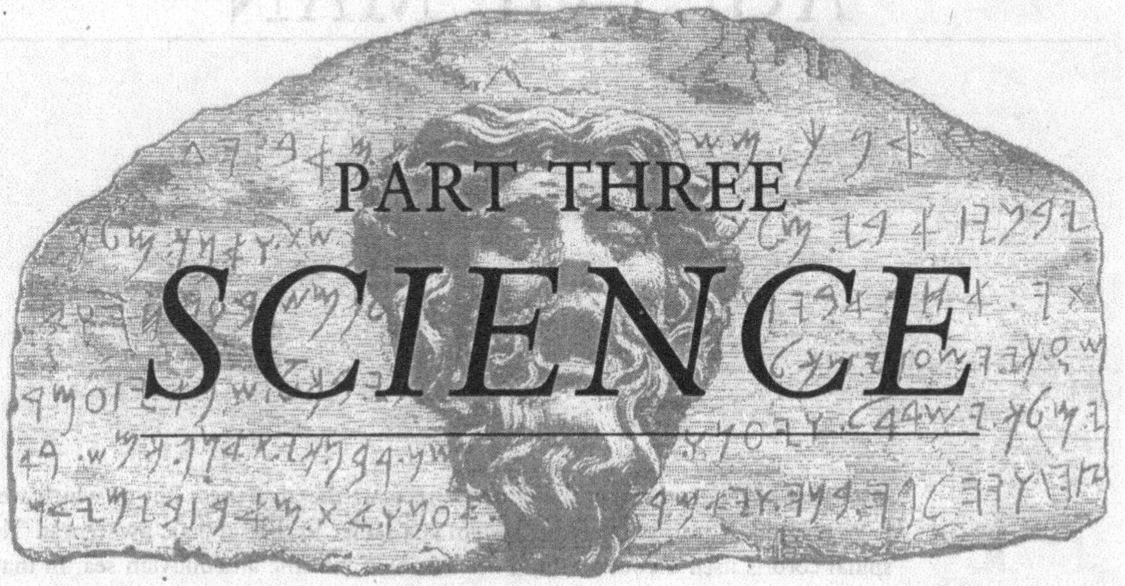

23

THE THREE AGES OF MAN

A beginning has been made in the effort to recreate the awareness out of which we have evolved. Your own nervous system is a tether to that archaic awareness. The spinal cord is itself a connection, a net let down into the antediluvian sea. In that sea our past is adrift. What sunders us from the past is not primarily time or space but awareness. To alter consciousness through trance is to don seven-league boots and foreshorten aeons with intuitions snatched from the nervous system.

What is called the development of thought or the evolution of the species or progress or time itself is a stealthy journey up the spinal cord, from coccyx to crown of head. The irreversibility of time is the hierarchy of consciousness. The evolutionary dynamic provoking our proprioceptive odyssey can be compared with a particular electronic circuit: a resonance in parallel with a negative resistance, also known as an oscillator. This is trance. The resonant element is the spinal cord. The telencephalon or forebrain is the element of negative resistance. In theory such a system could oscillate forever. It is the narcissism of the race and, to one degree or another, a factor in every experience, be it exalted cognition or lewd sensation.

Because the oscillator—or tank circuit—is part of a so-called living system, it grows. It integrates into itself other inductances and capacitances, altering the parameters of oscillation. There are also feedback properties present, amplification and gain. Experience alters. But the tank circuit has high impedance. The increase in proprioception is virtual, that is to say, it is imperceptible. An enormous amount of time—let's say four million years—has brought us to where we are now, at the parietoöccipital fissure. We have, each of us, recapitulated evolution that far, put one foot, as it were, into the third world, the sattvic world.* Yet all the while, evolution precedes awareness, and all the while the system oscillates. All the while we've been—we are—in deepest trance.

◆◆◆

* Sattva guṇa, roughly speaking, is the mode of cognition or intellect, the third world.

We have skirted a number of sticky questions that can be grouped under the category of *epistemology*, a somewhat daunting word that means "theory of knowledge." "To know," in the sense of epistemology, is very general. It means "to be aware of," and that specifically includes so-called subliminal awareness. Epistemology asks how is it we can know anything at all. For instance: What is subjective knowledge? What is objective knowledge? More pertinent: Is knowledge gained through sight distinct from what is known through touch? What about hearing? What about thought?

Our brains are crammed with nerves connecting one specialized region to another. Thus, sensation (perception) is linked neurologically with thought (cognition). Of course, that's not really news. Usually, whether we like it or not, if we see something, we also think and feel something. The message of yoga, however, is that we can isolate awareness. You can customize your epistemology, pick just what you want to know at a given moment and nothing else. Analogously, in your home you can close doors at will, so that the noise of the kitchen, say, does not interfere with the TV in the den. So too, according to yoga, can one isolate sight from sound, taste from touch, and so forth. That is sublime trance.

The analogy can be pressed too far. In your home each room is formally equivalent to any other room. The den may be smaller or larger than the kitchen or bathroom, it may be carpeted and air-conditioned where they are not, but it is still a room of the house, having walls, floor, and ceiling. In transiting from seeing to thinking, however, we make a qualitative "movement." One looks with one's eyes at a yardstick and sees all of its thirty-six inches precisely etched. One can also imagine a yardstick, and rather clearly too. Yet who can say that the yardstick one imagines in one's mind is thirty-six inches long? Who can honestly say that a *concept of length,* be it imagined ever so vividly, is the same as a length perceived by the eyes and measured by the hand in the world "out there"?

To say that seeing is qualitatively different from thinking means that one mode of experience cannot be converted into the other in the same way that feet convert to inches, for instance. In technical terms, vision and cognition are *incommensurable.* Hearing and cognition also are incommensurable. For that matter, so too are hearing and vision, touch and vision, and so on. The current assumption among biologists, especially biochemists and biophysicists, is that any experience can be reduced in principle to chemical combinations of matter. Yet even if we ignore the fact that the concept of matter is at present wholly ambiguous, we recognize in the reductionist assumption merely the fond hope of materialist science, one that is far from having been verified even in its own terms.

And it is precisely the terms of the debate that are at issue. Scientists frequently use words like *model* or *picture* in explaining their theories. Such words are second-world epiphenomena. They are visually defined categories that analogize appearance, phenomenon, and so on, so we can talk about them. Yet at the same time that scientists speak in terms of visual models, they refuse to assign to them any validity per se. And that is especially true if the objective of the theory is knowledge of an imperceptible entity such as an atom or molecule.

Bedrock epistemological confusion is unavoidable. The present understanding of scientific knowledge does not recognize qualitative schisms within the very nervous system that created science. It must therefore promiscuously mingle cognition with perception, even with stereognosis, which is awareness of that most mysterious of all physical concepts: *mass*. The triumph of the newtonian model has made words like *subjective* and *interior* suspect. Yet "inside" and "outside" are themselves spatial categories—hence, superlatively perceptual—and thus ipso facto without intrinsic application to, or explanatory value for, cognition and stereognosis.

Such an attitude was not handed down from on high but is rooted in deeply felt prejudices about the way the universe *should* behave. It is part and parcel of an antimystical, antireligious, anticlerical tradition going back to the early eighteenth century. Since the days of Bishop Berkeley* and Sir Isaac Newton, pure perceptions, taking the form of the motions of a pointer on a meter of one sort or another, have been the sole arbiters of scientific verification. To be scientific has come to mean to be "perceivable."

The pillars of science are its units of measurement: the pound, the foot, and the second, which allow the scientist to quantify mass, space, and time, respectively. At present, only the category of space (second world) is unambiguous. Why does time "flow" in only one direction when according to the newtonian model it could just as well run backward? Why have gravity waves—a patent perceptualization of mass—never been detected? The reason is that our current categories of mass and time are but second-world shadows of the real thing, perceptual representations of the literally imperceivable.

What that all comes down to is that our science is an *incomplete* science, incomplete because, fundamentally, it is only a second-world science. We not only see with our eyes, but we interpret everything by the rules of sight and naïvely call such an interpretation "objective": *Current scientific theory is strongly correlated with the dynamics of perception and defines verification wholly by perception.*

Second-world knowledge includes the experience of (1) light, which is massless, and (2) sound and (3) odor, which are phenomenologically massless. It is important to recognize, however, that all experience is mediated by light inasmuch as every nerve, whether serving a stereognostic, perceptual, or cognitive function, transfers electromagnetism, which is light, from one place in the body to another. In the case of hearing, for example, once the vibrating air molecules have set in motion certain hairlike filaments lining the labyrinth of the ear, the mechanical motion of the air is converted into an electromagnetic/chemical signal in the auditory nerve. Similarly for smell. Through stereognosis—the experience of the mass of the body—you experience your weight, which is the net gravitational force of all other masses in the universe acting on your mass. Yet the neural proprioceptors (in the conventional sense of the word) that convey the feeling of weight are also light-bearing nerves.† Obviously the same is true for cognition.

Analogously, in rāja yoga the mediation of electromagnetism in experience is described as *prakāṣāvaraṇa*, "the covering of light," which "wastes away" when the "formless" (akalpitā) is experienced. (Form, it should be noted, is a second-world category.) Light is here conceived as something that veils rather than illuminates. As we have seen, the encounter of the Greek hero Odysseus with the nymph Calypso is a description of entanglement with prakāśāvaraṇa.

In admitting the obvious, namely, the mediation of awareness by light, we should beware of embracing it too zealously. If we understood cognition and stereognosis by their own "lights," rather than by light per se, we could redefine awareness—be it internal, external, or neither—as all first world or all third world. For it is not obvious that the criteria of scientific truth *must* be based solely in perception. One can either deny that thought and feeling exist, the hysterical approach taken by so-called radical empiricists, or one can somehow incorporate them into the paradigms of science on an equal footing with perception. We would then define cognition as a proprioception of the diencephalon, for example, vision as a proprioception of the eyes, hearing of the ears, and so on. Instead of everything being perception in principle, everything, in principle, is proprioception. Alternatively, any experience can be redefined as a cognition. The objective thus becomes subjective. Frankly, it has been all along. Yet that is not to embrace solipsism. To admit that all we ever experience is our own

* George Berkeley (1685–1753) is perhaps most famous for the aphorism *esse est percipi*, "to be is to be perceived," which ratchets Descartes's existential criterion from cognition to perception.

† In his recent book, *The Emperor's New Mind* (New York, 1989), British physicist Roger Penrose speculates that specialized sensors of the brain respond only to "quantum gravity," i.e., to a nonelectromagnetic stimulus.

body is not remotely to admit that there is nothing apart from our own body. Indeed, by positing a body we have posited a world. It is the epistemological implications of body and world that must be explored critically.

The three cosmœ—cognition, perception, and stereognosis—are not accidental to our species or even to terrestrial organisms in general but inhere in all matter. The tripartite epistemology of the human body is a true universal and is summed up by the Biblical verse "So God created man in his *own* image, in the image of God created he . . . them."*

That the image of God referred to was of the nature of a triad is seen in the venerable Christian myth of the Holy Trinity, in the constant division into threes found in all ancient religions, indeed, in the very notion of the Three Worlds. The division is apparent to anyone who scrutinizes his or her own awareness. How far in spirit is such straightforward self-scrutiny from the opaque Trinity of dogmatic theology, from the glib metaphor mongering of psycholinguistic and symbolical approaches to myth. The myth of the Three Worlds is no more a symbol than feeling, seeing, and thinking are symbols: They are phenomenological facts. But we are making prematurely heavy epistemological weather for our purposes. For now, a summary statement is all that is needed: *Science equals epistemology.*

That is not to say merely that science treats incidentally of modes of knowledge—a statement with which few scientists could disagree—but that the essential subject matter of science *is* "knowing," a far more radical stance.† Science, we intend to show, is a description of the faculties of knowledge: seeing (electricity), hearing (magnetism), stereognosis (gravity), and so forth.

◆◆◆

Before the Perceptual Age was the Stereognostic Age, the age of Homer, Hesiod, and Epimenides, semimythical figures whose work is clearly mythical. Their criterion of knowledge was the law of the first world: *What is real is what one feels.*

The aeons prior to 700 B.C. we define as the Stereognostic Age. From approximately 700 B.C. to approximately A.D. 1900 was the Perceptual Age. Since 1900 we have been in the Cognitive Age. The Stereognostic Age is the age of authentic mythmaking. Myth springs from descriptions of internal states, and the first world, the realm of pure stereognosis, is purely internal. Thus, the narcissism of the species (cultural autism) implies that the first explorations of the universe—of awareness—must occur in the first world. In stereognosis are found the prototypical experiences of fire, air, earth, and water—the body is warm, buoyant, dense, palpably fluid—that led, inevitably, to the early speculations of the presocratic philosophers, the first perceptualists.

Anaximenes, for example, used a patently anthropomorphic model when he described the primordial element in the creation of the universe as air. He speaks of air moving ceaselessly throughout the world just as breath pervades the body. Thales believed that water was the primordial "world stuff." That too can be traced to experiences of the fluidity of the body, particularly of the first world. Heraclitus concentrated his attention on fire. Aristotle integrated all of the above traditions but also set the course of a retrograde antiempiricism that was to confuse natural philosophy until the time of Galileo. It was only during the Enlightenment, an apt self-pun indeed, that perceptualism became rigidly the ideology of modernism. The Enlightenment was therefore the fruition of centuries of thought about the world and humankind's proper place within it. Myth and science are first of all modes of awareness, and the two dozen centuries between Pythagoras and Clerk Maxwell, quite possibly the most brilliant expounder of perceptually biased science in history, witnessed an ever accelerating transition between the two modes.

The sea-island-sea paradigm is useful in defining the "three ages of man." Once mankind experienced in oceanic terms. That means in

* Genesis 1:27, emphasis added.

† Science < L. *scire*, "to know"; cf., Gk. *epistamæ*, "to know."

mythicoreligious terms. That means inwardly. But beginning in the late seventh century B.C., human awareness seems to have undergone a remarkable outward reorientation.* It was the era of Thales and Anaximenes, who first groped toward a recognizably scientific conception of our universe. The phenomenon was worldwide. In China, India, and Persia also there were the stirrings of an externally oriented consciousness and the beginnings of science. This outward reorientation was the beginning of the Perceptual Age. The shibboleth of the Perceptual Age was *clarity*, and the proudest fruit of perceptualism was the mechanical model of the universe, which emerged like an island of clarity from the visceral and temperamental sea that gave it birth. In the nineteenth century, however, scientists recovered the oceanic perspective not because they wanted to but because they had to. Driven to the concept of the *field*, they have been reluctant witnesses to the sinking of the island of clarity ever since. Quantum mechanics, a product of our century, marks the first science of the Cognitive Age.

***

The Three Worlds, mysteriously copresent in our awareness, lie at the bottom of the several descriptions of myth and science. Science is at present evolving theories that undermine its own perceptual biases and challenge the present uncritical understanding of ***empiricism***. The successes of such theories retrospectively verify the conclusions of myth: the Three Worlds are an illusion. But the Crack in the Cosmic Egg is not a mere crack until the Fall has been reversed. Until then it is the "wide-wayed world." Patañjali poses the dilemma as that of the confusion of seen with seer, of mistaking prakṛti for puruṣa. When, by kriyās, the yogi abstracts from all worlds, all three experiences are seen as one—coplanar as it were—then the illusion of perception is broken. But the perceptual illusion is only the grossest illusion, which is why it is broken first. The cognitive and stereognostic illusions must be broken as well. The hold of the first and third worlds is much more tenacious. It is not so simple as distinguishing seer from seen. The knower must not be confused with the known. The thinker must be proprioceptively separated from his thoughts. Patañjali tells us that then the guṇas are harmonized. The sages liken that moment to an awakening, a rapture that comes in the twinkling of an eye. In the union of Zeus and Hera on Crete, myth suggests that the creation at large enjoys this harmony habitually, but also, in the Trojan War, that the human organism is ever discordant. In the universe at large the stereognostic, perceptual, and cognitive faculties are harmonized in a peace that passes all understanding. In the human being alone, they are out of balance. Each individual human organism sees through a glass darkly what is otherwise crystalline clear. The sages tell us that this essential clarity cannot be described in words. Yet, having awakened to it, they sing its praises:

> The Lord is my shepherd, I shall not want. He maketh me to lie down in green pastures: he leadeth me beside the still waters. He restoreth my soul: he leadeth me in the paths of righteousness for his name's sake . . . thy rod and thy staff they comfort me. . . . Thou annointest my head with oil.

Infinite yearning, ever infinitely fulfilled—God Almighty. That is the reality of the liberated soul.

* This watershed century has been called the Axial Age by historians of science.

24

ON THE POSSIBILITY OF AN A PRIORI EXPERIENCE

Pygmalion, king of Cyprus, was in love with Aphrodite. The goddess, however, would not consent to lie with him even for a single night. Desperate, Pygmalion fashioned an ivory image of her and placed it in his bed, with a prayer that she might in some way show pity toward him. Entering into this image Aphrodite brought it to life, as Galatea, on whom Pygmalion promptly sired Paphus and Metharme.

That much we know from Ovid's *Tenth Metamorphosis* (verses 243ff.). The myth is interesting for several reasons, not least of which is Aphrodite's role in the creation of life. It is possible that her possession of such powers (normally exercised exclusively by Zeus)* is a vestigial mythic restatement of her role in the *Theogony*, where, as we've seen, she is born from the Castration of Uranus and with her companions, Eros and Himera (Love and Desire), helps animate the second world even before the appearance of Zeus. The setting of the myth of Pygmalion and Galatea is Cyprus, which is (1) an island, (2) sacred to Aphrodite, and (3) reducible to *kpr = kr*, so we have a constellation of evidence that the myth concerns the second world.

Hesiod also tells us that Aphrodite emerged from the foam of the sea, near the Ionian island of Cythera. Hence her epithet, *anadyomene*, meaning "upon the waves." The correspondence is elaborated by the names of Pygmalion's children. *Paphus* means "foamy" and *Metharme* "change."† Galatea, whose name translates as "milky," is also the name of a nereid, a mythical creature often linked with the frothy crest of a wave. The choice of ivory for the statuette follows naturally from bone.

Whatever Aphrodite's creative power is, it is similar to a nereid's. She is clearly not Galatea's mother nor her sister nor any other conventional relation that we might name. Nor is Galatea simply Aphrodite incognita. If the goddess had returned Pygmalion's love personally she could either have come to him as Aphrodite or else changed herself into a mortal for a short while, something all the

*** Very occasionally by Apollo.**

† Changeability being an attribute of foam.

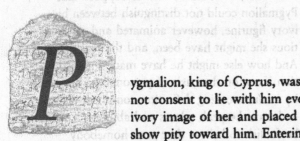

Olympians do whenever it suits their purpose. But she did neither of those things. Instead, she animated a body already fashioned for her. Presumably she was not trapped therein, for it is unreasonable to think that so unmaternal a deity would have remained inside Galatea for nine months. (We do not even know that Paphus and Metharme were twins.) But though Galatea is not Aphrodite in disguise, she is Aphrodite in some sense, because the point of the myth is that Pygmalion desired to lie with the goddess. Hence our final surmise must be that whatever Aphrodite's power is, it allows her to be Galatea's life without being her individuality, not to mention her mortality.

If all of that is eerily reminiscent of some of the doctrinal disputes that wracked early Christianity, particularly that of Monophysitism versus Nestorianism, it is no accident. For we are here faced with a similar conundrum: How is it that a creature may be both mortal and divine? Very briefly, Monophysitism taught that Christ had only one nature (physis) after his incarnation as Jesus of Nazareth, while Nestorianism considered that both before and after the Incarnation the divine and human personalities (prosopa) were utterly distinct. The Council of Chalcedon condemned both views as heretical and tried to draw the line between them in the following way: Christ had two natures, that of the Logos, which is divine, and that of Jesus of Nazareth, which was human, in the union (hypostasis) of one divine person.*

Whether the above formulation is truly helpful is open to question, for without a definition of nature or personality it is difficult to grasp what is being taught. The prosaic meaning of *personality* is a set of traits, or characteristics, that allow for differentiation among human beings above and beyond physiognomy. Personality therefore particularizes. *Nature*, on the other hand, is a unifying concept, for example, when we speak of human nature as a certain propensity shared by all people. The interpretation would seem to accord with Aristotle's use of *physis* as the being of living organisms. Of all the mind-contorting concepts with which metaphysics delights in amusing itself, that of *being* is probably the least amenable to particularization. Since we are here dealing with a Greek myth, let us adopt Aristotle's usage of physis/nature as our own.

If we now look at the relationship between Galatea and Aphrodite in light of our definitions of personality as particularization and nature as being, we find ourselves forced to a conclusion that differs markedly from that drawn by Chalcedon. Clearly Aphrodite's personality differs from Galatea's, if only because Aphrodite has a horror of domesticity while Galatea, from what little we know of her, does not. (After all, she does raise two children to adulthood.) Moreover, it would be rash to suppose that Pygmalion could not distinguish between his ivory figurine, however animated and rambunctious she might have been, and the real thing. And how else might he have made the distinction if not on the basis of personality? Personality in our working definition comprises traits; and traits bespeak talents and abilities; it would be foolish to believe that poor homebody Galatea could, in times of stress, wrap herself in a cloud and waft to Olympus or Ida or some other heavenly spa at a moment's notice, as Aphrodite could and often did. Their personalities must have been very different, as distinct as a housewife is from a goddess.

Then what of their natures? Are they also different? Because we have allowed ourselves to be straitjacketed within only two notions, which is to say personality and nature, and because we have admitted already that there must be some commonality between these women while at the same time eliminating a common personality, we must say that in some sense their natures are identical. (Either that or manufacture some third category the form of which, at the moment, is not at all apparent.) In a pinch, we turn to Aristotle for clarification, for our purpose is not to rest with a simple assertion of natural identity but to specify ever more clearly what that nature is.

Recall that for Aristotle the concept of

* J. M. Carmody and T. E. Clarke, *Word and Redeemer* (Glen Rock, N.J., 1966), pp. 82–106.

physis was merely a didactic tool, useful in discussing such recondite topics as being and becoming. For Aristotle there was only *ousia* (pure being), and physis is ousia. Reasoning analogously, can we not then say that Galatea's nature bears the same relationship to Aphrodite's that physis bears to ousia? That there is only an apparent difference between them? And if we say that, is our problem solved? Well, no. For we have yet to describe more usefully what quality is essential to either physis or ousia.

Now it is obvious that whatever this quality is, it will have to be metaphysically fundamental, because even to speak of ousia as having attributes is to tread a thin line between the profound and the banal. Hence this quality—call it *q*—will pertain exclusively to ousia and to nothing else. It may be possible to express *q* as an adjective or a noun, but if so its expression will have to be very nearly empty of meaning. But to be very nearly empty of meaning is not to be totally meaningless. We need only cite the usual translation of *ousia*, namely, "being," to see this. It is not possible to define being qua being, which makes it functionally or empirically meaningless. And yet we still cannot entirely shake a sense that there is something, if not meaningful then significant, about it. Perhaps a similar situation obtains with *q*. If so we can only hope that when we come to express it the idea will contribute something new to our understanding, something that is not entirely tautological. In other words we must hope that we do not end up saying, with Aristotle, that the quality of being is being, that not only is physis ousia but also that ousia is ousia, which would make our entire argument unnecessary. But before we close on our quarry let's look once again at the myth of Pygmalion and Galatea.

In fashioning his beloved, Pygmalion actually did very little. He sculpted a block of ivory into what was, presumably, a reasonable facsimile of a good-looking woman, and that was it. It was left to Aphrodite to do the rest, the really hard stuff. We have already decided that the "stuff" must have been the transmission to Galatea of Aphrodite's ousia. Now whether we call that act the giving of life (or soul) is unimportant at that stage. What is important is that she somehow did it.

Let us now assume that Pygmalion was a bit more talented than we find him in Ovid. Let us suppose that he'd had a premonition of what the goddess was about to do and that being a conscientious sort he decided to help her out. And let us further suppose that he was capable of technical feats that elude even our own science. What we now have, after a mountain of supposition, is not simply a whittler of ivory but a superlative biochemist (with several advanced degrees, no doubt), penetrating physicist, gifted engineer, and, last but not least, a first-rate mechanic, together with all the useful appurtenances of such: computers, libraries, laboratories, and assistants.

On the night that Aphrodite is due to arrive and administer the pièce de résistance, we find Pygmalion and his minions hard at work synthesizing nucleic acids, congealing proteins, putting the pep into polypeptides, and doing at least a million other necessarily spectacular things, all in preparation for the big moment (which, for the sake of melodrama, we shall fix at midnight). Looking up from his centrifuge, Pygmalion spies the incomparably lovely Galatea, eyes closed, stretched upon the amphitheatre operating table, and he heaves a sigh of undisguised longing. "If only," he thinks, "if only I didn't have to wait for Aphrodite. Where in Hades is she anyway?" Leaning on a rheostat he muses aloud to an assistant. "Bathos, my boy," he says (a note of quiet pride in his voice), "I do believe I could've done the whole business myself."

Bathos, who in all things save his ability to pose discomfiting questions is something of a dullard, replies by asking: "But Master Pyg, how'd you know if you had?" Before the disturbing implications of this question may seep into Pygmalion's lascivious reverie, he notices a look of horror stealing across Bathos's wizened face. "Have a care, Pyg!" Bathos cries. But it's too late. The rheostat on which Pygmalion has been so carelessly leaning slips forward an inch or two, sending a jillion jolts of potent ousia energy coursing through the supine Galatea. And before either of them can reset the device or do anything more than croak "Oh no!" she sits up and, in a lovely contralto, asks for a glass of water.

It is a long moment before Pygmalion can find words to speak, and Galatea is forced to ask twice for her water. Then, realizing that something truly stupendous has occurred, he breaks out the twelve-year-old Chian and pours a toast all around. Yet before he can grow really self-satisfied Pygmalion recalls Bathos's innocuous question. And it begins to nag at him. Observing his beloved more closely, he sees that the simpleton has a point. How can he be certain that Galatea is truly alive? After all, the awful thought crosses his mind, she might just be a robot, mightn't she? A highly complex and egregiously successful robot, it is true, but a robot all the same. Wringing his hands, he decides to try to dispel his doubts.

He begins by questioning Galatea, asking her this and that, striving to be pleasant, but all the while anxious lest she make some telltale robotic misstep and dash his hopes. He finds, much to his satisfaction, that Galatea appears to be a surprisingly articulate young woman, who knows when she is too warm or too cold, when something tastes good and when it doesn't, all of which is highly encouraging. Finally he stops beating around the bush. "My dear child," he says, somewhat nervously, "I was just wondering. But are you really human?"

Galatea smiles winningly. "Why you foolish, foolish man, you," she replies. "Of course I am. As human as you and you and you." And she singles out several of those around her. Turning to Bathos, Pygmalion snidely whispers: "You see. That settles that!"

But Bathos is unconvinced. Scratching the few hairs on his head and nudging Pygmalion in the ribs, he says: "What if she's lying?"

Pshaw! Pygmalion is about to retort, then thinks again. "What if she *is* lying?" To know that would be equivalent to knowing if she's human, so he's right back where he started from. Feeling glum, he dismisses everyone except Galatea and goes back to the drawing board.

Taking out a sheet of graph paper, he lays off two coordinate axes, labeling the abscissa *i*, for the amount of information he possesses about Galatea's technology, and labeling the ordinate *I*, for the amount of information concerning her "true feelings" that he is certain of. He tries to plot one against the other and at first assumes that as *i* increases from zero so too will *I*. But before long he realizes that, to be perfectly honest about it, there is no relationship between *I* and *i*. Absolutely none! His graph consists of a straight line lying on the axis of abscissae. Picking up a sheaf of papers on which he had written the many and extraordinarily detailed differential equations of state used in constructing Galatea, he stares fretfully at them for a moment before tossing them into the wastebasket. It is then that he notices Galatea has fallen asleep on the operating table, a thin smile wreathing her face. "If only," he thinks. "If only I'd foreseen this problem at the beginning. Why, I'd probably never have gone to all this trouble." Wincing inwardly he recalls the many days and nights of intense effort that went into fashioning his beloved. And for all of that he is left with a smiling enigma.

Pygmalion is about to turn in himself when who should appear but Aphrodite herself, right at the stroke of midnight. She floats down from a cloud that has drifted into the amphitheatre through an air duct and hovers callipygously an inch or so off the floor, a knowing look on her gorgeous puss. Of course she has divined his difficulty and, without uttering a word, goes right to work. What she does exactly is not easy to tell. Pygmalion can only watch bemusedly as the goddess transforms herself into a golden vortex, spinning off sparks and stars and pinwheels, moving faster and faster, until only her ears are discernible at the periphery of the whirl of stardust she has become, looking like a diaphanous, long-necked jug turning on the wheel of some celestial potter. And then, to the rhythmic sound of *braka-kyax-ko-ax-ko-ax*, she zips into Galatea's right nostril and disappears. Pygmalion watches breathlessly as Galatea stirs in her sleep, opens her violet eyes, and purrs, "Darling, please come to bed." Which is exactly what he does.

The point of our fairy tale should be obvious: Galatea's "true feelings" are as opaque to Pygmalion as the dark side of the moon. Nor is this news especially. What Pygmalion was led to discover so obliquely is a well-known problem of metaphysics, what might be called the solipsistic dilemma: How can we know if anyone other than ourselves is conscious? Our purpose here is not to answer this question once and for all but, rather, to exploit it.

If we accept the hypothetical evidence* of Pygmalion's graph of $I(i)$,† we must conclude that there is no causal connection between what may be observed to be true of an organism (what we've been calling *i*) and our knowledge of the experience of that organism (namely, *I*). Another way of putting it is to say that there is no such thing as empathy, except, perhaps, accidentally. The psychological state known as *empathos* is, sadly, a laudable fiction.

It is possible to have any number of responses to this discovery. Positivist-minded philosophers and psychologists are notorious for being utterly unmoved by it. Their attitude may be summed up in two words: So what? At most they would describe it as a pseudoproblem, unworthy of serious investigation. And there is no way, it must be admitted, to fault them on strictly logical grounds, though we may perhaps diagnose them as suffering from a lamentable lack of curiosity. Still others, for whom there is no agreed-upon title, persist in believing that the problem of consciousness is simply an unsolved problem, which future discoveries in biochemistry and biophysics may one day lay to rest. But by allowing Pygmalion to have access to all conceivable information *i* about the organism, we have formally precluded such a hope. The problem of consciousness cannot be reduced to lack of data. It is an epistemological problem, one that reaches deep into even the possibility of knowledge.

A salient feature of the biochemical-biophysical approach to the problem of consciousness is its perverse equation of consciousness and mind. This results in the so-called mind-body problem, what Schopenauer termed *die Weltknaut*, "world knot," the problem whose resolution precedes in importance all other problems. But we have seen that yogically the mind is a collection of proprioceptions and very definitely not, in and of itself, the locus of consciousness. In yoga, thoughts are pratyaya, that is, contents of consciousness, which is called puruṣa, and are in no wise epistemologically more significant than perceptions or visceral proprioceptions. Hence even were Schopenhauer's world-knot "untied" it would cast no light whatsoever on the problem of consciousness.

If we eliminate both the positivist and biochemical-biophysical approaches to consciousness as fundamentally inadequate, what are we left with? The answer, of course, is aristotelian ousia. Not only, we suggest, is ousia ousia, but ousia is consciousness, what we might call pure awareness, without any content (pratyaya) and in fact not requiring any. And it is toward the experiencing of such a pure awareness that yoga is ultimately directed. What we are saying, in effect, is that consciousness is transcendent, by which we mean nothing too spooky, but only that no causal relationship exists between consciousness and the object(s) of consciousness, between puruṣa and pratyaya. The presocratic philosopher Parmenides was perhaps intimating this possibility when he asserted that "reality is knowledge" (*Fragmenta* 5), not the object(s) of knowledge but pure knowing.

Ousia reduces to *s*, a sibilant, as does *puruṣa* (*ps*; the *r*, falling between two vowels, almost certainly is intervocalic). And we have seen that Aristotle, following the example of Anaximenes, considered that the stuff of soul, which is the true locus of consciousness, was air. In fact, there is no Greek word for our idea of pure consciousness, so it may be that *ousia* is legitimately translated as such, especially since there is already a perfectly good Greek word for "being," *on*. Given the primitive animism out of which every race, including the Greeks, has

* "Hypothetical" because it derives from technical discoveries not yet made by our science.

† Read as "*I* as a function of *i*" or more succinctly "*I* of *i*."

evolved, it should not be unexpected that a word such as *ousia*, which is usually translated as "being" or "essence," should partake of consciousness.

Which brings us back to our *q* factor. We were originally led to posit *q* to conceptualize more usefully the nature of Aphrodite's ousia (and hence Galatea's physis). We now propose that *q* is *consciousness*, because only consciousness fulfills our criteria for ousia exactly. Consciousness is a quality that pertains exclusively to ousia, is almost meaningless, yet adds a new element to our understanding of the word. The meaninglessness of consciousness stems from its supreme indeterminacy (as the fairy tale of Pygmalion's workshop tried to demonstrate), rather than from its lack of significance. Like the concept of being, it is validated in its significance for us only by our intimate inner relationship with it. As has been said before: "We do not know what 'Being' means. But even if we ask, 'What is "Being"?' we keep within an understanding of the 'is,' though we are unable to fix conceptually what that 'is' signifies."*

We now assert that a similar statement holds for consciousness and that consciousness, in its applications and significance, is coextensive with *being*, a position that Indian philosophy has maintained for thousands of years and the truth of which yoga claims can be experienced practically. By eliminating all pratyaya, be they cognitive, perceptual, or stereognostic, a yogi ipso facto experiences his or her puruṣa (or soul or self or consciousness—it hardly matters what one calls it), which has *been there* all along, but which has been obscured by its contents.† We therefore have both a theory of consciousness (Sāṃkhya/Vedānta) and a technique for experiencing pure consciousness practically (yoga); given these, the requisite verification of the congruency of consciousness with being is to understand the one while practicing the other.

The proprioceptive hypothesis, it should be noted, contains the above arguments implicitly. By positing the organism's awareness of its body *ad minutias*, the hypothesis makes awareness or consciousness transcendent, which is to say, not causally relatable to the body, including the brain. We must not leap to the frantically beckoning conclusion that consciousness is a quality of space and time, but must agree with Kant in saying that those concepts are synthetic judgments concerning phenomena, namely, pratyaya, and not of *noumena*, namely, puruṣa. Space and time are experiences of particular configurations of the organism's sensoria and are themselves contents of consciousness. We seem to be saying, in other words, that the locus of consciousness is not "in" the body at all. But then too it cannot be "out" of the body either. The absurdity is only apparent, however, and springs directly from the fact that both "in" and "out" are also pratyaya. They are posterior to consciousness, not prior to it. We cannot even ask "Where is consciousness?" because "where" also is pratyaya. All of that comes down to saying that consciousness is a priori. It bears the same relationship to phenomena as Chaos does to the Three Worlds in Greek myth: *Consciousness is a priori experience.* But before pursuing the idea further, let us return to the relationship of Galatea and Aphrodite.

The quality that Aphrodite implanted in Galatea was her (Aphrodite's) consciousness. But the next question is, How came Aphrodite to be conscious? If we follow Hesiod's genealogy our answer is clear: through Uranus. Aphrodite's physis is Uranus's ousia is his consciousness. If we now ask whence Uranus's physis derives we are on uneasy grounds scripturally, for Hesiod merely tells us that Gæa (Mother Earth) "first bore starry Uranus, equal to herself" and at once mated with him to produce the Titans. That would seem to indicate that Uranus's physis derives from Gæa's ousia. But the phrase "equal to herself" vitiates such a conclusion and in fact refers to Uranus's formal origins. Uranus comes into existence tautologically; that is, the creation of the second world (Gæa) deduces the appearance of the third (Uranus). For Uranus's substantive origins we must look elsewhere. He is not

* M. Heidegger, *Being and Time*, trans. J. Macquarrie and E. Robinson (New York, 1962), p. 25.

† Cf., Heidegger's *Dasein*, "there being" = uniquely human consciousness.

infrequently referred to as *Acmonides,* "son of Acmon." The proper noun *Acmon* is almost assuredly not Greek (it seems closest to Old Persian). Possibly it is cognate with Sanskrit *acman,* "stone."* Aboriginal imagery is always extremely concrete; the most obvious characteristic of the thing described drives the image. The characteristics of stone are hardness and immovability. And it is the latter characteristic that interests us here.

In Vedānta the supreme reality, brahman, is often described—when it is referred to at all—as "unmoving." Brahman pervades all reality, manifest and unmanifest. As a consequence of the extreme monism taught in the *Upaniṣads,* it is not possible or even desirable to cite brahman's attributes. Indeed, Vedānta even eschews the use of the term *conscious* when speaking of it. We must keep in mind, however, that Vedānta is infinitely more sophisticated, philosophically, than Greek myth. So it is barely possible to correlate Acmon, the unmoving, with brahman, the unmoving, and still retain notions of consciousness in the former.

We how have the following regression into ousia: Galatea from Aphrodite from Uranus from Acmon, the unmoving. The consciousness of each link in the chain derives from the consciousness of the previous link, until it concludes in a state of pure consciousness, undifferentiated and unmanifested; but it is essentially the same consciousness throughout. If we liken consciousness to a light, our sequence is comparable to a set of filters of varying colors laid over that light. From our previous analysis of mythic colors we may even speculate what the order of the colorings might be. Starting with the inconceivable color of consciousness itself—for the sake of a name we'll call it Sufic black—which corresponds to Acmon, we have indigo (Uranus), gold (Aphrodite), and white (Galatea). That is the reverse of the sequence a yogi experiences as the trance state deepens. In the reversed order we observe the progressive lightening of the visual field as the meditator emerges from trance, culminating in the bright light of eyes-opened, second-world awareness.

Aphrodite links the second world to what might be called the *sea of consciousness,* the underlying reality of the mystic seas of the first and third worlds. Because of her Nereid-like significance as a goddess of the spray off those seas, Aphrodite's gift of consciousness to Galatea is in reality a symbol of the presence of consciousness in the second world—the sea of consciousness in the second world, for the sea of consciousness underlies perception also, as Poseidon's stern rulership suggests. The mythic embodiment of the immanence of consciousness in perception is Galatea herself. She is the manifestation of the *oceanic experience* present in each one of us a priori.

◆◆◆

The sun Helius, offspring of the Titan Hyperion and the Titaness Thea, figures in a number of important Greek myths, notably those concerning Persephone, the nymph Rhode, and Phæthon (Helius's son), but he is himself a minor god overall. Indeed, the sun itself does not seem to have captured the hellenic imagination as much as the moon (whom the Greeks personified by the goddess Selene). As a sun god, Helius is associated with the second world, which he illuminates, and indeed, just as violet is the color of the third world and black that of the first, gold—the sun's color—describes the second. In the myth of Asopus and Sisyphus, we learned that the river god caused a sacred spring to bubble up beneath the temple of Aphrodite in Corinth. Pausanias relates that by the second century A.D., the shrine was emblazoned with an image of Helius and EROS THE ARCHER, the bow deriving from the shape of the eyebrows and, of course, the eyes themselves having an intimate relationship with sunlight.† The spring was called the Fountain of Pyrene. Pyrene mated with Ares (Eros) to produce Cyncnus, whose name means "swan."

* Rose, *A Handbook of Greek Mythology,* p. 20.

† Pausanius, *Description of Greece,* trans. W. H. S. Jones (London, 1921), 2.5.

The *Upaniṣads* of Indian Vedānta are perhaps the richest source of ancient sun lore. In general they refer to the sun as either Āditya or Surya (very occasionally as Pusan), the former derived from a root denoting infinity and the latter from a Sanskrit word for air. But the *ādityas* are also a group of eight solar deities, among whom the better known are Varuna, Mitra, and Vivasvat.

In the myth of Galatea we considered matters from the viewpoint of the organism, which we've treated as a vehicle for experience or consciousness. The organism provides eyes so that consciousness may see. It provides ears so that consciousness may hear, and so on for the other senses, and for voiceless speech (intellect) as well. The organism provides a brain so that consciousness may think.

Now what if we reverse the perspective and consider matters from the point of view of that which is perceived, thought, viscerally proprioception? What if we consider the pratyaya, in other words, rather than the puruṣa? Might we not now say that thoughts, sights, sounds, feelings, and so forth, are equally indispensable for experience? If a yogi gazes at the sun, there exists a profound relationship between an object of consciousness, the sun, and consciousness itself, the yogi's puruṣa; there is in fact a species of equivalency between them. Consciousness is ever equal to what it is conscious of. As the one changes so does the other. If, for example, a light shines into the eyes of the organism, the parameters of the light—its frequency, intensity, dispersion, and so on—are matched by a specific experience. If these parameters are varied, if, say, the intensity of the light is increased, there occurs an equivalent intensification in the experience. The stimulus may become so intense as to destroy the perceptual vehicle, in this case the eyes, but that is not to say that the experience or even vision is destroyed. Intensification may lead to pain, but pain is an experience too, and, in the event, it is a visual pain. The visual field is radically altered, namely, perception as such ceases, but vision does not cease. Vision cannot cease. Yet how intense may it become?

Because, on the proprioceptive hypothesis, gods and goddesses must ultimately derive from bodily proprioceptions, the mythic sun is not necessarily identical with the sun of astronomy; instead, in the body itself there exists a golden "divine" light, a source of proprioccepted photons. Patañjali speaks of a light that is experienced beneath the crown of the head,* and in the *Maītri Upaniṣad* we are told (by the sage Śākayānya): "He who is the yonder person in the sun, I myself am he. Verily, that which is the sunhood of the sun is the Eternal real."†

What is "the sunhood of the sun" in proprioceptive terms? The question is epistemological and springs from the very fact of proprioception: When one looks at the sun, what is it that one sees? If, for the sake of argument, we adopt a strictly materialist point of view, that is, if we assume that consciousness is not a transcendent phenomenon but arises out of the neurology and chemistry of the brain, we also are forced to conclude that the sun as experienced is a only a *representation* of the astronomical sun, one produced by the interaction of a stimulation of the retinal cells with neurons of the occipital cortex. But the stimulus alone is not enough to account for the sight of the sun, since someone who is blind cannot see it regardless of the external stimulation of the eyes. Moreover, in dreams sunlight is "seen" even without such stimuli.‡ Therefore, within the brain is a neural process capable of producing brilliant white light. When one looks at the sun that process is proprioccepted. The same process is activated when any light whatsoever is perceived.

Again, from the *Upaniṣads* (speaking of "the self"):

> The sun does not shine there nor the moon and the stars, nor these lightenings, much less this fire. After Him, when He

* *Yoga-Sūtra, Vibhūti Pāda*, sutra 33.

† *Maītri Upaniṣad* 6.35.

‡ See, e.g., C. G. Jung, "Individual Dream Symbolism in Relation to Alchemy," in: *The Portable Jung*, ed. J. Campbell (New York, 1971), p. 335.

shines, everything shines, by His light all this is illuminated.*

> In the highest golden sheath is brahman without stain, without parts; Pure it is, the light of lights. That is what the knowers of Self know.
>
> He [the purified soul] knows that supreme abode of brahman, wherein founded, the world shines brightly.†

The neurophysiological processes of the brain that allow for vision are bound up with an experience of identity or selfhood. The "sunhood of the sun" is therefore what has long been called the soul, the vision of the self (ātman), and the ability to experience it is the ability to "find" the neurological sun within the brain, to concentrate upon it at will and at length, ultimately to perform saṃyama on it. Similarly at the start of the Yaqui Deer Dance, the dancer fastens the head of the deer to his head. In that moment, we surmised, the deer is present. What can that mean practically, nonsymbolically, other than that to see a deer's head—any deer's head, anywhere, anytime—excites those circuits of the brain that represent (in the kantian sense of *vorstellen*) a deer?

In discussing the oceanic experience we speculated that when the organism is presented with a sufficiently chaotic external stimulus it represents the stimulus by substituting an experience—a proprioception—of the nervous system, or at least of a particular sensorium within the nervous system. Thus, when gazing at the myriad branchings of a shrub there is a level of ramification at which the organism becomes aware of the myriad ramifications of the brain itself. This is certainly *not* a static process because it involves the incorporation of proprioceptions of neuronal groups as required, almost ad hoc. The model of neuronal functioning that can do justice to our hypothesis must be dynamic, plastic, and multivalent. Neurons must be capable of entering into and dropping out of many representational and self-representational schemes simultaneously.‡ The transition to the oceanic experience is not arbitrarily concise but varies with the individual organism.

The manifest intricacies of the brain, on such a view, are a palette of configurations, all but numberless, that conform percepts with the nervous system. Yet the palette must be understood, not abstractly, but concretely: to experience a circle (not an oceanic experience) must involve a literal circle of neurons in the brain. To experience a tree involves proprioception of the brain's own arborizations, including the spinal cord: the anamorphic trunk-cum-roots of the perceptual tree. If one intersects a sagittal section of the brain passing through the frontal suture, a horizontal section through the gasserian ganglion, and a coronal section through the sinuses, the result is a *cross* centered on the interorbital space and—somewhat posteriorly—the optical chiasmus. Thus, proprioception of the optical chiasmus is central to the experience of any cruciform percept; and we might wonder if the historic power of certain symbols derives principally from their proprioceptive relationship with neuroanatomical structures that figure prominently in esoteric praxis (in the above case, the frontal suture, gasserian ganglion, and sinuses). The famous *yin-yang* symbol, which, in a wholly abstract sense, has been interpreted as connoting vague masculine and feminine "principles," may actually describe, albeit fancifully, the shapes of the cerebral hemispheres, for which there is evidence of differential functioning by sex. Other—and the same—structures could apply to the yantras and mandalas of Buddhism, the lotus of Hinduism, the Judaic *mogen David*, the solar disk and ankh of Egyptian religion, and the pagan thrysus. On our hypothesis, the mingling of percept with proprioception does not depend on whether an individual has been initiated. Initiation, followed by praxis, would

* *Śvetāśvatara Upaniṣad* 6.14.

† *Mundaka Upaniṣad* 2.2.12, 3.2.1.

‡ Something akin to this process is called "somatic selection" by Edelman in his *Bright Air, Brilliant Fire: On the Matter of the Mind.*

then heighten and make explicit the relation of perceptual symbol to proprioception.*

Saṃyama is deep trance, an experience in which the bīja becomes intimately known and understood. We can generalize this concept in light of the above discussion in the following way. Because *all* knowledge—be it stereognostic, perceptual, or cognitive—is perforce representational, all knowledge exists somewhere within the brain, in the sense that the nervous system is irremovably involved in its experience. In kantian terminology, we are skirting the boundary between his famous Ding an sich and its Vorstellung (representation). But can that boundary be crossed? Consider the following verses from the *Upaniṣads*:

> In the midst of the sun stands the moon, in the midst of the moon the fire, in the midst of the fire stands pure being; in the midst of pure being stands the indestructible one.†

The phenomenological commonality among sun, moon, and fire is light; and it makes sense to assume that the same neurophysiological processes are involved to one degree or another in the experience of those various "lightenings." As the trance deepens, the meditator goes through the sunhood of the sun to the moonhood of the moon to the firehood of fire and thence to the ineffable (what Kant would call the *numinal*). The last can be interpreted as meaning a very subtle proprioception of the undifferentiated energy of the brain, perhaps even as far as knowledge of a limiting quantum-mechanical field that, scientifically, cannot be precisely localized but overlaps with every other field in the universe. Ātman *is* brahman.

* Modern brain-scanning technology could be used to test the hypothesis. Tomographic techniques, which provide a literal visualization of the brain, as well as magnetic-resonance imaging (MRI), should be used rather than an electroencephalogram (EEG), a measure of neurological output, not structure. A calibrated EEG could be used to determine precisely when to apply MRI, CAT scans, and so on.

† *Maītri Upaniṣad* 6.38.

Starting with *āditya* (sun), which reduces to *dt* = *t*, a first-world phon,‡ we next get *candra* (moon), *knt* = *ktn*, which has an upper-second-world structure, and then *agñi* (fire), which reduces to *gn*, pronounced in Sanskrit as *ny* (or *ñ*), a third-world phon. The phons are the internal auditory parallels with the sequence of optical trance states (photons) of saṃyama. Sunhood means not only light but sound as well;§ seeing the moon involves the neurophysiology of the ear as well as the eye; the light of the third world resembles a fire that burns with a whine (agñi). Neither faculty of the trance state is in any sense subordinate to the other, and that holds for every other sense as well. Each is a different aspect of the integrated experience of selfhood.

The yogi who proclaims "That sun, I myself am it," seems also to imply that the experience of vision may go on indefinitely, that whenever we look at the sun and are able to see it we are vouchsafed a glimpse of how intense vision can become. If, through some miracle, the sun itself were to appear in all its splendor an inch in front of our eyes, there is no doubt that we would experience the limits of vision. In the split second before vaporization we shall have known the vision of the self. We shall have seen the light brighter than ten thousand suns that Kṛṣṇa revealed to Arjuna in the *Bhagavad Gītā*, what Semele beheld when Zeus in all his panoply appeared to her, what Odysseus glimpsed when he passed near Charybdis, that "deathless bane," as Homer calls her, that opening to oblivion. And might not Homer reply, if we put our questions to him, Are not the gods *athanatœ*, "deathless"? And is not vision a god? Then vision too is deathless, even as Ares. And hearing. And thought. All are states of consciousness. And consciousness is a priori.

Zeno of Elea (d. ca. 430 B.C.), a disciple of Parmenides, devised a famous conundrum—all

‡ Cf., ibid. 6.1–2.

§ Cf., *Iliad* 3.277, where Helius, first-world light, is described as he that "beholdest and hearest all things," the source, perhaps, of the Oxen of the Sun myth.

Eleans are liars—that is essentially a Greek koān. Rather than interpret it as an example of illogic *gratia* illogic, as is often done, we might better understand it as Zeno's attempt at indicating the disjunction between puruṣa and pratyaya, or, in a parmenidean context, between reality and illusion, in an aristotelian sense between ontological and ontic, in a heideggerian one between being and time. We cannot know if someone is lying without being that person, without inhabiting his or her consciousness, which, because of the covering of light separating us from them, transcends our knowledge. It is precisely the transcendent quality of consciousness that equilibrates the puruṣa with its pratyaya. We shall call the hypothesized equilibration the *symmetry of consciousness* and give it a special name: S_0. Not only is puruṣa aware of pratyaya, but pratyaya is aware of puruṣa. The one condition requires the other, which removes Zeno's paradox. Because consciousness is aterior, neither inside nor outside the organism, it matters not in a formal or substantive sense how we assign the so-called locus of awareness. What matters is that we be consistent once a choice is made. If we look at pratyaya as puruṣa, then we must look at puruṣa as pratyaya. We claim, with the Buddhists, that reality is either nirvāṇa (consciousness) or saṃsāra (objects of consciousness) and that "nirvāṇa is saṃsāra."*

There is no such thing as a *pathetic fallacy*. When we see a light the light sees us. When we hear a sound the sound hears us. When we smell an odor the odor smells us. When we touch a thing the thing touches us. When we taste food the food tastes us. And when we think a thought the thought thinks us.

* *Lankavatara Sūtra* 3, in Goddard, *A Buddhist Bible*, pp. 291–92.

Psychoscience comes down to this: Consciousness is omnipresent. Every so-called object is also a so-called subject. To paraphrase Parmenides: from existence only existence and from nonexistence only nonexistence. Existence and nonexistence are two aspects of the unity of puruṣa-pratyaya. Equivalently—*pace* nothing buttery*—consciousness cannot be "built up" out of nonconscious elements, chiefly because there are no such things, objects, or entities. All entities are conscious because they exist and exist because they are conscious. Consciousness is congruent with existence. Thus, a new physics, *psychoscience*, must be invented that conforms with a priori consciousness

Psychoscience asserts that all entities are *fully* conscious. For when we speak about consciousness as pratyaya we always speak about specific sights, sounds, odors, and so on. Everything has a soul, and the gods are *athanatœ*, "deathless." In the moment of germination of a single flower is the foundation of the orgasm: the Union of Zeus and Hera on Crete. Whether we speak of the experience of a human being, a rock, a grain of sand, an atom, or even of a subatomic particle, we speak of a complete experience comprising every faculty from feeling to thinking, from first world to third.

Furthermore, all faculties are present in all things simultaneously. Because of the dynamic nature of experience no faculty is capable of being "switched off"; it is always "on," though it will be useful to approximate an *off mode* whenever the intensity of a particular stimulus is weak in comparison to others. Thus it is possible to speak of an entity as being "deaf" when, compared to its visual reaction, its auditory reaction is negligible. (The same reasoning holds for cognition and proprioception as well.) We shall refer to such approximations as *limiting cases* of psychophysical dynamics.

The symmetry of consciousness (S_0) is a hypothesis. As was the case with the proprioceptive

* The inclination to explain away something as "nothing but [fill in with any inanity]"; e.g., life is *nothing but* not being dead.

hypothesis at the start of our investigation into myth, we need a body of data against which to test the truth or falsity of the hypothesis. For the investigation of S_0 the data are the laws of science: Newton's laws, Maxwell's equations, matrix quantum mechanics, and so on. We intend to show that significant features of those laws can be deduced from S_0 and its implications. The first implication is that if an entity is conscious, it is conscious of itself, which could be called the law of the *reflexivity of consciousness* (R_0). Specifically, we shall try to demonstrate that there is a univalent, which is to say a one-to-one, correspondence between the faculties of conscious experience and the laws of science. That will be equivalent to establishing that there truly is a model of consciousness embedded in the structure of scientific law. The organizing paradigm will be the Three Worlds. To many scientists, sedulously bent on midwiving grand unified theories—GUTs in current jargon—a tripartite physical core structure will seem retrograde. A consolidating step "backward" is necessary, however, before again setting out for *the* GUT. We hope to impress a fundamental coherence upon the laws of science, one that is at present lacking. Further, by elaborating the paradigm we hope to suggest the form of scientific laws not yet discovered and to make at least one substantive prediction that can be rigorously verified.

Our first task will be to produce semiquantitative descriptions of experiential faculties, starting with proprioception and concluding with cognition, and to apply them to the abovementioned limiting cases of conscious interactions.

Second, we shall compare the semiquantitative descriptions with Newton's mechanics and Maxwell's electrodynamics, and we shall try to discern a pattern in the analysis that will allow us to extend the experiential model into scientific areas that are either conceptually incomplete, such as quantum mechanics, or are as yet a complete mystery, such as gravity.

Finally, pursuing the inevitable vector of scientific knowledge, we shall scrutinize the insights of biology insofar as they have been set down in the theory of darwinian evolution.

25

MASTER MECHANIC ISAAC NEWTON

“God said, ‘Let Newton be,’ and all was light” (Pope). Newton was the ideal thinker of the Enlightenment. His theories were so perfectly expressed, attaining in elegance and clarity to every standard a humane rationalism might impose, that he was all but worshiped within a generation of his death in 1727. To Voltaire (d. 1778) and Diderot (d. 1784), he was a god—or, at the very least, a man who had peeked into God’s chapbook.

His three laws of mechanics can be expressed as follows:

N1. Every object in constant motion or at rest continues in motion or remains at rest unless acted on by an outside force.

N2. If a force act on an object, the force is the greater, the greater the mass of the object and the greater the acceleration of the object.

N3. If two objects interact, the reaction of one object to the interaction is equal and opposite to the reaction of the other object.

All the science of mechanics, on which rests the greater part of physics and engineering, is contained in those three laws.

The equivalent assertions of psychoscience, regarding the trance of an *entity*, are as follows:

P(N)1. An entity in trance tends to remain in trance unless distracted by another entity.

P(N)2. If an entity in trance is distracted, the distraction is the greater, the greater the stereognosis of the entity and the greater the change in the audition of the entity.

P(N)3. If two entities are mutual distractions, the resulting trance of one entity is symmetric with the trance of the other entity.

A semiquantitative demonstration of P(N)1–P(N)3 is given in appendix A.

◆◆◆

Newton brought the science of perception to maturity. He had long investigated optics, inventing the reflecting telescope in 1671. His first published scientific works were the "Hypothesis Explaining the Properties of Light" and the "Explanation of the Colors of Thin Plates and of Natural Bodies," both appearing in 1675 when he was thirty-two years old. His masterwork, the *Principia*,* demonstrated the three laws of mechanics (N1–N3) almost wholly through the plane geometry of Euclid. Newton was familiar with algebra but was also very conservative. He could not conceive of framing his theories other than through geometry, which had an apodictic rigor not as yet demonstrated for algebra, as well as nearly two thousand years of tradition to recommend it. René Descartes (d. 1650) had already invented *analytic geometry*, an ingenious marriage of algebra and geometry, publishing his results in 1637, five years before Newton was born. Newton was familiar with Descartes's discoveries but makes minimal use of them in the *Principia*.

Euclid's geometry is perceptualized mathematics. Its arguments are proved entirely by comparing his famous postulates with the visible results of using a compass and unruled straight edge. Newton believed that light is corpuscular because it seems to travel in a straight line; in other words, it behaved like a geometer's straight edge—no mere quibble, because a mathematical line cannot be drawn.† Perhaps Newton glimpsed in the straight-line motion of light a way past that limitation, a way that was nonetheless rigorously perceptual. Newton's conviction of the truth of the corpuscular theory provoked a scientific quarrel with Christian Huygens (d. 1695), who proffered an exclusively undulatory theory of light that was highly convincing until this century. At bottom the quarrel was an epistemological one, because on the undulatory hypothesis the perceived straight-line behavior of light results from its wavelength being imperceptible. Thus, the wave nature of light can only be inferred from experiments—chiefly on diffraction—not observed, something uncongenial to the mature Enlightenment understanding of scientific truth, an understanding that Newton was perhaps the first to acquire.

Yet in practice the three laws of motion are not so much about light as they are about mass and balance. Thus, the senses they appeal to empirically are stereognosis, which apprehends mass, and hearing. It is the imbalance of the fluid of the inner ear that allows perception of acceleration. Without acceleration, motion is nugatory. It can be made to vanish simply by closing one's eyes, which Einstein pointed out to great effect in his theory of relativity, at once the final refinement and dying gasp of perceptual science. All three laws of motion might have been discovered by a blindman, never by someone without an inner ear or the sense of touch. What vision does bring to the three laws is a means of demonstrating them rigorously, which is to say, geometrically. Vision is therefore a metalanguage for stereognosis and *audition*, a word we introduce to encompass both external hearing and proprioception of the inner ear.

The one area in which Newton worked that is not quite in plumb with perceptualism was gravity. Gravity alike holds objects on the earth and the earth in its orbit. Engineers have calculated that to hold in orbit a massive sphere the size of the earth, moving at the speed of the earth relative to the sun—as one would hold a whirling ball at the end of a tether—would require braiding strands of the strongest steel yet forged into a cable eight thousand miles thick and ninety-three million miles long. Yet the space between the earth and the sun is a near-perfect vacuum! No material or immaterial medium for the transmission of gravity has ever been detected. For want of anything better,

* *Philosophiæ naturalis principia mathematica* (London, 1686).

† Georg Mohr (d. 1697), the "Danish Euclid," demonstrated that even a straight edge was superfluous to geometric proof, something overlooked by Euclid.

Newton suggested the notion of *action at a distance*: the distant sun acts on the earth, and vice versa. Because, apparently, there is nothing to transmit the pull of gravity, it perforce acts instantaneously. By every standard of enlightened empiricism it was an intolerable situation, and Newton himself was quite grave on the subject. "That one body," he wrote to a fellow Englishman, "may act upon another at a distance through a vacuum without the mediation of anything else . . . is to me so great an absurdity that I believe no man who has in philosophical matters any competent thinking can ever fall into it."* Strong stuff.

Gravity is simply a fact, and the law of gravity does not explain the fact of gravity, it describes it. In and of itself, that is no objection to his theory. Most of "scientific law" is in the nature of a description rather than an explanation. The law of universal gravitation is a better description than most, for it allows astronomers to predict the positions of the planets and the occurrence of eclipses with astonishing precision (it certainly astonished the philosophes of the Enlightenment). Yet with gravity, unlike other phenomena described by scientists, it is not even known what is being described, unless it be motion itself, which would make redundant—you pick—either the three laws of motion or the law of universal gravitation. Yet such a reduction is so counterintuitive that we must strongly question it.

Einstein proposed a solution in his general theory of relativity, in which he concludes that gravity is a description of space. Whether or not his solution is correct, it is certainly a perceptualist solution, for space is apprehended only in perception. The problem for empiricism is that gravity is apprehended stereognostically. Unless one is willing absolutely to reduce stereognosis to perception, the present status of gravity as a scientific theory would seem to be one of epistemological confusion.

* Letter to the polymathic Richard Bently, 25 February 1692/3, in: H. R. Trumbull, ed., *The Correspondence of Isaac Newton*, vol. 3 (Cambridge, 1961), p. 253.

Clearly the difficulty lies in the nature of what scientists call *mass*. The three laws of motion and the law of gravity use a concept of mass that is defined only perceptually: *A mass of one pound is that mass, which being acted upon for one second by a force of one poundal, moves at a speed of one foot per second.* Just so, but in practical experience the measure of mass is taken simply by holding it. The equations of physics, bound hand and foot and cast by Newton into the maw of geometry, in no manner reflect that practical reality. As a result, the mass—denoted by *m*—haunts the equations like Banquo's ghost. It sits there autistically, interacting with nothing but itself, like the emperor of Japan, a surly algebraic nonentity waiting patiently to be canceled from the calculations.

The mass of an object is proper only to the first world of the object. Hence it must fall outside of any spatiotemporal volume, because such are given primarily in perception not stereognosis. Thus, when applied to physical entities, mass is always a *singularity*, a literal vanishing point in the visual metalanguages of analytic geometry and the calculus. The point bears stressing. *The mass of an object exists nowhere.* Rather, all the mass of the universe is concentrated in a singularity. The so-called inertial mass, the mass defined as above in terms of feet and seconds, is the mass associated with perception, a "ghost mass," *inferred* from the exchange of light between the object and the observer.

The implication therefore is that the nonghostly or mass qua mass of an object is invisible. Since the 1930s astrophysicists have recognized that the vast bulk of the mass of the universe is *not* visible. The whereabouts of the *missing mass* is currently the most hotly debated topic in physics. Visible mass can be likened to the snow on a mountaintop at night: all that can be seen of the huge bulk of the mountain. Because telescopes by their nature give us only the *visible* universe, astrophysics must be full of singularities that reveal the missing mass. Such singularities are called *black holes*. On our hypothesis, black holes are distributed uniformly throughout the galaxies, each being a perceptual singularity on a grand scale to which all the local mass, the mass within an immense ellipsoidal volume, can be referred, as the files of subdirectory in the memory of a digital computer can be related to a single directory. The subdirectories, in turn, comprise subsubdirectories, and so on until the individual mass of an atom is filed. Thus each atom contains at its center a low-order black hole.* The singularities arise from the incommensurability of mass and space, of stereognosis and perception. Conversely, any high-order black hole can be related to a black hole of higher order, until the mass of the highest order, that of the universe *in toto*, is located. It is perhaps amusing that the local black hole of highest order appears to lie in the constellation Cygnus, the Swan, a swan (haṃsa) being not only the ancient description of the soul in Vedānta but also a son of Ares, whose wings converge on the meditative vanishing point between the brows.†

The classical definition of matter is *that which has mass* and *occupies space*. The "and" here is not a trivial choice of coordinating conjunction. Mathematically "and" indicates not an intersection of the concepts mass and space in a concept of matter but their union. The intersection is null. The proper definition is *matter is that which has mass* or *occupies space*—and a bit more, as we'll see.

* Or high-order black hole, depending on how one scales the singularities. To describe the mass of a hydrogen atom as a zeroth-order black hole is perhaps more consistent overall.

† Hindus refer to such cosmic puns as *lila*, "[God's] play."

26

CLERK MAXWELL WAVES GOODBYE

When, someday, the history of perceptual science is written, the role played by the British Isles in its many triumphs will bestride the contribution of all other races like a colossus. What was it—and still is—about perfidious Albion that so draws its denizens toward light? The Celts seem to have invented unwoolly thinking. Since the days of Roger Bacon (d. ?1294) and William of Occam (d. ca. 1349), Anglo-Irish scientists have led the world in the debunking of metaphysics. Put together Francis Bacon, Thomas Hobbes, John Locke, David Hume, George Berkeley, Isaac Newton, and Robert Boyle; to be absolutely thorough, toss in Cavendish, Hamilton, Watt, Kelvin, Rayleigh, Thomson, and Rutherford. You have assembled the most unsentimental, clearheaded, tough as nails, down to brass tacks, no nonsense, believing is seeing, facts-is-facts aristocrats of prognathously combative common sense the world has ever seen—all come and gone in the space of three centuries. Empiricism has found no happier playground than in Britain, continuing in the work of Russell, Moore, and Ayers. And to mention the Americans of Anglo-Saxon extraction who toiled in the perceptualist vineyard would be as superfluous as it would be longwinded. It is no less ironic, therefore, that the man who, all unknowing, turned out the lights on the happy day of empiricism was a Scot.

James Clerk Maxwell (1831–79) was the most precociously gifted physicist who ever lived. In his *Treatise on Electricity and Magnetism* (1862) Maxwell compressed two thousand years of patient observation into four partial-differential equations. If Newton gave us the industrial revolution, it was Maxwell who gave us the technological revolution. Maxwell also fatally undermined the mechanical worldview. His four equations demonstrated that light is not a mechanical vibration but, rather, the vibration of crossed electric and magnetic *fields*.*

Translated from his mathematics, Maxwell's equations state:

* The field concept was invented by the chemist Michael Faraday (d. 1867). Maxwell made it rigorous.

M1. Electricity is monopolar in all media.

M2. Magnetism is bipolar in all media.

M3. If the magnetism changes, any nearby electricity changes.

M4. If the electricity changes, any nearby magnetism changes.

Equation M1 means that electricity behaves like a faucet without a drain; there are places where electric *charge* appears but not necessarily places where it disappears. Equation M2 states that magnetism behaves like a faucet *and* drain; every magnetic source is necessarily accompanied by a magnetic sink. The last two equations (M3, M4) tell us that electricity and magnetism are dynamically coupled.

Just as subversive was Maxwell's use of vector and scalar *potentials* in deriving his equations. Potential theory had been given mathematical rigor by Siméon Poisson (d. 1841). The dilemma for newtonian mechanics was that Maxwell's potentials can be thought of in mutually exclusive ways. They specify the distribution of electromagnetic sources and sinks, or else they are specified *by* the sources and sinks. Physicists can rationalize the chicken with the egg only by moving the sources and sinks "from infinity," where the potentials vanish (by definition), into the lab, where they are measured, thus giving preeminence to the chicken, um, charge. The procedure is entirely ad hoc. The same ambiguity taints the EM (electromagnetic) field, derived from the potentials. But the EM field is at least observable. The potential *field* is wholly nonperceptual. It is a cognitive Trojan horse innocently introduced into perceptual physics, without which Maxwell could not have solved his celebrated equations.*

Unlike gravity, Maxwell's electric and magnetic fields could be detected, focused, diffracted, and refracted. Huygens was vindicated—for the moment. Visible light, it now appeared, was but a narrow range of vibrations within a much broader phenomenon: the electromagnetic spectrum.

The equivalent assertions of psychoscience are:

P(M)1. Vision focuses to achieve trance.

P(M)2. Audition balances to achieve trance.

P(M)3. Visual trance is distracted by audition.

P(M)4. Auditory trance is distracted by vision.

The characteristic of vision with which Maxwell's equations conform is its topological continuity. There are no holes in the visual field, or at least none that we are aware of visually (the "blind spot" at the tip of the nose can be removed simply by closing one eye). The word *field*, describing both the content of visual perception and the set of all values of the electromagnetic force within a spatiotemporal volume, is the linking concept between electrodynamics and the psychophysics of perception. The word was coined by Faraday, one of the many untutored geniuses of British empiricism. It had long been known that electricity and magnetism acted in a vacuum, so whatever the nature of the electric and magnetic fields, they permeated all space and were stronger the closer one got to a source of electricity and magnetism and decreased as one moved away from such a source. While trying to explain the influence of electricity and magnetism at a distance, Faraday supposed the existence of a physical medium, the field, that carried the electric and magnetic force. Faraday also investigated the work of the Danish physicist Hans Ørsted (d. 1851) and the Frenchman André Marie Ampère (d. 1836), who had discovered different aspects of the connection between electricity and magnetism, Ørsted going so far as to identify them, at least in the case where one or the other was changing in strength. Maxwell took Faraday's discoveries and by a brilliant generalization showed how the field concept could be extended continuously from a vacuum into a so-called material object. The resulting four differential equations, when solved, indicated that electromagnetism—the

* As practiced, physics can often be described as a search for an *exact differential*, i.e., a path-independent (nonperceptual) potential.

unified electricity and magnetism of Ampère—most generally propagated in the form of sinusoidal waves. Using data on the behavior of electromagnetism in a vacuum, he was able to calculate the speed of propagation of EM waves in a vacuum. To his astonishment, electromagnetic waves moved at the speed of light ($c \approx 3 \times 10^8$ m/s).*

In the most general case, the electric- and magnetic-field vectors, respectively denoted by D and B, vibrate at right angles to one another within an ellipsoidal volume (roughly, the shape of a football with rounded extremities) articulated in space and time. Ellipses are the most commonly encountered shapes in physics. The solutions for the motions of the planets of the law of universal gravitation are ellipses. The dynamical cause of such solutions is the inertia of a moving body. But that is just the first-world equivalent of the second-world elliptical solutions to Maxwell's equations. In psychoscience the cause is the focusing property of vision. Thus, M1 cannot be a clear statement of the situation. Electricity focuses—or integrates—*two* fields and thus only appears to be monopolar. The two fields correspond to the left and right "eyes" of psychoscience. Equivalently, the Minkowski cone is not circular in cross-section but elliptical. The cone converges on the eyes (the facial rectangle) in a roughly elliptical space rather than a true mathematical point. All the vanishing points of perceptualist physics, of which there must be many because of its epistemological incompleteness, insofar as they are singularities are instances of the breakdown of a purely visual model. Such breakdowns are always associated with mass points.

When Maxwell analyzed his field equations, he realized that the electric charge (q) of an object, which enters into both electricity and magnetism, was expressible in units of the meter, kilogram, and second, a rather unwieldy denotation for a quantity so fundamental as charge. Physicists get around the awkwardness by defining a unit of charge called the *coulomb* and positing that it is as fundamental as the measures of space, time, and mass, but the procedure is as artificial as it is ad hoc. In a psychophysical model, however, the combination of the units that express charge is a natural consequence of experiential dynamics, specifically, of the integrating properties of vision versus the differentiating properties of hearing. The charge is a portmanteau concept describing the sound, sight, and self-feeling of an elemental entity, the electron historically considered (see appendix B).

* Throughout, "m" is the abbreviation for meter, "s" for second, and "kg" for kilogram; but "*m*" and "*s*" are the algebraic symbols for mass and space, respectively. The confusing orthography has only its long history to recommend it.

27

HEISENBERG ISN'T SURE

After Maxwell came Einstein (d. 1955), who was the last great perceptualist. Because he would not relinquish a visual prejudice, Einstein after 1916 was unable to participate wholeheartedly in the physics of the Cognitive Age that began with the discoveries of Max Planck (d. 1946). Einstein spent the balance of his career in a fruitless search for an epistemological unity among gravity and electromagnetism, which, on our hypothesis, cannot be done consistently because of the equipotency of the Three Worlds.

Planck was led to posit the existence of discrete bundles of electromagnetic energy he called *quanta*. His concern was with the manner in which energy was absorbed and radiated, but it was shown (by Einstein) that the energy also traveled in a discrete bundle to which was given the name *photon*. The discovery unseated the wave theory of light, which had been put into play by Huygens in the seventeenth century and seemed established as unassailable fact after the work of Maxwell. Now all of this can be traced to the breakdown of the mechanical theories of Newton—it merely took time for the larger epistemological consequences of electrodynamics to be realized.

The first to tackle the problem in an entirely new way was the Danish physicist Niels Bohr (d. 1962). Bohr made the quantum a structural principle of physics as well as a dynamical one. The Bohr atom, with its quantized energy levels and orbiting electrons modeled after the solar system, is well known. One of the inescapable consequences of Bohr's model is the notion that the electron, in passing from one orbit to the other, strictly speaking has vanished from space and time—the presenting symptom of further epistemic malady. The seeming paradox arises because with atoms we are at last dealing with entirely cognitive entities, entities that are literally imperceptible. Indeed, their imperceptibility is enshrined in physics as the famous uncertainty principle of Werner Heisenberg (d. 1976), a precept from which there is no appeal. The Copenhagen school of the philosophy of science (founded by Bohr) takes the uncertainty principle as a postulate and properly eschews the search for hidden (perceptual) variables that might allow one to dispense with it. In extremis, Copenhagenites claim that not only is a thing unknown before measurement, it also is nonexistent before measurement, thus blithely predicating nonexistence and plunging into circularity. The germ of truth in their argument is that the necessity of a measurement is the necessity of consciousness, for we have hypothesized that consciousness and existence are one and the same, are ousia. If a tree falls in the forest, does it make a sound? Of course it does. Who hears it? The tree hears it (and feels it!) *and* the tree nearby and the forest as a whole—at whatever system level one cares to isolate, a magnetic dipole implies audition. Trees and forests have net magnetic dipoles. Ergo, trees and forests hear. The self-awareness of all matter is a self-measurement; thus the two ideas can be reconciled.

The physics of the Cognitive Age is called quantum mechanics. Because it is a cognitive science, it is chiefly a mathematical science, and whereas one might press into service visual models to discuss its abstruse conclusions, no epistemological verisimilitude can be attached to them. The relationship of quantum mechanics to psychophysics is basically this: whereas in perception, the physical evolution of an entity can be described by requiring equality of the energy of an entity at the start with its energy at the terminal point of its evolution, in cognition, the strict equality is replaced by a principle of *similitude*. The starting and ending points of the evolution of the entity only must be sufficiently similar to one another. The necessity of strict equality in perceptual physics derives from the properties of vision. One can lay one circle over another circle in perfect visual congruence, which is to say, homeomorphically. Indeed, that is the essence of Euclid's fourth axiom in the *Elements*, from which enormously influential work perceptual science has historically derived its logical structure.* In cognition a circle can never simply be equated to another circle, for their relationship is essentially *isomorphic*, which is to say, of the nature of a mathematical metaphor. We see this in quantum mechanics chiefly in terms of its fuzziness or indistinctness, which the uncertainty principle requires. Thus, what is being conserved is not just perceptual energy but cognitive *meaning* as well. A system will evolve cognitively towards another configuration that is equally meaningful to it. Of course, *meaning* must be defined for the present purposes.

Yet quantum mechanics has not quite shaken off its perceptualist origins and clings to the concept of a conserved energy (called the hamiltonian) to guide the system and to select out of all possible outcomes only those having energies equal to the initial energy. In doing so, it begs the fundamental epistemological issue because energy is a wholly perceptualist concept. It is defined as the "ability to do work," and work is in turn defined as the "application of force over a perceptual length of space and time." What quantum-mechanical calculations, on such a basis, eventually select as permissible states of the entity, then, are perceptual states, instances when the entity happens solely to be seeing or hearing or both. Seeing-hearing states are only particular conditions in the evolution of the entity, the attention of which is cycling through all three worlds. More concretely, they are the quantum levels of the EM spectrum. If our experimental apparatus could be retuned so as to couple with the cognitive and stereognostic states of the electron, we would see not a quantized universe but a unity of experience.†

How such a retuning could be accomplished is at present unclear. We know only that it must primarily be a mathematical procedure. The mathematical technique known as *conformal mapping*, in which complex variables are used to transform one image to another, may offer opportunities (see appendix C). The gist of our argument thus far is that quantum mechanics is a mathematical description of the cognition of the observer, which is to say, it is the objectification of cognitive states without their simultaneous perceptualization. Additionally, invoking S_0, we claim that the mind of the observer and the mind of the observed are fundamentally identical.

* It is just the euclidean sense of congruence that is cast into question by the "non-euclidean" geometries of Gauss et al.

† Albeit, a continuum that is itself flickering on and off subject to *kramaḥ* (Skt. "moments").

If mass is not "in" space and time, space and time are not "in" cognition. The empirical truth of this assertion can be discovered in our experiences of dreams but more systematically by performing saṃyama on *sattwa guṇa* (cognition). So-called everyday awareness is a union of the three fundamental worlds. None is usually an isolated experience. In its investigation of imperceptibles, however, modern physics has in a practical sense performed dhāraṇā on the third world, so it is hardly surprising that in the process space and time—originally and properly defined only perceptually but carried over uncritically into the world of imperceptibles—have been compromised. It is sometimes said by adherents of the Copenhagen school that the best interpretation of the quantum-mechanical wave function (Ψ) is a repository of all the physical observations ever made of the system associated with Ψ. We should say that Ψ is the *awareness* or, more usefully, the *attention* of the system. Under any guise, is the Copenhagen interpretation so very far from introducing a comprehensive system *memory*?

Memory in the cognitive sense is a good candidate for what we have termed meaning. Yet the term meaning must be made still more specific if it is to be psychoscientifically useful. Here we could introduce the psychological concept of *association* as used in learning theory. When the system is presented with stimulus C, its response is influenced by $\{c_j\}$, where $\{c_j\}$ is the set of associations of C in the system's memory. Since the 1920s, all attempts to find the associational center of the cortex have failed.* There does not seem to *be* any locus of memory in the brain. Rather the entire brain is equipotent† with regard to memory, corroborating our guess that memory and meaning are intimately linked and indicating again that memory, like mass, is not "in" space-time and has no quality of *thereness*.

In linguistics a comprehensive cognitive science has been put forward by Noam Chomsky.‡ Can the syntactical structures of chomskyan linguistics and the mathematics of quantum mechanics be correlated? The mathematics of quantum mechanics can be classified as a noncommuting algebra of operators with bases spanning a Hilbert space (after the German mathematician David Hilbert [d. 1943] who first explored the properties of such a "space"). Chomskyan linguistics uses *transformational grammars* operating on base subsystems to convert one meaningful sentence into another. Simply put: Is language a Hilbert space? We refrain from making facile comparisons, which come readily to mind.§ Nevertheless, transformational-grammar lingusitics relies heavily on the notion of a "linguistic module" genetically hardwired into the brain. Language, in other words, seems to be inevitable, at least among *Homo sapiens*. The problem is then in separating out language from other cognitive functions, namely, to locate the language module of the mind. Our approach is somewhat more radical. We hypothesize that the third world, *in toto*, is the linguistic module and that all essentially cognitive functions are essentially linguistic functions.#

The brain revealed in autopsy, with which all—or nearly all—cognitive, perceptual, and stereognostic functions can be correlated, is itself

* The pioneer in experimental memory research was Karl Lashley (d. 1958), an admirer of John B. Watson (d. 1958), the founder of American behavioral psychology. After years of piecewise ablation of the rat cortex to see if he could defeat learning, Lashley simply gave up. So long as any cortex remained, the rat could still learn—to decipher a maze, say—although it would take longer. J. Tolman, Lashley's collaborator, came reluctantly to the personal conviction that learning was predicated on the reward offered having "meaning for the rat" and so abandoned behaviorism.

† "Hologrammatic" also has been used in this sense; for awhile anyway, it was trendy to do so.

‡ N. Chomsky, *Syntactic Structures* (The Hague, Netherlands, 1957).

§ For example, a Hilbert space is a linear space in which all Cauchy sequences converge. Analogously, a linguistic space is an infinite collection of concepts (words), all of which can be expressed in terms of concepts in the space.

R. Montague, *Formal Philosophy* (New Haven, Conn., 1974).

only a percept, and the only experiences that can reasonably be located therein are perceptions because only perceptions have the quality of localizability. Yet certain structural aspects of the brain are of the nature of singularities, for example, the optic chiasmus and even the progressively finer and finer structure of neuronal axons and dendrites in the neocortex tending toward *imperceptibility*. The latter characteristic is complementary with the staggering density of the neuronal net, which takes on *fractal* characteristics (see appendix C). Beyond a certain point both fineness and density are singularities in perception, raising the question of whether any artificial intelligence (AI) machine *must* design structural singularities into its hardware configuration as a prerequisite to achieving true cognitive states. In that regard, two sutras of Patañjali:

> The transformation from one . . . kind into another is by overflow of *natural tendencies*.
>
> The incidental cause does not stir . . . the natural tendencies into activity; it merely removes the obstacles, like a farmer (irrigating a field).*

The sutras are somewhat technical, but their purport is roughly this: The varieties of experience, of which cognition is but one, are not created so much as they are *permitted* to manifest in matter. Patañjali illustrates this very general and somewhat unexceptional statement with a metaphor—something very rare in the *Yoga-Sūtra*, so we must assume it is his attempt at describing an experience he has had: Just as a farmer when irrigating does not create the pressure of the water in the reservoir supplying his field but simply brings that pressure to bear by opening a sluice gate, so too the cogntive "tendencies" in matter appear when a structural obstacle is removed from the perceptual substratum. In varying degrees, AI experts assume just the opposite in designing the hardware and software of so-called cognitive engines. Clever simulacra of cognition encoded as software are insufficient, what is needed still is a sluice gate. Cognition is as much form as content, as much geometry as algebra. The perceptual substratum is not, as the Buddhists insist it is not, distinct from experience—be it cognition, perception, or stereognosis—it is experience embodied, experience as "the seen." The perceptual substratum, in other words, is just the "covering of light." What it covers is the cognitive-stereognostic singularity inhering in every conceivable entity.

Can the perceptual substratum be other than a living, breathing human nervous system? Although he does not specifically address the issue—the very notion of a thinking machine would have been outlandish in his time—Patañjali's aphorisms do not rule out the possibility in principle. Cognitive states cannot, however, be fashioned from whole cloth. Instead, what is necessary is to configure the substratum so as to *reveal* its antecedent cognitive states. Here, we suggest, the human CNS can be a useful guide insofar as its structural singularities are concerned, a very few of which were noted above. In general though, the engineering of current AI cognitive machines (computers) would seem to be on the wrong track. Computer chips are linked in rectangular arrays and are themselves roughly the shape of rectangular prisms. Having said that is very far from supplying a useful prescription for a computer engineer to follow. In appendix C we examine a possibly fundamental *psychogeometry* that, with immense effort, might someday prove useful.

Finally, there is the old controversy in quantum mechanics over the existence of so-called hidden variables. Dissatisfied with the essentially probabilistic interpretation of quantum reality, several eminent scientists, Einstein among them, devoted a good deal of ingenuity to showing that quantum mechanics is an *incomplete* theory. On that view, the statistical algorithms of the theory serve only to mask real properties that if known would yield a com-

* *Yoga-Sūtra*, *Kaivalya Pāda*, sutras 2–3, emphasis added; the parenthesis is Taimni's.

pletely determined physics à la Newton and Maxwell. We should say that the hidden variable is the wave function itself, which is not considered a "real" entity in quantum mechanics but only a mathematical device. If the wave function is thought of as a conceptualization of the awareness of the system—a step most physicists would be unwilling to take—it can be thought of as a variable that has been hiding in plain sight.

A well-known result of quantum-theoretical research is Bell's theorem,* which states that quantum mechanics can be reconciled with hidden variables only at the expense of *locality.* Locality here essentially means causality and slower-than-light transmission. We have seen that mass qua mass is a nonlocal concept, in other words, a nonperceptual variable, which is precisely the sense of hidden variable. Cognition too is nonperceptual, hence nonlocal. Thus, in psychophysics, the prerequisites for eliminating a probabilistic interpretation of quantum reality are already present. All the paradoxes of quantum mechanics can be removed by positing some sort of nonlocalizable a priori elementary awareness in any physical system.

In appendix C the idea is developed further along mathematical lines, but we have already argued that because consciousness is not a predicate, neither is unconsciousness. It is therefore a metaphysical decision which of the two to adopt a priori. Scientists, however, implicitly predicate unconsciousness as a fundamental property of physical reality, treating it like color or weight. So what we are talking about, in a shopworn phrase, is a paradigm shift, one in which assuming a consciousness in the universe—without predicating it—can have very many useful consequences for rationalizing physical theory.

* J. S. Bell, *Speakable and Unspeakable in Quantum Mechanics* (Cambridge, 1988).

28

DARWIN AND THE TEMPLE OF SOLOMON

Charles Darwin (b. 1809) was twenty-four years old when he joined the crew of the *Beagle* as ship's naturalist on its epochal journey round the world. The observations he made, meticulously recorded in his notebooks, and the brilliant hypothesis he inferred therefrom were announced in *The Origin of Species* of 1859. Darwin waited so long to publish his celebrated theory of evolution because he recognized from the start how extraordinarily controversial were its conclusions. The title says it all: the origin of *species*. The so-called descent of man was only a part of it. Darwin aspired to explain the mechanism of speciation in general and, in the manner of a bridge player finessing a king, "explain" *Homo sapiens* en passant.

In biology, a species is a classification of plants or animals taxonomically lower than a genus but higher than a subspecies or variety. The members of a species possess in common distinct traits and usually will mate only within the species. Crucial to darwinian evolution is the mechanism of *natural selection:* In a given environment or ecosystem, certain traits, either structural or functional, may render to an individual member of a species a reproductive advantage over his fellows. The trait, following rules of inheritance, can be expected to appear in the offspring, and until such time as the environment changes, the offspring will possess the same reproductive advantage. Hence, in time, the offspring will tend to crowd out other offspring not similarly endowed, the trait will become distinguishing, and a new species more perfectly adapted to its environment will have emerged. That simple model, which has so much of common sense to recommend it and in hindsight seems so obvious, has momentous consequences, as Darwin was quick to grasp.

Prior to the nineteenth century, the notion of speciation that held sway—clearly for religious reasons—was what might be called *creation in place*: God had created each species already perfected and occupying its own ecological niche, reflecting a sort of leibnizean preëstablished harmony of the natural world. Darwin's theory is often summed up in the careless phrase "survival of the fittest," careless because "fittest" must here be construed quite narrowly, for it really means *fit to reproduce*, at a minimum, fit to survive long enough to reproduce. Judged solely by that criterion, bacteria (which are plants) are perhaps the fittest organisms on the planet because of their rapid maturation and explosive reproductive rates. Also regnant are mosquitos, mice, and rabbits.

The virtue of darwinian natural selection, and the plain source of its appeal for many scientists, is its apparent dispensation of teleology: evolutionary artifacts, it is claimed, support nothing like a divine agenda for the planet. For that very reason natural selection was a curiously anachronistic theory, biology playing catch-up, because well before 1859 the natural sciences had freed themselves from explicit superordination of any sort. David Hume (d. 1776), in his tendentious *Dialogues Concerning Natural Religion*, was perhaps the first to nudge God from his driver's seat by attacking the medieval Argument from Design for the existence of God, also known as the Watchmaker Argument. While physics and chemistry had gone the way of godlessness, biology remained in good odor with public morality until the work of Darwin (who nevertheless remained a devout Christian till his death in 1882). In natural selection, we appear to have a theory based in random events that satisfactorily accounts for the methodical arrangements of nature.

The "random events" required for natural selection to work upon a given species are *genetic mutations* in the gametes of an individual. Darwin was the child of country gentry—he never had to work a day in his life—and particularly knowledgeable about the principles of animal husbandry. He knew well how livestock breeders were able to "create" new varieties of cattle and horses by selectively mating individual animals so as to reinforce the likelihood of desirable traits in the offspring. But of course the breeder clearly knows beforehand what traits he wants the offspring to exhibit, which is certainly superordinative of the process and definitely *not* natural selection. The work of the Austrian monk Gregor Mendel (d. 1884) is the historical source of the genetic theory of heredity but received little notice until around 1900. Mendel had shown that separate traits are inherited independently of each other, from which the existence of some "atom" of heredity, or gene, can be inferred. (The existence of genes was unknown to either Darwin or Mendel.) Lacking a genetic theory or its equivalent, Darwin could not account for speciation, and he knew it. The lack of such a unit of heredity in the biology of his day was a serious problem, and at one point he despaired of distinguishing, in principle, his theory from teleological theories. His opponents, who were numerous and vocal, could easily adapt evolution based on natural selection to evolution based upon divine selection. Although convinced of the truth of natural selection, Darwin was unable to demonstrate its fundamental mechanisms, and he went to his grave with a puzzle surrounding his theory. It was not until the work of the Dutch botanist Hugo de Vries (d. 1935), who rediscovered Mendel, that the role of chromosomes and genes in heredity was validated and natural selection put on a solid biochemical basis. Since that time, darwinian evolution—rechristened Neodarwinism—though repeatedly modified, has had no serious competitor for the attention of biologists.

Yet natural selection, even when predicated upon genetic mutation, has always presented other problems. For one thing it appears grossly to violate one of the elemental standards of sound theory, which is the consonance between the presuppositions of the theory and their consequences. How, it will be asked, can a principle that aspires to no standard more demanding than reproductive fitness account for the appearance of species that in their capabilities far outstrip the *objective* requirements of such a standard? In other words, why has a natural world governed solely by natural selection bothered to go beyond the bacterium? At the macroscopic level the appearance of the human species, with its long, delicate delay of puberty, seems to violate the sacred second law of thermodynamics, which insists that a physical system will always use the bare minimum of energy in its evolution. The system seems overdetermined, and the whole doth outstrip the sum of its parts. Given the talents of our species, the teleologist asks, from engineering, to abstract algebra, to lyric poetry, does it not seem at least possible that natural selection has all along been serving some other biological imperative?

Let us admit at the outset that such an objection is directed more to the plausibility of natural selection than toward its consistency, which is beyond cavil. But allied with the above objection are several others. For example, natural selection is a theory of differentiation, which is why it strictly applies only to species. Natural selection will explain why the eyes of hawks are set far apart whereas the raccoon's are close together but not why hawks or raccoons have eyes to begin with. It can explain the length of the giraffe's neck but not the neck itself. It does no good to sift back through the fossil record for the appearance of eyes and necks because as far as we can tell species have always had eyes and necks. The pattern of two eyes, two ears, a single mouth, and so on was set at least half a billion years ago—a point of enormous significance that evolutionists airily ignore.*

Another objection to natural selection is its reliance on *beneficial* mutations. The use of mutations to explain the origin of life is the linchpin binding together theories of biological evolution, such as Darwin's, and more contemporary theories of *chemical* evolution. Both disciplines rely entirely upon chance mutations and are in all important respects parallel vis-à-vis hypotheses and presuppositions. The one is practiced by biologists and sociobiologists, the other by organic chemists, but we shall refer to both groups as evolutionists.

The human genome, namely the assemblage of genes strung together as deoxyribonucleic acid (DNA), is at least one billion bases long. Each string is structurally coordinated with another string in the famous double helix. The geometrical constraints on structure alone are extraordinarily demanding and precise. Proteins will *not* form in the presence of water, rather hydrolysis acts immediately to decompose them. (Remember: all occurs in that enchanted kingdom, the primeval ocean.) Furthermore, most mutations, the sole source of this colossally precise convergence of matter and form, are indifferent to adaptivity or are maladaptive, hence lethal. The rate of mutations in species is not well known. Yet both neodarwinian and chemical evolution are predicated on the regular occurrence not simply of mutations but of adaptive mutations, and not simply adaptive mutations but adaptive germ-cell mutations in the parental organism (genetic mutations in somatic cells will not be passed on to offspring, yet in any individual organism the germ cells are far fewer in number than somatic cells), and not simply adaptive, germ-cell gene mutations but adaptive, germ cell, structural-gene mutations. A healthy skepticism towards extravagant teleology is one thing, to react with the credulity of a happy-go-lucky imbecile quite another. We have here an edifice of randomness that dwarfs the cathedral at Chartres, which is yet one of its productions. *Credat Judæus Apelles.*

The only appeal that the evolutionist can make in the face of this improbable concatenation of improbabilities is to the great length of time that has passed since the formation of planet earth in the so-called Azoic Time, to wit, some five billion years. This apparent safeguard of the theory leads to the most elaborate delusions, because in appealing to the sheer *bulk* of time past the evolutionist departs from the path of science like a drunkard falling down a long flight of stairs. The vast epochs that precede the present era are nowadays a reservoir of events, *any* chance event necessary, for "explaining" the intricate diversity of living organisms. The past beomes a mere commodity, indistinct and cheap, a deep, dark sack into which one reaches as for a lottery token. Here we discern a myopia to rival that of Mr. Magoo. What is right in front of the evolutionist's face is plain as paint; what is farther away in time is hazy and so can be taken to be whatever one wishes it to be. The statistical rate of occurrence of beneficial mutations is a matter of utter conjecture—and that

* The fossil record also reveals organisms having five eyes, e.g., the genus *Opabinia*, but such creatures died out more than half a billion years ago. See S. J. Gould, *Wonderful Life: the Burgess Shale and the Nature of History* (Boston, 1990).

assuming there is something to be mutated! Once one has nucleic acids, then at least there is something coherent upon which chance may operate. As to what sequence of impinging chemical billiard balls would give us DNA, the spans of time necessary are not known even conjecturally. The theory, in other words, is inherently unfalsifiable so long as it is predicated on randomness, thus not a science at all but more a lubriciously supple variety of wish fulfillment.

Such overreaching is understandable. Natural selection is a powerful tool for explaining speciation. Yet Neodarwinism has *zero* capacity for deriving that upon which selection may work its wonders. That cannot be repeated often enough. The numerous successes of microevolution recorded in zoology journals can be likened to a miser's collection of pennies, impressive so far as it goes. At some point, however, the evolutionist *will* set aside five pennies and claim "Now I have a nickel." In fact he has no such thing. He has what can be traded for a nickel or for what a nickel itself can be traded, but even had he five hundred pennies or five million pennies he would not have nickel, only copper.* Species and organism are as distinct as two elements or two parallel lines. All of that is so obvious it could be left unsaid if evolutionists, tumescent with the excitement of all those learned journals, didn't keep sighting the fabled crossroads. Of course we must do more than naysay and presently shall try to suggest what was that zeroth species upon which selection acted de novo.

The most famous example of the *Shazaam!* approach to evolution implicit in such theories is an experiment (performed in the 1950s) in which water vapor and various chemicals were mingled and electrified.† Upon inspection, the electrocuted "primordial soup" was found to contain amino acids! Hysteria set in, and the minds of the electrocutioners were permitted to run for the goal posts. For as surely as night follows day, genes, nucleic acids, and enzymes could now be expected to conjure themselves from the corpse, proteins and chromosomes to rush in, and archaeozoic hermaphrodites to swim happily in the oceans awaiting the next pass of the wand. Or perhaps it was the proteins that came came first, then the nucleic acids. Not to worry. And not since Mary Wollstonecraft Shelley was stirred by the galvanic effects of a voltaic pile on frog legs into imagining the birth of Frankenstein's monster had so miniscule a grain of truth seasoned such a dish. The relationship between amino acid and eukaryotic cell is that of raw silicon to mainframe computer. The inevitability of this tantalizing sequence is as likely as that wet clay, by chance uncovered in a riverbed and dried and baked by the sun, should thereby rise into the entablature of a parthenon—sooner or later. We must suppose it will be much later. And yet, the silly hope has been ardently embraced and even, in the final delusion, turned insidiously to buttress itself. For now the cry is wholesale "contingency."‡ We are encouraged to wallow in cynical wonder of the monstrosity: Is it not amazing that life has evolved when all could have been entirely different? And indeed, we may well ask, is it not amazing? But is it the amazement of a sunrise or the amazement of a two-headed calf? The capacity for amazement is a remarkable gift that

* Pushing the analogy a wee bit further, a penny is not legal tender so one cannot trade five of them for a nickel—which is—without first gulling someone to take them at face value.

† For an account of Stanley Miller and Nobel laureate Harold Urey's famous experiment (first published in *Science*, May, 1953), see S. Miller, "First Laboratory Synthesis of Organic Compounds under Primitive Conditions," in: *The Heritage of Copernicus*, ed. J. Neyman (Cambridge, Mass., 1974), p. 228. Miller found the amino acids glycine and alanine.

‡ See Gould, *Wonderful Life*, passim; although *freakish* would be truer to the spirit of this book than "wonderful." See also the representative nothing-buttery of Heinz Pagels (d. 1988), in H. Pagels, *The Cosmic Code: Quantum Physics As the Language of Nature* (New York, 1983), p. 187: "Life appears simply to be a 'disease of matter'"; also, à la Tertullian, "The idea of evolution is too implausible to have been *imagined*. It had to be *discovered*" (emphasis in original). We might charitably call that the Fallacy of Defective Honesty. In fact, what has been discovered—simply—is *only* implausibility.

humans seem to share with no other species. One may cite a hundred instances in every day that call forth this sentiment without restraining it to the quality of shocked amusement one experiences when one has drawn the ace of trumps in a game of bridge.

It is worth repeating that the metaphysical presuppositions that comfort the neodarwinian evolutionist are yet one more vestige of the Enlightenment's reflexive irreligiosity. Evolutionist ideas can be found in Aristotle, yet in Greek thought they are linked to an etiology in which the beginning of a process is but an anticipation of its end. The decision to exclude the end of the evolutionary process, to ridicule every consideration that there even might be an end, is wholly a philosophical one. A certain, noticeably petulant, foot-stamping temperament is absolutely required. Such an attitude has been called *nothing-buttery*. To the nothing-butterist life, art, religion, science are nothing but this and nothing but that. To explain is indeed to explain away. This puerile iconoclasm too has its origins in the Enlightenment, flagrantly so in the works of Auguste Comte (d. 1857) and Étienne de Condillac (d. 1780), the one a sociologist, the other a psychologist. A little knowledge is a truly dangerous thing. One searches in vain through the works of respectable scientists of the era—men like Laplace, Lagrange, Poisson, and Cavendish—to credit so demeaning a philosophy of nature.

Lest it seem we are insufficiently awed by the mysterious interplay of time and chance, which in orthodox evolutionary terms are essentially one and the same, it should be noted that the incipience of life on this planet, as revealed in the constantly accumulating fossil record, is regularly pushed back in time. Whereas once, chance had the majestically round sum of four billion years in which to shazaam "cold, dead matter" into vivaciousness, the time available appears now to be somewhat less expansive, perhaps 200 million years, subject of course to revision. Scarce had the planet cooled to room temperature, it seems, but the sea was bringing forth life. The great carpet of time under which the embarrassing improbabilities could be swept without a care is shrinking to throw-rug dimensions, getting a bit lumpy in spots the while.

Yet we are faced with the inevitable question: With what might natural selection be supplanted? There is no need, however, to remove natural selection root and branch. The theory has proven its utility in countless instances. The workings of chance can be accommodated over relatively brief time intervals. The principle is general: microscopic indeterminacy complementing macroscopic determinism. In the small—defined relatively—chance is a useful concept. In the large, its significance shrinks to invisibility. For example, in physics the motions of imperceptibly small molecules are *in principle* indeterminate; the motion of planets and suns, however, can be determined with stupefying precision. In biology it is not possible to speak of the individual cells of a mitochondrial organelle as having an individually determined structural locus. Yet, if the organelle be cut into numerous parts with a microtome, the parts will inevitably rearrange themselves into an overall organelle structure.* Here one could have few qualms in speaking of a superordinating electromagnetic- gravitational field—indexed by antecedent potential fields—as guiding the process and determining its outcome from the moment the organelle is dismembered.

It is one thesis of this book that in the transition from so-called cold, dead matter to life the antecedent potential field of the Three Worlds has guided the process: Matter strives to conform to the dynamic template of the universe: *hyle, kinesis, nous.* The word "strives" is not a circumlocution. Consciousness is a priori experience, and *striving* is perhaps as good a word as any to characterize the feelings of so-called inorganic matter. To remove the capacity to feel from inorganic matter is to eviscerate the unity of the Three Worlds. It is, analogously, to sever not simply the root system of, say, a lily but its germinating flower as well, leaving a

* See P. A. Weiss, "The Living System," in: Koestler and Smythies, eds., *Beyond Reductionism: The Alpbach Symposium.*

gorgeous, purposeless relic that has neither beginning nor end and will wither and die within the hour. Having thus ruthlessly truncated the totality of the lily, what will be left to explain it apart from chance?

Chance is *līla*, "[God's] play." Yet there is never any doubt about the outcome, howsoever great the diversity of paths that lead to it. Many possibilities does not mean anything is possible, a distinction that the biologist with a taste for serendipty would do well to maintain before settling on utter chaos as the womb of life. If we honestly reflect upon the multifarious capabilities of our species—our obssessive curiosity, our affinity for beauty, harmony, justice, and compassion, our mental agility—we find the darwinian, sociobiological explanation strangely artificial, inadequate, and rather too dependent on our good faith that in a fabulous bygone age a chain of happenstance blessed us with such gifts. It does not seem that "all could just as well have turned out differently." If walking erect, an opposable thumb, and binocularity can be leveraged into brains that fathom quantum field theory and compose haiku, does it not seem that those tokens of "reproductive fitness," however acquired, were like keys turning the lock of floodgates behind which was dammed an ocean of perfections even the angels might envy?

A recent modification to darwinian natural selection that has gained general approval (and disapproval) is that of *punctuated equilibrium*: The appearance of new species is not the gradualist phenomenon that might be expected (and Darwin believed). Instead, the fossil record demonstrates, in certain epochs new species appear suddenly and in great numbers, after which relatively quiet periods ensue. It has happened again and again, for example, at the Ordovician-Silurian, Permian-Triassic, and Cretaceous-Tertiary geological boundaries. Punctuated equilibrium is very difficult to reconcile with a theory predicated upon randomness alone. One cannot simultaneously appeal to the great reservoir of time needed for chance to expropriate a finished product (i.e., *Homo sapiens sapiens*) and at the same time credit evolutionary inhomogeneities, because, over the long haul, the events being randomized (i.e., adaptive mutations) must be smoothed out, which is to say, must approach a constant rate of occurrence.* So according to the theory, the notion of "punctuation" is closely linked to catastrophic changes in the environment: neutral mutations accumulate during the quiet periods and then are selected during ecological upheaval, leading to accelerated speciation. Yet, as with all Neodarwinism, the argument has the aroma of circularity. Mutation and environment are *not* separable concepts in natural selection. The one is as stochastic as the other. If, in a game of cards, the table is accidentally overturned and the cards gathered up and redealt, shall we then imagine that the number of strong hands has increased because of it? As an alternative metaphor, imagine a game of chess in which the pieces are drawn randomly by the players from a sack—containing many things besides chessmen—and placed on the board. Nothing will happen, the pieces sit inertly in place, until *both* kings are drawn. At that point the random events instantaneously become highly ordered. Here is an interplay between chance and order that can be applied to natural selection. Certain mutations—call them *conformal* insofar as they further the conformation of matter with the Three Worlds template—will be highly adaptive and lead to accelerated speciation. A temporary stability will be achieved that will be undone by the next, more conformal mutation.

To cite one example of conformation, as we have seen, Maxwell's equations associate every magnetic field with a dipole; that is, one never finds a north magnetic pole in isolation from a south magnetic pole. This holds right down to the level of elementary particles. Evolution is a theory of differentiation, and one of the problems of evolution is that it leaps over the question of the evolutionary origins of what is being differentiated by selection pressures, be they biological or chemical. On our hypothesis,

* This seemingly paradoxical result parallels the ergodic theorem of statistical mechanics.

it is just the magnetic dipole, axiomatized in Maxwell's equations, that over the course of billions of years became the human ears. Further, an electric field tends to be oriented at right angles to its associated magnetic field, which, when operated on by selection, results in the orthogonal seeing-hearing axes of most species and especially of humans. Conformation with the Three Worlds template means that out of the myriad ways that the seeing axis *could* be oriented with respect to the hearing axis in an organism, what is ultimately selected is orthogonality. That this is not necessarily the case is illustrated many times over in nature. Fish exhibit seeing-hearing axes that are practically collinear. The seeing-hearing axes of many species of birds are obliquely oriented; that is, the axial relationship falls somewhere between collinearity and orthogonality. In that sense then, birds are more conformal than fish, and humans more conformal than birds. It is not necessary that the fundamental magnetic-electric system be conscious—there is no necessary epistemology of consciousness—yet because in the fossil and chemical record we cannot find a sudden injection of awareness into matter but rather, at all levels, from electron to *Homo sapiens,* (from *Particula electronis,* family Lepidae, to *Homo sapiens* of the Hominiae)* find appetitve activity and response to environment, the most elegant and simplest hypothesis consistent with the evolutionary record is that the starting configuration was itself conscious. In the cruciform microwave quadropole moment of the cosmic-background radiation, a slowly fading image of the universe in its infancy, we can already discern the human face grinning back at us like the smile of a Cheshire cat.

The process is far from over. If you would know the "missing link," gaze in a mirror. You are not quite human yet. Whereas the first world–second world relationship might already have been finalized in three mutually orthogonal axes—vertical notochord (basically the spinal cord) orthogonal to mutually orthogonal seeing-hearing axes—the relationship of the third world to that configuration is far more complex and indeed would seem to defy any spatiotemporal model to do justice to it. Evolution continues its main work on cognition, specifically on the neocortex, which is orthogonal neither to the notochord nor to the optical-auditory axes but is curvilinear and complexly so.† Yoga claims that the billion-year program of evolution toward *Homo perfectus* can be compressed into a single lifetime! The ultimate design is already present within the endocrine system, but latently so, and it is the endocrine system that the kriyās of rāja yoga affect irreversibly.

◆◆◆

And the Lord spoke to King Solomon:

> Now mine eyes shall be open, and mine ears attent unto the prayer that is made in this place. For now have I chosen and sanctified this house, that my name may be there forever; and mine eyes and mine heart shall be there perpetually.‡

With the building of the First Temple, Solomon fulfilled the covenant that the Lord had made with his father, King David. There is the clear sense that the mission of the people of Israel had at last been achieved. On our hypothesis, the LAND OF ISRAEL is the human body. Consider that the "house of Jacob" has the power of locomotion:

* Because a human organism comprises electrons, our fanciful cladistics must generate a new category, higher than the kingdom, which might be called the *imperium,* and having just two taxa: Visibilia (including hominids) and Invisibilia (leptids).

† In the very earliest stage of embryogenesis, within days of conception, a *kink* appears in the developing notochord, a bending away from the vertical that soon ramifies into the cranial nerves and various second-world sensoria, which are primarily oriented not up-down but left-right and forward-backward. This kink (kn) is an embryological analogy to the Fall, and although it only becomes apparent when there is a notochord to examine, it is present notionally from the moment of conception as a genetically preordained event.

‡ 2 Chronicles 7:15–16.

O house of Jacob, come ye, and let us walk in the light of the Lord.*

The Twelve Tribes of Israel are the parts of the body; the most sacred structure of human physiology is the frontal suture, the entrance to the TEMPLE OF SOLOMON:

The Lord loveth the gates of Zion more than all the dwellings of Jacob.†

The "dwellings of Jacob" are the several breaths of the body, which places Jacob and Odysseus in a parallel mythic status. The Temple of Solomon is the skull above the eyebrows, the KINGDOM OF JUDEA is where the wing-shaped brows meet:

And he [Solomon] set the cherubim [angels] within the inner house: and they stretched forth the wings of the cherubim, so that the wing of the one touched the one wall, and the wing of the other cherub touched the other wall; and their wings touched one another in the midst of the house.‡

But the wings of the "inner chamber" are more likely the lateral ventricles.

The Three Worlds template for the Temple of Solomon is found in the Old Testament:

The nethermost chamber was five cubits broad, and the middle was six cubits broad, and the third was seven cubits broad.§

This is the shape of a pyramid, that is, the body seated in meditation.

This is the thing that ye shall do; A third part of you entering on the sabbath, of the priests and of the Levites, shall be porters of the doors; And a third part shall be at the king's house; and a third part at the gate of the foundation: and all the people shall be in the courts of the house of the Lord. But let none come into the house of the Lord, save the priests.#

Note, the priests are "porters," that is, they decide who to admit into the topmost chamber; they control initiation. Ultimately, the power was Solomon's. Before his temple was built, Solomon had a dream in which the Lord says "Ask, what I shall give thee." Solomon's reply reveals again the connection between esoteric *child* and initiate:

I am but a child: I know not how to go out or come in.**

Entry into the Temple of Solomon therefore speaks to a special condition of the organism: the status of initiate into the Holy Name of God. This then is the purpose of the creation, that one place might be set aside for remembering the Name of God. Yet note, the Lord warns that he will carefully weigh "the prayer that is made in this place" (where he dwells in "thick darkness" = Wine-Dark Sea). The status of initiate is probationary and a fall from sacred knowledge more damnable than the sin of the uninitiate or gentile:

But if ye turn away, and foresake my statutes and my commandments, which I have set before you, . . . then will I pluck them up by the roots out of my land which I have given them; and this house, which I have sanctified for my name, will I cast out of my sight. . . . And this house,

* Isaiah 2:5; Jacob was renamed Israel after seeing God "face to face"; the renaming follows upon Jacob's insistence that he learn the Holy Name of God (Genesis 32:26–30).

† Psalms 87:2.

‡ 1 Kings 6:27; cf. figure 5.

§ 1 Kings 6:6.

\# 2 Chronicles 23:4–6.

** 1 Kings 3:5–7. Cf., the version of Solomon's dream in 2 Chronicles 1:10–11: Solomon explicitly asks for "wisdom and knowledge, that I may go out and come in before this people," for which reason alone the Lord makes him king, confirming the caesaropapism of Judaism that most likely was modeled on the Egyptian pharaoh.

> which is high, shall be an astonishment to everyone that passeth by it; so that he shall say, Why hath the Lord done this unto this land, and unto this house? And it shall be answered, because they forsook the Lord God of their fathers, which brought them forth out of the land of Egypt.*

Thus, without knowledge of the statutes and commandments—the gnosis that, *au fond*, is knowledge of the Ineffable Name of God—the embodied human soul is a marvel without a purpose, an Ozymandian hulk, a monument to vanity, spiritual emptiness, alienation, and desperate decay.†

Upon what, we must ask, had the Lord established his temple? Out of which elements was it formed? What, in other words, is the esoteric pedigree of the human organism? The contrast between Solomon and his father David is noteworthy. Whereas David builds a house for himself, Solomon builds a house for the Name of God. The Lord tells David that the building of the temple will be left to his son because David has shed blood in war, yet it is David who initiates the sequence of events that lead to the founding of the temple. He tells the prophet Nathan that whereas he lives in a house of cedars, the Lord dwells "under curtains," a reference to the Ark of the Covenant in which were kept the Tables of the Law brought down from Mount Horeb by Moses. That night Nathan has a dream in which the Lord speaks to him:

> For I have not dwelt in a house since the days I brought up Israel unto this day; but have gone from tent to tent, and from one tabernacle to another. . . . Saith unto my servant David, thus saith the Lord of hosts, I took thee from the sheepcote, even from following the sheep, that thou shouldst be ruler over my people Israel.‡

The Lord, it seems, has lived in the fields and among the beasts of the field. The esoteric message is that until a human being is perfected by remembering the Holy Name, a human being is but an animal, an animal, in the case of the Twelve Tribes of Israel, that is being prepared for something greater but an animal nonetheless. The reference to sheep singles out once again the sacredness of the place between the brows, upon which the Kingdom of Judea, the esoteric cranium and David's throne, is founded. David is the son of Jesse, and so we find the breath tied to this sacred spot yet again. In 2 Chronicles 2, Solomon selects Mount Moriah in Jerusalem for the site of the temple. Not coincidentally, this is the location of the attempted SACRIFICE OF ISAAC (Genesis 22:2–4), where Abraham's hand was stayed by the sight of a "ram caught in a thicket."§ As previously noted, the Sacrifice of Isaac and the Death of Absalom are recapitulations of prāṇāyāma with root gazing. The introduction of the Temple of Solomon indicates that both techniques are associated with the kriyā for calling on the Name of the Lord, the secret of secrets, the end of human evolution.

◆◆◆

In this book we have sought to establish the scientific basis of mythology and the mythological basis of science. It should come as no surprise that the two disciplines are united within the human body, which is both the body of myth and a physical body that has evolved in conformity with the laws of nature. When one gazes at the night sky one gazes at an infinity that *must also* be within oneself, for where else could the oceanic experience be? The night sky, as the astronomers tell us, is the past—indeed it is a multiplicity of pasts—but the experience of

* 2 Chronicles 7:19–22.

† Ozymandias is another name of Ramses II (d. 1225 B.C.), the pharaoh who held the Hebrews in bondage "down in Egypt" (*Egypt* = *kpt*, the second world).

‡ 1 Chronicles 17:1–7.

§ In Islamic tradition, the sight of Jacob's dream and Muhammad's ascent to Heaven as well.

that immense volume is immediately present to us and a part of our very natures.

A further aim of this book has been to redeem the human past and to recognize the accomplishments of our ancestors. Our civilization is a consequence of the archaic gnosis. The ancient religions of the world proceeded from a discovery of the practical means of isolating that internal "vasty deep," of maintaining it in a moment-to-moment experience that abides with the individual organism as would a dear companion. In the Sermon on the Mount, Jesus says that the "pure of heart . . . shall see God," nor does he scruple to add *after they are dead*. Lacking any knowledge of the true baptism, it is difficult to see how latter-day orthodoxy could construe the verse as it was intended. "Pure of heart," as we have seen, refers not simply to a metaphorical state of purity but to a heart physically altered by practice of gnosis. The circumstances of the Beatific Vision are physical as well as spiritual, therefore the heart must be physically purified beforehand. David's heart was impure—its natural function had been modified in the instant he summoned the anger necessary to kill his enemies. Therefore, it was left to Solomon to realize the "beatific vision." At the end of the *Yoga-Sūtra*, Patañjali discusses this event in a series of powerfully moving verses:

> Then, verily, the mind is inclined towards discrimination [between the real and the unreal] and gravitating towards kaivalya.
>
> In the intervals [between discrimination] arise other pratyayas from the force of saṃskāras.
>
> Their removal like that of kleśas . . . has been described.
>
> In the case of one, who is able to maintain a constant state of renunciation even towards the most exalted state of enlightenment and to exercise the highest kind of discrimination, follows *dharma-megha-samādhi.**

* *Yoga-Sūtra*, *Kaivalya Pāda*, sutras 26–29, parentheses added.

Dharma-megha-samādhi: "the cloud-of-virtues trance." The final obstacle to the goal is "the most exalted state of enlightenment"; in other words, the archangel Lucifer, who appears at this moment as he did to Jesus in the wilderness, must be renounced. Jesus went into the desert immediately following his baptism in the Holy Name by John the Baptist, his guru:

> And straightaway coming up out of the water, he saw the heavens opened, and the Spirit like a dove descending upon him: And there came a *voice* from heaven, saying, Thou art my beloved Son, in whom I am well pleased. And immediately the Spirit driveth him into the wilderness.†

Lucifer is the voice that whispers to us in our brains, a hissing serpent (Apocalypse 12:9) who manages to confuse us as to who we really are because he can whisper that most deadly, most pernicious lie: *I*. He was a liar from the beginning (John 8:41).

At the same time, Lucifer is radiant Athena. He is the "Wisdom" of cabala, the highest of the *sephiroth*, "emanations" of the deity. He is the highest faculty that nonperfected beings possess, our rationality and our pride in our rationality (1 Timothy 3:6). Because the wish is ever father to the deed, he is the "prince of this world" (John 12:31, 14:30). The practical function of initiation is to provide a moment-to-moment choice of where to place one's piety. Without initiation we can turn merely from one part of our mind to the other—"No man cometh unto the Father, but by me"‡—from one idea of God to another idea of God, from sentiment to sentiment, hope to hope, yet all the desperate while the abiding presence of the almighty within the human form, subtly betokened in the life-giving rise and fall of the breath, goes unnoticed:

† Mark 1:10–12, emphasis added; "voice" here means esoteric sound, the Word.

‡ John 14:6.

> Did ye never read in the scriptures, the stone which the builders rejected, the same is become the corner: this is the Lord's doing, and it is marvelous in our eyes?*

Even the same stone of Sisyphus, which must be raised up and set in place for the cornerstone of the temple that is built in heaven, the CNS transformed, the NEW JERUSALEM—*that* is the requisite task: Place the mind in the breath and thus subdue Lucifer. *That* is what the true baptism, the rāja yoga, the yoga of yogas, offers *ya evam veda*, "to him who knows," as the *Upaniṣads* say again and again and yet again. Whatever the failings of orthodox Christianity—and they are many and egregious—the Church has always insisted on the *full* humanity of Jesus of Nazareth. Against Arian and Nestorian, *contra* Monophysite and Monothelite, the Church has preserved the plain sense of these words of Jesus, almost in spite of itself, across two millennia: "What I have done, you can do. Yea, and greater things!"

* Matthew 21:43; cf., Psalms 118:22–23 and Isaiah 28:16

APPENDICES

APPENDIX A

Newton's Three Laws

We begin with a simple description of visceral proprioception, which, throughout the discussion, will be referred to as *stereognosis.** Stereognosis is that faculty which allows an entity to be aware of its materiality. That is perhaps inelegant, but it will have to do for now. Visceral proprioception is an experience compounded of a sense of mass and energy, and it is the same duality that we now define as "materiality."

Now the most striking aspect of stereognosis is its constancy. Short of killing the organism/entity, it is impossible to extinguish visceral sensation. It is a first principle of proprioception that such inextinguishability is common to every faculty, what we have repeatedly referred to as "the dynamic nature of experience." And yet the principle still seems to be particularly applicable to stereognosis.† The reason has to do with our previous characterization of visceral proprioception as a sort of touch and with the almost synonymous use of the words *touching* and *feeling* colloquially; and *feeling* is itself virtually a synonym for experience in general. We thus have a chain of meaning from stereognosis to touch to feeling to experience and from these to the assertion that *every entity feels itself continuously,* which follows not only from the dynamic nature of experience but from the congruency of awareness (consciousness) with existence. In the absence of external stimuli, the cessation of stereognosis in the entity means that the entity has ceased to exist. The statement comes down to an assertion that feeling is always reflexive.

Given the duality inherent in stereognosis and given that touch is one member of this duality, what sort of experience might the other member be? Obviously taste, for with touch it is the predominant faculty of the first world. We have seen that taste here refers to a quality of first-world experience: pleasure-pain. Now according to both Vedānta and Buddhism, existence qua existence is associ-

* Literally, "solidity knowledge."

† Even in cases of severe neurological trauma such as quadraplegia, when the spinal cord has been cut, it is not a case of no feeling but rather of a "numbness," which is still a true feeling.

ated with an experience of suffering. If we permit ourselves a slight oversimplification we may say that suffering is contingent on a craving for pleasure, which, in accordance with the so-called law of karma, inevitably leads to pain. It is not unreasonable, therefore, to imagine the craving for the experiences of the Three Worlds as an impelling force, in fact as an *energy*. By looking at things in this light we can come to the following conclusions: (1) taste is closely involved with existence (as craving); (2) taste is energy. If we then make the plausible correlation of touch with *mass* we can describe a stereognostic experience as one of mass-energy or touch-taste, wherein both faculties are existentially necessary. Those ideas frame our assertion that every entity feels itself continuously.

Adopting a yogic point of view, which is to say, the puruṣa-pratyaya paradigm, we now ask if taste and touch aren't combined in the "feeling" of stereognosis in the same way that puruṣa and pratyaya are linked by the symmetry of conciousness (S_0.) Is taste the puruṣa for the pratyaya that is touch, and vice versa? Stereognosis is somewhat challenging to symmetry because a proprioccepting entity functions as both puruṣa and pratyaya. We have refined the argument by asserting that consciousness is reflexive (R_0), that is, every entity is conscious of itself.

The compound feeling of taste-touch can serve as a practical model of "reality" (we are forced to use the word *reality* here because we are rapidly running out of concepts). We cannot say that taste-touch is a model for existence, for we have already decided that existence is coextensive with consciousness, namely, the puruṣa, which, depending on the viewpoint adopted, is either taste or touch. If we say that taste is the puruṣa or existence, what is touch, what is pratyaya? The conclusion is that it is nonexistence. The assertion is rescued from paradox if we recall that yogically what exists is only puruṣa, whereas pratyaya qua pratyaya is an illusion. To use the phraseology of the Buddhists, pratyaya is "void." Thus, by equating existence with consciousness we can make the concept of existence more useful metaphysically, the same for nonexistence. Existence and nonexistence are useful signifiers of the a priori experience that is consciousness.

When Parmenides claims that from an existent subject there may only evolve another existent and that from a nonexistent comes only a nonexistent, he is not just blowing balloons filled with hot air but is speaking plainly about the relationship between the puruṣa and its pratyaya; he is concretizing—making useful—ultimately indeterminate concepts. Puruṣa is existence and pratyaya is nonexistence and by S_0 puruṣa is pratyaya. "Nirvāṇa is saṃsāra." Similarly, when Thales states that reality is water and that (the) earth "floats" in this reality he is imaging the puruṣa-pratyaya model as well. Water is an age-old symbol for feeling, and the earth is none other than Mother Earth (Gæa) sandwiched between the first and third worlds, the realm of illusion or pratyaya.*

Our description of stereognosis is complete. Stereognosis is really internal touch combined with internal taste, so the logical subject for analysis is now external touch and external taste. We shall consider them separately.

The most obvious feature of external touch (from now on shortened simply to touch) is its reciprocity. If two entities, call them A and B, make contact, A touches B and B touches A. That is just S_0, here appearing so obviously because touch is so basic a faculty, as fundamental as symmetry is a concept. Moreover, because A is the puruṣa when B is pratyaya and vice versa and because there are no other pertinent factors in the limiting case, the experience of A touching B is equivalent to that of B touching A.

Again, an interesting possibility arises. If we repeat the above argument for taste (and there is no reason why we may not) and if we remember that taste-touch parallels puruṣa-pratyaya, we can say that if A and B are brought into contact, A tastes B and B tastes A and vice versa. Because everything is subsumed by the categories

* Cf., Cancer (the Crab), the zodiacal sign associated with touch, also the first water sign.

puruṣa and pratyaya, there being no third possibility, and because taste-touch still parallels puruṣa-pratyaya, the implication is that taste and touch stand in an antipodal relationship to each other. Hence it is reasonable to say that in the abovementioned limiting case the experience of A touching (tasting) B is opposite to the experience of B touching (tasting) A.

With external touch and taste a new factor enters the picture: time. Whereas in stereognosis the constancy of the experience precludes the entity's development of a "sense" of time (in the limiting case), in external (or perceptual) touch-taste the probability that the contact between A and B is intermittent does allow for temporality. Also possible are ancillary concepts of frequency, periodicity, and rate. A complete sense of time by the entity obviously requires cognition,* but in the limiting case that faculty is absent. Hence the understanding of time with which we are here concerned must be described as incomplete. There is a "sense" of time in the entity, but no more than that. Clearly some such sense is necessary for a complete concept, yet just as clearly it is insufficient. To refer to an insufficient limiting experience we shall call it a negative-order temporality, in which we appeal to that meaning of negation that implies a lack.

Temporality is a consequence of the transition from stereognosis to perception that occurs when internal touch-taste (feeling-appetite) is replaced by external touch-taste. Those faculties are intermediate modes of experience, straddling the first-to-second-world boundary in consciousness. And yet even when considered perceptually, they maintain their intimate relationship. Clearly it is not possible for taste to occur without touch; and the converse is also true, though less obviously, because every actual touching is either pleasurable or painful, what the taste faculty participates in most irremovably.

The pleasure-or-pain capacity allows us to characterize negative-order temporality more usefully. Consider three entities, A, B, and C, which are brought into contact in the following manner: A touches B, then touches C. And let's suppose that the A-B contact is pleasurable to A, while the A-C contact is painful. Then from A's point of view the sequence is pleasure then pain. Furthermore, because the sequence is intermittent, it will contribute to a sense of time in A. If we now run the sequence backward, namely, A touches first C then B, the result is pain then pleasure. Loosely put, in the first instance A's end experience may be characterized as one of shock, in the second as one of relief. What all of this comes down to is that A's sense of time (negative-order temporality) is irreversible. Whether or not negative-order temporality is always irreversible, which is to say, can never be run backward to reach the same experience in the entity as obtained initially, is unclear. But we can say that negative-order temporality is generally irreversible and that situations to the contrary are special cases, for which a unique set of conditions are required.

Our next topic is spatiality. Again, it is evident that in the limiting case stereognosis alone cannot contribute to the development in the entity of a "sense" of space. With perceptual touch-taste, however, the question is more problematic. It might be that the experience of touching-tasting another entity implies a sense of spatiality; but that is not a cognitive implication. Rather it is a *shading* of the entity's experience that derives from a feeling of apartness and that is also contingent upon the intermittency of external touch-taste.

The "feeling of apartness" is fully established only in visual perception. Hence the sense of space developed by touch-taste is insufficient for the experience of true spatiality, though it is probably necessary. In analogy to our temporal argument, let us refer to this insufficient sense of space as negative-order spatiality. And here it is necessary to point out a crucial difference between temporality and spatiality. The former experience is completed in cognition, whereas the latter is completed in perception. Hence time is more of a concept than space and space is more of a percept than time, although, because

* Equivalent to Kant's assertion in his *Critique of Pure Reason* that time is "a synthetic judgment a priori."

of the dynamic nature of experience, neither is solely one or the other.*

We are now almost ready to examine the faculties of the second world: hearing, vision, and smell. But a number of prefatory remarks are necessary.

We've seen that for a variety of reasons perception has become the criterion of objectivity in popular thinking. In such a view, unless an entity possesses perceptual "reality" it may not possess objective reality. All other experiences are relegated to the realm of mere subjectivity, are, in behavioral (second world) parlance, epiphenomenal as opposed to phenomenal. The yogic division of reality into puruṣa and pratyaya itself reflects that prejudice. We could even say that the terminology was tailored to perception, although it did not stop there, as we've seen. And short of dispensing altogether with perception as a concept, which is perhaps not impermissible from a purely proprioceptive point of view, we have no choice but to adhere to the distinction between puruṣa and pratyaya somewhat more stringently than we have in our previous descriptions of first-world faculties, even though we must keep in mind the preeminence of the principle of S_0 overall. What this comes down to in practice is that our application of the principle must be explicit rather than implicit. In other words, we must objectivize it, treat it as if it were just another second-world fact of experience, while remembering that this is simply a device.

We consider hearing first. Unlike stereognosis and touch-taste, hearing is bipolar. The left-right aspect of hearing is essential to its functioning, and any description, however qualitative, must take it into account. As we have been at pains to stress throughout this book, even were the entity deaf in one ear, that ear still "hears" internally, as, for instance, in the sound of one hand clapping. And just as a sound is most audible when the source is in direct line with one of the ears, so too *directionality* is inherent to our hearing model. Moreover, we know from neuroanatomy that the left and right auditory nerves are connected, respectively, to the left and right sides of the brain. It is also known that the two hemispheres of the cerebrum serve different functions; and because the auditory connections are ramified into those hemispheres, it is plausible to assume that the different functions affect the ears and in some way, however subtly, distinguish the hearing of the left ear from that of the right.

Another obvious sensory factor with regard to hearing is balance. As is well known, the ears participate in an individual's sense of equilibrium to such an extent that disturbances of the inner ear such as infections sometimes result in an inability to stand erect unaided. The mechanisms of this balancing function lie within a portion of the inner ear known as the osseous labyrinth, in the three semicircular canals containing a clear fluid called the liquor Cotunii. In addition the walls of these canals, as well as those of other components of the inner ear, for example, the cochlea, are lined with myriad hair cells that are exquisitely sensitive to vibration and motion.†

Directionality and balance, are obviously

* Kant referred to space as "the form of external sense."

† An interesting sidelight on the discussion is the well-known myth of THESEUS AND THE MINOTAUR. The Minotaur, half man–half bull, was the offspring of Zeus (in the guise of a white bull) and Pasiphaë, wife of King Minos of Crete. With the help of Ariadne, Minos's daughter, Theseus slew the monster in its labyrinth on Crete. That this is a myth about the meditative control of hearing is likely. Not only is Theseus guided to Crete by Aphrodite, but he also gives to Ariadne the crown of the goddess, which he received from Thetis. Also while on Crete, he beds down with Peribœa and Pherebœa, respectively, "among the cows" and "cowherdess," and was advised by Ariadne to seize the Minotaur by his hair (the cilia?). The labyrinth is probably the cochlea and the locale (Crete) is the second world. Theseus, who was an Athenian, dallied with Ariadne on Cyprus. Proprioceptively it can be understood as a description of the split between the third world (Athens) and the second (Crete-Cyprus; Cyprus was sacred to Aphrodite, who is often styled "the Cyprian"). Ariadne, who wears Aphrodite's crown and ends up living on Aphrodite's island, where a cult was established for her, cannot complain if we identify her with Aphrodite herself. Theseus is no one if not Athena, and his hardheartedness toward Ariadne parallels the hostility between the goddesses so common in myth, particularly in Homer. Yet the esoteric point of the myth is that the mind must be joined to hearing in meditation by means of a mantra.

linked. The positioning of the ears at the sides of the cranium establishes both a preferred direction for audition and, in the manner of someone balancing on a wire with arms outspread, defines a plane of equilibrium that passes through the Cotunian fluid. In evolution, the ears developed from position-sensing organs on the sides of fish.

In myth too we find a clear relationship between hearing and balance. Aphrodite, as we've seen, has rulership over the zodiacal sign of Taurus (the Bull = hearing), but she also rules Libra, the Balance. In astrology the various parts of the body are assigned to different signs of the zodiac. Thus Taurus is associated with the ears and Libra with the kidneys. In ancient psychological usage the kidneys were believed to be the seat of passion, and the idea survives in the archaic expression "to be of a certain kidney," which is to say, of a certain emotional temperament. The fact of the Balance's rulership of the kidneys would seem to suggest a harmonizing control over the passions, a moral stance so important in antique philosophy, for example, Stoicism and Epicureanism. Indeed, the symbolism derives from proprioceptions of activity within the kidneys during states of extreme emotional disturbance.* But whatever the explanation, Aphrodite's dual role as ruler of Taurus and Libra explicitly ties together hearing and balancing.

Perceptual or external hearing is phenomenologically *passive*—phenomenological because no sense is ever functionally passive but may appear to be so; passive because sounds come *to* the ears, which cannot "look" for stimuli as can the eyes or the teeth (talented sorts who can wiggle their ears notwithstanding). This passivity is reflected in hearing's being a goddess, hence feminine, with all the qualities of receptivity that the term traditionally implies. An equivalent way of phrasing this is to say that hearing is phenomenologically reactive. It cannot initiate perceptions.

* If there are neurological connections between the kidneys and the cerebellum, which regulates balance, they are as yet unknown to neuroanatomy.

At this point it might be useful to combine the three aspects of hearing discussed so far—directionality, balance, and passivity—in a single illustration. Imagine a limiting case of two entities, A and B, that can only hear. Also imagine that A hears B and that the experience is pleasurable to A. Finally, let us suppose, in response to the pleasurable sound of B, that A moves toward B. (B is somehow constrained, so we need not consider its reaction to A.) What, we now ask, will be the characteristics of A's motion given our qualitative description of hearing? To begin, let's assign the names positive and negative to, respectively, the right and left poles of A's hearing axis. It might help to think of A as a blindfolded, olfactory-less dog, where B is its master's whistle. In the most general case, we cannot assume that the axis is aligned along a preferred direction for audition, of which there are always two. In fact, given the distinction between right hearing and left, the axis may be oriented anywhere within 360 degrees of solid angle† (of space) immediately surrounding A. Implicit in the arrangement is the idea, were the axis aligned preferentially, that A would know in which direction B lies and would at once move toward B along a straight line. Similarly, if the axis happened to fall exactly perpendicular to the straight-line course, then A could not hear B and the result would be no movement on A's part. All other possible motions for A thus fall between the two extremes, and it is the other motions, being the most probable, that we must describe.

We distinguish two cases: (1) when the signal (sound) from B is intermittent, with the signal time being of the same order of magnitude as A's response time, but of a lesser order of magnitude than the interval between signals, and (2) when the signal is continuous. In case 1 the signal will obviously fall unequally on the positive and negative poles of the hearing axis. It is assumed

† A solid angle is a three-dimensional angle, e.g., the apex angle of a pyramid; if one thinks of the image of the dog and whistle the angle is planar, but the same reasoning applies throughout the following discussion.

that A seeks to go to B, so it will be necessary for A to adjust its axis so as to align it with the straight-line heading. That will happen when the signal falls either entirely on the right or entirely on the left pole, thus giving A a precise fix on B. The signal time is short, so A might not be able to get a fix on B within that time or, in the case of a particularly alacritous entity, A might even overshoot the straight-line heading.

In either case, when the signal vanishes the entity will presumably follow the heading it is on at that moment, not correcting it until the next signal burst, at which time it will either get a fix on B or will again follow a heading that deviates from the direction in which it wants to go but presumably not by as much. Thus it will approach its target by a series of course corrections and if we, observing the process, were to plot A's path it would look decidedly ragged (figure A1, top). The number of divagations necessary to bring A to B depends on several factors (A's response time, auditory acuity, the signal time, interval between signals, etc.), none of which needs explaining particularly.

In case 2, assuming that (1) the signal acts continuously and (2) A reacts immediately, waiting no longer than its response time,* the path will be curvilinear (figure A1, bottom), over the course of which A will continually correct its heading until the poles of its hearing axis are preferentially aligned, at which point the plot of the motion will revert to a straight-line approach.†

Two aspects of the above description (valid in both cases) stand out especially clearly. First, the entity automatically strives to minimize its divagation times and hence its total time of approach. Second, the means of achieving the minimization is for the entity to maximize the degree of signal imbalance with respect to its positive and negative poles of hearing. Actually, both factors function in tandem and neither is

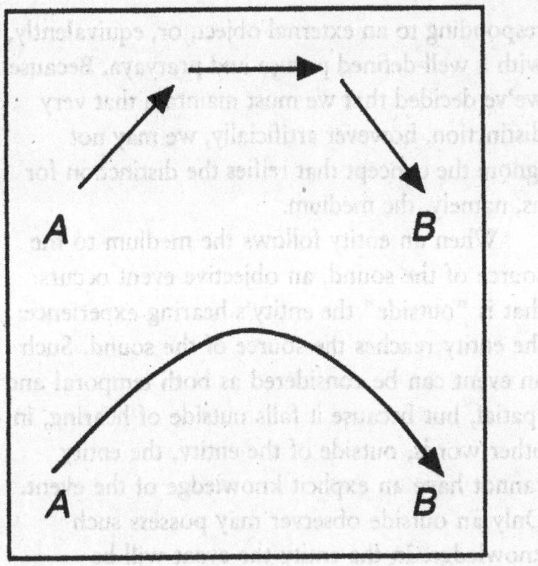

Figure A1. Auditory Course Corrections

more nor less important than the other.

Before closing our discussion of hearing it is necessary to consider the temporality and spatiality of our model. At first glance, it would seem that since we have introduced a pleasurable psychological response to sound in the entity, our conclusion, in analogy with perceptual touch-taste, must be that the temporality of hearing is irreversible. But that would be to ignore a crucial difference between the two models: the medium.

Touch-taste has no external medium necessary for its operation, whereas that is not the case with hearing. Now it is true that from a purely proprioceptive standpoint we may ignore the medium of sound, which, in the dog-whistle model, is air. In such a model we could focus exclusively on the entity's experience of pleasure or pain.‡ But in that case we shall have expanded perception into proprioception and defeated our purpose, which was to treat perception as it is commonly understood: with an internal subject

* Tacitly assumed in case 1.

† By a technique of the calculus known as *variation of the integral*, the shape of the path can be rigorously demonstrated.

‡ Were the sound painful, A would proceed *away* from B in a manner identical to cases 1 and 2.

responding to an external object, or, equivalently, with a well-defined puruṣa and pratyaya. Because we've decided that we must maintain that very distinction, however artificially, we may not ignore the concept that reifies the distinction for us, namely, the medium.

When an entity follows the medium to the source of the sound, an objective event occurs that is "outside" the entity's hearing experience: the entity reaches the source of the sound. Such an event can be considered as both temporal and spatial, but because it falls outside of hearing, in other words, outside of the entity, the entity cannot have an explicit knowledge of the event. Only an outside observer may possess such knowledge. In the entity the event will be implicit, which is to say, will coincide with some coordinate of its own spatiotemporal sense (negative-order spatiotemporality) but will not necessarily be identical with it.

Moreover, the new spatiotemporality is clearly reversible. If we rotate our frame of reference through 180 degrees (equivalent to A and B trading places), then A will execute the exact same motion in reverse until it reaches B, with the same amount of new spatiotemporal measurement having elapsed as in the original situation (for both cases). The new spatiotemporality forms a unity and in fact is identical to what is known as the space-time continuum of relativity theory; but we postpone an elaboration of the identity until the third portion of our argument.

The phrase *zeroth-order spatiotemporality* is suggested in analogy to negative-order spatiality and negative-order temporality, but primarily because the entity has zero explicit knowledge of events referred thereto for measurement. For the first-world faculty of taste-touch, temporality and spatiality are kept distinct because the irreversibility of negative-order temporality and negative-order spatiality, rooted in subjective states of the entity, does not allow us to mechanically, which is to say, objectively, equate space with time. It is only because, in the limiting case, a hearing entity is explicitly ignorant (implicitly aware) of the new spatiotemporal events that we may qualitatively and then quantitatively unite them. In other words, ignorance, like negative spatiality and negative temporality, is a subjective state of the entity, and because it applies to both the new space and the new time of our hearing model, it allows for the requisite qualitative unity. Quantitative unity then follows as a matter of course.

A distinction between negative and zero orders arises only because we are adhering to an explicitly perceptual paradigm, in which, because of the nature of perception qua perception, we require both an external observer and an internal subject, something possible only in a model that sunders puruṣa from pratyaya absolutely. In speaking of the entity's pleasure or pain states, we are in fact speaking of taste-touch and not of hearing per se. If we decide (as we have) not to expand hearing into taste-touch then we cannot allow pleasure-pain to play so crucial a role in defining spatiotemporality. Our use of such subjective states in cases 1 and 2 is a device—one that accounts for the entity's inclination to move—but not a description of the motion, which can only proceed from properties of hearing alone, namely, directionality, balance, and passivity.

If pleasure-pain is merely a device (in a hearing model), we should be able to find another, better device to account for the entity's inclination to move. At least one such device exists: the Doppler shift. The Doppler shift is a phenomenon of hearing in which the apparent frequency of sound emitted by a moving source shifts markedly relative to an observer. (In our model, it is immaterial whether we regard A as moving toward B or vice versa.)

For motion toward the observer, the apparent frequency increases; for motion away from the observer it decreases.* If observer and source are on a straight line relative to the observer's hearing axis, the Doppler shift will be maximal. If we now assume that A seeks to maximize the Doppler shift relative to B, we have an explana-

* Anyone who has stood on the shoulder of an expressway and noticed the variation in sound from a rapidly moving freight truck as it passes has experienced a Doppler shift firsthand; the sound goes from a higher to a lower pitch.

tion for A's inclination to move that does not involve pleasure or pain explicitly.

Yet we cannot escape entirely a nagging doubt that such an explanation begs the question. For why should A "seek" to maximize the Doppler shift, which is to say, to move? Are we not at least implying that A takes pleasure in so doing? The answer is, yes and no.

By hypothesis, A is a conscious entity, and it is also a given that all faculties, hearing included, are intimately connected with touch-taste. The medium for hearing does *touch* the eardrum in transmitting the sound, so it is not unexpected that A experiences either pleasure or pain in hearing. But again, that is to expand perception into proprioception. Pleasure (or pain) is simply too general a notion to account for A's inclination to move. We have not begged the question, though we have still not answered it.

What is the necessity for A to move? Recall our prefatory remarks in the situation of A hearing B. In them we isolated two extreme positions of A's hearing axis. In the second case the axis is aligned perpendicularly to the straight-line course to B. When the axis was in that position, we decided, A could not hear B. But does that mean that A has ceased to hear? Obviously not: it may still hear itself; it can still hear proprioceptively, which we've called *audition*. That is an extrapolation from the stereognostic axiom that every entity feels itself continuously: the case in which *feels = audits*. It is also a possibility not explicitly excluded by our adoption of the limiting case of hearing alone.

What, we now ask, is a relevant description of an entity experiencing only itself and in only one way? The answer is *trance*. And yet we know from yogic texts that the seed for trance (the bīja) may legitimately be a perceptual stimulus, for instance, a sound. The yogic preconditions necessary for trance (samādhi) are (a) concentration (dhāraṇā) and (b) contemplation (dhyāna), which essentially means that all stimuli in the yogi's awareness save the pertinent bīja are suppressed (though *ignored* might be a better word). In adopting a limiting-case model, however, we have automatically fulfilled the yogic criteria for entity A. Hence, A's experience of the sound of B should very rapidly become a trance state focused on that sound.

We have already speculated that the human nervous system could be likened to a well-known electrical mechanism: an oscillator tank circuit. Experience of the Three Worlds has an irremovable oscillatory character. We've also seen that a trance state is achieved through a repetitional technique, for example, through a mantra. Making an inductive leap, might we not conclude that it is the oscillatory, back-and-forth operation of the nervous system that renders trance possible in our species? Moreover, does that not imply as well that trance is supremely natural in our species, that whenever we concentrate on any stimulus, be it of internal or external origin and ever so fleeting, we are approaching—nay are *in*—a state of trance? On such a view, all our experiences, our so-called stream of consciousness, are a succession of trance states of varying depth and duration. What distinguishes each trance state is an instant of *comprehension*. An example of a relatively deep trance state that occurs quite often is arithmetical calculation: adding, subtracting, multiplying, and so forth. A superficial trance state might be noting the time on a clock.

Applying these remarks to the hearing model, we can say that when A hears (and only hears) B it is entranced. Because the natural tendency of the uninterrupted trance state is to grow deeper and deeper, A's trance must grow deeper and deeper. But what can "grow deeper and deeper" mean practically? What are the objective correlates to A's ever-deepening subjective trance state?

It is hard to avoid some notion of *intensification* in the meaning of "deeper and deeper." In the case of hearing, that means an increase in the volume of the sound, its frequency, or both. Both quantities can most practicably be increased by moving toward the source of the sound on the straight-line course. From the entity's point of view, no perceptual motion occurs, only an intensification of the stimulus instigated by the entity's natural tendency to deepen its state of trance. The intensification shows up as a Doppler shift, a descriptive device well-suited to hearing because it involves both directionality and balance explicitly. We have thus accounted for the entity's inclination to move toward a source without appealing exclusively to the pleasure-pain paradigm.

What of the case when the entity moves away from the source? How can it intensify the trance state then? One answer is that the entity, in moving away from the source, simultaneously and ipso facto deepens its auditional *self-trance*, that is, hears itself more and more intensely until, at some point, it is far enough away from the source as to be unable to hear it at all. Thus, the entity is ever in a state of trance, either internally or externally, which follows from the dynamic nature of hearing: the entity must always hear something in a limiting case. How distinguish between the two possible motions; how account for the entity's "choice" of auditing itself and moving away from the source or, alternatively, of hearing the external stimulus and moving toward the source? That there are only two choices resulting in opposite motions suggests a solution involving the *polarity* of the entity's hearing, namely, the positive and negative poles of the hearing axis. The right-left poles reflect a division in the entity's perceptual apparatus, which we shall refer to as the difference between right hearing and left hearing, respectively.* If that is true for an arbitrary entity such as A, it must also be true for B.

Now apply S_0 to the situation. When A hears B, B hears A. That means there is a univalency between the sound from B and the hearing of A and vice versa; practically speaking, it comes down to a univalency between the hearing axis of A and the sound from B and vice versa. But if the univalency means anything, it means that there is also a right-left quality to the sound from A when B hears it. In other words not only is the hearing of an entity polarized, but its own sound is polarized as well.

To illustrate polarization without introducing new parameters, posit that, whenever B's positive pole is aligned toward A, the sound that A hears is a sound possessing the quality of *rightness*, and that when B's negative pole is aligned toward A then the sound that A hears possesses the quality of *leftness*, and vice versa.

So far we've said nothing concerning the alignment of A's hearing axis. Before specifying so crucial a parameter, let's make one final assumption in the interests of simplification. Let's assume that with respect to hearing, A and B are identical entities, that there exists some abstract quality that, when measured relative to A, gives the same value as when measured relative to B. The abstract quality, which we have yet to name, can be thought of as being a measure of the strength of an entity's hearing and hence, by S_0, of the strength of the sound of that entity as well.

Now return to the question of the alignment of A's hearing axis and note two salient factors. First and most importantly, prior to A's perception of B, it (A) must be in a state of auditional trance. Second, either A's positive or its negative pole is closer to B and hence detects B's signal more clearly/strongly. If the signal from B is a *dexter* sound, that is, one possessing the quality of rightness, and if it is A's positive pole that is closer to B and given that A and B are identical hearing-wise, then the effect of the sound of B will be to repeat the sound that A is already hearing at that pole internally. But that is equivalent to deepening A's trance state, which, we've already seen, means that A must move away from B. Reversing the poles of A means that the dexter sound from B will disrupt A's internal hearing (again given that they are identical), shifting A into a hearing trance state, the seed of which is the sound from B, and causing A to move toward B in order to deepen it. A similar argument holds if we assume that the sound from B is a *sinister* sound, that is, one possessing the quality of leftness.

If we now remove the constraints from B so that it too is free to move, the above arguments can be repeated to demonstrate that its motion

---

* The division is qualitative and related to the more general concept of *handedness* encountered in physics and chemistry.

will correlate positively with A's, because to say that B is emitting a dexter sound or a sinister sound is equivalent to specifying the alignment of B's hearing axis. Obviously the effect will be maximized whenever the axes are preferentially aligned relative to the straight-line course between the entities. For alignments deviating from the preferred direction the effect will be weaker and will result in what we may call mixed states of internal and external trance, but which will resolve quickly into a preferred alignment on the basis of whatever pole happens to be closer to the source. Such *mixed states* appear as divagations in the motion.*

Whenever the entity (A or B) is in the condition of auditional trance, its status is analogous to a state of equilibrium. The effect of the external sound, then, is to tip the scales and precipitate a state of disequilibrium in the entity that manifests as motion either toward or away from the source. Although we have made the entities A and B identical with respect to hearing strength, our conclusions would still hold were one stronger than the other, for the disequilibrium would be commensurately greater the greater the strength of the stimulus.

The application of ideas of trance to the hearing model suggests that those notions could be extended to our previous descriptions of stereognosis and touch-taste. Our stereognostic axiom might then be restated in the following way:

Every entity in a state of self-trance [stereognosis] tends to remain in a state of self-trance.

If we put together this assertion and what we've learned from the hearing model, we arrive at the even more general axiom:

An entity in a state of self-trance tends to remain in a state of self-trance until it experiences an external stimulus, and an entity in a state of external trance [perception] tends to remain in external trance until it experiences an internal stimulus.

We have said nothing concerning the deepening of either the self-trance or the external trance. The intensification of the trance state relates to psychophysical *dynamics*, whereas the above axiom describes a state of what could be called psychophysical *equilibrium* (statics).

According to Patañjali, the result of transforming the trance state is "fusion" (samāpattiḥ) of puruṣa with pratyaya known as saṃyama—a restatement of S_0. In the hearing model, A can be thought of as the puruṣa and the stimulus as a pratyaya. But the stimulus is in reality the medium. Hence, it is correct to say that whenever A hears the medium the medium hears A. The medium is as conscious as A and B. In the limit, B becomes the medium. The conclusion underscores once again the importance of S_0. Without it, none of the conclusions we have reached is possible.

Because symmetry renders immaterial the distinction between puruṣa and pratyaya it also dissolves the distinction between internal and external. That fact allows us to restate our general axiom even more simply:

An entity in trance tends to remain in trance.

* Clearly the sense of "mixing" intended *cannot* be that the entity is simultaneously in an internal and external trance state. Rather, what is implied is that the entity rapidly alternates between them until a resolution is attained. The notion of mixed states will prove useful (appendix C).

APPENDIX B

Maxwell's Equations

The next topic for discussion is vision. Obviously, the eyes function differently from the ears, but not so differently that we may not, in a formal sense, carry over insights garnered in our analysis of hearing. There we saw that directionality was critically involved in the qualitative model. It will also be true for vision, because the eyes, though much freer to move than the ears, tend to be limited in their perspective to a direction that is roughly perpendicular to the axis of hearing. There is, however, one major difference between the two senses: Whereas in the case of hearing the ears define a line that lies exactly along the preferred directions for audition, in the case of vision any axis joining the eyes will be perpendicular to the line of sight. Hence, vision cannot be thought of as functioning by means of a balancing mechanism, but, rather, by means of a focusing one.

Practically speaking, the mobility of the eyes is used to pick out a particular point in the visual field. Thus, we may not speak of a *preferred* direction for vision—other than to the front. The eyes can select a single point from an infinity of possible points of focus, each of which defines a visual axis that is neither more nor less valid than any other axis so defined.

The property of focus can be more usefully characterized if we take into account certain implicit meanings of the word. In Latin, *focus* means "a hearth fire," the center of ancient home life. *Focus* therefore has the meaning of "pulling together" or "centering"; to focus means "to join together" or "unite." Analogously, when the eyes are brought to focus on a stimulus, their mutual action "reinforces" their separate activities, a situation much different from that of hearing, where the contributions of the ears balance one another and are more compared than consolidated.

The distinction is evident in neuroanatomy. The auditory nerves never link up with each other directly, but instead "lose" themselves in the right and left temporal lobes, respectively, whereas the optic nerves emerging from the back of each eyeball do literally join together back of the optic thalamus, from where they travel together to the occipital cortex (cortical area 17), often called the visual cortex, at the rear of the skull.

Summarizing: *Hearing differentiates; vision integrates.*

The synthesizing property of vision shows up most plainly in a phenomenon called pattern recognition. Given an amorphous visual stimulus, say the ink blots on a Rorschach test, the percipient will see numerous designs, of varying subjective clarity, spontaneously appearing within the stimulus field. Pattern recognition is closely allied with another visual peculiarity known as figure-background conversion, in which certain elements of a pattern appear to stand out from the rest, which are ignored, with an irregular alternation of attention between these groups occurring nearly always.*

Clearly such phenomena possess a high degree of cognitive input. So high, in fact, that it is almost impossible to say where cognition begins and perception leaves off in such experiences. And yet, if we are to adopt a limiting-case model for vision, fixing the division between the two faculties is rather important.† Toward that end, therefore, let us examine more closely the operation of figure-background conversion.

The device of a Necker cube is often used to demonstrate the phenomenon (figure B1). Studying the cube, we notice that the apparent face containing the circle alternates between the one stereographically closest to the percipient and the one farthest away. Equivalently, in the first case the circle is in the foreground, hence "stands out," in the second it is in the background and recedes. The percipient can either make the switch occur by mental effort or wait for it to happen spontaneously. Furthermore, by concentrating, one may hold to either perspective indefinitely. The cognitive contribution would seem, then, to lie in a sort of choice that the cognitor makes to see the circle one way or the other. It is only a *sort* of choice because often it appears to have been made after the fact.

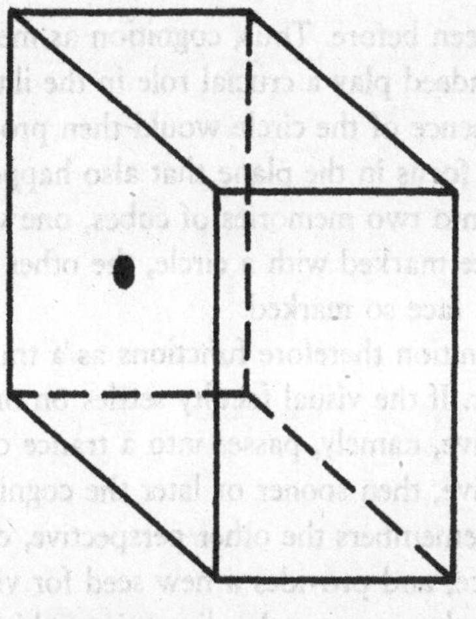

Figure B1. Necker Cube

As a first step toward the limiting case, assume that cognition enters into the experience only at the instants of conversion, before and after which purely perceptual states hold; of these there are but two: (1) circle stereographically closest, (2) circle farther away. Now obviously both faces are at the same perceptual distance from the viewer. It is only the stereographic way the cube is constructed that allows for an illusion of depth. As is well known, depth perception is a consequence of binocularity; the perceptual field as seen through only one eye is more planar, less solid. Only when the eyes are functioning in tandem do we see in three dimensions. In fact, so far as our qualitative model is concerned, focus and depth bear the same dynamical relationship to one another in vision as do balance and directionality in hearing. They will be fundamental parameters in any description of sight.

And yet, if the distance to the faces (the focal length) is constant, how is it that we experience depth when gazing at the cube? It is easy enough to dismiss the whole thing as an illusion or trick, but such a judgment tells us nothing useful. One possible explanation is that the arrangement of the lines in parallels looks *like* a three-dimensional figure we remember

* R. L. Gregory, *Eye and Brain: The Psychology of Seeing* (New York, 1973), pp. 7–12.

† Neurologically the eyes are a development of the cerebrum. They are a morphological evagination (unsheathing) of the prosencephalon. During embryogenesis they first appear as protuberances on the first cerebral vesicle. It's as though cognition pokes its way into perception via the eyeballs.

having seen before. Thus, cognition as memory would indeed play a crucial role in the illusion. The presence of the circle would then provide a point of focus in the plane that also happens to be tied into two memories of cubes, one with the front face marked with a circle, the other with the back face so marked.

Cognition therefore functions as a trance disrupter. If the visual faculty settles on one perspective, namely, passes into a trance on that perspective, then sooner or later the cognitive faculty remembers the other perspective, disrupts the trance, and provides a new seed for visual trance, only to repeat the disruption a bit later. This interpretation squares with our assumption that cognition functions only at the instants of conversion. And it also agrees with the yogic pronouncement that by concentrating (i.e., dhāraṇā, which has the sense of "deliberate ignorance" in Sanskrit) the seed can be kept constant. As Patañjali puts it: Yoga is the suppression of the modifications of the mind.* In the present case, the modifications can be characterized as *similitudes*, namely, likenesses, between the stimulus/seed and prior experiences held in the memory of an organism.

Similitudes make any attempt to maintain the seed very difficult—as the experience of daydreaming shows—because they tend to confuse different but similar seeds. Thus, a complete analysis of the model, be it of hearing, vision, or what have you, must take into account the chain of resemblances that cognition automatically initiates. But by hypothesis, we are here dealing with an incomplete situation, which is to say, a limiting case. Hence, to separate cognition from vision it is necessary only to preclude any disruption of the visual trance that arises from the influence of memory. And we may postpone considerations of similitude until we take up the cognitive model.

Let us now assume the existence of two entities, A and B, separated by some distance *d.* The entities possess the faculty of vision (internal and external) and only that faculty. Let us also assume that at the outset both entities are in the dark: There is no external sight occurring. Hence they must be seeing internally. Moreover, as a consequence of the extremely general axiom with which we concluded the discussion of hearing, this internal vision is a trance state.

In analogy to the hearing model we cannot assume that the entities are "facing" each other, that is, aligned in such a way relative to the direction in which they perceive visually that, were they to begin perceiving, they would see each other at the centers of their respective visual fields. If for the sake of argument we assume that the entities' visual fields are similar to our own, the fields are roughly circular in cross section and, considered three dimensionally, are shaped like *elliptic cones* truncated close to the vertices. Truncated cones are called frustra in solid geometry. As figure B2, top, illustrates, in the most general case the cones need not intersect. The entities cannot see each other and will remain in a state of internal trance. In figure B2, bottom, the frustra intersect. The volume of intersection of the frustra of two conical ellipses can be shown to be an ellipsoid.

The ellipsoid is the shape of the bounding volume described by the vibrating crossed D and B fields of Maxwell's electrodynamics while they propagate through matter. The crossed nature of the electric and magnetic vectors is a parallel to the rectangle formed by the intersection of the mutually perpendicular hearing and seeing axes in an organism. Moreover, just as we have associated hearing with changes in motion, so too does a static magnetic field act only on a moving charged particle in a direction perpendicular to its direction of motion. The dynamics are summed up in the Lorenz force law:

$$F = (q/\varepsilon)D + q(v \times B),$$

where ε is a constant that takes account of the properties of the particular medium in which an electromagnetic field is present and **v** is the velocity of the charged (q) particle on which the field exerts a force F. The Lorenz force law tells us that if the particle is stationary in the pres-

* *Yoga-Sūtra, Sādhana Pāda,* sutra 2.

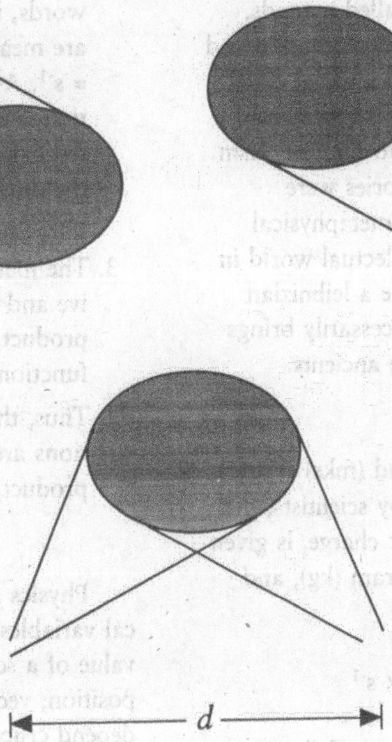

Figure B2. Conic Frustra

ence of electric and magnetic fields directed at right angles to each other, the particle will "feel" only the force exerted by the electric field vector (**D**) and will move in a direction parallel to the field. Once it begins to move, however, the magnetic field (**B**) will exert a force on it that will tend to curve the trajectory to one side.

The action of a field on a particle such as the electron goes to the epistemological heart of psychoscience. Scientists have always placed quotation marks around *feel* and *sense* when used in reference to charged particles: the electron "feels" the charge on the nucleus that holds it in orbit, the proton "senses" the presence of a magnetic field in a cyclotron, and so forth. The intention is to avoid an elaborate and inadequate circumlocution. Orthodoxy has not accepted the a priori nature of consciousness, hence the quotation marks. Yet the question remains, if the electron in some sense does not "really"—"actually"? "truly"?—feel the electrostatic field of the nucleus, what does take place? Rather, what takes place that is different from the electron *feeling* the electromagnetic field? Physics delves somewhat deeper and posits the exchange of photons of the quantized fields, but the exchange of quanta must also, in some manner, be *sensed* by both electron and field, so the question has merely been postponed. Given the philosophical prejudice of modern science, which we might call the pining for a *cold, dead universe*, the question is infinitely postponable and a solipsistic retreat into "pure" mathematics inevitable.

In the seventeenth century, the German philosopher Gottfried Wilhelm von Leibniz (d. 1716), a devout Lutheran, attempted to refute the mechanistic philosophy of Descartes in his celebrated *Monadology*. On Leibniz's view, the universe consists of an infinite collection of incorporeal simple substances called monads, which have the capacity for both perception and appetition, namely, external and internal experience. To achieve his synthesis of science and philosophy, Leibniz went back to the causalism of Aristotle. As a result, his theories were ignored in the onslaught of antimetaphysical positivism that gripped the intellectual world in the eighteenth century. To revive a leibnizian perspective, as we are doing, necessarily brings us back to the worldview of the ancients.

◆◆◆

In the meter-kilogram-second (mks) system of measuring units used by many scientists, the coulomb (C), the unit of electric charge, is given in terms of the meter (m), kilogram (kg), and second (s) by

$$C = m^{3/2} \times kg^{1/2} \times s^{-1}$$

The argument from experience is as follows:

1. Two eyes are necessary for a perception of a volume (V), which involves the third power of the spatial unit: $[V] = m \times m \times m = m^3$ (the notation $[V]$ reads "measuring unit of V"). Because the eyes integrate, the proper mathematical operation is multiplication. Thus the contribution of each eye is $m^{3/2}$, that is, $m^{3/2} \times m^{3/2} = m^3 = [V]$.
2. Hearing differentiates, or balances, by comparing the signals falling on each ear. But it does so per unit time interval; in other words, it recognizes frequencies (ν), which are measured in units of inverse seconds: $[\nu] = s^{-1}$. A subtraction is implied. The subtraction is actually the operator of the differential calculus: D_t or ∂_t, which appear in all the differential equations of perceptual physics.
3. The mass (self-touch) of an object is reflexive and also modeled mathematically by a product. The appropriate operator for that function is $kg^{1/2}$, that is, $kg^{1/2} \times kg^{1/2} = kg$.
4. Thus, the three elemental experience functions are $m^{3/2}$, $kg^{1/2}$, and s^{-1}, which, as a product, equal C.

◆◆◆

Physics recognizes two categories of dynamical variables: scalars and vectors/tensors. The value of a scalar is independent of direction or position; vectors (shown in boldface type) depend crucially on both. Because direction and position are essentially percepts, the use of vectors in all equations is widespread. Yet they are promiscuously mingled in the equations of perceptualist physics with nonperceptual categories such as mass and temperature, both scalars. It would therefore seem necessary to separate scalars from vectors to achieve a rationalized physics. The failure to do so leads to experimental observations that are inexplicable within a solely perceptal paradigm. In appendix C, we shall look at the epistemological problems more closely.

APPENDIX C

Quantum Mechanics and Psychogeometry

The hydrogen atom is the elemental paradigm of both perceptual physics and psychoscience. In an atom, all the mass is virtually contained in a one-proton nucleus, which has virtually no volume. Virtually all the space is occupied by a single electron, which has virtually no mass. The disjunction is a singularity following on the breakdown of the perceptual model when applied to imperceptible atoms. The conjunction of proton-electron is the stereognosis-perception dyad in the Three Worlds structure of the atom (cognition needs specification). An electron is essentially a charged volume; it is only virtually a charged mass particle. Conversely, a proton is essentially a charged mass particle; it is only virtually a charged volume. The same paradigm can be scaled up to galactic dimensions and higher. The space of a galaxy is defined by its visible light, which is analogous to the electronic volume of the atom. The most recent discoveries of astronomy confirm the inhomogeneous, shell-like distribution of galaxies (around a high-order black hole). The mass of the galaxy is all concentrated within the local black hole, to which all so-called individual masses in the galaxy are ultimately referable. Thus, by extrapolation, because hydrogen and helium comprise nearly 99 percent of the visible mass of the universe, a weighted combination of the ratios 1:1836 and 1:3672, the ratios of the electron-to-nucleon mass in hydrogen and helium, must hold for the universe as a whole to within 1 percent. To six places then, dark mass makes up 99.952887 percent of the universe.*

The above can perhaps be reconciled with Einstein's general theory of relativity by noting that the minute degree of curvature of a light beam in the vicinity of a star is a measure of the local visible mass-to-missing-mass ratio.

◆◆◆

* The Hubble space telescope, launched in 1991 and repaired in 1993, is calibrated to look for enormous numbers of so-called brown dwarf stars to account for the missing mass. On our hypothesis, it will find few if any.

Beginning with the well-known fact from quantum mechanics that the uncertainty in the energy (ΔE) is at a minimum when the first time derivative of the action (I) is a constant, one shows by straightforward, albeit somewhat lengthy, differentiation that, in the limit,

$$dE = 5T - U - \tfrac{1}{2} \int \left(\frac{\partial^2 U}{\partial t^2} \right) t dt,$$

where dE is the energy gain or loss, t is the elapsed time of measurement, T is the relativistic kinetic energy, and U is any local potential-energy operator. Perceptualist physics assumes that $dE = 0$, namely, that the net loss or gain of energy in an isolated system is zero.

The term $5T - U$ is of especial interest. In applying classical newtonian physics, the three laws of motion often are not the most general or useful form in which to solve mechanical problems. During the eighteenth century exhaustive analysis of Newton's three laws of motion showed that the ad hoc function $L = T - U$ is the governing dynamical variable in the evolution of a physical system. The function L is known as the *lagrangian* after the French astronomer Joseph Louis Lagrange (d. 1813), who first pointed out its significance in his *Mécanique analytique* of 1787. The kinetic energy (T) is the most sensitive gauge of purely perceptual motion in mechanics. As its name suggests, it is the energy of *motion*, a category having only perceptual data as its referents in current science, even though relativity theory has shown that, because it depends on mass, kinetic energy is an ambiguous dynamical variable. The potential energy (U) describes all other energy in the isolated system. Their difference ($T - U$) controls the evolution of the system. The difference can be likened to a tension between where the system is and where it *could* be. A lagrangian-like term, $5T - U$, appears in our equation for the decrement of the energy (dE). The factor of 5 indicates that the kinetic energy is scaled up by the total number of perceptual stimuli operating, namely, the five senses of the physical system. The product is then compared to the overall potential energy in the vicinity. The difference is the tension driving the system to a state of constant motion in accordance with Newton's first law of motion.

The foundation of perceptualist physics is the law of the conservation of energy: $T + U =$ a constant (E). The integral term,

$$\tfrac{1}{2} \int \left(\frac{\partial^2 U}{\partial t^2} \right) t dt,$$

sums up the changes in the potential energy over time. Changes in the potential energy with time indicate a gain or loss of energy. The necessary equality, we have speculated, is a result of the properties of vision, by which true congruencies can readily be demonstrated. If, however, the potential energy describes, at least in part, nonperceptual energy, the question of congruency is moot. Therefore, the integral term *can* describe an absolute loss of energy within the isolated system. Yet the energy cannot simply vanish, which would violate a principle more fundamental still: from something only something, from nothing only nothing—which might be called the *parmenidean principle*. The energy must be converted into something else, something more general than energy.

The necessary and sufficient condition that the integral term not vanish is

$$\frac{\partial^2 U}{\partial t^2} \neq 0,$$

(first noting that the integrand is a monotonically increasing function of t). We can strengthen this assertion further by requiring that

$$\frac{\partial^2 U}{\partial t^2} = M,$$

where M is a constant, and we posit that M is a third-world operator yet to be specified. Acceleration in the potential energy is constant, not merely explicitly in the equations of physics but implicitly. That would seem to be a condition on the psychophysical stability of the Three Worlds, particularly the second world. In the first world it is encountered as the constancy of one's weight; in the second it shows up as the constant acceleration of gravity ($g = 9.8\ m/s^2$). The operator M is therefore a true parameter, one that we define to be the *meaning* of the isolated physical system.

The simplest, normalized time-varying potential of mathematical physics—also one frequently encountered—is $U = e^{-i\omega t}$, where e is the basis of the natural logarithms, $i = \sqrt{-1}$, and ω is the angular frequency of variation in the potential with time. Differentiating gives

$$\frac{d^2U}{dt^2} = i\omega \frac{d^2\omega}{dt^2} U - \omega^2 \frac{d\omega}{dt} U = M.$$

Although we cannot solve the equation without more knowledge of the crucial relationship between ω and t, we can deduce useful information about M. We must first look more closely at the number i, the square root of -1 and the basis vector for an infinite set of numbers called the imaginaries, collectively symbolized by $\mathfrak{I}$.

Imaginary numbers were introduced in the sixteenth century by the Italian mathematician Rafael Bombelli (d. 1573), who used them to solve cubic equations. Important contributions were made by the Swiss mathematician Leonhard Euler (d. 1783), the German Carl Friedrich Gauss (d. 1855), and the Frenchman Augustin-Louis Cauchy (d. 1857). Imaginary numbers have proved enormously useful in solving physical problems yet are assigned no "real" status. The word *real* in this context can be misleading. It has both a technical sense and a colloquial sense. Imaginary numbers are numbers for which no perceptual model exists. *Perceptual* here means *geometrical*. The counting numbers (1, 2, 3, . . .) can be represented by line segments. Surds too can be drawn, although only indirectly, and negative numbers. Thus, whereas -1 can be modeled as a mirror image of 1, $\sqrt{-1}$ bears no such easy relationship to $\sqrt{1}$. If real numbers are numbers that correspond to visualizable models, then imaginary numbers correspond to nonvisualizable cognitive or stereognostic models. Hence, in psychophysics, imaginary numbers are the numbers that scale the nonperceptual sources of energy. Their persistence in the equations of quantum mechanics, where they are treated merely as intermediary forms to be eliminated in arriving at so-called real results, is another indication of the maladroitness of a physics based solely in perception when applied to imperceptible physical systems. We now assume that $\omega \in \mathfrak{I}$; that is, ω is an imaginary number. The form of the differential equation then indicates that M too is either imaginary or *complex*: having both real and imaginary parts. Whereas the magnitude of M remains constant, its projection onto the visual axis varies. The technique of determining the projection of M onto the real axis is called by physicists *diagonalization of the matrix* or *solving the eigenvalue problem.*

In effect we are positing not a perceptual space as the domain of application of physical laws but an *experience space* ($\mathfrak{E}$) modeled on the Three Worlds: I, II, and III (figure C1). The perceptual space of physics (Minkowski space) is a subset of $\mathfrak{E}$ occupying the median (s,t)-plane of vanishingly small thickness, ΔZ. Experience space involves functions of four fundamental variables: s, t, m, and M, respectively, space, time, mass, and meaning. The space variable s is in fact a triplet (x,y,z), where x, y, and z are the usual cartesian space coordinates (denoted by $\mathfrak{R}^3$), giving a six-dimensional space overall.

In current practice, the quantum-mechanical theorist calculates the eigenvalues for the energy of the physical system under investigation. He then delivers those numbers to an experimental physicist who, in the most usual case, verifies them in the spectrum of the physical system. The spectra are a series of discrete frequencies of light emitted by the system when stimulated. The spectral frequencies are directly related to the eigenvalues of the energy operator (sometimes called the hamiltonian). The final result is a photographic plate showing a series of lines spaced according to an empirically determinable formula. The spectral lines appear against a black background.

The classical quantum mechanics of Bohr, Schrödinger, and Heisenberg, which could more properly be called quantum electrostatics, and

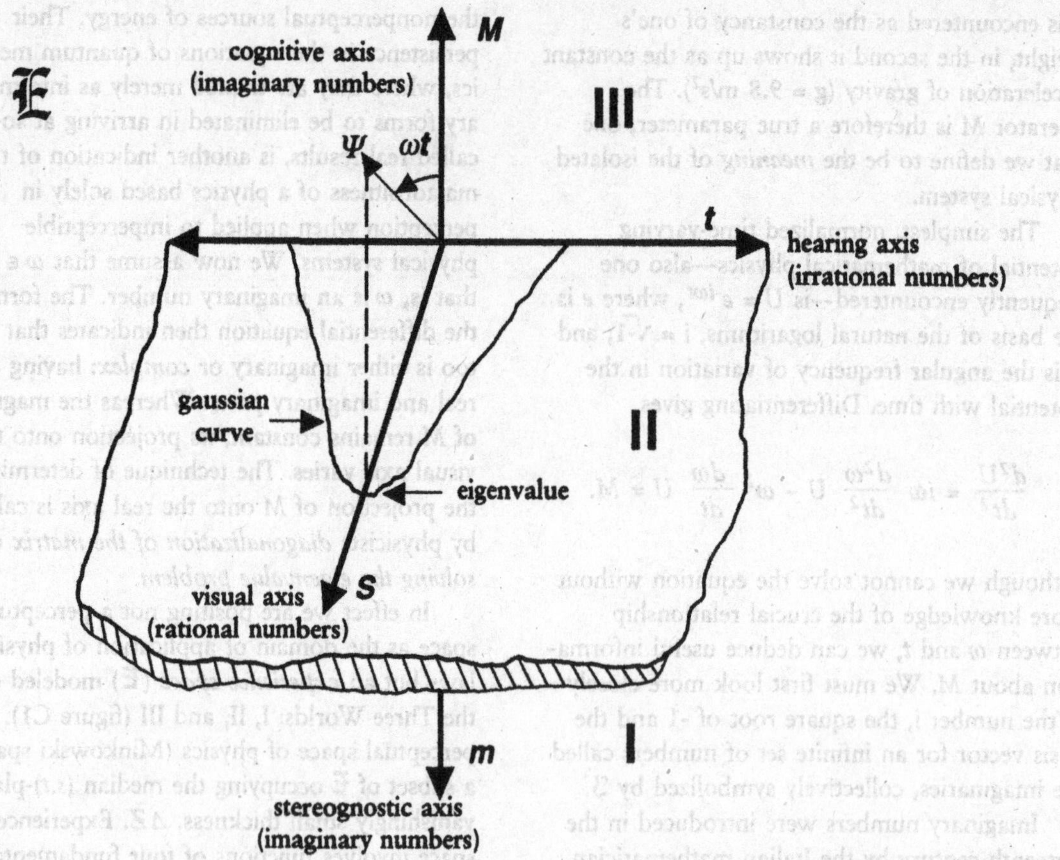

Figure C1. Experience Space (Ɛ)

quantum electrodynamics (QED), its talented stepchild, have proven outstandingly successful in predicting the spectral lines for various elements—for example hydrogen and helium—as well as the so-called fine structure and hyperfine structure of the spectra. Because the mode of experimental interaction is an electromagnetic (i.e., seeing-hearing) entity called a photon, the perceptual bias in the equations leads to accurate results. Our attention is drawn, however, not to the spectral lines but to the gaps *between* the lines. Those gaps are associated with the nonperceptual, internal states of the physical system. As the state vector Ψ rotates through the three worlds of the system, it regularly enters a purely perceptual mode characterized by an absorbed photon. It then emits another photon and passes into an internal state. The frequency of rotation of the state vector is just ω, and the product *ωt* measures the Ɛ arc swept out as Ψ rotates. The motion of the state vector through the three worlds is analogous to the "dynamic template of the universe" previously introduced:

ὑλε ↔ κινησις ↔ νοος
(hyle ↔ kinesis ↔ noös)
$m \leftrightarrow T(s,t) \leftrightarrow M,$

or

I ↔ II ↔ III.

The process can be scaled up to the cosmic level. The vast blackness of the heavens observed at night is related to the internal state of the universe at large. The visible stars correspond to perceptual states of the universe. The black void is therefore the placeholder, as it were, for the greater portion of the mass of the universe, the so-called missing mass. Because mass is fundamentally nonperceptual and nonlocalizable, it "appears" as a void in perception. Stars and voids in the larger universe are related as electrons and protons in an atom, namely, two worlds (perception-stereognosis).

The rotation of Ψ describes the cyclical awareness of the physical system. All awareness involves a degree of focus, what Patañjali calls *ekāgrāta*, or one-pointedness. It is only in exceptional cases that true one-pointedness occurs. Because no faculty of awareness is ever truly "off," there will always be a diffuseness to experience, a spreading out analogous to figure-background awareness. In physics, this manifests as peaks in the quantum-mechanical wave function or state vector (Ψ). There is, in general, a gaussian curve ($e^{-\alpha t^2}$) of awareness in which the experiential field drops off exponentially around the focus. The width of the spectral lines can be directly related to the degree of spreading, just as the peak region of focus can be related to a particular eigenvalue of Ψ. Figure C1 shows the measured eigenvalue as falling directly on the *s* axis. That means the eigenvalues are real numbers in the mathematical sense. The spread of the wave function is shown in the figure as a typical gaussian curve projected onto the (s,t)-plane. In quantum-mechanical theory there is a strange concept called the "collapse of the wave packet." Before a measurement is taken, the physical system is not in any distinct state. The state vector Ψ in the most general case is represented as a linear combination of n eigenvectors ψ_i such that

$$\Psi = \sum_{i=1}^{n} c_i\psi_i = c_1\psi_1 + c_2\psi_2 + \ldots + c_k\psi_k + \ldots + c_n\psi_n$$

In other words, Ψ is obtained by adding together the eigenvectors $\{\psi_i\}$; the set of complex coefficients $\{c_i\}$ specify how much of each eigenvector is needed to sum to Ψ. The process is analogous to constructing a stick of a given length using only multiples (0, 1, 2, . . .) of a finite set of smaller sticks.* Which set of eigenvectors depends on the physical system, particularly on the nature of the potential-energy operator U. In the general case, current theory holds, the system is in no definite eigenstate but rather in the combination (mixed state) described above. At the moment of measurement, through some transcendentally inscrutable process, the wave function collapses into a definite eigenstate—call it ψ_k—characterized by a particular eigenvalue E_k. It is like polling a heterogeneous population of millions and getting only a single opinion from one member of the group. From a psychophysical perspective, however, the collapse is less mysterious. The set of eigenvectors $\{\psi_i\}$ describes the mixed states of awareness of the system and comprises all faculties from cognition through stereognosis—as well as all combinations thereof. Taking a measurement by using a photon is a means of focusing the awareness of the system in a seeing-hearing mode. The result is a single rational or irrational eigenvalue. Mathematical physicists describe this as the diagonalization of the matrix. It is the cognitive correlate of perceptual focus.

It should be stressed that the evolution of Ψ is merely *analogous* to a rotation because $\mathfrak{E}$ is a six-dimensional space and a perceptual model of a system that is not solely perceptual. Quantum mechanics has long made use of a model that bears striking similarities to $\mathfrak{E}$. To specify Ψ completely, one need only specify $|\Psi|$ and Ψ_z, where Ψ_z is usually shown as the vertical component of the state vector and $|\Psi|$ is the "length" of the vector in Hilbert space. The similarity is merely coincidental, but it illustrates that the structure of the space of eigenvectors reflects the psychophysical reality. The perpendicular constraint on Ψ_z is related to the apparently vertical arrangement of the Three Worlds. It hardly matters whether it is Ψ_x, Ψ_y, or Ψ_z that characterizes the quantized vertical compo-

* In many cases of interest the set of eigenvectors is infinite and forms the basis of what physicists call a Hilbert space.

nent. What is interesting is that there exists a preferred direction of quantization that is normal to the perceptual (x,y)-plane.

The question of course is how to interact with a physical system apart from the exchange of photons. Gravity is one such exchange, a mass-to-mass interaction. In practice, however, the gravitational interaction is only inferred through a perceptual process—the exchange of photons between the interacting bodies—which allows a specification of trajectories and orbits. For that reason, the form of the law of universal gravitation (Newton's law) is identical to the form of the law of electrostatic attraction (Coulomb's law). We are dealing with a perceptual simulacrum, as it were, of the true gravitational interaction.

Because, as we have speculated, mass is not a perceptual entity—in Patañjali's phrase, it is *antaraṅgaṃ*, "internal"—hence not a spatial entity, any law of interaction such as Newton's law that depends essentially on spatial separation is misleading insofar as it describes the action of gravity. In perceptual terms the most accurate description of mass is that *all* the mass of the universe is located at one point—a singularity—but that point can be taken to be anywhere in the universe, as expressed in the so-called virial theorem. The law of universal gravitation itself depends crucially for its validity on the assumption that the mass of an object acts *as if* it were concentrated in one point, known as the *center of gravity*.* The concept of a center of gravity illustrates that singularities are inescapable when integrating an essentially nonperceptual entity (mass) with a perceptually based theory.

In mechanics the center of gravity is generalized into the *center of mass*. The localized center of mass of perceptual physics is only a (local) window, as it were, onto the infinite mass of the universe. The theory of special relativity demonstrates how that window is widened as the mass particle under consideration is accelerated to higher and higher velocities, essentially a kinematic phenomenon. Because of the finite value of the maximum speed (c) of perceptual-information transfer between the mass particle and the observer, the localizability of the mass of the particle fails as its speed approaches c. The measured center of mass then approaches the infinite mass of the entire universe. The nature of the failure is expressed in the famous Einstein formula $E = mc^2$, where the mass m is also a function of the speed of the particle. For nonkinematic mass—that is, mass per se—we must look elsewhere. The most obvious candidate is the so-called strong force, which binds the nucleus of an atom together. The nucleus, as we have seen, is an essentially nonperceptual entity, or at best, a virtually perceptible entity. When one splits the atom, one is chipping at the infinite mass of the universe, so vast stores of mass energy are released into the perceptual realm.

Quantum electrodynamics is the advanced theory that accounts for the observed properties of the interaction of light with matter—photons with electrons. In the first approach to QED in the 1920s, Heisenberg encountered difficulties when the mass of the electron was introduced into the equations of the quantized electromagnetic field: the mass took on values approaching infinity. The solution to the problem was to "renormalize" the field—in an ad hoc way—by sweeping under the rug an infinite amount of mass. The failure of the earlier, unrenormalized QED, so current thinking holds, was ascribable to an epistemological dead zone, inhabited by "ghost particles," surrounding electrons at infinitesimal distances. That is only half right. The electron is itself the quantum of space, and the ghost particles are the traces of its irreducible volume (i.e., the second world cannot be closed off). The failure to resolve the physics for lengths smaller than the putative electron diameter ($\sim 10^{-13}$ m) is a result of the epistemological disjunction of stereognosis and perception. There is no mass *there*, thereness and mass being utterly disjunct categories. The current rationalization, which implicates the uncertainty introduced by momentum transfer between the photons used to probe both the electron volume

* Newton delayed publishing his law of universal gravitation until he could rigorously establish the principle of a center of gravity. To do so, it was necessary for him to perfect the integral calculus.

and the electron mass, is a *pons asinorum*: only those audacious enough to disregard common sense are permitted to cross the bridge into the wonderland of spaceless mass. Experimental high-energy physics demonstrates that each attempt to find a true mass point reveals volumes within volumes. For example, Rutherford showed that the atom was mostly empty space. So-called atom smashers then revealed that the nucleus was mostly empty space. Nucleons are believed to be composed of *quarks*. Although no one has ever observed a quark directly, experimental evidence suggests that a quark is not structureless either. Everything is *void*, and we can almost hear the Buddha laughing. All attempts to found a physics on the localizability of mass must lead to paradoxes such as renormalized quantum fields or merely logical dilemmas like the position-momentum uncertainty principle.

The nonperceptual part of a complete physical system is expressed in the use of statistics to describe, for example, nuclear breakdown. Statistics is an essential tool in analyzing all imperceptible systems, from the nuclear to the molecular level. In the nineteenth century, before the advent of quantum mechanics, this fact was recognized in the development of statistical mechanics by the Austrian physicist Ludwig Boltzmann (d. 1906) and used in his kinetic theory of gases. There is something antithetical to perception about probability and statistics, so the crucial role they play in modern physics is not surprising. Any statistical analysis of a physical system can be interpreted psychophysically as a cognitive interaction with the system.

In the current view, there is a theoretical continuum from quantum mechanics, including QED, to quantum chromodynamics (the study of nuclear forces), to quantum gravity. All interactions are conceived of as taking place *in* space-time. On our view, quantum mechanics-cum-QED is the transitional science linking perception to congnition. Introducing Ɛ space, however, we have fragmented the continuum. When one introduces irremovable boundaries, however, one simultaneously introduces quantization, which becomes necessary if one is to match the solutions of Ψ across the I-II, II-III, and III-I boundaries (and vice versa).* The result is a set of six subatomic particles that describe the transitions.

The conclusion toward which we are groping is that the dynamical principle driving events in Ɛ space is incessant creation and destruction of the second world. Systems experiencing unaccelerated motion represent trance states: closure of the Crack in the Cosmic Egg. Because volume, a wholly geometric concept, is the defining variable for perceptual states, the dynamical principle that opens and closes space must be a kinematic one; but the physical variable that best describes the overall *excitability* of a physical system is charge (q). Therefore, a satisfactory dynamical equation must involve

$$\frac{dq}{dt},$$

the time rate for change of the charge. In present theory the charge of a physical system is a fundamental quantity. We have adopted the notion that charge is a portmanteau concept of space, mass, and time, as suggested by the units used to scale it: $m^{3/2} \times kg^{1/2} \times s^{-1}$. When two charged entities interact, the result is q^2, where $[q^2] = m^3 \times kg \times s^{-2}$, which can be interpreted as the *materialization* of the system, a kind of mass-volume acceleration. The acceleration involved becomes even more recognizable if we consider the charge as a ***unit experience vector*** $\mathfrak{e} = (s^{3/2}, m^{1/2}, D_t)$. Thus, the Ɛ vector,

$$\frac{dq}{dt}$$

has one component of the form D_{tt}: conventional newtonian acceleration, a prime desideratum of any comprehensive dynamical equation. Once established, matter is maintained by the available energy against cognitive-

* The I-III-I boundary cannot be illustrated because it is completely nonperceptual.

sterognostic pressures to obliterate it. When a state of unaccelerated motion is attained, the free energy dissipates, the crack closes, and the system passes into internal trance. It is then, in a sense, *asleep*.

◆◆◆

As a mathematical exercise we offer the following conjectures. The disjunction between the rational and irrational numbers, which together make up the set of so-called real numbers ($\mathfrak{R}$), is strictly related to the disjunction of the vision and audition of the universe. ("Audition," it may be recalled, is both perceptual, as hearing, and stereognostic, as balance.) Thus, there must be an intimate relationship between the irrational numbers (surds) and the imaginary numbers. The relationship is specified by Euler's formula:

$$i = -e^{i\pi}.$$

Here, the square root of -1 is an implicit function of two irrational numbers, e and π.

In $\mathfrak{E}$ the set of irrational numbers ($\mathfrak{I}$) are used to scale the temporal, left-to-right axis. The rationals ($\mathfrak{Q}$) are used to scale the spatial, out-of-the-page axis. For simplicity's sake, we have characterized the two axes by s and t (or ct), whereas the axes are actually two elemental-experience functions:

$$\tau(t) = \Delta t \rightarrow dt \text{ and } \upsilon(s) = s^{3/2}.$$

The left-to-right axis in figure C1 is an axis of periods; the out-of-the-page axis is an axis of root volumes. The operators V and ν then act on this function space:

$$V(s) = s^3, \text{ the cubic operator,}$$

and

$$\nu(t) = D_t = \frac{d}{dt}, \text{ the differential operator.}$$

Bear in mind that $\mathfrak{E}$ is only a model. Immediately, it is a model of the space "within" which we are conscious. Less immediately, because we have postulated the a priori nature of consciousness, it is a model of the universe in the large and small. Experience space is a model of the union of cognition, perception, and stereognosis in whatever system we are investigating. Specifically, the (s,t)-plane of figure C1 is actually what mathematicians call a *hyperplane* (it is not contained in ordinary cartesian three-space but contains it); a hyperplane is the locus of certain projections of a Minkowski *hypercone* with vertex at the $\mathfrak{E}$-space origin.

The ancients considered the sphere to be the paradigm for the cosmœ. Following proposition 34 in *On the Sphere and the Cylinder,* Archimedes demonstrates that the volume of a cylinder is three-halves the volume of its inscribed sphere. Within the sphere, a cone can be further inscribed with volume one-half that of the sphere. Therefore, the volume of the cylinder is three times that of the cone.* Archimedes was so pleased with proposition 34 that he asked that after his death his tomb be crowned with a model of a sphere inscribed in a cylinder on which $\frac{3}{2}$ was engraved.†

Given his numerous and revolutionary contributions to mathematics, which include a determination of the area of a circle and a quite serviceable value for π, we might well inquire why Archimedes was so taken with this particular proposition. More to the point, is the solid geometry of $\mathfrak{E}$ just this same archimedean sphere

* W. Dunham, *Journey through Genius* (New York, 1991), pp. 103–105; Archimedes, *On the Sphere and the Cylinder*, props. 33–34, in *The Works of Archimedes*, trans. Sir T. L. Heath (New York, 1953).

† The story is probably not apocryphal. Archimedes was killed when the Romans besieged Syracuse (in Sicily) in 212 B.C. Two centuries later, Cicero located the grave and reported in his *Tusculan Disputations* that, indeed, although disfigured by time, it had been designed just as Archimedes wanted. It is tempting to speculate that the factor of $\frac{3}{2}$ is somehow related to the exponent of the elemental vision operator $s^{3/2}$. Cognition, then, could be thought of as a logarithmic space of events over the spatio-temporal field $\mathfrak{R} = \mathfrak{Q} \cup \mathfrak{I}$.

within a cylinder?* As a perception, the vertical human form then defines the axis of the cylinder, and the sphere is "the sphere of awareness," apparently centered on the skull.† Is that the psychogeometry of the universe, the outward form that the laws of physics have patiently evolved since the Big Bang of eighteen billion years ago? If so, and if that geometry could be designed into a microprocessor, a strong-AI cognitive engine would emerge almost necessarily.

In its ground state (lowest energy) a hydrogen atom is a sphere. The radius of the atom, denoted by a_0 (the Bohr radius), can be likened to the focal length of the atomic visual faculty, the minimum distance at which the volume of the atom is "in focus" and the place where a "spread out" electron wave function defines the volume of the system. The electron is thus a second-world link found in the chemical bonds that reflect light to form perceptible entities. The second world can be likened to an *image* in a mirror, which has no mass. The great liability of its "free" electrons is responsible for a metal's ability to reflect an image.

The atomic volume is associated with a frequency of revolution ν_0 of the electron about the nucleus, which describes the hearing faculty of the atom. All physical frequencies are associated with the irrational number π through the equation defining the period (τ) of revolution: $\tau = 2\pi / \omega$. Hence, all frequencies are irrational numbers. The factor of ω in the denominator is the so-called angular frequency of rotation. In effect, ω perceptualizes a nonspatial category, that of frequency, by mapping it onto a full 360-degree arc.

The essential irrationality of time scales derives from the lack of an adequate perceptual model for an interval of time. Whereas a spatial point of demarcation can easily be constructed, with time there is only an interval denoted by Δt. To use the hands of a clock to mark an interval of time spatially is to beg the question. Vision is fundamentally timeless, so for systems approaching the speed of light—the intermediary of vision—time must slow down. Hearing, on the other hand, is fundamentally spaceless; at the speed of light, lengths contract to zero in the direction of motion, which is the direction of frequency of Doppler shifting. (In mathematical terms, spatial intervals are closed sets, temporal intervals are open sets.)

The characteristic time interval of a physical system is the period of oscillation of the system, implying that $\Delta t \geq \tau$. All change within the system is compared to that interval. The comparison is of the nature of a change per period of oscillation of the state vector through $\mathfrak{E}$. In perceptual physics, the quantity whose change is measured is the total energy E. Thus, in quantum mechanics, the energy operator or hamiltonian (H) is a function of

$$\partial_t = \frac{\partial}{\partial t},$$

which is basically a frequency (i.e., $[\partial_t] = s^{-1}$).‡ All perceptual measurements are made in space and time. The set of rational numbers mark off spatial intervals, the irrationals mark off temporal intervals. The two sets are united in

* Or ellipsoid of negligible eccentricity. Like Thales before him, Archimedes was notorious in antiquity for being absorbed in thought most of the time; in other words, he spent most of his time in the third world. Might he have got insight into psychogeometry from prolonged abstraction? According to Plutarch, he died because he would not—could not because entranced?—take his attention from a theorem to heed a Roman soldier. As a young man, Archimedes studied in Alexandria, so he must have been exposed to the mystical numerology of the Pythagoreans. The question of whether he was ever initiated is impossible to answer.

† We have not used a bounding cylinder in constructing $\mathfrak{E}$ of figure C1, but the notion can be illustrated by the irrotationality of electric and magnetic fields (D & B); i.e., $\nabla \times D = \nabla \times B = 0$. Irrotational fields also are called *solenoidal*, "cylindrical," i.e., the fields circulate in a plane around an axis of symmetry normal to the plane but cannot be rotated out of the plane (i.e., all torques vanish). Irrotationality is a condition for the existence of an EM potential; in mechanics it is a necessary and sufficient condition for conservation of energy.

‡ The exact energy-operator function is $H = -i\hbar \frac{\partial}{\partial_t}$, where $\hbar$ is Planck's constant divided by 2π.

the three-world experience of the entity (what Kant refers to as the "transcendental unity of apperception"). They cannot be united in a one-dimensional visual model such as the real-number line without violent paradoxes ensuing.

The topology of $\mathfrak{E}$ leads to some curious results, although for reasons of space we can discuss only a few:

1. We have already spoken of the length of the state vector Ψ. The state vector can be thought of as the *attention* of the system under investigation. Because attention is only with great difficulty focused completely on one stimulus (in yogic terms, *ekāgrāta* or one-pointedness is rare), in general attention is of the figure-background sort: a certain stimulus occupies the bulk of system attention but not all of it. The eigenfunction expansion of any $\mathfrak{E}$ operator describes the linear partitioning of system attention. Quantum mechanics, as with all perceptually biased science, does not recognize the a priori nature of consciousness, so the only way it can partition the state vector is probabilistically, namely, for each c_i (complex) in the orthonormal expansion of Ψ, $|c_i^2| \in [0,1]$ and $\Sigma c_i^2 = 1$. The psychophysical parallel would be to require normalization of every experience to *unity* when summed over the figure-background attention of the entity, in other words, attention is conserved.

2. Because no irrational number equals a rational number, the length of the state vector in the plane ($/\Psi/^2 = \Psi_s^2 + \Psi_t^2$) can never be such that $s = c\Delta t$ (so long as $c \in \mathfrak{I}$), an insufficient condition for restricting the speed (c) of energy transfer throughout $\mathfrak{E}_{II}$, where the subscript denotes the second world. Yet note, though $s \neq c\Delta t$, both $s < c\Delta t$ and $s > c\Delta t$ are possible. The speed of light is invariant if and only if c is transcendental.

3. The stereognostic or mass axis is an ordinate of negative imaginaries. Mass-mass interactions, therefore, must be attractive (negative) because $(-i)^2 < 0$.

4. Because $0 \notin \mathfrak{I}$, $t \neq 0$ and $\Delta t \neq 0$; that is, there is no zero point of time, which is what might have been expected if time is essentially a frequency. The second inequality is just the time-energy uncertainty principle. It is an interesting question whether the two inequalities are tautological.

5. Perhaps most important, the incommensurability of the visual rationals and auditory irrationals means that each $\mathfrak{E}_{II}$ axis is full of "holes." Thus, in constructing nonpathological functions of space and time, certain states will necessarily be excluded, leading to discontinuities related to quantum states. A *metric* is an abstract length in the vector space. We have thus far restricted the discussion to the (s,t)-plane to simplify matters, but the actual $\mathfrak{E}$ metric will be a complex number. For useful physics, it is crucial that a unique metric be definable between any two points in $\mathfrak{E}$. In defining a metric for $\mathfrak{E}_{II}$, a *double* quantization is necessary because $s \in \mathfrak{Q} \Leftrightarrow s = [(2m + 1) \div (2n)]^{\pm 1}$, where m and n are integers. Under the ordinary operations of algebra (+, −, ×, and ÷), the set $\mathfrak{Q}$ is closed, but irrationals ($\mathfrak{I}$) can map either to rationals or to irrationals. Given that the elemental vision operator involves extracting a root, rationals can be mapped to irrationals in $\mathfrak{E}_{II}$, but such a map will have visual meaning only for certain space values—for example, those of the form $s = q^{2n}$, where $n = 0, 1, 2, \ldots, q \in \mathfrak{Q}$. Thus quantization and uncertainty, on our hypothesis, are not so much antecedents as they are consequences of number *plus* the qualitative distinction between vision and audition. The concept of a physical unit becomes superfluous. Thus, a *meter* is uniquely defined by a rational number, a *second* by an irrational, and a *kilogram* by a negative imaginary, which taken together might be called the "kwy" (qwi) or pythagorean system of units. The wave

function of orthodox quantum mechanics is dimensionless. Indeed, $\Psi(s,t,m,M)$ can be redefined as a *vector charge* describing the disposition of the system to interact (psycho)physically. The temporal (left-right) axis is also the hearing axis, and we have already correlated hearing with magnetism. Thus, the lack of magnetic monopoles may explain why time has a preferred direction, that is, is irreversible or nonsymmetric. If the universe is permeated by an intergalactic magnetic field, an "arrow" of time is automatically established. At any hierarchical level, however, a local time scale is established by a local magnetic field. Thus, on earth, the magnetic north–magnetic south dipole establishes terrestrial time.

6. The nodes of the state vector obtained from the Schrödinger wave equation for spatiotemporal position (or momentum) are those points in the domain of Ψ (or Φ) at which the vector vanishes. On our hypothesis, there should be some relation between the nodes of Ψ and the set $\mathfrak{W}$ because each instance of $\Psi(s,t) = 0$ is a point of space-time where the measured physical system cannot be found. In fact, that is just the case. The nodes of any wave equation fall at rational multiples of π, which is not only irrational but *transcendental* (a nonzero rational multiple of an irrational number is always irrational). Decomposing the real number line into two axes constitutes the physics of psychophysics and cannot be justified deductively, only experimentally.*

7. One concept of perceptual physics abandoned in psychophysics is *hermiticity*. A hermitian operator has only real eigenvalues. Electric and magnetic fields are represented by hermitian operators in $\mathfrak{E}$. When the system is aware of an electric field, the operator associated with D acts to rotate Ψ onto the axis of rational real numbers (Stark effect). The operator for B similarly rotates the state vector onto the axis of real irrationals when the entity hears a magnetic field (Zeeman effect). Because we allow the state vector to rotate "above" and "below" $\Re^3$, imaginary eigenvalues are possible. The operator associated with the gravitational field is *not* hermitian because it rotates Ψ onto the axis of negative imaginaries, analogously for the memory (third world) operator. In quantum-mechanical jargon, all such rotations can be interpreted as *projections* onto one-dimensional subspaces of $\mathfrak{E}$ giving rational real, irrational real, and imaginary eigenvalues. Eigenvalues cannot, in general, be complex. Note, we have not specified whether the imaginary eigenvalues for the first- and third-world operators are rational or irrational. In summary, a psychophysical operator need only be *unitary*.

It has been long known that the important equations of physics fall into three categories: ***parabolic***, ***elliptical***, and ***hyperbolic*** partial differential equations, designations chosen by analogy between the form of the differential equations—considered as second-degree operator polynomials—and the form of the algebraic equations of the parabola, ellipse, and hyperbola in a plane. Yet the analogy may conceal a deeper correspondence with the Three Worlds. Solutions to elliptical equations—for example, Maxwell's equations—are closed ellipsoids, suggesting the inherent boundedness of vision and the second world. Parabolic and hyperbolic equations are most often encountered in problems of diffusion and heat conduction. The one involves mass, the other internal energy, in particular the *loss* of perceptual energy through little-understood dissipative processes such as friction. The solutions are open-ended surfaces: hyperboloids and paraboloids. As a first, tentative step, we might assign parabolic equations like the diffusion equation to the first world because it involves

* Because there are an infinite number of holes in both $\mathfrak{E}_{II}$ axes, an astute reader might conclude that *all* points of the (s,t)-plane are excluded, a very serious objection. A possible resolution may lie in the fact that the cardinality of $\mathfrak{Q} = \aleph_0$, whereas the cardinality of $\mathfrak{W} > \aleph_0$; i.e., the irrationals are much more dense than the rationals. (A rigorous demonstration of this conjecture has eluded me.)

mass.* Hyperbolic equations are then left to the third world. Only close investigation can reveal the ultimate wisdom of these choices.

The closed nature of second world—i.e., electromagnetic—solutions is a consequence of the form of the wave equation:

$$\nabla^2 U = 0$$

Here

$$\nabla^2 U = \frac{\partial^2 U}{\partial s^2} + \frac{\partial^2 U}{\partial (ct)^2},$$

and c is the speed of propagation of the wave (in the EM case, c is the speed of light). Essentially then, the wave equation states that when U "accelerates" with respect to s, it "decelerates" by an algebraically equal and opposite amount with respect to t—and vice versa—which turns the solution space in on itself and closes it.

To solve the wave equation, theoretical physicists often can introduce a function of a complex variable ($z = s + ict$) having the potential U as its imaginary part.† The potential is a cognitive variable from which perceptual variables, such as a force, are readily obtained using $\nabla U = -F$. The technique is known as the method of conformal mapping. Its efficacy depends on the existence of a superordinating potential (as defined by the Cauchy-Riemann equations) having a constant component *perpendicular* to the plane of physical interaction, in other words, for solenoidal fields.

A classic example is the determination of the electrostatic field between the plates of a condenser.‡ A condenser is a tantalizingly apt model of the Three Worlds. One has the "emergence" of a measurable electric field into a perceptual volume from two point sources (the places where the positive and negative electrodes are attached to the plates). The point sources, being singularities, are not perceptual and bound the perceptual volume on two sides, which, for consistency with the Three Worlds structure, we can take as meaning *above* and *below*. It is therefore doubly interesting that the potential—which strictly speaking *cannot* be perceptually measured—should be introduced as an imaginary number in capacitance problems. Nor is the imaginary character of U at all arbitrary. It is the immediate result of a well-known physical fact that at the surface of a conductor the potential energy must be a constant.

Without scaling the potential by an imaginary number, many problems of electrostatics and hydrodynamics would be impossible to solve save numerically. It is true that the technique of conformal mapping can only be applied in a plane, but most problems of theoretical physics display a symmetry with respect to at least one spatial dimension, allowing it to be ignored in calculations. In experience space, the problem never arises because the three space variables (x, y, and z) are combined into a single variable $s^{3/2}$. Conformal mapping uses imaginary numbers to map one image into another, suggesting its possible utility for relating perceptual states to cognitive states. In physical problems that means transforming a force into a potential, which are related as percept is to concept under the all-important condition that percepts and concepts are equally objective states of the universe in the large and small. Clearly a neologism is needed to formalize the objective equality of the Three Worlds, and *isoöbjective* or the kantian *apperceptual* might do for now.

We might generalize the above by introducing the mathematical notion of a *category*. A category is a collection of objects and relationships among the objects. Generalized transformations from one category to another category are called *functors*. Experience space is composed of three categories: I, II, and III. In II, we place all percepts (sights, sounds, smells, etc.) The rela-

* An interesting speculation would be to rewrite the Einstein equation as

$$m = \lim_{v \to c} E(1/v)^2,$$

a parabola in $1/v$. Infinite invisible mass transforms to finite visible mass by *cosmic diffusion* (i.e., from the first world into the second). The energy (E), when held constant, is a coefficient of diffusion of mass into velocity.

† In this context, z is not a third space variable.

‡ In the present case, the dynamical wave equation is a two-dimensional Laplace equation, a partial-differential equation of elliptical type.

tionships between the percepts are called *morphisms*. Morphisms make use of *scale factors*, operations, and operators (both linear and nonlinear). For generality, they are indicated by arrows. For example, Maxwell's equations are morphisms of the percepts D and B: $D \rightarrow B$, $D \rightarrow D$, $B \rightarrow B$, and $B \rightarrow D$, where we explicitly include *inverses* among the morphisms, operations that transform D into B and back again. We have already characterized the morphisms of II: they are isometric homeomorphisms, that is, strict equivalencies. The simplest category-II morphism is *homothety*, congruency achieved without rotation, an example of which is the galilean transformation. In III, the morphisms are isomorphisms.* In I, the morphism is particularly simple; it is the reflexive relationsh $m \leftrightarrow m$ or, possibly, $f(m) \leftrightarrow m$, where f is some operation over $\mathfrak{I}$. Psychophysically, morphisms specify how the attention (Ψ) of the system under investigation "rotates" within a single category, functors between categories. An example of a functor already discussed would be the Einstein equation, $E = mc^2$, which specifies how a category-I variable (mass) transforms into kinetic energy (II).

What concerns us now are the general properties of psychophysical functors. As we proceed, it will become increasingly apparent that we must solve what theoretical physicists refer to as a *boundary-value problem*, of which there are basically two kinds: Dirichlet- and Neumann-type problems. Loosely speaking, in a Dirichlet-type boundary problem one analyzes an element of the category at some boundary; in a Neumann problem, the *dynamics* of the element at the boundary—for example its rate of change—is the focus. Which boundary-value problem best models the relationships between feelings, percepts, and cognitions? To usefully limit a very complex discussion, we restrict it to the back-and-forth relationship between II and III.

How does a percept transform into a memory, and how does a memory transform into a percept? We have already made two, nonindependent suggestions regarding II-III transitions: conformal mapping and Hilbert space transformation. Those very general characterizations can be made more specific and to a certain extent unified in the notion of a *fractal*. A fractal is a point set that, apart from scale, does not vary under the action of some morphism. Thus, fractals exhibit self-similarity: they look the same at any level of magnification. Although fractals have geometrical representations such as the Mandelbrot set and von Koch's curve, they are also adamantly cognitive entities. For instance, fractals have fractional dimension—hence their name—something for which no adequate perceptual model exists.

Physiologically, fractoid behavior is found in the progressively finer neuronal branchings of the CNS, tending to imperceptibility. Metaphorically, fractals describe the transition from the covering of light (II) to interiority (III), from perception to cognition. We hypothesize that morphisms over fractals are functors. The main obstacle to such a formulation is that the image of an element of the fractal set S under a given morphism is also a member of S, by definition. Thus it would seem impossible to map a percept into a cognition. One way out of the difficulty is not to apply the functor—call it f—an infinite number of times but only a ***sufficiently large*** number of times, that is, given f^n (f applied n times to S), then $n \gg 1$ and $n \neq \infty$. There is thus created a fuzzy region of $\mathfrak{E}$ space in which the codomain of images is not wholly equivalent to some subset of S. If we start with a real, rational element $s \in S$ of II and let f be a functor that maps s to some *complex* element M in III, then M cannot be wholly a member of S, although its real part might be. Alternatively, in what might be called the platonic approach, one could start with the third-world form of the fractal and map to the second world, eliminating the imaginary component in the mapping.

Also of interest is system stability, that is, images converging to some definite, fixed image

* More precisely, they are *homomorphisms*, where a homomorphism should not be confused with a homeomorphism. Homorphisms are abstract relations between algebras, hence cognitive. Homeomorphisms are topologically based concepts; topology, with its "rings," "balls," and "coverings," is hopelessly perceptual.

in the codomain—sometimes called an *attractor*—rather than endless "free association." It turns out that the crucial element in the analysis is f', the rate of change (derivative) of f with respect to s.* To put it concretely, in the psychophysical transition from *seeing* a circle drawn, say, on a chalk board to *remembering* a halo, it is the dynamical state of the percept that is conformally mapped: Is it moving, shrinking, growing, and so forth?† All of which leads us to suspect that we are dealing with a Neumann-type boundary-value problem. Such problems are common in the solution of elliptical differential equations involving the electromagnetic field propagating through mixed media (e.g., the field inside a condenser made of alternating layers of conductors and insulators). Psychophysically, as Ψ crosses from II to III, it is the derivative of the associated functor that is continuous across the boundary. That is not entirely surprising, for we have already seen that sensory awareness is always awareness of *difference* not substance. How does all that relate to fractals? First, the solutions to Maxwell's induction-driven equations certainly *resemble* fractals, with each point of the wavefront generating wavelets ad infinitum and almost recursively. Second, the tripartite division of $\mathfrak{E}$ can be likened to a complex phase space and certain fractals typically show up as boundaries in the complex plane. In particular, the Julia fractal is a conformal mapping and hence well suited to complex numbers. (When the various Julia fractals, all of which exhibit left-right symmetry, are represented geometrically, the resulting images can be eerily suggestive of the human face.)

Summing up, in going from II to III, homeomorphisms in II become homomorphisms in III, which can now be characterized as a fuzzy region of $\mathfrak{E}$ space. Classical newtonian orbits in II become set partitions in III. In a quantum-mechanical context, the result is a peak in the wave function or, equivalently, a diagonalization of the matrix associated with f.‡ System attention is focused discontinuously, but its rate of change or *distraction* is continuous. A circle becomes a halo.

As a final illustration of our fundamental psychogeometry, we return to the volume traced by the EM-field wave vector generated by a charged simple harmonic oscillator as the wave moves through space. As previously noted, the vector traces an oscillating ellipsoidal volume, but it is a solenoidal volume as well because the wave propagates in a direction perpendicular to the plane of vibration of the field vector. It is as if the photon associated with the wave is "following its head [the perpendicular, cognitive-potential direction]" as defined from moment to moment by the EM potential. There is an echo here of the "pilot wave" hypothesis advanced by David Bohm in his nonprobabilistic variety of quantum mechanics.§ Bohm posited the existence of an undetectable quantum potential that guides a particle, essentially by seeing into the future. Pilot waves are not very popular among physicists because they obviously require nonlocal, faster-than-light physics. In the realm of imperceptibles, however, we have been at pains to stress that *location* is a frivolous concept, so there is no objection to a quantum potential from this quarter.

We conclude with a conjecture that is very definitely facile but that can at least be tested. The shape of the DNA molecule, as is well known, is a double helix. If it could be shown that the volume obtained by revolving the two helices around the molecular axis is of varying but elliptical cross section, we might then speculate as follows. The chemical evolution of

* H. Lauwerier, *Fractals: Endlessly Repeated Geometrical Figures*, trans. S. Gill-Hoffstädt (Princeton, N.J., 1991), p. 178.

† The halo here intended is purely notional and excludes perceptual halos like the ring around the moon.

‡ In practice, one calculates either the matrix elements of the similarity transformation in the f representation—which is tantamount to specifying f uniquely—or the eigenfunctions and eigenvalues of Ψ from a Schrödinger-type wave equation.

§ D. Bohm, *Causality and Chance in Modern Physics* (Philadelphia, 1957). Bohm revived an idea of Prince Louis de Broglie (d. 1989), a pioneering quantum mechanic, who early demurred from the theory's probabilistic basis.

life has been guided by the same dynamics that constrains the EM wave vector as it propagates through space. The length of the DNA molecule is not as important as the length between any two sequential nodes of the helices. Each such length defines a Three Worlds template, with the nodes playing the part of the requisite vanishing points of the second world into the first and third.

It has been calculated that *without* a guiding template, the odds of a mere 100-nucleotide sequence randomly assembling itself is 1 in 10^{32}! The earth could be a trillion years old and not a fraction of the time necessary to capitalize such a long shot will have elapsed. Perhaps, in Archimedes' favorite geometry, the guiding template has been identified. Recently it has been discovered that a special set of genes called Hox genes determine overall somatic structure during embryogenesis. Amazingly enough, the Hox genes are arrayed along the DNA strand analogously to the arrangement of the body, from feet to head, in the form of a *homunculus*, a genetic recapitulation of the Three Worlds.*

* N. Angier, "Making an Embryo: Biologists Find Keys to Body Plan," *New York Times* (22 February 1993) pp. C1, C9.

BIBLIOGRAPHY

Æschylus, *Complete Works*, 2 vols., trans. H. W. Smyth, Cambridge, Mass., 1922–26.

Allegro, John M., *The Sacred Mushroom and the Cross*, New York, 1971.

Anaxagoras, in: Frederick M. Cleve, *The Philosophy of Anaxagoras*, New York, 1949.

Apollodorus, *Bibliotheca*, in: *Apollodorus: The Library*, trans. Sir J. G. Frazer, Cambridge, Mass., 1922.

Apollonius Rhodius, *Argonautica*, in: *Apollonius Rhodius*, trans. E. P. Coleridge, London, 1889.

Archimedes, *On the Sphere and the Cylinder*, in: *The Works of Archimedes*, trans. Sir T. L. Heath, New York, 1953.

Aristotle, *Metaphysics*, in: *The Philosophy of Aristotle*, ed. R. Bambrough, trans. J. L. Creed and A. E. Wardman, New York, 1963.

———, *Nichomachean Ethics*, in: Andrew G. Oldenquist, *Moral Philosophy: Text and Readings*, Boston, 1978.

Athenæus, *Depnosophistæ*, 7 vols., trans. C. B. Gulick, Cambridge, Mass., 1957.

Autenrieth, George, *A Homeric Dictionary*, trans. R. P. Keep, rev. ed. I. Flag, Norman, Okla., 1958.

Bateson, Gregory, *Mind and Nature: A Necessary Unity*, New York, 1980

Bede, *A History of the English Church and People*, trans. L. Shirley-Price, rev. ed. R. E. Latham, London, 1968.

Bell, John S., *Speakable and Unspeakable in Quantum Mechanics*, Cambridge, 1988.

Bémont, Charles, and G. Monod, *Medieval Europe: From 395 to 1270*, New York, 1903.

Bentov, Itzhak, *Stalking the Wild Pendulum*, Rochester, Vt., 1988.

Bhagavad Gītā, in: *The Song of God*, trans. Swami Prabhavananda and C. Isherwood, New York, 1960.

Bohm, David, *Causality and Chance in Modern Physics*, Philadelphia, 1957.

Borowski, E. J., and J. M. Borwein, *The Harper Collins Dictionary of Mathematics*, New York, 1991.

Brauer, G. C. , Jr., "Alexander in England: the conqueror's reputation," *Classical Journal* 76, no. 1 (1980): 34–47.

Brown, J. E., "Modes of Contemplation through Actions: North American Indians," in *Traditional Modes of Contemplation and Action*, Tehran, 1977.

Campbell, Joseph, *The Mythic Image*, Princeton, N.J., 1974.

———, *Myths to Live By*, New York, 1973.

Carmody, J. M., and T. E. Clarke, *Word and Redeemer*, Glen Rock, N.J., 1966.

Childes, Gordon, *The Aryans*, London, 1925.

Chomsky, Noam, *Syntactic Structures*, The Hague, Netherlands, 1957.

Cicero, *Tusculan Disputations*, in: *The Basic Works of Cicero*, trans. M. Hadas, New York, 1959.

Clement I, in: *Early Christian Writings: The Apostolic Fathers*, trans. M. Staniforth, rev. ed. A. Louth, London, 1987.

Clement of Alexandria, in: *Clement of Alexandria*, trans. G. W. Buttersworth, London, 1968.

Cole, Susan G., *Theoi Megaloi: The Cult of the Great Gods at Samothrace*, Leiden, 1984.

Cook, A. B., *Zeus: A Study in Ancient Religion*, vol. 1, Cambridge, 1914.

Coulson, Michael, *Sanskrit: An Introduction to the Classical Language*, Oxford, 1976.

Daly, L. W., *Æsop without Morals*, New York, 1961.

DiCara, Leo, "Learning in the autonomic nervous system," *Scientific American* 1(1970): 30–39.

Dilthey, Wilhelm, *Gesammelte Werke*, bd. 8, Stuttgart, 1926.

Diogenes Laërtius, in: *Diogenes Laertius*, vol. 2, trans. R. D. Hicks, London, 1925.

Dumézil, Georges, *Mitra-Varuna*, trans. D. Coltman, New York, 1988.

———, *The Destiny of the Warrior*, trans. A. Hiltebeitel, Chicago, 1970.

Dunham, William, *Journey through Genius*, New York, 1991.

Edelman, Gerald, *Bright Air, Brilliant Fire: On the Matter of the Mind*, New York, 1992.

Einstein, Albert, *Relativity*, New York, 1961.

Eliade, Mircea, *Shamanism: Archaic Techniques of Ecstasy*, Princeton, N.J., 1964.

———, *Yoga: Immortality and Freeedom*, 2d ed., Princeton, N.J., 1969.

Encyclopedia of World Religions, London, 1975.

Euripides, in: *Euripides: Collected Works*, vol. 2, trans. W. Brynner; vol. 4, trans. W. Arrowsmith; vol. 5, trans. W. Arrowsmith, Chicago, 1955.

Eusebius, *Ecclesiastica Historia*, vol. 1, trans. Kirsopp Lake, Cambridge, Mass., 1980.

Fechner, George, *Elements of Psychophysics*, vol. 1, trans. H. E. Adler, New York, 1966.

Feyerabend, Karl, *Classical Greek-English Dictionary*, Berlin, 1990.

Field, George B., and Eric J. Chaisson, *The Invisible Universe*, New York, 1985.

Finley, Moses I., *The World of Odysseus*, New York, 1976.

Flanagan, Dennis, ed., *The Brain*, San Francisco, 1979.

Frazer, Sir James George, *The Golden Bough: A Study in Magic and Religion*, 12 vols., London, 1911–15.

Fuller, E., ed., *Bulfinch's Mythology*, New York, 1962.

Giere, Ronald N., *Understanding Scientific Reasoning*, New York, 1979.

Gill, Brendan, "Face of Joseph Campbell," *New York Review of Books*, 28 September 1989.

Gladstone, Sir William Ewart, *Studies on Homer and the Homeric Age*, 3 vols., Oxford, 1867.

Gleick, James, *Chaos: Making a New Science*, New York, 1987.

Goddard, D., ed., *A Buddhist Bible*, Boston, 1970.

Gould, Stephen J., *Wonderful Life: The Burgess Shale and the Nature of History*, Boston, 1990.

Graves, Robert, *Goodbye to All That*, London, 1923.

———, *The Greek Myths*, 2 vols., rev. ed., London, 1960.

Graves, Robert, and R. Patai, *Hebrew Myths: The Book of Genesis*, London, 1964.

Gray, Henry, *Human Anatomy*, New York, 1977.

Green, Elmer, and Alyce Green, *Beyond Biofeedback*, New York, 1977.

Gregory, R. L., *Eye and Brain: The Psychology of Seeing*, New York, 1973.

Greiner, Walter, *Quantum Mechanics: An Introduction*, vol. 1, Berlin, 1989.

Hambidge, J., *The Parthenon and Other Greek Temples: Their Dynamic Symmetry*, New Haven, Conn., 1924.

Harper's Dictionary of Classical Literature and Antiquities, ed. H. T. Peck, New York, 1965.

Heidegger, Martin, *Being and Time*, trans. J. Macquarrie and E. Robinson, New York, 1962.

Hesiod, *Homeric Hymns*, in: *Hesiod and the Homeric Hymns*, trans. H. G. E. White, Cambridge, Mass., 1977.

———, *The Homeric Hymns*, 2d ed., ed. T. W. Allen, W. R. Halliday, and E. E. Sikes, Oxford, 1936.

———, *Theogony*, in: *Hesiod and Theognis*, trans. D. Wender, London, 1973.

Homer, *Iliad*, 2 vols., trans. A. T. Murray, London, 1924.

———, *Odyssey*, 2 vols., trans. A. T. Murray, London, 1926.

———, *Odyssey*, trans. S. H. Butcher and A. Lang, New York, 1950.

Hope, Thomas, *Costumes of the Greeks and Romans*, New York, 1962.

Horace, *Horace: Odes and Epodes*, trans. C. E. Bennett, Cambridge, Mass., 1927.

———. *Satires, Epistles, and Ars Poetica,* trans. H. Rushton Fairclough, rev. ed., London, 1929.

Huang, Kerson, *Statistical Mechanics*, New York, 1963.

Hughes, R. I. G., *The Structure and Interpretation of Quantum Mechanics*, Cambridge, Mass., 1989.

Hyginus, *Fabularum liber*, in: *Hyginus*, untrans., New York, 1976.

Ignatius of Antioch, in: *Early Christian Writings: The Apostolic Fathers*, trans. M. Staniforth, rev. ed. A. Louth, London, 1987.

Isherwood, Christopher, and Swami Prabhavananda, trans., *How to Know God*, New York, 1974.

———, *The Song of God*, New York, 1960.

Iverson, Leslie L., Susan D. Iverson, and Solomon H. Snyder, eds., *Handbook of Psychopharmacology*, New York, 1978.

Jacobson, Marcus, *Developmental Neurobiology*, New York, 1978.

Jung, Carl Gustav, in *The Portable Jung*, ed. J. Campbell, New York, 1971.

Katz, B., *Nerve, Muscle, and Synapse*, New York, 1966.

Keleman, Stanley, *Emotional Anatomy*, Berkeley, Calif., 1985.

Kerényi, Karl, *Hermes, Guide of Souls*, Dunquin Series, No. 7, Bern, 1976.

Koestler, Arthur, and J. R. Smythies, eds., *Beyond Reductionism: The Alpbach Symposium*, Boston, 1969.

Kovach, Judith E., "Contemplation in Movement: The Significance of Walking in Zen Meditative Practice," Master's Thesis, UCLA, 1990.

Lashley, Karl, *Brain Mechanisms and Behavior*, New York, 1927.

Lauwerier, Hans, *Fractals: Endlessly Repeated Geometrical Figures*, trans. Sophia Gill-Hoffstädt, Princeton, N.J., 1991.

Lindsay, J., *Blast Power and Ballistics: Concepts of Force & Energy in the Ancient World*, New York, 1974.

———, *Origins of Astrology*, New York, 1971.

Littleton, C. S., *The New Comparative Mythology*, rev. ed., Berkeley, Calif., 1973.

Marcus Aurelius, *Meditations*, trans. Maxwell Staniforth, New York, 1964.

Migne, Abbé Jean-Paul, *Patrologia*, vol. 6, Paris, 1846.

Miller, Neil, "Learning of visceral and glandular responses," *Science* 163 (1969): 434–45.

Miller, Stanley, in *The Heritage of Copernicus*, ed. J. Neyman, Cambridge, Mass., 1974.

Minucius Felix, *Octavius*, trans. G. H. Rendall, Cambridge, Mass., 1977.

Mommsen, Theodor, *Römische Geschichte*, bd. 1, Leipzig, 1854.

Monier-Williams, Monier, *A Sanskrit-English Dictionary*, Oxford, 1899.

Montague, Richard, *Formal Philosophy*, New Haven, Conn., 1974.

Mylonas, George D., *Eleusis and the Eleusinian Mysteries*, Princeton, N.J., 1972.

Newton, Sir Isaac, *Philosophiæ naturalis principia mathematica*, trans. A. Motte, rev. ed. F. Cajori, Berkeley, Calif., 1934.

———, *The Correspondence of Isaac Newton*, vol. 3, ed. H. R. Trumbull, Cambridge, 1961.

Ovid, *Metamorphoses*, trans. F. J. Miller, Oxford, 1968.

———, *Metamorphoses*, trans. M. M. Innes, London, 1955.

———, *Fasti*, trans. Sir J. G. Frazer, Cambridge, 1919.

Pagels, Heinz, *The Cosmic Code: Quantum Physics As the Language of Nature*, New York, 1983.

Parmenides, in: Willem J. Verdenius, *Parmenides: Some Comments on His Poem*, Groningen, Netherlands, 1942.

Patañjali, *Yoga-Sūtra*, in: *The Yoga-Sūtra of Patañjali*, trans. George Feuerstein, Rochester, Vt., 1989.

———, *Yoga-Sūtra*, in: *The Science of Yoga: Commentary on the Yoga-Sūtras of Patañjali*, 3d ed., trans. I. K. Taimni, Madras, 1968.

Pausanias, *Description of Greece*, trans. W. H. S. Jones, London, 1921.

Penrose, Roger, *The Emperor's New Mind*, New York, 1989.

Philostratus, *Life of Apollonius of Tyana*, in: *Philostratus*, vol. 1, trans. F. C. Conybeare, New York, 1917.

Pindar, *The Odes of Pindar*, 2d ed., trans. Sir J. E. Sandys, Cambridge, Mass., 1919.

Plato, *Gorgias*, *Phædrus*, and *Republic*, in: J. A. Stewart, *The Myths of Plato*, London, 1905.

———, *Apology*, *Crito*, and *Phædo*, in: *Plato: Euthyro, Apology, Crito, Phædo, Phædrus*, trans. H. N. Fowler, Cambridge, Mass., 1911.

Plutarch, *Moralia*, in: *Moral Essays*, trans. Rex Warner, London, 1971.

———, *Parallel Lives: Alcibiades* and *Themistocles*, trans. B. Perrin, Cambridge, Mass., 1901?

Pool, Phoebe, *Impressionism*, New York, 1973.

Pugh, Emerson M., and Emerson W. Pugh, *Principles of Electricity and Magnetism*, Reading, Mass., 1960.

Radhakrishnan, S., *The Principal Upaniṣads*, London, 1953.

Reynolds, L. D., and N. G. Wilson, *Scribes and Scholars*, 3d ed., Oxford, 1991.

Ṛg Veda, in *Hymns from the Rig-Veda*, trans. J. LeMee, New York, 1975.

Robinson, J. H., *Readings in European History*, 2 vols., Boston, 1904.

Rose, H. J., *A Handbook of Greek Mythology*, New York, 1959.

Śaṇkara, *The Crest Jewel of Discrimination*, trans. Swami Prabhavananda and Christopher Isherwood, Hollywood, Calif., 1947.

Schaya, Leo, *The Universal Meaning of the Caballa*, Baltimore, 1973.

Smith, Edward B., *The Dome: A Study in the History of Ideas*, Princeton, N.J., 1950.

Smith, Morton, *Clement of Alexandria and a Secret Gospel of Mark*, Cambridge, Mass., 1973.

———, *The Secret Gospel: The Discovery and Interpretation of the Secret Gospel According to Mark*, New York, 1973.

Smith, Richard, ed., *Nag-Hammadi Library*, 3d ed., San Francisco, 1988.

Sophocles, *Œdipus Rex*, trans. C. R. Walker, New York, 1966.

Staniforth, Maxwell, *Early Christian Writings: The Apostolic Fathers*, rev. ed. A. Louth, London, 1987.

Strabo, *Geographica*, vol. 6, trans. H. L. Jones, Cambridge, Mass., 1929.

Tertullian, *Apologia and De Spectaculis*, trans. T. R. Glover, Cambridge, Mass., 1977.

Theocritus, *Idylls*, in: *The Greek Bucolic Poets*, trans. J. M. Edmonds, London, 1935.

Thomas, George B., Jr., and Ross L. Finney, *Calculus and Analytic Geometry*, 5th ed., Reading, Mass., 1982.

Tikhonov, A. N., and A. A. Samarskii, *Equations of Mathematical Physics*, trans. A. R. M. Robson and P. Basu, New York, 1990.

Ushenko, A. P., *The Philosophy of Relativity*, London, 1937.

Virgil, in: *Virgil's Works*, trans. J. S. Mackail, New York, 1934.

Upaniṣads, in: S. Radhakrishnan, *The Principal Upaniṣads*, London, 1953.

Wilhelm, Richard, and C. F. Baynes, eds., *T'ai I Chin Hua Tsung Chih*, in: *The Secret of the Golden Flower*, trans. R. Wilhelm and C. F. Baynes, commentary by Carl Gustav Jung, New York, 1962.

Zeller, E., *Outlines of the History of Greek Philosophy*, Cleveland, 1965.

INDEX

children: description of uninitiated, 33, 245, 309; and mythopœsis, 32; sexuality of, 267
children of Israel, 33, 253
China, 276
Chios, 122, 129
Chiron, 123, 125
chlamys, 87
Chomsky, Noam, 299
Chosen People, 253
Christ. *See* The Christ
Christian myth. *See* Judeo-Christian myth
chromosomes, 303, 305
Chryse, 161
Chryseis, 161
Chryses, 92
church hierarchy, 230
churches, 154, 222
Cicero, Marcus Tullius, 3, 197
cipher, a symbol of static, 18
Circe, 167
Cisseus, 266
cistæ, 142, 147, 154, 204, 214
cisterns and Essene baptism, 237
citadel cults, 197
cittā, *55*, 106, 116
clarity and Perceptual Age, 276
Clashing Rocks. *See* Cyænean Rocks
classical era, 2, 33, 40
Cleanthes, 92
Clement I, 229
Clement of Alexandria, 2, 223, 227, 232; and Carpocratians, 223; and Mysteries of Eleusis, 204; Protrepticon, 223; and secret gospel, 223, 225, 226, 237; Stromateis, 223
clicking, second-world phonics, 165
Clio, 263, 264
Clodius (Publius Clodius Pulcher), 42
cloisters, 230
Clymene, 175
Clytemnestra, 97, 134, 160
CNS, 158; human, 17; neurons of, 21; never "off", 13; singularities of, 300; and Thrysus of Dionysus, 75; and Zeus, 101
cock, theriomorphism of vision, 57, 82, 131
Cœus, 91, 175, 177
Cognition, 69, 188, 301
cognition, *55*, 103, 106, 111, 118, 136, 12, 176, 180, 183, 202, 273, 274, 288, 289, 298, 299; and artificial intelligence, 300; cognitive engines, 300; cognitive lengths, 219, 273; externalization of, 34; illusion of, 276; and language, 299; Mount Olympus, 171; not perception, 78; placeless, 299; not symbolic, 275; and olfaction, 96; and scientific theory, 273, 274; third world, 68; transmogrif-ications of, 193; wedded to perception, 177; and Zeus, 101
Cognitive Age, 275, 276, 297, 298; defined, 275; and quantum mechanics, 276
cohanim, 30
Colchis, 140, 216, 218
collective unconscious, 6
Colonus, 175
Colophon, 129
Columella, 53
columns, 142, 145, 147, 151, 172
commensurability, 148, 273
Commodus, 197
complex variables, 298
computers, 300, 305
Comte, Auguste, 306
concentration, 24, 28, 36, 114; dhāraṇā, 26, 106; at moment of death, 210
Condillac, Étienne de, 306
cone of light, 77
Coney Island cutout, 33, 234
confessionals, 230
confirmation, 229, 230, 240; and epoptea, 207, 208
conformal mapping, 298
Consciousness, 189, 288; a priori experience, 282, 306; undefinable, 235
consciousness, 98, 106, 186, 188, 276, 283, 298, 301; aboriginal, 193; archaic, 114; as brahman, 25; and irreversibility of time, 272; and metempsychosis, 201; and mind, 105; noncontingency of, 8; not a thing, 7; and pratyaya, 281; reflexive hypothesis, 289; symmetric hypothesis, 287, 288; uncreated, 234; and Word of God, 235
consonants, 221
Constantinople, 226, 229
contemplation, 125; dhyāna, 26, 106
contiguity, principle of, 155, 156, 254
contingency in natural selection, 305
Copenhagen school of philosophy of science, 297, 299
Corinth, 47, 90, 130, 132, 138, 163, 283; in sacred geography, 134, 140; phonics of, 134
Corinthian, 168; capitals, 154, 172; order, 142
cormorant, theriomorphism of vision, 57
Cornelius, 253
cornice, 145; third world, 146
Corē, 71, 76, 210, 211, 214; and Hades, brother of Zeus, 201; and Mysteries of Eleusis, 197; parallels with The Christ, 256. *See also* Persephone
corollary to Axiom II, 67
Coronus, 217
Corot, Jean Baptiste, 183
corpus callosum, 172, 266
cortex: auditory, 15; cerebral, 21, 122; neocortex, 141, 300; occipital, 8, 15, 106, 176, 218, 284; occipital, What does it look like?, 19; olfactory, 167; and sensoria, 15; somatic sensory, 89; visual, 15, 58
Cosmic Egg, 96, 158, 170, 276
cosmic-background radiation, 17, 18, 41
cosmogony, 99
cosmos, 69, 190
Cottus, 178
coulomb, 296
covering of light, 165, 167, 274
cow: and khecarīmudrā, 173; theriomorphism of hearing, 57, 82
crab: fourth sign of zodiac, 64; theriomorphism of touch, 64, 188
Crack in the Cosmic Egg, 79, 126, 170, 276
crackling, second-world phonics, 177
Cranaus, 102
cranial nerves, 15, 16, 114, 137, 145, 157, 207, 248, 254; auditory nerves, 15; and Calypso, 167; as EM waveguides, 15; glossopharyngeal nerve, 19; modulated by other nerves, 15; and mythic war, 88; olfactory nerves, 19, 94, 96; optic, 15; and prāṇa, 239; sensory, 15; as serpents of Gorgon's Head, 36; trigeminal nerve, 94; vagus nerve, 23. *See also* auditory nerves; olfactory nerves
cranium, 17, 80, 85, 98, 114, 115, 139, 140, 172, 196, 237, 238, 241, 252, 310; as ark, 90; Ark of the Covenant, 239; as Argo, 217; bones of and Troy, 158; dilations of, 219; etymology, 102; and Hephæstus, 74; and movement of prāṇa, 220; Noah's Ark, 238; Pandora's Box, 79; and prāṇāyāma, 48; and skullcaps, 123; and Titans, 85
creation myths, 68, 70, 99, 170, 188
crepidoma, 145
Crete, 39, 110, 156, 158, 171, 182; and Minoan architecture, 145; in sacred geography, 131, 132; as second world, 97, 101; trysting place of Zeus and Hera, 72, 104, 276, 288
Creus, 175
cricket, theriomorphism of internal sound, 165
Crocus, 203
Cronus, 71, 75, 80, 159, 179, 184; castrates Uranus, 178; crooked-scheming, 175; dethroned by Zeus, 101; grim reaper, 167
Cross, 239, 240, 256
cross, 211, 247
Crown of Glory, 135
Crown of Life, 256
Crown of Thorns, 61, 89, 90, 135, 242
Crown of Victory, 46
crowns, 135; and Demeter, 198
Crucifixion, 89, 128, 169, 175, 232, 241, 242, 245, 248, 253, 254
cults, 226
cultural autism, 27, 275
Cumæ, 42
currents, piezoelectric, 16
cuttlefish, theriomorphism of first world, 123
Cyænean Rocks, 216, 218
Cyclopes, 84, 178, 179
Cygnus, constellation, 293
Cyncnus, 82, 283
Cyprus, 277
Cyril of Alexandria, 226, 227, 231
Cythera, 166, 182, 277
Dædalus, 213
dancing, 114; Yaqui Deer Dance, 54, *55*
darkness and proprioceptive light, 193
Darwin, Charles, 302, 303, 307
Daulis, 175
David, 310, 311; and Absalom, 241; and Goliath, 241; throne of, 310

empiricism, 235, 274, 276, 292, 294, 295
En Soph, 118
encephalon, 107; EM energy of, 114; self-modulating, 16
endocrine system, 21, 180, 308
energy, 189, 193, 298; as awareness, 72; and natural selection, 303; neurological, 183
Enlightenment, 3, 269, 275, 290, 291, 306
enstasy, 27. *See also* samādhi
entablature, 145, 146, 156
entasis, 145, 146
entity, 290, 298
entropy, 18. *See also* static
environment, 302; and catastrophes, 307
enzymes, 305
Eos, 176, 177, 203; and Ares, 177; anthropomorphism of second-world light, 176; mates with Ares, 82; and Tithonus, 177
Ephesus, 121, 155
Ephialtes, 84, 205
Ephyre, 139
Epicureans, 207, 233
Epidaurus, 200
epilepsy, 169; as uncontrolled trance, 211
Epimenides, 121, 275
Epimetheus, 85, 126
epiphenomenalism, 105, 181
epistemology, 105, 273; of electromagnetism, 296; equals science, 275; of gravity, 292; and theories of light, 291; of the Three Worlds, 78; tripartition of, 275
epoptea, 42, 207, 208, 240; and Mysteries of Cabiri, 207; and opening of cistæ, 214; vision of the self, 208
Er, myth of, 46, 213
Erasmus, Thomas, 264
Erebus, 193
Erechtheum, 142, 154
Erechtheus, 196
Ereuthalion, 162
Eribœa, 205
Erichthonius, 102, 103, 127
Erinyes, 187
Eris, 157; and Apple of Discord, 125
Eros, 170, 171, 277, 283; birth of, 178
Erymanthian Boar, 58, 61
Erysichthus, 195, 196
Esau, 32
esoteric, 29; description, 100; distinguished from esoterical, 43; rites of American Indians, 39
esoterical, 43
esoterism, 36, 38, 40, 230; and cabala, 251; Celto-Christian, 228; and definition of a myth (Axiom I), 36; failures of, 226; and fairy tales, 32, 38; Greco-Roman, 39, 43; Judaic, 231, 232; Judeo-Christian, 232; and monsaticism, 228; and Mysteries of Eleusis, 203, 214
Essenes, 232, 237
Ethiopia, 83, 177
ethnology, 3
eucharist, 173, 230, 240
Euclid, 108, 291; Elements, 298
Euhemerism, 2
Eumæus, 168
Eumenides, 178, 187
Eumolpids, 30
Eumolpus, 196
Eurasia, 68
Euripides, 3; Heracles, 203; Iphigenia in Aulis, 125; Iphigenia in Tauris, 151
Europe, 66, 109, 255; and internecine war, 61
Eurus, 140
Eurydice, 184
Eurypylus, 110
Eurystheus, 89, 139
Eusebius, Ecclesiastical History, 223
Eve, 79, 126, 127, 186
evolution, 272, 302, 308; chemical, 304, 306; darwinian, 302, 307; evolutionists, 304
existentialists, 5
Exodus, 33
experience, 193, 288; a priori experience, 180; as configuration of nervous system, 183; as karmic seed, 182; and quantization, 298; and reductionism, 273; usurped by perception, 266
exteriority, 76
external sound, 15, 16
extreme unction, 230
Eydothea, 107
eyes, 28, 77, 79, 109, 110, 137, 157, 160, 182, 189, 194, 218, 241, 252, 274, 284; and Atlas, 85; of Cyclopes, 178; define length, 273; and epoptea, 208; filled with light, 9; and Girdle of Venus, 167; and heart, 188; and the Mass, 231; and Maxwell's equations, 296; and Newton's laws, 291; proprioception of, 114; ruled by a male god, 82; and scientific theory, 274; and second-world pain, 80; and speciation, 304; and sun, 284; and Theogony, 171; and Titans, 85, 86; and trigeminal nerve, 127; and volutes of Ionic order, 145; What do they look like?, 19; and Wine-Dark Sea, 100
Ezekiel, vision of, 252
fables, 43, 56
face, 149, 159, 177, 296
face of parents, 100
fact and second world, 77
faculties, 229
fainting, 28, 52
fairy tales, 32, 38
faith: in death, 23; insufficiency of for gnosis, 29; and praxis, 242, 244
fakirism, 28
Fall, 86, 127, 158, 159, 187, 188, 252, 276; in Hesiod, 179
Fall of Troy, 160, 164, 217, 254
fancy, as vṛtti, 55
fane, 40, 140
Faraday, Michael, 295
fasting, 208; during Mysteries of Eleusis, 204; heightens internal awareness, 46
fate, 101
Fates, 97, 123, 193; and Zeus, 101
Father God, 85, 109, 118, 225, 235, 238; and hour of death, 255; and Mysteries of Eleusis, 197; nothingness of brahman, 235
fathers, and reincarnation, 250, 251
fathers of the Church, attitudes toward pagan myth, 40
fauns, 3, 38
feedback: in breath control, 51, 103; negative, 158; oscillatory, 272
feeling, 99, 288; bottomless, 71; and inorganic matter, 306; invisible, 70; not perception, 69, 78; not symbolic, 275; and pleasure as touch and taste, 73; as proprioception, 20; as stereognosis, 69; synonymous with touching, 73; of vascular flow, 76. *See also* ichor
Feet of the Lord, 172, 174, 245
female: anthropomorphism of bodily orifice, 86; anthropomorphism of sensation, 112; and Holy Spirit, 85
fennel, 79, 126
fetishes, 27, 37, 38; and Thrysus of Dionysus, 75
fetus and first-world proprioceptions, 76
fibers: dendritic, 17; dorsal, 20; nonmedullated, 96; thalamocortical, 96, 219
field, 276; electromagnetic, 295; EM, 306; gravitational, 306; visual, 283, 295
Field of Ares, 82
fifty, numerology of, 111, 112, 131, 167, 174, 216
fillets, 46
Fionn mac Cumail, 228
fire, 137, 188, 207, 230, 286; baptism by, 208, 237, 240; creative fire, 121; as description of thoracic proprioception, 46; elemental, 118, 136, 137, 275; and fuel as taste and touch, 72; and Hephæstus, 73; and Prometheus, 126; and samāna breath, 74; in Tartarus, 76
firmament, 70, 87, 139
first world, 70, 77, 137, 158, 163, 164, 166, 185, 288; antagonistic to perception, 81; defined, 69; entrance to, 99; fluidity of, 76, 182; Great Mother, 136; in Greek architecture, 146; as infinite void, 79; and kumbhaka, 97; and Mysteries of Eleusis, 197, 201, 202; as mystic sea, 69, 70, 71, 74; phonics of, 121, 126; and river Alpheus, 138; united with third world, 99
fish, theriomorphisms of first world, 186
fissures, cranial, 175
five, 187; numerology of, 109, 110, 112, 174, 188, 217
Flood, 78, 254, 255
foam: and Aphrodite, 202; and birth of Aphrodite, 277; and Nemean Lion, 177; and Nereids, 185
focusing, 296
folklore, 3, 43
foot: anthropomorphism of second world, 172, 266; unit of measurement, 274
foramina, 131
force, 37, 298; electromagnetic, 295; and pneuma, 191
forehead, 156, 159; and Hecuba, 174; and

Mithraism, 226
Mitra, 284
Mnemosyne, 175; and Muses, 263, 264
models, scientific, 273
modes of awareness, 176, 275; voiceless speech as, 28
modifications of the mind, 55, 56, 105; phonics of, 116
Moiræ, 101, 123, 125, 159, 201, 255
mokśa, 243
moldings, 145, 147
molecules, 273, 274, 306
monasticism, 228, 231
Monet, Claude, 183
money, 180
Mongols, 61
monkey, theriomorphism of mind, 51
monoamines, 181
Monophysites, 225, 278, 312
monopoles, 295
monotheism and Homer, 70
Monothelites, 312
Montaigne , 264
Montanism, 226
Montanus, 226
moon, 89, 176, 177, 283, 286; in Genesis, 188
morality, 247; and meditation, 98; of darwinism, 303
Moses, 33, 239, 251, 310; and Burning Bush, 239; and Sisyphus, 239; receives Torah, 232
Mother Earth, 71, 178, 179, 182, 282; and birth of Titans, 175; in Theogony, 171
motion, 37, 185, 189, 291; and emotion, 37; in creation myths, 171; Newton's laws, 290, 291
motor roots, action on muscle, 15
Mount Atlas, 252
Mount Caucasus, 126; in sacred geography, 135
Mount Cyllene, 252
Mount Dictys, 101
Mount Gargarus, 157, 158, 252
Mount Horeb, 130, 239, 310
Mount Ida, 72, 104, 130, 171, 278
Mount Meru, 130
Mount Moriah, 310
Mount Nebo, 33, 232
Mount Nysa, 133
Mount Olympus, 79, 81, 130, 170, 175, 205, 278; etymology, 171; third world, 69
Mount Ossa and esoteric north, 138
Mount Pelion, 125, 130, 138; and Alœdes, 205
Mount Pœcilon, 202
Mount Sinai, 232, 239
mountains, 140, 175, 240, 252; and Judeo-Christian esoterism, 232; in sacred geography, 130; in Theogony, 171, 175
mouse, theriomorphism of perception, 94
mouth, 74, 110; and Judeo-Christian numerology, 110; and speciation, 304
Moyers, Bill, 7
Muhammad, 248
mule, theriomorphism of respiration, 92, 161, 241
Müller, F. Max, 3
mūrdha jyotiṣi, 140, 208, 240; Burning Bush, 239
muscle, 15
Muses, 125, 263, 264
music, Hindu, 117
music of the spheres: and Pythagoras, 41; as static, 18. *See also* static
muskrat, theriomorphism of smell, 97
mutations. *See* genes
Mycenæ, 88, 92, 107, 130, 148, 161, 248; architecture of, 145; in sacred geography, 134, 135, 140
myeis, 42
Myrmidons, 194, 195
mystagogue, 224
mysteries, 227, 230, 231; Christian, 225; propagation of, 228
Mysteries of Cabiri, 42, 202, 218; epoptea, 207
Mysteries of Eleusis, 40, 41, 76, 88, 129, 139, 142, 154, 196, 215, 240, 256; Antheria, 198, 201, 208; and esoterism, 42, 43; fifth day, 201, 203; first day, 199; first-world myth, 197, 202; fourth day, 200; Greater Mysteries, 197; and Judeo-Christian mysteries, 214; Lesser Mysteries, 198; magistrates of, 200; an open secret, 42; origins of, 196; and overcoming death, 209, 210; and Pelasgians, 62; as practice in dying, 211; and prāṇāyāma, 50; preparations for, 199; purpose of, 208, 214; sacrifice of pigs, 199; sacrifices during, 201; second day, 199, 200; and second world, 201; Sisyphus betrays, 48; telesterion, 197; teletē, 203, 207; third day, 200
mystery, religious, 38
mystes, 197, 198, 207, 208; and praxis, 211; searches for Persephone, 210; skull of, 214
myth, 33, 39; as acculturated description of samādhi, 39; alien to philosophy, 114; as allegory, 2; and animals, 53, 64; and archetypes, 6; and architecture, 268; and art, 268; and astrology, 63; and biblical exegesis, 3; and canonical scriptures, 33; Celto-Christian, 228; and citadels, 197; cosmogonies, 99; as cultural artifacts, 27; cultural determinants contrasted, 61; and demons, 184; as description, 37; distinguished from history, 264; Egypto-Semitic, divisions of, 8; an enigma, 1, 9; as esoteric description, 36, 100; and esoterism, 38; and ethics, 174, 194; etymology, 1; Euhemerism, 2; and fairy tales, 32; and females, 86; as folklore, 3; formalism of, 32, 100; and frontal suture, 48; Hindu, 58, 109, 120; and history, 265; and hunting, 61; and ichor, 76; as ignorance of science, 3; and imagination in Plato, 2; Indo-European, 32, 221; Indo-European, divisions of, 8; influence on Western culture, 269; intentionally mysterious, 38; and internal visualization, 35; islands, straits, and isthmi, 69; and isthmi, 47; and Jesus, 40; Judeo-Christian, 256; and koāns, 26; and magic, 37, 38; and mantra, 116, 128; and marriage, 72; as metaphor, 4; as mode of awareness of, 214; motivation for, 36; mythopœsis, 37, 40; and New Testament, 233; and nineteenth-century imperialism, 4; Norse, 85, 109; numerology of, 109, 112; of Œdipus in modern psychology, 40, 265; and Old Testament, 33; and parables, 222, 223, 231; and pastoralism, 2; and patricides, 80; and Pelasgians, 218; and perception, 79; and philosophy, 140, 225, 269; physiological definition of, 36; and physis, 278; and the priest class, 40; as primitive catechism, 32; and psychoanalysis, 4, 265; and psycholinguistics, 4; Rationalism, 2; and recapitulation, 65, 67, 110; and riddles, 29; and saṃyama, 107; as story, 85; as symbol, 4, 5; and symbolism, 265, 275; teleology of, 183; three categories of (Axiom III), 108; transition to religion, 38; and Victorianism, 4; and virginity, 99; and war, 61, 79, 81, 88, 89, 104, 169; and Western literature, 268; and yogis, 37; worldwide similarities of, 5
mythographers, defined, 3
mythologists, 3, 5
mythology: brief history of, 5; redefined as esoteric physiology, 68; scientific basis of, 310
mythopœsis, 37; and esoterism, 39, 40; mythopoetic age, 39; mythopoets, 34, 43, 100; and numerology, 110; and Presocratics, 33, 34
mythopoets, 159; Homer and Hesiod, 218
nadi, 45
næads, 184, 217
Nag-Hammadi, 231
nails, image of perceptual pain, 175, 245
Name. *See* Name of Jesus; Name of God; Word of God
Name of God, 235, 236, 237, 240, 309, 310; and sound of breath, 236; ineffable, 236
name of God, 233
Name of Jesus, 233, 235, 237, 248
naos, 98, 153, 207
narcissism: cultural autism, 275; and survival, 37
Narcissus, 133
Narrow Gate and Sisyphus, 47
Narrow Way, 69
nasal bone, 85
nasal spine, 89; and egg-and-dart molding, 147; as spear, 59, 104
nasopalatine nerve, 92
Nathan, 310
Native Americans. *See* American Indians
natural philosophy, 33
natural selection, 278, 302, 304, 307; appeal for scientists, 303; chess analogy, 307; problems of, 303, 305; and randomness, 303, 306, 307; theory of differentiation, 304
nature, divine and human, 278

skull, 15, 130, 155, 156, 168, 239; bones of and Troy, 158; Cave of Calypso, 86; Cave of Nemean Lion, 90; and crown cakra, 173; and Greek temples, 145; and Jason and the Argonauts, 218; as mountaintop, 232; Mount Olympus, 175; orifices of, 86, 89, 109, 123, 130; and pineal body, 89; and Plato's allegory of the Cave, 41; sutures of, 89, 102; and udāna breath, 91
skullcap, 51
sky, 70, 171; mates with earth, 85; oceanic experience, 310; as sea, 99; and Zeus, 100, 101;
Slavs and Indo-European migration, 61
sleep, 193; as vṛtti, 55
sling, image of brows, 241
smell, 161, 196, 274; and Artemis, 99, 205; and herbs, 188; and Hesperids, 138; and John, 238; and karma, 180; and khecarīmudrā, 173; and Mysteries of Eleusis, 200; and numerology, 110; and pituitary catastrophe, 173, 254; and proprioception of olfactory bulbs, 166; second world, 69, 78; theriomorphisms of, 57; and Trojans, 88
smoking, 52
Smyrna, 227
snake: theriomorphism of taste, 202
snow and Mount Olympus, 171
sādhaka, 29, 96, 114, 115 140, 164, 169, 208, 217, 234, 239, 244, 245; begins inward journey, 219; deals with distractions, 81; Heracles, 121; and khecarīmudrā, 204; and laying on of hands, 230; robed during initiation, 207
sādhana, 26, 114, 219
Sāṃkhya philosophy, 25, 29, 88, 105, 109, 180, 234
sociobiology, 304, 307
Socrates, 2, 5, 184, 189, 207, 247, 251; and anamnesis, 213; death of, 194; differences with Anaxagoras, 33; initiated at Eleusis, 197; and perception, 79; and ringing in ears, 41; and Tartarus, 76
Solinus, 97
Solomon, 308, 310, 311; his dream, 309; and initiation, 309; temple of, 166
soma, 173, 204
Son of God, 85, 109, 210, 226, 235, 249
Son of Man, 249
Son of man, 254
sons and reincarnation, 250, 251
Sophocles, 3, 203; initiated at Eleusis, 197; and Œdipus cycle, 40; Œdipus rex, 265
sorcerer. *See* shaman; shamanism
soteriology, 41; Buddhist, 88
soul, 34, 98, 110, 158, 160, 166, 167, 168, 183, 189, 192, 193, 194, 217, 235, 243, 244, 249, 250, 256; arrival in Hades, 75; and breath, 58; confronts Ker, 209; and death dream, 202; and heart, 198; and hegemonicon, 190; and Helen of Troy, 158; in Homer, 34; incarnated in Temple of Solomon, 310; incarnates in animal bodies, 252; and karma, 180, 186, 201; led by Hermes to judgment, 88; and metempsychosis, 200; performs saṃyama at moment of death, 211; redefined as the unconscious, 6; reincarnation of in Plato, 80; separates from body, 209; and sin, 267; snared by perception, 80; takes refuge in Word of God at death, 256; transmigration of, 113, 196; in yoga, 26
sound, 15, 118, 274
sound made by the Bow of Odysseus, 43
sound of God, 234
sound of grass growing, Zen koān, 14
sound of life, 18. *See also* sound of one hand clapping
sound of one hand clapping, 12, 16, 24, 100, 233, 237; as auditory static, 14; as aural nothingness, 21; and Beethoven, 14; decrypted, 14; not a memory, 15; not an imagined sound, 14; as static, 17, 18
sound of snow falling, Zen koān, 14
sound of your soul, 16. *See also* sound of one hand clapping; static
south, esoteric, 92, 136, 138
space, 272, 296, 298; and cognition, 299; and electromagnetic field, 295; measure of, 274; only apprehended in perception, 292
Sparta, 66, 97, 159
spear, 162, 163
Spear of Peleus, 137
species, 302, 303, 304, 307
spectrum, 298; electromagnetic, 295
sphenoid bone, 154
Sphinx, 156
spinal cord, 181, 272; and proprioception, 20; and Thrysus of Dionysus, 75, 173, 202
spirit, 34, 77, 201, 311; ancestral, 200; of God, 185; lost esoteric knowledge of, 28; sin against, 196; of spirits, 38, 98; in yoga, 26
spirit world, 27, 29. *See also* spirit
springs, in sacred geography, 130
squamous fissure, 219
squamous suture, 85
stag: and olfactory nerves, 59; theriomorphism of smell, 57, 58, 196
static, 14, 16, 17, 18, 116
steam engine, 37
Stephen, 241; death recapitulates Crucifixion, 242
Stepteria, 137
stereognosis, 106, 111, 136, 162, 171, 183, 188, 274, 275, 292, 293, 300; of electron, 298; first world, 68, 69; and gamma afferent, 21; as gravity, 275; illusion of, 276; and mass, 291; and mechanics, 291; and Newton's laws, 290; and scientific theory, 273, 274; and Stereognostic Age, 121; visceral proprioception, 20
Stereognostic Age, 190, 275, 276
Steropes, 178
Stoics, 92, 190, 191, 233; Hymn of Cleanthes, 233
stomach, 105; in sacred geography, 136
stone as description of stopped heart, 36
Stone Age, 53
Strabo, 171, 264
strait, 140; and frontal suture, 48; image of second world, 69; in sacred geography, 130
Straits of Messina, 130
Stream of Ocean, 99
Stymphalian Marshes, 130
Stymphalus, 138
Styx, 76, 130
subconscious, affects of archetypes on, 6
subjectivity, 183, 184; in science, 193; and scientific theory, 273, 274;
sublime trance, 24, 26, 36, 45, 55, 168; enstasy, 27; initiation into, 29; and Noah's Ark, 79
subliminal sound, 16
substance of Schwann, 96
suffering and second world, 77
Sufism, 193
sulci, 131
Sumerians, sky lore, 63
sun, 99, 104, 140, 160, 176, 283; in Genesis, 188; and gravity, 291; as mythic inner light, 284; the self, 284; and vision, 105
Suovetaurilia, 200
superior maxillaries, 85
supraorbital arches, 57, 59; and Titans, 85
surds, 112, 149
survival of the fittest, 302
Surya, 284
sutures: illus., 90; line of, 89
svarga, 69
swan, 293; and recapitulation, 67; theriomorphism of nasal breath, 58, 283
swine, theriomorphisms of nasal breath, 58, 139
swoon, 28, 52, 217, 243
sword, 156
Sybil of Cumæ, 42
Sybilline oracle, 34
syllabary, 115, 221
syllogism, 108
symbolism, 225, 265; and experience, 275
symbols, 32, 37; and archetypes, 6, 7; and myth, 4, 5, 275
symmetry, dynamic, 148
sympathetic magic, 54, 55, 60
sympathetic nervous sytem, 69
symplegades. *See* Cyænean Rocks
synagogues, skull-shaped, 51
synapses, 21
syntax, 114
Syria, 225
syrinx, 86

Tacitus, Caius Cornelius, 3
tank circuit, 272
Tantalus: dismembers Pelops, 138; and myth of Sisyphus, 47, 49
tantra, 25, 27, 28, 91
tantrism, 28, 169, 208; and cakras, 79
Taoism, 236
Tartarus, 75, 132, 136, 167, 170, 201; first world, 71; phonics of, 125; as thorax, 76